THE SOCIAL INFLUENCE PROCESSES

ALDINE TREATISES
IN SOCIAL PSYCHOLOGY
edited by
M. BREWSTER SMITH
University of California, Santa Cruz

THE SOCIAL INFLUENCE PROCESSES

EDITED
BY
JAMES T. TEDESCHI
STATE UNIVERSITY OF NEW YORK AT ALBANY

ALDINE•ATHERTON   CHICAGO•NEW YORK

ABOUT THE EDITOR

James T. Tedeschi is Professor and Director of the Social Psychology Program, State University of New York at Albany, and is the author of numerous theoretical and research papers on the topics of power and influence. He received his Ph.D. in psychology from the University of Michigan in 1960 and is a fellow of the American Psychological Association.

Copyright © 1972 by James T. Tedeschi

All rights reserved. No part of this publication may
be reproduced or transmitted in any form or by any
means, electronic or mechanical, including photocopy,
recording, or any information storage and retrieval
system, without permission in writing from the publisher.

First published 1972 by
Aldine • Atherton, Inc.
529 South Wabash Avenue
Chicago, Illinois 60605

ISBN 0-202-25012-1
Library of Congress Catalog Number 79-169507

Printed in the United States of America

Contributors

Darcy Abrahams, Department of Sociology, University of Wisconsin, Madison, Wisconsin

Thomas V. Bonoma, Department of Psychology, State University of New York at Albany, Albany, New York

Steven H. Chaffee, Mass Communications Center, University of Wisconsin, Madison, Wisconsin

Howard L. Fromkin, Department of Psychology, Purdue University, Lafayette, Indiana

Svenn Lindskold, Department of Psychology, Ohio University, Athens, Ohio

Jack M. McLeod, Mass Communications Center, University of Wisconsin, Madison, Wisconsin

H. Andrew Michener, Department of Sociology, University of Wisconsin, Madison, Wisconsin

Henry L. Minton, Department of Psychology, University of Windsor, Windsor, Ontario, Canada

Barry R. Schlenker, Department of Psychology, State University of New York at Albany, Albany, New York

Siegfried Streufert, Department of Psychology, Purdue University, Lafayette, Indiana

Robert W. Suchner, Department of Sociology, Northern Illinois University, DeKalb, Illinois

James T. Tedeschi, Department of Psychology, State University of New York at Albany, Albany, New York

Elaine Walster, Department of Sociology, University of Wisconsin, Madison, Wisconsin

Preface

The current status of theory and research in the areas of social power and influence is clearly inadequate from almost anybody's point of view. Hypotheses are ambiguously stated, research programs continually end up in cul-de-sacs, and experiments take on the character of isolated one-shot studies. During a period when social psychology has invented a revolutionary set of techniques to investigate social psychological phenomena little accumulation of knowledge has been achieved. The chief goal of the present effort is to provide some new beginnings and to stimulate new directions for social psychological research. The emphasis is upon the development of scientific theory.

The contributors were chosen because they represent the new voices in sociology and social psychology. Most of them have been out of their own graduate training programs one decade or less. Each is a prodigious contributor to the research literature in his or her topic area. All of the chapters offer explicit suggestions for important but as yet almost untouched research areas.

In their introductory chapter Tedeschi and Bonoma review some of the theoretical discussion of social power. Most of the definitional problems concerning the concept of power are identified as philosophical or prescientific. Arguments about what power is too often hide the complicated social influence relationships that "connect" persons in interaction. The authors therefore provide an analysis of the types of connections that can exist between persons and suggest the major variables of interest for anyone who wishes to develop a scientific theory of the social influence processes. The modes of influence are those that exist between two persons—the source of influence and his target. The characteristics of the two parties may facilitate influence or produce resistance to it. Most of the subsequent chapters can be categorized within the cubbyholes provided by Chapter 1.

In Chapter 2, McLeod and Chaffee come to grips with the old but unsolved problem of how people define the psychological situation. Their juxtaposition of the individual's perception of the situation with the group's consensus of the same situation puts the discussion of the nature of social reality on the scientific level of discourse—a clear gain for those who like to evaluate their conclusions by the impartial judgments of Nature. The integration of the authors' definitions with Newcomb's A-B-X system and with socialization analyses of cognitive styles of evaluating information and constructing social reality are quite provocative.

In Chapter 3, Henry Minton views personality as a power construct. Expectancies, dispositions, and aspirations produced by a person's experiences are directly implicated in the source's attempt to gain influence and the target's resistance to influence. The roots of such personal power are embedded in the development of the individual, particularly his early childhood socialization. Minton's discussion of the possible developmental factors opens an entirely new perspective and suggests a number of future research possibilities.

In Chapter 4, Streufert and Fromkin review the various notions of cognitive complexity that have been presented by theorists in the last few years. Their contribution is an explicit extension of complexity theory to some of the traditional problems of attitude research. The result is a speculative series of hypotheses offered as scientifically testable. Of course the focus is upon the individual difference factor of cognitive complexity but the evidence gained by testing the hypotheses should throw some light upon fundamental factors involved in the social influence processes.

Walster and Abrahams shift the direction of the book away from individual difference factors associated with cognitive styles, information evaluation, motivational dispositions, and cognitive complexity to the relationship between the source of influence and the target individual. The degree or type of attraction between the two parties is considered to be based on certain antecedent conditions and has subsequent impact on the outcomes of social interactions. Thus, the authors move away from the research emphasis on the development of attraction to the effects of attraction (once it exists) on the social influence processes.

Michener and Suchner view social power within the context of exchange theory. After carefully explicating the basic principles they have borrowed from elementary economics, the authors examine the tactics people use to implement their interpersonal goals or to block

Preface

the tactics used by others. Four basic tactics are examined: (1) a threat may be used as a deterrent or blocking action, (2) the group may be expanded to include new members, who can then be included in powerful coalitions, (3) formation of norms limit power on the one hand, but freeze the status quo on the other, and (4) the conferral of status renders the person high in the hierarchy dependent upon those lower in the hierarchy, who, in effect, bestow the social reinforcements. These tactics are integrated within the terminology of exchange theory with the result that a number of explicit research hypotheses are generated.

Tedeschi, Schlenker, and Lindskold focus upon the source of influence and attempt to answer a series of questions: (1) Who influences? (2) Why is a particular target chosen? and (3) How do situational factors affect the source's choice of an influence mode? The utilization of the language of decision theory provides a loose integration for the chapter and serves to generate a large number of researchable questions, which for the most part have not even been asked by social psychologists.

In the final chapter, Tedeschi, Bonoma, and Schlenker attempt to provide a general theory of the social influence processes as they affect the target individual. All interpersonal interactions are interpreted in terms of tacit or explicit communications of threats, promises, warnings, or mendations. Each type of message is shown to have probability and value components, which are assumed to mediate influence as a direct effect of their product. Source characteristics of attraction, status, prestige, and esteem are assumed to bias either upwards or downwards the target individual's estimates of a message's probability component. A comprehensive review of the research literature is offered to indicate the integrating power of the theory.

We originally planned to have Israel Goldiamond write a chapter devoted to the social engineering approach developed from operant techniques. Unfortunately, Professor Goldiamond was involved in a serious automobile accident and could not complete his manuscript. We truly miss his contribution.

Each of the contributors has been patient and cooperative despite the fact that arbitrary deadlines were set and chapter titles constituted the only hint that they were given about the editor's expectations. The usual stylistic uniformities and certain space limitations provided the only other editorial restrictions upon the authors. Otherwise, each was asked to do his "own thing."

The personal debts of the editor are many since he is neither bashful nor hesitant in seeking help and advice from others. Past and present students have been the best teachers of all. They have asked the most probing questions, owe the least allegiance to the prejudices of the past, and hence offer the sharpest criticism of received answers. More importantly, they have made the hard work fun and they have forced me to develop with them. Among my "mentors" are Daniel Aranoff, Tom Bonoma, Bob Brown, Tom Faley, Jim Gahagan, Bob Helm, Joann Horai, Brooks Jones, Don Lewis, Svenn Lindskold, Dick McClain, Gordon MacLean, Chuck McKeown, Bill Pivnick, Barry Schlenker, Bob Smith, and Matt Steele.

This book owes a great debt to Bob Wesner of Aldine Publishing Company, whose confidence in the editor provided total freedom in the selection of topics, authors, and final editing. Much of the typing and tedious work of checking references was accomplished with dispatch by Terry Stapleton. The final proving grounds for my work rests upon the intelligent criticisms of my wife, Peg.

Contents

CONTRIBUTORS v

PREFACE vii

1. Power and Influence: An Introduction
   James T. Tedeschi and Thomas V. Bonoma — 1
2. The Construction of Social Reality
   Jack M. McLeod and Steven H. Chaffee — 50
3. Power and Personality
   Henry L. Minton — 100
4. Cognitive Complexity and Social Influence
   Siegfried Streufert and Howard L. Fromkin — 150
5. Interpersonal Attraction and Social Influence
   Elaine Walster and Darcy Abrahams — 197
6. The Tactical Use of Social Power
   H. Andrew Michener and Robert W. Suchner — 239
7. The Exercise of Power and Influence: The Source of Influence
   James T. Tedeschi, Barry R. Schlenker, and Svenn Lindskold — 287
8. Influence, Decision, and Compliance
   James T. Tedeschi, Thomas V. Bonoma, and Barry R. Schlenker — 346

INDEX 419

THE SOCIAL INFLUENCE PROCESSES

1

James T. Tedeschi and Thomas V. Bonoma

Power and Influence: An Introduction

In his analysis of the structure and development of scientific disciplines, Kuhn (1962) has postulated that it is possible to subdivide the development and growth of any body of scientific knowledge into two characteristic phases: the preparadigm and paradigm stages. The general trend of investigation and research in the former phase is characterized by "nearly random activity," emphasizing rival but diverse and unorganized subfields of inquiry, and a lack of theoretical or empirical direction. The paradigm stage is said to occur when the accumulation of knowledge is reorganized logically and theoretically to define a coherent, integrated new approach to the field as (1) "unprecedented enough to attract and maintain an enduring group of adherents" who are convinced of the significance of this "new look," but at the same time (2) "sufficiently open-ended to leave all sorts of problems for the redefined group of practitioners to solve" (p. 10). It is the paradigm state, then, which provides for "particular coherent traditions of scientific research."

The "state of the art" of social psychology is quite evidently in the preparadigm phase of development. Social psychological theory as such does not exist; rather, there are a multitude of competing "local" conceptualizations each of which provides some semblance of construct-data correspondence within its subfield of inquiry. The use of common sense language and trial-and-error forays into research areas suggested by disconnected, ambiguous hypotheses have produced an anarchy of concepts and empirical data. What seems to be necessary is the kind of revolution that Cubism brought

The present chapter was supported in part by Grant Number GS-27059 from the National Science Foundation to the senior author and by Grant Number ACDA-0331 from the U. S. Arms Control and Disarmament Agency (National Research Council) to the second author.

to the arts. We need to fractionate and break apart present forms to discover their fundamental properties, and then restructure them so that we can see them more profoundly and in their proper relationships.

The present chapter attempts to break down and restructure much of social psychology by analyzing the fundamental concepts of power and influence. A minimum set of influence relationships are proposed which we think exhaust the kinds of dyadic interactions persons can experience, and which may serve as the basis of a novel and coherent perspective of social psychology. An attempt will be made to relate the major research interests of contemporary social psychology to one aspect or another of the social influence processes. The intended result is an overview of the writings in this book. No attempt will be made to fill in the theoretical details, or with few exceptions, to evaluate the theoretical assumptions by an examination of empirical data. In short, we hope to provide a unified perspective of the problems of social psychology and a foundation from which a paradigm may eventually be developed.

Macht

The concept of power, or Macht, has generated a great deal of controversy among social scientists of all disciplines. One reason is that the concept includes so much of the content of interest to each discipline. A number of writers have concluded that the study of power and influence may well be coextensive with their particular field of interest. Lasswell (1966), for example, asserts that the study of politics is equivalent to the study of influence and the influential. Karl Deutsch (1966) has defined political science as the study of how compliance is obtained. Bazelon (1965) has demonstrated that economics can be conceived of as a system of threats and promises. And Homans (1958), drawing from the principles of elementary economics, views sociology as based on processes of social exchange.

One possible reason why the concept of power encompasses so much aggregate data and so many dissimilar disciplines is that it has developed from a series of intuitive analyses spanning several centuries, and with each new analyst criticizing, revising, and extending the previous analyst's position so that one more crucial class of events could be added in order to gain greater scope and utility. Such defining, refining, and redefining has been particularly intense during the last two decades, during which both Grand Theorists (Dahl, 1957; Parsons, 1967) and mathematical modelers (Harsanyi, 1962a; Shapley & Shubik, 1954) have attempted classification and summation. Often these theoretical efforts have fallen prey to the nominalistic error, which assumes that once a set of events has been named, they have been explained. Also, there is the danger of assuming that the greater the number of events which can be subsumed under the rubric "power," the greater the theoretical achievement. Perhaps the generic relationship between the words "power" and "energy" has given the social scientist the illusion that power has the same theoretical status in social science as does energy in physics.

The definitions of power to be examined include the notions of power as interpersonal causation and as coercive influence. Neither of these definitions has produced a scientific theory of power, but explication does help provide an analytical breakdown of the problems encountered in the construction of a scientific theory.

Power as Interpersonal Causation

Morgenthau (1960), in presenting a realist theory of international relations, relies upon a concept of power to analyze the problems of diplomacy, war, and other political processes. He defines power as "anything that establishes and maintains the control of man over man. Thus, power covers all social relationships which serve that end, from physical violence to the most subtle psychological ties by which one mind controls another" (p. 9). Unfortunately, Morgenthau's far-reaching definition raises difficulties in specifying a form of interpersonal interaction which is *not* power.

Robert Dahl (1957), another political scientist, has defined power in terms of interpersonal causation—the powerful person, P, has power over the weak person, W, to the extent that P causes W to do something that W would not otherwise do. More formally, Dahl's definition states that the amount of power P has over W with respect to response x is a function of (1) the probability that, when P does y, W does x, minus (2) the probability that, when P does not do y, W does x (Riker, 1964). Dahl's definition requires that P make some "power attempt" *and* that as a result of this attempt, P changes W's behavior. Dahl's own insistence that the exercise of power requires that P manifest an intention to influence W is softened somewhat by his suggestion that if W imputes an intention to P, and W shapes his behavior to meet the intentions he imputes to P, then power has been manifested. Empirically, it has been demonstrated that the attribution by W that P intends to influence him makes a considerable difference in the outcome of the interaction (Walster & Festinger, 1962).

One could speculate that when intentions are falsely attributed to

P by *W*, different consequences will follow from the interaction than if *P* actually possessed the intentions imputed to him. False or nonveridical attributions may lead to communication problems which would not result if each party was clear about the other's intentions (White, 1965). Analysis of power relationships by Dahl's requirements, then, would require that a causal connection be discovered between *P*'s behavior and *W*'s behavior, even when it is the latter's misattributions which cause the change in *W*'s behavior (Nagel, 1968). The essential point to be made is that while Dahl's definition of power represents a delimitation of Morgenthau's all-pervasive construct of control of "man over man," the inclusion by Dahl of the requirement that *P intend* to influence *W* introduces the novel but equally complex problem of determining the attributions and intentions of the participants involved before the presence or absence of power can be determined.

A number of social scientists have noted that the assertion "*P* has power over *W*" may be synonymous with "*P*'s behavior causes *W*'s behavior" (for a detailed treatment relating power to causation, see Cartwright, 1959; Dahl, 1968; Heider, 1958; Simon, 1957). As with Morgenthau's concept of "control," the concept of "cause" includes *at least* all of social psychology within its domain, and does not differentiate subsets of independent variables as functionally related to subsets of dependent events. The experience of psychology has been that such all-pervasive sovereign concepts are not only vague, but are immune to empirical evaluation (Allport, 1954). It is a truism to comment that men partially control or determine each other's behavior, but it does not further scientific understanding to label all such interpersonal causation as power. Thus, if the concept of power is to be rescued as a scientific construct, the referent events must be carefully delimited.

Power as Coercion

There has been a growing consensus among social scientists which accepts a series of qualifying conditions regarding those types of interpersonal relationships which may be considered power-relevant. Weber (1947), for example, was careful to distinguish power from other forms of social control in which cooperation is crucial. For Weber, power (Macht) is the probability that one actor in a social relationship will be in a position to carry out his own will *despite resistance*, regardless of the basis on which this probability rests. Hence, in the exercise of power, resistance and conflict in one degree or another are considered as common or probable. In this sense, Weber's conception of power implies a process of *overpowering*.

Bendix (1962) has perceptively observed that Weber's concept of power is very similar to Clausewitz' (1962) definition of war.

Harsanyi (1962a, 1962b) has applied Weber's ideas to bargaining situations. Harsanyi views most power as bilateral in nature where each person has some control over the behavior of the other. The amount of P's power in P and W's joint policy with respect to some controversial issue X is defined as the probability of P's being able to get the joint policy X_p adopted when P favors this policy and W favors a different policy X_w. Harsanyi further specifies that power relations become relevant in a social group when two or more individuals have conflicting preferences, and a decision must be made as to whose preferences will prevail. Thus, power is considered to be relevant only where social conflict exists between P and W. Parenthetically, Chein (1967) poses an interesting paradox by combining Dahl's notion that where there is no intent there is no power with Harsanyi's and Weber's contention that, where there is no resistance there is no power. The Paradox of Unconditional Omnipotence states that any person who is omnipotent must at the same time be powerless, for he can have neither occasion to want anything nor any resistance to overcome!

Both Weber and Harsanyi agree that power is relevant only under conditions of social conflict. Accepting this primary restriction, Bachrach and Baratz (1963) have limited the domain of power to an event set of even smaller size. They argue that there are three relational characteristics associated with power: power exists (1) when there is a *conflict of interests* or values between two or more persons or groups; (2) only if W actually *complies* with P's demands; and (3) only if P can *threaten to invoke sanctions*. Thus, power is the process of affecting the policies of others with the help of threatened deprivations for nonconformity with the policies recommended.

The insistence that power should only be equated with *successful coercion* leads Bachrach and Baratz to provide some hypotheses about the conditions of such success. The threat of sanction, though necessary, is not considered a sufficient condition of power. It is insufficient because the availability of sanction endows P with power over W only when certain conditions are met: (1) W must be aware of what P wants, presumably through clear communications between P and W; (2) the threatened punishment must be perceived as costly by W; (3) the cost of W's nonconformity to P's wishes should be greater than the costs of conformity; and (4) W must believe that P will probably punish nonconformity. These propositions are clearly testable, and, in fact, have been generally supported by the evidence (Tedeschi, 1970). At the same time, it is equally clear that these propositions are much too simple to explain the entire domain of power even if the limited definition provided by Bachrach and Baratz is adopted.

The actual application of sanctions for nonconformity is considered by Bachrach and Baratz to be a property of force, rather than power, a differentiation with which a number of other theorists concur (e.g., Gamson, 1968; Lasswell & Kaplan, 1950; Parsons, 1963, 1967). Force is considered to be associated with manipulation rather than with power, though potential force is the basis for the successful exercise of power. Further, Bachrach and Baratz assert that the absence of any threat of sanctions coupled with an attempt to control or change the behavior of W is what differentiates power from persuasion. Since threats imply the intent by P to procure compliant behavior from W, Bachrach and Baratz apparently agree with Dahl that without source intent there is no power relationship.

The implications for both P and W when P employs force are quite different from the employment of other forms of influence. A person's scope of decision making is radically curtailed under force. Once the bullet or missile has been fired, the target person is no longer in the position of choosing between compliance or noncompliance. As Chein (1967) has pointed out, in a power relationship it is W who chooses what to do, while in a force relationship it is P. Similarly, Simmel (1950) has noted that in power relationships, the "weak" target of influence has much more latitude of behavior than is commonly ascribed to him, for he may *choose* to comply or not comply with the source of influence. Both Tedeschi (1970) and Fisher (1969) have noted that, from an ahistorical viewpoint, punishment of W for noncompliance to a threat may be considered a nonrational action on the part of P, since the noncompliance has already occured and cannot be abrogated by subsequent punishment. Similarly, once W has complied to a contingent promise of future gain, P can gain no more by actually rewarding W; in fact, costs are incurred by P when he keeps his promises. Of course, the actual application of sanctions or rewards does establish the credibility[1] of P's threats and promises and may serve to enhance or decrease P's effective power or influence in the future, either with respect to W or to third parties. Doubt about P's actual power potential may be engendered if P does not maintain high credibility for his power

---

1. Credibility, as used here, does *not* refer to a notion of expertise or trustworthiness of the source (Hovland, Janis, & Kelley, 1953), but rather to an objective probability which may be attached to a source's influence messages. Credibility is operationally determined as the proportion of times the source follows his words with deeds. Thus, a promisor who always rewards compliance or a threatener who always punishes noncompliance has a credibility of 1.0; a source who never backs up his threats of promises with sanctions and rewards, respectively, has 0.0 credibility. See Tedeschi, Bonoma, and Brown (1971) for a more detailed discussion of credibility.

attempts; indeed, the employment of sanctions and rewards may be considered a declaration of the existence of potential power. Such displays of credibility, however, can only be effective with regard to future interactions of P and W. The exercise of force, therefore, is essentially future-oriented (Fisher, 1969; Lehman, 1969; Tedeschi, 1970).

Clearly, persons often comply with the commands and requests of others in society without the threat of punishment or the promise of reward. Indeed, the commands are often given quickly and without justification or elaboration—on an assembly line, for example, or in the middle of a surgical operation. The compliant or conforming individual does as requested because he feels he *ought* to do so. Thus, as both Gamson (1968) and Goffman (1963) have noted, legitimacy is vested in the office or socially prescribed role, and not in the man serving the office. The study of authority structures is essentially a sociological problem, but the establishment of legitimacy is a social psychological process.

Apparently a consensus has been growing among social theorists that *power* refers to the threat of sanctions, *force* refers to the applications of sanctions for nonconformity, and *authority* refers to compliance based on the target's perception of the legitimacy of the request. The parties in a power relationship are believed to have different preferences for the outcomes of interdependent behaviors, though this condition is not necessary for an authority relationship. Some theorists suggest that *influence* is the more general concept, subsuming within this category authority, power, and force in order of decreasing generality. Whether P intends to influence W, or whether W must be aware of P's intent to influence are essentially philosophical questions of exclusion or inclusion regarding the boundaries of the field of power and influence, but which do not mitigate the necessity of exploring all such possibilities since they do occur among interacting individuals.

Once basic conceptual lines are drawn, questions of measurement arise. Dahl (1968) has listed some parameters of interest to anyone studying social power. Questions of social structure and social change are related to the distribution of power—how many Ps and Ws there are, who are they, where are they, how many Ws does P control and who are they, and how does this structure and distribution change over time? Such sociological inquiries are beyond the scope of the present discussion. More pertinent are questions which focus upon dimensions important for measuring power as indicated by W's responses. Questions raised by Dahl include: (1) what is the range or scope of P's power over W; that is, what class of W's activities are controlled by P; (2) with what probability will W comply to P's influence attempt; (3) what is the amount of change in W's position, attitudes, or psychological state; (4) with what speed or latency does W change; and (5) what is the reduction in the size or set of outcomes or behaviors available to W? Intuitively, it would be expected that these factors would be highly intercorrelated, and that they may be alternative operationalizations of the same concept. Learning theorists (cf. Kimble, 1961) have demonstrated that such response properties as probability, latency, and magnitude are positively interrelated as long as the responses measured occur under the same conditions (e.g., a straight-alley runway). The experience of learning theorists implies that one should not expect such correlations between the disparate conditions of power, authority, force, and other forms of influence.

Conclusion

The arguments concerning the "correct" definition of power are *not* scientific ones, and power is not a scientific construct. Though an occasional commentator has made the nominalistic error in the use of the power label, more often the definitional attempts reviewed constitute prescientific (preparadigmatic) efforts to carve out a set of events amenable to study.

Social power has been defined grossly as coextensive with all interpersonal causation (social interactions). Other definitions attempt to delimit the set of interpersonal events that would be subsumed under the label. Arguments have arisen regarding whether power is potential or actual influence (or both), whether power should be conceived as separate from force, whether conflict is a necessary condition for the relationship of power, and whether the source must affect the target intentionally.

While it is clear that *all* of social psychology cannot profitably be conceived of as the study of social power, it is equally clear that a significant portion of the field of inquiry may be considered as one or another aspect of the social influence processes. The remainder of the chapter attempts to (1) identify a limited number of different influence *means* which together are considered as important basic forms of social interactions; and (2) examine the nature of *source* and *target characteristics* as these modify the basic influence interactions.

The Means of Influence

To focus upon the means by which one person can influence another is tantamount to examining all of the basic types of social

Power and Influence: An Introduction

interactions which can take place. It is not easy to separate the means of influence from the conditions of their success in gaining the source's objectives, nor indeed from the source himself, since the latter's role position, relationship to the target, and other characteristics may themselves produce the conditions of successful influence and help determine the means employed. However, at least ideally, several different means of influence may be delineated.

A source may attempt to utilize information to convince the target that it would benefit the latter to carry out certain actions or to hold certain attitudes, or that the target ought to change his attitudes. Alternatively, as we have already seen, a source may threaten the target with punishments, and if this power attempt fails, may resort to force as a means of changing the target's other behaviors. Similarly, the source might issue promises of reward to the target, and actually provide these rewards when certain target attitudes are expressed or responses emitted. All of these influence means are used intentionally, though not necessarily consciously, by the source.

Separate categories of influence may be used to indicate that the source does not intend to influence the target, but nevertheless does so. The source may serve as a model for the imitative responses of a target individual, and the source may neither intend such influence nor be aware of it;[2] in fact, the source may not even be aware of the target's existence. For instance, a movie star may be the source of certain gestures, fashions, or other behaviors without knowing anything about the fan who has performed the imitative responses. Similarly, the mere presence of a person may facilitate or amplify responses—social contagion. Thus, the influence processes of modeling and contagion may not involve intent on the part of the source even though he has been a causative agent in determining the behavior of another individual.

The source may adopt a strategy calculated to prevent the target from becoming aware of the influence relationship. Mills (1956) has referred to such clandestine attempts at influence as manipulation. Manipulatory techniques may be discovered by the target without the source's awareness that he has been found out. The critical feature of manipulatory influence attempts is that the source intends to keep the target "in the dark" about the nature of their relationship and believes that the target is unaware of the source's intentions. The manner with which information and reinforcements are utilized will be significantly affected by whether influence is intended to be open and aboveboard or clandestine and manipu-

---

2. Of course, the source may *both* fully intend and be aware of his modeling effects on the target. In such cases, the influence mode would probably fall into the class of techniques termed manipulation, discussed below.

latory. Deliberate refusal to make decisions—a type of implicit veto power over new initiatives and involving a kind of psychology of nondecision-making (Bachrach & Baratz, 1963; Fisher, 1969)—may also have far-reaching consequences and is therefore listed as an influence technique. However, it must be established that the nondecision was deliberate and was intended to bring about a certain kind of change in attitude or behavior in a referent person.

Finally, much social interaction takes the form of curiosity behavior. The individual makes forays into his social environment to reconnoiter, probe, and discover who has what he values, who will offer resistance to influence, and hence who would be the best person to try to influence. Little will be said about probes in this chapter, although such activities are undoubtedly important to the study of social influence.

Figure 1.1 presents the minimum set of influence processes discussed above.[3] Each of these processes will be considered in more detail and their interrelationships explored. We will also attempt to demonstrate that contemporary research areas in social psychology significantly correspond to the modes of influence shown in Figure 1.1.

Deterrence, Inducements, Persuasion, and Activation of Commitments

Parsons (1963) has characterized influence as "ways of getting results in interaction." The four ways offered by Parsons are deterrence, inducements, persuasion, and activation of commitments. Deterrence includes power and force, threats and negative sanctions. Inducements are based on positive social exchanges and include promises and rewards as mediators of target compliance. Persuasion constitutes an attempt to change or restructure the goals or attitudes of the target individual through the use of argument, propaganda, or special knowledge, but not through the employment of either deterrence or inducements. Activation of commitments involves an appeal to normative values in order to cause a reassessment by the target of what he *ought* to do in a given situation. As with the process of persuasion, successful activation of commitments is presumed to be a pure information effect and does not require the supportive use of deterrence or inducements.

Inducements involve the addition of advantages to the situation for W or the promise to do so, regardless of the resources actually

---

3. The case in which the target imputes desires to the source and then acts in conformity to his own (the target's) anticipations (cf. Friedrich, 1963) will not be considered here as a form of social influence, since no "connection" takes place between the alleged source and the target.

Power and Influence: An Introduction 11

used, while persuasion may be considered a case of exchange in which *P* maintains control of the resource being used. Thus, persuasion involves some change in the minds of the targets without adding anything new (such as rewards and punishments) to their situation. Successful persuasion leads *W* to prefer the outcomes *P* wants *W* to prefer.

Each of these influence processes has drawn considerable empirical interest. The study of threats and promises is becoming a major interest of scientists from a number of disciplines (cf. Tedeschi, 1970). Attitude formation and change, concerns of those focusing upon the process of persuasion, have long held the interest of social psychologists.

A question may be raised regarding the existence of research concerned with the activation of commitments. However, Berkowitz and Daniels (1963, 1964) have shown that persons will perform actions based on the needs and dependencies of others. Schopler and Bateson (1965) have argued that self-reference in terms of "powerlessness" or dependency may in fact be the basis of an individual's

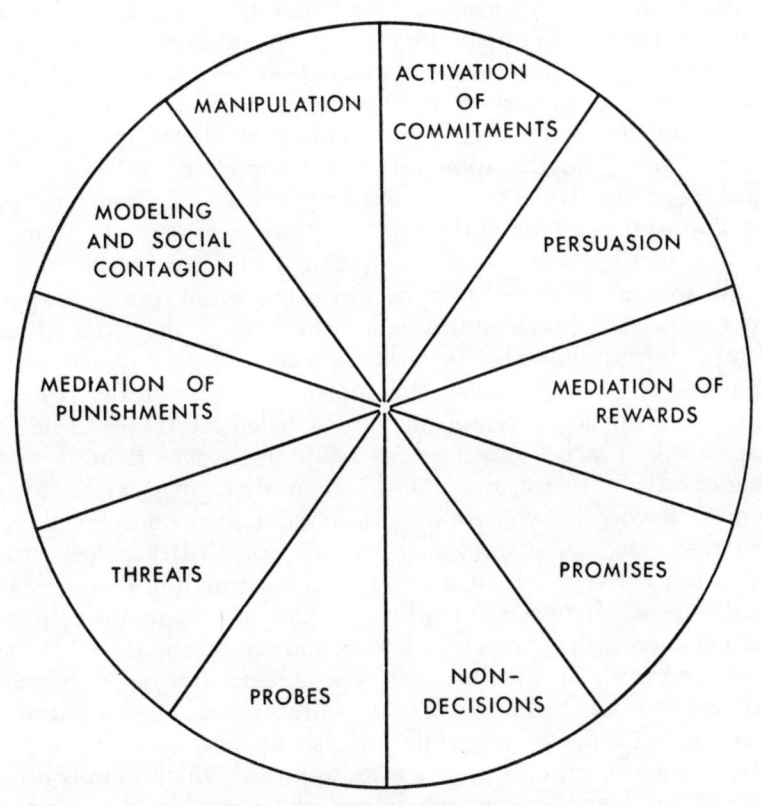

Figure 1:1

power. Hence, a beggar can appeal to the conscience of a rich man in order to gain sufficient funds for a cup of coffee. Conversely, where social responsibility is not an important norm or where anonymity or diffusion of responsibility exists, the individual finds that the power of dependence evaporates (Latané & Darley, 1968). Recent evidence indicates that the power of dependence may derive from the activation of commitments, related to the notion of the "good samaritan" (Piliavin, Rodin, & Piliavin, 1969). Support for the idea that behavior can be activated on the basis of "oughtness" is provided by Collins and Raven (1969), who speculate that helping a dependent individual may actually derive from reciprocity for past help or be rendered in the expectation of future assistance or exchange. Either one of these latter explanations rests at least partially on normative commitments; in the one case to debts owed and in the other to trusting that the other person will do as he ought in repaying his debts.

Although areas of research generally correspond to Parsons' types of influence, close examination does raise some questions about their purity. Fisher (1969) has suggested that threats seldom are transmitted without accompanying offers of reward for compliance. Gamson (1968) notes that the distinction between influence types may be more a matter of the phenomenological experience of the target than the tactics used by the source. He illustrates his point by focusing upon social approval and disapproval as rewards and punishments available for use as power resources. Gamson suggests that approval may be influential for two reasons: (1) it may be regarded by the target as a tacit promise of future rewards, and/or (2) the source's approval may be intrinsically rewarding. If approval is perceived as a tacit promise by the target, then the influence attempt corresponds closely with Parsons' category of inducement; but if the target experiences the approval as intrinsically rewarding, then the influence attempt may be labeled persuasion. Similarly, disapproval may be perceived as an implicit threat, or it may be experienced as intrinsically punishing. In the former case, deterrence (Gamson's word is "constraint") is the tactic being employed, and in the latter case, persuasion. Blau (1964, pp. 66 ff.) makes a similar distinction between extrinsic and intrinsic attraction. Blau notes that the difference between intrinsic and extrinsic attraction "parallels that between artistic creation and economic production." He views social approval in extrinsic attraction relations as a bargaining resource, to be promised as an inducement or its withdrawal threatened as a deterrent, while intrinsic attraction, when employed in the influence processes, generates approval which entails no costs to P and no obligations to provide material rewards and punishments.

Although verbal discriminations are sometimes tedious and nonproductive, at other times they can be important for reconceptualizing events or for explaining what appear to be contradictory empirical results. Gamson's distinction between a warning and a threat may be important for both reasons. He views a warning as an act of persuasion, and a threat as an act of deterrence. In the former, the source has no control over whether the dire consequences will occur. For a message to be a threat, on the other hand, the source *must* be the manipulator of the disadvantages, not merely the predictor of them.

Tedeschi (1970) has carried the analysis somewhat further. Finding no word in the dictionary to catch the meaning of the event, Tedeschi coined the term "mendation" to indicate an influencer's positive prediction of a contingency between a target's behavior and a favorable outcome, where the outcome is not controlled or affected by the source of influence. A mendation is to a promise as a warning is to a threat.

Clearly, warnings and mendations are psychologically more complicated for a target than are threats and promises. The target must consider the intentions and capabilities of the source, and whether in fact the source does have influence over the contingency he points out, whether the source is deliberately using deception, whether in fact the contingency is probable, and the magnitude of the consequences. Furthermore, the target must also consider the intentions, capability, and influenceability of a third party, if the latter controls the administration of the reward or punishment specified in the mendation or warning. However, from the source's point of view, warnings and mendations may be simpler than threats and promises, since with the employment of the former no obligation or responsibility rests with the source except perhaps as a monitor of events and an accurate perceiver of the contingencies involved. There may be some difficulties for the source in terms of making his intentions clear because of the necessity of disconnecting his own actions from the contingencies involved in a warning or mendation. On the other hand, the source might want to connect his actions to the outcomes of a mendation to convert environmental contingencies into perceived inducements. Then, too, it may be to the source's advantage to cause the target of the influence message to believe that a threat is really a warning, that *P*'s actions are beyond his own control or are forced by the environment. An example of this kind of thinking may be seen in the advocation of some deterrence theorists that the Pentagon automate a trip-wire nuclear retaliatory strike. The basis of this suggestion is that the credibility of a second-strike would be seen to be beyond human will or intentions and retaliation would be certain to occur should the enemy be the first to attack. Similarly, it is a common tactic of many trial lawyers to attempt to convert human intentions into excusable conditions under the law (*Mens rea*); thus, it is not uncommon, and often expected in cases involving capital punishment, to be faced with arguments of justifiable homicide, temporary insanity, involuntary manslaughter, etc.

Manipulation

It is possible to identify three basic concerns of psychologists interested in the techniques of behavior modification: (1) the manipulation of the cues affecting the person's specific decisions; (2) control of the environment and hence the context of behavior; and (3) the direct modification of behavior. We will examine each of these techniques separately.

1. Decision Theory. Influence may be gained, according to March (1955; 1957) indirectly and without regard to reinforcements. If P is aware that a particular stimulus or cue reliably elicits response x from W, then P can control response W_x by controlling the discriminative stimulus. In effect, by gaining control over the discriminable stimuli, P narrows the range of possible outcomes which W may attain. This type of cue-control depends upon P's ability to predict W's behavior.

P can also gain control over the behavior of W by manipulating the elements of decision, the values of each element, and the probability connections between the elements. For March, there are four basic means which can be employed for influence purposes. Threats of punishment or promises of reward, along with simple causal descriptions of the environment (i.e., warnings and mendations) have the effect of changing the probability connections between the elements of decision. For example, threatening to deprive a teenager of the use of the family car over the weekend if he does not perform his chores may change his expectancies relating mowing the lawn to having a good time Friday evening. The values attached to the elements may also be manipulated by P either by changing the information relevant to the elements (e.g., manipulating the appraised value of a diamond ring), or by affecting W's states of deprivation. Studies by Aronson and Carlsmith (1962), Turner and Wright (1965), and Freedman (1965) have all shown that a mild threat of punishment leads children to devalue an attractive but forbidden toy. Similarly, the risky-shift phenomenon may be due to persons who are greater risk-takers, more persuasive and influential in the group (Kelley & Thibaut, 1969), and who thus change the expectancies regarding a group decision for the other group members.

March's theory of influence demonstrates a sensitivity to learning theory, and, although a different language is employed (i.e., individual psychology rather than social psychology), his views are not unlike those already discussed. One consequence of March's analysis is to re-emphasize that influence may occur without W's awareness. Those who are unaware they are being influenced are in no position to offer resistance. In addition, controlled ignorance and secrecy serve as bases of power because they limit the perceived alternatives and affect the values of the decision-maker.

2. *Environmental Control.* Roundabout controls refer to the manipulation of general aspects of the environment, which in turn produce general behavioral effects (Dahl & Lindblom, 1953). Unlike March's more specific notion of controlling clearly predictable and identifiable responses through the control of particular discriminable stimuli, roundabout controls refer to more total effects on the individual of a more unpredictable character. The goals of roundabout control include affecting W's personality, social roles or his "agenda" of decisions. For example, a decision by the Federal Reserve Board to tighten the money supply by increasing the interest rate on loans may be made to fight inflation. One consequence of such a decision is ordinarily an increase in unemployment rates. Hence, a decision can be deliberately made that will have unknown effects upon the lives of a rather sizable group of people. Those who make the decision are aware that unemployment rates will increase but they do not know specifically who will be affected. Those who are affected are often not aware that a deliberate decision was made which caused their unemployment.

Bachrach and Baratz (1963) describe a type of environmental control which they term the "psychology of nondecision-making." This means that within an organization or status hierarchy of any kind, subordinates usually have the "less important" jobs of determining whom the superior will see, what material will reach his desk, what items will be considered on the agenda of a meeting, etc. Bachrach and Baratz aptly point out that such control over the items which do or do not reach the decision-making stage is a potent form of influence indeed, often resulting in greater control by the subordinate than by the superior.

When P has the ability to control critical aspects of W's environment in such a way that the new environment will bring about a desired change in W's behavior, then P has "ecological" control over W. Cartwright's (1965) definition is sufficiently ambiguous to allow inclusion of both March's notion of controlling discriminable stimuli and Dahl and Lindblom's concept of roundabout control. It is clear from Cartwright's examples that he intends to relate influence to the notion of behavior settings (Cartwright & Zander, 1968, p. 222; Wright & Barker, 1949). Public places have been categorized according to the kinds of behaviors they typically elicit from the great majority of persons who enter them. A behavior setting is usually organized around behavior objects, which elicit the behaviors for that setting. If one can contrive a public event, such as a boy scout camping trip or a PTA meeting, or can provide behavior objects such as a toy or a movie projector, then one gains control over the behaviors of those who are enveloped within that behavior setting.

The study of behavior settings does have some interesting implications for the general understanding of influence relationships. Barker and Wright's investigations have indicated that there are more behavior settings per capita in the United States than in Great Britain, and that this difference exists across all age levels of the population. Barker (1965) has concluded that a critical factor about the ecological environment in America is the paucity of people available to participate in the nation's numerous behavior settings. One of the principles relevant to behavior settings is that each one requires an optimal number of participants; if there are too few, each person must assume a correspondingly greater number of functions within each setting. For example, it has been found that churches with small congregations have proportionately more participation per member and require far more activity time per member than do churches with large congregations. If Barker is correct about the small ratio of people to settings in the United States, then it follows that Americans should actually have more opportunity to exercise influence, more reason to exercise influence, and should also be more influenced than their British counterparts.

Ecological control considerations also raise questions about the constraints which act upon all decision makers, whatever their status or position. Rose (1967) has called attention to several such constraints: (1) large-scale historical forces, often of an economic or technological character, which limit and push any society in ways beyond the control of human intentions. These forces include geography, technology, economic organization, and the basic institutions of the family and religion. The operation of such pervasive forces reminds one of Halle's (1965) comment that diplomacy is like down a rapids in a canoe: one does not consider controlling the ion of the canoe for it takes all one's effort just to keep it right . In this context, Tedeschi (1966) has labeled the myth that trols his environment, rather than vice versa, the Principle of

Sisyphus—to the degree that man does gain control over one phase of his environment, he tends to lose control over another. (2) Cultural values are subject only to limited manipulation. The everyday norms of mutual expectations set limits on rational behavior despite the considerable ability of some articulate spokesmen to rationalize and/or distort those rules and ideals for their own purposes. (3) Finally, the countervailing power of competing groups and individuals functions in such a manner that a decision maker's range of alternatives is often drastically limited. The sum of these three constraints considerably reduces the area of decision even for the President of the United States, which might otherwise be based on his ideological predilections or personal idiosyncrasies (Smith, 1962).

3. Control over Behavior. Skinner (1938, 1950) has been relentless in his pursuit of techniques for manipulating behavior via reinforcements and punishments. Skinner views the entire domain of psychology in terms of power or the "control" of behavior. Aversive stimulation as a technique for manipulating behavior involves providing a negative reinforcement prior to the occasion for the target's individual compliant operant, with the promise that the aversive stimulus will be removed when the correct response is forthcoming. This form of control has been referred to as "distress" or "promise of relief" by A. Kuhn (1963). The technique of deprivation lowers the target's resistance to influence, while the technique of satiation increases resistance with regard to a particular reinforcer.

Secondary reinforcement principles could be used to explain the acquisition of source factors related to successful influence, such as attraction. In a manner similar to Parsons' activation of commitments, the source of influence might attempt to establish emotional predispositions toward himself or the desired action so that the target will be more likely to comply. Perhaps the most obvious example of this sort of manipulation is the experimental technique of "shaping" or successive approximations, in which the experimental animal is predisposed to make the correct operant response through a process of successively more stringent reward contingencies with regard to the final desired behavior. The entire social reinforcement literature can thus be viewed as part and parcel of the study of influence and power (Tedeschi & O'Donovan, 1971). Further, by the direct manipulation of stimuli a particular behavior might be eliminated by eliciting incompatible responses, a form of inhibition not unlike the activation of commitments (Marwell & Schmitt, 1967). It can be seen that Skinner is much more interested in *how* to go about gaining compliance than in *why* people (or rats, for that matter) comply to influence.

Perhaps more applicable for influencing human behavior, the techniques of behavior therapy (Bandura & Walters, 1963) and desensitization therapy (Wolpe, 1958) represent rather direct transformations of classical and operant conditioning paradigms. Bandura and Walters postulate several methods of producing behavioral change in humans through the employment of Skinner's operant conditioning procedures. The extinction of undesirable behaviors (Ayllon & Michael, 1959; Williams, 1959), the acquisition of normal behavior patterns in socially deficient subjects through reward training (King, Armitage, & Tilton, 1960), and the acquisition of responses through the observation of a model's behavior (Bandura, Ross, & Ross, 1963a, 1963b, 1963c; Slavson, 1950a, 1950b) are methods by which the learning and performance of behaviors can be influenced by manipulation of the reinforcements contingent upon W's responses. For example, Ferster (1961) has demonstrated that, contrary to usual diagnoses, autistic children have no serious learning decrements and can respond to generalized conditioned reinforcers in reward training. Similarly, Dittes (1957a, 1957b) has presented experimental evidence that favorable outcomes in conventional interview therapy sessions may be due to the therapist's extinguishing the client's anxiety.

Desensitization therapy may be seen as a special case of Bandura and Walter's fourth technique of behavior modification, counterconditioning. Counterconditioning "involves eliciting in the presence of fear-arousing stimuli responses that are incompatible with anxiety or fear reaction; through the classical conditioning of these incompatible responses to fear-arousing cues, anxiety is eliminated or reduced" (Bandura & Walters, 1963, p. 231-232). Employing this technique with individuals suffering from severe fears or anxieties, Wolpe (1958) first compiles a list of stimuli to which the client reacts with increasing degrees of anxiety. Clients are subsequently hypnotized and given relaxation suggestions.⁴ When thoroughly relaxed, the client is asked to imagine the first item on the anxiety-arousing list. If relaxation remains unimpaired, the therapist moves on to the next item on the list, until all items which were originally fear producing are reconditioned to evoke feelings of relaxation. Even with a limited number of therapy sessions Wolpe has been able to achieve significant and stable reductions of fear reactions through the ~yment of desensitization techniques. Both Bandura and Wald Lazarus (1960) report additional evidence regarding the of counterconditioning procedures with both adults and

longer uses the technique of hypnosis.

Conclusion

Several basic influence means have been specified and divided into two major classes: (1) those means employed by a source to change a target's behavior or attitudes in an intentional and undisguised effort to exercise *control*, and (2) those tactics employed by the source to *manipulate* the target's behavior, without the latter's awareness of the influence relationship. The former class includes the Parsonian categories of inducements, deterrence, persuasion (i.e., warnings and mendations), and activation of commitments, while the manipulatory modes include the manipulation of decision criteria, environmental control, and direct conditioning techniques.

Seldom will one influence mode be used to the exclusion of other modes. Persuasion tactics meant to convey the source's resolve are likely to accompany his threats and promises; additional information may be utilized for the purposes of asserting the moral "rightness" of the source's requests and actions. However, a single influence tactic will usually dominate a given social interaction. Which mode is emphasized often depends upon the characteristics of the source of influence.

Source Characteristics and Social Influence

If a source chooses to use threats as a means of influence in lieu of other more cooperative tactics available to him, it is likely that the target will perceive P's intentions as exploitative or hostile, no matter who the source is or what the source is like (Nardin, 1968). However, even when the means employed by the source are most determinative of the target's reactions, the holistic nature of the interaction renders it highly probable that P's characteristics will, in some measure, affect W's reactions. Hence, as compared with a liked threatener, a disliked threatener may be perceived as more likely to enforce his threats, perhaps because he is seen as more hostile (Schlenker et al., 1970).

The predilection for defining power or influence as a *capacity* of the source stems from observations like those of DeKadt (1965) that power can be directly perceived and measured with respect to the resources, values, or characteristics which contribute to the capacity of persons or groups to affect the behavior of others. Simon (1957) has suggested that if we could measure the magnitude of the influence base, we could infer from this the magnitude of influence. For example, if wealth is the principal influence base in a particular situation, then in that situation influence should be indirectly measurable by an index of monetary resources. The assumption that capacity is related in a one-to-one fashion to actual influence has led some to adopt a Marxist interpretation of a power elite in America (Domhoff,1967; Lundburg, 1968; Mills, 1956). Schulze (1958), however, warns against the assumption of "any neat, constant, and direct relationship between *power as potential for determinative action and power as determinative of action, itself*" (p. 9).

The literature on persuasion and attitude change (Cohen, 1964; Hovland, Janis, & Kelley, 1953; McGuire, 1969) makes it evident that there is more to the capacity of a source than his material possessions. The value position of the source may constitute an important part of his influence base. Values may be considered to be commodities useable in exchange, as in Homans' (1961) theory of social behavior. Values may be used by P to reinforce a desired behavior of W. Insofar as a value succeeds in producing desired behaviors, of course, influence has occurred, and the base of influence is the relevant value dimension. Any condition which gives P influence potential is likely to become a positive value for P. Extending this hypothesis, it might be predicted that any condition which gives influence potential to P would similarly become a positive value for W. This latter hypothesis is consistent with the arguments of Cartwright (1959) and Blau (1964) that where the base of P's influence is irrelevant to the needs of W, there can be no influence of P over W. Hence, if P possessed only wealth as an influence base, and W did not evaluate money positively or had values preventing him from accepting bribes, P would be unable to influence W's behavior. Two conditions, then, must be met if something is to be viewed as a resource: (1) the commodity or attribute must be controlled or possessed by the source; and (2) the source must be able to bring the commodity to bear on the target in interaction.

A whole range of personal characteristics may be relevant to the exercise of influence, even when the person makes decisions as a representative of a group, organization, or nation. Further, cultural factors may be important in determining which of these source characteristics will function as influence bases. One might expect, for instance, that a society emphasizing worldly success will differ from one emphasizing asceticism and a "sackcloth and ashes" philosophy. Considering the patterns of influence within an American community, Dahl (1961) includes as bases of influence the distribution of wealth, social standing, popularity, control over jobs and information, and access to the legal apparatus. It may be seen that each of these bases ensures that the individuals possessing them achieve personal worldly success, perhaps reflecting a basic American cultural orientation. In any case, for Dahl, potential influence is synonymous with the control of resources, a conception that concentrates on the potency and activism of the source and the passivity or lack of contribution to the process by the target.

Lasswell and Kaplan (1950) developed an early and still very viable exchange theory of influence. They viewed social interactions as controlled through the mediation of values by one party for another, and speculated that there are eight basic values which can be subdivided into two groups of four. Those values which emphasize deference or ascribed position are power, respect, rectitude, and affection; those that deal with welfare include wealth, well-being, skill, and enlightenment. Whenever P has influence over W, P enjoys a favorable position with respect to some value, and by his actions can increase or decrease the value position of W. The amount and type of these values which P controls for W serves as the basis of P's power over W, and are termed "base values." Those of P's own values which W can be induced to increase by his actions or by transfer of his possessions in exchange for P's base values are referred to as "scope values." Base values are exchanged for scope values. Each of the eight basic values may be useful in improving P's position regarding the other values; this conclusion has received empirical support in studies of status congruence (Sampson, 1969). The implication is that preferred outcomes, once attained, have the value of resources. Hence, the conclusion of Tin Pan Alley in the less affluent Thirties has found theoretical expression: "the rich get richer and the poor get poorer."

Lasswell and Kaplan had an almost immediate influence upon the group of social psychologists at Yale University. Hovland and his colleagues began systematically to study source credibility effects in the persuasion process. At the end of the Fifties, a typology of the bases of social power was devised by French and Raven (1959) which has had important effects on subsequent psychological interest in the influence processes. French and Raven discuss the influence processes from the viewpoint of the target; however, their typology is based most heavily on source characteristics. Their postulated bases of power included information influence, the expertise and legitimacy of the source, the attraction for the source, and the amount of reward and punishment power possessed by the source.

Source-Esteem

French and Raven have classified all influence as either socially dependent or independent of the source.[5] Informational influence, a

---

5. To avoid confusion, the concept of source esteem will be employed in place of source credibility or source expertise. In this context, source esteem denotes much the same combination of source expertise and trustworthiness as does Hovland, Janis and Kelley's (1953) notion of credibility.

source-independent base of social power, may be best described as a pure form of Parsons' category of persuasion. Exercise of informational influence results in a change in W's cognitive structure. As Raven (1965) has noted, in information influence, "it is the content of the communication that is important, not the nature of the influencing agent" (p. 372). However, Raven's statement is incorrect to the degree that P must first gain access to W before attempting influence. Obviously, P's status, expertise, and style of communication will, to a large extent, determine whether or not W will expose himself to P's influence attempt.

Drawing from Heider (1958), Kelley (1967) and Kelley and Thibaut (1969) have postulated an individual need for attribution stability. Persons infer that the behaviors of others are guided by motives. These attributions allow the individual to perceive others as rather stable and illustrate the Gestalt principle of constancy in social perception. High stability of attribution would characterize a person who is quite capable of discriminating between social entities and yet capable of perceiving any given person as highly invariable and constant. W is considered to be informationally dependent on P if the latter can raise W's stability of attribution about the intentions of others more than alternative source of information. Kelley and Thibaut state that information dependence may be defined objectively, in terms of actual information effects on W's attribution stability, or subjectively, in terms of either experienced or anticipated effects.

Attribution instability and consequent susceptibility to influence is considered to be a product of the same factors which Schein (1958) viewed as causing the "unfreezing" of attitudes and beliefs: lack of social support, poor or ambiguous information, factors related to low self-confidence, etc. P's influence effectiveness may derive from the confidence and strength associated with his style of presentation, demonstrated expertise, information provided about social consensus, or information provided W for attribution stability through the content of P's communications.

The generally accepted definition of social reality is often the product of a vigorous power struggle over the control of information. A person who has a gatekeeper function in the flow of communications has an important persuasion resource: he can define the nature of issues and alternatives. Carl Schmitt, the famous Nazi constitutional lawyer, has stated this principle most succinctly—"sovereign is he who decides the emergency situation." The implication is that analyses of the generally accepted picture of reality (survey research) or of communication flows could reveal important clues about who has power in society (Deutsch, 1966). Societies may be so structured that the same interlocked institutions or groups (elites) tend to control both the flow of information and the allocation of rewards and punishments. Studies in which both these controls were rather stringent include those made of the brainwashing of American POW's in Korea, and of the conditions in convents, monasteries, and military academies. Schein, Schneier, and Barker (1961) have adopted the term "coercive persuasion" to emphasize the complete control that influence agents may have over both communications and the administration of rewards and punishments.

Schattschneider (1960) argues that the definition of alternatives is the supreme instrument of power, while Lasswell (1966) views the giving and receiving of orientation as the fundamental characteristic of the leader-follower relationship. At its most basic level, control over information constitutes control over the target's focus of attention. As Lasswell puts it: "Leaders are signal towers who provide the cues that release the predispositions of those involved" (p. 215). Information control may be considered as synonymous with authority. The individual possessing legitimate authority has achieved the right to prescribe for targets what *is*, as well as what ought to be.

Social psychologists have often demonstrated that people are persuaded by a communication not because of its compelling logic or empirical grounds but because the communicator is considered prestigious. Asch (1948) argued that prestige suggestion was effective not because of irrational considerations such as dulling of the critical faculties (Bowden, Caldwell, & West, 1934), but rather was due to a reinterpretation of the *message* by the target as a function of the identification of the source. Hovland, Janis, and Kelley (1953) postulated two source factors that determine the extent to which information is accepted by the target: (1) the expertise of the source, and (2) the trustworthiness of the source. A source is considered an expert to the degree that the target accepts the source's messages as containing valid content. A source is considered trustworthy to the extent that the target perceives that the intent of the source is to communicate the most valid message: the source is considered to be merely a mediator of fact. Expertise may be inferred because the source has special training or experience, education, history of success in problem solution, or from general attributes such as age, position, seniority, or social background. Trustworthiness is directly related to the perception by the target of the source's intentions. If the communicator is perceived as having a vested interest in influencing the target, the latter will presumably not trust the former. Both expertise and trustworthiness contribute to source esteem.

A number of interesting hypotheses have been derived from this simple framework. One is that the delivery of a communication by a source which is blatantly against his own interests may raise the esteem, and thus the effectiveness, of the source's influence attempt (Walster, Aronson, & Abrahams, 1966). Studies of source esteem have been limited to the influence process of persuasion, though it is clear that research related to the use of activation of commitments by priests or educators, the use of threats by police or military strategists, and the use of inducements by parents and politicians could be quite interesting.

French and Raven (1959) viewed expertise as an important base of social power. The degree of power derived from expertise, or expert power, that P has depends upon how much knowledge or ability W attributes to P, the amount of knowledge which W perceives himself as possessing, and the relevance of the knowledge to the object being judged or the problem being solved. To distinguish expert power from informational influence, Raven (1965) has used the example of a student-teacher relation. If a student accepts a teacher's advice in applying a particular formula to solve a mathematics problem and does so because of an understanding of why the solution is applicable, informational influence has occurred. But if the student accepts the formula because the teacher "knows best," then expert power is the basis of influence. The more expert power W attributes to P, the more likely it is that W will use P as a source of information about which values, goals, beliefs, or behaviors W should adopt.

Exchange theorists (Blau, 1964; Homans, 1961) have postulated that expert influence may be especially vulnerable to counter-influence or balancing tactics employed by W. If approval is exchanged for help and the conferral of approval implies inferiority on the part of the grantor, then the exchange requires that W perform deferent, status-conferring behaviors in relation to P. Approval and deference may act as rewards for P, who then becomes reciprocally dependent upon W for them. Hence, P's power advantage, which is gained through his special knowledge or skills (or at least the perception that P has such expertise), is counterbalanced by W's ability to produce social reinforcements for P. The result is mutual behavior control and the apparent paradox that leaders are often the most conforming members of a group (Homans, 1961).

Referent Power

Referent power (sometimes referred to as attraction power) stems from W's wish to maintain similiarity with P, and is equivalent to

Deutsch and Gerard's (1955) notion of normative influence, Thibaut and Strickland's (1956) concept of group set, and Kelman's (1961) mechanism of identification. The influence base paralleling referent power is perhaps most clearly illustrated by the process of identification, and corresponds to an internalization of values, attitudes, and behaviors constituting compliance to influence attempts from a value-congruent rather than sanction-mediated basis. Raven (1965) notes that many of the studies of balance, congruence, or dissonance may be reinterpreted as instances of referent influence. The Festinger and Hutte (1954) finding that an individual who discovers that two persons he likes dislike one another may reject one or both of them can be seen as taking on the attitudes of the strongest referent person or the attitudes of both referent persons. If his friends like one another, the individual is more apt to continue his friendly relations with each of them.

Festinger's (1954) theory of social comparison is also relevant to considerations of referent power. Festinger postulates that individuals have a need to evaluate their beliefs about themselves, and about the nature of social reality. Since social reality (e.g., the opinions, values, and beliefs of others) must have some basis upon which its validity rests, and since objective standards for assessing this validity are lacking, Festinger proposes that "an opinion, a belief, an attitude is 'correct,' 'valid,' and 'proper' to the extent that it is anchored in a group of people with similar beliefs, opinions and attitudes" (p. 272). Consensual validation requires that W accept some individual or group as a referent.

Bandura (1965) and Bandura and Walters (1963) propose an alternative approach to the study of referent power. They present evidence for a "no-trial" learning theory in which new responses may be learned simply from observation of the behavior of a model. It appears that such socially-mediated responses as aggression (Bandura, 1962), dependency behavior (Radke-Yarrow, Trager, & Miller, 1952) and opinions and attitudes, including racial prejudice (cf. Bandura & Walters, 1963) may be acquired by subjects simply through the observance of these behaviors in models. Although Bandura and Walters are careful to note that the selection of a model may be based upon source characteristics, such as P's height (Miller & Dollard, 1941), they also insist that the acquisition of observed responses may be accounted for in strict contiguity terms, and without the additional assumption of a prior attraction or comparison relationship between P and W. However, the subsequent *performance* of these learned responses by W is presumed to depend to a large extent upon the nature of the outcomes (rewards and punishments) received by the model for his behavior. Bandura and Walters believe that theories of imitation, identification, and attraction power may be most parsimoniously explained by contiguity theory. The issue for Bandura and Walters, then, is whether the modeling effect occurs independently of attraction between P and W and whether learning occurs without the use of rewards and punishments. If Bandura's interpretation is correct, attraction may be the consequence of modeling behavior, rather then its cause.

In a closely related area of research, Lippitt, Polansky, Redl, and Rosen (1952) have proposed the term "behavioral contagion" to refer to changes in W's attitudes, beliefs, or behaviors which stem from unintended influence from a popular or high-status P. Children attending summer camp rated their peers on five characteristics designed to measure social power (fighting ability, independence of social pressure, etc.). Observers then unobtrusively rated the activities of each camper over an extended period of time. The results indicated that not only were group members more likely to accept direct influence attempts from a high-power member, but were also more likely to spontaneously emulate high- rather than low-members. The authors hypothesize that such imitation of P's behavior by W often has the function of being a vicarious reinforcement to the low-power member. Hence, individuals often imitate the behaviors of leaders and popular persons within a social setting.

The relation of attraction to influence has not been firmly established (Simons, Berkowitz & Moyer, 1970). Taguiri and Kogan (1960) have postulated four possible relations of liking and influence: (1) some persons like best those with whom they share mutual influence; (2) others like best those they feel they influence; (3) some like best those who influence them; and (4) some persons display only a weak relationship between preferences in liking and influence. Given prior analysis and the complexity of the events involved, it seems unlikely that any of these propositions are independent of either other source characteristics or the type of influence process involved. However, in general, those who are highly attracted are apt to have similar attitudes and values (Byrne, 1961, 1969), a fact that would enhance normative influence pressures and the credibility with which values could be used to activate commitments. Those who like one another interact frequently (Homans, 1961), yielding more opportunities for influence. The norm of reciprocity (Gouldner, 1960), which states that a person should help those who help him, derives from the general proposition of balance theory that "you should like those who like you," and probably limits influence attempts in relations of interpersonal attraction to inducements, persuasion, and activation of commitments. The use of coercion is certainly not expected in a friendship relation, though it may be quite appropriate for those we love (e.g., children, wives; cf. Blau, 1964).

Referent power may derive from normative influence or through a process of identification, modeling, or contagion. The individual's need for a firm anchor or frame of reference to gain consensual validation for his theory of social reality, a kind of attribution instability, may give others influence over the person. On the other hand, it is likely that the person will select referent groups on the basis of perceived similarity and as a consequence encapsulate and protect his present values, attitudes, and behavior patterns. A crucial factor in changing influence relations and in changing the individual will be the rewards and punishments he experiences.

Conclusion

In addition to the offers of rewards or threats of punishments, French and Raven have suggested several other bases of social influence. *Informational influence* is said to arise from P's transmission of knowledge or data to W such that a permanent change in W's cognitive structure occurs. While informational influence is presumed to be independent of the attributes of the particular source, it is clear that a prime determinant of W's initial exposure to a source of information may be the demonstrated expertise, communication style, or status of the communicator. *Expert power* (source esteem) resembles informational influence in that W seeks knowledge from P; however, expert power is socially dependent on the continued presence of the source mediating the relevant data. Expert power presents opportunities for counterinfluence by W; W's expressions of deference and status-conferring behavior toward P may serve to make P reciprocally dependent upon the exchange of assistance for deference.

Finally, referent or *attraction power* stems from W's wish to maintain similarity with P. The adoption of a referent may serve to validate conceptions of social reality through the comparison of beliefs, values, and attitudes.

A significant amount of the theory and evidence relevant to the social influence processes has concentrated solely upon the manipulation of source characteristics and has often relegated the target to a passive and recipient role during the influence interaction. It is evident, however, that characteristics of W may to a great extent cause him to be more or less resistant to influence attempts, notwithstanding either the tactics or resources P employs to ensure compliance.

Target Characteristics and the Influence Processes

The theoretical and empirical interest directed toward the target of influence has differed in both nature and scope from the approaches so far discussed. From the time of Weber (1947) to date, theorists have consistently qualified definitions of social power as the ability to implement one's will *despite resistance*. The "implementation of will" has been considered a joint function of the tactics, resources, and characteristics of P, while the resistance of the target of influence has been defined as a joint function of the means which W may employ to minimize P's influence plus the characteristics and/or resources of W which make W more or less susceptible to influence attempts.

Focusing upon the target of influence, three general classes of inquiry may be proposed: (1) what characteristics, resources, or orientations of W lead P to choose W for influence purposes, and why; (2) how do W's stable expectations and personality predispositions modify the nature of the W-P interaction; and (3) what tactics or resources may W bring to bear on P in order to minimize the effect of P's influence? In a like manner, three classes of theory focusing upon aspects of these general questions may be identified: (1) theories emphasizing motivational processes, (2) theories emphasizing cognitive processes, and (3) theories relevant to counterinfluence and resistance tactics.

Target Motivations

Social influence may occur and be effective for a number of reasons and may arise out of a host of different motivations or orientations. Deutsch and Gerard (1955), drawing from Kelley's (1952) analysis of the functions that reference groups play in the determination of a person's attitudes, have differentiated between normative and informational influence. The enforcement of group standards or norms characterizes the former, and the frame of reference provided by the group for self-comparisons constitutes the latter. A similar distinction has been made by Thibaut and Strickland (1956), who have referred to the means of maintaining group membership as group set and the need to attain cognitive clarity about the environment as task set. The individual is considered to be dependent upon others as "mediators of fact" in the case of informational influence or task set. Both constructs reflect the influence of Festinger's (1954) assumption that individuals need and seek consensual validation for their constructions of social reality since objective, physical standards are unavailable. Such consensual validation is itself assumed to be reinforcing, a point used by Gamson (1968) in the distinction between the two effects of social approval.

Informational influence is more likely to lead to public conformity and private acceptance, while normative influence presumably would lead only to public conformity without private acceptance of the standards or evaluations involved (Asch, 1956; Deutsch & Gerard, 1955; Levy, 1960). Furthermore, Deutsch and Gerard argue that most studies of conformity are concerned with informational influence, because subjects merely respond in the presence of others without sharing group goals or mutual expectations. Informational influence should be more effective the more confused or ambiguous the stimulus situation, or the more vague the criteria for assessing the "nature of reality" (Luchins, 1945; Walker & Heyns, 1962; Wiener, 1958). For example, a greater shift in attitudes might be expected in conformity studies utilizing the autokinetic phenomenon (Sherif, 1947) as the research tool rather than the classical line-judgment tasks (Asch, 1956).

The process of producing change in an individual's attitudes or behaviors as a function of group manipulation has been described by Lewin (1947a; 1947b) as involving three stages: (1) unfreezing the attitude or behavior under consideration, (2) modifying the attitude, and (3) refreezing the newly developed patterns. Cartwright (1951) has described how deeply imbedded an individual is in his groups: "how aggressive or cooperative a person is, how much self-respect and self-confidence he has, how energetic and good he is, what he loves or hates, and what beliefs and prejudices he holds, all these characteristics are highly determined by the individual's group memberships" (p. 388). Schein and his co-workers (Schein, 1958; Schein, Schneier, & Barker, 1961) point out that a breakdown of such firm group relationships could quickly lead to unfreezing. Hence, isolation from friends, removal of self-defining titles or status, breakdown of hierarchical authority, substitution of value-incongruent information, and the engineering of feelings of guilt can lead to the unfreezing of fixed positions and remove resistance to change. It could be expected, therefore, that a change in group membership with the concomitant modification of norms and informational inputs, would be a powerful means of unfreezing old attitudes and behaviors, providing the stimulus for change and subsequent refreezing of new patterns. Marginal men, because they lack social anchors, should be prone to change and be disposed to join social movements (Hoffer, 1951.) Anxieties within a group generated by external dangers should encourage group cohesiveness and confidence in leaders as a means of reducing fear (Mulder & Stermerding, 1963). Hence, leaders apparently gain charisma only at times of social crisis (Gerth & Mills, 1953). On the other hand, it could be predicted that as group cohesiveness increases, the individual's resistance to influence attempts by persons outside the group would increase.

There are wide differences between persons in the degree of conformity, influenceability, or suggestibility which they demonstrate in their interactions (Cohen, 1964; Crutchfield, 1955; Hovland, Janis, & Kelley, 1953; McGuire, 1969). Definitions of power which specify that P must overcome resistance by W (e.g., Harsanyi, 1962a; Weber, 1947) imply a need to know more about the kinds of resistance which W will present to P if a prediction of P's probable success in interaction is to be made.

A number of specific motivational states of W have been identified with increased resistance to influence attempts. For example, Kelman (1950) and Hochbaum (1954) have demonstrated that W's experience of a task success prior to receiving a persuasive appeal heightened W's resistance to P's arguments. Gelfand (1962), in a related investigation, found that W's experience of prior success on some task was effective in inducing resistance to persuasion even though the task experience was irrelevant to the subsequent appeal by P. Apparently it is W's immediate history of general competency, and not W's chronic past experience in similar influence situations which increases resistance to persuasive appeals.

The needs of W mediate the utility of P's resources as reinforcing agents to W and contribute to W's overall susceptibility to influence. Hence, if W is very hungry and P attempts to use motive-irrelevant praise as a reinforcement, W is likely to be unresponsive to P's influence attempt. In fact, motivation theorists have often used the concept of motive to refer to a class of reinforcers (Atkinson, 1964). Deprivation operations have been associated with the salience or prepotency of classes of reinforcements. An aroused motive not only increases the prepotency of a reinforcing stimulus, but also broadens the class of stimuli which will be evaluated as reinforcing. If a person is relatively hungry, he may eat a hamburger or a steak, but if he is starving, he may also eat a dog, horse, or even another human being. Hence, an increase in the strength of a motive (however established) decreases the person's resistance to the influence attempt of another person who offers a relevant reinforcement, and increases the probability that the other person will possess a relevant reinforcer.

Kelman (1961) has related the means of influence to the kinds of changes sought by P, and has evaluated both means and outcomes in terms of the ongoing motivational processes operative in the target of influence. He postulated three combinations of processes and ends achieved: compliance, identification, and internalization. The crucial factors in W's acceptance or rejection of influence as well as the type of influence which occurs are presumed to be largely a function of W's motivational set. Compliance is a behavior by W consistent with P's wishes (or W's perception of P's wishes) which W performs because he hopes to achieve a favorable response from P—the delivery of a reward or the removal of a punishment. Identification refers to conforming behavior performed by W which serves the function of maintaining a desired relationship with P. Identification behaviors may refer to attempts by W to maintain or increase his attractiveness in the eyes of P, or to meet role requirements which are essential for continued interactions with P. Kelman postulates that "to the extent that he [W] is concerned with the social anchorage of his behavior, influence will tend to take the form of identification" (p. 58). Internalization, the third type of means-ends relation, represents conformity to P's influence by W because the induced changes are consistent with W's existing value system. W's motivation for adopting and internalizing P's behaviors is presumed to be concern over the value congruence of his own and P's behaviors, and as such, W accepts P's communications as consistent with W's own value system.

There is some question, however, whether the motivational bases of W and the means of influence employed by P actually yield three separate and distinct interactive outcomes. Most instances of social influence appear to be the result of the contribution of all three motivational processes operative in W. Thus, if W is concerned about the social effects (rewards or punishments) of his behavior, and simultaneously, W wishes to maintain his attractiveness to P as a social anchor, then both compliance and identification may occur. Kelman's three classes of behavior by W may be seen to constitute a target-oriented counterpart to French and Raven's (1959) reward and coercive power, referent power, and legitimate power, respectively, as well as Parsons' categories of inducements and deterrents, persuasion, and activation of commitments. The clarification by Kelman that private opinion and public conformity of W may be incongruent except when internalization is involved is a distinction generally accepted by those who study conformity behavior and attitude change (Kiesler & Kiesler, 1969; Walker & Heyns, 1962; Zimbardo & Ebbesen, 1969). Perhaps the most unique facet of Kelman's analysis is that it suggests that the different tactics of influence employed by *P* may not be determinant of *W*'s behavior unless *W* possesses a suitable motivational base disposing him to respond in a compliant manner.

Target Cognitions

The cognitive basis of influence consists of the generalized expectancies which individuals develop through the social learning processes, and which may lead *W* to accept or resist *P*'s influence. Riesman (1954) believes that interpersonal expectations may be one of the primary determinants of influence attempts. If an individual, whatever his resources, feels weak or dependent upon others, then in all likelihood he *will* be weaker than another person who has strong feelings of independence. Charles de Gaulle has demonstrated that the will to resist influence attempts can have important effects despite the fact that the target is relatively short on resources. This latter observation is consistent with Horwitz' (1958) proposition that among equals, the individual with the greatest need will gain deference from the person with the least need concerning some interpersonal outcome. These propositions could be rephrased to read: the person with the greatest expectation of success, and the strongest self-perception of strength relative to the person to be influenced will gain deference with respect to the policy at issue, whatever the objective conditions.

Research has indicated that a person's level of aspiration is used as a basis of comparison for judging his own failures and successes (Lewin et al., 1944). Thibaut and Kelley (1959), drawing from level-of-aspiration theory, have postulated a relationship between influence and comparison level (CL). The CL is defined as the level of reward, or positive outcomes, that a person expects based on his previous interactions. The optimistic and self-confident individual should have a generally high CL, while the pessimistic and anxious person should have a generally low CL. The latter person should be satisfied with much less in the way of outcomes than the former person. Thus, the CL may be used to determine a rough index of the likelihood with which any individual will exert or resist influence.

While the concept of CL serves as a reference point for the value of outcomes in social interaction, Rotter's (1966) social learning theory introduces a term to represent the generalized expectancy than one *can* produce intended effects. Thus, CL represents the value of an outcome, while internal-external (I-E) control could be said to refer to the subjective probability of attaining that outcome.

Within Rotter's theory, a person who has an orientation of internal control tends to believe that he can determine his own outcomes, and that his abilities are such that he can affect and control his social and physical environment in specific ways. A person who is high in external control orientation, on the other hand, has the general expectancy that his rewards and punishments are not connected to his own actions, but rather that they occur by chance, luck, fate, or powerful others. Obviously, if a person does not feel that he can affect his environment, he will not attempt to affect it, and, as a consequence, will not affect it—a self-fulfilling prophecy. Gore and Rotter (1963) and Strickland (1965) have found that I-E scale scores do predict who will participate as social activists in an attempt to effect social change. Conversely, Odell (1959) and Crowne and Liverant (1963) have demonstrated a relationship between externality and conformity.

Harvey, Hunt, and Schroder (1961), in their theory of cognitive development, relate the means of parental control and the kind of orientation developed by the child. If the parents exercise nearly total control over all aspects of the child's behavior, the child will develop a dependence upon external sources of control. The internally controlled individual, who has a very complex cognitive structure, is assumed to have been the recipient of training which emphasized rewards for the display of effectance motivation. Harvey, Hunt, and Schroder (1961) note that the dimension of concreteness-abstractness is of prime importance in the subsequent development of cognitive structure and cognitive needs. If, as Jones and Gerard (1967) and Cohen (1964) have suggested, the development of conceptual structures is a matter of progression from concrete to abstract methods of categorization, then it might be expected that individuals high in needs for cognitive clarity or concreteness would be more responsive to definitive influence communications than those individuals capable of tolerating a high level of ambiguity. Kelman and Cohler (1959) and Baron (1963) have confirmed this hypothesis using persuasive communications as the influence mode.

The composite picture derived from these separate theories is that the highly resistant target is confident of his own abilities to affect his environment and those around him, he has a complicated and highly differentiated cognitive structure, is heterogeneous in his view of other individuals, and has "expensive" tastes (high CL). The deferent target may suffer from feelings of anomie or normlessness, does not feel that he can control his own reinforcements and is likely to attribute causation to the environment rather than to himself, has a rather uncomplicated, clearly segmented cognitive structure, is homogeneous in his views of others, and has "beer" tastes (low CL).

Resistance Forces

Fritz Heider (1958) has presented a "common sense" view of power with keen insight. Heider extended Lewin's (1941) theoretical concept of the space of free movement, which consists of those regions within a person's life space that are accessible because the person has the requisite abilities to move from one region to another. Lewin postulated two constraints on the space of free movement that are due to environmental forces: quasi-physical barriers, or those tasks which are too difficult for the person, and quasi-social barriers, or those activities which are socially forbidden to the person. In agreement with the arguments of Harvey et al. (1961) and with Piaget (1954), Lewin believed that the space of free movement increased with increasing cognitive complexity (i.e., differentiation of the life space).

Heider specifically equated personal power with ability. For Heider whether a person *can* carry out an intention depends upon the ability of that person, how hard he tries, and the difficulty of the task or the environmental resistances present. Since *can* is a function of both personal ability and environmental difficulty, there are both intrapersonal impediments to influence, such as lack of eyesight or lack of knowledge, and constraints presented by the environment, or other individuals composing the social environment (e.g., *P*). *Trying* is also separable into two aspects: intention and exertion. Heider believes that *can* influences *trying*; thus when a person can do something, he may develop a desire to do so. This hypothesis is similar to that proffered by Singer (1963) as the basis for attributions in threat systems. A nation which has the capability to do great harm will be perceived as also having malevolent intentions.

Heider postulates that exertion varies directly with the difficulty of the task and inversely with the ability of the person. From these intuitions, Heider offers the following definition:

$$\text{power} = f \left[\frac{\text{difficulty}}{\text{exertion}} \right]$$

In describing this equation, Heider implicitly offers an interesting potential measurement of power. He states that if two people exert themselves to the same degree, the one who solves the more difficult task has greater power. Further, holding task difficulty constant, the person who exerts himself least is the most powerful. This latter measure emphasizes that power, like intelligence, is a relative matter.

The power of W to resist P's influence attempts, then, is a joint function of W's ability and intent. Personal ability is determined by the resources which W controls as well as those cognitive characteristics (e.g., internal control orientation) which render W generally resistant to influence. The amount of environmental difficulty which W encounters in pursuing his policies is a function of the strength of influence exerted by P. The means of influence employed, the amount and kind of resources controlled, and the characteristics of the source will all affect the amount of environmental difficulty experienced by W. To the extent that W's personal ability exceeds the net environmental difficulties which P may impose on W in interaction, W will be resistant to influence.

Similarly, W's intent is a function of both exertion and trying. To the extent that W is capable of performing a more difficult task than P, or if W can perform an equally difficult task with less effort than P, W will be highly resistant to influence attempts. Trying refers to the chronic or acute motivational states of W which mediate W's degree of susceptibility and involvement in interaction. These motivational states may have a multiplier effect on exertion. For example, the more motivated W is to resist influence, the greater exertion W might be willing to expend on counterinfluence tactics, and consequently, the greater W's resistance to influence.

In sum, Heider's "naive psychology" predicts that W may successfully pursue his personal policies in an influence situation to the extent to which (1) the resources or cognitive characteristics of W enable him to surmount the difficulties imposed by P, (2) W is capable of performing more difficult tasks with less exertion, and (3) W is motivated to resist influence attempts. Heider thus manages to combine the motivational and cognitive approaches in discussing the personal power of the individual.

If power is considered as the ability of P to gain assent to his policies from W, then holding P's ability constant, P can gain his policy to the degree that W does not provide resistance. It follows that if W is dependent upon P, and as a consequence, does not provide resistance to P's influence attempts, P will have power over W. Emerson's (1962) theory of power as dependency pursues this particular trend of thought. He defines dependence of W upon P as: (1) directly proportional to W's motivational investment in goals mediated by P; and (2) inversely proportional to the availability of those goals to W outside the W-P relationship. The power of P over W is equivalent to the dependence of W on P. This first factor (W's motivational investment) is very general, and corresponds to all those abilities and resources of P that can produce significant outcomes for W, or that produce information which convinces W that P can serve as a positive or negative mediator of goals or values.

Emerson's second component of dependency appears to be identical with Thibaut and Kelley's (1959) concept of comparison level for alternatives (CL_{alt}). CL_{alt} may be defined as the lowest level of outcomes which W will accept given the available alternatives. The lower the CL_{alt}, the higher W's dependence on his present relationship with P. If, in fact, dependency is defined as functionally tied to the range of outcomes which P can mediate for W, then Emerson's concept of power becomes identical with Thibaut and Kelley's definition. This notion of choosing between alternatives at all times has also been discussed at length by Homans (1961) and Blau (1964), for whom forgone alternatives constitute the costs of any interaction.

As do other theorists (e.g., Harsanyi, 1962a; Nagel, 1968), Emerson hypothesizes that two individuals can be equal in power but still exercise very significant influence over each other. If power is balanced, neither party will dominate the other, but neither will the power "cancel itself out." Rather, each party may have considerable influence over the other's behavior, as in the case of lovers. A rather potent relationship may occur in a case of reciprocal power when each party is dependent on the other. That person who is most dependent is least powerful, and the person who is least dependent is most dominant. Thus, Blau (1964, pp. 78ff.) refers to the dilemma of love: an individual in a love relationship is expected to express affection and approval, but doing so too early, too freely, or too much will depreciate the value of such approval and erode power by making the other person less dependent on the relationship.

Just as conflicting and equal power may not be dismissed as a cancellation of influence, a relationship of zero power will not necessarily produce vectors towards the development of power. However, an unbalanced relationship in which P is dominant over W produces forces toward balance. The forces toward balance constitute counter influence techniques employed by W to reduce the P-W power disparity, and includes: (1) Cost reduction or reduction in motivational investment by W in the goals mediated by P. One means for implementing this balancing method is for W to change his value structure; another is for W to simply withdraw love or some other sentiment which makes him dependent upon P. (2) W may also reduce the power disparity by cultivating alternative social relationships in order to reduce his dependence on P. The operation of this counter influence tactic leads to an increase in the number of interactive participants and to attempts at coalition-formation by W. (3) W can attempt to increase P's dependence upon W. One method suggested by Emerson is status conferral. When W confers status upon P, the latter is given a larger portion of the rewards which are allocated jointly—more credit and social approval for a job well done or a larger share of the financial rewards, etc. Ego-rewards, such as social approval, signs of deference and respect are often highly valued by recipients, while they cost W little to bestow. Thus, conferral of status increases P's dependence upon W and more evenly distributes power between them. (4) The dominance of P over W can be broken if W is successful in extending the group and/or forming coalitions with other members against P. Thus, as W seeks alternative social relationships (balancing mechanism 2), he extends the group, and then subsequently attempts to set the group against P. The stabilization of coalitions within groups takes place through the development of group norms. The demands of these stable coalitions over the formerly powerful individual are called role-prescriptions, the specifications of behaviors which are expected or demanded of P by the group. The norms and prescriptions define implicitly the membership of the coalition which would either support or oppose any member if he were to perform any action relevant to those rules.

Various features of the social structure operate to discourage the development of mutual dependency through the use of counter-influence tactics. Blau (1964) notes that while power disparities tend to dissipate through the operation of balancing mechanisms, one function of the existing social structure is the prevention of this dissipation through the institutionalization of power disparities. The caste system of the American south required (and still informally requires) that Blacks use separate fountains and rest rooms, restaurants, beaches, and schools to prevent the development of mutual dependencies and the reduction of power disparities.

Legitimacy and Authority

Through socialization, each person learns what he ought to do and what he ought not to do. In American society, as in most others, one of the important values that a person learns is that he should play according to the rules of the game. Although on occasion there will be disputes about an interpretation of the rules, once a judgment is established, the person is expected to abide by them. The rules of a group or organization are analogous to those of a game. They prescribe how problems will be solved and how conflicts will be settled, they prescribe the proper channels of information and decision, and they identify who should accept which suggestions of which other persons or organizations (Goffman, 1962, 1967; Szasz, 1961). The internalization of these rules and the willingness to abide by them constitute the power of legitimacy (Simon, Smithburg, & Thompson, 1970). The more legitimate the source's attempt at influence is perceived to be, the more likely it is the target will acquiesce to it.

Legitimacy may be said to have the property of "requiredness" (Asch, 1952; Kohler, 1938; Wertheimer, 1935). W feels that he ought to perform the behaviors requested of him when the source is legitimate. Hence, for Weber (1947), authority refers to the probability that P can secure obedience from designated others. Blau (1964, p. 200) has noted that only legitimate authority yields truly willing compliance, even in the absence of inducements to do so and even when compliance is costly.

Authority is distinguished from inducement and coercion by the absence of rewards or punishments, and from persuasion by the fact that people a priori suspend their own judgments and accept that of the legitimate authority without having to be convinced of the accuracy of his view. Parsons' (1963) category of activation of commitments and French and Raven's (1959) concept of legitimate power directly reflect this sort of one-way interaction. Similarly, Bachrach and Baratz (1963) have stated that neither individuals nor groups defer to the wishes of an authoritative source for fear of negative sanctions, but rather they do so because compliance can be rationalized in terms of their own value systems.

Friedrich (1963) has defined legitimate authority in terms of potentiality for "reasoned elaborations." Although a surgeon in the middle of an operation cannot take the time to explain to his nurse why she should promptly obey each of his commands, he could with time elaborate all the reasons why the nurse should suspend her judgments and comply with his requests. Authority relies upon a set of symbols, myths, legends, documents, and slogans for its legitimacy and rationalizes its requests on the basis of such paraphernalia. When persons in official positions need to rely upon deterrence or inducements for their influence, they are not acting as legitimate authorities (Gamson, 1968). Since the failure of authority usually degenerates into the use of coercion, legitimate communications often involve the component of tacit threat as part of P's right to prescribe W's behavior (Lehman, 1969).

Blau (1964) views the development of legitimate influence as a direct outgrowth of a situation in which one participant possesses more authority (and thus can allocate significant resources). When P

uses his authority to mediate rewards for *W*, *P* creates social obligations for *W*, which extends *P*'s scope of influence. Using the example of a factory supervisor, Blau hypothesizes that if the supervisor uses his position to obtain rewards for his staff such as coffee or smoking breaks, a feeling of obligation to the supervisor will be engendered in the workers, and the supervisor's demands over an extended scope of behaviors will be complied with and enforced by the members of the staff themselves as a way of "paying off" the social obligations incurred.

Hollander (1964) takes a somewhat different view of the development of legitimacy, leadership, and authority. A leader earns his position through compliance with the normative structure of the collectivity and by contributing significantly to the achievement of group goals. As a reward for his contributions, the leader is given positive credits which allow for future idiosyncratic, non-normative responding without jeopardizing his authority position. These idiosyncrasy credits are presumed to be expendable in a way analogous to the leisure-time entertainment expenditures of earned income. The overextending of credits by a great frequency of nonconforming actions may result in the loss of legitimacy by the leader. Hence, for Hollander (1964), authority in a group situation is earned through conformity and contributions to group goals and is dissipated through nonconformity.

It is unlikely that authority relations would ever develop from dyadic interactions alone. Addition of *n*th parties to an interaction opens up possibilities of coalition formation (Gamson, 1964), the reduction of the absolute influence of any one party over another because of the availability of alternative relationships (Blau, 1964; Thibaut & Kelley, 1959), and the legitimization of authority for decision-making and the allocation of resources (Goffman, (1967; Homans, 1961; Thibaut & Kelley, 1959). At least one function of "broadening the field" by the addition of *n*th individuals to the basic dyadic interaction is the generation of a new form of influence—legitimate authority. In this context, Thibaut and Kelley (1959) have noted that one function of societal norms is to decrease the range of negative outcomes which one party can prescribe for the other. Norms, therefore, serve a damping function on the severity of sanctions applicable for deviance.

Although authority would not develop within dyadic interactions, the relation of authority is essentially dyadic in nature. One does not interact with City Hall, one interacts with the mayor, councilman, police officer, or clerk representing that agency and deriving his legitimacy from the office he holds in the collectivity. Hence, it may be said that an individual is granted authority by the collectivity of which he is the chosen representative. The authority derives from the office and not the individual (Blau, 1963; Goffman, 1962, 1967).

In summary, legitimate authority derives its influence effectiveness from two sources: (1) the socialization process which inculcates deference patterns regarding various structures of authority, the office holders who have the capacity for reasoned elaboration in regard to the value systems of their constituents, and (2) the delegation of authority within collectivities for the purpose of coordinating activities and allocating resources. Authority is granted as a form of equity restoration and as a means of rendering the authority dependent upon those who legitimize his office.

Conclusion

The theories proposed which focus on the motivational state of the target can be subdivided into two major classes: those which emphasize the chronic states of the organism, and those which concern themselves with the target's situational needs at the time of influence. The former class can offer little more than the postulation of some psychoanalytically oriented self-determination of "will to power" existing in the target. The latter raises the important consideration that the situational needs and state of deprivation of W direct and determine which classes of reinforcers will be effective in interaction. Thus, regardless of P's characteristics or the means he employs, his influence may not be effective unless W possesses a suitable motivational base disposing him to comply.

Theories focusing upon the cognitive bases of target resistance are concerned with the generalized expectancies of W developed through the socialization process. The composite derived from several theories indicated that the highly resistant target is confident of his abilities to affect the environment, has a complicated and differentiated cognitive structure, and has a high Comparison Level. The individual susceptible to influence, on the other hand, is likely to feel that he cannot control his own reinforcements and may have an undifferentiated cognitive structure and low Comparison Level.

An examination of the theories which focus on W's explicit counterinfluence tactics indicates that the "weak" party in interaction is not so weak after all. W, in addition to the alternatives of compliance or noncompliance to P's attempts, has as counterinfluence tactics at least the options of withdrawal, alternate social relations, coalition formation, and status conferral.

All three classes of theorists concerned primarily with the target of interaction serve to underscore the *relativity* of social power in influence relationships—at the very minimum, whether P is in fact powerful with respect to W will depend on the motivational state of the target, his past history of socialization, and the range of resistance tactics W can employ to negate P's influence.

Finally, the collective nature of social life broadens the types of influence that may be employed between persons. A need for consensual validation of a person's perception of social reality provides the basis for informational influence, while the need for group rewards provides the basis for normative influence. The activation of normative commitments supports the distribution of authority, which is legitimized by collective decision or acquiescence and supported by the socialization process.

Conclusions

The redefinition of social psychology as the study of the influence processes re-emphasizes the social character of the science. Unfortunately, much of the discipline still draws its explanatory concepts from individual psychology. For example, despite the fact that an individual is placed in a social setting and his attitudes are compared with another individual's as in balance theories, the subsequent explanation for attitude change is based on the individual's strain for balance, reduction of tension, reduction of dissonance, etc. Similarly, theories of interpersonal attraction focus upon effectance motivation, drive reduction, and secondary reinforcement, while explanations of aggression include frustration, displacement, cue-response learning, and other individual or personality mechanisms. In contrast, the viewpoints of Lewin, Heider, Homans, and others have attempted to produce "social" explanations of social behavior. This latter approach requires the use of concepts representing the relationships *between* actors, such as social space, unit relations, and social exchange.

The preparadigm state of social psychology is indicated by the apparent meanderings of research and the lack of even miniature theories of a hypothetico-deductive nature. The literature reveals bursts of activity directed toward the investigation of variables currently in vogue, the search only to be abandoned when inadequate theory has reached the inevitable cul-de-sac.

The task of ordering the phenomena studied in social psychology is indeed a formidable one. Yet, when these phenomena are viewed as aspects of various social influence processes, the outlines, at least, of an integration become visible. Further, a reconceptualization of much social psychology as centered around the social influence processes has great heuristic value in its suggestions of new hypotheses and new areas of research. For example, the development of interpersonal attraction can be viewed as a power-enhancing tactic to gain "credit" for use in interaction with others at a later time. If reinforcement principles explain why attitude similarity is an important factor in the development of attraction, they do not adequately explain why we like to be liked. The latter question requires a social answer: those who like us can be expected to refrain from using some types of influence (e.g., deterrence or punishment) and at the same time may be expected to be predictable mediators of reward. Then, too, those who like one another interact frequently, which implies that friends influence one another more than do strangers or enemies. In other words, we influence those who like us and are influenced by them, and we like those we influence and those who influence us. Attraction, then, is not only a determinant but also an important consequence of social influence. The present chapter has been an attempt to demonstrate the heuristic value of viewing many areas of social psychology as part of the social influence processes.

Once a social influence orientation is adopted, two major tasks clearly emerge, one with convergent and the other with divergent consequences. The first task is a systematic comparison, across the social influence processes, of the principles found within research areas. If these comparisons reveal a high degree of similarity across processes, it may raise hopes of the development of a general theory of social psychology. The second task is a by-product of the first. Insofar as the principles of the various research areas cannot be integrated with one another, then to that extent does it become necessary to build separate miniature theories. Actually, there is no reason why both convergent and divergent trends should not continue simultaneously, as long as encapsulation within narrow areas does not persist.

Finally, it should be noted that at least portions of all the social sciences are concerned with the influence processes. Any theory of deterrence will be applicable not only to social psychology, but to military science, political science, economics, sociology, and history. Whatever trends there may be for interdisciplinary integration within the social sciences focus around problem areas, the chief characteristics of which are the potential for social influence and social change.

References

Allport, G. W. The historical background of modern social psychology. In G. Lindzey (Ed.), *Handbook of social psychology.* Vol. 1. Reading, Mass.: Addison-Wesley, 1954. Pp. 3-56.

Aronson, E., & Carlsmith, J. M. Performance expectancy as a determinant of actual performance. *Journal of Abnormal and Social Psychology,* 1962, 65, 178-182.
Asch, S. E. The doctrine of suggestion, prestige, and imitation in social psychology. *Psychological Review,* 1948, 55, 250-277.
Asch, S. E. *Social Psychology.* New York: Prentice-Hall, 1952.
Asch, S. E. Studies of independence and conformity: a minority of one against a unanimous majority. *Psychological Monographs,* 1956, 70, (9, Whole No. 416).
Atkinson, J. W. *An introduction of motivation.* Princeton: Van Nostrand, 1964.
Ayllon, T., & Michael, J. The psychiatric nurse as a behavioral engineer. *Journal of Experimental Analysis of Behavior,* 1959, 2, 301-305.
Bachrach, P., & Baratz, M. S. Decisions and nondecisions: an analytical framework. *American Political Science Review,* 1963, 57, 632-642.
Bandura, A. Vicarious processes: a case of no-trial learning. In L. Berkowitz (Ed.), *Advances in experimental social psychology.* Vol. 2. New York: Academic Press, 1965. Pp. 1-55.
Bandura, A. The influence of rewarding and punishing consequences to the model on the acquisition and performance of imitative responses. Unpublished manuscript, Stanford University, 1962.
Bandura, A., Ross, D., & Ross, S. A. Imitation of film-mediated aggressive models. *Journal of Abnormal and Social Psychology,* 1963, 66, 3-11. (a)
Bandura, A., Ross, D., & Ross, S. A. A comparative test of the status envy, social power, and the secondary reinforcement theories of identificatory learning. *Journal of Abnormal and Social Psychology,* 1963, 67, 527-534. (b)
Bandura, A., Ross, D., & Ross, S. A. Vicarious reinforcement and imitation. *Journal of Abnormal and Social Psychology,* 1963, 67, 601-607. (c)
Bandura, A., & Walters, R. H. *Social learning and personality development.* New York: Holt, Rinehart, 1963.
Barker, R. G. Explorations in ecological psychology. *American Psychologist,* 1965, 20, 1-14.
Baron, R. M. A cognitive model of attitude change. Unpublished doctoral dissertation, New York University, 1963.
Bazelon, D. T. *The paper economy.* New York: Random House, 1965.
Bendix, R. *Max Weber: an intellectual portrait.* New York: Doubleday, 1962.
Berkowitz, L., & Daniels, L. R. Responsibility and dependency. *Journal of Abnormal and Social Psychology,* 1963, 66, 429-436.
Berkowitz, L., & Daniels, L. R. Affecting the salience of the social responsibility norm: effects of past help on the response to dependency relationships. *Journal of Abnormal and Social Psychology,* 1964, 68, 275-281.
Blau, P. M. Critical remarks on Weber's theory of authority. *American Political Science Review,* 1963, 57 (2), 305-316.
Blau, P. M. *Exchange and power in social life.* New York: Wiley, 1964.
Bowden, A. D., Caldwell, F. F., & West, G. A. A study in prestige. *American Journal of Sociology,* 1934, 40, 193-204.
Byrne, D. Interpersonal attraction and attitude similarity. *Journal of Abnormal and Social Psychology,* 1961, 62, 713-715.
Byrne, D. Attitudes and attraction. In L. Berkowitz (Ed.), *Advances in experimental social psychology.* Vol. 4. New York: Academic Press, 1969. Pp. 35-89.
Cartwright, D. Achieving change in people: some applications of group dynamics theory. *Human Relations,* 1951, 4, 381-393.
Cartwright, D. A field theoretical conception of power. In D. Cartwright (Ed.), *Studies in social power.* Ann Arbor: University of Michigan Press, 1959.

Cartwright, D. Influence, leadership, control. In J. G. March (Ed.), *Handbook of organizations.* New York: Rand McNally, 1965. Pp. 1-47.

Cartwright, D., & Zander, A. *Group dynamics: research and theory,* 3rd. ed. New York: Harper & Row, 1968.

Chein, I. On the concept of power. Paper presented at the meetings of the American Psychological Association, Washington, D. C., September 3, 1967.

Clausewitz, K. von. *War, politics, and power.* Chicago: Henry Regnery Co., 1962.

Cohen, A. R. *Attitude change and social influence.* New York: Basic Books, 1964.

Collins, B. E., & Raven, B. H. Group Structure: attraction, coalitions, communication, and power, In G. Lindzey & E. Aronson (Eds.), *Handbook of social psychology,* 2nd ed. Vol. 4. Reading, Mass.: Addison-Wesley, 1969. Pp. 102-204.

Crowne, D. P., & Liverant, S. Conformity under varying conditions of personal commitment. *Journal of Abnormal and Social Psychology,* 1963, 66, 547-555.

Crutchfield, R. S. Conformity and character. *American Psychologist,* 1955, 10, 191-198.

Dahl, R. A. The concept of power. *Behavioral Science,* 1957, 2, 201-218.

Dahl, R. A. *Who governs.* New Haven, Conn.: Yale University Press, 1961.

Dahl, R. A. Power. *International Encyclopedia of the social sciences.* Vol. 12. New York: Macmillan, 1968. Pp. 405-415.

Dahl, R. A., & Lindblom, E.C. E. *Politics, economics, and welfare.* New York: Harper & Row, 1953.

DeKadt, E. J. Conflict and power in society. *International Social Science Journal,* 1965, 17, 454-471.

Deutsch, K. W. *The nerves of government.* New York: Free Press of Glencoe, 1966.

Deutsch, M., & Gerard, H. G. A study of normative and informational social influence upon individual judgment. *Journal of Abnormal and Social Psychology* 1955, 51, 629-636.

Dittes, J. E. Extinction during psychotherapy of GSR accompanying "embarrassing" statements. *Journal of Abnormal and Social Psychology,* 1957, 54, 187-191. (a)

Dittes, J. E. Galvanic skin response as a measure of patient's reaction to therapists permissiveness. *Journal of Abnormal and Social Psychology,* 1957, 55, 295-303. (b)

Domhoff, G. W. *Who rules America?* Englewood Cliffs, N. J.: Prentice-Hall, 1967.

Emerson, R. M. Power-dependence relations. *American Sociological Review,* 1962, 27, 31-41.

Ferster, C. B. Positive reinforcement and behavioral deficits in autistic children. *Child Development,* 1961, 32, 437-456.

Festinger, L. A theory of social comparison processes. *Human Relations,* 1954, 7, 117-140.

Festinger, L., & Hutte, H. A. An experimental investigation of the effect of unstable interpersonal relations in a group. *Journal of Abnormal and Social Psychology,* 1954, 49, 513-532.

Fisher, R. *International conflict for beginners.* New York: Harper & Row, 1969.

Freedman, J. L. Long-term behavioral effects of cognitive dissonance. *Journal of Experimental Social Psychology,* 1965, 1, 145-155.

Friedrich, C. J. *Man and his government.* New York: McGraw-Hill, 1963.

French, J. R. P., Jr., & Raven, B. The bases of social power. In D. Cartwright

(Ed.), *Studies in social power.* Ann Arbor: University of Michigan Press, 1959. Pp. 150-167.

Gamson, W. A. Experimental studies of coalition formation. In L. Berkowitz (Ed.), *Advances in experimental social psychology.* Vol. 1. New York: Academic Press, 1964. Pp. 81-110.

Gamson, W. A. *Power and discontent.* Homewood, Ill.: Dorsey Press, 1968.

Gelfand, D. M. The influence of self-esteem on the rate of verbal conditioning and social matching behavior. *Journal of Abnormal and Social Psychology,* 1962, 65, 259-265.

Gerth, H. H., & Mills, C. W. *Character and social structure.* New York: Harcourt, 1953.

Goffman, E. *Asylums.* Chicago: Aldine, 1962.

Goffman, E. *Behavior in public places.* Glencoe, Ill.: Free Press, 1963.

Goffman, E. *Interaction ritual.* Garden City, N. Y.: Doubleday, 1967.

Gore, P. M., & Rotter, J. B. A personality correlate of social action. *Journal of Personality,* 1963, 31, 58-64.

Gouldner, A. W. The norm of reciprocity: a preliminary statement. *American Sociological Review,* 1960, 25, 161-178.

Halle, L. J. *The society of man.* New York: Harper & Row, 1965.

Harsanyi, J. C. Measurement of social power, opportunity costs, and the theory of two-person bargaining games. *Behavioral Science,* 1962, 7, 67-80. (a)

Harsanyi, J. C. Measurement of social power in n-person reciprocal power situations. *Behavioral Science,* 1962, 7, 81-91. (b)

Harvey, O. J., Hunt, D. E., & Schroder, H. M. *Conceptual systems and personality organization.* New York: Wiley, 1961.

Heider, F. *The psychology of interpersonal relations.* New York: Wiley, 1958.

Hochbaum, G. M. The relation between group members' self-confidence and their reactions to group pressures to uniformity. *American Sociological Review,* 1954, 19, 678-687.

Hoffer, E. *The true believer.* New York: New American Library, 1951.

Hollander, E. P. *Leaders, groups and influence.* New York: Oxford University Press, 1964.

Homans, G. C. Social behavior as exchange. *American Journal of Sociology,* 1958, 63, 597-606.

Homans, G. C. *Social behavior: its elementary forms.* New York: Harcourt, Brace, 1961.

Horwitz, M. The veridicality of liking and disliking. In R. Tagiuri and L. Petrullo (Eds.), *Person perception and interpersonal behavior.* Stanford, Cal.: Stanford University Press, 1958. Pp. 191-209.

Hovland, C. I., Janis, I. L., & Kelley, H. H. *Communication and persuasion.* New Haven, Conn.: Yale University Press, 1953.

Jones, E. E., & Gerard, H. B. *Foundations of social psychology.* New York: Wiley, 1967.

Kelley, H. H. The two functions of reference groups. In G. E. Swanson, T. M. Newcomb, & E. L. Hartley (Eds.), *Readings in social psychology,* 2nd ed. New York: Holt, 1952. Pp. 410-414.

Kelley, H. H. Attribution theory in social psychology. In D. Levine (Ed.), *Nebraska symposium on motivation.* Lincoln: University of Nebraska Press, 1967. Pp. 192-240.

Kelley, H. H., & Thibaut, J. W. Group problem solving. In G. Lindzey and E. Aronson (Eds.), *The handbook of social psychology.* 2nd ed. Vol. 4. Reading, Mass.: Addison-Wesley, 1969. Pp. 1-101.

Kelman, H. C. Effects of success and failure on "suggestibility" in the autokinetic situation. *Journal of Abnormal and Social Psychology*, 1950, 45, 267-285.

Kelman, H. C. Processes of opinion change. *Public Opinion Quarterly*, 1961, 25, 57-78.

Kelman, H. C., & Cohler, J. Reactions to persuasive communications as a function of cognitive needs and styles. Paper read at the Thirtieth Annual Meeting of the Eastern Psychological Association, Atlantic City, N. J., 1959.

Kiesler, C. A., & Kiesler, S. B. *Conformity*. Reading, Mass.: Addison-Wesley, 1969.

Kimble, G. A. *Hilgard and Marquis' conditioning and learning*. New York: Appleton-Century-Crofts, 1961.

King, G. F., Armitage, S. G., & Tilton, J. R. A therapeutic approach to schizophrenics of extreme pathology. *Journal of Abnormal and Social Psychology*, 1960, 61, 276-286.

Kohler, W. *The place of value in a world of facts*. New York: Liveright, 1938.

Kuhn, A. *The study of society: a unified approach*. Homewood, Ill.: Dorsey Press, 1963.

Kuhn, T. S. *The structure of scientific revolutions*. Chicago: University of Chicago Press, 1962.

Lasswell, H. D. Conflict and leadership: The process of decision and the nature of authority. *Ciba Foundation symposium on conflict in society*, A. S. de Reuck and J. Knight (Eds.). London: Churchill, 1966. Pp. 210-228.

Lasswell, H. D., & Kaplan, A. *Power and society*. New Haven, Conn.: Yale University Press, 1950.

Latane, B., & Darley, J. M. Group inhibition of bystander intervention in emergencies. *Journal of Personality and Social Psychology*, 1968, 10 (3), 215-221.

Lazarus, A. A. The elimination of children's phobias by deconditioning. In H. J. Eysenck (Ed.), *Behavior therapy and the neuroses*. New York: Pergamon, 1960.

Lehman, E. W. Toward a macrosociology of power. *American Sociological Review*, 1969, 34 (4), 453-465.

Levy, L. Studies in conformity behavior: a methodological note. *Journal of Psychology*, 1960, 50, 39-41.

Lewin, K. Regression, retrogression and development. *University of Iowa Studies of Child Welfare*, 1941, 18, 1-43.

Lewin, K. Frontiers in group dynamics. *Human Relations*, 1947, 1, 5-41. (a)

Lewin, K. Group decision and social change. In T. M. Newcomb and E. L. Hartley (Eds.), *Readings in social psychology*. New York: Holt, 1947. Pp. 330-344. (b)

Lewin, K., Dembo, Festinger, L., & Sears, P. S. Level of aspiration. In McV. Hunt (Ed.), *Personality and behavior disorders*. New York: Ronald Press, 1944. Pp. 333-378.

Lippitt, R., Polansky, N., Redl, F., & Rosen, S. The dynamics of power. *Human Relations*, 1952, 5, 37-64.

Luchins, A. S. Social influences on perception of complex drawings. *Journal of Social Psychology*, 1945, 21, 257-273.

Lundberg, F. *The rich and the super-rich*. New York: Lyle Stuart, 1968.

March, J. G. An introduction to the theory and measurement of influence. *American Political Science Review*, 1955, 49, 431-451.

March, J. G. Measurement concepts in the theory of influence. *Journal of Politics*, 1957, 19, 202-226.

Marwell, G., & Schmitt, D. R. Dimensions of compliance-gaining behavior. *Sociometry*, 1967, 30, 350-364.
McGuire, W. J. The nature of attitudes and attitude change. In G. Lindzey & E. Aronson (Eds.), *Handbook of social psychology*. 2nd ed. Vol 3. Reading, Mass.: Addison-Wesley, 1969. Pp. 136-314.
Miller, N. E., & Dollard, J. *Social learning and imitation*. New Haven, Conn.: Yale University Press, 1941.
Mills, C. W. *The power elite*. New York: Oxford University Press, 1956.
Morgenthau, H. *Politics among nations*, 3rd ed. New York: Knopf, 1960.
Mulder, M., & Stermerding, A. Threat, attraction to group, and need for strong leadership. *Human Relations*, 1963, 16, 317-334.
Nagel, J. H. Some questions about the concept of power. *Behavioral Science*, 1968, 13, 129-137.
Nardin, T. Communication and the effect of threats in strategic interaction. Peace Research Society (International). *Papers*, 1968, 9, 69-86.
Odell, M. E. Personality correlates of independence and conformity. Unpublished master's thesis, Ohio State University, 1959.
Parsons, T. On the concept of influence. *Public Opinion Quarterly*, 1963, 27, 37-62.
Parsons, T. *Sociological theory and modern society*. New York: Free Press, 1967.
Piaget, J. *The construction of reality in the child*. New York: Basic Books, 1954.
Pilliavin, I. M., Rodin, J., & Pilliavin, J. A. Good samaritanism: an underground phenomenon. *Journal of Personality and Social Psychology*, 1969, 13 (4), 289-299.
Radke-Yarrow, M., Trager, H. G., & Miller, J. The role of parents in the development of children's ethnic attitudes. *Child Development*, 1952, 23, 15-53.
Raven, B. H. Social influence and power. In I. D. Steiner and M. Fishbein (Eds.), *Current studies in social psychology*. New York: Holt, 1965. Pp. 371-382.
Riesman, D. *Individualism reconsidered*. Glencoe, Ill.: Free Press, 1954.
Riker, W. H. Some ambiguities in the notion of power. *American Political Science Review*, 1964, 58, 341-349.
Rose, A. M. *The power structure*. New York: Oxford University Press, 1967.
Rotter, J. B. Generalized expectancies for internal versus external control of reinforcement. *Psychological Monographs*, 1966, 80 (1, Whole No. 609).
Sampson, E. E. Studies of status congruence. In L. Berkowitz (Ed.), *Advances in experimental social psychology*. Vol. 4. New York: Academic Press, 1969. Pp. 225-270.
Schattschneider, E. E. *The semi-sovereign people*. New York: Holt, Rinehart & Winston, 1960.
Schein, E. H. The Chinese indoctrination program for prisoners of war: a study of attempted "brainwashing." In E. Maccoby, T. Newcomb, & E. Hartley (Eds.), *Readings in social psychology*, 3rd ed. New York: Holt, 1958. Pp. 311-334.
Schein, E. H., Schneier, I., & Barker, C. H. *Coercive persuasion*. New York: Norton, 1961.
Schlenker, B., Bonoma, T., Tedeschi, J. T., Lindskold, S., & Horai, J. Induced interpersonal attraction as a determinant of compliance to threats and promises. Mimeographed manuscript, State University of New York at Albany, 1970.
Schopler, J., & Bateson, N. The power of dependence. *Journal of Personality and Social Psychology*, 1965, 2, 247-254.

Shapley, L. S., & Shubik, M. A. A method for evaluating the distribution of power in a committee system. *American Political Science Review*, 1954, 48, 787-792.

Sherif, C. W. Variations in judgment as a function of ego-involvement. Paper presented at the Annual Meeting of the Eastern Psychological Association, Atlantic City, N. J., 1947.

Simmel, G. *The sociology of Georg Simmel.* K. H. Wolff, Ed. New York: Free Press, 1950.

Simon, H. A. *Models of man: social and rational.* New York: Wiley, 1957.

Simon, H. A., Smithburg, D. W., & Thompson, V. A. Why men obey. J. H. Kessel, G. F. Cole, & R. G. Seddig (Eds.), In *Micropolitics.* New York: Holt, Rinehart & Winston, 1970. Pp. 580-589.

Simons, H. W., Berkowitz, N. N., & Moyer, R. J. Similarity, credibility, and attitude change: a review and a theory. *Psychological Bulletin*, 1970, 73, 1-16.

Singer, J. D. Inter-nation influence: a formal model. *American Political Science Review*, 1963, 57, 420-430.

Skinner, B. F. *The behavior of organisms.* New York: Appleton-Century-Crofts 1938.

Skinner, B. F. Are theories of learning necessary? *Psychological Review*, 1950, 57, 193-216.

Slavson, S. R. *Activity group therapy* (16 mm. sound film). New York: Columbia University Press, 1950. (a)

Slavson, S. R. *Analytic group psychotherapy with children, adolescents, and adults.* New York: Columbia University Press, 1950. (b)

Strickland, B. R. The prediction of social action from a dimension of internal-external control. *Journal of Social Psychology*, 1965, 66, 353-358.

Szasz, T. S. *The myth of mental illness.* New York: Dell, 1961.

Tagiuri, R., & Kogan, N. Personal preference and the attribution of influence in small groups. *Journal of Personality*, 1960, 28, 257-265.

Tedeschi, J. T. Prediction, control, and the multiple-environment problem. *Psychological Record*, 1966, 16, 409-418.

Tedeschi, J. T. Threats and promises. In P. Swingle (Ed.), *The structure of conflict.* New York: Academic Press, 1970.

Tedeschi, J. T., Bonoma, T. V., & Brown, R. A paradigm for the study of coercive power. *Journal of Conflict Resolution,* 1971, 15, 197-224.

Thibaut, J. W., & Kelley, H. H. *The social psychology of groups.* New York: Wiley, 1959.

Thibaut, J. W., & Strickland, L. H. Psychological set and social conformity. *Journal of Personality*, 1956, 25, 115-129.

Turner, E. A., & Wright, J. C. Effects of severity of threat and perceived availability on the attractiveness of objects. *Journal of Personality and Social Psychology*, 1965, 2, 128-132.

Walker, E. L., & Heyns, R. W. *Anatomy for conformity.* Englewood Cliffs, N. J.: Prentice-Hall, 1962.

Walster, E., Aronson, E., & Abrahams, D. On increasing the persuasiveness of a low prestige communicator. *Journal of Experimental Social Psychology*, 1966, 2, 325-342.

Walster, E., & Festinger, L. The effectiveness of "overheard" persuasive communications. *Journal of Abnormal and Social Psychology*, 1962, 65, 395-402.

Weber, M. *The theory of social and economic organization.* New York: Oxford University Press, 1947.

Wertheimer, M. Some problems in the theory of ethics. *Social Research*, 1935, 2, 353-367.

White, R. K. Images in the context of international conflict: Soviet perceptions of the U. S. and the U.S.S.R. In H. C. Kelman (Ed.), *International behavior: a social psychological analysis.* New York: Holt, Rinehart & Winston, 1965. Pp. 236-276.

Wiener, M. Certainty of judgment as a variable in conformity behavior. *Journal of Social Psychology,* 1958, 48, 257-263

Williams, C. D. The elimination of tantrum behavior by extinction procedures. *Journal of Abnormal and Social Psychology*, 1959, 59, 269.

Wolpe, J. *Psychotherapy by reciprocal inhibition.* Stanford, Cal.: Stanford University Press, 1958.

Wright, H.F., & Barker, R. G. Day-long records of children's behavior as a research tool. *American Psychologist*, 1949, 4, 248.

Zimbardo, P., & Ebbesen, E. E. *Influencing attitudes and changing behavior.* Reading, Mass.: Addison-Wesley, 1969.

II

Jack M. McLeod and Steven R. Chaffee

The Construction of Social Reality

Why Social Reality?

Each of us likes to think of himself as being rational and autonomous. Our ideas seem to be peculiarly our own. It is hard for us to realize how little of our information comes from direct experience with the physical environment, and how much of it comes only indirectly, from other people and the mass media. Our complex communication systems enable us to overcome the time and space limitations that confined our ancestors, but they leave us with a greater dependence on others for shaping our ideas about how things are in the world. While becoming aware of places and events far from the direct experience of our daily lives, we have given up much of our capacity to confirm what we think we know.

This dependence on communication would have little impact on the study of social influence processes were it not for certain other aspects of the way we typically construct our view of the world. First, it appears that much of the information obtained from others is given the status of *reality*, as if it were no less valid than if it had been a direct observation of physical reality. The personal and tentative nature of our information may be forgotten as the material becomes absorbed into our cognitive structure. This tendency to treat information as reality is reinforced by the fact that a large

Much of our own research reported in this chapter was supported by Grant GS-1874 from the National Science Foundation; by contracts from the national Institute of Mental Health; by grants from the Graduate Research Committee of the University of Wisconsin from funds supplied by the Wisconsin Alumni Research Foundation; and by a grant to the University of Wisconsin Computing Center from the National Science Foundation. We would like to thank our colleagues and former students whose research is represented here, especially Brian Donnelly, H. S. Eswara, Jose Guerrero, Oguz Nayman, Robert Nwankwo, Gary O'Keefe, Ramona Rush, Vernon Stone, Leonard Tipton, Daniel Wackman, and Scott Ward. The help of our current students, Charles Atkin, William Elliott, George Pasdirtz, and Rebecca Quarles is gratefully acknowledged.

proportion of unverified information is shared by others around us. That is, they seem to have the same information and ideas we do, and we may find ourselves agreeing that everyone "ought to" see things the way we do. This normative sharing of "oughtness" is often referred to by the term *social reality*.

It is widely held that the influence process is greatly affected by the beliefs, attitudes, and values brought to an influence situation by its participants. These intrapersonal factors help determine the amount of influence attempted and received, as well as the patterns of interaction that occur in an interpersonal encounter. One's prior beliefs, attitudes, and values form a frame of reference — a kind of cognitive map for interpreting reality that precedes and controls the exchange of information and influence. To the extent that one's definition of a situation is derived from communication with other people rather than from his direct experience, we can say that it describes *his* social reality. Since individuals differ considerably in their communication experiences, we can expect that their maps of social reality will also vary greatly. This individual variance in pictures of social reality makes the concept an attractive one for social scientists, because it provides an index of the outcomes of social processes.

If the frequency with which social scientists employ a term is taken as an indicator of its pragmatic utility, then social reality would seem to be a very useful concept indeed. It is invoked not only in describing social influence processes, but also in explaining a variety of other forms of social behavior. Almost every textbook on social psychology contains some reference to it, as do many classic essays in the field. But in almost every instance, the notion of social reality is used only to provide post-hoc explanations of unaccounted-for social process. Rarely, if ever, has it been used directly as an organizing concept in devising research. Why has such an appealing idea remained simply a descriptive teaching concept, and not become a seminal research concept? Why is the term no more than a facile label for factors that the researcher has not studied—but apparently "knows" are there? Before research will be focused on social reality, some explicative decisions need to be made about the most useful definition of the concept and how it should be measured.

Problems in Defining Social Reality

One Term, Two Concepts

No one who has spent much time in the social sciences is surprised to find definitional problems. Pure theoretical terms such as "ego," "role," "life-space," "alienation," "mass culture," and "empathy" have proven stubbornly resistant to systematic empirical research—partly because their widespread use has meant that they refer to very different things in different verbal contexts, or in the employ of different writers. Common-language symbols such as "poverty," "generation gap," "decline in morality," and "the middle majority" can provide powerful stimuli to social action, but are far too vague to permit the clear operational definitions required for social research. And so it has been with "social reality." In fact, this term has been frequently used to refer to ideas that are not simply different, but are almost incompatible.

There have been writers concerned with *social* reality, and writers concerned with social *reality*. The first group takes the cognitive system of the *individual* as its unit of analysis, and lets social reality refer to the person's frame of reference in a social situation (Berger & Luckmann, 1966; Berlo, 1960; Cooley, 1909; Scheff, 1968). A vastly different conception is held by others who examine the *social system* as their unit of analysis, and look on social reality as the actual degree of agreement or consensus among the members of that system (Cartwright & Zander, 1968; Katz & Lazarsfeld, 1955; Newcomb, 1953, 1959, 1965). For convenience in this rather confusing state of affairs, we will use the label Sr to refer to the first (individual cognitive system level) concept, or social reality. The second (social system level) concept, social reality, we will call sR.

Within these two mutually exclusive conceptual traditions, there is still a great deal of variance in usage, and neither general definition provides clear enough guidelines for data-gathering to make social reality a viable research concept as it stands. Let us examine each definitional approach in some detail.

SOCIAL REALITY (Sr) AS A COGNITIVE SYSTEM VARIABLE

Generally, the cognitive system approach to Sr places a heavy emphasis on the "unreality" that pervades an individual's unique construction of "reality" as it emerges through interaction. Cooley (1909, p. 119), for example, defining society as a relation among what he calls personal ideas, comments that "the immediate social reality is the personal idea." Berlo (1960), even more extremely, equates social reality with strictly personal or autistic meaning—i.e., meaning that is *not* shared with others through denotative agreement in the verbal community.

Scheff (1968) takes a more concrete approach; his social reality is shared, but in an explicit dyadic situation. In the psychiatrist-patient relationship, for example, the psychiatrist rejects many of his patient's statements about the sources of his problems and accepts others. Since the psychiatrist controls the situation, the patient tends to incorporate only the accepted statements into *his* social reality. Unfortunately from a research standpoint, this conception gives us few clues as to how to compare one dyadic actor's personal social reality with someone else's. No statements are offered regarding expected norms of social realities across, say, the population of psychiatrist-patient relationships, nor about factors that might explain systematic variations among realities.

Berger and Luckmann (1966) offer perhaps the best single treatise on social reality. They provide considerable insight into the ways in which social reality emerges from habituation and becomes institutionalized into the social structure. They give us less help toward understanding how different views of Sr become embedded in different parts of the social system. Their choice of introspection, or self-insight, as the exclusive source of data will send those who require "hard" empirical evidence elsewhere in their search.

The root problem with the cognitive system approach is that it is not specific regarding the origins of Sr in the social structure. Even if we examine a person's Sr in endless detail, we will be unable to distinguish those elements of it that are based on direct observation from those that have been learned socially. We will be unable to attribute it to specific parts of the social system, or to specific social groups or institutions among the many with which the person is involved. We can hardly expect the person himself to reveal these important matters to us, since Sr presumably has for him a "self-evident and compelling facticity" (Berger & Luckmann, 1966, p. 23). To him, Sr is all of a piece; to account for it then, we must compare it with the social reality of others in his social environment—that is, with sR.

SOCIAL REALITY (sR) AS A SOCIAL SYSTEM VARIABLE

A social system approach to the definition of social reality holds out the promise of describing the distribution of perspectives throughout a social system. The criterion of consensus is clearly stated by Newcomb (1965, p. 234): "Cognitive norms that do not correspond to any physical reality have effects that are just as real as those that do. Insofar as they are generally shared they come to constitute a kind of reality known as *social reality*." This statement goes well beyond the usual social system (sR) definition of social reality as agreement about what the situation is; Newcomb also adds two significant requirements: that the members feel that others in the group should feel as they do (i.e., that their beliefs carry normative sanctions), and that each person is aware that the others feel this way.

This type of definition of sR is quite satisfactory under certain conditions: when the group is small and its boundaries are clear cut; when the group is relatively isolated from competing constructions of social reality; when the norms at issue are very close to the core values of the group; and when independent, external validation via direct observation of reality is very difficult. In, for example, Newcomb's studies of Bennington college girls and of male rooming-house boarders (1943, 1961, 1967), these conditions were maximized.

But can sR as a state of consensus in the social system provide as useful a concept in field situations that fall short of these criteria? Can we, for example, validly talk of consensus in a national society, or in a megalopolitan community? It seems obvious that we cannot expect to find complete or even widespread agreement about anything of consequence in such large, permeable, and heterogeneous social systems. How, then, should we go about defining boundaries of groups in which consensus can be found? Assuming that we will have to accept a level of agreement which is less than perfect, but which we can regard as a consensus social reality, how can we set any empirical criteria for determining that level? These are not easy questions. Somehow we must pay closer attention to individual adaptations to Sr in order to be able to deal with sR in other than an arbitrary fashion.

Different Theories Imply Different Questions

Apart from the Sr-sR confusion that grows out of the use of different levels of abstraction, convergence in the use of social reality is made even more difficult by the fact that different theorists seek answers to rather different questions. No one writer seems attentive to all these questions. They can be stated as three general queries: (1) *What* is the content of social reality, and how is it structured? (2) *Why* do people construct it (Sr), or accept it (sR)? (3) *How* do people construct Sr, or accept sR? It should come as no surprise that the answers to each of these questions exhibit considerable variation.

WHAT IS SOCIAL REALITY?

The main divergence in answers to the content question is between those who are concerned with *belief* and those who stress *meaning*. In the first group belong Newcomb's (1965) idea of consensus as shared beliefs; Berger and Luckmann's (1966) interest in what is real; and Cartwright and Zander's (1968) concept of "acceptable beliefs." Writers on meaning have put it in terms of meanings for ambiguous situations (Katz & Lazarsfeld, 1955), personal connotative meaning (Berlo, 1960), and definition of the situation (Scheff, 1968). In none of these cases is the organization or structure of these beliefs and meanings made sufficiently clear. Nor can one find evidence, in these conceptions of content, of the common assertion that social reality anticipates experience.

WHY DO PEOPLE ACCEPT IT?

Three general classes of explanation are offered for the acceptance of social reality: motivational states within the person; situational factors; and forces that arise in the group.

Festinger (1954) typifies the first approach. He posits a basic drive to evaluate one's own opinions, i.e., for the person to determine that he is correct. When physical reality-testing is impossible, this leads to a drive toward social comparisons of oneself with others. Worried that he might not be quite right, the individual looks to others for validation of his views. Later writers (Schachter, 1959; Scheff, 1968) have shifted the stress from cognitive to emotional uncertainty.

Situational determination of reality seeking is the explanation offered by Jones and Gerard (1967). Rejecting Festinger's motivational drive for evaluation, they instead see the force coming from requirements for action within the social situation. The person needs to know the various courses of action, and the probability of each. So he seeks information from the most *reliable* source (rather than from the most familiar source, as Festinger would have it). Newcomb (1953) implies that he might also tend to seek an "attractive" source.

Earlier, Festinger (1950) discussed pressures toward uniformity that arise in the group. Newcomb (1965) also sees group pressures increasing acceptance of social reality, through positive and negative sanctions that reflect shared cognitive norms.

HOW DOES IT DEVELOP?

The "how" of social reality, the exact nature of the processes by which it comes about, has been given less attention than have the "what" and "why" questions discussed above. One major distinction that has been made is between learning through communication with other people and learning from observing the behavior of others. Jones and Gerard (1967) call these two modes of social learning "reflected appraisal" and "comparative appraisal," respectively. Aside from this distinction, the literature has little to tell us about the parameters of, or variations in, the communication-learning process. For example, is the learning of Sr based on the imitation of what others do, or on social reinforcement of what one does himself? Or is the "learning" of one Sr structure simply the inevitable result of the *absence* of competing Srs within the social system? These questions of micro process are not posed in the literature although they suggest potentially major issues.

Different Concepts with Similar Meanings

We have so far been emphasizing the problem of dealing with one core concept, social reality, that has many different definitions. The opposite problem further confuses the situation: there are many names for some very similar concepts. For example, in discussing the cognitive individual-level conceptions of social reality (Sr), we have already used four terms that are not easily distinguishable: *frame of reference, cognitive map, definition of the situation* and *perspective*. To this list might well be added some other widely used concepts: *weltanschauung, image, conformity*, and *reference group behavior*. Similarly, at the social system level (sR), we find other nearly synonymous concepts: *consensus, consensual validation*, and *common value system*.

It would be convenient if we could ignore these overlapping concepts and substitute our own language and definitions. But these terms will not simply go away. They are embedded in a rich and varied literature that will continue to guide social theorists. If we are to come up with a clear, researchable conception of social reality, then, we must consider each of these terms and distinguish among them.

SIMILAR COGNITIVE CONCEPTS

The term *cognitive map* refers to the structure of the person's total thinking, including not only "social reality" material learned from others in ambiguous situations, but things learned from direct experience and observation as well. Thus social reality (Sr) is part of, but not the whole of, one's cognitive map.

The term *frame of reference* has a more specific meaning than the general notion implied by "cognitive map." One's frame of reference *precedes* social interaction, and determines the ways in which his experience in the interaction will be organized in his thinking. Thus it involves his general "approach" or "mental set" toward the situation; the attributes he will use to evaluate what is important or valuable in that situation; the things he will look for and the relations he will expect to find between these things.

Construction of Social Reality

One's frame of reference is, theoretically, applied rather consistently, over time, to a variety of different situations. It is a kind of "personality" trait. By contrast, the concept of *definition of the situation* refers to the specific frame of reference that one applies to a particular situation. Rokeach (1966-1967), in discussing social attitudes, makes an analogous distinction between one's "attitude toward the situation" and his "attitude toward an object in the situation." To the extent that a person's general frame of reference, or his specific definition of a given situation, is systematically related to frames of reference that are lodged in some social system, it can be thought of as Sr.

As an example, let us consider two hypothetical voters and their views of an upcoming election in which a "dove" is challenging a "hawkish" incumbent congressman. Both voters consider the war in Vietnam as the overriding issue in the election; that is, they will cast their votes on the basis of the relative positions of the candidates regarding the war. One of the voters is a Quaker pacifist, works in a community service organization, and for the past few years has contributed 10 percent of his salary to organizations devoted to peace. The other voter holds the view that the war should be won, and that it would be won if citizens supported the war effort. Now we may say that these two voters share approximately the same definition of the situation. They do not, however, have the same general frame of reference, since as reflected in their attitudes toward the war, their ways of thinking are clearly very different. These two gentlemen would find it very difficult to achieve any sort of political *consensus*, a topic that is taken up under social system concepts (sR) below.

The term *perspective* comes to us from an intellectual tradition almost completely separate from the American social-psychological background that has given us the other concepts we have been discussing. The use of "perspective" to describe the situation where human thought or cognitive structure is tied to specific elements of social activity or social structure, finds its roots in the sociology of knowledge, a European branch of scholarship begun by Scheler (1925). The best-known exponent of this approach is Mannheim (1936), who devotes considerable attention to the ways in which social reality (Sr) distorts one's perception of "real" social conditions.

Much of the sociology of knowledge literature grows out of Karl Marx's twin concepts of *ideology* (ideas serving as weapons for social interests) and *false consciousness* (thought alienated from the real conditions of life). So it is not surprising that we find writers in this tradition who see perspectives as if they were attached solely to narrow economic interests. But if we interpret the term more broadly, recalling its origins in the context of social conditions and institutions, then the concept of perspectives is very close to our general cognitive-level Sr. Until very recently, however, the parallel traditions of social psychology and the sociology of knowledge—each with major implications for the analysis of social reality—have coexisted with little intellectual interchange (cf. Berger & Luckmann, 1966).

Weltanschauung means one's philosophy or conception of the world and of life. It reflects the European concern with the person's fundamental values rather than with the specifics of cognitive structure that are implied by such concepts as frame of reference. A much overused (and misused) term, *image* is used by Boulding (1961) as apparently synonymous with frame of reference. He also uses the term *public image* for the situation where the same image is shared by many persons, analogous to cognitive level Sr. Boulding gives no hint of how to measure an image, but his highly readable work makes a good case for the importance of the concept, and even coins the term "eiconics" for the science of image study.

Since social conformity is a behavior determined by the behavior of other people, it bears at least a superficial resemblance to social reality. The term *conformity*, however, refers to overt behavior rather than to the less accessible cognitive structure. And too, conformity can take place for a variety of reasons, including purely instrumental acquiescence without any corresponding changes in cognitive structure. A person can, in other words, publicly conform to a group standard without privately believing that what he is doing corresponds to a veridical perception of reality.

In the well-known conformity experiments by Asch (1951), for example, approximately one-third of the subjects overtly conformed to a unanimous group judgment about the relative lengths of a set of lines, even though that judgment was clearly contradictory to the physical facts of the situation. Some of these subjects said they expressed a conforming judgment although they knew it was erroneous, simply to avoid any social stigma in this rather bizarre situation. Others reported that they had actually doubted their own judgment, reasoning that if "everyone else" saw the facts differently, then "everyone else" might well be right. Of these two processes of conformity, only the second would be considered as an instance of Sr.

Reference group behavior presents a somewhat similar situation. Only one of its three varying definitions listed by Shibutani (1955) involves accepting group viewpoints as reality. When reference group behavior is taken to mean the use of the group's modal view as a point of reference in making comparisons or contrasts, the person clearly need not see the group members' beliefs as real, or even desirable. Such is the case in the classic study of "relative deprivation" analyzed by Merton and Kitt (1950). They found that the judgments of rear-echelon soldiers overseas concerning their future varied, depending upon whether they compared themselves to men at home or to combat soldiers.

The second concept of "reference group" is as a group to which the person aspires to gain or maintain acceptance. This implies that the person sees a difference between the desired group and some other one; hence, it is unlikely that he would mistake the perceived beliefs of the former for reality.

Only in the third usage of "reference group," as *perspective*, does the person accept a frame of reference as reality. Shibutani makes the interesting observation that this group need not be one in which the person desires acceptance; even though he dislikes it in some cases, it may serve to structure the way he views the world.

SIMILAR SOCIAL SYSTEM CONCEPTS

The social system definition of social reality, sR, involves fewer terms that overlap in meaning. As we have already indicated, *consensus* as used by Newcomb (1965) appears to be synonymous with sR. *Consensual validation*, a key term for Sullivan (1953), designated a symbol that comes to have a standard meaning. While this bears some resemblance to sR, there is no implication that sharing must include awareness that others have the same meaning. Nor are cognitive norms involved in Sullivan's concept. Finally, the popular term *common value systems* is somewhat analogous to the concept of *weltanschauung* discussed earlier. Each deals more with general values or philosophies than with specific cognitive structures.

Possibilities for Research on Social Reality

Although there are, as we have seen, many competing concepts of social reality, few of those who have used this or the related terms reviewed above have provided instructions for measuring their concepts. To convert this vague notion into a research concept, we will have to begin with some arbitrary choices among definitions. Fortunately there is a fair amount of convergence around the two modal concepts we have called Sr and sR. If we can specify acceptable research procedures for each of these, it will matter little which one is thought of as the "real" social reality.[1]

Our search of definitions, or "meaning analysis" in Hempel's (1952) terms, convinces us that a set of data must meet three basic requirements if social reality is to become a research concept:

1. There must be an assessment of the person's cognitive mapping or, more specifically, his frame of reference.
2. A comparable assessment must be made for others within his social "system"—that is, his milieu, membership or reference groups, or other collectivities or social categories that might be of research interest.
3. A correspondence must be shown between the first and the second sets of data, to provide an estimate of the social derivation of the person's cognitive structure.

These requirements refer to the form of the data. We will defer questions about the content of the data until a later section of the paper.

Interpersonal Unit of Analysis

As we have set out our requirements for data, it seems clear that an individual, or atomic, unit of analysis is inadequate. At the other extreme, data gathered at the macrosystem, or molar, level of analysis could easily prove to be socially and psychologically unrealistic. It is preferable to employ a level of analysis that is complex enough to meet our data requirements, but no more complex than that. On this reasoning, we have chosen to approach social reality at the *interpersonal*, or molecular, level. We will refrain from generalizing to larger social units except where this can be shown to be a valid procedure.

For example, in analyzing the social reality of a college senior, we are likely to find rather quickly that his frames of reference have not simply grown out of personal experience; so an individual unit of analysis is inappropriate. But if we attempt to correlate his definitions of situations with the social collectivity "college students," we will probably find that we have cast too wide a net. He does not, after all, interact with all college students, nor even share a common set of communication sources with all of them. Indeed, we will find that there is no "typical college student perspective" that our student could adopt even if he were in a mythical total-interaction system with that entire group. If, however, we limit

---

[1]. The search for operational definitions is the social scientist's basic test of the meaningfulness of a concept. For the student of social phenomena who seeks understanding rather than leads for empirical research, however, this sort of tearing-and-comparing of measurement procedures can become quite tedious. The general reader is, therefore, advised at this point to skip ahead to the summary of this section.

Construction of Social Reality

ourselves to a specifically interpersonal approach, we can begin to learn something by comparing his perspectives to those of his roommate, classmates, girlfriend; perhaps, teachers and parents; even his favorite newspaper, magazine, or film director.

Use of the interpersonal level implies that we will analyze social influence situations in rather different terms from those that have been used in the past. For example, instead of concepts that describe a person's customary individual behavior across a variety of social situations (e.g., he is "persuasible," or he "strives for consistency"), we will find ourselves making interpersonal inferences (e.g., he seeks information from high-power figures, or he adjusts his opinion-expression to the norms of the small group). We shall return to this point below.

THE COORIENTATION MODEL

We have found it most useful to examine interpersonal situations in terms of a very simple model of *coorientation*. This model combines Newcomb's (1953) *A*-to-*B*-re-*X* paradigm with the terminological and measurement approach of person-perception research (Tagiuri,

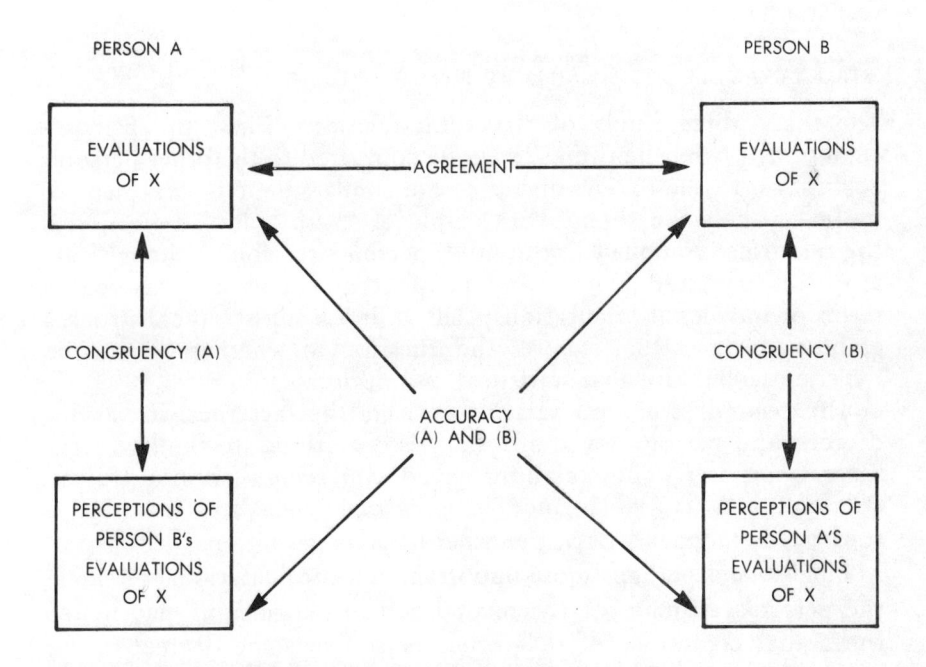

Figure 2.1. Components of a Coorientation Situation: Agreements, Accuracy, and Congruency

Bruner, & Blake, 1958). The simplest situation is one in which the person is focused on the same set of objects as is a second person; the two are then said to be "cooriented" with one another. Each of the persons in the situation has at least two distinguishable sets of cognitions: he knows what he thinks, and he has some estimate of what the other person thinks. In a two-person situation, then, there is a minimal set of four cognitions. The basic concepts in the model consist of relations between different pairs of cognitions from this total set. The model is shown schematically in Figure 2.1.

Describing Figure 2.1 in Newcomb's terms, the first person, A, and the second person, B, are simultaneously cooriented to one another, and oriented to some issue or set of objects, X. Newcomb treats these elements as *givens*, or as necessary conditions for the social influence process he characterizes as a "strain toward symmetry." We will later discuss these elements as *variables*, which may be either more or less salient (and therefore more or less operative) in a given coorientation situation. We will also deal at considerable length with the nature and dimensionality of the "Xs" of Newcomb's paradigm when we discuss the content of communication and coorientation. Here, we are mainly concerned with the two persons (A and B) and the structural relations among their cognitions about X and about one another.

STRUCTURAL RELATIONS AND DERIVED MEASURES

There are three kinds of structural relations. First, the person's cognitions ("what he thinks") can be compared to the other person's cognitions; to the extent that they are similar, there is *agreement* or mutuality between them. This simple or "zero-order" definition is the one usually applied in the multi-person situation. Although data are often gathered from many people, agreement is measured in terms of individual orientations; that is, it is a statistical construct, a grand reification that ignores the question of whether there is an experiential base for that statistical assumption.

The second structural relation reflects the fact that, in varying degrees, the person may think that his cognitions are similar to the second person's. This relation, called *congruency*, is not truly a coorientational variable since it is *intrapersonal* and its value is statistically independent of the other person's cognitions.

Finally, and perhaps most important for coorientational research, the person's estimate of the second person's cognitions may match the actual cognitions of that other person in some degree; to the extent that this is the case, *accuracy* is involved.

In any coorientation situation, therefore, the person is described by two coorientational measures, agreement and accuracy, and by one orientational measure, congruency. The measure of agreement is shared between the two persons, while each person has his own set of measures on the other two indices. Thus, there are five sets of relational scores based on the four measures in a two-person situation.

Of course, the set of four structural relations with the five measures derived from them could be expanded infinitely. The generalization from Scheff (1967) takes the following form:

Zero order: What do I think?
First order: Do I know what he thinks?
Second order: Does he know what I think he thinks?
Third order: Do I think he knows what I think he thinks?
Nth order: etc.

The point is, at what point does this series of queries become empirically irrelevant? Scheff suggests that an extension to higher orders is necessary to index thoroughly the concept of consensus (our sR). He criticizes the use of a simple zero-order agreement—the comparison of the "What do I think?" from both persons—as not taking into consideration the perception of the conditions of agreement we call congruency.

The paradox of *pluralistic ignorance* illustrates the inadequacy of using simple agreement. The classic case of pluralistic ignorance came from Schanck (1932) who found considerable private violation of the "Elm Hollow" community norms against drinking and playing cards, even though each of the violators assumed he was virtually alone in his violation. That is, there was private *agreement* on the covert drinking and card playing behaviors, but low *congruency* and *accuracy*.

Newcomb (1961) also found pluralistic ignorance, among 17 students immediately after they had moved into a rooming house. The low level of congruency and accuracy resulted from the restricted communication of early acquaintance. Later, with more informal and open communication, congruency and accuracy increased as the students became aware that others felt as they did.

In a study of husband-wife coorientation, Pasdirtz (1969) found that prior congruency was an important determinant of both later agreement and later accuracy, when a discussion of current news issues was interposed between the two measures. It appears that two people are more likely to explain their values to one another when they think they agree.

Scheff's position is that we need to go to even higher levels of reciprocal cognition. Laing, Phillipson, and Lee (1966) present some evidence that the analysis of higher-order reciprocity is necessary to understand marital discord among couples who had applied for marriage counseling. Such an extension may be desirable when we restrict our interest to the dyad; however, when our interest is in larger numbers of people, as is most likely the case with social reality, the problems of obtaining and analyzing nth-order data are overwhelming.

Even in working with first-order relations, there are some rather severe operational problems that must be faced. The statistical dependence of the measures on one another means that controls cannot be used in a straightforward manner. In the area of person perception, the problems in measuring accuracy or "empathy" are well documented (Bender & Hastorf, 1953; Bronfenbrenner, Harding, & Gallwey, 1958; Cronbach, 1955, 1958; Gage & Cronback, 1955). The problem is somewhat lessened when the beliefs of others, rather than the characteristics of the other person himself, are being judged. Wackman (1969) has suggested some methods for analyzing coorientational change by means of partial correlations. However, his procedures require a large battery of items (each of which must be asked twice per respondent, for coorientational data), so that the basic correlations will be stable enough to be meaningful. More often, the researcher will content himself with a few items, analyzed in terms of mean deviations (D) or D^2 scores (see Osgood, Suci, & Tannenbaum, 1957).

One of the seeming strengths of the coorientational model for teaching purposes turns out to be a weakness for research purposes. If it is not intuitively obvious to the reader, it could easily be shown that a change in the value of any one of the three "legs" of the coorientational "triangle"—agreement, congruency, and accuracy—necessarily means that one of the other legs will change in a predictable direction if the third is held constant. Unsophisticated students in introductory "communication" courses sometimes mistake this unfortunate statistical interdependence for an insightful hypothesis about coorientational processes. For example, if congruency is low and agreement is high, any increase in accuracy implies that congruency will increase (assuming agreement remains constant). Or if congruency is high and constant, an increase in agreement means an attendant improvement in accuracy. These artifactual "hypotheses" that result from dependent measures are always present in coorientational process analysis. They only serve to make true hypothesis-testing a more difficult business than is the case with most types of social research. In advocating coorientational analysis in the face of this kind of difficulty, we are clearly willing to sacrifice some methodological elegance for what we consider a major gain in substantive validity. In situations where the existence of social reality in the sense we are defining it here is questionable or peripheral to the study, however, it would be foolish to force coorientational analysis on one's research design in the face of these inherent statistical shortcomings.

Generalization to Larger Groups: The Reification Problem

At first blush, the procedures for generalizing the general coorientational model to units of more than two persons might seem conceptually trivial and procedurally straightforward. In a three-person situation, for example, the analysis would consist of three coorientational pairings, AB, AC and BC, toward one or more objects X. Summary statistics for the triad could be constructed by summing across the three agreement, six accuracy, and six congruency measures, to provide three general descriptive indices. Analogous procedures are possible, in principle, for groups of any size. Indeed, one might even attempt to compare groups of various sizes in terms of coorientational criteria, in the manner of early small groups research (e.g., Bales & Borgatta, 1955). This kind of procedure, however, involves some assumptions about just whom the person is cooriented with, and the degree to which he reifies the group that is being analyzed.

ASSUMPTIONS IN STUDYING LARGER GROUPS

The simple summation of coorientation measures contains a hidden assumption that each person reacts to the group as a collection of individuals. There is, of course, an alternative formulation: that the person reacts to the group as a "generalized other," which is his internal *reification* of the other members of the group and their beliefs and products taken as a unit. This kind of reification is described by Berger and Luckmann (1966, p. 82): "Reification is the apprehension of human phenomena as if they were real things... Reification is the apprehension of the products of human activity *as if* they were something else than human—such as facts of nature, cosmic laws, or manifestations of divine will." We use such grand reifications as "American public opinion" in everyday speech as if it were a concrete and homogeneous entity. When we ask people in our research to make summary judgments about categories of people, we are assuming reification. Many of the classic studies of stereotyping (e.g., Katz & Braly, 1933) asked respondents to attach labels (e.g., dishonest, shrewd) to groups (e.g., Russians, Jews) thus forcing people to reify. Public agreement about the content of the stereotype of a particular group does not indicate, for example, that all or even most of the members of that group are seen as possessing that attribute. Clearly, the assumption of reification of the group is as hazardous as is the alternative assumption of independent perception of the group's members.

DEGREE OF REIFICATION AS A VARIABLE

If we are interested in treating the reification of groups as a measured variable rather than as an assumed property, it is important to state the conditions necessary to reification from the point of view of the person, and to develop appropriate operational definitions for the *degree of reification* in the person's judgment of a group or collectivity. While other properties might be desirable to include under reification, we should certainly consider as necessary the person's perceiving a high degree of agreement within the group in question. For relatively small groups, say a half-dozen members or less, this form of stereotyping might be indexed by a relatively low level of variance in the person's judgment of the position of individual members of the group across the various items of judgment. For larger groups where measures of judgments of other individuals becomes difficult or impossible, group reification might be indexed by asking each person to estimate the proportion of people in the group holding each position, rather than asking for the "average position" as is customarily done. The less the variance of this perceived distribution, the more valid the assumption of reification becomes.

This "group reification" is different from other forms of stereotyping, such as the fixedness, polarization, and homogenization of image elements discussed by Carter (1962). The last of these, which involves generalization across several attributes of one's judgment of another person, may actually be complementary to our "degree of reification," in that a low level of one may lead to a high level of the other. That is, making discriminations between group members (nonreification) may make intramember distinctions more difficult. The person may need to simplify his view of the internal qualities of each person, in order to make nonreified discriminations between persons.

There is a fair amount of research relevant to this question of the wisdom of treating the group as an assemblage of the perceptions of its members. Consider the accuracy of judgment as an example. It appears that the ability of a person to predict the typical responses of the group is uncorrelated with his ability to differentiate among the individuals in the same group (Bronfenbrenner et al., 1958; Cline & Richards, 1960).

Construction of Social Reality

In a three-person group, coalition-formation is often found; indeed, it is often necessary if the group is to come to any decision or action, under certain conditions. It is no reification for the group member who is excluded from the coalition to react to the coalition as a unit, rather than as two individuals. Accordingly, it would be no reification for the researcher to treat this as a dyadic unit for purposes of analysis.

The basic question is whether the reification is cognitively operative for the persons who are coorienting. If there is an empirical basis for inferring (1) that the necessary conditions of coorientation are met and (2) that the person is cooriented with a collectivity of more than one other person, then the assumption may be admissible. Of course, we have already made a second assumption that reification is a continuum, making "degree of reification" a meaningful term. An alternative assumption and one more in keeping with the formulation of Berger and Luckmann (1966) presented earlier, is that reification is an either-or phenomenon—something is either "real" or it's not for a given person. This alternative view would affect measurement and statistical procedures, but would make little difference for basic research strategies.

PROBLEMS OF LABELING GROUPS TO BE PERCEIVED

If we wish to take a coorientational approach to studying large noninteracting groups, we must first specify labels for these groups that satisfy two criteria: they must be psychologically meaningful to the population of people under study; and they must suggest boundaries for the groups such that the researcher can tell objectively who should be included and who should not. While the first criterion is obvious, the second is less so. It becomes a requirement because our research strategy calls for a check of the person's perception of the group's position, against the actual distribution of positions in the defined group. The seemingly infinite number of group labels fall into one or the other of Merton's (1957, p. 299) two categories of groups: *collectivities* whose members have "a sense of solidarity by virtue of sharing common values and who have acquired an attendant sense of moral obligation to fulfill role-expectations"; and *social categories*, "aggregates of social statuses, the occupants of which are not in social interaction." Examples of collectivities might include "ships' captains," "newspaper editors," and "sociologists"; by contrast, "adolescents," "the very rich," and "women" can be considered social categories. Of course, these examples are arguable and pretty imprecise, but the general distinction is operationally viable in most cases, if one is careful about the referents of his labels. The social category "women" can become a collectivity when we use the label "active member of a women's liberation movement," and an interacting group if we considered "women attending a NOW convention in Washington." Often in drawing samples for social research, an interacting group is treated as no more than a social category or collectivity. This can produce some unexpected findings on occasion, such as the puzzling "sleeper effect" in opinion change (Hovland et al., 1949).

The problem of selecting the most useful set of labels for collectivities and social categories is a difficult one. What is meaningful for the persons who are being studied may not be easy for the researcher to determine and sample. For example, the label "poor people" may have a clear referent (albeit a varied one from person to person), but establishing the proper cutting point for "poverty" is a question that researchers and politicians alike have been debating for some time. An opposite situation may also obtain. For example, the researcher can rigorously define and sample "scientists," but a considerable part of his public sample may think of pharmacists, dentists, and astrologers under this label. Theoretically relevant labels like "middle class" may pose problems for both the researcher and the person he is studying. The problem is even more complicated where we wish to determine the limits of reification by comparing the judgments of the designated "in-group" with a contrasting "out-group." In such a case, the two criteria must hold for the contrasting label as well (e.g., for "rich people" as well as for "poor people"); it has often been demonstrated that many perspectives vary from one social sector to another, and reification of social units is surely no exception.

Generalization Over Time

Let us suppose we find a high degree of agreement between a person's frame of reference (Sr) and the perspective of a particular group (sR). Let us further assume that he accurately perceives the group's position as being fairly close to his own and that he reifies this position as a "generalized other." We would like to believe the functioning of the group has "caused" him to accept its perspective; however, two alternative explanations are possible. One is that the reverse causal sequence is operating here; the person has influenced the group to hold his position. (This would be more plausible, of course, if the group consists of a single other person.) The second explanation is that there is no functional relationship, that the person's frame of reference and the group perspective were developed independently and at most were produced by some common external source.

Collection of research data at a single point in time does not allow us to choose between our social reality (sR) explanation and the two alternative formulations. If we repeat our measures across time, we can come closer to identifying functional relationships. If the person's judgments vary systematically and follow the positions of the group in time, we can be somewhat more sure the person's judgments depend upon social reality rather than vice versa. (For a discussion of the use of time-series data see Bohrnstedt, 1969.)

Generalization over time may be useful to study the possibility that the person's world is made up of "multiple realities" that shift from situation to situation. It would be useful to study the shift in judgment from situation to situation over time, to index this degree of shift.

Devising Appropriate Measurement Procedures

Up to this point, we have discussed the problem of who-rates-whom and how the derivative measures are used in the coorientational approach. There are additional questions about the *what* of measurement. In principle, the task of specifying content for judgment is rather simple. We pick material (attitude, belief measures, attributes, etc.) that is relevant to the person under study and/or to the group of which he is a member. If we are interested in studying the social reality function of the family for the adolescent, for example, we look for topics of mutual concern (e.g., educational plans, time for getting in at night, use of the car). Any list of topics is open to question and perhaps the best guideline is to over-sample topics to make sure some are relevant to all persons under study. It is generally advisable to check the assumption of relevance by permitting "don't know" (see Carter et al., 1968-1969).

A final measurement problem derives from the conceptual definition of *frame of reference* discussed earlier. The definition implies that the frame of reference "precedes and organizes" subsequent behavior. The easiest interpretation of this notion is that it merely indicates a summation of what the person "brings to" the situation that he has learned from his past experience. This is theoretically uninteresting, however, and doesn't really help us much in devising measures. It is more interesting to take a literal and restrictive view of the qualities "precedes" and "organizes." The former can carry the implication of time-order, where the "frame" cues an emphasis on certain elements in the subsequent situation at the expense of others. The "organized" aspect implies structure, with parts and sequences that help to make for differing levels of salience. While this construction of frame of reference is certainly no rigorous definition for measurement, it at least provides some hint of what to include and what to leave out. Later in this paper, we describe at length some studies of the ways in which the structure of parent-child communication "precedes and organizes" adolescent cognitive development in varying directions.

The quality of "structure" seems to imply greater emphasis on the form of cognition than on the content. A simple compilation of the person's beliefs or attitudes would seem inappropriate for this kind of emphasis. A structural emphasis calls instead for measurement less closely keyed to specific content. Rather than impose a single "school" solution, we will illustrate three rather different types of measurement that appear to be useful alternatives.

COGNITIVE STRUCTURE AND STYLE

The intellectual forerunner of the idea of cognitive structure was Lewin's (1936) concept of *life space*. His definition not only expresses the basic view, but also illustrates the difficulty of developing from it an adequate index:

> Life space is the totality of facts which determine the behavior of an individual at a certain moment. Structure of a region refers to the degree of differentiation of the region (that is the number of subparts); the arrangement of those parts; and the degree of connectedness among them. Region is simply part of life space.

Since Lewin's presentation, the attempts to measure cognitive structure and style have been many and varied. Zajonc (1954; 1960) represents the first explicit clarification. His concept of *cognitive universe* is equivalent to life space: the set of all concepts or attributes by means of which an individual can identify and discriminate objects and events. *Cognitive structure* is then an organized subset of the given cognitive universe. He identifies more than ten properties of cognitive structures from a topological model; however four of these are particularly relevant—*differentiation, complexity, unity*, and *organization*.

The number of subsets or attributes a person uses to discriminate and identify an object constitutes Zajonc's measure of *differentiation*. Wackman et al. (1970) used a similar measure in a study of political socialization. The respondents were read a list of paired political objects and asked to point out similarities and differences between them. Cognitive differentiation was indexed by the total number of attributes used in making comparisons.

The attributes a person uses to classify an object or set of objects may come from a single class or dimension, or they may represent many dimensions. For example, a person may judge another person (as an object) purely in terms of his physical attributes (e.g., height, weight) or he may mix classes of attributes (e.g., height, intelligence, honesty). Such attribute groupings may be further subdivided into smaller classes. The number of subdivisions is the index of cognitive *complexity*.

The components of the whole structure may be dependent upon one another to a greater or lesser extent. Dependency is the extent to which the presence of one attribute predicts the presence of another attribute. When summed across all the attributes a person uses, the dependency score represents the *unity* of the cognitive structure.

Finally, the degree of *organization* can be thought of as a guiding principle that controls the parts of the whole. To the extent that one part or cluster of parts dominates the whole, the whole is said to demonstrate *organization*.

Another group of researchers emphasize cognitive "style" rather than structure. (In practice, this distinction is often hard to maintain.) They focus on dimensions of cognitive functioning as an indicator of the person's personality. Kagan et al. (1963), for example, distinguish among three kinds of cognitive style used by subjects in their judgments of pictures. Persons with a *descriptive* style tended to respond to details of the pictures when they were asked to point out similarities. Persons with an *inferential* style tended to respond by attempting to impose a classificatory scheme, and those with a *relational* style tended to point out functional relations between objects in the pictures.

Another approach is that of Carter (1965). Here the emphasis is upon the use of attributes to compare two or more objects, in contrast with the customary models, which study people's judgments of single objects. Carter also shares with Lewin the stress on specific situations, rather than working with trans-situational concepts such as "attitude." Carter distinguishes between two structurally different types of person-object relations. A *salience* relation is the affective link between the person and a *single object*, presumably a function of past experience that determines the degree of "psychological closeness" in the particular situation. A *pertinence* relation is the affective discrimination *between two objects* when the person judges which object possesses the greater degree of a relevant attribute. Carter's concepts have been treated as a model of communication content by Chaffee (1967) and Tipton (1970).

While the measurement considerations of the model have not yet been fully worked out, Chaffee et al. (1969) have shown that the model can be usefully applied to cognitive discrepancy experiments on information-seeking and selective exposure problems. As applied to comparing social reality (Sr) among sets of persons, the model implies separate measures for various aspects of salience and pertinence. Salience measures include an index of: overlap among persons in the objects they hold in common; overlap in relevant attributes; and a ranking of the general utility of each. Pertinence comparisons use such indices as: the discriminatory power of various attributes; and the discriminations that can be made with various two-object, one-attribute pairs.

As an example of this approach, consider the possibility of a husband and a wife cooriented toward a decision about how they should spend their summer vacation. The husband would like to go to the mountains, primarily because he likes to fish. His wife, who cares little about fishing, would rather go to a seaside resort, where there will be swimming, sunbathing, and some pleasant social activities. Each spouse would be well-advised to attempt to appeal to the other on the basis of the attributes the other values. The wife might well point out the attractions of ocean sportfishing, while the husband describes the aquatic advantages of freshwater lakes and the wholesome social atmosphere so often found at mountain retreats. Thus, the content of communication focuses on the attributes that are the basis for judgment, rather than on the objects that are being evaluated.

If these attempts at counter persuasion fail, the couple is unlikely to look to an additional object for "new content"; that would probably only provide a compromise unacceptable to either. Instead, they can be expected to introduce new attributes. The husband may argue that the mountain trip would be much cheaper; or the wife might point out that the ocean resort is closer by a day's drive, thus affording more total vacation time. And so it will go, in this hypothetical model of connubiality and coorientation, until a joint decision is made. However unlikely such an egalitarian and rational marital situation may seem, it illustrates several general points. One is that it is the absence of a clear-cut choice in favor of one alternative (conflict) that triggers communication. Another is that effective communication strategies require a fairly high degree of coorientational *accuracy*. A third is that these strategies, and the resolution of conflict, depend on the relevance and discriminating power of various attributes of judgment. And a final, perhaps obvious, point is that such intense, continuous, and complete communication requires not only a cohesive (almost indissoluble) social system but a strongly cooriented one as well.

Anyone considering research on social reality should also consult other approaches to cognitive structure and style. A partial list would include: Bieri (1955); Gardner, Jackson, and Messick (1960); Cohen (1961); Ausubel (1962); Leventhal (1962); Scott (1962); Witkin et al. (1962); Leventhal and Singer (1964); Wyer (1964); and Donnelly (1968).

SCALING SOCIAL JUDGMENTS

Measurement procedures, ideally, are consistent with the major assumptions underlying the concepts involved. Sherif and Hovland's (1961) assimilation-contrast theory presents a possibility for measurement that appears responsive to the assumption that frame of reference precedes interaction in the influence situation. This theory contains four key sets of concepts: social reference scales, anchors, contrast and assimilation, and latitudes of acceptance and rejection.

Social reference scales are formed by persons in judging political, ethical, and other matters that can't be gauged against an objectively graded stimulus series. These scales are said to be based on "psycho-social actualities," which can be considered synonymous with sR. *Anchors* are stimuli that exert a disproportionate amount of influence on the person's judgments, such as the extreme items within a series. In an influence situation, the person's previous attitudes can act as an internal anchor, and the persuasive communication he receives can be thought of as an external anchor. *Assimilation* is defined as instances when the person shifts his judgment toward an anchor; *contrast* is the shift away from an anchor. The person's social reference scales are conceived as consisting of three regions: a latitude of *acceptance*, a latitude of *rejection*, and a neutral area in between.

The combination of these concepts forms a theory of attitude change. The amount of influence is thought to be a function of the discrepancy between the position of the persuasive communication and the person's latitude of acceptance. If the communication advocates a position within the person's region of acceptance, he will assimilate the message, by seeing it as being less extreme than it is considered by others, and by being more influenced by it. More discrepant communications will fall outside the latitude of acceptance and opposite results will be found. Within the region of acceptance, the greater the discrepancy, the greater is the predicted attitude change. In the region of rejection, on the other hand, greater discrepancy will lead to less attitude change. Overall, it appears that a curvilinear relationship is predicted between discrepancy and attitude change (Insko, 1967).

As a theory of attitude change, the assimilation-contrast formulation creates some serious methodological problems, and hypothesis-testing research has given only equivocal support. This does not limit its relevance to indexing frame of reference, because our interest is confined to the scaling of social reference scales. The measurement procedure used by Sherif and Hovland consists of presenting the person with a lengthy set of Thurstone-type scale statements to be judged according to their perceived position on a continuum.

Some rather interesting findings have come from this procedure. Sherif and Hovland show that the person's own position affects his placement of items. For example, those who are moderate on an issue sort items about equally spaced along a continuum; more partisan judges tend to place middle items more toward the opposite pole, away from their own positions. These findings might simply reflect the extremists' lack of ability to discriminate; however, Kelley et al. (1955) had earlier shown that all types of subjects were able to discriminate among these same items on a paired-comparisons test. When given the choice of creating any number of categories, partisan subjects used fewer categories than did those with more moderate positions.

The social reference scaling procedures could easily be adapted to our purposes of comparing the individual's frame of reference with the positions of various groups of people. Presumably the person could sort the items in terms of how he felt others would sort them, thus setting up the possibilities for coorientational analysis discussed earlier. Agreement, for example, would be indexed by the degree of similarity between the person's sorting and the modal sorting patterns of members of a relevant group. This would provide the large number of items required for the kind of coorientational measurement advocated by Wackman (1969).

STRUCTURE OF SEMANTIC JUDGMENTS

The strong emphasis on *meaning* in some definitions of social reality has already been discussed. A procedure for measuring the dimensions of meaning is clearly appropriate as an index of social reality in terms of the frame of reference. The semantic differential (Osgood, Suci, & Tannenbaum, 1957) serves this purpose, although a variety of other multidimensional instruments might serve as well. The multidimensional character is important because we wish to focus on the form and structure of meaning, rather than on specific content.

As is well known, the semantic differential technique requires that a person judge each concept on an extensive battery of seven-point scales. Each scale is described by a pair of adjectival antonyms (e.g., good-bad, active-passive). Factor analysis is used to determine the underlying dimensionality of "semantic space." The factor analysis can be calculated either one concept at a time, or by collapsing across concepts. Most often the factoring is based on the scale-by-scale correlation matrix, although it is possible to invert the matrix, and factor persons (Q-analysis). If enough replications across concepts and scales are possible, we can speak of the "semantic space" of a given person; more often several groups of people are involved, and one can compare groups by factoring each separately.

The basic idea is to use these multidimensional techniques to develop measures of similarity between people, or groups of people, with respect to their frames of reference. The requirements are similar to those involved in the measurement of socialization discussed by Tannenbaum and McLeod (1967). Three of the measures proposed in that paper are relevant here. The first, *similarity of factor structure*, is the most direct index of frame of reference. Lack of agreement between persons on the basic dimensions of meaning would, of course, make communication between them very difficult. A rough idea of factor similarity can be gained merely by inspecting the rotated factor matrices of two sets of persons to see if the same scales tend to load on the same factors for each. Correlation among factor loadings, as well as more formal descriptive statistics, can be used. Some of the applications of factor similarity and other derivative measures of meaning will be included in the later sections of the paper.

Two persons or groups of persons can share the same factor structure but give rather different degrees of emphasis to each of the dimensions. This second similarity measure, *relative factor salience*, can be indexed by the percent of common and total variance accounted for by each factor for each group of persons. A rough analogy might be made to the frame of reference, with the common factor structure representing the various elements in the frame and the factor salience providing the depth or nearness of each of the elements.

The third derivative measure of meaning involves the comparison of specific cognitive judgments within the various dimensions. Here *difference between judgments* can be indexed by the generalized distance function, D (Osgood et al., 1957). As is the case with our other two measures, the single score for similarity between sets of persons is difficult to interpret. We need a third set of persons for comparison, or an additional set of concepts, so that we can statistically compare the relative magnitude of similarity.

Once more, our coorientation strategy would call for each person to judge the concepts not only as he himself feels about them, but also in terms of how specific other reference persons judge them. In that way, one can speak of congruency and accuracy as well as agreement. Here the distance measure is a particularly meaningful descriptive measure of similarity between sets of persons and between the coorientation measures themselves.

These measures have been particularly useful in studies of mass media personnel and their audiences. Tannenbaum (1963) used an analysis of difference scores to show that the image of mental illness was most similar to the television communicator's *perceptions* of the audience, but rather different from the actual audience as well as from the communicator's own views. Several studies have found the measures of semantic judgment to be sensitive indicators of difference in meaning among various groups of professional journalists (McLeod & Nayman, 1970; McLeod & Rush, 1969).

Summary of Research Possibilities

Let us summarize our discussion of social reality to this point. We have found that although social reality is a very common term, social scientists don't use it as a research concept. It tends to be included in post-hoc accountings of human behavior as something we know is "there." Nobody has defined the term with sufficient clarity so that it could become useful in research.

To say that there is ambiguity in the meaning of social reality is to understate the case. A meaning analysis reveals that two incompatible definitions have been used. The first treats social reality as an attribute of the cognitive system of the person (Sr), roughly equivalent to his frame of reference. The second treats social reality as an attribute of the social system (sR), very close in meaning to a state of agreement or consensus among a group of persons. The situation is further complicated by the fact that various theorists tend to be answering different questions about social reality—why? what? how?—in their post hoc discussions of the concept. Finally, the definitional problems are increased by the many apparent synonyms for each meaning of social reality.

Our research suggestions are based on the following tentative definition: *social reality* is that part of the person's *frame of reference* which can be reliably attributed to the *perspectives* of specific interacting social groups, noninteracting collectivities, or social categories. This definition makes social reality an interpersonal concept by combining some of the essential elements of both the cognitive system (Sr) and social system (sR) definitions. It becomes a subset of the person's frame of reference that he shares with some part of the social system.

The task of measurement consists of three basic steps. First, we need a set of measurement procedures capable of indexing the person's frame of reference. Secondly, we must be able to investigate the state of various social systems to gauge the perspectives of those groups, collectivities, or social categories. Finally, we must devise ways to attribute parts of the person's frame of reference to the perspectives of the particular social system under study.

Three rather different possibilities were discussed for the measurement of frame of reference. Each emphasizes the attributes of structure and form implied by the frame of reference conception that sees it as "preceding and organizing" subsequent behavior. These three are: *cognitive structure and style* as treated by Zajonc (1960), Kagan, Moss, and Sigel (1963), and Carter (1965); *social reference scales* from Sherif and Hovland (1961); and *structure of semantic judgments* as adapted from Osgood et al. (1957) by Tannenbaum and McLeod (1967).

The second and third stages of our research strategy clearly require the adoption of an interpersonal unit of analysis. A model of coorientation was presented that satisfies the requirements of such a unit. The coorientation model requires that the judgmental data obtained from a particular person be compared with data from other persons within the social system. A simple comparison of the degree of overlap of the two sets of judgments constitutes the measure of *agreement*. Although agreement is a necessary condition, it is not in itself sufficient evidence to demonstrate the "reliable attribution" element of social reality. While conscious awareness that one is being influenced is certainly not necessary, reasonably high levels of perceived agreement (*congruency*) and accurate perception of the group's position (*accuracy*) are required. To obtain congruency and accuracy, of course, we must ask the person not only for his own judgments of "Xs", but also how he thinks other people in the particular group or system feel about these same things.

We have argued against uncritically accepting a simple summation of the individual judgments of a group's members as an adequate index of group perspective. The members' perceptions of one another is one additional element, and it may be necessary to consider others. Many theorists hold that the presence of norms—that others in the group *ought* to hold similar beliefs—is also a necessary element of social reality. We have suggested that, in extensions of the coorientation model to the multiperson situation, we might treat "reification" of the group or collectivity as a variable rather than assuming it is universally seen as a homogeneous entity. This element of social reality might be indexed by measures such as the judgment of the variation that is perceived in the judgments of others in the group; this would require somewhat cumbersome measurement procedures, but might be worth the effort where the degree of reification is obviously low but group cohesion is high.

Another potential use of social reality as a research concept is to study its origins and functioning in actual social systems. As we have argued earlier, social reality is derived from the communication of others, either directly or in mediated form through the mass media. In the next major section of the paper we will consider a constraint model of communication that brings together theories and research regarding social systems as points of origin for social reality. The family will be used as the main example, although the data requirements for measuring social reality are only partially met in research cited. Hopefully, an organized approach can help close some of the all-too-apparent gaps in research.

Social Reality in the Real World: The Cambodia Crisis

In the spring of 1970, most American colleges experienced a phenomenon that only a few had seen on a large scale before: the widespread "radicalization" of their students. In the last week of April, President Nixon had sent U.S. troops from Vietnam into neutral Cambodia, an act that was widely interpreted as an expansion of American military involvement in Indochina. The following week brought tumultuous antiwar demonstrations to many campuses. At Kent State University in Ohio, four students were shot and killed by National Guard troops. Within a week, more than 80 schools had been closed, some for the remainder of the academic year.

The merits of the President's military policy, and of the various reactions against it, will continue to be argued by politicians and historians. Here, however, we are concerned with the clues these dramatic events give us about the operation of processes we have referred to as social reality. Three features of the Cambodia crisis are especially pertinent:

1. The activism spread far beyond the "hard core" radicals who had been protesting the Vietnam war for so long. Previously inactive students suddenly found themselves marching, shouting, "trashing" stores and banks, boycotting classes, and endorsing rhetoric that would have sounded outlandish in a less inflamed context.
2. The process was not immediate. There was a lag of several days between the "stimulus" events in Asia and the "responses" on campus. In some cases the overt demonstrations did not reach their peak for a week or more after the U.S. entry into Cambodia and the angry reactions by "doves" in the U.S. Senate and elsewhere.
3. The reactions took very different forms on different campuses. A complete list of the things that were done is impossible here, but

it seems safe to say that no two campuses had identical experiences. Some were forced to shut down immediately, but others became centers of intense (if non-academic) activity. At a few, wanton property destruction became commonplace, while elsewhere it was disdained as simply another form of violence. From some campuses, deputations were sent to Washington, D.C., to register protest, while others dispatched teams into the local community, or organized letter-writing campaigns to family and friends, to spread the antiwar word.

We have no hard data on what was going on among students in this period. But let us try to imagine a plausible case, one whose personal experience would contribute to the overall social patterns described above. The hypothetical critical individual would be a "nonradical" student who abhors the war, but has not actively protested it, and who has looked to President Nixon to carry out his avowed intention to end the war. The campus crisis of early May 1970, which was triggered by the events at Kent State, was basically made up of hundreds of thousands of young people who roughly fit this description.

We can imagine that, prior to the Cambodian offensive, this student might well have seen the war in terms of an ordered set of attributes:

—Social morality, which defines property destruction as wrong.
—Loyalty, to the nation's chosen leaders.
—Safety, from the personal sanctions that might be brought against demonstrators.
—Doubt, as to just what was being done to extricate the U.S. from Vietnam.

The announcement of the deployment of U.S. troops to Cambodia removed most doubts; the American trend in Asia was toward a wider war, at least temporarily. Now, a college campus is a very close, and relatively closed, social system; so it would not be surprising that anywhere our hypothetical student might turn, he would find others who shared his negative reaction to the turn in U.S. policy. Thus does social reality begin to assert itself.

The next stage was not immediate, because it involved a more embedded attribute in the cognitive hierarchy: personal safety. Slowly at first, perhaps, but eventually quite rapidly the sentiment began to spread that "something has to be done" to oppose this spreading war. Suggestions for action would be widely approved in such an atmosphere, and probably encouraged some hitherto non-activists to advocate things they had never themselves taken part in. This tendency would give our hypothetical student a partly false sense of "safety in numbers"—if everyone demonstrated, then they all would probably be pretty safe. Note here that a temporary situation in which expressed intentions outran private certainties tended to create a social reality that was to become "real" because the combined overstatements of many were mutually so reassuring.

The crumbling of patriotic loyalty, and in some cases of moral strictures against vandalism, can be more easily understood in this context of social redefinition of cognitive structures. To some extent, both these values had already been compromised: the national leadership seemed to have failed to carry out its promises; and surely, it was often said, a bit of vandalism could not compare with the destruction being wrought in Asia. For our hypothetical student, even if he did not temporarily abandon them, these values would not be quite the same—nor would they be tied to the same set of related attributes—as when the crisis had subsided. And this readiness for cognitive restructuring would later render him extremely suggestible—and thus open to social influence by those around him. Because of this vulnerability and the intense communication situations on college campuses, it is quite probable that there was very high agreement (plus coorientational accuracy) among college students in the late stages of the crisis on the Cambodian issue.

That speculative account would explain why the reaction to U.S. Cambodian policy penetrated so deeply into student bodies, and why it took some time to reach its peak. But why were the overt reactions so different at various schools? That is, why was there so much behavioral diversity, when there was such strong agreement regarding "facts" and values? A likely explanation would rest on our assumption that college campuses are discrete social systems. Value-attribute structures can be communicated from campus to campus, but makeshift action requires physical interaction. It was crowds that closed campuses, not words. It was the sight of someone breaking a window that inspired others to do the same; such practices are not very contagious in print.

The process that we have outlined in this lengthy example can be considered as a set of hypotheses about the construction of social reality. Only data, carefully gathered during a campus crisis, can test these propositions. Yet we find ourselves in the curious position, as social scientists, of hoping that conditions and events comparable to those of the Cambodia crisis will not recur.

Communication and the Construction of Social Reality

To this point, we have spoken of communication as if it were an obvious and simple activity, which can be taken as "given" in social processes. It becomes immediately obvious that this is not the case, as one begins to examine communication in its own right. Communication, in fact, is an essentially imperfect form of human activity. Our daily efforts at conveying information produce disappointing results. When other people don't understand us, we say they aren't listening; when we can't understand them, we say they aren't making themselves clear. Our tendency is to place "blame" for our communication failures inside people, without seeing that the problem may lie in the basic *interpersonal* nature of the communication process and in the *relationships* we have with other people.

Perhaps it is our tendency to blame other people that allows us to believe that communication is potentially free and open, and capable of being perfected. From the standpoint of social reality, it should be no great problem to bring a person's frame of reference into line with the perspectives of his group affiliations; that is, accuracy and agreement should be easy to achieve. From the vantage point of "social engineering," it is sometimes even expected that "more communication," fostered by the new mass media technology, can achieve intergroup agreement across social and political boundaries (sR), which will produce "national development" and "international understanding" (see Lerner, 1965; Pye, 1963; Rogers, 1965; and Schramm, 1964). Communication may well help man reach such lofty goals, but it is doubtful that controlled research will uncover such straightforward effects. Complex interactive functions are more likely.

The mainstream of communication research has been built on an implicit assumption of "perfect transmission." For example, the seminal experimental studies of attitude change by Carl Hovland and his associates (1949) employed the strategy of holding "all other factors" constant while comparing variations in the form of a persuasive message. This procedure makes good sense in terms of the internal validity of the experiments (Campbell, 1957), but it is important to note that these "other conditions" are typically held at a *high level of constancy*. The messages are highly organized and focused on the topic of persuasion. The subjects are isolated, told to read or watch the materials carefully, and given nothing else to do. These ideal conditions rarely obtain in field situations. A model for the analysis of communication processes in the construction of social reality should incorporate the many impediments that make attempted communication less than perfectly effective.

Constraint Models of Communication

One alternative strategy is to focus on the social constraints that render communication imperfect. Although we might dignify this approach by giving it the name *constraint analysis*, it is not represented by any unified body of research. Rather, it is a common thread running through some extremely diverse kinds of inquiries. The core assumption is that communication is *nonrandom*, in that form, content, direction, and other characteristics of communication are shaped by constraining forces. This in turn shapes the effects of communication on social reality.

Examples of constraint analysis are not hard to find. Legal research on freedom of speech and of the press is clearly concerned with constraint. So is economic research on monopolistic mass-media institutions. At quite another level, the study of "selective perception" and "selective exposure" examines psychological constraints; the recent interest in "information seeking" implies more positive psychological constraints. Social barriers, such as role and status differences (e.g., Kelley, 1951; Strodtbeck, James, & Hawkins, 1958) and the ecological arrangements of living (e.g., Festinger, 1950), also constrain communication.

Perhaps the most interesting type of constraint, if also the most difficult to study, is that which grows directly out of the communication process itself. It seems almost paradoxical that barriers to effective communication may be erected by the habitual procedures we use to facilitate communication in our daily lives. The two best-known names connected with this kind of constraint theory are Benjamin Lee Whorf (1956) and Marshall McLuhan (1964).

Whorf's principle of "linguistic relativity" states that the structure of the language of a social system determines the structure of its "world view," i.e., the way in which the system's members characteristically think about themselves and their environment. In short, a person cannot think or communicate a thought for which he has no corresponding term or syntactic structure in his language.

McLuhan, borrowing freely from ideas advanced by Innis (1951) and others, has asserted that the habitual medium of communication determines the kind of thinking that will prevail in a society. Thus, post-Gutenberg society has been characterized by "linear" modes of thought, because of the reliance on print—which enforces a linear process of communication. By contrast, pre-Gutenberg "tribal" society and the contemporary world of electronic media produce "simultaneity" of thought because the person learns to process communication via several independent channels simultaneously.

There has been only a smattering of research on the Whorfian hypothesis, and practically none relevant to McLuhan's "theory." But the general notion that the structure of communication constrains the structure of thought is intuitively so appealing that Whorf's and McLuhan's theses are often treated as matters of fact, rather than as untested (and practically untestable) theory.

Construction of Social Reality

In a parallel vein, we too have looked for constraints on communication in the habitual structure of communication itself. Consistent with our acceptance of cognitive coorientation as a basic model for assessing communication, we have examined the constraints that develop in interpersonal discourse. The specific locus of communication in our studies has been the family, which we suspect is one of the most pervasive sources of constraint. We have attempted to differentiate empirically the basic types of family communication structure, and compare them as systems of communication and potentially as major socializing sources in the construction of social reality.

Family Communication Structure

Most descriptions of parent-child relations are one-dimensional portrayals of the power situation within the family. One finds such dichotomies as "autocratic-democratic," "controlling-permissive," and "traditional-modern." If the description is written by a social scientist, it is likely the first term in each of those dichotomies is thought to produce less desirable effects than the latter. On the other hand, a politician speaking in an election year is likely to portray the democratic-permissive-modern family as "the bad guys."

TWO DIMENSIONS OF COMMUNICATION STRUCTURE

Whatever the merits of these simple typologies for the analysis of power, with communication the case is not that simple. In half a dozen studies in a variety of social settings, we have consistently found that there are at least two uncorrelated dimensions of communication structure in families (Chaffee, McLeod, & Wackman, 1966; Eswara, 1968; McLeod, Chaffee, & Eswara, 1966; McLeod, Chaffee, & Wackman, 1967; McLeod, O'Keefe, & Wackman, 1969; Stone & Chaffee, 1970; Wackman, 1968).

The first dimension, which is roughly analogous to the types of social power referred to above, we have called *socio-oriented*. It is indicated by the frequency of (or emphasis on) communication that is designed to produce deference, and to foster harmony and pleasant social relationships in the family. For example, the child may be instructed to defer to his elders, or to give in on arguments rather than risk offending others.

The second dimension we call *concept-oriented*, because it involves positive constraints to stimulate the child to develop his own views about the world, and to consider more than one side of an issue. For example, the parents may encourage him to weigh all the evidence before reaching a conclusion, or may expose him to counterarguments—either by differing openly on an issue, or by discussing it with visitors in the home.

Our research has centered on these dimensions as they define the structure of parent-child communication. We have chosen to study only one set of the child's social relations; those with the parent. To obtain a complete picture of all the agents who might alter the child's construction of social reality, we would have to trace his other relations, with teachers, peers, and siblings. Nor have we made parallel investigations of husband-wife communication structure. But, while no family is perfectly consistent over time or persons in its socio- or concept-orientation, we have considerable evidence that there is enough homogeneity to justify us in treating these as attributes of the family as a definable communication system.

We find that families are about equally likely to stress either, neither, or both of these orientations (at least in the United States). Blue-collar homes show some tendency to stress the socio-orientation; white-collar families give more attention to the concept-orientation. The differences are not all that strong, however, and the relationships the orientations have to various consequences for cognitive processes do not seem explainable as simply manifestations of social class. Our limited evidence from less developed societies indicates a preponderance of socio-oriented communication, with relatively little concept orientation; presumably the direction of social change is away from this pattern. A change in modal family type would imply that one of the most pervasive and fundamental communication structures within society is changing.

FOUR PATTERNS OF COMMUNICATION STRUCTURE

We have found it useful to think of these relations in terms of Newcomb's (1953) *A-B-X* paradigm. As shown in Figure 2.2, we interpret the paradigm by making A the child, B the parent, and X the concept or idea that is the focus of communication. Rather than making the assumption that all three relations among A, B, and X are present and equally prominent, we have adopted the alternative assumption that each relation is variable in strength, and that any one could dominate the relationship. A socio-oriented communication pattern involves stress on A-B relations, whereas a concept-oriented pattern emphasizes A-X relations. Although each relation is conceived of as a continuous variable, it is easier to analyze the model if we assume each dimension is either present or absent. Thus, a four-fold typology of family communication is posited (Fig. 2.2).

Construction of Social Reality

Socio-Oriented Communication

	Low	High
Concept-Oriented Communication: Low	A B / X ↙ (dashed) — Laissez-fair	A ↔ B, X ↙ — Protective
Concept-Oriented Communication: High	A ↘ B ↙ X — Pluralistic	A ↔ B, ↘ X ↙ — Consensual

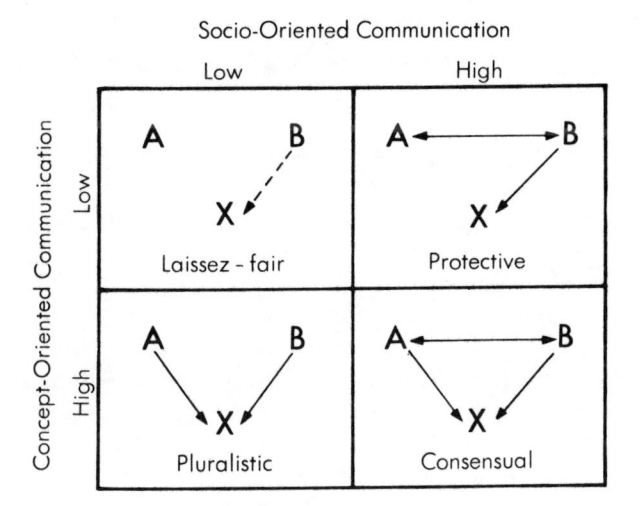

LEGEND: A = The child; B = The parent; X = Topic under discussion; arrows indicate relations in family communication system.

Figure 2.2. Family Communication Patterns in Terms of Newcomb's (1953) A-B-X Paradigm

Laissez-faire families are characterized by a lack of emphasis on either socio- or concept-oriented relations. For the most part, there is simply little parent-child communication; or more explicitly, an absence of coorientation. (A more intentional laissez-faire form, which might be called "true permissiveness," does not seem to be a very common pattern.) The child in the laissez-faire family appears to be relatively more influenced by external social settings, such as peer groups. For an analysis of communication structure and effects on social reality, this type of family is rather like an experimental "control group," and little can be said about its effectiveness.

In the *protective* family, obedience and social harmony (*A-B*) are prized and there is little concern with conceptual matters. We have used the term "protective" to indicate the goal, not the effect of this structure. Ironically, experiments have shown that the child from a protective home is highly susceptible to influence from external sources, such as persuasive messages (Eswara, 1968; Stone & Chaffee, 1970). The parental attempt to protect the youngster from controversy within the home has left him relatively unprotected against outside influences. This may be due in part to a lack of knowledge of effective counterarguments, and in part to a lack of practice at argumentation.

In the *pluralistic* family, the pattern is exactly the opposite of the protective home. The pluralistic environment encourages open communication and discussion of ideas (A-X), without accompanying (A-B) constraints. The emphasis in this communication structure seems to be on mutuality of respect and interests; the combination of an absence of social constraint plus a positive impetus to self-expression should foster both communication and competence. While this pattern tends also to produce independence of ideas, it does not appear to be the risky pattern a protective parent might fear. It is the pluralistic child who is most likely to say he would like to be like his parents when he grows up (Chaffee et al., 1966).

The *consensual* family seems to be, as our label for it implies, built on pressures toward agreement. The child in this family is faced with an incompatible set of combined A-B, A-X and B-X constraints. Thus the family is the full A-B-X system assumed by Newcomb, (1953). He is encouraged to take an interest in the world of ideas, yet to do so without disturbing the family's hierarchy of power and internal harmony. These conflicting pressures may induce the child to retreat from the parent-child interaction. There is some evidence of "escape" by consensual children, such as strikingly heavy viewing of television fantasy programs (Chaffee, McLeod, & Atkin, 1971; Chaffee, McLeod & Wackman, 1966; McLeod, Rush & Friederich, 1968). But to the extent that parent-child interaction is maintained, the child can meet both the socio- and concept-oriented constraints simultaneously by a "short-cut" strategy; he can learn what his parent's views are and simply adopt them.

An interesting parallel can be drawn between our work and that of Basil Bernstein (1964). Distinguishing between "restricted codes" and "elaborated codes" as different forms of speech systems, he sees the former as tuned to the status relationships of the interaction and as reinforcing that relationship by restricting the verbal signalling of differences. In coorientational terms, in a restricted code system we might expect an emphasis on congruency and agreement to be combined with a deemphasis on increasing accuracy. The reverse should be true for speakers using elaborated codes, where language is used as a set of theoretical possibilites available for transmission of unique experiences. Accuracy would become a dominant goal of the interaction.

Bernstein ties the two forms of speech codes to their origins in social class systems, where he sees different "normative systems creating different role systems operating with different codes of social control." Thus, middle-class children tend to be socialized in normative systems with elaborated modes; working-class children are more likely to be raised in systems limited to the restricted mode of speech. The middle-class child is likely to use both types of codes, while the working-class child's speech is more likely to be confined to the restricted code. Bernstein sees social class as an extremely crude index for these codes and acknowledges considerable variation in the use of codes within social classes. We see our family communication pattern typology as a closer approximation to predicting differences in coorientation, but as yet we have not made any direct examination of speech codes within the types of families. It remains an intriguing possibility for research.

COMMUNICATION STRUCTURE AND SOCIAL REALITY

We assume that each person learns a set of structural relations of communication in his family and that he uses that structure as a prototype in each new situation he encounters. Thus, communication structure can be seen as a frame of reference that guides the construction of social reality in new situations that require definition (see Fig. 2.2). As explained earlier, communication structure is determined by the presence or absence of each of two dimensions: socio-orientation $(A-B)$ and concept-orientation $(A-X)$. Their role in the construction of social reality can be seen best as implying different sets of questions that the person habitually asks about any undefined situation. The socio-oriented person $(A-B)$ asks: Who is involved? Do I like them? Do they like me? The concept-oriented person $(A-X)$ asks: What is involved? Is it a good idea? How does it compare to what I know?

Thus, children in each of the four types of families should approach ambiguous situations in rather different ways. We can make no predictions for those from laissez-faire families since neither type of orientation is present; presumably they have learned cognitive structures elsewhere. Those from protective homes should be sensitive to information in the situation that provides answers to the first set of questions; pluralistic children should look for information relevant to the second set. Both sets of questions are relevant to consensual children and, in addition, the interaction of the two may mean coorientational concerns come to the fore: How can I resolve the situation to my satisfaction, and theirs?

This formulation of the differences among the four family types could be tested directly if we could gather data on behavior of each type in actual social situations. We would also like to examine interfamily differences in frames of references, as indexed by the procedures discussed earlier. Unfortunately, most of our evidence is indirect because it was gathered for other purposes—to study political socialization, attitude change, information-seeking, etc. (However, we feel that the available divergent sources of indirect evidence does, in sum, illustrate consequences for the construction of social reality.) Three areas of difference can be examined: sensitivity to the cues of the situation; mass media content preferences; and cognitive differentiation and communication style.

The informational cues of the situation were manipulated in two experiments by Eswara (1968) when he varied the number of arguments in a set of messages given to adolescent subjects. In a reanalysis of these data, Wackman et al. (1970) examined differences among the four groups in their differential attitude change to high versus low levels of information (Table 2.1). The data from each experiment showed virtually the same result; children from pluralistic families had the highest level of differential attitude change. If we can assume that greater attitude change for the messages with more arguments indicates greater sensitivity to informational cues, then our social reality formulation is given support. One other finding was unexpected, however. Although the difference was not statistically significant, the laissez-faire subjects showed slightly more differential attitude change than did the consensuals—perhaps indicating that socio-orientation is at least as important in diverting attention from informational cues as is the concept-orientation in providing positive incentives.

The importance of the socio-orientation was also illustrated in a study by Stone and Chaffee (1970). Subjects were presented with a list of 20 topic areas and asked to indicate for each whether "who says it" or "what is said" is more important. Although more than one-third of the 75 subjects showed no consistent patterns, the high socio-subjects (protectives and consensual) among those showing a pattern were more "source-oriented" ("who says it") while the low socio-groups (pluralistic and laissez-faire) were more "message-oriented" (Table 2.1). When these same subjects were given messages in which the expertness of the source was manipulated, the high socio-oriented persons showed higher overall levels of attitude change; however, it was the concept-oriented subjects (pluralistics and consensuals) who changed their attitudes more for the expert source, as compared to an anonymous message. Again, this is consistent with the social reality formulation if we assume that expertness functions as an informational cue, rather than as a source cue per se. It can be said that pluralistics exhibit the highest change relative to the informational content of the message and to the expertness of the source; the protectives are least likely to behave in these ways. The contrasting reactions of these two "pure types" gives support to the hypothesis of informational cue differences.

The orientational patterns are also reflected in the mass media content preferences of adolescents. As shown in Table 2.1, children from pluralistic homes are again an extreme group, in spending the

Table 2-1. Child's behavior, by family communication pattern

Behavioral Index	Laissez-Faire	Protective	Pluralistic	Consensual
Reactions to Persuasion				
a. sensitivity to information in message[A]	high	low	very high	moderate
b. sensitivity to source expertness[B]	low	very low	high	very high
c. message vs. source orientation[B]	high	low	high	low
d. lowered self-esteem[C]	high	high	low	low
Cognitive Differentiation[D]	moderate	low	high	low
Political Competence[E]				
a. comparative political interest	very low	moderate	high	high
b. campaigning activity	very low	moderate	high	high
c. political knowledge	moderate	moderate	very high	low
School Activities[F]				
a. homework time	low	very low	high	high
b. grade average	moderate	very low	very high	moderate
c. extracurricular activities	low	low	very high	moderate
Mass Media Use[G]				
a. time with TV	moderate	very high	very low	moderate
b. TV public affairs viewing	very low	low	high	high
c. news reading	very low	very low	high	high
d. modeling of parental TV use	low	high	low	high

[A]From Wackman (1970) and Edwara (1968). [B]From Stone & Chaffee (1970). [C]From Ward & Wackman (1969). [D]From Wackman et al. (1970). [E]From Chaffee et al. (1970). [F]From Chaffee et al. (1966) and McLeod et al. (1967). [G]From Chaffee et al. (1971).

least time with television and yet being relatively high in viewing of television public affairs programs (Chaffee et al., 1966; Chaffee et al., 1971; McLeod et al., 1967). And apparently these communication preference differences go beyond simply greater interest in reliable information among the pluralistic children. Their parents (see Table 2.2) are most willing to request an opposition candidate's political pamphlet (Chaffee et al., 1969); the children (Table 2.1) themselves are considerably more likely than others to do political campaigning, to participate in student government and debate and other forms of "conflict" activities in school, and to read both newspapers in a town where each supports a different political party (Chaffee et al., 1966; Chaffee & McLeod, 1967, 1970). Apparently, the pluralistic families feel comfortable enough in the "heat" of the political kitchen. It is not surprising that both parents and children in pluralistic families are considerably better informed about politics than are their counterparts in each of the other three types of families (Chaffee et al., 1966).

Adolescents from consensual families present a surprisingly sharp contrast to the pluralistic pattern. While they are highly interested in politics and are apt to participate in partisan campaigning, they are well *below* average in knowledge of politics (Table 2.1). It appears that the dual socio- and concept-orientation presents a difficult conflict situation to the consensual child, which he solves with a "short-cut" strategy: he can learn what his parent's views are, and simply adopt them. This means he behaves overtly like the pluralistic youngster, but lacks knowledge to base his actions on. Significantly, he is more likely than other adolescents to know his parents' party, despite his lack of other types of political knowledge. His general conceptual problems seem reflected in his school work. While he spends an above-average amount of time with his homework, he is likely to be only average in his grades in school, and is below average in social studies courses.

Political knowledge and competence show considerable variation among the four communication patterns; however, these criteria are considerably removed from the "precedes and organizes" requirements of specifying a frame of reference. Somewhat more direct evidence is found in the measurement of cognitive differentiation (Wackman et al., 1970). Taking the total number of dimensions used in distinguishing between pairs of political objects as our criterion, we found that the pluralistic group showed more differentiation than either of the two high socio-oriented groups (Table 2.1). These differences could not be attributed either to educational level nor to the general level of political knowledge.

Differences among families with various communication structures should also be manifested in the sequences of interaction between

Construction of Social Reality

the members. In protective families, for example, we would expect considerable avoidance of conflict in dealing with external issues. In a study of husband-wife coorientation, Pasdirtz (1969) found this to be the case (Table 2.2). Congruency but not agreement increased more in the protective families than in any other type of family, when the spouses were asked to discuss controversial issues for a short period. It appears that agreement itself is not necessary;

Table 2-2. Parental behavior, by family communication pattern

Behavioral Index	Laissez-Faire	Protective	Pluralistic	Consensual
Changes in Coorientation During Discussion[A]				
a. accuracy increase	moderate	moderate	high	moderate
b. agreement increase	moderate	moderate	moderate	high
c. congruency increase	moderate	high	moderate	moderate
Requests for Pamphlets for Opposition Candidate[B]	moderate	low	high	moderate
Probable Responses to Unbalanced A-B-X Situation[C]				
a. direct communication	very low	moderate	high	moderate
b. indirect communication	very low	high	moderate	moderate
c. internal response	moderate	very high	low	low
d. direct withdrawal	high	high	very low	low
e. indirect withdrawal	very low	moderate	low	high

[A]From Pasdirtz (1969). [B]From Chaffee & McLeod (1967). [C]From McLeod et al. (1967).

harmony will be maintained so long as the family members think they hold the same orientations. Communication may well be discouraged, in fact, because it poses a threat to congruency. In the discussion these protective spouses apparently emphasize their points of agreement—at the expense of accurate communication. By contrast, real increases in agreement occurred most often in the consensual pairs—as the name we have given them would imply.

Pluralistic families show no tendency to avoid communication of disagreement. They were the family-type most likely to increase in accuracy, during the discussion studied by Pasdirtz. The combination of an absence of social constraint plus a positive impetus to self-expression appears to foster open communication. This pluralistic tendency to communicate and to confront situations directly was also found in responses given to a hypothetical conflict situation (McLeod et al., 1967). Adult respondents were asked to imagine that somebody in their neighborhood whom they liked very much, opposed a project that they (the respondent) thought would improve their neighborhood. They were then asked to indicate the likelihood that they would react with each of ten alternative behaviors, which can be grouped into five types of responses:

Direct communication: ask him why he feels that way; tell him why he's wrong.
Indirect communication: finding out what other people think; getting others to support my views.
Internal response: feel upset about it; feel angry at the neighbor.
Direct withdrawal: forget about the whole project; avoid talking with him.
Indirect withdrawal: find someone with authority to decide; ignore the criticism.

Communication responses were the most likely to be preferred by all types; however, pluralistic parents were clearly the most likely to confront conflict with direct communication to the source of the problem (Table 2.2). They saw themselves as being less upset by the situation, and both direct and indirect withdrawal was unlikely in the pluralistic case. This distinctive strategy of constructing social reality was unlike the patterns of other family types. Protective parents were the most upset by the situation and tended to solve the problem either by indirectly communicating with third persons or by direct withdrawal from the situation. Laissez-faire parents saw indirect withdrawal as very unlikely, but were also less likely than others to use either form of communication. Only on direct withdrawal were they relatively high. Indirect withdrawal was suggested more often by consensuals than by other parents; they were moderate to low on all other measures.

All the research on family communication cited to this point has involved measuring the communication dimensions in their natural state; this has meant exclusively correlational research designs. But we may also consider manipulating the two dimensions in an experimental design. Since we have assumed that communication patterns are more a product of experience in interaction situations than unalterable personality dispositions, such a step is of considerable theoretical importance. Only Ward and Wackman (1968) have reported an experiment where the communication norms of the situation were manipulated, by instructions to "naive" subjects. The subjects then discussed a controversial issue with a confederate of the experimenter and their behavior was coded according to the Bales (1950) system. As predicted, those in the socio-orientation conditions showed more solidarity and self-disparagement (Table 2.1), and complied more with the assertions of the confederate. Those in the concept-orientation condition asked for and gave more orientational and evaluative statements, and more frequently disagreed with the confederate.

In all, this collection of research findings provides a general pattern linking the structure of interpersonal communication in the family to the construction of social reality. Much of the evidence is indirect, however; a better description of the causal sequences of the process awaits future studies that manipulate, rather than simply measure, the dimensions of communication structure.

Can Social Reality be Reconstructed?

We must be careful not to treat social reality as a reification of our own, attributing to it an all-pervasive quality that determines the person's responses to every social situation. If we wish to avoid making it a rigid trans-situational concept, we must understand not only its origins but also its susceptibility to change over time. Shifts in the person's frame of reference may take either of two forms: recurrent variation among situations and groups in the person's environment; and systematic nonrecurrent change over time.

This first form of variation is called "multiple reality" by Berger and Luckmann (1966). They suggest that as the person moves from the reality of one group (or situational) perspective to another, he experiences a kind of shock, caused by a shift in attention. There is some question as to whether the person has different frames of reference for different situations, or whether the frame remains the same while demands of the situation vary. The question is an empirical one, and could be tested by studying the stability of frames of reference while systematically varying the situation.

No less important is the question of the extent to which

non-recurrent changes take place in the person's social reality over time. If such systematic changes do occur, we can explore the conditions that produce such fundamental alterations. Habituation probably plays a crucial role in his maintaining a stable frame of reference. In searching for the conditions producing important changes in his frame of reference, therefore, we should look for factors that break down habitual patterns of living, such as changes of role or location.

Changes in the person's role at critical junctures of his life force the person to solve problems anew, to reorder priorities, and to seek information relevant to the decisions he must make. Thus, we expect to find changes in frame of reference when the person begins college, takes a permanent job, gets married, has a child, buys a home, etc. It is probably no accident that insurance agents and other salesmen concentrate their influence efforts at such choice-points in the life cycle.

When the person's idea about what's expected of him in his future interaction with others change, he may accept information that will also serve to redefine his frame of reference. If he expects to use the information in the future, he may even seek information that is contrary to his own position (Atkin, 1970; Chaffee & McLeod, 1967). Crisis situations, such as the campus situation following the Cambodian incursion described earlier, operate to disturb the habitual patterns that maintain the person's frame of reference. Breed and Ktsanes (1961) found, for example, that as the opinion situation crystallizes during a crisis, accuracy increases due to greater communication. Prior to the crisis situation, judgments of public opinion erred in the direction of overestimating the acceptance of traditional conservative beliefs. Ultimately, the new communication needs may outrun the limitations of the particular social system. As Shibutani (1966) says:

> As long as there is a possibility of communication among those caught in a crisis, social reconstruction will to some extent depend upon the reactions of the victims to one another as well as upon their reactions to the events. It is by consulting each other and comparing their experiences that they alter their ways of acting. Rumor is an important part of this process of transformation. As such, it is not a pathological phenomenon, but an integral part of the process whereby men develop more adequate ways of coping with new circumstances.

The person's search for information to help him define ambiguous situations may also operate in noncrisis situations where the demands for action require some structuring of the situation. The influence of the press in election campaigns may operate in this fashion. The most likely effect of news coverage is not to change existing attitudes, but rather to specify and order the attributes of the candidates and issues to set the agenda of the campaign. The person's perception of the agenda can depend upon the newspaper he reads and he can be influenced thereby without directly changing attitudes (McLeod, 1965).

Another possible source of social reality reconstruction lies in the changing of the person's interaction patterns—who he talks to—and the structure of his communication patterns. It is likely the person's interaction patterns are selective in part according to congruency—he associates with those he sees as holding values similar to his own. But life is also comprised of situations where the person is thrust into groups with different sets of values. As a freshman in college he may meet alternative values for the first time. To an extent he may reject them, but the presence of alternative perspectives may mean that at times he will consider them, in seeking solutions to new and unfamiliar situations.

There are many circumstances, then, when social reality will be reconstructed. The relative stability of the person's role relationships, his action requirements, and his communication structures help to produce and maintain a habitually patterned frame of reference. This fact should not lead us to assume that his frame of reference never changes, nor that it can't be altered. The alternate picture, of a dynamic social reality, is an optimistic one for it presents man as actively coping with his environment rather than being a prisoner within his predetermined social perspectives.

References

Asch, S. E. Effects of group pressure upon the modification and distortion of judgments. In H. Guetzkow (Ed.), *Groups, leadership, and men.* Pittsburgh: Carnegie Press, 1951. Pp. 177-190.

Atkin, C. K. Communicatory utility and information seeking. Paper presented to Association for Education in Journalism, Washington, D. C., 1970.

Ausubel, D. P. A subsumption theory of meaningful verbal learning and retention. *Journal of General Psychology*, 1962, 66, 215-224.

Bales, R. F. *Interaction process analysis: a method for the study of small groups.* Reading, Mass.: Addison-Wesley, 1950.

Bales, R. F., & Borgatta, E. F. Size of group as a factor in the interaction profile. In A. P. Hare, E. F. Borgatta, & R. F. Bales (Eds.), *Small groups: studies in social interaction.* New York: Knopf, 1955. Pp. 396-413.

Bender, I. E., & Hastorf, A. H. On measuring generalized empathic ability (social sensitivity). *Journal of Abnormal and Social Psychology*, 1953, 48, 503-506.

Berger, P. L., & Luckmann, T. *The social construction of reality: a treatise in the sociology of knowledge.* Garden City, N. Y.: Doubleday, 1966.

Berlo, D. K. *The process of communication.* New York: Holt, Rinehart & Winston, 1960.

Bernstein, B. The ethnography of communication. In J. J. Gumperz & D. Himes (Eds.), *American Anthropologist Special Publication*, 1964, 66, 55-69.
Bieri, J. Cognitive complexity-simplicity and predictive behavior. *Journal of Abnormal and Social Psychology*, 1955, 51, 263-268.
Bohrnstedt, G. W. Observations on the measurement of change. In E. F. Borgatta (Ed.), *Sociological methodology 1969*. San Francisco: Jossey-Bass, 1969. Pp. 113-136.
Boulding, K. E. *The image*. Ann Arbor: University of Michigan Press, 1961.
Breed, W., & Ktsanes, T. Pluralistic ignorance in the process of opinion formation. *Public Opinion Quarterly*, 1961, 25, 382-392.
Bronfenbrenner, U., Harding, J., & Gallwey, M. The measurement of skill in social perception. In D. C. McClelland, A. L. Baldwin, U. Bronfenbrenner, & F. L. Strodtbeck (Eds.), *Talent and society*. Princeton, N. J.: Van Nostrand, 1958.
Campbell, D. T. Factors relevant to the validity of experiments in social settings. *Psychological Bulletin*, 1957, 54, 297-312.
Carter, R. F. Stereotyping as a process. *Public Opinion Quarterly*, 1962, 26, 77-91.
Carter, R. F. Communication and affective relations. *Journalism Quarterly*, 1965, 42, 202-212.
Carter, R. F., Ruggels, W. L., & Chaffee, S. H. The semantic differential in opinion measurement. *Public Opinion Quarterly*, 1968-1969, 32, 666-674.
Cartwright, D., and Zander, A. *Group Dynamics*, 2nd ed. Evanston, Ill.: Row, Peterson, 1968.
Chaffee, S. H. Salience and homeostasis in communication processes. *Journalism Quarterly*, 1967, 44, 439-444, 453.
Chaffe, S. H., & McLeod, J. M. Communication as coorientation: two studies. Paper presented to Association for Education in Journalism, Boulder, Col., 1967.
Chaffe, S. H. & McLeod, J. M. Coorientation and the structure of family communication. Paper presented to International Communication Association, Minneapolis, Minn., 1970.
Chaffee, S. H., McLeod, J. M., & Atkin, C. K. Parental influences on adolescent media use. *American Behavioral Scientist*, 1971. 14, 323-340.
Chaffee, S. H., McLeod, J. M., & Guerrero, J. Origins and implications of the coorientational approach in communication research. Paper presented to Association for Education in Journalism, Berkeley, Cal., 1969.
Chaffee, S. H., McLeod, J. M., & Wackman, D. B. Family communication and political socialization. Paper presented to Association for Education in Journalism, Iowa City, Iowa, 1966.
Chaffee, S. H., Stamm, K. R., Guerrero, J. L., & Tipton, L. P. Experiments on cognitive discrepancies and communication. *Journalism Monographs*, 1969, 14, 1-85.
Cline, V. B., & Richards, J. M. Accuracy of interpersonal perception—a general trait? *Journal of Abnormal and Social Psychology*, 1960, 60, 1-7.
Cohen, A. R. Cognitive tuning as a factor affecting impression formation. *Journal of Personality*, 1961, 29, 235-245.
Cooley, C. H. *Human nature and the social order*. Glencoe, Ill.: Free Press, 1956.
Cronbach, L. J. Processes affecting scores on "understanding of others" and "assumed similarity." *Psychological Bulletin*, 1955, 52, 177-194.
Cronbach, L. J. Proposals leading to analytic treatment of social perception scores. In R. Taguiri and L. Pertullo (Eds.), *Person perception and*

interpersonal behavior. Stanford, Cal.: Stanford University Press, 1958. Pp. 353-379.
Donnelly, J. B. Effects of cognitive tuning and source or target status on communication behavior. Unpublished master's thesis, University of Wisconsin, 1968.
Eswara, H. S. An interpersonal approach to the study of social influence; family communication patterns and attitude change. Unpublished doctoral dissertation, University of Wisconsin, 1968.
Festinger, L. Informal social communication. *Psychological Review*, 1950, 57, 271-282.
Festinger, L. A theory of social comparison processes. *Human Relations*, 1954, 7, 117-140.
Gage, N. L., & Cronbach, L. J. Conceptual and methodological problems in interpersonal perception. *Psychological Review*, 1955, 62, 411-423.
Gardner, R. W., Jackson, D. N., & Messick, S. J. Personality organization in cognitive controls and intellectual abilities. *Psychological Issues*, 1960, 2 (4).
Hempel, C. G. *Fundamentals of concept formation in empirical science.* Chicago: University of Chicago Press, 1952.
Hovland, C. I., Lumsdaine, A. A., & Sheffield, F. D. *Experiments on mass communications.* Princeton, N. J.: Princeton University Press, 1949.
Innis, H. *The bias of communication.* Toronto: University of Toronto Press, 1951.
Insko, C. A. *Theories of attitude change.* New York: Appleton-Century-Crofts, 1967.
Jones, E. E., & Gerard, H. B. *Foundations of social psychology.* New York: Wiley, 1967.
Kagan, J., Moss, H. A., & Sigel, I. The psychological significance of styles of conceptualization. *Monographs of the Society for Research on Child Development*, 1963, 28 (2).
Katz, D., & Braly, K. W. Racial stereotypes of 100 college students. *Journal of Abnormal and Social Psychology*, 1933, 28, 280-290.
Katz, E., & Lazarsfeld, P. F. *Personal influence: the part played by people in the flow of mass communication.* Glencoe, Ill.: Free Press, 1955.
Kelley, H. H., Communication in experimentally created hierarchies, *Human Relations*, 1951, 4, 39-56.
Kelley, H. H., Hovland, C. I., Schwartz, M., & Abelson, R. P. The influence of judges' attitudes in three methods of scaling. *Journal of Social Psychology*, 1955, 42, 147-158.
Laing, R. H., Phillipson, H., & Lee, A. R. *Interpersonal perception: a theory and method of research.* New York: Springer, 1966.
Lerner, D. *The passing of traditional society.* New York: Free Press, 1965.
Leventhal, H. The effects of set and discrepancy on impression formation. *Journal of Personality*, 1962, 30, 1-15.
Leventhal, H., & Singer, D. Cognitive complexity, impression formation, and impression change. *Journal of Personality*, 1964, 32, 210-226.
Lewin, K. *Principles of topological psychology.* New York: McGraw-Hill, 1936.
Mannheim, K. *Ideology and Utopia.* London: Routledge & Kegan Paul, 1936.
McLeod, J. M. Political conflict and information seeking. Paper presented to American Psychological Association, Chicago, Ill., 1965.
McLeod, J. M., & Nayman, O. B. *Professionalism and job satisfaction among journalists in four areas of the world.* In preparation. University of Wisconsin, Madison.

McLeod, J. M., & Rush, R. Comparative studies of professionalization: I. Latin American and U. S. journalists in contrast; II. Professionalization among Latin American journalists. *Journalism Quarterly*, 1969, 46, 583-590, 784-789.

McLeod, J. M., Chaffee, S. H., & Eswara, H. S. Family communication patterns and communication research. Paper presented to Association for Education in Journalism, Iowa City, Iowa, 1966.

McLeod, J. M., Chaffee, S. H., & Wackman, D. B. Family communication: an updated report. Paper presented to Association for Education in Journalism, Boulder, Col., 1967.

McLeod, J. M., Rush, R., & Friederich, K. The mass media and political information in Quito, Ecuador. *Public Opinion Quarterly*, 1968, 32, 575-587.

McLeod, J. M., O'Keefe, G. J., & Wackman, D. B. Communication and political socialization during the adolescent years. Paper presented to Association for Education in Journalism, Berkeley, Cal., 1969.

McLuhan, M. *Understanding media: the extensions of man.* New York: McGraw-Hill, 1964.

Merton, R. K. Continuities in the theory of reference groups and social structure. In R. K. Merton (Ed.) *Social theory and social structure.* Glencoe, Ill.: Free Press, 1957. Pp. 281-386.

Merton, R. K., & Kitt, A. Contributions to the theory of reference group behavior. In R. K. Merton & P. F. Lazarsfeld (Eds.), *Continuities in social research.* Glencoe, Ill.: Free Press, 1950. Pp. 16-39.

Newcomb T. M. *Personality and social change.* New York: Dryden, 1943.

Newcomb, T. M. An approach to the study of communicative acts. *Psychological Review*, 1953, 60, 393-404.

Newcomb, T. M. The study of consensus. In R. K. Merton, L. Broom, & L. S. Cottrell (Eds.), *Sociology today.* New York: Basic Books, 1959. Pp. 277-292.

Newcomb, T. M. *The acquaintance process.* New York: Holt, Rinehart & Winston, 1961.

Newcomb, T. M., Turner, R. H., & Converse, P. E. *Social psychology.* New York: Holt, Rinehart & Winston, 1965.

Newcomb, T. M., Koenig, K. E., Flacks, R., & Warwick, D. P. *Persistence and change: Bennington College and its students after 25 years.* New York: Wiley, 1967.

Osgood, C. E., Suci, G. J., & Tannenbaum, P. H. *The measurement of meaning.* Urbana: University of Illinois Press, 1957.

Pasdirtz, G. W. An approach to the study of communication processes. Paper presented to Association for Education in Journalism, Berkeley, Cal., 1969.

Pye, L. W. (Ed.), *Communication and political development.* Princeton, N. J. Princeton University Press, 1963.

Rogers, E. M. Mass media exposure and modernization among Colombian peasants. *Public Opinion Quarterly*, 1965, 29, 614-625.

Rokeach, M. Attitude change and behavioral change. *Public Opinion Quarterly*, 1966-1967, 30, 529-550.

Schachter, S. *The psychology of affiliation.* Stanford, Cal.: Stanford University Press, 1959.

Schanck, R. L. A study of a community and its groups and institutions conceived of as behaviors of individuals. *Psychological Monographs*, 1932, 43 (2), 1-33.

Scheff, T. J. Toward a sociological model of consensus. *American Sociological Review*, 1967, 32, 32-45.

Scheff, T. J. Negotiating reality: notes on power in the assessment of responsibility. *Social Problems*, 1968, 16, 3-18.
Scheler, M. *Die wissensformen und die gesellschaft.* Bern: Francke, 1925.
Schramm, W. *Mass media and national development.* Stanford, Cal.: Stanford University Press, 1964.
Scott, W. A. Cognitive complexity and cognitive flexibility. *Sociometry* 1962, 25, 405-414.
Sherif, M., & Hovland, C. I. *Social judgment.* New Haven, Conn.: Yale University Press, 1961.
Shibutani, T. Reference groups as perspectives. *American Journal of Sociology*, 1955, 60, 562-569.
Shibutani T. *Improvised news: a sociological study of rumor.* Indianapolis: Bobbs-Merrill, 1966.
Stone, V. A., & Chaffee, S. H. Family communication patterns and source-message orientation. *Journalism Quarterly*, 1970, 47, 239-246.
Strodtbeck, F. L., James, Rita M., & Hawkins, C. Social status in jury deliberations. In E. Maccoby, T. M. Newcomb, & E. L. Hartley (Eds.), *Readings in social psychology*, 3rd ed. New York: Holt, 1958. Pp. 379-387.
Sullivan, H. S. *The interpersonal theory of psychiatry.* New York: Norton, 1953.
Taguiri, R., Bruner, J. S., & Blake, R. R. On the relation between feelings and perception of feelings among members of small groups. In E. Maccoby, T. M. Newcomb, & E. L. Hartley (Eds.), *Readings in social psychology*, 3rd ed. New York: Holt, 1958. Pp. 110-116.
Tannenbaum, P. H. Public communication of science information. *Science*, 1963, 140, 579-583.
Tannenbaum, P. H., & McLeod, J. M. On the measurement of socialization. *Public Opinion Quarterly*, 1967, 31, 27-37.
Tipton, L. P. Effects of writing tasks on utility of information and order of seeking. *Journalism Quarterly*, 1970, 47, 309-317.
Wackman, D. B. Family communication patterns and adolescents' responses in role conflict situations. Unpublished doctoral dissertation, University of Wisconsin, 1968.
Wackman, D. B. A proposal for a new measure of coorientational accuracy or empathy. Paper read to Association for Education in Journalism, Berkeley, Cal., 1969.
Wackman, D. B., McLeod, J. M., & Chaffee, S. H. Family communication patterns and cognitive differentiation. Unpublished paper, University of Wisconsin, Madison, 1970.
Ward, L. S., & Wackman, D. B. An experimental test of the effect of norms on interpersonal communication behavior. Paper read to Association for Education in Journalism, Lawrence, Kan., 1968.
Whorf, B. L. *Language, thought and reality,* J. B. Carroll, Ed. New York: Wiley, 1956.
Witkin, H. A., Dyk, R. B., Paterson, H. F., Goodenough, D. R., & Karp, S. A. *Psychological differentiation: studies of development.* New York: Wiley, 1962.
Wyer, R. S. Assessment and correlates of cognitive differentiation and integration. *Journal of Personality*, 1964, 32, 455-509.
Zajonc, R. B. Cognitive structure and cognitive tuning. Unpublished doctoral dissertation, University of Michigan, 1954.
Zajonc, R. B. The process of cognitive tuning in communication. *Journal of Abnormal and Social Psychology*, 1960, 61, 159-167.

III

Henry L. Minton

Power and Personality

Power is a concept that transcends the boundaries of any one social science discipline. Even within a given discipline, such as psychology, power is a concept that bears relevance to a number of subareas of specialization. My purpose is to delineate the nature of power as a personality construct—first by understanding what power is, and then applying this working conceptualization to the area of personality.

Although power has been discussed by many social philosophers over the course of history, it is only within recent times that conceptual clarifications of power have appeared. Attempts by social scientists to define the concept began in the late 1930s and have gradually accelerated within the past two decades. The definitions advanced by Bertrand Russell and Max Weber represent two of the earliest attempts at conceptual clarification. Russell defined power as "...the production of intended effects" (1938, p. 35). Weber states, "In general we understand by 'power' the chance of a man or a number of men to realize their own will in a communal act even against the resistance of others who are participating in the action" (cited in Gerth & Mills, 1946, p. 180). Common to both of these definitions is a theme of power as the implementation of intentions. Also implied, particularly by Weber, is the ability to carry out one's intended effects against the resistance of others.

A variety of conceptual analyses of power, mostly by political scientists and sociologists, have appeared since the contributions of Russell and Weber. Several of these analyses are reviewed by Riker (1964), and they are generally consistent with the conceptualizations

---

The author wishes to express his appreciation to Stephen D. Karr, Gladys M. Kuoksa, Edward C. Simmell, and M. Brewster Smith, who read and commented on earlier portions of this chapter.

of Russell and Weber. Further congruence to the meaning of power is offered by a psychologist, Isidor Chein, who defines power ". . . as the ease with which an element in a social unit can carry out its will against resistance" (1969, p. 28). Accordingly, power can be conceptualized as the ability of a person or group of persons to overcome resistance in the course of obtaining intended effects.

There are a number of terms with meanings that closely approximate the meaning of power. In order to achieve conceptual clarity, it would be helpful to distinguish power from the related concepts of force, authority, control, and influence.

Force refers to the use of punitive or coercive methods by a person or group for the purpose of getting others to comply. Punishments are specifically administered in response to acts of noncompliance. Some theorists, such as Bierstedt (1950) tend to view force as the only way in which power can be exercised. However, other theorists, such as French and Raven (1959) consider coercion to be one of several means of exercising power. They refer to reward, legitimacy, attraction, and expertness as other possible bases of exercising power. Force can best be viewed as one of several means of obtaining intended effects.

Authority is often thought of as formal power, or in other words, power that is attached to statuses and norms rather than to persons (Bierstedt, 1950). When a person exercises the authority vested in his position, he makes use of norms of legitimacy in obtaining compliance from others. There is a problem, however, in viewing authority only from the perspective of the social system. One must assume that there is consensual agreement about the legitimacy of authority vested in the traditions, laws, or statuses of the social system. Indeed, as Flacks (1969) points out, there has been a growing (erosion of legitimacy) in acceptance of the values of American society as indicated by the black revolt and the challenges of many middle-class youths. A more viable conceptualization of authority is one that considers the relative nature of legitimacy. For example, Bachrach and Baratz view authority as implying ". . . rationality in the sense of [person] B deferring to [person] A . . . because A's command is reasonable in terms of B's values" (1963, p. 638). Thus, a policeman's badge or uniform is not representative of his authority; rather it is the reasonableness of his commands that represents authority. What is considered reasonable or authoritative is a product of the consensual norms between two persons or groups in a power relationship.

Control represents the successful exercise of power, that is, obtaining effects that are consistent with one's intentions. Thus, I would agree with Cartwright's (1959) conception of control as a change in person B which corresponds to the change intended by person A. He points out that Russell's (1938) definition of power as the production of intended effects might be restated as: A has power over B if and only if A controls B. If we assume that control represents the successful implementation of intentions, control should not be considered as an all-or-none phenomenon. One can effect partial control if there is some correspondence with antecedent intentions.

Influence and power have often been used interchangeably or synonymously in the literature (Dahl, 1957; March, 1955). There have been, however, a number of attempts to distinguish between the two terms (Cartwright & Zander, 1968; Lasswell & Kaplan, 1950; Lippitt, Polansky, Redl, & Rosen, 1952; Simon, 1953). Influence is typically viewed as one's *potential* to effect the outcomes of others, while power is viewed as one's *ability* to effect the outcomes of others. The implication is that power reflects previous evidence that a person has successfully carried out his intentions and overcome social resistance. In contrast, influence reflects the possibility that a person may have some effect on others. What seems to be the essential distinction between power and influence is the presence or absence of intentionality. Power, as opposed to influence, involves carrying out intentions. Power is therefore a more purposeful or deliberate social process than influence, and consequently usually involves overcoming a greater degree of social resistance. In a power interaction, A is an active agent in attempting to get B to comply with A's wishes. In a situation of influence, B may spontaneously wish to pattern his behavior after that of A because A possesses valued attributes, such as wealth, respect, and wisdom. Influence can be combined with power if A utilizes his personal attributes valued by B as a means of obtaining B's compliance.

At this point, I would like to return to my definition of power as the ability of a person or group of persons to overcome resistance in the course of obtaining intended effects. The next step is to consider how this conceptualization of power can be operationalized. A recurring problem in operationalizing power is that it can be measured in a variety of ways. For example, Simon (1953) refers to direct measures such as the actual behavior change one individual can effect on another, and indirect measures such as attitudes and expectations about the power of others. Rose (1967) expresses the view that the way power is defined is related to the way it is studied. He cites examples of power as potential and power as behavior; the former measured as attributes for wielding power, and the latter measured as participation in the decision-making process. Similarly, D'Antonio and Ehrlich (1961) indicate that one may focus upon power as a potential for control or, through its exercise, as control itself.

Thus, it is generally agreed that power can be measured from a number of perspectives. The issue is whether or not these various methods of measurement lead to a convergent validity (Campbell & Fiske, 1959) of power as a unitary construct. In discussing studies on community power, Rossi (1957) indicates a lack of convergent results due to the use of varying research designs. He cites three ways in which power has been measured in these studies: (1) potentials for power as measured by inventories of persons and organizations who are in a position to apply power, (2) power reputation based on the perceived power structure, and (3) actual power in terms of who determines outcomes. The tendency is for community power studies that utilize power potential or power reputation to produce results supportive of a power elite point of view, while studies that utilize measures of the actual exercise of power produce results supportive of a power diffusion point of view. This finding exemplifies a basic problem inherent in assuming that power is a unitary construct. Indeed, the confusion over the meaning and measurement of power is caused by overlooking the possibility that power may involve a set of variables which underlie the production of intended effects.

From the foregoing discussion, the most efficacious approach in operationalizing power is a multivariate one. I would like to propose that there are at least four relatively distinct aspects of power—motivational, manifest, subjective, and potential power. To illustrate these power variables, let us take an example of a husband-wife interaction. For a Saturday night's entertainment, the husband wants to go to a movie while the wife wants to go to a ballet performance. Analyzing the interaction from the point of view of the husband, we would first assume that he is motivated to obtain his wife's compliance. The desire to obtain social compliance is an example of *power motivation*. The husband is motivated to implement his intention of taking his wife to the movies thereby overcoming her resistance. If, in fact, the wife agrees to go to the movies, then the husband has exercised his power. The actual implementation of intentions is an example of *manifest power*. However, the husband may or may not subjectively feel that he was actually responsible for his wife's actions. *Subjective power*[1] refers to one's subjective evaluation of effectiveness in implementing personal intentions. Finally, if the husband has manifestly demonstrated his power in obtaining his wife's compliance, we could predict that on a

---

1. The term "latent power" was used in two previous papers (Minton, 1967, 1968) to refer to this variable. However, it is not as preferable a term because it can imply potential as well as subjective aspects of power.

subsequent occasion given the same set of alternative decisions the husband would again obtain his wife's compliance. *Potential power* refers to previously demonstrated instances in which intentions have been attained, thus allowing for predictions about a person's power in future situations.

In the above illustration, not all of the four power variables may correspond to one another. If the husband is motivated to exercise his power, he may be unable to overcome his wife's resistance. Consequently, he will not have demonstrated his manifest power in the situation. Even assuming that his wife objectively complies with his intended wishes, the husband may feel that he was not responsible for his wife's actions. Still further, if the husband has both manifestly and subjectively exercised his power, he may not choose to use his power in a subsequent situation. Although he possesses power, he may not choose to exercise it. Thus, with the possibility that differences may exist among measures of power it becomes necessary to consider a person's power in a given situation from several perspectives.

In conceptualizing the operation of power within the context of a two-person interaction, I have up to this point dealt only with the power of the person who initiates action. In a power interaction, both the person initiating attempts at gaining power (the *initiating agent*) and the person who is the recipient of these attempts (the *target person*) need to be considered. In our illustration, the wife will subjectively evaluate her husband's power. She will also evaluate her own power relative to her husband's, and may be motivated to counteract her husband's attempts at gaining her compliance. Consequently she may attempt to exercise her own power over her husband. In most ongoing social interactions an exchange of power exists: a person is at one time an initiating agent and at another time a target person.

A multivariate analysis of power is relevant to both an ongoing interaction between two or more social elements, such as persons or groups, and the consistency of a particular social element interacting with various other social elements across several situations. Thus, within the context of a person as a social element, power can be analyzed either in a given situation which involves some interaction with another person or persons (*social power*) or as a relatively consistent attribute of the person across situations (*personal power*). Personal power is most pertinent to a consideration of power as a personality construct.[2]

2. A comprehensive consideration of both personal and social power will be included in a forthcoming book by the author, entitled *Power: A Psychological Analysis*, to be published by The Macmillan Company.

Personal Power

The four power variables introduced in the first section can be conceptualized as dimensions of personal power. Individuals can be compared to one another along dimensions ranging from low to high levels of power motivation, manifest power, potential power, and subjective power. An individual's placement along a continuum of power represents a personal attribute which is relatively consistent across situations. For example, a person who possesses a high degree of subjective power is one who believes or feels that he can generally carry out personal intentions. Any situation which involves a person's attempt to implement intentions would contribute towards the development of generalized motives, beliefs, manifestations, and potentials of power. Thus, attempts at affecting the actions of others, or attempts at mastering impersonal tasks which have social significance would be specific examples of situations relevant to personal power dimensions.

Power Motivation

Motivation, itself, is a complex psychological construct with three components: (1) drive or need, the conditions that energize the organism towards satisfying some physiologically based requirement; (2) motivated behavior, the actual behaviors the organism manifests in seeking satisfaction; and (3) the goal, the specific object or objects that when attained lead to drive satisfaction. With reference to power motivation, motivated behavior is reflected by a person's actual attempts to overcome resistance and attain an intended effect—in other words, manifest power. If we are to consider power motivation as a variable or variables separate from manifest power, our concern is with the drives and goals that may or may not be translated into some degree of manifest power.

In a general sense at the level of human motivation, drives and goals can be distinguished from one another on the basis of what is universal across individuals and what is distinctive between individuals. Drives, being innate requirements, can be considered as universal human characteristics; while, specific goals can be considered as the distinctively learned means of satisfying drives. A similar distinction is made by Maddi (1968) in his analysis of personality theories. Maddi refers to general human requirements as the "core characteristics" of personality and motives (the anticipation of attaining specific goals) as a particular type of "peripheral personality characteristic." The distinction between drive and motive leads to two issues regarding the motivational basis of personal power. First, is there a physiologically based power drive or general human requirement for self-determined activity? Second, is a self-determination requirement translated into specific motives or anticipated goals of attaining power? The notion of a universal power drive, or *need for self-determination* cannot actually be considered as a dimension of personal power since it is general rather than distinctive across individuals. A *power motive*, on the other hand, is a power dimension that refers to variations across individuals regarding the extent to which one is motivated to attain specific goals of power.

Let us first consider the possibility of a universal or core need for self-determination. Several personality theorists have conceived of a core characteristic of self-determination. For example, Adler (Ansbacher & Ansbacher, 1956) viewed a "will-to-power," in the sense of striving for personal success or perfection, as the basic source of human motivation. The ego psychologist, Hendrick (1942) proposed an "instinct to master," which he characterized as an inborn drive to do and to learn how to do. More recently, Robert White (1959), whose theoretical approach has been influenced by the ego psychologists, proposed the concept of "effectance" to refer to the motivating state underlying success striving. White defines effectance as a need to interact effectively with the environment through one's own efforts. Another reflection of self-determination is Allport's (1955) concept of "propriate strivings," which refers to one's attempts at being an active self-initiating agent. The successful implementation of propriate strivings would result in one's ability to shape rather than be shaped by his environment. Both White and Allport contrast their variants of a self-determination core characteristic with the core tendency of biological survival needs, such as hunger, thirst, and pain avoidance. The implication is that effectance or propriate strivings contribute to the highest development or fulfillment of the person as opposed to mere physical survival.

The conceptualization of a core characteristic of self-determination is not limited only to personality theory. De Charms (1968), in his treatment of human motivation, proposes a core characteristic of "personal causation," which is identified as self-initiated behavior directed at producing environmental change. In the area of cognitive development, Bruner (1966) refers to man's capacity of a "will to learn" about his environment so as to achieve personal mastery.

White is the most explicit theorist regarding the citation of empirical support. He points out that an effectance drive is reflected in the exploratory and manipulatory behaviors that have been systematically observed in various animal species, and the play behavior of young children that has been investigated by Piaget. Unfortunately, White is rather vague as to the physiological basis of an effectance drive. There is, however, much to suggest from the recent theory and research on activation or arousal level (Berlyne, 1963; Fiske & Maddi, 1961; Hebb, 1955) that there are physiological regulatory mechanisms which govern levels of sensory input from the external environment. Consequently, an effectance drive could be based on the coordination between internal arousal level and sensory feedback from self-initiated or self-determined efforts by the person to effect purposeful environmental change.

A power motive, as previously stated, refers to the extent to which one is motivated to seek specific goals of personal power thereby satisfying the need for self-determination. However, two types of power goals exist. Consequently, two types of power motives should be considered. One motive is to seek power through the successful enactment of self-initiated efforts, while the other is to seek power as an objective reward resulting from but external to one's self-initiated efforts. The former is characterized by a reward of self-determination which is intrinsic to the successful implementation of one's efforts. The implication is that the person is motivated to seek personal power through the demonstration of skill or competence in performing a self-initiated task. A power motive in which the reward of self-determination is intrinsic to the act might therefore best be termed a *competence motive*. In contrast, the second type of power motive is characterized by a reward of self-determination which is extrinsic to one's efforts. Power is a by-product of an objective reward, such as wealth or status. If one strives for a position of high status the reward of being able to exercise power does not come from the status-striving behaviors themselves, but rather as a consequence of having attained the position of high status. At this point I will use the term, *power motive*, to refer only to power as an extrinsic reward and in contrast to *competence motive* which refers to power as an intrinsic reward.

There is as yet no direct measure of a competence motive dimension which would assess individual differences in expressing a desire to attain competence in self-initiated activities. Maddi (1968), however, has developed a conceptually related thematic apperceptive measure of a motive for variety, and reports preliminary research suggesting that individuals who have a high need for variety will manifest an active orientation in effecting environmental change. A considerable body of research exists on the power motive, which is based on a thematic apperceptive measure developed by Veroff (1957). In a review of these findings, Veroff and Veroff (1969) conclude that a high power motive occurs in status groups concerned about their weakness and at an individual level is correlated with poor social adjustment when other specific extrinsic motives, such as achievement and affiliation, are low. Positive social adjustment is indicated when an individual receives high scores on several extrinsic motive dimensions. What emerges from these results regarding a power motive is the suggestion that a person or group of persons may be highly motivated towards attaining extrinsic goals of power, such as status, as a means of compensating for the lack of self-determination that they both possess and feel. The frustration of not being in a position to satisfy self-determination may lead to an emphasis of trying to attain goals of extrinsic power. On the other hand, an orientation towards goals of competence or intrinsic power may be a reflection of one's successful attainment of a status position which provides opportunities for implementing self-determination. Generally, an inverse relationship may exist between a competence motive dimension and a power motive dimension.

The contemporary theme of "Black Power" and "Student Power" might exemplify the compensatory nature of a power motive. These themes reflect groups occupying social positions which provide little opportunity for the expression of self-determination. The goal for such groups is attaining a share of social power thereby overcoming the obstacles that have blocked self-determination.

Potential Power and Manifest Power

Both potential power and manifest power involve the actual exercise of power. The distinction is one of capability versus performance. Potential power refers to the capability of being able to overcome resistance and carry out an intended effect, while manifest power refers to the performance of overcoming resistance and carrying out an intended effect. Potential power implies that a person has previously manifested his power, and consequently has the potential to exercise his power in subsequent situations.

Measures of potential power are most often labeled "competence," reflecting an emphasis on the skills a person has acquired. The purpose of an overall measure of personal competence is primarily prognostic; that is, one's general level of skills and accomplishments should be predictive of one's future effectiveness as a self-determining agent equipped to cope with environmental demands. A measure of general personal competence has been developed by Phillips (1968) and includes a checklist of levels of achievement in such areas as education, occupation, marriage, social participation, and social responsibility. A similar measure has been developed by Lanyon (1967) to specifically assess competence in a college environment. Another kind of competence measure has emphasized internal personal attributes, such as personality traits, attitudes, and values, as predictors of effectiveness. Heath's (1968) factor analytic study of maturity among college males, and Smith's (1966) analysis of interview data from Peace Corps volunteers are examples of competence measures stressing internal characteristics. Validity studies of these various competence indices are still at a preliminary stage, but available evidence has been in the direction of predicted results.

Manifest power implies the effects of specific situations in interaction with skills and attributes one brings to a given situation. Measures of manifest power would therefore often serve as the criterion for the other dimensions of power, that is power motive, competence motive, potential power, and subjective power. However, manifest power can also serve as a measure of individual differences in behavioral response style. Manifest power as a dimension across individuals would vary in terms of how effective one's observed behavioral responses were in overcoming environmental resistance and implementing intended effects. For an *effective response style* to be considered as a personality characteristic, measurements are needed in several specific situations which would be functionally equivalent to one another. An example of assessing manifest power in terms of an effective response style is the study reported by Goldfried and D'Zurilla (1969) of effective behavior among college freshmen. The authors developed a questionnaire consisting of a number of problematic situations that are likely to occur in a college environment. Respondents are called upon to write out a description of how they would react to each problem situation. The authors report that validity studies are currently in progress.

Subjective Power

Most of the research relevant to personal power has emphasized self-conceptions of power, or subjective power.[3] Subjective power refers to one's subjective evaluation of effectiveness in implementing personal intentions. Subjective power, then, is a dimension that can vary from feelings or beliefs of powerlessness to feelings or beliefs of powerfulness. A number of theoretical concepts, including *internal versus external control, subjective probability,* and *Origin versus*

---

3. More comprehensive considerations of the other aspects of personal power will be included in the author's forthcoming book, *Power: A Psychological Analysis.*

Pawn, appear to share the notion of a continuum of powerlessness–powerfulness.

Internal-External Control

Rotter, as part of his social learning theory (Rotter 1954, 1966, 1967), has developed the concept of internal versus external control of reinforcement. The basic postulate of social learning theory is expressed by Rotter as follows: "The potential for a specific behavior directed toward a reinforcement to occur in a particular situation is a function of the expectancy of the occurrence of that reinforcement following the behavior in that situation and the value of the reinforcement in that situation" (1967, p. 117). Rotter points out that in order to be able to predict behavior in a specific situation the individual's past reinforcement experiences must be considered in addition to the situation-specific variables. Across specific situations the individual develops generalized expectancies or beliefs and sets of values or preferences (referred to as "need values") about behavior-reinforcement sequences.

Internal-external control is an example of a generalized expectancy, and refers to "...the degree to which the individual believes that what happens to him results from his own behavior versus the degree to which he believes that what happens to him is the result of luck, chance, fate, or forces beyond his control" (1967, p. 128). In other words, external control represents the individual's attribution of personal causality to environmental forces, while internal control represents the individual's attribution of personal causality to personal forces.

Comprehensive reviews of the variable of internal-external control have been presented by Rotter (1966) and Lefcourt (1966). Generally, there have been two approaches to the study of internal-external control: one, where the variable has been investigated in terms of situational factors; the other, in terms of individual differences.

SITUATIONAL COMPARISONS OF INTERNAL-EXTERNAL CONTROL

In a given situation the individual is disposed to interpret the locus of causality according to the generalized expectancy of internal-external control that has been developed across situations. However, as Rotter points out, the nature of the situation and the degree to which it is structured will also determine the individual's causal attribution. Thus, the more uniform a situation is and the more clearly it is structured, the less one's generalized expectancy will contribute toward causal attribution. In terms of situational determinants Rotter has hypothesized that perceived causal relations will be dependent on whether the task is structured as one of skill or one of chance. Rotter predicts that skill conditions lead to a belief of internal causality and chance conditions to a belief of external causality. Consequently, in a skill situation one's expectancies of future outcomes will be more contingent upon past reinforcement than in a chance situation.

Rotter and his associates have conducted several studies comparing expectancies for future reinforcement in skill and chance learning tasks. Most of these studies (Lefcourt, 1966; Rotter, 1966) have used an ambiguous task that has been introduced by the experimenter as being dependent upon either skill or chance. Expectancy is measured by the subject's reported probability of being correct on the succeeding trial. The general results of these studies indicate that reinforcements under skill conditions have a significantly greater effect in shifting expectancies in the direction of past reinforcements, which is consistent with an interpretation of internal causality. Under chance conditions there is a strong trend toward unusual shifts, that is, an increase in expectancies after failure and a decrease after success. Unusual shifts in expectancies are often referred to as the "gambler's fallacy" (Cohen, 1960), and are consistent with an interpretation of external causality.

In addition to demonstrating the effects of skill and chance conditions on shaping expectancies for reinforcement, Rotter has investigated the effects of skill and chance conditions on the rate of extinction of expectancies. The extinction of expectancies is accomplished by withholding the reinforcements that had been previously provided during the learning acquisition trials. In a study by James and Rotter (1958) partial (50 percent) and continuous (100 percent) reinforcement schedules during acquisition trials were each used under skill and chance conditions. The task involved a card-guessing problem, in which subjects reported verbal expectancies. The criterion for extinction was defined as a stated expectancy of 1 or 0 on a scale of 10 for three consecutive trials. Among the skill groups there was a trend toward greater resistance to extinction under 100 percent reinforcement, while among the chance groups there was a significantly greater resistance under 50 percent reinforcement. In comparisons between skill and chance, the number of trials to extinction under 50 percent reinforcement was significantly greater for chance than skill, whereas the number of trials to extinction under 100 percent reinforcement was significantly greater for skill than chance. These findings indicate that under continuous (100 percent) reinforcement, skill instructions are more consistent with the reinforcement schedule during acquisition trials and make it more difficult for the subject to accept the change in reinforcement during extinction. The conditions during partial (50 percent) reinforcement are reversed so that chance instructions serve as the condition more consistent with the reinforcement schedule. In general these findings demonstrate the interaction of reinforcement schedules and task structure as determinants of expectancies.

Rotter (1966) reports several other studies that are consistent with the findings of James and Rotter. Minton (1967), however, reports that in a study where a scorekeeper as well as the experimenter were present the effects of chance versus skill on extinction of verbal expectancies was not replicated.

Several studies cited by Rotter (1966) have investigated situational variables other than experimenter-instructions that could influence a subject's perceptions about the chance or skill nature of a task. Some of the conditions that account for a sequence of reinforcement as *not* being chance-controlled are significant deviations from a 50 percent reinforcement schedule in a right-wrong situation, reinforcements that have a definite pattern, and minimal variability of performance in tasks where a scoring continuum is provided. These findings indicate that a task can be structured as one of skill or chance on the basis of clearly defined stimulus patterns.

In summary, the above studies provide generally consistent evidence that the locus of causal attributions can be influenced by the way in which the situation is structured. The evidence is also generally supportive of the hypothesis that in a skill situation one's expectancies of future outcomes will be more contingent upon past performance than in a chance situation.

THE MEASUREMENT OF INDIVIDUAL DIFFERENCES IN INTERNAL EXTERNAL CONTROL

Individual differences in a generalized expectancy of internal-external control are measured by a forced-choice questionnaire referred to as the Internal-External Control (I-E) Scale (Rotter, 1966). The I-E scale consists of alternative expectancy statements; one representing an internal locus of control, the other an external locus of control. The scale is scored in the external direction. The items were developed from a set of logical content areas. For example, external control statements represent beliefs that the locus of personal causality is based on factors of chance, luck, or fate.

An item analysis of internal-external control items, carried out around 1960, revealed high intercorrelations among specific content areas. The internal-external control variable has thus been considered to be unidimensional. However, recent factor-analytic studies of the I-E scale have generated two factors. Mirels (1970) using a student sample from a large Midwestern state university, and Gurin, Gurin, Lao, and Beattie (1969) using student samples from several Negro colleges in the South, report factorial distinctions based on items stated in the first person versus those stated in the third person. First person items have been labeled "Personal Control" and third person items have been labeled "Control Ideology." The Personal Control factor appears to be closer to Rotter's notion of internal-external control and the meaning of subjective power, since the emphasis is on the person's evaluation of his own power rather than, as implied by the Control Ideology factor, a cultural belief about self-initiative. Unfortunately, almost all of the research with the I-E scale has been based on the assumption that it is unidimensional. Thus, a problem appears in being able to clearly interpret the results of studies that have used the I-E scale. The discrepancy between the factor-analytic results represents a ten-year time span, which suggests the possibility that a Personal Control factor as distinct from a Control Ideology factor could be a reflection of changing times. At least with reference to college population, events during the decade of the Sixties have alienated a great number of students. As a consequence of this alienation many students who hold to a cultural belief that one can get ahead through one's own efforts might not feel that such a belief holds true in their own case. In conclusion, much more caution needs to be placed on interpreting the results of I-E studies (especially those relevant to political behavior) that have been carried out in the late Sixties as opposed to the early Sixties. At any rate, I would recommend that subsequent studies utilizing measures of the internal-external control variable consider the personal-ideological distinction. Unless otherwise indicated, the following review of I-E studies contains results based on the assumption of unidimensionality.

Rotter (1966) and Hersch and Scheibe (1967) report extensive data on the I-E scale indicating a consistently high level of reliability. Relationships to measures of intelligence show low and nonsignificant correlations. Normative data indicate approximately equivalent distributions of scores for several college samples. Sex differences among college students appear to be minimal. However, Wolfe (1966), using adult samples drawn from several communities, found that females tended to be more external on the I-E scale, and this difference reached statistical significance when the samples were combined. There is the suggestion, then, that sex differences may be more characteristic of noncollege than college samples. More normative data is needed with noncollege adult samples.

Measures of the internal-external control variable have also been developed for children and adolescents. Bialer (1961) has constructed a Locus of Control Scale for children which is an orally administered true-false scale. Crandall, Katkovsky, and Preston (1962) developed a forced-choice questionnaire for children, titled the Intellectual Achievement Responsibility Questionnaire, which measures responsibility attribution in achievement situations. A projective-type test for children that consists of cartoons with verbal statements to be filled in by the child has been developed by Battle and Rotter (1963). The cartoons represent lifelike situations involving responsibility attribution. Jessor, Graves, Hanson, and Jessor (1968) have adapted the I-E scale for use with high school students.

CORRELATES OF INTERNAL-EXTERNAL CONTROL

The internal-external variable has been studied in relation to a number of personality dimensions. These correlational studies have involved samples of college students. Hersch and Scheibe (1967) studied the relation of the I-E scale to two multidimensional personality measures—the California Psychological Inventory and the Gough Adjective Check List. They found that internal scorers described themselves as more active, striving, achieving, powerful, independent, and effective. The results also indicated greater homogeneity or agreement in self-descriptions by internal scorers. Consistent with the contellation of a striving and achieving self-description by internal scorers, Minton (1967) reports a significant and moderately negative relationship between external control and a self-descriptive achievement scale (one of the scales of the Jackson Personality Research Form). Feather (1967a), however, found no significant relationship between the I-E scale and the TAT measure of need achievement. Method variance between a questionnaire and a projective measure might account for Feather's lack of replicating the relationships found among questionnaire measures of the control and achievement dimensions.

Anxiety in relation to internal-external control has been investigated through several indices of anxiety. Butterfield (1964) using the I-E scale and two questionnaire measures of anxiety-related variables found that external control was related to nonconstructive problem-solving responses (as measured by the Child-Waterhouse Frustration Reaction Inventory) and debilitating test anxiety (as measured by the Alpert-Haber test anxiety scale). In contrast, internal control was related to constructive problem-solving responses and facilitating test anxiety. Other evidence of a relationship between external control and the debilitative form of test anxiety is reported by Watson (1967) using the Alpert-Haber measure of test anxiety, and by Ray and Katahn (1968) using the Sarason Test Anxiety Scale. A relationship between external control and the Taylor Manifest Anxiety Scale (a less situation-specific index of anxiety than test anxiety) is also reported in the Watson and Ray and Katahn studies. Theoretical consistency appears in the findings that external control is positively related to debilitating test anxiety and negatively related to need achievement, as exemplified by Atkinson (1957) who posits a negative relationship between the need to achieve and the need to avoid failure.

Consistent with the relationship between external control and anxiety are results which indicate that there is some relationship between external control and measures of maladjustment. Rotter (1966) hypothesized that there would be a low linear correlation between external control and maladjustment for relatively homogeneous and normal groups such as college students. However, in a study with college students where scores on the I-E scale were compared with an index of maladjustment on the Rotter Incomplete Sentences Blank, a rather complex curvilinear relationship was found. In another study with college students, Hersch and Scheibe (1967) did find a consistently low but significant linear relationship across three measures of maladjustment in which external scorers were more maladjusted. The indices of maladjustment included the same incomplete-sentence form Rotter had used, the Psychasthenia scale from the MMPI (a measure of a neurotic syndrome), and a discrepancy score between self- and ideal-self-descriptions. Other support of a linear relationship between external control and maladjustment among college students is provided by Feather (1967a), who reports significant correlations between external control and neuroticism (as measured by the Maudsley Personality Inventory).

Another means of investigating the relationship between the control variable and maladjustment would be to compare seriously maladjusted groups with normal groups. Whether locus of control scores for maladjusted subjects can be interpreted in the same way as for normal subjects is questionable. Although we would generally expect maladjusted subjects to score more externally, extreme internal scores could reflect a pathological distortion of one's belief in personal control. As yet, no evidence exists relating extreme internal scores to a distorted view of personal control. However, some evidence indicates that samples of maladjusted subjects score more externally than normal subjects. Cromwell, Rosenthal, Shakow, and Zahn (1961) found that schizophrenics were significantly more external than a group of normal control subjects. Other interesting evidence differentiating the two groups is also reported. As predicted, normal subjects performed better in a reaction-time task under internal control conditions, whereas schizophrenics performed better under external control conditions. Consistency appears between these results and those reported by Rotter and Mulry (1965) with normal subjects in which internal scorers took more time to make a decision in a skill condition than in a chance condition, while external scorers manifested a reverse trend. Agreement in results by Watson and Baumal (1967) is shown in which internal scorers made more errors when they anticipated not having control, whereas external scorers made more errors when they anticipated having control. These studies suggest that the most effective performance takes place when the individual is in situations that are congruent with generalized expectancies of locus of control.

For seriously maladjusted individuals situational congruency might be reflected by a need to seek out those environmental conditions which will reinforce their beliefs that what happens to them is beyond their control. Receiving confirmation of an external locus of control might also serve the function of reducing anxiety over personal responsibility. Although evidence exists of a relationship between anxiety and external control, research is needed to investigate the function of external control as an anxiety-reducing mechanism.

The relationship between internal-external control and social status has been investigated in several studies using noncollege populations. It would be expected that one's position or status in society would have some affect on one's belief in personal control. As we would predict, the results consistently demonstrate that the lower one's social status the greater one's belief in an external locus of control. For example, Battle and Rotter (1963) found a general relationship between lower social class and external control in comparing Negro and white sixth- and eighth-grade children. The projective-type test of internal-external control was used, and the general social-class effect was obtained with race and intellectual level controlled. In more specific comparisons, lower-class Negroes were significantly more external than middle-class Negroes and lower-class or middle-class whites. Similar findings were obtained in a study by Lefcourt and Ladwig (1965) of Negro and white prisoners. With most of the prisoners categorized in the lower socioeconomic class, Negroes had higher external score than whites. Jessor et al.

(1968) in a study of high school students in a tri-ethnic community in the Southwest reported that whites were the most internal, followed by Spanish-Americans, with Indians being the most external.

BEHAVIORAL PREDICTIONS OF INTERNAL-EXTERNAL CONTROL

Generally, internal-external control measures have been used as predictors of four types of behavioral criterion situations: performance in controlled laboratory tasks; attempts to control the environment; achievement situations; and reactions to social influence.

Predictions of individual differences in performance within tasks that are defined as either skill- or chance-based has been only partially successful. Rotter (1966) reports that the generally consistent finding has been the tendency of externals to produce more unusual expectancy shifts than internals within a given task condition of skill or chance. Apparently, task structure is a more salient determinant of performance than the generalized belief in personal control that the subject brings to the task. In less controlled or more ambiguous situations we would expect a generalized expectancy of locus of control to have some influence on behavior.

The hypothesis that individuals who are more internal will demonstrate more initiative and effort in shaping their environment has received considerable empirical support. One aspect of initiating control is information-seeking, and the results of several studies show that internals learn more about their environmental setting than externals. Seeman and Evans (1962), using a scale adapted from the I-E scale and controlling for occupational status, education, and ward placement, found that internals sought out and acquired more information in a hospital setting. In a study with reformatory inmates in which level of intelligence was controlled, Seeman (1963) found that internals knew more about their institution, the parole system, and long-range factors that could affect them after leaving the reformatory. Within a laboratory setting involving a problem-solving task, Davis and Phares (1967) found that internals were superior to externals in actively seeking information. Similarly, Phares (1968) reported that internals make better use of information in solving problems.

Other evidence in support of a relationship between internal control and attempts at initiating environmental control is provided by studies of collective social-action behavior. Gore and Rotter (1963), in a study with students at a southern Negro college, found a relationship between internal control and paper-and-pencil commitment to various civil rights activities. Consistent with these results, Strickland (1965) found that activists in a Negro civil rights movement were significantly more internal than nonactive Negroes who were matched for education and social class. In a sample of Negro college students from three predominantly Negro colleges in the South, Escoffery (1968) found that internals held a larger number of memberships in civil rights organizations. However, more refined results are contained in a study by Lao (1970), which while also invloving Negro college students included a separate analysis of the I-E items that had high loadings on the Personal Control factor reported by Gurin et al. (1969). In addition, the I-E scale was extended to include several forced-choiced items referring to the race situation. Unlike the results of previous studies with the total I-E score, high or internal Personal Control was not related to measures of collective social action. Among the race-related items, a relationship was found between an external Control Ideology (blaming the social system instead of personal inadequacies of Negroes) and the collective social-action measures of active participation in civil rights activities and preferences for collective as opposed to individual action and protest as opposed to negotiation. An interaction was found in terms of low Personal Control-high System Blame and the preference for militant protest action. The results of the Lao study, then, tend to be inconsistent with those reported results of a relationship between internal control and collective social action. However, as previously stated, discrepancies may reflect time variations when data was collected. Differences in sampling and item analysis also have to be considered as contributing to these variations in results.

A recent study by Thomas (1970) provides further indication of the difficulty of interpreting the relationship between the total score and collective social-action behavior. Among a sample of white college students, left-wing activists scored more externally than nonactivists, who in turn scored more externally than right-wing activists. Thomas interprets these results as reflecting a politically conservative bias in the I-E scale. It may be that the conservative bias is due to the Control Ideology factor, that is, the belief that people-in-general can get ahead by their own effort and therefore the system is not the source of social problems. In any event, unless the personal-ideological distinction is considered in using the I-E scale as a predictor of political activism, results will be ambiguous.

Another realm of action-taking behavior that may bear relevance to the control dimension is attempts at self-change. In an interesting finding Phares, Ritchie, and Davis (1968) reported that internals showed a greater willingness to engage in attempts at self-change when confronted with personal shortcomings. In this study, action-taking behavior was defined as a personal commitment to taking therapeutic steps, such as attending a lecture on mental health, attending a small group discussion on the stresses of college life, and making an appointment for personal counseling. The findings by Phares, Ritchie, and Davis were obtained under laboratory-induced conditions. It remains for further research to demonstrate the degree of internal control and relative attempts at overcoming personal deficiencies. There is some evidence on the relationship of the control dimension to changing a specific behavior pattern, namely smoking. James, Woodruff, and Werner (1965) found that among male smokers, internals were more successful in quitting. The relationship did not hold for female smokers. In a related finding, both James and his associates, and Straits and Secrest (1963) reported that nonsmokers were significantly more internal than smokers.

With respect to the relationship of the control dimension to performance in achievement situations, it has already been pointed out that internals tend to describe themselves as more striving and achieving than externals. Relevant to overt performance in achievement situations, very striking evidence of a relationship between internal control and actual achievement is shown. This evidence comes from a report by Coleman and his associates (1966), conducted under the auspices of the United States Office of Education. The study included 645,000 pupils in grades 3, 6, 9, and 12 in 4,000 American public schools and the data was gathered in the fall of 1965. Scores of a sense of control were based on three agree-disagree items, which were very similar to the theme of the I-E scale. A measure of verbal ability was used as the criterion for school achievement. In summarizing the study, Coleman and his associates state:

> A pupil attitude factor, which appears to have a stronger relationship to achievement than do all the school factors together, is the extent to which an individual feels that he has some control over his own destiny.... The responses of pupils to questions in the survey show that minority pupils, except for Orientals, have far less conviction than whites that they can affect their own environments and futures. When they do, however, their achievement is higher than that of whites who lack that conviction (p. 23).

The relationship between internal control and achievement was more marked for children from disadvantaged groups. The control dimension accounted for about three times as much variance in the achievement test scores of disadvantaged children as of advantaged children. As with the correlational findings of external control and low societal status, the findings of the Coleman report indicate the saliency of the objective social environment in relation to one's sense of control or power. The causal sequence of the control dimension and school achievement cannot be directly assessed from these correlational findings. Whether sense of control affects achievement or achievement affects sense of control is unknown. Most likely both of these causal relationships are involved. Most striking is the strong relationship among disadvantaged children between low academic achievement and a sense of external control.

Another important finding in the Coleman report was the assessment of school factors in relation to the control dimension. Generally, school characteristics showed little relationship to sense of control. However, among Negro children a significantly greater feeling of internal control was found for those children in schools which had a higher proportion of white-to-Negro students. Coleman and his associates comment: "This finding suggests that the direction such an attitude [sense of control] takes may be associated with the pupil's school experience as well as his experience in the larger community (p. 23)."

Several other studies provide evidence of a relationship between the control dimension and achievement behavior. McGhee and Crandall (1968) used the Intellectual Achievement Responsibility Questionnaire with subjects in grades ranging from elementary school through high school and found that children who were highly internal (in terms of assigning self-responsibility) consistently had higher course grades and higher achievement test scores. Girls' academic performance scores were consistently related to self-responsibility ascription for both success and failure situations, while boys' performance scores related more consistently to self-responsibility ascription for failure situations. Crandall, Katkovsky, and Preston (1962) using the same responsibility questionnaire with early-grade-school-age children found that the assignment of self-responsibility was predictive of boys' free-play achievement behavior and achievement test scores. Self-responsibility among girls was unrelated to achievement behaviors in this study. Crandall and McGhee (1968), with subjects ranging from junior high school to college age, found a positive relationship between various measures of expectancy of reinforcement and academic course grades and achievement test scores. The findings of these studies are consistent with the general finding that one's expectancy of academic success is related to one's actual academic success (Battle, 1966; Todd, Terrell, & Frank, 1962; and Uhlinger & Stephens, 1960).

Evidence of a relationship between the Personal Control factor of the I-E scale and indices of achievement is indicated in Lao's (1970) study of Negro college students. Students who scored high on Personal Control as opposed to those who scored low had higher entrance test scores and grade point averages, as well as greater self-confidence in attaining grades and higher educational aspirations. The total I-E scores, however, were not predictive of the achievement indices, thus indicating the necessity of partialing out the Control Ideology items for the sample of Negro college students.

Rotter (1966) reports that studies investigating the effects of deliberate social influence as related to the control dimension have shown that internal persons are more resistant to subtle attempts that are not to their benefit. However, if given a conscious choice, the internal person may conform. These results were obtained in studies using verbal conditioning and in an Asch-type yielding situation involving social pressure. Evidence of a relationship between internal control and effectiveness in influencing others is indicated in a study with college students by Phares (1965). The findings showed that internally-controlled subjects were significantly more successful than externally-controlled subjects in their attempt to change the attitudes of other college students. With respect to situations of deliberate social influence we can conclude that the individual who believes in an external rather than an internal locus of control is more easily influenced and less effective as an influencing agent.

External individuals may be more suspicious about being a target of manipulation. Miller and Minton (1969) hypothesized that externals would be more suspicious than internals of deception in an experimental setting. In support of this hypothesis it was found that external subjects (only males were used) engaged in more violations of experimental instructions when not under the surveillance of the experimenter. Other evidence of an attitude of suspicion on the part of externals is provided in a study by Hamsher, Geller, and Rotter (1968). The findings showed that external males (but not females) had significantly greater attitudes of disbelief of the Warren Commission Report on the death of President Kennedy. In addition, for male subjects a significant negative relationship was found between external control and the Rotter Interpersonal Trust Scale.

Empirical support is impressive for the generalized expectancy of internal-external control as a predictor of conceptually relevant behaviors. The individual with a belief in an internal locus of causality tends to be an active, effective, influential, and initiating person. On the other hand, the individual with an attitude of external control tends to have a passive orientation to his environment. Nevertheless, the emergence of a personal-ideological distinction in recent factor-analytic studies of the I-E scale raises questions about the predictive validity of present unidimensional measures of internal-external control. Consideration of the possibility of multidimensionality should be taken into account in further research with I-E measures. Some suggestion also appears of a more heterogeneous set of relationships with external than with internal control. Hersch and Scheibe (1967) recommend the need for more differentiation of the concept of externality as an important area for future research.

Subjective Probability

Subjective probability generally refers to an individual's evaluation of the degree of success attainable in a given situation and is equivalent in meaning to Rotter's use of "expectancy." Several theorists in addition to Rotter have conceived of goal-directed behavior as a function of both value or incentive and expectancy or subjective probability. For example, Lewin, Dembo, Festinger, and Sears (1944) concluded that goal-setting behavior (level of aspiration) was based on the value and subjective probability of success or failure. Edwards (1954) postulated that decision-making is based on subjective probability and subjective value. Tolman (1955) considered performance to be a function of expectancy and valence or value.

In a series of studies bearing close relationship to the situational comparisons of the internal-external control variable, Atkinson and his associates (Atkinson, 1964; Atkinson & Feather, 1966) have studied subjective probability as it relates to achievement motivation. The major difference between the positions of Rotter and Atkinson is that Rotter views expectancy and reinforcement value as theoretically independent, while Atkinson makes the contrary assumption. Rotter (1954) points out that expectancy and value may influence one another depending on the situation, but there is no necessary influence independent of the situation. Contrarily, Atkinson (1964) assumes that the incentive values of success and failure at a task are not independent of the corresponding subjective probabilities of success and failure. The specific relationship postulated is that as the positive incentive of success increases, the subjective probability of success decreases, and as the negative incentive of failure increases, the subjective probability of success increases. In other words, the incentive of success is high in a difficult-task situation where the probability of achieving success is low, while the incentive of success is low in an easy-task situation where the probability of achieving success is high. Heider's (1958) discussion of attribution of causality in relation to task difficulty is consistent with the above. Success in a difficult task is attributed to the person, whereas success in an easy task is attributed to the situation.

Atkinson has investigated individual differences in relation to the subjective probability of success through a consideration of achievement motivation. A number of studies reported by Atkinson and Feather (1966) have shown that subjects with a strong motive to approach success (a high score on a need achievement measure) and a weak motive to avoid failure (a low score on a debilitating test anxiety scale) have a preference for moderate levels of probability or risk-taking. Subjects with a strong motive to avoid failure and a weak motive to approach success tend to prefer either very high or very low probability levels. For example, Atkinson and Litwin (1960) using college males found that in a ring-toss game subjects with high need achievement (as assessed by a graphic measure, the French Test of Insight) and low anxiety (as assessed by the Mandler-Sarason Test Anxiety Questionnaire) took significantly more shots from an intermediate or moderate risk-taking position than subjects with low need achievement and high anxiety.

In an extension of the Atkinson and Litwin study, de Charms and Davé (1965) assessed the actual probabilities of success for each subject. The subjects included fourth, fifth, and sixth-grade boys, and the task was to shoot a volleyball into a basket placed on the floor. Neither the TAT need achievement measure nor the Mandler-Sarason Test Anxiety Questionnaire were related to risk-taking behavior. However, a measure of hope of success and fear of failure derived from the TAT stories was related to risk-taking. Subjects with a high hope of success and a high fear of failure took more moderate risks and achieved more success in the task. The investigators interpreted this finding as indicating that subjects concerned with both success and failure have a more realistic outlook than subjects who are concerned only with success or failure. Apparently, the measures of hope of success and fear of failure are more sensitive to personally determined probabilities of success than achievement and anxiety measures.

The studies using a ring-toss game involve the role of achievement motivation in a situation of skill. The Atkinson model has also been applied to a situation of chance. In a gambling situation involving college males, Littig (1963) hypothesized that high need achievement-low anxiety subjects (assessed by the TAT and Test Anxiety Questionnaire) would take moderate risks. However, the results were not supportive of the hypothesis. To what extent an achievement orientation is related to moderate risk-taking in chance situations needs further clarification. For, as de Charms (1968) points out, the Littig study excluded subjects high or low on both the achievement and anxiety measures.[4]

Several studies have been conducted by Feather (1961, 1965, 1967b) in which both motive and task-defined expectancy have been varied simultaneously. These studies included the TAT measure of need achievement and a questionnaire measure of test anxiety. Feather (1961) found that high need achievement-low anxiety subjects persist longer at an achievement task when it is presented to them as easy (high probability of success) rather than as difficult (low probability of success). The reverse was found for low need achievement-high anxiety subjects. In a subsequent study, Feather (1965) assessed subjective probability estimates of success by subjects prior to task performance. A significant positive relationship was found between need achievement and initial probability estimates in a task defined as moderately difficult, while significant negative relationships were found between test anxiety and initial probability estimates for both a moderately difficult and an easy task. These relationships between the personality variables and initial probability estimates were not demonstrated when estimates were assessed during the middle and terminal stages of task performance. Apparently, expectations of success become more influenced by present performance than by preperformance orientations of success and failure—an assumption consistent with the findings of the internal-external control variable, where situational factors are more dominant in shaping probability estimates than individual differences in a generalized belief of personal control.

Feather (1967b) has also investigated probability estimates under conditions defined as skill or chance. The results indicated that when success or failure is attributed to skill rather than chance, subjective probability estimates are higher. Subjective probability was found to be unrelated to the personality measures of need achievement, test anxiety, and internal-external control in support of previous findings concerning the dominant influence of situational factors, such as the way a task is structured. Feather (1968) did find a relationship

---

4. Internal-external control has also been related to risk-taking behavior in chance situations, and as with need achievement the results need further clarification. Liverant and Scodel (1960) found that among college males internal scorers on the I-E scale took more moderate risks in a betting situation. However, in a replication of the Liverant and Scodel study, Strickland, Lewicki, and Katz (1966) found that high school male subjects who were internal scorers on the I-E scale took high-level risks rather than moderate risks. The Strickland et al. study is difficult to interpret because of the low reliability found among the high school subjects on the I-E scale. The low reliability may have been due in part to the college-level orientation of the I-E scale.

between subjective probability estimates and I-E scores in a situation in which subjects were given an initial experience of success or failure. Consistent with Rotter's (1966) reported findings, external subjects had a lower frequency of expectancy shifts in the direction of past experience.

It is difficult to draw overall conclusions about the research on subjective probability because this variable has been assessed in different ways. In studies where actual probability estimates are assessed, the results appear to be generally consistent with the findings of those internal-external control studies which also include actual probability or expectancy estimates. What is needed for future research is more convergence among studies derived from the Rotter and Atkinson models. For example, subjective probability or expectancy has been shown to be related to individual differences in need achievement and test anxiety in some studies, and to individual differences in internal-external control in other studies. The relation of subjective probability to the combined constellation of need achievement, test anxiety, and internal-external control needs to be considered. Such studies would also provide more insight into an apparently complex relationship between achievement motive and belief in personal control.

The Origin-Pawn Variable

The Origin-Pawn concept has been developed by de Charms (1968), who notes the similarity between his conception and Rotter's internal-external control. De Charms describes Origin-Pawn as a dimension representing the attribution of causality. The Origin end of the continuum reflects an internal locus of causality, while the Pawn end of the continuum reflects an external locus of causality.

In comparing the Origin-Pawn variable with the control dimension, de Charms (1968) makes the following comments:

> In general, the studies of internal and external control constitute an impressive series. In our view, however, basing the "internal-external" concept on reinforcement is a barrier to confrontation with the basic issue of personal knowledge that is clearly implied by Rotter's stress on the perceived contingency between behavior and results. The important results of behavior are not always objectively measurable as hinted by Rotter's statement that the "internal" person "has a stong belief that he can control his own destiny." We suspect that the most appropriate way to measure the Origin-Pawn variable is the technique of thought sampling, i.e., tapping spontaneously emitted thoughts, rather than eliciting controlled responses on a questionnaire such as the I-E scale (p. 323).

De Charms (1968) reports the results of two studies designed to manipulate the Origin-Pawn variable. In one study, each subject performed similar tasks under both an Origin and a Pawn condition. The tasks involved constructing models using standard sets of Tinkertoys. Under the Pawn condition the subject was given very detailed instructions to create an atmosphere of constraint and a dependency upon proscribed guidelines. Under the Origin condition an orientation of self-directedness was emphasized. The results indicated that on a post-task questionnaire subjects reported feelings about the extent of personal freedom which were congruent with the direction of the manipulated Origin-Pawn conditions. In a further study along similar lines, the congruency between feelings of personal freedom and task orientation was replicated. In addition the results indicated a more positive attitude towards the work conducted under the Origin condition than under the Pawn condition. In both studies it was found that the Rotter I-E scale did not relate to any of the measures used to compare the Origin and Pawn conditions. Consistently, other findings have shown that individual differences in the control dimension do not predict performance in tasks that are structured as being based upon an internal or an external locus of causality.

The results of de Charms' studies demonstrate that conditions representative of the Origin-Pawn continuum can produce congruent attitudes and feelings. De Charms, however, has not as yet developed a measure of individual differences along a continuum of Origin-Pawn orientation. He has presented the challenge that a technique of thought sampling is a more appropriate way of assessing locus of causality or subjective power than a questionnaire method, because thought sampling is more directly related to obtaining personal knowledge. A need exists to compare a unidimensional questionnaire measure and a thought-sampling measure of subjective power. Subjective power assessed in different ways may lead to relatively high agreement in terms of behavioral predictions. On the other hand, subjective power assessed by a questionnaire may be something quite different than subjective power assessed by a thought-sampling technique.

Other Concepts of Subjective Power

In addition to internal-external control, subjective probability, and Origin-Pawn, there have been other concepts presented that reflect feelings, beliefs, and attitudes about personal power.

Mastery is a concept discussed by Strodtbeck (1958), who indicates that it represents an individual's concern for demonstrating personal control over the environment. Mastery is one of two factors derived from a scale of achievement-related values (the V-scale). The other factor is independence of family. Three items, stated in the third person and relating to a rejection of fate, have a high loading on the mastery factor. Strodtbeck found with a sample of third-generation Italian and Jewish male adolescents that Jewish boys had higher achievement-related responses than Italian boys. Two of the three mastery items showed significantly greater rejection of fate on the part of the Jewish boys. A significant relationship between internal control and mastery has been reported by Liberty, Burnstein, and Moulton (1966) who administered both the I-E scale and the V-scale to a sample of servicemen.

The concept of alienation has been related to a subjective dimension of power by Seeman (1959). He points out that one of the meanings of alienation is a feeling of powerlessness, which is conceptually distinct from four other meanings—isolation, normlessness or anomie, self-estrangement, and meaninglessness. Seeman equates powerlessness with Rotter's external control, and has adapted the I-E scale for use with noncollege samples. [5] Although Seeman uses a form of the I-E scale to measure powerlessness, Dean (1961) has constructed an independent questionnaire of alienation, which includes scales of powerlessness, normlessness, and isolation. The powerlessness scale consists of items (some stated in the first person and some stated in the third person) reflecting an attitude of powerlessness and the respondent indicates to what extent he agrees with these statements. The scale thus differs from the I-E scale which consists of forced-choice expectancy statements. The powerlessness and I-E scales are, however, closely related as indicated by Lefcourt's (1963) report of a significant correlation between the two scales for a sample of Negro males. Lefcourt and Ladwig (1965) also report that Negroes as compared to whites had higher scores on the powerlessness scale, which was consistent with the differences found on the I-E scale.

Another measure which seems conceptually similar to the dimension of internal-external control is an assessment of personal preferences for skill- or chance-determined outcomes. Bortner (1964) has developed a Skill-Chance Preference Scale, which provides the respondent with a choice between a skill-determined outcome and a chance-determined outcome. With a sample of males at a VA domiciliary, Bortner found that although most respondents shifted their preferences according to the odds for each choice which varied across the items, some respondents maintained consistent choices. Using those respondents with a highly consistent chance or skill preference, results indicated that individuals with a skill preference

---

5. Seeman's studies have been discussed in the section on internal-external control.

showed greater ego strength on a projective measure of impulse-control. Although it measures task preference rather than expectancies, the Skill-Chance Preference Scale appears to be similar to the I-E scale. A recent study by Schneider (1968) provides evidence that there is a close relationship between task preference and generalized expectancy. College students were given the I-E scale and a forced-choice activity preference scale. The hypothesized relationship between internal control and skill-preference and between external control and chance-preference was obtained for males but not females.

The concept of hope seems to be similar in meaning to expectation or subjective probability about goal attainment. Stotland (1969) in a treatment of the psychology of hope defines hope as a person's perceived probability of achieving a goal. Hope or hopefulness has been discussed in a variety of contexts. In studies of animal behavior, Richter (1957) has referred to a loss of hope and Mowrer and Viek (1948) to a sense of helplessness in accounting for reactions to conditions where animals had no control over what happened to them. Bettelheim (1960) describes the following reactions of concentration camp inmates in Nazi Germany who came to believe that their plight was hopeless:

> Prisoners who came to believe the repeated statements of the guards—that there was no hope for them, that they would never leave the camp except as a corpse—who came to feel that their environment was one over which they could exercise no influence whatever, these prisoners were, in a literal sense, walking corpses.... They were people who were so deprived of affect, of self-esteem, and every form of stimulation, so totally exhausted, both physically and mentally, that they had given the environment total power over them (p. 151).

Bettelheim reports that these prisoners did not try to get food for themselves and soon died.

Stotland (1969) postulates that an individual's hopelessness about important goals leads to anxiety. He cites Goldstein's (1940) observations that an individual experiences marked anxiety in reaction to conditions of environmental stress that are beyond the individual's control. Similarly, Grinker and Speigel (1945) in describing the emotional reactions of soldiers in World War II noted that anxiety was related to the individual's concern about mastery and freedom of activity. Mowrer (1960) has noted that in animal studies a sense of hopelessness about escape from pain leads to reactions of anxiety. Hence, consistent evidence exists of a relationship between hopelessness and anxiety in extreme conditions of threat where the organism lacks control over the environment. Under less extreme conditions, internal-external control studies indicate that there are individual differences in the desirability of personal control over the environment. Where personal threat is not involved, individuals with a belief in external control seem to prefer situations where they do not have to assume personal control. Perhaps, hopelessness becomes a source of anxiety in extreme situations because these situations are appreciably divergent from individual expectancy. The anxiety may be due to the marked reduction in personal control.

A conceptual problem with the use of the term "hope" is that it can refer to an expectancy of idealized outcomes as well as anticipated outcomes. One's hopes may not always be equivalent to one's actual expectancy.

This difference between expectancy and hope is illustrated in a study by Harvey and Clapp (1965). College subjects indicated the kinds of ratings they would expect from another person, as well as the kind of ratings they would hope to receive. The subjects were then exposed to fictitious ratings from the other person that deviated from their own expectancies, but tended to either confirm or refute the ratings they hoped to receive. The results indicated that subjects responded differently to the feedback of confirmed or refuted hope. When the term "hope" is used or assessed, a distinction should be made between anticipated and idealized outcomes. The same problem may also exist when you ask someone what they expect. The response to such a question may be given either in terms of actual anticipation or preferable occurrence.

Conclusions

This section has illustrated that one's subjective evaluation of personal power can be conceptualized and assessed from a number of theoretical vantage points. Conceptual convergence from these theoretical points of view indicates that subjective power (via the various labels that are used) is a product of both one's immediate environmental structure and one's past experiences in attempts to carry out intended effects.

It remains for future research to clarify the relationship among these various methods of assessing subjective power. Perhaps a beginning to this end is to note the conceptual similarities and the relatively consensual results across investigations that use different conceptual labels. In clarifying the meaning of any concept it is necessary to understand the dimensionality of the concept. Whether subjective power is unidimensional or multidimensional needs to be investigated to gain a more meaningful understanding of the role of subjective evaluation in personal power.

The consistency is striking between one's feelings of power and one's actual attempts to be powerful or effective. If one believes that he is controlled by forces beyond his control, he tends to act on this belief by assuming a passive orientation to his environment. On the other hand, if one believes that he is master of his fate, he tends to assume an active orientation to his environment. One's evaluation of how powerful or powerless he feels seems to be an important determinant of the action he will take. The congruency between subjective and manifest levels of power should not, however, be considered as a relationship that holds in all cases. One may develop subjective feelings of being omnipotent as a defense against being behaviorally ineffectual or one may compensate for feelings of powerlessness by striving towards behavioral effectiveness. Individual differences and situational conditions which might lead to compensatory relationships between subjective and manifest power need to be investigated.

The Development of Personal Power

How does the individual acquire the motives, feelings, and skills that enable him to be an effective agent in his social environment? The infant at birth is in a situation of complete powerlessness. With increasing experiences in environmental transactions the growing child is able to achieve greater levels of personal power. In addition to the increasing number of facilitating environmental experiences to which the child is exposed, experiences also exist which may retard or interfere with the development of personal power.

A number of recent research trends are beginning to provide some insights about the developmental antecedents of personal power. These trends are brought together in a comprehensive and integrative paper by Smith (1968). With reference to progress and retardation in the development of personal power, Smith states:

> Launched on the right trajectory, the person is likely to accumulate successes that strengthen the effectiveness of his orientation toward the world while at the same time he acquires the knowledge and skills that make his further success more probable. His environmental involvements generally lead to gratification and to increased competence and favorable development. Off to a bad start, on the other hand, he soon encounters failures that make him hesitant to try. What to others are challenges appear to him as threats; he becomes preoccupied with defense of his claims on life at the expense of energies to invest in constructive coping. And he falls increasingly behind his fellows in acquiring the knowledge and skills that are needed for success on those occasions when he does try (p. 277).

Smith is suggesting a benign circle of favorable power development in

Power and Personality

which success begets further success, and a vicious circle of retarded power development in which failure begets further failure. Two contrasting consequences seem to emerge: (1) with a history of personal efforts leading to successful outcomes, the individual tends to develop an active self-initiating orientation to his environment; (2) with a history of personal efforts leading to unsuccessful outcomes, the individual tends to develop a passive and avoidant orientation to his environment.

Figure 3.1 represents what might be called a wheel of power. Essentially, a benign circle of power development is one in which personally achieved success (A) leads to a feeling that one can be successful (B) which leads to intended efforts to achieve success (C) which leads to further success (A) and the reinforced repetition of the same benign circle. A vicious circle of power development would be schematized in the same way, except that failure would be substituted for success in phases A and B and phase C would most likely be represented by intended efforts to avoid striving for success, which in turn would lead back to phase A represented by a deficiency or lack of achieved success. If the individual does strive for success in phase C, his previous failure may significantly decrease the likelihood of his achieving success, which would then complete the vicious circle.

We now consider the kinds of developmental antecedents during

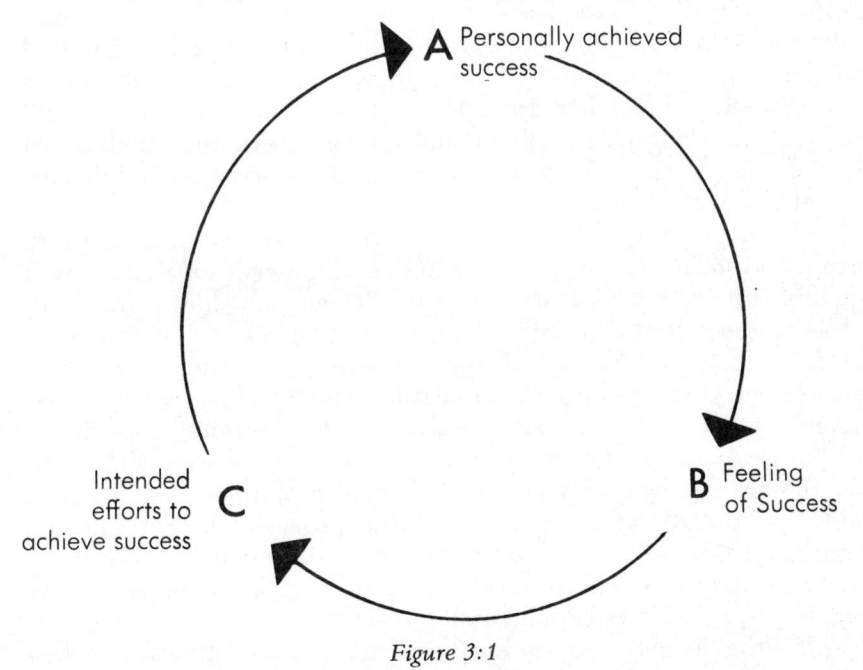

Figure 3:1

three age periods which might be critical in shaping the development of personal power.

The First Two Years

Piaget (1930, 1954) in his observational studies has provided an analysis of the acquisition of sense of personal causation by the age of two. Through cumulative sensory-motor experiences the child gradually learns to anticipate the outcomes that are produced by his own efforts. Thus reflex movements begin to be replaced by intentional movements. By the time the child is approximately two years of age, he has acquired the ability to conceive of himself as a causal agent who can produce intended environmental effects. Concomitant with acquiring a sense of personal causation the child acquires specific skills, such as directed grasping and active looking, which are utilized in attaining personal mastery. Thus, the child's cumulative experiences in interacting with his environment lead to increasing degrees of power at both the subjective and manifest levels.

Piaget does not explicitly deal with the motivational basis of power development. However, several theorists have pointed to Piaget's general developmental theory as being consistent with an underlying motivational striving to interact effectively with one's environment. For example, White (1959), as previously pointed out, refers to Piaget's observations of the child's accommodating to and assimilating environmental stimulation as supportive evidence for his concept of an effectance drive. Hunt (1965) and de Charms (1968) complement Piaget's developmental analysis with the inclusion of intrinsic motivation, the process of successfully assimilating information derived from environmental stimulation.

Following along the lines of Piaget's empirical investigations, Bruner (1968) has carried out a series of observational studies of infants up to two years of age. Bruner concludes from his observations that the infant learns to control his environment through the development of specific areas of competence, which include sucking, looking, manipulating, and speaking. Like Piaget, cumulative sensory-motor activities and eventual symbolic operations within the context of environmental interactions are seen as the basis for the development of increasing personal power. Bruner, however, adds a motivational component to the process of environmental mastery. In a similar vein with effectance and intrinsic motivation, Bruner refers to a "will to learn" about one's environment to achieve competence in that environment.

With the inclusion of motivation, the critical causative factors which might relate to a favorable or retarded rate of power development begin to appear. The reinforcement for an effectance drive or will-to-learn is provided by the feedback the infant receives in his attempts at personal control. A benign circle of favorable power development would seem to be based on the infant's acquisition of specific skills which enable him to receive successful feedback regarding personal control. More specifically, the infant learns to anticipate the outcomes produced by his own effort. Cumulative successes in the feedback of personal control serve as reinforcements for further attempts at effecting personal control. Gradually on the basis of past successes the infant will acquire realistic expectancies about his own personal control while engaged in environmental transactions. The more personal control the infant acquires, the higher his expectations. Not all attempts at effecting personal causation will be successful, and some infants may receive little positive reinforcement for their efforts.

Infant studies carried out by Burton White and his associates (described in B. White, 1967, 1969) provide some insight into environmental factors which may be associated with the development of personal power. Specific areas of competence, such as visual attention and prehension, were studied in relation to variations in the amount of environmental stimulation. The general results indicated that infants (studied from birth to four months of age) who were exposed to enriched environmental conditions exhibited a more rapid development of the various visual-motor skills than a group of control infants. Such results suggest that environmental enrichment during infancy can be facilitative to the development of increasing levels of personal control. Through the acquisition of specific areas of competence which are facilitated by an enriched environment the infant should develop a greater sense of personal control and be consistently motivated to strive towards carrying out self-initiated activities. On the other hand, conditions of relative deprivation of environmental stimulation apparently lead to a retarded development of skills necessary to effect personal control and the gradual decrement of attempt to carry out self-initiated activities. More longitudinal data is needed to clarify the long-range effects of stimulation during the first two years.

Another environmental factor which may be relevant to the development of personal power in infancy is the style of mothering. Kagan (1968) investigated attentional behaviors, such as fixation time and heart-rate changes, in first-born Caucasian infants from families with different social-class backgrounds. The infants were observed at 4, 8, 13, and 27 months of age. Social-class differences in attention began to clearly emerge by 13 months, with middle-class children manifesting more fixation time and less cardiac deceleration (a response to tension and novelty) than lower-class children. Kagan suggests that the social-class differences are a reflection of the middle-class mother spending more time stimulating and entertaining her baby. Some data relevant to this hypothesis is indicated in a recent study by one of Kagan's graduate students (reported by Pines, 1969). Middle-class mothers as compared to lower-class mothers spend more time entertaining their babies by way of face-to-face talking, smiling, and playing. Particularly critical to the development of a child's sense of personal power may be the availability of immediate face-to-face contact with the mother. The middle-class child may more often have the advantage of this contact. As Kagan states: "When a mother tends to a child in distress as soon as he cries, this leads the child to believe there is something he can do ... He learns he can have an effect upon the world—make things go or stop. If he is not tended he will learn helplessness" (quoted by Pines, 1969).

Research into the roots of personal power during infancy is still at a very preliminary stage. Some promising leads seem to be indicated by the investigations of environmental stimulation and mothering style. The mother's role in being able to provide a stimulating environment appears to be a central factor in determining whether the child will begin to move in a direction of successfully mastering his environment. However, other factors remain to be investigated, such as the role of the father, the presence or absence of other siblings, the continuity of stimulation and mothering style from infancy to later periods of development, and the interaction of genetic and prenatal factors with early developmental conditions.

Early Childhood

Until recently, the development of personal power during early childhood received little attention. Murphy and her associates (Murphy, 1962) conducted an exploratory study with a small group of preschool children ranging from two to five years of age who had been observed in infancy. Substantial correlations were found between infancy and preschool ratings of both mastery skills and strivings for mastery.

A comprehensive study into the development of competence among preschool children is currently being carried out by Burton White and his associates (White, LaCrosse, Litman, & Ogilvie, 1969). The general methodological approach has been observing children as they go about their natural activities. From an initial set of observations with six-year-old children, two groups of children were selected as representatives of high and low overall competence in terms of coping with their daily experiences. A list of abilities that appeared to distinguish these two groups of children was then developed. The distinguishing abilities represented two broad areas of competence: nonsocial abilities, such as linguistic skills, intellectual skills, and attentional ability; and social abilities, such as interpersonal skills in relating to adults and peers.

In subsequent observations, some three year olds were more advanced in the ability dimensions than six year olds. It was decided to focus on children between the ages of one and three, when signs of developmental divergence begin to clearly emerge. Continuing the ecological approach to data collection, researchers observed children's activities and mother-child interactions in the home. From these observations a maternal behavior scale was developed. Currently, only preliminary data with the scale is available. So far the identification of five prototype mothers has emerged. The "Super-Mother" is one who accepts her role, enjoys and approves of her child, and is able to achieve a good balance between activities she initiates and those initiated by the child. The other four maternal patterns that have been identified all tend to fall somewhat short of the Super-Mother criteria. These patterns include mothers who are overwhelmed by life's circumstances and therefore have little time to interact with their children, mothers who are rigid and controlling, mothers who "smother" their children with attention and mother-initiated activities at the expense of spontaneously relating to their children, and mothers who accept their children but are confused and often unable to meet their children's needs. Preliminary data indicate that it is the Super-Mother who is most effective in raising the child well developed in overall competence.

Further verification of the relationship between types of mothers and children's competence is currently in progress. The point of reporting the still preliminary results of the White project reflects the appearance of efficacious and comprehensive research toward understanding the development of levels of personal power during the preschool years. The nature of mother-child interactions seems to be a very critical variable underlying different rates of acquiring components of competence.

Data on the child-rearing practices of both mothers and fathers in relation to their child's level of competence are contained in studies of preschool children by Baumrind (1967) and Baumrind and Black (1967). Three and four year olds in a nursery-school setting were rated on social abilities, such as self-reliance, self-control, and degree of affiliation. Observations of parent-child interactions were obtained through home visits. The results indicated that parents of highly competent children tended to receive high ratings on child-rearing practices reflecting control, maturity demands, communication, and nurturance. In contrast, parents of less competent children tended to be either uncontrolling and relatively warm, or detached and relatively controlling.

The picture of the kind of parental behaviors most conducive to effecting high levels of competence in the preschool child that emerges from the White and Baumrind studies is a mixture of nurturance and control. As a tentative summary Smith (1968), commenting on Baumrind's findings, states:

> For engendering competence, it is clear, love is not enough, though it matters. Challenge, respect for the child, perhaps even some abrasiveness in relations with the child that provokes his assertiveness, good communication with an emphasis on reasons for directiveness—these would seem important too (p. 310).

Another source of significant research on parent-child interactions at the preschool level of competence is the series of studies conducted by Hess and Shipman (1965, 1967) using Negro mothers and children. The mothers were observed interacting with their four-year-old children as the children performed various tasks. The social-status of the subject pairs included upper-middle, upper-lower, and lower-lower groups. The researchers were interested in the relationship between maternal teaching styles and children's learning styles. Results indicated that middle-class mothers' teaching styles tend to make use of subjective appeals where the personal qualities and feelings of the child as well as instructive appeals related to the demands of the task are emphasized. In contrast the lower-class mother tends to rely more on an imperative and normative approach where unqualified commands are emphasized. Additional data indicated that the subjective and instructive teaching styles were positively related to the child's level of competence in verbal tasks, while the imperative-normative style was inversely related to performance on the verbal tasks.

The role of the social-class environment on a preschool child's developing competency seems to be most directly mediated by the teaching style of the mother. Complementing Hess and Shipman's results are the previously discussed findings by Kagan (1968) of middle-class mothers tending to spend more time attending to their infants. It is maternal style, however, rather than social status which is directly related to children's performance. Social-class differences merely lead to varying probabilities regarding the kind of mothering style that may be adopted.

Although there is no direct data, the Hess and Shipman studies also suggest a possible relationship between mothering style and the child's sense of his own power or competence. An imperative-normative teaching style on the part of the mother with its emphasis on external factors, such as status and authority, would seem to be a precursor to the development of a belief of powerlessness or external control on the part of the child. In contrast, a child's belief in internal control or a sense of personal power would seem to emerge from encounters with a mother who encourages her child to be sensitive to both his subjective feelings and objective task demands—in other words, an emphasis on internal standards and relative rather than absolute external standards. It would also seem that Burton White's "Super-Mother" would be the maternal prototype most facilitative of a developing sense of personal power during the preschool years.

The School Years

Consistent with the trend of studies regarding the relationship between parent-child interaction and competence is a study by Bee (1967) with school-age children and their parents. Two groups of nine-year-old boys and girls were selected on the basis of their ability to resist distraction—an ability which would seem to be a critical component of competence at the school-age level. Home observations were obtained of situations where the child carried out intellectual tasks under the guidance of his parents. The parents of nondistractible children, in constrast to the parents of distractible children, provided more positive encouragement, paid more attention to their child's contributions in decision-making interaction, gave less specific suggestions regarding ways of accomplishing the task, and made relatively more evaluative comments than suggestions. This pattern of providing encouragement, offering feedback, and emphasizing the child's own efforts seems generally in agreement with the parental styles noted as facilitative of preschool competence.

Complementary data is also available on the relationship between parental style and the school-age child's sense of power. Katkovsky, Crandall, and Good (1967) used a sample of children between the ages of six and twelve.[6] They compared the child's scores on the Intellectual Achievement Responsibility Questionnaire (a measure of

---

6. Relevant to the wide cross-section of age in this study is evidence reported by Crandall, Katkovsky, and Crandall (1965) of the relative stability of scores on the internal-external control dimension across samples ranging from the third through twelfth grades.

internal-external control in achievement situations) with home-visit ratings of mother-child interactions as well as interview and questionnaire data from the parents. The findings generally indicated that children's beliefs in internal control were associated with parents who were characterized as warm, praising, protective, and supportive—a pattern consistent with the parental styles positively associated with children's competence.[7]

A factor to consider in the family setting, in addition to parental style, is the role of siblings. In the studies of preschool competence (e.g. B. White et. al., 1969) the presence of other siblings is suggested as critical for second and later-born children, since unlike the first-born or only child, much of the interaction is with siblings rather than with parents. At the school-age level, Crandall, Katkovsky, and Crandall (1965) provide data on the relationship of ordinal position to sense of power. Findings indicated that in the upper grades (sixth through twelfth) first-born children had a greater sense of internal control than later-born children. Further in the upper grades children from smaller families (one or two children) had more internal control responses than children from larger families (three or more children). No differences were found for the relationship between ordinal position or family size and internal control for children below the sixth grade. These results suggest that during preadolescence and adolescence the child in a smaller family has a greater likelihood than the child in a larger family to receive encouraging support from his parents and be involved in family decision-making.

Beyond the characteristics of the family setting the school environment has an important impact on developing personal power. The most striking disparity in levels of competent performance occurs between white and minority group children (except for Orientals) on indices of academic achievement. For example, in the Coleman survey (Coleman et al., 1966) of American public schools across grade levels and geographic regions, average Negro scores on achievement tests were about one standard deviation below average white scores. In addition, as referred to in the section on subjective power, the Coleman survey indicated that minority group children as a group had a greater sense of powerlessness than white children. When minority group children did express a sense of their own personal power, their achievement was higher than that of whites who expressed a sense of powerlessness.

The correlational findings of Coleman indicate that there is an

---

7. This pattern is also consistent with internally controlled college students' retrospective reports of parenting (Davis & Phares, 1969; MacDonald, 1969).

inverse relationship between minority status and academic achievement. This relationship cannot be explained by correlational findings. Much controversy concerns the relative effects of the home and school environments in producing academic failure among minority group children. Hunt (1968) places considerable weight on the "cultural deprivation" of the home environment of lower-class children. He emphasizes the need for compensatory programs for parents and children before the child begins his formal schooling. Clark (1965), on the other hand, feels that the school environment is primarily responsible for the academic failure of minority children. Clark further points out that the term, "cultural deprivation" with its implications of the irreversible effects of the home environment, has served as a rationalization for educational neglect. However, little argument exists about the cumulative effects of deprivation in both the home and school situations. If discouragement, which starts at home, is continued by teachers and administrators, then a reduction in attempts at striving for competence, feelings of powerlessness, and incompetent levels of performance will be further reinforced. Indeed, compensatory programs are needed at both the school and preschool levels.

Some insight into the specific sources of incompetent performance among Negro school children is provided in a study by Katz (1967). In studying fifth-and sixth-graders in a predominantly Negro school in Detroit, Katz found that low-achieving boys were more self-critical of their performance than high-achieving boys. Most interesting is that the self-evaluations were not related to the actual quality of performance, which was equivalent for both groups of boys. The relationship between self-evaluation and level of achievement was not found for girls—a finding consistent with the generally reported sex differences in achievement-related behaviors. The findings for low-achieving boys indicate a generalized tendency to be self-discouraging regardless of the actual level of performance. Katz suggests that this self-discouragement to accept one's own performance as adequate results from a history of punitive reactions to the child's achievement efforts. To assess the effect of possible punitive reactions by parents, Katz obtained data from a questionnaire about children's perceptions of their parents. Low-achieving boys reported a pattern of parental disinterest and punitiveness, while high-achieving boys reported generally favorable parental experiences. These perceived differences in parental reactions are in accord with the previously discussed findings of actual parent-child interactions, where parental encouragement and support were associated with competent performance and feelings of internal control.

The consistent findings of a relationship between parental characteristics and children's feelings and manifestations of personal power would suggest a similar relationship when teacher characteristics are considered. Perhaps, a teacher who can provide support and encouragement in the school situation may counteract the debilitating effects of parents who do not engage in facilitative interactions with their children. Further, incompetent teachers may counteract the positive effects of competent parents. Although no data directly show the interactive effects of teachers and parents on children's feelings and manifestations of personal power, some findings indicate the significant impact a teacher can have on a child's attitude about his own competence. Sarason and his colleagues (Sarason et al., 1960) conducted classroom observations in white middle-class schools and reported considerable variation in the degree of support and encouragement that teachers provided. In some cases, the response to a child's lack of progress increased the child's feeling of inadequacy; in other cases, the response did not make him feel that the teacher was derogating him.

Variations among teachers are particularly marked across schools reflecting varying social-class enrollments. In a study based on interviews with teachers and principals, Herriott and St. John (1966) found that the higher the social-class standing of the school the more positive the attitude expressed by the teachers and principals about their jobs and about the motivation and behavior of their pupils. In addition, based on the reports of principals, the higher the social-class rating of the school, the greater the proportion of teachers who were rated as being competent.

Teacher characteristics appear to be an important contributing factor to children's attitudes and manifestations of academic competence. It would be unfair, however, to place the blame for inadequate school environments solely on teachers. Particularly in the case of schools with predominantly Negro enrollments, the prevailing conditions also reflect a lack of general administrative and financial support.

Reviewing studies relevant to the development of personal power uncovers the importance of encouragement, challenge, evaluative feedback, and support from socialization agents, such as parents and teachers. The challenge is to provide a school environment to foster facilitative teacher-student interactions, regardless of the social-status level of the student.

Personal Power Through the Life Span

The role of socialization agents as facilitators in the development of personal power during the formative years must be seen within the context of the societal structure. To become a self-determined agent functioning in society one must have access to positions of social power. Thus, the individual who has had the exposure of competent socializing agents, such as parents and teachers, may still not be able to manifest his personal power if societal obstacles prevent him from attaining positions of social power. Discouragement in an environment of social inequality can counteract the encouragement by socializing agents.

Beyond the formative years of childhood and adolescence, the power of the individual is continually being affected by his social environment. Indeed, throughout the life span the individual is continually engaged in attempts at overcoming resistance and implementing self-determination though the kinds of tasks and environmental demands change.

Erik Erikson's (1950) theory of psychosocial development provides a guideline for the social problem-solving situations the individual must master at successive stages and the kinds of personal characteristics needed to bring about successful resolutions. For Erikson, competent problem-solving would be expressed first through the development of trust, then autonomy, and then initiative and responsibility at the earliest stages of childhood. Industry follows during the early school years and preadolescence, identity during adolescence, intimacy during young adulthood, generativity during middle adulthood, and ego integrity during old age.

The individual's expression of personal power may not always conform to societal expectations. The "generation gap" between adolescents/young adults and middle-aged adults is based on conflicting expectations about personal responsibility and power assumed by each group. Greater accelerations in education and social and technological change have resulted in greater sophistication at younger ages. Consequently, youths want more personal involvement in shaping their destinies. Obstacles to expressing personal power based on age status can discourage strivings for self-determination and lead to unnecessary power struggles between age groups. The transition to competent adulthood requires opportunities for engaging in gradually increasing levels of personal responsibility from early childhood through adolescence and young adulthood.

Our society, often characterized as youth-centered even though it may not really allow much self-determination for the young, has also tended to neglect the needs of its senior citizens. Many researchers in the area of social gerontology, such as Cumming (1964), have pointed to the inverse relationship between manifestations of personal competence and aging during the later years. As some people age, the loss of competence and the growing sense of powerlessness can be traumatic experiences. The transition from middle-adulthood to old age should be accompanied by opportunities for the utilization of available competencies. The challenge for society is providing opportunities in self-determination for both young and old.

Increasing Personal Power Through Social Engineering

Up to this point the development of personal power has been considered within a long-range longitudinal context. However, one's personal effectiveness can also be responsive to immediate environmental conditions. If the social environment has produced obstacles to the development of personal effectiveness, then the removal of these obstacles should provide greater opportunities for individuals to overcome their feelings and manifestations of powerlessness. The need, then, is for societal institutions to become more responsive to the requirements of minority group members and other alienated segments of our society by providing educational and training opportunities, and economic political power.

The term "social engineering" refers to planned programs of environmental intervention. Goals include development of training programs or achievement of greater political participation for a target population which has been confronted with externally imposed restrictions. Some interesting evidence shows that intervention programs can have an effect on feelings of personal power. Hunt and Hardt (1969) found that among high school students enrolled in an O.E.O. Upward Bound summer program for disadvantaged youths there was a general change toward an attitude of greater internal control. Studies by Gottesfeld and Dozier (1966) and Levens (1968), although limited to cross-sectional data, report findings that members active in poverty-related community action programs are more likely to have greater feelings of mastery and control than matched groups of either nonmembers or new trainees who had not previously participated in the program. These findings suggest that if one is actively engaged in trying to shape his social environment, he will begin to develop a greater sense of his own power of effectiveness. It is, however, important that such efforts lead to some positive feedback of change in expected directions. False hopes after one has already committed himself will produce frustration and a greater sense of powerlessness.

The purpose of this chapter has been to conceptualize a model of the person as an active social agent in his environment. Such a model, then, is relevant not only to an analysis of personal power, but also to dyadic social-power interactions, social-power interactions in groups and organizations, and the role of the individual in the social system. Consideration of personal power can only be a part of an analysis of power processes.

References

Allport, G. *Becoming: basic considerations for a psychology of personality.* New Haven, Conn.: Yale University Press, 1955.
Ansbacher, H. L., & Ansbacher, R. R. (Eds.), *The individual psychology of Alfred Adler.* New York: Basic Books, 1956.
Atkinson, J. W. Motivational determinants of risk-taking behavior. *Psychological Review*, 1957, 64, 359-372.
Atkinson, J. W. *An introduction to motivation.* Princeton, N.J.: Van Nostrand, 1964.
Atkinson, J. W., & Feather, N. T. *A theory of achievement motivation.* New York: Wiley, 1966.
Atkinson, J. W., & Litwin, G. H. Achievement motive and test anxiety conceived as motive to approach success and avoid failure. *Journal of Abnormal and Social Psychology*, 1960, 60, 52-63.
Bachrach, P., & Baratz, M. S. Decisions and nondecisions: an analytical framework. *American Political Science Review*, 1963, 57, 632-642.
Battle, E. S. Motivational determinants of academic competence. *Journal of Personality and Social Psychology*, 1966, 4, 634-642.
Battle, E. S., & Rotter, J. B. Children's feelings of personal control as related to social class and ethnic group. *Journal of Personality*, 1963, 31, 482-490.
Baumrind, D. Child care practices anteceding three patterns of preschool behavior. *Genetic Psychological Monographs*, 1967, 75, 43-88.
Baumrind, D., & Black, A. E. Socialization practices associated with dimensions of competence in preschool boys and girls. *Child Development* 1967, 38, 291-327.
Bee, H. L. Parent-child interaction and distractibility in 9-year-old children. *Merrill-Palmer Quarterly*, 1967, 13, 175-190.
Berlyne, D. E. Motivational problems raised by exploratory and epistemic behavior. In S. Koch (Ed.), *Psychology: A study of a science.* Vol. 5. New York: McGraw-Hill, 1963. Pp. 284-364.
Bettelheim, B. *The informed heart.* Glencoe, Ill.: Free Press, 1960.
Bialer, I. Conceptualization of success and failure in mentally retarded and normal children. *Journal of Personality*, 1961, 29, 303-320.
Bierstedt, R. An analysis of social power. *American Sociological Review*, 1950, 15, 730-738.
Bortner, R. W. Personality differences in preference for skill or chance determined outcomes. *Perceptual and Motor Skills*, 1964, 18, 765-772,
Bruner, J. S. *Toward a theory of instruction* Cambridge, Mass.: Harvard University Press, 1966.
Bruner, J. S. *Processes of cognitive growth.* Barre, Mass.: Barre Publishing Co., 1968.
Butterfield, E. C. Locus of control, test anxiety, reactions to frustration, and achievement attitudes. *Journal of Personality*, 1964, 32, 298-311,
Campbell, D. T., & Fiske, D. W. Convergent and discriminant validation by the multitrait-multimethod matrix. *Psychological Bulletin*, 1959, 56, 81-105.

Cartwright, D. A field theoretical conception of power. In D. Cartwright (Ed.), *Studies in social power*. Ann Arbor, Mich.: Institute for Social Research, 1959. Pp. 183-220.

Cartwright, D., & Zander, A. Power and influence in groups: Introduction. In D. Cartwright and A. Zander (Eds.), *Group dynamics*, 3rd ed. New York: Harper & Row, 1968. Pp. 215-235.

Chein, I. On the concept of power. Paper presented at the meeting of the American Psychological Association, Washington, D. C., 1969.

Clark, K. B. *Dark ghetto: dilemmas of social power*. New York: Harper & Row, 1965.

Cohen, J. *Chance, skill and luck*. Baltimore: Penguin Books, 1960.

Coleman, J. S., Campbell, E. Q., Hobson, Carol J., McPartland, J., Mood. A. M., Weinfeld, F. D., & York, R. L. *Equality of educational opportunity*. Washington, D. C.: Office of Education, 1966.

Crandall, V. C., Katkovsky, W., & Crandall, V. J. Children's beliefs in their own control of reinforcement in intellectual-academic achievement situations. *Child Development*, 1965, 36, 91-109.

Crandall, V. J., Katovsky, W., & Preston, A. Motivational and ability determinants of young children's intellectual achievement behaviors. *Child Development*, 1962, 33, 643-661.

Crandall, V. C., & McGhee, P. E. Expectancy of reinforcement and academic competence. *Journal of Personality*, 1968, 36, 635-648.

Cromwell, R., Rosenthal, D., Shakow, D., & Zahn, L. Reaction time, locus of control, choice behavior, and descriptions of parental behavior in schizophrenic and normal subjects. *Journal of Personality*, 1961, 29, 363-379.

Cumming, M. E. New thoughts on the theory of disengagement. In R. Kastenbaum (Ed.), *New thoughts on old age*. New York: Springer, 1964. Pp. 3-18.

Dahl, R. A. The concept of power. *Behavioral Science*, 1957, 2, 201-218.

D'Antonio, W. V., & Ehrlich, H. J. (Eds.). *Power and democracy in America*. Notre Dame, Ind.: University of Notre Dame Press, 1961.

Davis, W. L., & Phares, E. J. Internal-external control as a determinant of information-seeking in a social influence situation. *Journal of Personality*, 1967, 35, 547-561.

Davis, W. L., & Phares, E. J. Parental antecedents of internal-external control of reinforcement. *Psychological Reports*, 1969, 24, 427-436.

Dean, D. G. Alienation: Its meaning and measurement. *American Sociological Review*, 1961, 26, 753-758.

de Charms, R. *Personal causation: the internal affective determinants of behavior*. New York: Academic Press, 1968.

de Charms, R., & Davé, P. N. Hope of success, fear of failure, subjective probability and risk-taking behavior. *Journal of Personality and Social Psychology*, 1965, 1, 558-568.

Edwards, W. The theory of decision making. *Psychological Bulletin*, 1954, 51, 380-417.

Erikson, E. H. *Childhood and society*. New York: Norton, 1950.

Escoffery, A. S. Personality and behavior correlates of Negro American belief in fate-control. Paper presented at the meeting of the Eastern Psychological Association, Washington, D. C., 1968.

Feather, N. T. The relationship of persistence at a task to expectation of success and achievement related motives. *Journal of Abnormal and Social Psychology*, 1961, 63, 552-561.

Feather, N. T. The relationship of expectation of success to need achievement

and test anxiety. *Journal of Personality and Social Psychology*, 1965, 1, 118-125.
Feather, N. T. Some personality correlates of external control. *Australian Journal of Psychology*, 1967, 19, 253-260. (a)
Feather, N. T. Valence of outcome and expectation of success in relation to task difficulty and perceived locus of control. *Journal of Personality and Social Psychology*, 1967, 7, 372-386. (b)
Feather, N. T. Change in confidence following success or failure as a predictor of subsequent performance. *Journal of Personality and Social Psychology*, 1968, 9, 38-46.
Fiske, D. W., & Maddi, S. R. (Eds.). *Functions of varied experience*. Homewood, Ill.: Dorsey Press, 1961.
Flacks, R. Protest or conform: Some social psychological perspectives on legitimacy. *Journal of Applied Behavioral Science*, 1969, 5, 127-15 0.
French, J. R., Jr., & Raven, B. H. The bases of social power. In D. Cartwright (Ed.), *Studies in social power*, Ann Arbor, Mich.: Institute for Social Research, 1959. Pp. 150-167.
Gerth, H. H., & Mills, C. W. (Eds.). *From Max Weber: Essays in sociology*. New York: Oxford University Press, 1946.
Goldfried, M. R., & D'Zurilla, T. J. A behavioral-analytic model for assessing competence. In C. Spielberger (Ed.), *Current topics in clinical and community psychology*. Vol. l. New York: Academic Press, 1969. Pp. 151-196.
Goldstein, K. *Human nature in the light of psychopathology*. Cambridge, Mass.: Harvard University Press, 1940.
Gore, P. M., & Rotter, J. B. A personality correlate of social action. *Journal of Personality*, 1963, 31, 58-64.
Gottesfeld, H., & Dozier, G. Changes in feelings of powerlessness in a community action program. *Psychological Reports*, 1966, 19, 978.
Grinker, R. R., & Speigel, J. P. *Men under stress*. Philadelphia: Blakiston, 1945.
Gurin, P., Gurin, G., Lao, R. C., & Beattie, M. Internal-external control in the motivational dynamics of Negro youuth. *Journal of Social Issues*, 1969, 25(3), 29-53.
Hamsher, J. H., Geller, J. D., & Rotter, J. B. Interpersonal trust, internal-external control, and the Warren Commission Report. *Journal of Personality and Social Psychology*, 1968, 9, 210-215.
Harvey, O. J., & Clapp, W. F. Hope, expectancy, and reactions to the unexpected. *Journal of Personality and Social Psychology*, 1965, 2, 45-52.
Heath, D. H. *Growing up in college*. San Francisco: Jossey-Bass, 1968.
Hebb, D. O. Drives and the C.N.S. (Conceptual Nervous System). *Psychological Review*, 1955, 62, 243-254.
Heider, F. *The psychology of interpersonal relations*. New York: Wiley, 1958.
Hendrick, I. Instinct and the ego during infancy. *Psychoanalytic Quarterly*, 1942, 11, 33-58 .
Herriott, R. E., & St. John, N. H. *Social class and the urban school*. New York: Wiley, 1966.
Hersch, P. D., & Scheibe, K. E. On the reliability and validity of internal-external control as a personality dimension. *Journal of Consulting Psychology*, 1967, 31, 609-614.
Hess, R. D., & Shipman, V. C. Early experience and the socialization of cognitive modes in children. *Child Development*, 1965, 36, 869-886.
Hess, R. D., & Shipman, V. C. Cognitive elements in maternal behavior. In J. P. Hill (Ed.), *Minnesota symposia on child psychology*. Vol. 1. Minneapolis: University of Minnesota Press, 1967. Pp. 57-81.

Hunt, D. E., & Hardt, R. H. The effect of Upward Bound programs on the attitudes, motivation, and academic achievement of Negro students. *Journal of Social Issues*, 1969, 25(3), 117-129.

Hunt, J. McV. Intrinsic motivation and its role in psychological development. In D. Levine (Ed.), *Nebraska symposium on motivation 1965*. Lincoln: University of Nebraska Press, 1965. Pp 189-282.

Hunt, J. McV. Toward the prevention of incompetence. In J. W. Carter, Jr. (Ed.), *Research contributions from psychology to community mental health*. New York: Behavioral Publications, 1968. Pp. 19-45.

James, W. H., & Rotter, J. B. Partial and 100% reinforcement under chance and skill conditions. *Journal of Experimental Psychology*, 1958, 55, 397-403.

James, W. H., Woodruff, A. B., & Warren, W. Effects of internal and external control upon changes in smoking behavior. *Journal of Consulting Psychology*, 1965, 184-186.

Jessor, R., Graves, T. D., Hanson, R. C., & Jessor, S. L. *Society, personality and deviant behavior*. New York: Holt, Rinehart & Winston, 1968.

Kagan, J. The many faces of response. *Psychology Today*, 1968, 1 (8), 22-27, 60.

Katkovsky, W., Crandall, V. C., & Good, S. Parental antecedents of children's beliefs in internal-external control of reinforcements in intellectual achievement situations. *Child Development*, 1967, 38, 765-776.

Katz, I. The socialization of academic motivation in minority group children. In D. Levine (Ed.), *Nebraska symposium on motivation, 1967*. Lincoln: University of Nebraska Press, 1967. Pp. 133-191.

Lanyon, R. I. Measurement of social competence in college males. *Journal of Consulting and Clinical Psychology*, 1967, 31, 495-498.

Lao, R. C. Internal-external control and competent and innovative behavior among Negro college students. *Journal of Personality and Social Psychology*, 1970, 14, 263-270.

Lasswell, H. D., & Kaplan, A. *Power and society*. New Haven, Conn.: Yale University Press, 1950.

Lefcourt, H. M. Some empirical correlates of Negro identity. Unpublished doctoral dissertation, Ohio State University, 1963.

Lefcourt, H. M. Internal versus external control: A review. *Psychological Bulletin*, 1966, 65, 206-220.

Lefcourt, H. M., & Ladwig, G. W. The American Negro: a problem in expectancies. *Journal of Personality and Social Psychology*, 1965, 1, 377-380.

Levens, H. Organizational affiliation and powerlessness: a case study of the welfare poor. *Social Problems*, 1968, 16, 18-32.

Lewin, K., Dembo, T., Festinger, L., & Sears, P. S. Level of aspiration. In J. McV. Hunt (Ed.), *Personality and the behavior disorders*. Vol. 1. New York: Ronald Press, 1944. Pp. 333-378.

Liberty, D. G., Jr., Burnstein, R., & Moulton, R. W. Concern with mastery and occupational attraction. *Journal of Personality*, 1966, 34, 105-117.

Lippitt, R., Polansky, N., Redl, F., & Rosen, S. The dynamics of power. *Human Relations*, 1952, 5, 37-64.

Littig, L. W. Effects of motivation on probability preferences. *Journal of Personality*, 1963, 31, 417-427.

Liverant, S., & Scodel, A. Internal and external control as determinants of decision-making under conditions of risk. *Psychological Reports*, 1960, 7, 59-67.

MacDonald, A. P., Jr. Internal-external locus of control: parental antecedents. Unpublished paper, West Virginia University, 1969.

McGhee, P. E., & Crandall, V. C. Beliefs in internal-external control of reinforcements and academic performance. *Child Development*, 1968, 39, 91-102.

Maddi, S. R. *Personality theories: A comparative analysis.* Homewood, Ill.: Dorsey, 1968.

March, J. G. An introduction to the theory and measurement of influence. *American Political Science Review*, 1955, 49, 431-451.

Miller, A. G., & Minton, H. L. Machiavellianism, internal-external control, and the violation of experimental instructions. *Psychological Record* 1969, 19, 369-380.

Minton, H. L. Power as a personality construct. In B. A. Maher (Ed.), *Progress in experimental personality research.* Vol. 4. New York: Academic Press, 1967. P. 229-267.

Minton, H. L. Contemporary concepts of power and Adler's views. *Journal of Individual Psychology*, 1968, 24, 46-55.

Mirels, H. L. Dimensions of internal versus external control. *Journal of Consulting and Clinical Psychology*, 1970, 34, 226-228.

Mowrer, O. H. *Learning theory and behavior.* New York: Wiley, 1960.

Mowrer, O. H., & Viek, P. An experimental analogue of fear from a sense of helplessness. *Journal of Abnormal and Social Psychology*, 1948, 43, 193-200.

Murphy, L. et al. *The widening world of childhood: paths toward mastery.* New York: Basic Books, 1962.

Phares, E. J. Internal-external control as a determinant of amount of social influence exerted. *Journal of Personality and Social Psychology*, 1965, 2, 642-647.

Phares, E. J. Differential utilization of information as a function of internal-external control. *Journal of Personality*, 1968, 36, 649-662.

Phares, E. J., Ritchie, D. E., & Davis, W. L. Internal-external control and reaction to threat. *Journal of Personality and Social Psychology*, 1968, 10, 402-405.

Phillips, L. *Human adaptation and its failures.* New York: Academic Press, 1968.

Piaget, J. *The child's conception of physical causality.* New York: Harcourt-Brace, 1930.

Piaget, J. *The construction of reality in the child.* New York: Basic Books, 1954.

Pines, M. Why some 3-year olds get A's and some get C's. *The New York Times Magazine*, July 6, 1969. Pp. 4, 5, 10, 12-17.

Ray, W. J., & Katahn, M. Relation of anxiety to locus of control. *Psychological Reports*, 1968, 23, 1196.

Richter, C. P. On the phenomenon of sudden death in animals and man. *Psychosomatic Medicine*, 1957, 19, 191-198.

Riker, W. H. Some ambiguities in the notion of power. *American Political Science Review*, 1964, 58, 341-349.

Rose, A. M. *The power structure: political process in America.* New York: Oxford University Press, 1967.

Rossi, P. H. Community decision making. *Administrative Science Quarterly*, 1957, 1, 415-443.

Rotter, J. B. *Social learning and clinical psychology.* Englewood Cliffs, N. J.: Prentice-Hall, 1954.

Rotter J. B. Generalized expectancies for internal versus external control of reinforcement. *Psychological Monographs*, 1966, 80, (1, Whole No. 609).

Rotter, J. B. Beliefs, social attitudes and behavior: a social learning analysis. In R. Jessor & S. Feshbach (Eds.), *Cognition, personality and clinical psychology.* San Francisco: Jossey-Bass, 1967. Pp. 112-140.

Rotter, J. B., & Mulry, R. C. Internal versus external control of reinforcement and decision time. *Journal of Personality and Social Psychology*, 1965, 2, 593-597.

Russell, B. *Power: A new social analysis*. London: Allen and Unwin, 1938.

Sarason, S. B., Davidson, K. S., Lighthall, F. F., Waite, R. R., & Ruebush, B. K. *Anxiety in elementary school children*. New York: Wiley, 1960.

Schneider, J. M. Skill versus chance activity preference and locus of control. *Journal of Consulting and Clinical Psychology*, 1968, 32, 333-337.

Seeman, M. On the meaning of alienation. *American Sociological Review*, 1959, 24, 783-791.

Seeman, M. Alienation and social learning in a reformatory. *American Journal of Sociology*, 1963, 69, 270-284.

Seeman, M., & Evans, J. W. Alienation and learning in a hospital setting. *American Sociological Review*, 1962, 27, 772-782.

Simon, H. Notes on the observation and measurement of political power. *Journal of Politics*, 1953, 15, 500-516.

Smith, M. B. Explorations in competence: A study of peace corps teachers in Ghana. *American Psychologist*, 1966, 21, 555-566.

Smith, M. B. Competence and socialization. In J. A. Clausen (Ed.), *Socialization and society*. New York: Little, Brown, 1968. Pp. 270-320.

Stotland, E. *The psychology of hope*. San Francisco: Jossey-Bass, 1969.

Straits, B. C., & Secrest, L. Further support of some findings about characteristics of smokers and non-smokers. *Journal of Consulting Psychology*, 1963, 27, 282.

Strickland, B. R. The prediction of social action from a dimension of internal-external control. *Journal of Social Psychology*, 1965, 66, 353-358.

Strickland, L. H., Lewicke, R. J. & Katz, A. M. Temporal orientation and perceived control as determinants of risk taking. *Journal of Experimental Social Psychology*, 1966, 2, 143-151.

Strodtbeck, F. L. Family interaction, values, and achievement. In D. McClelland (Ed.), *Talent and society*. Princeton. N. J.: Van Nostrand, 1958. Pp. 138-195.

Thomas, L. E. The I-E scale, ideological bias, and political participation. *Journal of Personality* 1970, 38, 273-286.

Todd, F. J., Terrill, G., & Frank, C. E. Differences between normal and under-achievers of superior ability. *Journal of Applied Psychology*, 1962, 46, 183-190.

Tolman, E. C. Principles of performance. *Psychological Review*, 1955. 62, 315-326.

Uhlinger, C. A., & Stephens, M. W. Relation of achievement motivation to academic achievement in students of superior ability. *Journal of Educational Psychology*, 1960, 51, 259-266.

Veroff, J. Development and validation of a projective measure of power motivation. *Journal of Abnormal and Social Psychology*, 1957, 54, 1-9.

Veroff, J., & Veroff, J. B. Power motivation reconsidered. Unpublished paper, University of Michigan, 1969.

Watson, D. The relationship between locus of control and anxiety. *Journal of Personality and Social Psychology*, 1967, 6, 91-92.

Watson, D., & Baumal, E. Effects of locus of control and expectation of failure control upon present performance. *Journal of Personality and Social Psychology*, 1967, 6, 212-215.

White, B. L. An experimental approach to the effect of experience on early human behavior. In J. P. Hill (Ed.), *Minnesota symposia on child psychology*. Vol. 1. Minneapolis: University of Minnesota Press, 1967. Pp. 201-225.

White, B. L. Child development research: an edifice without a foundation. *Merrill-Palmer Quarterly*, 1969, 15, 49-79.
White, B. L., La Crosse, E. R., Litman, F., & Ogilvie, D. M. Pre-School Project, Laboratory of Human Development, Harvard Graduate School of Education. Syposium presented at the meeting of the Society for Research in Child Development, Santa Monica, Cal., March, 1969.
White, R. W. Motivation reconsidered: the concept of competence. *Psychological Review*, 1959, 66, 297-333.
Wolfe, R. N. Situational determinants of anomie and powerlessness. Paper presented at the meeting of the Eastern Psychological Association, New York, 1966.

IV

Siegfried Streufert and Howard L. Fromkin

Cognitive Complexity and Social Influence

The further one moves from the realm of the physical toward the social sciences, the more one finds the scientist concerned with the "quality" of his research methodology. The reason for this concern is a good one. Researchers in several subspecialties of physics, for example, manipulate one variable at a time with relative ease. They can be reasonably sure that all other variables are randomized, held constant, or capable of being viewed as orthogonal or otherwise irrelevant. We know much less about the covariates of human behavior, and consequently we find ourselves in danger of neglecting to identify or manipulate casual relationships in social science research designs. Our defense against these uncontrolled complexities of social science has produced a movement toward "infinite regress"; we attempt to analyze smaller and smaller components of behavior, and as soon as we are successful in isolating still smaller segments, we apply our molecular research approaches to them. This approach is certainly "safe," and it leads to a wealth of data. For instance, in social influence research we are able to look at specific message components, and we might even reduce the message to mathematical statements about the interactions among values of adjective combinations. Similarly, we may look at the source or at the receiver of the message specifically in terms of one single characteristic, for instance, their respective "referent powers," without viewing any other characteristic. There is little question that this approach to social influence has value. However, a number of questions may be raised by those who find pure science a matter of little interest. Two questions seem particularly relevant: (1) can we find real-world parallels for the social influence experiment which was designed for laboratory research, and (2) if such parallels exist, would the effect of some message from a source on a receiver be the same in the laboratory and in the real world?

The first question might be asked for all laboratory research. It is up to the experimenter, if he has the interest and the ingenuity, to make the research relevant to real-world settings and yet maintain the tightness of quality experimental design. But even when the parallel (or the relevance) of lab setting and real world does exist, we will find the second question much harder to answer. Even, "relevant" lab research usually employs a relatively simple message. Laboratory environments in which the interaction among source and target is measured tend to be simple themselves because visually and intellectually austere environments avoid many experimental confounds. Further, to avoid noise or error produced by confounding variables, experimenters generally limit the contact between source and target. Social influence in the real world generally has a quite different flavor: messages are complex confounds of various communications, contacts between source and target are often extensive and repetitive, and messages frequently are sent in both directions, so that the positions of source and target are interchangeable to some degree. In other words, settings for laboratory research on social influence and real-world settings can be quite different. Can one expect that the laboratory's limited source characteristic, the limited quantity and dimensionality of its message characteristics, and the constraints it places on the target or recipient of the message, interact to produce the same outcomes as their equivalent units in the real world? Is a simple stimulus similiar to a complex stimulus? If complex stimuli are qualitatively different from simple stimuli, is it possible to assemble—theoretically as well as for the purpose of data interpretation—many simple stimuli through some summing or averaging process into a more complex stimulus compound? In other words, can one simply reverse the process of infinite regress by adding the parts of a molecular analysis back together (e. g., by testing for interactions among the components of social influence)? The processes of analysis toward molecular views and synthesis toward a more molar approach may or may not be inversions of each other. For instance, one might argue that some components of social influence originate at the level of the confound, producing new influence characteristics that cannot be predicted from the sum or average of their parts. Social influence processes may be based on more than one dimension (cf. Marlowe & Gergen, 1969), and, moreover, on dimensions that may be neither linear nor orthogonal. If this is so, then analyzing social influence from the vantage point of small factors influencing some component of the source-message-target chain may be insufficient. Even though a molecular approach may be very useful, it may need comparisons with, and possibly validation by, a molar, multidimensional approach. This chapter is concerned with a multidimensional view of social influence. The interaction between source, message, and target is viewed from the vantage point of complexity theory.

Writers who have been concerned with complexity theory have repeatedly emphasized that they are interested in the *structure* of stimulus arrays or in the structure of human cognition (human information processing). They are *not* interested in stimulus or cognitive *content*. In other words, they are talking about the dimensionality of stimulus material, or about the dimensions of cognitions which a person utilizes when he is engaged in perception or in task performance. Those complexity theorists who have been concerned with the interaction of stimulus and person, for instance, discuss the way a person utilizes stimulus dimensionality through discrimination on stimulus dimensions (viewing shades of gray), through differentiation among dimensions (looking at the same thing from various points of view), and through integration of differentiated dimensions (combining the various points of view into the currently most appropriate—often strategic—action with reference to an intent).

Approaching social influence from a complexity viewpoint makes it impossible to view segments of the influence process in isolation. Rather, the interaction of source, message, and target is seen as a total process where the characteristic of each component is likely to affect the others. Since it is the target that is potentially influenced, the focus would necessarily be on the source characteristics, the message characteristics, or the target characteristics as they produce potential changes in the target. Before social influence predictions based on complexity views can be advanced in this chapter, a more explicit statement about complexity theory is necessary.

Theoretical Approaches to Complexity

Psychological theory and research has viewed the concept of "complexity" in a number of ways. To some, the term refers to the modality, irrelevance, order, or frequency of stimuli received by a subject who may be engaged in a signal detection, concept formation, decision-making, or choice preference task (e.g., Berlyne, 1964; Dunham, Guilford & Hoepfner, 1968; Eisenmann & Platt, 1968; Heckhausen, 1964; Houston & Garskof, 1965; Streufert, Driver & Haun, 1967; Terwilliger, 1963). Complexity, in other words, is some characteristic, or set of characteristics, in the environment: a form of stimulus configuration. Others have viewed complexity as a cognitive (personality) characteristic of a subject who is engaged in responding to his environment (e.g., Bieri, Atkins, Briar, Leaman, Miller, & Tripodi, 1966; Crockett, 1965; Harvey, Hunt, & Schroder, 1961; Streufert, 1966; Witkin, Dyk, Goodenough, Faterson, & Karp, 1962). In this case complexity is not a stimulus function, but becomes evident and measurable in a subject's response to certain standardized kinds of stimulation.

Environmental, personality, and behavioral views of complexity have varied widely in their theoretical conceptualization and in their research methodologies. Identity or complementarity of theoretical constructs and measures have often been assumed (e.g., Witkin et al., 1962) but have been difficult to establish in experimental or correlational studies (cf. Streufert, in press; Vannoy, 1965; Wiggins, 1968; Zajonc, 1968). Further, since the various theoretical and experimental approaches have focused on specific differing components of the S-O-R chain, complementarity cannot necessarily be assumed. In the following section of this chapter some of the approaches to complexity that have relevance to social influence are reviewed.

Response Complexity: Individual Differences in Personality Structure

Although theorists concerned with personality structure argue that complexity is a characteristic of the conceptual dimensionality which a subject uses to *process* information, measurement of information processing occurs by necessity at the response end of the S-O-R chain. Individual differences in complexity have been described as a function of the degree of discrimination, differentiation, and integration of cognitive concepts or dimensions in perception and performance. Persons who demonstrate on tests or on behavioral indices that their perceptual concepts, or the concepts they use in performance (e.g., decision making), are highly differentiated or integrated (multidimensional) have been described as complex. Persons who operate on the basis of fewer concepts (more unidimensional) have been described as simple.

A number of reviewers (e.g., Wiggins, 1968; Zajonc, 1968) have pointed out that the personality approaches to complexity are yet highly dissimilar. This conclusion is based on the divergent research methods employed by complexity theorists, on the lack of theoretical relationships between some of their concepts, and on the lack of comparability of their personality measures (cf. Vannoy, 1965). This criticism applies in good part to the two most prevalent theories of structural complexity. One of these approaches is concerned with psychological differentiation (e.g., Bieri et al., 1966; Crockett, 1965; Harrison, 1966; Irwin, Tripodi, & Bieri, 1967; Leventhal & Singer, 1964; Miller & Bieri, 1965; Rigney, Bieri, & Tripodi, 1964; Signell, 1966; Tripodi & Bieri, 1966; Witkin et al., 1962). The other approach emphasizes integration (e.g., Crano & Schroder, 1967; Harvey et al., 1961; Karlins & Lamm, 1967; Streufert, 1966; Suedfeld & Hagen, 1966; Tuckman, 1966). Both views are concerned with (and measure complexity on the basis of) the dimensionality into which subjects sort stimulus information. Yet the conceptualizations are, at least in part, dissimilar. According to Witkin et al. (1962), complexity, or differentiation, refers to the specialization of perceptual functions, in other words, the degree to which information processing occurs through a heterogeneous conceptual state. In contrast, Harvey et al. (1961) refer to complexity, or integration, as a synthesis of specialized functions similar to the Hegelian synthesis of thesis and antithesis. On first view, it appears that the two approaches are not far apart: differentiation is conceived as a precondition for integration. However, is integration necessarily (always) associated with differentiation? Witkin et al. (1962) state that development toward greater differentiation must be accompanied by successively more complex reintegration of the (perceptual or decision-making) system. Theorists who are more concerned with integration (e.g., Harvey et al., 1961) view differentiation as a necessary but quite insufficient precondition for integration.

No matter which view of the relationship between differentiation and integration is correct, one should expect some covariance between them, in other words, some positive correlation between personality measures for the two concepts. However, tests of integration—the Sentence Completion Test (SCT) of Schroder and Streufert (1963), for example, or the Impression Formation Test of Streufert and Driver (1967)—have shown little relationship to various versions of the best known measure of differentiation—Kelly's Role Concept Repertoire (REP) test as used by Bieri. For instance, Vannoy (1965) reports a correlation of +.05 between the SCT and the REP test. Research of the present authors has shown that these correlations are consistently low. The probable reason for this apparent inconsistency is a characteristic of complexity tests: integrators produce fewer integrated dimensions (concepts) on the REP test, and differentiators score moderately low on the SCT, since that test is primarily geared to measure degrees of integration.

Stimulus Complexity: Effects of the Environment

Considerable research has been concerned with the effects of environmental (stimulus) complexity on signal detection, concept formation, preferences, attitudes, decision making, and so forth. These research approaches have been widely divergent.

Schroder, Driver, and Streufert (1967) have studied the effects of environmental complexity on differentiation and integration in complex performance. These authors have suggested that increasing environmental complexity (increasing frequency of varied stimuli) should produce initially increasing, and then decreasing, complex performance characteristics (e.g., differentiation and integration in perception, attitude formation, communication, etc.): in other words, they should produce an inverted U-shaped curve. Much of the research on stimulus complexity, however, is not related to performance measures that show any relationship to differentiation and integration. In other words, Schroder et al.'s inverted U-curve hypothesis need not apply. Rather, researchers concerned with areas of signal detection or concept formation have often measured "accurate" responding. Nevertheless, the inverted U-shaped curve showing optimal performance at some midlevel of stimulus complexity appears to hold for at least some of that research also. Data collected in settings that represent generally simple tasks or environments tend to show improvement in performance with increasing stimulus or task complexity (e.g., Weiner & Feldman, 1967, in a signal-detection task; Bourne & Parker, 1964, and Dörner, Everding, & Kötter, 1967, in concept-formation tasks; Monty, Karsh, & Taub, 1967, in a problem-solving experiment). Research in more complex settings or tasks generally has produced performance decrements with increasing stimulus or task complexity (e.g., Howell, Johnston, & Goldstein, 1966, and Mackworth, 1965, in signal-detection tasks; Blanchard, 1966, and Kepros & Bourne, 1966, in research on perception and selective attention; Byers, 1964, Byers & Davidson, 1968, Haygood & Stevenson, 1967, Kirloskar & Parameswaran, 1967, Pishkin, 1965, and Wolfgang, Pishkin, & Lundy, 1962, in work concerned with concept learning and concept formation; and Campbell, 1968, in problem-solving research). A third group of researchers has reported both increments and decrements in performance when stimulus characteristics were varied. As a rule, their research includes both low and high (or a range of low to high) levels of stimulus or task complexity (e.g., the work of Broadbent & Gregory, 1965, and Hsia, 1968, in signal detection; Morgan & Alluisi, 1967, with stimulus discrimination; Archer, 1962, Braley, 1962,

Krossner, 1966, Laughlin, 1968, and Wolfgang, 1967, with research on concept learning, identification, or formation; and finally, Berry, 1967, Ranken & Dowling, 1965, and Ranken & Wang, 1965, in cognitive or thinking tasks).

Complexity as a Personality and Stimulus Variable: Interaction

An attempt to relate environmental complexity and complexity in personality structure was made by Driver and Streufert (1966, 1969), Schroder, Driver, and Streufert (1967), and Streufert and Driver (1967). These authors proposed that the degree of differentiation and integration (in both perception and performance) can be represented as a family of inverted U-shaped curves. Perceptual and performance levels should be low when environmental stimulus complexity is either high or low. Perceptual and performance levels should be high when environmental complexity is moderate (optimal). However, differentially high levels should be reached, depending on individual differences in the subjects' (or group of subjects') complexity of conceptual structure. Complex subjects should reach higher levels of differentiation and integration when optimal environmental complexity is given.

According to Schroder et al. (1967), environmental complexity consists of at least three components: (1) information load, or the quantity of information (stimulation) received by subjects per unit time, (2) noxity, or the failure proportion of that information, and (3) eucity, or the success proportion of that information. The theory has been tested and generally supported (Streufert, in press; Streufert & Schroder, 1965; Streufert, Streufert, & Castore, 1969).

Since social influence is concerned with both stimuli (in the message) and with cognitions (in source and target), the interactive approach to complexity might be the most applicable to influence research. In addition, that approach has the advantage of combining the theoretical views and research methodologies taken by several researchers.

How Unitary Is Complexity?

If the concept of complexity is viewed in the interactive fashion proposed by Driver and Streufert (1966; 1969), Schroder et al. (1967), and Streufert and Driver (1967), then the theoretical approaches to the concept may be less divergent from each other, and we may find we can make more generally useful predictions. Yet would a prediction, for instance, for a complex person who is placed in a complex situation, hold in all cases? Can we speak of a general cognitive style that would have the same effects for all segments of a particular person's cognitive structure? For instance, if he perceives information in a complex way, will he always make complex decisions? Not necessarily.

An individual may not possess the same level of complexity in all segments of his cognitive structure or across all points in time. In addition, several different *kinds* of complexity may be present in the same person at the same point in time. Not all kinds of complexity are necessarily relevant to the social influence process. In the section below, the different forms of structural complexity are outlined, and the degree to which they affect the social influence process is considered.

LEVEL OF COMPLEXITY

Differences between differentiative and integrative complexity have already been discussed. For the present, individual differences in the complexity of cognitive structure may be viewed along one developmental dimension: from *very "simple,"* where a person uses a single judgmental dimension and identifies incoming information only with the endpoints of that dimension, to *less simple*, where he is able to discriminate along his single dimension, to *differentiated*, where the person can employ various dimensions simultaneously (but independently) to place a stimulus, to *complex integrative*, where the person can combine discriminated judgments based on the stimulation on various differentiated dimensions into a meaningful whole. It should be pointed out that the differences in the complexity of stimulus (message) perception are not correlated with any intelligence measures, whether verbal or quantitative; rather they appear to be perceptual styles that an individual has learned.

PERCEPTUAL VERSUS EXECUTIVE COMPLEXITY

The measurement of cognitive complexity has most frequently occurred at the response end of the *S-O-R* chain. This procedure has provided researchers with a wealth of data for the effects of complexity on decision making, in other words, on executive complexity. Although one might assume that there should be some relationship between the complexity of perception for the target of an influence attempt and his complexity of subsequent decision-making behavior, Streufert and Driver (1965, 1967) have shown that there is certainly no one-to-one relationship. The effect of any social influence attempt should be first of all determined by the target's perceptual complexity. Consequently, it is that form of complexity which is emphasized in later pages of this chapter.

HIERARCHICAL VERSUS FLEXIBLE COMPLEXITY

When one views cognitive integration, one could view a person's cognitive structure as fixed or as flexible. If it were fixed (hierarchical in organization), then a stimulus would have to perfectly fit one of a number of available integrated dimensions before it may be "absorbed" into the system without distortion. Stimulus arrays (messages) containing nonmatching information would require distortion or selective attention. If the system were flexible (flexible integration), then the dimensions themselves, and the relationships among dimensions, might be modified or rearranged as an effect of an incoming stimulus (message). The hierarchical complex cognitive structure differs from the simple cognitive structure merely in the number of components on which information may be placed. It is similar to the simple system in its lack of flexibility, in other words, its inability to consider alternative interpretations of stimulus material and its inability to generate change within itself. For the purpose of social influence processes, the simple system and the hierarchical complex system may not be distinguishable: both produce constant and predictable response patterns. The predictions made below for simple structural systems should hold in most cases as well for hierarchical complex system of cognitive structure.

SOCIAL VERSUS NONSOCIAL COMPLEXITY

Another distinction can be made between social and nonsocial complexity. Social influence processes normally occur in an interpersonal context. The concern in this chapter is consequently limited to social complexity (cf. Streufert & Driver, 1967).

OPENNESS VERSUS CLOSEDNESS

A final distinction might be made between openness and closedness. Rokeach (1960) considered open persons those who approach information in nondogmatic ways: they are able to view concepts in novel ways and see them in novel relationships to each other. Closed persons, on the other hand, take familiar approaches to information. They are unable to attach new meaning to familiar concepts, and consequently they would be unable to relate familiar concepts in more than one way. Their approach to information is, in other words, dogmatic. The concepts of openness and closedness are viewed somewhat differently by the present authors. It is assumed that openness and closedness are not generalized across all areas of human information processing, rather *either* openness *or* closedness might occur at a number of points in a person's cognitive structure. For instance, a person might be open as a perceiver of information but might be closed in his decisions. That pattern might be reversed, and, of course, he might be open or closed in both perceptual and decision-making areas. Openness in perception defines the degree of receptivity to information (whether the system is willing to receive information, but not necessarily whether the system will absorb the information or be modified in line with the information). Openness-closedness in decision making is concerned with a person's willingness or ability to close for action after some conclusion has been reached as a function of the stimulation. If he remains open, he would likely vacillate without being able to settle on any particular decision, even a temporary one. This form of decision-making openness, of course, would most often be a characteristic of some complex systems, since it is easier to act on the basis of a single unidimensional judgment than it is to act on the basis of a multitude of differentiated dimensional judgments, or on the basis of various integrated dimensional judgments. Again, because of the concern with perception of social messages, the emphasis of this chapter is on openness-closedness on the perceptual end of a person's cognitive structure. For those who are familiar with the views of Schroder, Driver, and Streufert (1967), one more view of the current authors needs to be emphasized. While Schroder et al. saw complex systems as necessarily open to information, they are not necessarily viewed in that fashion in this chapter. Both simple and complex systems are seen as potentially open or closed, and, as recent research has demonstrated (Streufert & Castore, in press), under certain environmental conditions simple systems might be considerably more open to incoming information than complex systems are.

INCIDENCE OF COMPLEXITY

Only few people (about 10 to 15 percent of the population) are complex. (From now on the term complex will be used to describe integrators and the term simple to describe those who are unidimensional in social perceptual attributes.) How "adaptive" complexity is would depend on environmental requirements. Complexity is useful in a quickly changing world, but in a more stable world it will bring accusations from less complex persons of wishy-washyness. For that matter, it might be maladaptive to be in a state of complex cognitive flux when one must live in an environment that requires stability and unwavering knowledge of "what is right and what is wrong."

The Measurement of Complexity

Stimulus Complexity

Stimulus complexity—whether in signal detection, concept formation, perception, or personality research—has generally been defined in terms of the *number* of specific elements contained in the stimulus array to which a person is exposed within a limited period of time or within a limited physical space. When dealing with a message sent by another person (or a researcher who is simulating another person), stimulus complexity may be viewed as the number of dimensions on which a message is presented. For example, a message stating that "Kentucky Blue Grass looks good" contains one judgment on only one dimension. In contrast, if the statement is extended to read "Kentucky Blue Grass looks good and grows slowly," there would be two dimensions. In cases of such relatively terse messages, one need merely count the number of communicated concepts that can *potentially* be placed on separate dimensions. Certainly, not all persons *would* view such a message on two dimensions, e.g., slow growth could mean "bad," good looks probably would mean "good," and the combined unidimensional judgment might be intermediate. However, on how many dimensions a message is perceived is not an aspect of the message; the dimensionality of the message merely sets an upper limit for the target's perceptual dimensionality. More multidimensional messages, particularly if they contain many sentences, would have to be scaled (using linear or curvilinear multidimensional scaling techniques) to determine their maximum dimensionality. However, scaling, no matter how quantitatively sophisticated, represents merely a more refined way of stimulus counting, using a number of individuals as referees.

Information Theory

The reader might ask whether information theory techniques can be employed in this kind of research. Several attempts to measure complexity and predict behavior of simple and complex persons based on information theory concepts have been made (e.g., Scott, 1963). However, there has been no wide use. The difficulty in applying information theory is in part due to its proposition that a single item of information should either increase uncertainty, decrease uncertainty, or leave it unaffected. It should not do two or even all three of these things. Information theory defines information quantitatively as "one bit" if it decreases uncertainty by one half. Such a quantification would be impossible, or at least of little use, if one bit of information would have a variable net effect.

As long as information received by a target is unidimensional, and relates to only one concept in his cognition, there can be either uncertainty reduction or uncertainty induction based on the information, but not both. If the information is multidimensional (whether or not it consists of no more than a single statement), it may increase uncertainty on one dimension while it decreases uncertainty on another. If the target must utilize both dimensions to make a single decision, then the information theorist might find it difficult to determine the net effect of the information. An example might be useful. A national decision maker who is involved in recommending policy for his nation's involvement in a Vietnam-type war receives information that a recent military venture by his nation was highly successful: all enemy units and all agricultural production in a certain region held by the enemy were wiped out. Should he recommend more actions of the same kind? Militarily, certainty is increased. Destruction of enemy units seems desirable and likely. However, destroyed farmland and decreased or eliminated agricultural production may have an adverse effect: the local population becomes hungry, increasingly hostile, and may in turn strengthen the enemy's guerilla operations. In that area the uncertainty is increased.

Cognitive Complexity

Cognitive (personality) complexity has been measured in a number of ways. Theorists and researchers who have been primarily interested in differentiative complexity (the number of dimensions on which an incoming stimulus array can be placed) have most frequently used Kelly's (1955) Role Concept Repertoire (REP) test. Researchers concerned with integrative complexity have primarily used Schroder and Streufert's (1963) Sentence Completion Test (SCT) and Streufert and Driver's (1967) Impression Formation Test (IFT).[1] Both these tests are subjective rather than objective but have yielded interrater reliabilities as high as +.95. Several attempts to develop objective measures of integrative complexity have until

---

1. Scored sample responses for the SCT may be found in Schroder, Driver, and Streufert (1967) and for the IFT in Streufert and Driver (1967).

recently yielded disappointing results. Although they are subjective, SCT and IFT scores are highly reliable and have predicted a wide range of behavioral differences. Unfortunately, considerable rater training is often necessary to assure high interrater reliabilities.

Complexity and Social Influence

Social influence requires a source of information, a message of some kind, and a receiver of that message, whose opinions, attitudes, or behavior might potentially be influenced. Most views of the message emphasize specifically "what" is being communicated, in other words, information content. For instance, if the source states that "Kentucky Blue Grass looks good," he probably intends for the target (the receiver of the message) to purchase Blue Grass rather than some other variety. There are, however, except in some sterile laboratory settings, other simultaneous communications. There may be personality or status characteristics of the source, the seriousness with which the message is presented, demand characteristics inherent in both source and setting, other (if the message is not terse) verbal communications, and so forth. Rather than representing a single stimulus point on a single dimension, the message reaching the target may be a complex stimulus configuration on a number of potentially orthogonal or oblique dimensions. Consequently, even though the experimenter intended to expose the subject to a single stimulus on a single dimension, he may inadvertently have presented him with considerably more stimuli and more dimensions.[2] Where his intent may not have permitted predictions based on complexity theory, the need for interpretation of his results in the light of complexity may nevertheless become necessary. Of course, if we are concerned with social influence in real-world settings, rather than in laboratory settings, multidimensionality is a sine qua non.

It was pointed out before that the message (stimulus) characteristics merely set the upper limit for the complexity with which the message is perceived by the target. Whether or not he does perceive the message in a complex (multidimensional) or simple (unidimensional) way depends on his specific cognitive complexity and other current situational constraints under which he operates.

2. Interpretation of research data collected in experiments concerned with some content component of social influence often hinges on the complexity of the message that the experimenter has employed. Data should vary potentially with the dimensionality, and results of one experimenter may not be comparable to that of another if their message complexity differs, even if both varied content in exactly the same way. Inconsistent results between various experiments may consequently not be surprising.

For instance, he may or may not single out the intended message for consideration. For that matter, he may as well single out some other component of the stimulus array. What he does should to a great extent depend on (1) the complexity (dimensionality) of the stimulus configuration (including but not exclusively consisting of the intended message) that he is exposed to, (2) internally- or externally-induced physiological stimuli which occur simultaneously with the message, (3) the content of his current cognitions, including attitudes, openness, and so forth, and (4) the dimensionality (simplicity or complexity) of his cognitive structure in the realm of the stimulus configuration. The specific impact of any communication (again including the message) on a receiver should be determined by an interaction of these environmental, physiological, and personality factors. Certainly we cannot know all the factors affecting laboratory experimentation, and we cannot expect to "read" the current physiological state of, for instance, a negotiator of the other side in international negotiations. However, an estimate of the cognitive structure of a target may be helpful in at least clearing up some of the difficulties we may experience. In other words, a better "matching" of source and target at the complexity level of the communication might have great advantages.

Matching Source and Target via Message Complexity

Theory

The theoretical position proposed in this chapter grows out of the interactive view of Driver and Streufert (1966), Schroder, Driver, and Streufert (1967), and Streufert and Driver (1967), particularly as represented in the recent modifications proposed by Driver and Streufert (1969). Environmental stimulus characteristics (including message complexity) are seen as interacting with an individual's complexity of cognitive structure (here specifically perceptual social complexity) to produce a particular complexity of message perception. If the message is simple, i.e., unidimensional (and if other stimulus characteristics are absent or do not add dimensionality), then perception would have to be unidimensional no matter what the complexity level (dimensionality) of the receiver. If the message is complex (multidimensional), it would be perceived unidimensionally by a person with simple cognitive structure, and multidimensionally by a person with (relevant) complex cognitive structure. If the message is overly complex (contains many more dimensions and judgments than the receiver can utilize), cognitive complexity would tend to become depressed, and both simple and complex individuals would tend to perceive the information contained in the message in simple (unidimensional) fashion. The predictions from the theory are presented in Figure 4.1.

Assuming that message and environmental characteristics permit optimal message conditions, then differences between cognitively simple and cognitively complex individuals would be at their highest. At this point, the complex individual would be able to utilize more dimensional information than his simple counterpart, and he would utilize information on more dimensions than he himself would under less favorable conditions. Research on complexity effects on infor-

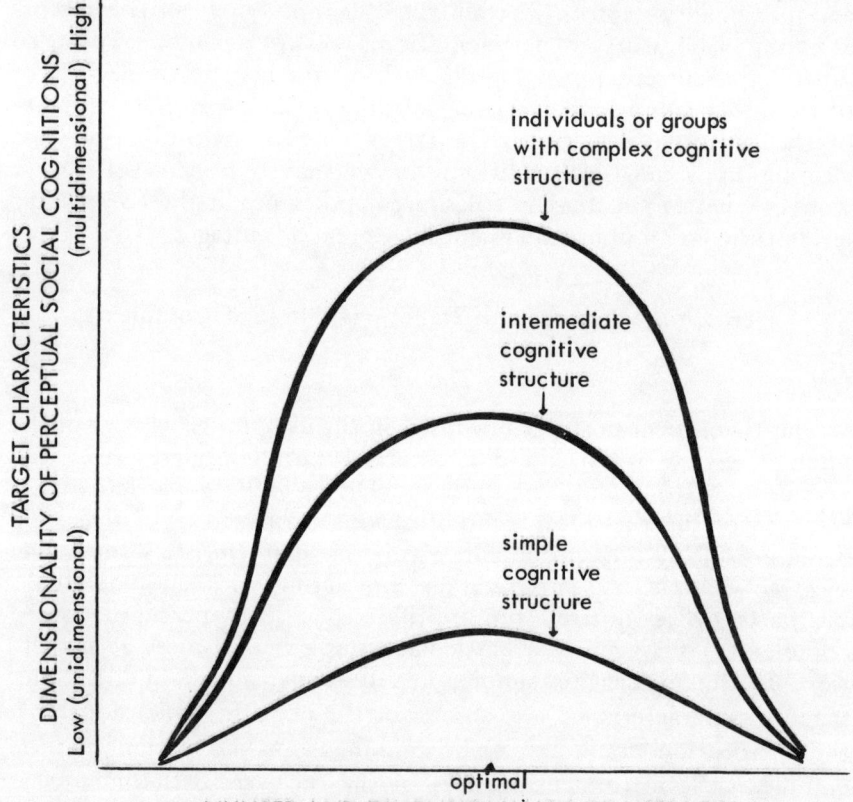

Figure 4.1. The Theoretical Relationship Between Message and Target Characteristics for Individuals or Groups of Various Levels of Cognitive Complexity.

mation search (cf. Streufert, 1970) suggests that individuals strive —and are mostly successful—in producing optimal message conditions. A simple (unidimensional) message received by a complex person under optimal conditions would contain too limited information, and the person would be interested in either seeking additional relevant information or would seek a more appropriate (more complex) source to gain similar but "better" (more multidimensional) information. In contrast, a simple person who is the target of a complex (multidimensional) message would either read the message in terms of the most salient dimension included in that message [3] or would seek a "better" (more simple) source for that information. In this way, complex persons who are unsatisfied with information contained in a message frequently talk about "getting more points of view" on the subject, while simple individuals frequently talk of "finding out the truth from an authority on the subject." In other words, a simple (unidimensional) message is easily perceived by a subject with simple cognitive structure. A complex message tends to be distorted or not understood by him. A simple message tends to be understood by a complex subject, but tends to prove unsatisfactory to him, and a complex message tends to be well understood by him. One should note, however, that understanding is not the same as preference, nor does it produce agreement with or a response of some specific kind to the message. In general, one may propose that persons of similar complexity of cognitive structure would prefer to receive messages from each other, and if source and target communicate at their own complexity levels, then simple sources and complex sources can be understood (accurately in terms of their intent) by complex targets, but only complex sources can be understood accurately by complex targets (always assuming that complexity exists in both source and target specifically with regard to the subject of the message and that the message reflects the

---

3. Schroder, Driver, and Streufert (1967) have proposed that a person of simple (unidimensional) cognitive structure should be more subject to information salience than a complex person. If a simple person has only one dimension on which an incoming stimulus (components of a message) can be placed, then the part of the message that is relevant to that particular dimension would be salient and would determine any effects the message might have. Similarly, if the person should have more than one dimension that could be used for stimulus (message) evaluation, but normally operates simply (unidimensionally), then one—the most salient—dimension should be called upon for placement of the information contained in the message. Which dimension would be most salient might depend on the current cognitive characteristics of the person (e.g., if he is currently concerned with moral issues, he might seek a placement of a good-bad dimension) or on some demand characteristic inherent in the message itself (what is perceived as a "demand" would, of course, again depend to some extent on the individual who is receiving the message).

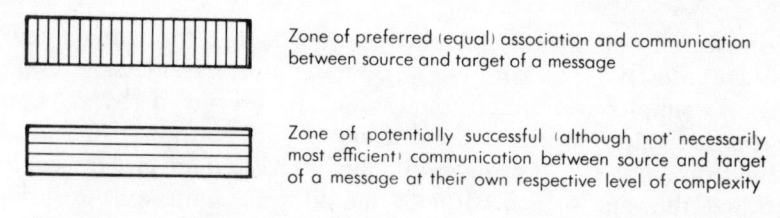

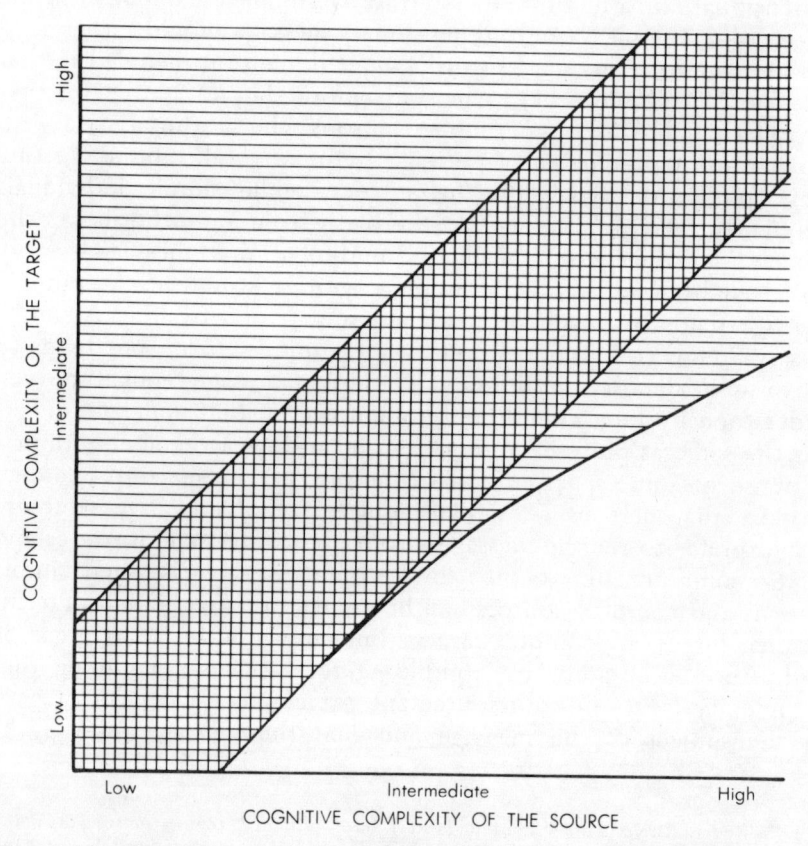

Figure 4.2. Cognitive Complexity and Communication Between Source and Target.

complexity level of the source's cognitions). These predictions are presented graphically in Figure 4.2.

Data on Perception of Complex Information

As suggested earlier, the dimensionality of information tends to determine the upper limit of perceptual dimensionality. Simple information, in other words, cannot (by itself) produce anything but simple cognitions (human information processing). Complex (multidimensional) information, on the other hand, might have a quite divergent effect on persons who are perceptually complex and perceptually simple. Streufert and Driver (1965, 1967) presented subjects in a complex decision-making task with a series of messages. Each message was unidimensional; however, the different messages represented various dimensions. The results indicated that (1) persons with complex conceptual structure perceive and utilize more dimensions of information than persons of simple conceptual structure, and (2) differences between simple and complex persons are greatest under intermediate (optimal) environmental conditions (when a new unidimensional item of information was presented every three minutes, rather than more or less frequently).

Data on Preferred Association of Source and Target

There has been some discussion on whether complexity is a style, an ability, a preference, or some combination of these (cf. Driver & Streufert, 1969). The current consensus appears to place the construct into the style category. However, some preference characteristics appear to exist. One might suggest that a target would be most open to information that is dimensionally most understandable and satisfying, suggesting the matching of source and target by means of the message for greatest success in communication as well as for greatest attraction due to similarity (cf. the work of Byrne and associates, e.g., Byrne, 1969). To test for an attraction due to similarity (in complexity) effect, Streufert, Bushinsky, and Castore (1967) asked 32 female freshman who had been exposed to each other in an introductory class for two semesters to list those others in the group whom they would like to (1) talk to at a party, (2) lead, (3) be led by, and (4) work with on an academic task. Although some shifts of choices across the areas of potential interaction did occur, simple subjects generally preferred to associate with other simple subjects. Similarly, complex subjects preferred their own kind. Only subjects of intermediate complexity level appeared to switch their preferences. These data, as well as those of Streufert and Driver (1965, 1967) cited above, suggest that matching of source, message, and target may be important if optimum attraction and influence is to be achieved.

Unfortunately, research that has *specifically* examined the effect of source complexity, message complexity, and target complexity is very limited. Much research appears needed to test for the usefulness of complexity theory for predicting and explaining social influence effects. This lack of pertinent data, however, is not a shortcoming of the theory itself. Specific predictions for complexity effects on social influence can be made. The following section contains several propositions about complexity and influence. Most of them are purely theoretical and lack empirical demonstration. Many of the proposed relationships, in other words, are so far speculative and invite empirical test.

Complexity of Target and Influence

The effect that the source has on the target is in good part determined by the characteristics of the target. If one intends to study complexity effects, then the role of the target is even increased; a simple target cannot perceive the complexity of the source's intent (if any), nor is he sensitive to potential complexity of a message. The focus of any discussion of complexity effects on the social influence process is consequently directed at (1) source effects on the target, (2) message effects on the target, and (3) target characteristics per se.

Source Factors

A burgeoning area of persuasion research focuses on variation in opinion change due to differences in the characteristics of the source of the message. Most relevant literature can be circumscribed within Kelman's (1958; 1961) tricomponential analysis of source characteristics and related dynamics of persuasive impact. According to this analysis, the persuasive impact of a message will vary with the degree of source *credibility*, source *attractiveness*, and source *power*. The opinion change produced by the three classes of source characteristics are linked to three different psychological mechanisms of opinion change: internalization, identification, and compliance, respectively. When a person is motivated to attain a veridical position on some issue, opinion change in a direction advocated by a credible source is referred to as internalization. When a person is motivated to initiate and/or maintain a favorable interpersonal relationship (either actual or fantasy), acceptance of position advocated by an attractive source is referred to as identification. The tertiary mechanism, compliance, represents the person's acceptance of the position advocated by a powerful source without private acceptance of it.

CREDIBILITY

Hovland and his colleagues (e.g., Hovland & Weiss, 1951; Kelman & Hovland, 1953) are frequently cited as the first to research communicator credibility. Their initial view of credibility focused on the communicator's perceived expertise with regard to the facts surrounding the issue. For example, a world-famous professor of international economics and trade would be a more "credible" communicator than a world-famous professor of music on an issue such as "America should increase import duties." In the Hovland and Weiss (1951) study, college students read excerpts from newspaper and magazine articles on several topics such as the feasibility of an atomic submarine. The articles were attributed either to a highly credible source (e.g., a famous American nuclear physicist) or to sources low in credibility (e.g., Pravda). When measured immediately after subjects read the articles, opinion change in the direction advocated by the messages was greater for articles attributed to highly credible sources than for articles attributed to less credible sources. In contrast, delayed retests of opinion change, four weeks later, revealed that the magnitude of opinion change for the two credibility groups was almost equivalent. The high credibility groups had decreased to the magnitude of change obtained for low credibility sources.

In the Kelman and Hovland (1953) study, high school students listened to a tape-recorded educational program featuring a speaker who advocated extreme leniency for juvenile delinquents. The introduction to the program varied the characteristics of the speaker. A positively-valenced source group was informed that the speaker was a highly respected, honest, well-informed judge who had the public interest at heart, and so forth. A negatively-valenced source group was informed that the speaker, who appeared to be of questionable character, was chosen at random from the studio audience. For the neutrally-valenced source group the speaker was introduced as a person chosen at random from the studio audience and no other information about the speaker was provided to this group. Although the prerecorded speeches were identical, measurement of opinion change immediately following the presentation of speeches showed that groups hearing the message from positive sources were more favorably disposed toward leniency than were the groups hearing speeches from negative sources. The neutral groups were closer to the positive source groups. Three weeks later, the source was reintroduced to half of the subjects by playing the introduction that was used during the original program. For the remaining subjects opinion measurement was obtained without "reinstatement" of the source. In the no-reinstatement group, the difference in opinion between positive and negative source conditions had decreased considerably. Under conditions of reinstatement, opinion change was greater for positively-valenced sources and lower for negatively-valenced sources. The latter findings were consistent with the results obtained by Hovland and Weiss (1951).

The diminishing effect of credibility demonstrated in the above two studies has been called the "sleeper effect" (cf. Cohen, 1964; Hovland, Janis, & Kelley, 1953) or the "discounting cue" effect (McGuire, 1969). According to this explanation, when source credibility is high, the persuasive situation has two immediate effects. The first effect is an "information effect" which is a result of the substantive content of the message, i.e., the nature, number, and kind of persuasive arguments. The second effect is the "communicator effect." A positively-valenced source is presumed to enhance the listener's desire to agree and to diminish the receiver's desire to listen and/or critically examine the message contents. A negatively-valenced source is presumed to decrease the receiver's desire to agree and to enhance the receiver's desire to listen and/or to critically examine the message contents. With the passage of time, the recollection of source diminishes and the net persuasive effect is that the positively-valenced and negatively-valenced sources lose their advantages and disadvantages, respectively. This explanation has not been accepted without some skepticism. For example, the variations of source credibility in the above studies confounded communicator "expertise," i.e., his knowledge about the facts relevant to the issue and "trustworthiness," i.e., his desire to communicate the facts in an unbiased manner (cf. a discussion by Hovland, Janis, & Kelley, 1953).

More recently, a number of studies have focused on the latter component of credibility or the communicator's "intent to persuade" (cf. a review by McGuire, 1966).

At the very least, it is clear that the dynamics of source credibility are too complex to permit a simply stated generalization to account for the phenomenon of communicator credibility. It appears that a number of components may contribute to the effect that has been attributed to source credibility. These various components may represent in turn various dimensions (not to speak of the dimensionality inherent in the message characteristics that have arisen in this research area). For instance, when a speaker is introduced as "having the public interest at heart" and another is merely introduced as "a person taken from the audience," differences in dimensionality necessarily arise. Further, the prerecorded speeches used in experiments are not controlled for dimensionality. What differences can be expected for complex and simple persons?

Persons with simple cognitive structures tend to respond only to the salient stimuli in their environment (see above). Furthermore, simple people often make judgments about the stimuli in a bifurcated manner, i.e., either good-bad, or correct-incorrect, or relevant-irrelevant, and so forth. Consequently, it seems reasonable to predict that simple people should respond either to the source of the message *or* the message content, i.e., to whichever is most salient, but not to both inputs. If the message source is most salient, simple people should either agree with the position advocated by a positively-valenced source or disagree with the position advocated by a negatively-valenced source without listening carefully and without critically evaluating the message content. If so, opinion measurement immediately following reception of the message should yield a main effect with more change in the direction advocated by the message occurring for positive sources than negative sources. If disassociation of the source from the message content or recollection of source occurs with the passage of time, then delayed retest of opinions should produce less differences between positively and negatively valenced sources, i.e., the "sleeper effect." Alternatively, if message content is the most salient stimulus, simple people should not be more persuaded by positive sources than by negative sources because the message content is identical for both conditions. Furthermore, this effect should not be changed by temporal factors. The above predictions may be seen in Figure 4.3 below.

Unlike simple people, persons with complex cognitive structures tend to respond to many dimensions of stimulation in their environment at the same time. In the present persuasion situations, complex people should evaluate and weight *both* the source credibility as an input and the dimensionality, number, and content of the arguments contained in a message. Furthermore, although the complex person should listen to and critically evaluate the message arguments, the persuasive impact of the message arguments will be enhanced by attribution to a positive source and diminished by attribution to a negative source. Therefore, we are predicting that the immediately tested persuasive impact of messages attributed to positive and negative sources for complex persons will be at least the same as, or greater than, the difference which occurred for simple persons (see Fig. 4.3). In order to generate predictions about the effects of delayed measurement for complex persons, we will briefly consider the manner in which complex persons manipulate information (as different from the mere "agreeing or disagreeing" response of simple persons).

Cognitively complex persons should act upon information in at least three ways. First they would process incoming information (message components) by placing it on any relevant dimension that is present in their cognitive system (i.e., rehearsal process). Second, the

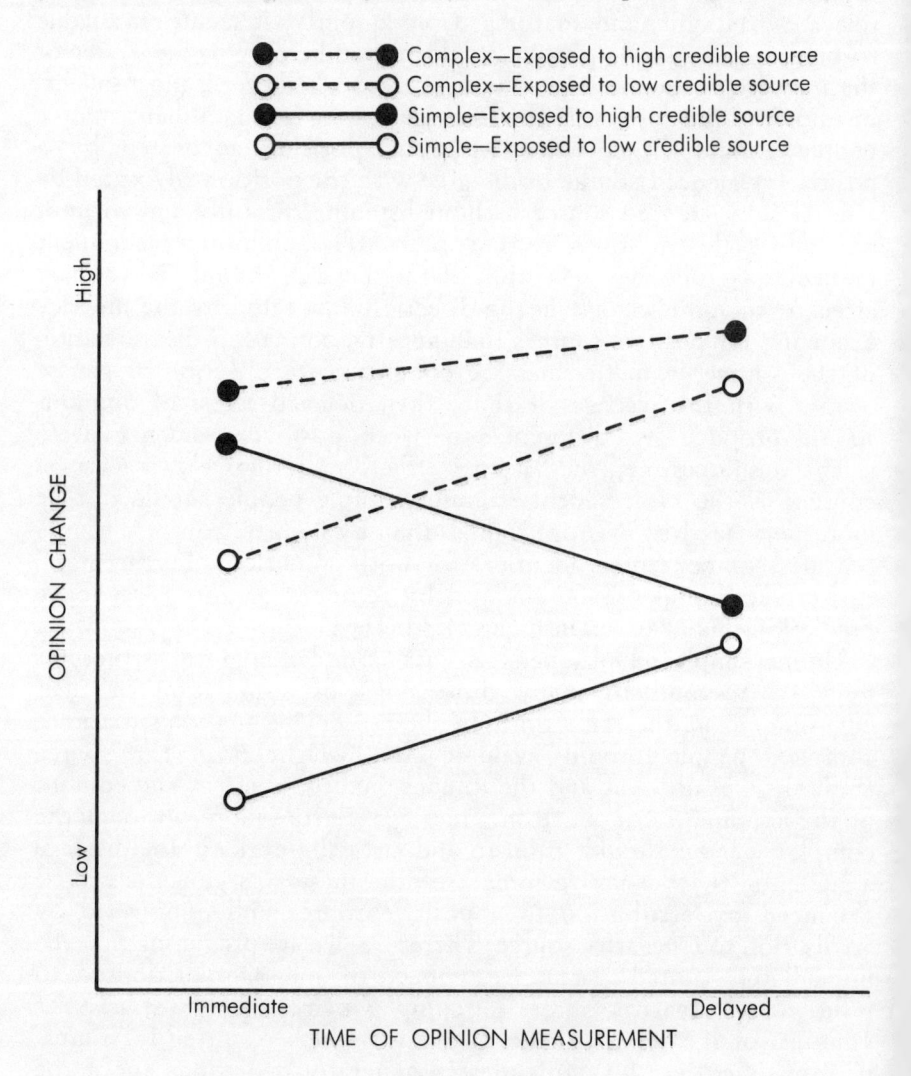

●-----● Complex—Exposed to high credible source
○-----○ Complex—Exposed to low credible source
●———● Simple—Exposed to high credible source
○———○ Simple—Exposed to low credible source

Figure 4.3. Effects of Complexity of Cognitive Structure on Opinion Change in Response to Messages from High and Low Credibility.

information should be integrated with the existing information and lead at this point to potential changes in cognitive dimensionality or in the placement of previously coded information on existing dimensions. Third, the newly integrated information should be available in the future for further integration with information received at that time.

One often observed characteristic of complex cognitive systems is a specific information search characteristic (cf. Schroder, Driver, & Streufert, 1967). Information that has modified previous dimensionality or has modified information placement on existing dimensions often results in openness to similar information, or even in information search in that area. Consequently, if a change in the complex target is produced by a message, then the target is likely to be receptive to message-relevant information in the near future. Given these arguments, and assuming the message content is veridical, the complex person should show further attitude change in the direction advocated by the source after a time delay.

No specific tests of complexity effects on source credibility are known to the current authors. Whether or not the predictions made here will hold will have to await relevant research.

ATTRACTIVENESS

A source may be attractive to a target for a number of reasons. He may simply be liked, or he may be liked because he has referent power (French & Raven, 1959). No matter what the reason, a positive attitude toward the source should produce greater social influence, and a more negative attitude should produce less social influence (Berkowitz, 1957; Osgood & Tannenbaum, 1955). Complexity should affect either influence or attitudes similarly as it did for source credibility. One would expect only slight to moderate differences between simple and complex persons when attitudes or influence are measured immediately after exposure. Only when additional dimensions are introduced would major differences be expected. An experiment by Streufert (1966) determined the effects of cognitive complexity on attitudinal judgments of a source by persons exposed to agreeable or disagreeable messages by that source. Streufert found that simple and complex individuals did not differ in their respective ratings of the source when the subjects were merely asked to "rate the person" who just presented a message. Sources presenting agreeable messages were rated favorably by complex as well as simple individuals, and sources presenting disagreeable messages were rated negatively. Streufert then asked the subjects in his experiment to rate the sources again (in randomized sequence) if they were (1) just introduced as next year's college roommate, (2) would participate with the subject in a debating task lasting a short time, and (3) would merely be seen by the subject in the cafeteria of another college, sitting far off with a few other persons of their own age and sex. Ratings for the three hypothetical situations provided the *potential* for judgments on two dimensions: (1) attitude similarity and (2) degree of hypothetical interaction. It was assumed that attitude similarity would be more salient than an imaginary future interaction, so that simple subjects would base their responses on the first, rather than the second, dimension. Streufert predicted that the judgments of complex subjects would be determined by both dimensions of information jointly. In other words, simple subjects who were exposed to the agreeable message should like the source and should not modify their attitude, no matter what the interaction distance. Similarly, simple persons exposed to the disagreeable message should dislike the source and should not change their attitudes if interaction distances change. Complex subjects on the other hand should dislike the source of a disagreeable message most when interaction distance was close and should dislike the source less when interaction distance was not close. They should like the source of the agreeable message most when interaction distance was close and like that source less as interaction distance increased. The predictions were supported in the research. A simplified version of the data obtained by Streufert (1966) is presented in Figure 4.4.

POWER

A number of different types of source power have been proposed in the psychological literature. Among these are coercive power (ability to punish the target for nonacceptance of the influence attempt), reward power (ability to reward the target for acceptance of the influence attempt), referent power (ability to present the target with social rewards), expert power (competence of the source in the task area may help the target achieve a goal), and more (French & Raven, 1959). Much research has shown that coercive, reward, and referent powers have strong but not always reliable effects (e.g., Berkowitz, 1962; Ring & Kelley, 1963; Solomon, 1964; Zander & Curtis, 1962; Zipf, 1960). In any case, these forms of power would likely produce specific unidimensional compliance, leaving little room for differences between simple and complex individuals.

Expert power presents a somewhat different situation. An expert is a highly credible source of information: an authority source. The predicted responses of simple and complex persons to authority sources have been discussed above. There is, however, yet a somewhat different kind of expertise. After repeated exposure, some information sources prove to be consistently accurate; others prove to be consistently inaccurate. An example of this form of source expertise was created by Kennedy for use in his Simulation of Business and Industrial Games (SOBIG) laboratory at Princeton in the early Sixties. Kennedy exposed simple and complex subjects to four sources of predicted stock market quotations. One of the sources was consistently accurate; the others were not. Simple subjects

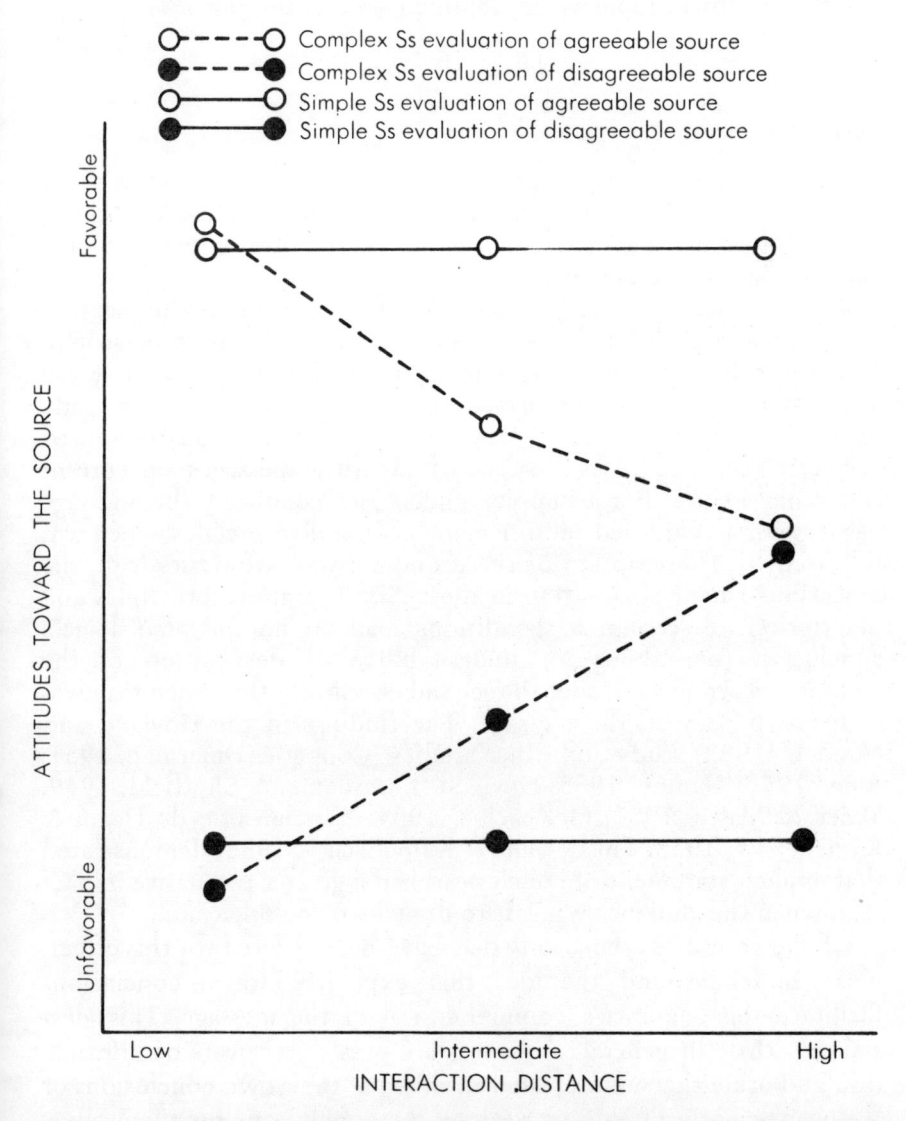

Figure 4.4. *Effects of Cognitive Complexity on Evaluative Attitudes Toward Sources of Agreeable and Disagreeable Attitudinal Information.*

bought and sold stocks on a simulated market entirely in line with the predictions made by the accurate source. Complex subjects also discovered the accurate source but were unwilling to stick with it. They were sure that there must be some element of truth in the other three sources and attempted to combine (integrate) the predictions of the four sources in various ways. Their efforts necessarily failed. Here, then, is one of the cases where cognitive complexity (in a simple world) represents a disadvantage.

Message Factors

EXPLICIT VERSUS IMPLICIT CONCLUSIONS

The above discussion isolated characteristics of the source for consideration. We now turn to characteristics of the mesage, without regard for source characteristics or for interactions between source and message characteristics.

We focus first on the question that has plagued communication engineers and their predecessors for centuries. Is it more persuasive to allow the audience to draw its own conclusions or to make the conclusions explicit in the persuasive appeal? A direct experimental approach to the question (Hovland & Mandell, 1952) presented subjects with one of two types of identical messages on current economic issues. For example, under one condition the message began with a simplified set of general economic principles which was followed by a description of the economic state of affairs (e.g., the precarious financial situation in the U.S.). The above principles and description of economic conditions lead to an *unstated* logical conclusion (desirability or undesirability of devaluation of the American currency). Under the second condition, the conclusion was *stated* explicitly in the message. The findings in the Hovland and Mandell (1952) study and other studies (Cooper & Dinerman, 1951; Fine, 1957; Hadley, 1953; Hovland, Lumsdaine, & Sheffield, 1949; Maier & Maier, 1957; McKeachie, 1954; Thistlewaite, de Haan, & Kamenetsky, 1955; Thistlewaite & Kamenetsky, 1955) demonstrated that explicit statement of conclusions had a greater persuasive impact than when the audience was left to draw its own conclusion.

Of the various explanations that have been offered for this effect, most center around the idea that explicitly drawn conclusions facilitate the audience's comprehension of the message. This view assumes that, in general, audiences are passive receivers of information and are either uninterested in drawing their own conclusions or are insufficiently intelligent to draw the conclusions for themselves.

Therefore, when the conclusion is not contained within the message, the audience "misses the point" (cf. McGuire, 1969, p. 209). Indeed, indirect evidence suggests that, with the exception of the Hovland and Mandel (1952) study, when subjects are intelligent enough (Cooper & Dinerman, 1951; Thistlewaite, de Haan, & Kamenetsky, 1955) or motivated enough (Marrow & French, 1945; Thistlewaite & Kamenetsky, 1955) or when the issues and arguments are familiar enough (cf. Cohen, 1964, p. 7) to draw their own conclusions, subjects who do so are more persuaded. An intriguing extension of the above ideas may be found in McGuire's logical model of attitude organization (McGuire, 1960a, 1960b; also Dillehay, Insko, & Smith, 1966).

It appears likely that the greater persuasive impact of explicitly drawn conclusions will vary with source characteristics, the degree of complexity or familiarity of the issue and the arguments, time factors, and individual differences. Furthermore, it appears likely that the above variables will interact with each other to produce higher-order interactions. Again one can make predictions from complexity theory. As discussed previously, simple persons are likely to search for the most salient cue in their environment to help identify the "correct" position on an issue (assuming they are open to the communication). In general, certain source characteristics (e.g., credibility) and certain message characteristics would likely serve as the basis for selecting the salient attribute. A statement by a credible source should produce considerable opinion change, with a fairly strong subsequent sleeper effect. But what about these effects when information about the source is not given, when the source is minimized, unidentified, or ambiguous? Under these conditions the simple person would be forced to pick the salient cues from the information presented in the message, something he should find difficult to do when a conclusion is not drawn for him. Complex information is too multidimensional, too confusing, and so forth, so that a common effect (picking the same message component as salient) cannot be expected for each one of several simple persons. In addition, simple persons may only respond to extraneous cues contained in the message or may not respond at all. For these reasons, one would expect that a message with implicit conclusions (unless the message is indeed unidimensional) presented without salient source characteristics would produce little opinion change in simple persons and would result in negligible sleeper effects.

Unlike the simple person, cognitively complex individuals respond to more than one cue or more than one component of the message. When the message source is unidentified, minimized, or ambiguous, the complex persons should respond to each premise and to the conclusion of a message. Indeed, the conclusion likely would not be weighted more heavily than each premise. If we assume that the premises are relevant and moderately compelling, then an explicitly stated conclusion should have only a slight advantage (if any) over a message that does not draw an explicit conclusion. After time delay, during which the complex individuals are again able to rehearse the

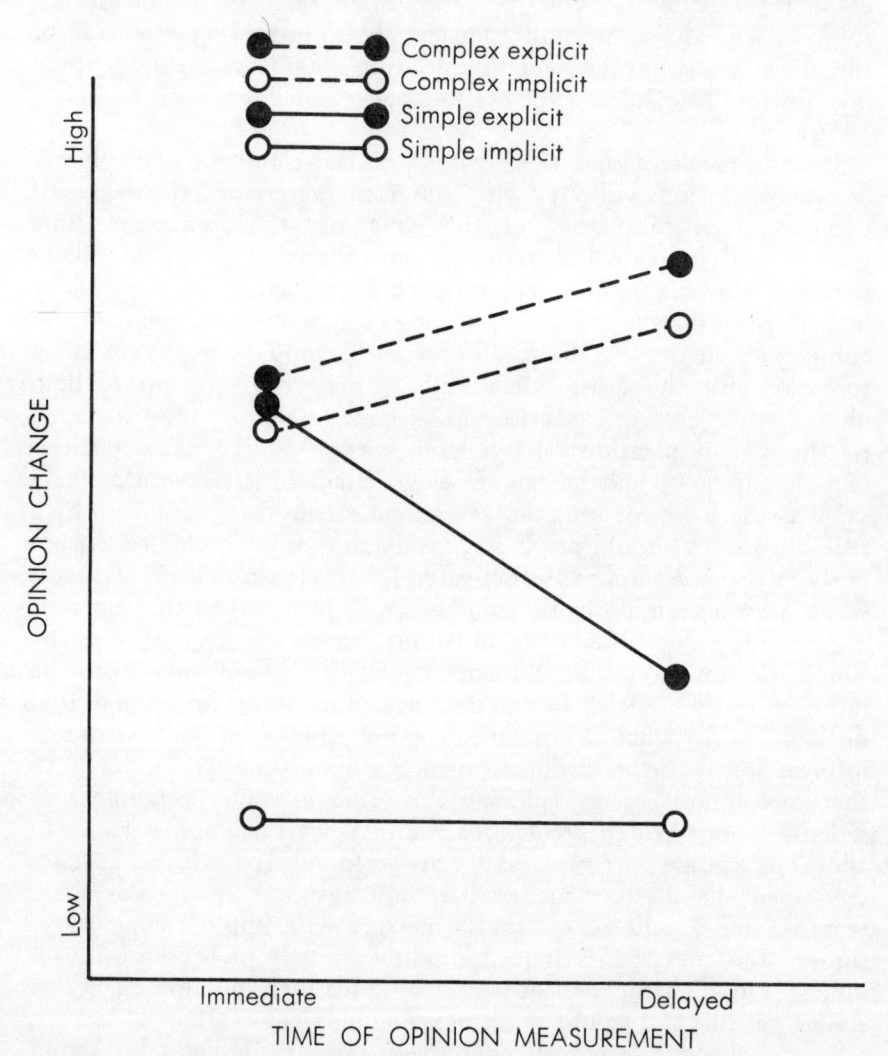

Figure 4.5. Effects of Cognitive Complexity on Opinion Change When the Message Does or Does Not Contain an Explicitly Drawn Conclusion, and When the Message Source is Unidentified

information and might seek for (or be open to) additional information on the same topic, an increasing effect of the message would be expected, whether explicit or implicit.[4] Since the message with an explicit conclusion in effect contains more information, it probably would maintain any advantage in terms of opinion change that it had immediately after the message was received by the target. These predictions are presented in graphic form in Figure 4.5.

The present authors are not aware of any research that has related complexity theory to the above predictions. Whether the predictions will be supported remains, of course, to be seen.

PRIMACY-RECENCY

Research on attitude formation based on the sequence of information presentation has been quite extensive and appears to be, if anything, on the increase. In this realm of social influence we usually have two different sources attempting to influence the target, sources who have different and often opposite intent to persuade. Most research has demonstrated a primacy effect: the first message has more of an influencing effect than a subsequent message of opposite content (e.g., Anderson, 1965; Anderson & Barrios, 1961; Asch, 1946; Luchins, 1957a; Stewart, 1965). This effect is explainable as derivatives of learning theory (Hovland, Campbell, & Brock, 1957; Hovland & Mandell, 1957; Miller & Campbell, 1959) or perceptual theory (Asch, 1946; Luchins, 1942). These theoretical formulations and others (e.g., adaptation level theory) have permitted manipulations of data to produce the opposite effect: greater influence of the recent message (e.g., Anderson & Hubert, 1963; Luchins, 1957b; Stewart, 1965). All of these manipulations and theories assume that either a primacy or a recency effect should indeed occur. Complexity theory would make a quite divergent prediction. Again, it would be expected that simple persons would focus on (and perceive and/or learn) the more salient cues in the message (or other parts of the environment). This cue, particularly if no previous attitude is present, would certainly be the initial information to which the subject is exposed. Later conflicting information would require modification of the now existing placement of the previous information on a unidimensional judgment and consequently can be hardly expected. Of course, one might (as some experimenters have

---

4. The above discussion assumes that the message information is veridical and that its effects would consequently be enhanced by the complex person's search for information between test and retest. If the information is not veridical, or if considerable information on several dimensions would be at variance with the message content, the sleeper effect should show the standard decrease in opinion change toward the base line.

done) manipulate the experimental design to increase the salience of the information presented in the recency condition and obtain a recency effect for simple subjects.

However, what about complex persons? One of the measures of perceptual social complexity is precisely based on primacy-recency in impression formation: the Impression Formation Test (IFT) of Streufert and Driver (1967). This test employs one of a series of adjectives which are presented three at a time. For instance, a subject may be told that a person is intelligent, industrious, and impulsive and is then asked to write a descriptive statement about that person. Subsequently he is asked to write a description of another person who is critical, stubborn, and envious. Finally, he is asked to combine the six adjectives. All are now ascribed to one person, that is, someone who is intelligent, industrious, impulsive, critical, stubborn, and envious. [5]

Cognitively simple individuals find it very difficult to deal with an incongruent series of six adjectives. They usually described the first (intelligent, industrious, impulsive) individual as a good guy. The critical, stubborn, and envious person they described as a bad guy. How can someone be both bad and good, if you can view him only on one (e.g., the evaluative) dimension of cognitive judgment? The usual solution for simple subjects is to either omit, reject, or bifurcate some of the adjectives. For instance, they may now describe someone who is impulsive, critical, stubborn, and envious, and omit intelligent and industrious. Or they may state that he is intelligent, industrious, and impulsive at work and describe him there, and say that he is critical, stubborn, and envious at home, also with a relevant description.

The usual outcome of the impression formation task for cognitively simple persons is a primacy effect: the evaluatively favorable characteristics are weighted higher, and the unfavorable characteristics (in the example we presented here stubbornness is most often unfavorable) are omitted or excused. For some individuals, of course, there is a recency effect. A person who is perceived as partially bad must be all bad.

Complex individuals have a much easier time with the impression formation task. For them there is neither a primacy nor a recency effect. All the characteristics can be integrated and the intelligent, industrious, impulsive, critical, stubborn, and envious person may turn out to be very well described, as, for example, an industrial executive, still on the way up but practically there, who has used all

5. This particular set of adjectives is drawn from the Asch's work with primacy and recency. Other adjective sets producing the same effect are available (cf. Streufert & Driver, 1967).

these characteristics to his advantage. In other words, complexity theory would predict that—as other theories do—all other things being equal, a primacy effect may be expected, unless experimental characteristics are varied to specifically produce a recency effect. This proposition should hold for most but not all persons. Some persons should experience a recency effect (the difference between the two groups should be primarily determined by a discrimination style). However, for (the outnumbered) complex individuals there should be neither a primacy nor a recency effect, rather there should be an "integration effect" where all information is weighted equally or nearly equally.

In a test of that proposition by the present authors, 100 complex individuals (selected on the SCT) and 100 simple individuals were presented with a description of a person (Mr. Walter) by one source using the key words "intelligent, industrious, and impulsive." Another source described that person in a statement including the key words "critical, stubborn, envious." Order of presentation was counterbalanced. After the presentation, subjects were asked to rate the described person on semantic differential scales containing five scales with evaluative meaning (correlating +.85 or higher with the good-bad scale). Data analysis revealed a significant ($p < .05$) primacy effect for simple subjects and no effect for complex subjects. More interesting, however, was the effect obtained when the groups receiving the unfavorable message first and those receiving the favorable message first were combined. Complex subjects rated the described person intermediate on the evaluative dimension, while simple subjects viewed him as either more good or more bad.

In other words, the issue of whether primacy or recency is a better method of social influence (depending on the setting and related constraints) is useful only when the influence attempt is intended for persons of simple cognitive structure.

Target Factors

The number of target factors that might be included in a discussion of social influence is rather extensive, particularly if one takes an interactive view of source, message, and target. Among these factors are a host of individual difference variables. From the vantage point of complexity theory, most of the relevant target factors would include personality structure effects, e.g., what kind of complexity at what point in a person's cognitive structure has what kind of an effect?

The previous discussions of complexity effects on source and message have repeatedly considered target complexity. It appears unnecessary to return to those predictions and findings at this point. There is, however, one target characteristic that has not been previously covered from a complexity viewpoint, neither in this chapter nor in other writings by complexity theorists: selective exposure.

SELECTIVE EXPOSURE

The principle of selective exposure has received devout attention as a determinant of the effectiveness of mass communication (cf. Klapper, 1949, 1960) and as a core proposition of dissonance theory (Brehm & Cohen, 1962; Festinger, 1957, 1964). Indeed, "One of the most widely accepted principles of mass communication and social psychology is that voluntary exposure to information is highly selective. People seek out information that supports or reinforces their previous beliefs, and avoid information that challenges their opinions" (Freedman & Sears, 1965, p. 59).

In general, efforts to experimentally examine the selective exposure principle have favored two kinds of experimental paradigms, either "free-choice" situations or "exposure" situations. In the former, subjects were selected or segregated on the basis of their purchase of a new automobile (Ehrlich, Guttman, Schönback, & Mills, 1957), their belief in hereditary or environmental theories of child development (Adams, 1961), their preferences among gubernatorial candidates (Freedman & Sears, 1963), and their preferences for multiple-choice or essay type exams (Mills, Aronson, & Robinson, 1959; Rosen, 1961). The experimental manipulations consisted of providing subjects with a choice of reading literature that was supportive or unsupportive of their initial position. The dependent variables were the subjects' rated interest in each of the articles and the rankings of their reading preferences. In "exposure" situations (Allyn & Festinger, 1961; Brodbeck, 1956; Davis & Jones, 1960; Jecker, 1964; Maccoby, Maccoby, Romney, & Adams, 1961; Mills & Ross, 1964) subjects were exposed to information that was either consistent or inconsistent with their beliefs or behavior, and the dependent variables were measures of subjects' modes of reducing the inferred cognitive dissonance. The findings, in general, suggested that the phenomenon of voluntary selective exposure consists of at least two different mechanisms: seeking supportive information and avoiding nonsupportive information.

There is evidence, albeit somewhat ambiguous, that individuals do seek supportive information (cf. Adams, 1961; Ehrlich et al., 1957; Freedman & Sears, 1963; Rosen, 1961). With the exception of Festinger (1957, pp. 162-176) and Cohen, Brehm, and Latané

(1959), the avoidance postulate, however, has received mixed support (Feather, 1962, 1963; Mills, Aronson, & Robinson, 1959; Steiner, 1962) and theoretical supplementation (Brock, 1965). At the very least, "Clearly, experimental evidence does not demonstrate that there is a general tendency to avoid nonsupportive and to seek supportive information" (Freedman & Sears, 1965, p. 69). More recent empirical developments have demonstrated that it is more fruitful to search for conditions which interact with the nature of the information (i.e., supportive versus nonsupportive) to submerge or enhance the information-avoidance tendency.

Confidence. Festinger (1964) hypothesized that seeking or avoiding discrepant information will depend upon how confident a person is that his position is correct. In situations when the individual is very confident that he is correct, he can reduce dissonance by seeking out the opposing information and refuting it. In situations when the individual lacks confidence in his position, he will avoid opposing information and reduce dissonance by some other mode (e.g., derogation of the source of the information). Inquiries into the validity of this proposition yielded inconsistent findings (Mills & Ross, 1964; Sears, 1965; Sears & Freedman, 1965). For example, a direct experimental test by Canon (1964) was not replicated by Freedman (1965). In these studies, high degrees of confidence were induced by informing subjects that their solutions to three different business school case studies were correct while the solutions offered by most of the other students were incorrect. Low degrees of confidence were induced by informing subjects that their solutions to the case studies were incorrect while most of the other students were correct. Next, subjects made a decision about a fourth case study (without correct or incorrect feedback) and were led to expect to write an essay about the fourth case. Subjects rated their preferences for reading five articles (two supported their decision, two opposed their decision, and one was a neutral article) which would allegedly help them to write their essay about the fourth case. Although Freedman (1965) found no differences, Canon (1964) found that high confidence groups preferred nonsupportive information and low confidence groups preferred supportive information. The findings from the above and related studies appear encouraging but suggest the need for more factors to be considered with confidence (cf. Freedman & Sears, 1965).

Utility and Novelty of Information. Characteristics of information such as perceived usefulness or the degree to which it is familiar information may be more influential determinants of information receptivity than supportiveness. Studies have been conducted utilizing information which the person expects will serve a practical purpose for some ongoing or future activity, such as information which will help prepare for a forthcoming debate (Canon, 1964; Freedman, 1965) or information which will help prepare for a forthcoming test (Brock & Balloun, 1967).

In the Canon (1964) and Freedman (1965) studies, discussed above, subjects were led to believe that they would either have to present the reasons for their case decisions for which supportive information would be more useful or that they would have to debate in favor of their decisions for which nonsupportive information would be useful in refuting opponents' arguments. Useful information was preferred to nonuseful information, but usefulness did not affect receptivity to supportive or nonsupportive information. In contrast, no preferences for useful information were found in three studies by Brock and Balloun (1967).

More recent commentaries on information receptivity have agreed that the novelty-familiarity dimension of information input may be a powerful determinant of voluntary selective exposure (Festinger, 1964; Freedman & Sears, 1965; Rhine, 1967). Sears (1965) exposed subjects to biased case reports of criminal trials (favoring the defense or prosecution position) and varied subjects' expectations about the degree of their familiarity with arguments contained in forthcoming defense and prosecution summations. The dependent variable was rated preferences for supportive and nonsupportive information (prosecution or defense summations) which contained either familiar or novel arguments. Information-seeking behavior reflected greater preferences for familiar nonsupportive information than for novel nonsupportive information. Other studies (Brock & Balloun, 1967; Brock & Fromkin, 1968; Sears & Freedman, 1965) found little or no effect of information familiarity. Most recently, Brock, Albert, and Becker (1970) varied commitment to a position, supportiveness of information, usefulness of information, and novelty of information in an ingenious experimental contrivance. Commitment to a decision was varied by having subjects swallow a gelatin capsule allegedly containing a "drug" which they had previously chosen (commitment) or by having subjects swallow an empty gelatin capsule (no commitment). Subjects were given an opportunity to audit one of several tape-recorded communications which contained information about the side effects of the "drug." The communications were constructed to include all possible combinations from one of two levels of information supportiveness (supportive versus nonsupportive), information familiarity (novel versus familiar), and information usefulness (useful versus useless). The major findings, obtained on several different dependent variables, showed that supportive information was preferred by committed subjects when the information was unfamiliar.

Lastly, some success in accounting for information receptivity has been found with individual difference variables such as educational level and socioeconomic class (Lazarsfeld, Berelson, & Gaudet, 1948; Star & Hughes, 1950; Steiner, 1963) and situational variables such as the individual's expected role in the communication process (Brock & Fromkin, 1968).

Selective exposure theory has required several recent modifications (Feather, 1967; Festinger, 1964) and may yet require additional changes in both theoretical approaches and in research method. Most of the difficulties appear to involve questions of motivation: when, why, and how is an individual motivated to seek (or to selectively expose himself) to supportive (consistent) or nonsupportive (inconsistent) information? Driver and Streufert (in press) have shown that selective exposure occurs to both consistent and inconsistent information. Which of the two (or some combination of them) does occur appears to depend on (1) certain personality characteristics of the individual (Driver & Streufert, in press) and on (2) the situational constraints imposed on the individual.

How does complexity relate to selective exposure? Earlier formulations of complexity theory (e.g., Schroder et al., 1967) suggested that complex individuals should be more open to information, particularly to inconsistent or nonsupportive information. Research of Streufert (in press) and Streufert, Suedfeld, and Driver (1965) has demonstrated that the relationship between complexity and exposure is not all that simple. It appears that the differences in openness to supportive and nonsupportive information are not greatly affected by complexity, rather complexity appears to determine how the received information is utilized in relating the message received by an individual to his current attitudes. The selective exposure research has not generally made a distinction between information reception and information processing. It appears that both complex and simple persons request and seek information that may or may not be consistent with their existing views (Streufert, Suedfeld, & Driver, 1965), but that complex individuals request more different kinds of information (Karlins & Lamm, 1967) and consequently would thereby increase the possibility of exposure to inconsistent or nonsupportive information. Once exposed to nonsupportive information, simple and complex individuals use quite different resolution processes. Crano and Schroder (1967), for instance, have demonstrated that simple individuals tended to use a single way of reducing the attitudinal conflict that was induced by a nonsupportive message. Complex individuals, on the other hand, tended to use more than one way of reducing conflict. Further, Streufert (1966) has shown that exposure to counterattitudinal messages results in fixed (stable) attitudes in simple individuals and in flexible attitudes in complex individuals.

The characteristics of simple individuals, particularly their unidimensional responding to salient information, of course, makes them much more subject to prediction. For example, the dissonance reduction characteristics or selective exposure propositions of dissonance theory should fit simple individuals quite well, particularly if the experimenter designs his experiment to make one way of reducing dissonance much more salient than any other. Complex individuals, on the other hand, should be difficult to predict with any of the consistency theories. Not only do they tend to respond in various (internally and externally determined) ways to information but also salience appears to affect them only slightly. There are, of course, as discussed above, situational (information) factors interacting with complexity: under certain conditions one would expect complex individuals to behave more like simple individuals.

As more and more (or more inconsistent) information is presented to a simple person, he should engage in more selective exposure for supportive information. The same effect for the more complex person should be attenuated, for two reasons. First, the complex person should be able to cope with more inconsistent information (through integration), and second, the complex person should be much more able to "select" (after exposure!) relevant information from a given information quantity, and consequently should not have to cope with as much total information. Research on complexity and information search by Karlins and Lamm (1967) provides a good example for this proposition. Nonetheless, under extreme overload conditions (when the amount of information received by an individual per unit time is exceedingly large, or when he receives more nonsupportive information than could possibly be utilized in an integrative fashion), one should expect no differences between complex and simple individuals. No differences would also be expected under extreme information deprivation (cf. research reported by Streufert & Schroder, 1965; Streufert & Driver, 1965). However, the moment information conditions change toward less extreme overload or less extreme deprivation conditions, the differences between complex and simple individuals should immediately re-emerge (cf. Suedfeld, 1964).

Some Final Thoughts

Complexity versus Personality Content Effects on Social Influence

In this chapter complexity has been viewed both as an individual difference variable which affects source and target and as a stimulus variable defining message (and environment) characteristics. Differences in individuals' complexity of conceptual structure has been further subdivided into several different kinds of structural characteristics (e.g., perceptual and executive complexity, differentiation and integration). The various kinds of complexity were postulated to have different degrees of divergent effects upon the social influence process. The effect of any influence attempt was seen as being in part determined by the interaction of target complexity with source and message complexity.

This view has not considered other individual difference variables, that is, personality content characteristics which may be ascribed to the target as well. What would happen if such variables were added into theoretical predictions or research designs that employ complexity as one individual difference variable?

Marlowe and Gergen (1969) have warned of the possible high-level interactions when several situational and personality variables are used simultaneously. One might make predictions for the outcome of complex interactions among several situational and personality variables. One does, however, encounter problems in interpreting results once they are obtained. Even the most skilled interpreter would find it difficult to explain the precise meaning of significant five- or six-way analysis of variance (ANOVA), analysis of covariance (ANCOVA), or multi-variance analysis of variance (MANOVA) results. Does that problem place an artificial limit on potential "personality content by complexity by environment" designs?

Fortunately, complexity research has been able to avoid these problems in most cases. There appears to be very little, if any, common variance between complexity and content of personality measures. Effects of personality content variables and of complexity variables on several measures of perception and decision making have demonstrated orthogonality of personality content and structural complexity. Past research has produced few and only low-order interaction effects that include both sets of variables. These results suggest that personality content effects on the social influence process can probably be treated independently from complexity effects without an inordinate loss of information.

Predictions for Simple Subjects and for Populations

The predictions made in this chapter for the behavior of simple subjects may appear quite familiar. They were often similar to predictions made by other theories that do not consider individual differences. This similarity is hardly surprising. The majority of persons from any previously tested population have been structurally simple, no matter what their intelligence level, or their social-occupational status. In past research complex persons have never made up more than 30 percent of a test population. As a rule the incidence of complex individuals has been between 5 and 25 percent.

If so few persons are complex, then why should one be concerned with cognitive complexity effects on social influence? If one's interest is in influencing a large number of persons within a population (but not the entire population), then a concern with the complexity of each individual target is probably superfluous. However, if one is interested in influencing specific individuals, then their complexity should be considered. This should hold particularly if the position the target holds in society would permit or require some level of complexity.

Current societies, particularly in the developed nations, appear to be in a continuous state of rapid fluidity; the demands made on influential individuals, the premises for these demands, and outcomes tend to change frequently. Simple individuals, because of their unidimensionality, emphasis on salience, and frequent inflexibility are often hard put to maintain (not achieve!) positions of key influence. If those persons who can maintain key positions in spite of flux are likely to be complex, then any influence directed toward them should consider target complexity. As Streufert, Streufert, and Castore (1969) have shown, complex leaders do respond differently from simple leaders, both as sources and as recipients of messages.

Complexity, Affect, and Influence

This chapter has taken a cognitive approach to social influence. Any theory that is concerned with "cold cognition" is necessarily quite different from one that deals with "warm affect." Should affect be considered when complexity predictions are made?

It may be fairly safe to assume that some affect will be generated when an influence attempt is made where attitudes are central in the target's cognitions. Affect is likely to interact with cognition. Past research has repeatedly demonstrated that increasing affect is associated with decreasing complexity. When affect levels are exceedingly high, little differences between the behavior of complex and simple persons can be obtained. As long as social influence remains free of affect "interference," as long as the target operates under "ideal" conditions (acts rationally), matching source, target, and message complexity is of great value for optimal social influence. As affect rises to high levels, simple communications between source and target are probably as effective as—and possibly more effective than—complex ones.

References

Adams, J. S. Reduction of cognitive dissonance by seeking consonant information. *Journal of Abnormal and Social Psychology*, 1961, 62, 74-78.
Allyn, J., & Festinger, L. The effectiveness of unanticipated persuasive communications. *Journal of Abnormal and Social Psychology*, 1961, 62, 35-40.
Anderson, N. H. Primacy effects in personality impression using a generalized order effect paradigm. *Journal of Personality and Social Psychology*, 1965, 2, 1-9.
Anderson, N. H., & Barrios, A. A. *Primacy effects in personality impression formation. Journal of Abnormal and Social Psychology*, 1961, 63, 346-350.
Anderson, N. H., Hubert, S. Effect of concomitant verbal recall on order effects in personality impression formation. *Journal of Verbal Learning and Verbal Behavior*, 1963, 2, 379-391.
Archer, E. J. Concept identification as a function of obviousness of relevant and irrelevant information. *Journal of Experimental Psychology*, 1962, 63, 616-620.
Asch, S. E. Forming impressions of personality. *Journal of Abnormal and Social Psychology*, 1946, 41, 258-290.
Berkowitz, L. Leveling tendencies and the complexity-simplicity dimension. *Journal of Personality*, 1957, 25, 743-751.
Berkowitz, L. *Aggression: a social psychological analysis.* New York: McGraw-Hill, 1962
Berlyne, D. E. Objective and phenomenal complexity: comments on Heckhausen's note. *Canadian Journal of Psychology*, 1964, 18, 245-248.
Berry, C. Timing of cognitive responses in naming tasks. *Nature*, 1967, 215, 1203-1204.
Bieri, J., Atkins, A. L., Briar, S., Leaman, R. L., Miller, H., & Tripodi, T. *Clinical and social judgment: the discrimination of behavioral information.* New York: Wiley, 1966.
Blanchard, W. A. Relevance of information and accuracy of interpersonal prediction: a methodological note. *Psychological Reports*, 1966, 18, 379-382.
Bourne, L. E., Jr., & Parker, B. K. Differences among modes for portraying stimulus information in concept identification. *Psychonomic Science*, 1964, 1, 209-210.
Braley, L. S. Some conditions influencing the acquisition and utilization of cues. *Journal of Experimental Psychology*, 1962, 64, 62-66.
Brehm, J. W. & Cohen, A. R. *Explorations in cognitive dissonance.* New York: Wiley, 1962.
Broadbent, D. E., & Gregory, M. Effects of noise and of signal rate upon

vigilance analyzed by means of decision theory. *Human Factors,* 1965, 7, 155-162.
Brock, T. C. Commitment to exposure as a determinant of information receptivity. *Journal of Personality and Social Psychology,* 1965, 2, 10-19.
Brock, T. C., Albert, S. M., & Becker, L. A. Familiarity, utility, and supportiveness as determinants of information receptivity. *Journal of Personality and Social Psychology,* 1970, 14, 292-301.
Brock, T. C., & Balloun, J. L. Behavioral receptivity to dissonant information. *Journal of Personality and Social Psychology,* 1967, 6, 413-428.
Brock, T. C., & Fromkin, H. L. Cognitive tuning set and behavioral receptivity to discrepant information. *Journal of Personality,* 1968, 36, 108-125.
Brodbeck, M. The role of small groups in mediating propaganda. *Journal of Abnormal and Social Psychology,* 1956, 52, 166-170.
Byers, J. L. Rate of information acquisition in concept attainment. *Psychological Reports,* 1964, 15, 111-117.
Byers, J. L., & Davidson, R. E. Relevant and irrelevant information in concept attainment. *Journal of Experimental Psychology,* 1968, 76, 283-287.
Byrne, D. Attitudes and attraction. In L. Berkowitz (Ed.), *Advances in experimental social psychology.* Vol. 4. New York: Holt, Rinehart & Winston, 1969.
Campbell, A. C. On introducing supraminimal data to items whose solution demands the use of indirect procedures. *British Journal of Psychology,* 1968, 59, 211-217.
Canon, L. K. Self-confidence and selective exposure to information. In L. Festinger (Ed.), *Conflict, decision and dissonance.* Stanford, Cal.: Stanford University Press, 1964. Pp. 83-96.
Cohen, A. R. *Attitude change and social influence.* New York: Basic Books, 1964.
Cohen, A. R., Brehm, J. W., & Latane, B. Choice strategy and voluntary exposure to information under public and private conditions. *Journal of Personality,* 1959, 27, 63-73.
Cooper, E., & Dinerman, H. Analysis of the film "Don't be a sucker:" a study in communication. *Public Opinion Quarterly,* 1951, 15, 243-264.
Crano, W. D., & Schroder, H. M. Complexity of attitude structure and processes of conflict reduction. *Journal of Personality and Social Psychology,* 1967, 5, 110-114.
Crockett, W. H. Cognitive complexity and impression formation. In B. A. Maher (Ed.), *Progress in experimental personality research,* Vol. 2. New York: Academic Press, 1965.
Davis, K., & Jones, E. E. Changes in interpersonal perception as a means of reducing cognitive dissonance. *Journal of Abnormal and Social Psychology,* 1960, 61, 402-410.
Dillehay, R. C., Insko, C. A., & Smith, M. B. Logical consistency and attitude change. *Journal of Personality and Social Psychology,* 1966, 3, 646-654.
Dörner, D., Everding, I., & Kötter, L. Zum Einfluss erhöhter Reaktionsunbestimmtheit auf den Konzepterwerb. (On the influence of increased reaction uncertainty upon concept learning.) *Zeitschrift für experimentelle und angewandte psychologie,* 1967, 14, 89-116.
Driver, M. J., & Streutert, S. Group composition, input load and group information processing. Purdue University: Institute for Research in the Behavioral, Economic and Management Sciences. Institute Paper No. 142, 1966.

Driver, M. J., & Streufert, S. Integrative complexity: an approach to individuals and groups as information processing systems. *Administrative Science Quarterly*, 1969, 14, 272-285.

Driver, M. J., & Streufert, S. *Cognitive approaches to motivation.* Homewood, Ill.: Dorsey Press, in press.

Dunham, J. L.,Guilford, J. P., & Hoepfner, R. Multivariate approaches to discovering the intellectual components of concept learning. *Psychological Review*, 1968, 75, 206-221.

Ehrlich, D., Guttman, I., Schönbach, P., & Mills, J. Post-decision exposure to relevant information. *Journal of Abnormal and Social Psychology*, 1957, 54, 98-102.

Eisenman, R., & Platt, J. J. Complexity-simplicity, experience, and incongruity. *Perceptual & Motor Skills*, 1968, 26, 615-619.

Feather, N. T. Cigarette smoking and lung cancer: a study of cognitive dissonance. *Australian Journal of Psychology*, 1962, 14, 55-64.

Feather, N. T. Cognitive dissonance, sensitivity and evaluation. *Journal of Abnormal and Social Psychology*, 1963, 66, 157-163.

Feather, N. T. An expectancy-value model of information-seeking behavior. *Psychological Review*, 1967, 74, 342-360.

Festinger, L. *A theory of cognitive dissonance.* Stanford, Cal.: Stanford University Press, 1957.

Festinger, L. (Ed.). *Conflict, decision and dissonance.* Stanford, Cal.: Stanford University Press, 1964.

Fine, B. J. Conclusion-drawing, communicator credibility and anxiety as factors in opinion change. *Journal of Abnormal and Social Psychology*, 1957, 54, 369-374.

Freedman, J. L. Confidence, utility, and selective exposure: a partial replication. *Journal of Personality and Social Psychology*, 1965, 2, 778-78.

Freedman, J. L., & Sears, D. O. Voters' preferences among types of information. *American Psychologist*, 1963, 18, 375.

Freedman, J. L., & Sears, D. O. Selective exposure. In L. Berkowitz (Ed.), *Advances in experimental social psychology.* Vol. 2. New York: Academic Press, 1965. Pp. 58-97.

French, J. R. P., Jr., & Raven, B. The bases of social power. In D. Cartwright (Ed.), *Studies in social power.* Ann Arbor, Mich.: Institute for Social Research, 1959.

Hadley, H. D. The nondirective approach in advertising appeals. *Journal of Applied Psychology* 1953, 37, 496-498.

Harrison, R. Cognitive change and participation in a sensitivity training laboratory. *Journal of Consulting Psychology*, 1966, 30, 517-520.

Harvey, O. J. Hunt, D. E., & Schroder, H. M. *Conceptual systems and personality organization.* New York: Wiley, 1961.

Haygood, R. C., & Stevenson, M. Effects of number of irrelevant dimensions in nonconjunctive concept learning. *Journal of Experimental Psychology*, 1967, 74, 302-304.

Heckhausen, H. Complexity in perception: Phenomenal criteria and information theoretic calculus—a note on D. Berlyne's "Complexity effects." *Canadian Journal of Psychology*, 1964, 18, 168-173.

Houston, J. P., & Garskof, B. E. The informational basis of judged complexity. *Journal of General Psychology*, 1965, 72, 277-284.

Hovland, C. I. Campbell, E. H., & Brock, T. The effect of commitment on opinion change following communication. In C. I. Hovland (Ed.), *Order of presentation in persuasion.* New Haven, Conn.: Yale University Press, 1957. Pp. 23-32.

Hovland, C. I., Janis, I. L., & Kelley, H. H. *Communication and persuasion.* New Haven, Conn.: Yale University Press, 1953.

Hovland, C. I., Lumsdaine, A. A., & Sheffield, F. D. *Experiments on mass communication.* Princeton, N. J.: Princeton University Press, 1949.

Hovland, C. I., & Mandell, W. An experimental comparison of conclusion-drawing by the communicator and by the audience. *Journal of Abnormal and Social Psychology*, 1952, 47, 581-588.

Hovland, C. I., & Mandell, W. Is there a law of primacy in persuasion? In C. I. Hovland (Ed.), *Order of presentation in persuasion.* New Haven, Conn.: Yale University Press, 1957. Pp. 13-22.

Hovland, C. I., & Weiss, W. The influence of source credibility on communication effectiveness. *Public Opinion Quarterly*, 1951, 15, 635-650.

Howell, W. C., Johnston, W. A., & Goldstein, I. L. Complex monitoring and its relation to the classical problem of vigilance. *Organizational Behavior and Human Performance*, 1966, 1, 129-150.

Hsia, H. J. Effects of noise and difficulty level of input information in auditory, visual, and audiovisual information processing. *Perceptual & Motor Skills*, 1968, 26, 99-105.

Irwin, M., Tripodi, T., & Bieri, J. Affective stimulus value and cognitive complexity, *Journal of Personality and Social Psychology*, 1967, 5, 444-448.

Jecker, J. D. Selective exposure to new information. In L. Festinger (Ed.), *Conflict, decision and dissonance.* Stanford, Cal.: Stanford University Press, 1964. Pp. 65-81

Karlins, M., & Lamm, H. Information search as a function of conceptual structure in a complex problem-solving task. *Journal of Personality and Social Psychology*, 1967, 5, 456-459.

Kelly, G. A. *The psychology of personal constructs.* New York: Norton, 1955.

Kelman, H. C. Compliance, identification and internalization. *Journal of Conflict Resolution*, 1958, 2, 51-60.

Kelman, H. C. Processes of opinion change. *Public Opinion Qarterly*, 1961, 25, 57-78.

Kelman, H. C., & Hovland, C. I. "Reinstatement" of the communicator in delayed measurements of opinion change. *Journal of Abnormal and Social Psychology*, 1953, 48, 327-335.

Kepros, P. G., & Bourne, L. E., Jr. Identification of biconditional concepts: effects of number of relevant and irrelevant dimensions. *Canadian Journal of Psychology*, 1966, 20, 198-207.

Kirloskar, S., & Parameswaran, E. G. Effect of irrelevant material on concept formation. *Research Bulletin of the Department of Psychology*, Osmania University, 1967, 3, 18-25.

Klapper, J. T. *The effects of the mass media.* New York: Bureau of Applied Social Research, Columbia University, 1949.

Klapper, J. T. *Effects of mass communication.* Glencoe, Ill.: The Free Press, 1960.

Krossner, W. J. Density and dimensionality in the attainment of conjunctive concepts. *Psychonomic Science*, 1966, 6, 265-266.

Laughlin, P. R. Conditional concept attainment as a function of if factor complexity and then factor complexity. *Journal of Experimental Psychology*, 1968, 77, 212-222.

Lazarsfeld, P. F., Berelson, B., & Gaudet, H. *The people's choice*, 2nd ed. New York: Columbia University Press, 1948.

Leventhal, H., & Singer, D. L. Cognitive complexity, impression formation and impression change. *Journal of Personality*, 1964, 32, 210-226.

Luchins, A. S. Mechanization in problem solving: the effect of Einstellung. *Psychological Monographs*, 1942, 54 (248).

Luchins, A. S. Primacy-recency in impression formation. In C. I. Hovland (Ed.), *The order of presentation in persuasion*. New Haven, Conn.: Yale University Press, 1957. Pp. 33-61. (a)

Luchins, A. S. Experimental attempts to minimize the impact of first impressions. In C. I. Hovland (Ed.), *The order of presentation in persuasion*. New Haven, Conn.: Yale University Press, 1957. Pp. 62-75. (b)

Maccoby, E. E., Maccoby, N., Romney, A. K., & Adams, J. S. Social reinforcement in attitude change. *Journal of Abnormal and Social Psychology*, 1961, 63, 109-115.

Mackworth, J. F. Deterioration of signal detectability during a vigilance task as a function of background event rate. *Psychonomic Science*, 1965, 3, 421-422.

Maier, N. R. F., & Maier, R. A. An experimental test of the effects of "developmental" versus "free" discussion on the quality of group decisions. *Journal of Applied Psychology*, 1957, 41, 320-323.

Marlowe, D., & Gergen, K. J. Personality and social interaction. In G. Lindzey and E. Aronson (Eds.), *The handbook of social psychology*. Reading, Mass.: Addison-Wesley, 1969.

Marrow, A. J., & French, J. R. P. Changing a stereotype in industry. *Journal of Social Issues*, 1945, 1, 33-37

McGuire, W. J. A syllogistic analysis of cognitive relationships. In C. I. Hovland and M. J. Rosenberg (Eds.), *Attitude organization and change*. New Haven, Conn.: Yale University Press, 1960. Pp. 65-111. (a)

McGuire, W. J. Cognitive consistency and attitude change. *Journal of Abnormal and Social Psychology*, 1960, 60, 345-353. (b)

McGuire, W. J. Attitudes and opinions. *Annual Review of Psychology*, 1966, 17, 475-514.

McGuire, W. J. The nature of attitudes and attitude change. In G. Lindzey and E. Aronson (Eds.), *The handbook of social psychology*. Vol. 3. Reading, Mass.: Addison-Wesley, 1969. Pp. 136-314.

McKeachie, W. J. Individual conformity to the attitudes of classroom groups *Journal of Abnormal and Social Psychology*, 1954, 49, 282-289.

Miller, H., & Bieri, J. Cognitive complexity as a function of the significance of the stimulus objects being judged. *Psychological Reports*, 1965, 16, 1203-1204.

Miller, N., & Campbell, D. T. Recency and primacy in persuasion as a function of the timing of speeches and measurement. *Journal of Abnormal and Social Psychology*, 1959, 59, 1-9.

Mills, J., Aronson, E., & Robinson, H. Selectivity in exposure to information. *Journal of Abnormal and Social Psychology*, 1959, 59, 250-253.

Mills, J., & Ross, A. Effects of commitment and certainty upon interest in supporting information. *Journal of Abnormal and Social Psychology*, 1964, 68, 552-555.

Monty, R. A., Karsh, R., & Taub, H. Keeping track of sequential events: irrelevant information and paced rehearsal. *Perceptual & Motor Skills*, 1967, 24, 99-103.

Morgan, B. B., & Alluisi, E. A. Effects of discriminability and irrelevant information on absolute judgments. *Perception & Psychophysics*, 1967, 2, 54-58.

Osgood, C. E., & Tannenbaum, P. H. The principle of congruity in the prediction of attitude change. *Psychological Review*, 1955, 62, 42-55.

Pishkin, V. Dimension availability with antecedent success or failure in concept identification. *Psychonomic Science*, 1965, 2, 69-70.

Ranken, H. B., & Dowling, W. J. Language and thinking: the interaction of naming with relevance and concreteness. *Psychonomic Science*, 1965, 3, 459-460.

Ranken, H. B., & Wang, H. S. Language and thinking: the interaction of amount of pretraining and relevance in the effect of naming on problem solving. *Psychonomic Science*, 1965, 3, 461-462.

Rhine, R. J. Some problems in dissonance theory research on information selectivity. *Psychological Bulletin*, 1967, 68, 21-28.

Rigney, J., Bieri, J., & Tripodi, T. Social concept attainment and cognitive complexity. *Psychological Reports*, 1964, 15, 503-509.

Ring, K., & Kelley, H. H. A comparison of augmentation and reduction as modes of influence. *Journal of Abnormal and Social Psychology*, 1963, 66, 95-102.

Rokeach, M. *The open and closed mind*. New York: Basic Books, 1960.

Rosen, S. Post-decision affinity for incompatible information. *Journal of Abnormal and Social Psychology*, 1961, 63, 188-190.

Schroder, H. M., Driver, M. J., & Streufert, S. *Human information processing*. New York: Holt, Rinehart & Winston, 1967

Schroder, H. M., & Streufert, S. The measurement of four systems of personality structure varying in level of abstractness: sentence completion method. Princeton University: ONR Technical Report No. 11, 1963.

Scott, W. A. Cognitive complexity and cognitive balance. *Sociometry*, 1963, 26, 66-74.

Sears, D. O. Biased indoctrination and selectivity of exposure to new information. *Sociometry*, 1965, 28, 363-376.

Sears, D. O., & Freedman, J. L. The effect of expected familiarity with arguments upon opinion change and selective exposure. *Journal of Personality and Social Psychology*, 1965, 3, 420-426.

Signell, K. A. Cognitive complexity in person perception and in nation perception: a developmental approach. *Journal of Personality*, 1966, 34, 517-537.

Solomon, R. L. Punishment. *American Psychologist*, 1964, 19, 239-253.

Star, S. A., & Hughes, H. M. Report on an educational campaign: the Cincinnati plan for the United Nations. *American Journal of Sociology*, 1950, 55, 389-400.

Steiner, G. A. *The people look at television*. New York: Knopf, 1963.

Steiner, I. D. Receptivity to supportive versus nonsupportive communications. *Journal of Abnormal and Social Psychology*, 1962, 65, 266-267.

Stewart, R. H. Effect of continuous responding on the order effect in personality impression formation. *Journal of Personality and Social Psychology*, 1965, 1, 161-165.

Streufert, S. Conceptual structure, communicator importance and interpersonal attitudes toward deviant and conforming group members. *Journal of Personality and Social Psychology*, 1966, 4, 100-103.

Streufert, S. Complexity and complex decision making: convergences between differentiation and integration approaches to the prediction of task performance. Journal of Experimental Social Psychology. 1970, 6, 494-509.

Streufert, S., Bushinsky, R. G., & Castore, C. H. Conceptual structure and social choice: a replication under modified conditions. *Psychonomic Science*, 1967, 9, 227-228.

Streufert, S., & Castore, C. H. Information search and the effects of failure: a test of complexity theory. *Journal of Experimental Social Psychology*, 1971, 7, 125-143.
Streufert, S., & Driver, M. J. Conceptual structure, information load and perceptual complexity. *Psychonomic Science*, 1965, 3, 249-250.
Streufert, S., & Driver, M. J. Impression formation as a measure of the complexity of conceptual structure. *Educational and Psychological Measurement*, 1967, 27, 1025-1039.
Streufert, S., Driver, M. J., & Haun, K. W. Components of response rate in complex decision making. *Journal of Experimental Social Psychology*, 1967, 3, 286-295.
Streufert, S., & Schroder, H. M. Conceptual structure, environmental complexity and task performance. *Journal of Experimental Research in Personality*, 1965, 1, 132-137.
Streufert, S., Streufert, S. C., & Castore, C. H. Conceptual structure, increasing failure and decision making. *Journal of Experimental Research in Personality*, 1969, 3, 293-300.
Streufert, S., Suedfeld, P., & Driver, M. J. Conceptual structure, information search and information utilization. *Journal of Personality and Social Psychology*, 1965, 2, 736-740.
Suedfeld, P. Attitude manipulation in restricted environments: I. conceptual structure and response to propaganda. *Journal of Abnormal and Social Psychology*, 1964, 68, 242-247.
Suedfeld, P., & Hagen, R. L. Measurement of information complexity: conceptual structure and information pattern as factors in information processing. *Journal of Personality and Social Psychology*, 1966, 4, 233-236.
Terwilliger, R. F. Pattern complexity and affective arousal. *Perceptual & Motor Skills*, 1963, 17, 387-395.
Thistlewaite, D. L., de Haan, H., & Kamenetzky, J. The effects of "directive" and "nondirective" communication procedures on attitudes. *Journal of Abnormal and Social Psychology*, 1955, 51, 107-113.
Thistlewaite, D. L., & Kamenetzky, J. Attitude change through refutation and elaboration of audience counterarguments. *Journal of Abnormal and Social Psychology*, 1955, 51, 3-9.
Tripodi, T., & Bieri, J. Cognitive complexity, perceived conflict and certainty. *Journal of Personality*, 1966, 34, 144-153.
Tuckman, B. W. Interpersonal probing and revealing and systems of integrative complexity. *Journal of Personality and Social Psychology*, 1966, 3, 655-664.
Vannoy, J. S. Generality of cognitive complexity-simplicity as personality construct. *Journal of Personality and Social Psychology*, 1965, 2, 385-396.
Weiner, B., & Feldman, P. Information processing related to stimulus novelty and complexity in a signal detection paradigm. *British Journal of Psychology*, 1967, 58, 69-75
Wiggins, J. S. Personality structure. *Annual Review of Psychology*. Vol. 19. Palo Alto, Cal.: Annual Reviews, Inc., 1968. Pp. 293-350.
Witkin, H. A., Dyk, R. B., Faterson, H. F., Goodenough, D. R., & Karp, S. A. *Psychological differentiation*. New York: Wiley, 1962.
Wolfgang, A. Effects of social cues and task complexity in concept identification. *Journal of Educational Psychology*, 1967, 58, 36-40.
Wolfgang, A., Pishkin, V., & Lundy, R. M. Anxiety and misinformation feedback in concept identification. *Perceptual and Motor Skills*, 1962, 14, 135-143.

Zajonc, R. B. Cognitive theories in social psychology. In G. Lindzey and E. Aronson (Eds.), *The handbook of social psychology*. Vol. 1. Reading, Mass.: Addison-Wesley, 1968. Pp. 320-411.

Zander, A., & Curtis, T. Effects of social power on aspiration setting and striving. *Journal of Abnormal and Social Psychology*, 1962, 64, 63-74.

Zipf, S. G. Resistance and conformity under reward and punishment. *Journal of Abnormal and Social Psychology*, 1960, 61, 102-109.

V

Elaine Walster and Darcy Abrahams

Interpersonal Attraction and Social Influence

Personally attractive individuals often have a remarkable ability to influence others.

> Delilah, an early spy for the Philistines, was assigned to uncover the secret of Samson's strength. After much nagging she finally succeeded in learning Samson's secret and depriving him of his strength. The Bible's terse language reveals little of Delilah's technique (other than continual harassment), yet we may safely assume the presence of attraction and social influence.

> When most Russians looked at Rasputin they saw a physically repulsive peasant. But Tsar Nicholas II and his Tsarina did not see the flaws in Rasputin which to others were as obvious as his outstanding odor. The Romanoffs insisted that Rasputin was personally attractive, and proved their devotion to him by acceding to all his requests. They even allowed Rasputin to control Russian policy, in spite of the outraged opposition of Russian citizens.

The preceding examples suggest that interpersonal attraction and social influence are sometimes intimately related. In this chapter we will explore the relationships between interpersonal attraction and social influence. In the first section, we will review the antecedents of interpersonal attraction. In the second section we will review the antecedents of social influence. Finally, in the third section, we will speculate about the relationship between these variables.

Antecedents of Interpersonal Attraction

Definitions

This chapter will focus on two forms of attraction: liking and romantic love. *Liking* has been defined by a number of researchers (e.g., Newcomb, 1961; Homans, 1950); most definitions agree that liking is one person's positive attitude toward another, evidenced by the person's tendency to approach and interact with the other. Unusually intense liking between two persons is sometimes designated *companionate love*.

Researchers have tried a number of techniques to detect how much people like one another. In 1884, Francis Galton became convinced that metaphorical expressions often mirror physical reality. He proceeded to investigate "the inclination of one person toward another" (Webb et al., 1966, p. 151). On the basis of his observations of people seated next to each other at dinner, Galton concluded that the more the dinner partners were attracted to one another, the more they leaned toward one another. Galton evidently believed that insults could be discreetly traded in an upright position, but that sweeter words might best be spoken at an angle of less than 90°.

How close one stands to another, how much his pupils dilate when gazing at the other, how often he looks into the other's eyes, whether he chooses the other as a work partner, and his self-reports have all been used to assess how he feels about the other. (See Webb et al., 1966, for an intriguing description of the wide variety of unobtrusive techniques which have been used to determine how people feel about one another.)

Researchers have spent little time defining or investigating *romantic love*. Most theorists have simply assumed that love is simply very intense liking. A few researchers have suspected that love may be a unique emotional state. For example, Schachter (1964) might argue that a person is "in love" only if (1) he is in a physiologically aroused state when contemplating the loved one, and (2) he labels his feelings as "love."

Reinforcement Theories

The principle which is most often cited to explain interpersonal attraction is the *principle of reinforcement*. This principle states that people learn to like those who reward them and to dislike those who punish them. Several theorists have elaborated upon the relationship between reinforcement and interpersonal attraction. For example, Homans (1961) proposes that how much we like others depends entirely on how often and how much they reward us. He observes,

> A man's esteem depends upon the relative rarity of the services he provides ... If he has capacities of heart, mind, skill, experience, or even strength that they do not have, and he uses these capacities to reward others, he will get esteem from them. But if his capacities are of a kind that they also possess, or if these capacities are widely available in the group, he will not get much esteem even if he uses them in such a way as to reward others (p. 150).

The open secret of human exchange is to give the other man behavior that is more valuable to him than it is costly to you and to get from him behavior that is more valuable to you than it is costly to him (p. 62).

Byrne, London, and Reeves (1968) propose that there is an exact correspondence between reinforcement and attraction. They state: "Attraction toward X is a positive linear function of the proportion of positive reinforcements received from X or expected from X."

Other reinforcement theories have been proposed by Thibaut and Kelly (1959); Lott and Lott (1961); and Blau (1967).

All theorists agree that we like those who reward us. Unfortunately, as Berscheid and Walster (1969) lament:

> While it is generally accepted that "we will like those who reward us and dislike those who punish us," we must note that this statement does not, to any great extent, increase predictability in the area of interpersonal attraction. We have no equation which will permit us to add up all the reward a stimulus person will provide and balance them against the punishment which he will inflict and thus arrive at a total reward index which will tell us how much others will like him: A multitude of things may be rewarding or punishing to any individual at a given time. In addition, it is often the case that "one man's meat is another man's poison" individuals differ in what they find to be rewarding or punishing (p. 31).

Since it is impossible to calculate exactly what each individual will find rewarding at each point in time, researchers in interpersonal attraction have chosen a simpler strategy. They have concentrated on pinpointing reinforcers which are rewarding to most people most of the time. Such universally valued reinforcers are labeled *transituational reinforcers*.

A reinforcer can be universally valued for two reasons: (1) Everyone is deprived of that specific reward nearly all the time. For example, in an overpopulated world, habitually hungry people may come to value food under a wide variety of conditions. (2) The reinforcer is capable of reducing a wide variety of needs. For example, money properly spent can be used to relieve hunger, boredom, thirst, etc. In the following section we will review three of the rewards which have been found to be potent transituational reinforcers.

ANXIETY REDUCTION

When individuals are anxious, frightened, lonely, or unsure of themselves, the presence of others is particularly reinforcing. Schachter (1959) demonstrated that the cowardly crave company. Schachter invited college girls to participate in an experiment. After arriving at the experiment, some girls made the alarming discovery that the experiment involved extremely painful electric shocks. Other girls made the reassuring discovery that although they would be exposed to electric shock in the course of the experiment, the intensities involved were so very low that the "shocks" could best be described as mild tickles.

Once the girls had been frightened or calmed, Schachter then gave all of the girls an opportunity to affiliate with others. They were told that they could wait for the experiment to begin either in a private cubicle or in a cubicle shared with other girls. Schachter found that frightened girls were most inclined to seek the company of others. Sixty-three percent of the very frightened girls chose to wait with others: only 33 percent of the calm girls chose to affiliate. Additional support for this hypothesis comes from Gerard and Rabbie (1961); Sarnoff and Zimbardo (1961); Zimbardo and Formica (1963); and Darley and Aronson (1966).

Why do people seek company when they are frightened? Schachter examined several alternative explanations of this behavior: (1) *Escape.* When one is reluctantly trapped in a frightening situation he may seek company in the hope that others will be able to figure out a way to avert the cause of fright. (2) *Cognitive Clarity.* Volunteering for an experiment and then discovering that you will be severely shocked is a once in a lifetime experience. Individuals in this ambiguous setting may seek company in the hope of gaining a better understanding of this unsettling event. (3) *Indirect Anxiety Reduction.* Individuals may seek company in order to take their minds off the forthcoming shock. (4) *Direct Anxiety Reduction.* Frightened subjects may hope that their fellow students will give them emotional support. (5) *Self-Evaluation.* When individuals are placed in confusing situations they generally worry about whether or not their reactions are "normal." High-anxiety subjects undoubtedly experience a variety of conflicting emotions when they discover they are about to be shocked. They may feel frightened, curious, angry, timid, etc. Very frightened girls may seek out company in the hope of receiving information which will enable them to better label and identify their own ambivalent feelings.

On the basis of subsequent research, Schachter concluded that frightened individuals choose to associate with others for two reasons: they hope to receive direct anxiety reduction (reassurance) and they hope to receive information which will allow them to evaluate the normality of their feelings.

A physiological explanation of the fact that individuals seek company when they are frightened is also available. According to Bovard (1959), both physical and psychological stress produce dramatic physiological changes. They both produce a pituitary-adrenal response which stimulates carbohydrate metabolism and protein breakdown. Bovard argues that this pituitary-adrenal response is maladaptive; it diminishes the individual's chances of coping with the stressful situation. However, this maladaptive response can be dampened in a very simple way; the individual can seek out the company of a companion. Research has documented that the presence of a comrade will markedly reduce the physiological disturbance of a stressed individual, and thus increase his chances of survival. Individuals should quickly learn that when they are frightened, they will be better able to handle difficult situations (both physically and psychologically) if they surround themselves with agreeable companions.

ADMIRATION

As Homans (1961) points out, social approval is the epitome of a transituational reinforcer. Individuals value the esteem of others highly and will generally exert a great deal of effort to attain this reward.

When one has been deprived of affection, the approval of others becomes especially reinforcing. A number of investigators have demonstrated that deprived individuals are especially responsive to social approval (e.g., Stevenson and Odum, 1962). Of course, the converse is also true: deprived individuals become unusually frustrated when they seek social approval and are rejected.

The principle that deprived individuals react to rewards and punishments with unusual strength, suggests that the social relations of unpopular individuals might be especially volatile. According to the preceding reasoning, unpopular adolescents might be especially susceptible to falling in love with any suitor who professes his own infatuation. Scarce resources are valuable and, to the unpopular youth, an admiring date is rare and valuable indeed. But woe to the suitor who is caught feigning interest. The insecure adolescent who is desperately seeking admiration will hate the date who humiliates her.

Support for the proposition that individuals with low self-esteem (those who receive little social approbation) will be especially appreciative of dates who proffer affection and especially resentful of those who do not, comes from Dittes (1959), Walster (1965), and Jacobs, Walster, and Berscheid (1970).

CONFIRMATION THAT OUR BELIEFS ARE CORRECT

Festinger (1954) argues that people discover early in life that holding incorrect opinions can be punishing or even fatal. Thus, they soon develop a drive to evaluate (and evidently to affirm) the correctness of their opinions and beliefs. When one discovers that someone else agrees with his attitudes and opinions, he is given support for the notion that his opinions are correct. This presumably is a pleasant experience. When another disagrees with his opinions, it is a punishing experience. Byrne (1961) observes "disagreement raises the unpleasant possibility that we are, to some degree, stupid, uninformed, immoral, or insane" (p. 713).

Byrne and his associates have demonstrated in numerous experiments that when one discovers that another shares his opinions, he increases his liking for the other. Evidently everyone behaves a bit like the Disraeli character who unashamedly affirmed: "My idea of an agreeable person . . . is a person who agrees with me."

Byrne, Ervin, and Lamberth (1970) found that in natural settings, individuals quickly discover whether or not potential dates share their attitudes, and, on that basis, decide whether or not to be friends. The authors selected two types of couples to go out on brief coffee dates. Half of the couples selected were similar in personality and attitudes. Half were dissimilar in personality. All of the couples went out for coffee. Even in the brief amount of time they were allowed for conversation, students soon detected whether or not they had similar attitudes. Similar couples became much more attached to one another in the course of conversation than did dissimilar couples. Similar couples liked each other better, stood closer to one another, judged each other to be more physically attractive, and more often wished to continue dating one another than did dissimilar couples.

There are obviously many other transituational reinforcers besides those we have detailed. Many of these are elucidated in Berscheid and Walster (1969).

In summary, research makes it clear that we will like those who provide us with rewards, who cooperate with us in our attempts to attain rewards for ourselves, or who are physically present when we are rewarded. The complement of this observation is also true: we will dislike those who punish us, who frustrate our attempts to obtain rewards, or who are present when we are punished (Dollard et al., 1939; Berkowitz, 1962).

The Exchange Theories

Thus far, we have been writing as if individuals are most content when attaining as many rewards as possible at the least possible cost to themselves. We will see that this perspective is too limited. Even if one assumes that a man is completely selfish, one must acknowledge that it is not in any man's self-interest to remain oblivious to the needs and feelings of others. When everyone is competing for the same rewards, a man who refuses to compromise and tries to hoard all the valuables would not be expected to survive for long. The necessity for accommodating oneself to others' needs is so universal that every culture has institutionalized a system for equitably apportioning scarce resources among its members (Levi-Strauss in de Jong, 1952). Of course, the definition of what is equitable varies enormously among cultures.

In spite of the fact that different societies have established surprisingly different procedures for apportioning their resources, a general principle has been found useful in characterizing what is equitable. Homans (1961), Blau (1967), Adams (1965), and Walster, Berschied, and Walster (1970) have contributed to this formulation.

These theorists define an equitable relationship as one in which everyone receives what he "deserves"—or in the terms of equity theory—when everyone receives outcomes appropriate to his inputs. If anyone receives more rewards or fewer rewards than he deserves, the relationship is inequitable and uncomfortable for its participants.

Participants in inequitable relationships have been found to handle their discomfort in one of two different ways: (1) They try to correct the inequitable conditions. For example, an uneasy boss may encourage his underpaid and overworked secretary to take a day off. Or, the exploited secretary may herself demand time and a half for overtime. (2) They do nothing to correct the inequity, but they attempt to justify it. Human beings seem to be surprisingly adept at distorting reality in order to reassure themselves that the world is as they wish it to be. Research indicates that both the exploiter and the exploited often respond to inequities by denying they exist.

The statement that *exploiters* often justify their exploitation is not too surprising to us. It is a common observation that people easily rationalize the harm they do to others. Even those who commit atrocities are able to devise complex rationalizations for their behavior. Several are especially popular: denigration of the victim, minimization of his suffering, and denial of one's responsibility for his suffering.

That harmdoers will often denigrate their victims was evident to the ancients. Tacitus observed, "It is a principle of human nature to hate those you have injured." Experimental support for this insight comes from Davis and Jones (1960), Glass (1964), and Walster and Prestholdt (1966). According to Sykes and Matza (1957) juvenile delinquents often defend their victimization of others by arguing that those they rob or "mug" are homosexuals or bums. In tormenting others, the delinquents claim to be the restorers of justice rather than harmdoers.

Sykes and Matza (1957), and Brock and Buss (1962) found that harmdoers consistently underestimate how seriously they have injured another. Brock and Buss found that college students who administered electric shocks to other students generally denied that their fellow students suffered or that the shocks they administered really hurt. In daily life, denial of responsibility seems to be a favorite strategy of those who are accused of exploiting others. That harmdoers will often deny their responsibility for harmdoing has been documented by Sykes and Matza (1957) and by Brock and Buss (1962, 1964).

Victims also sometimes justify inequitable relations. Generally, exploited individuals are persistent in their attempts to secure restitution. Sometimes, however, the victim finds that he is not able to secure it. The impotent victim is then left with two options: he can acknowledge that he is exploited and that he is too weak to do anything about it; or, he can justify his exploitation. Often, victimized individuals find it less upsetting to distort reality and justify their victimization than to acknowledge that the world is unjust and they are too impotent to elicit fair treatment (Lerner and Matthews, 1967).

Victimized individuals have been found to justify their own exploitation in several ways. Victims sometimes console themselves by imagining that their exploitation has brought compensating benefits.

Sometimes they try to convince themselves that the exploiter actually deserves his excessive outcomes. Recent data document that the exploited engage in such systematic distortions. Jecker and Landy (1969), Walster and Prestholdt (1966), and Hastorf and Regan (personal communication) pressured students into performing a difficult favor for an unworthy recipient. They found that the abashed favor-doer would try to justify his misguided philanthropy by convincing himself that the recipient was especially needy or worthy.

Reformers who work to alleviate social injustices are often at a loss when they discover that the exploited are themselves sometimes vehement defenders of the status quo. Integrationists encounter "Uncle Toms," who defend white supremacy. Women's Liberation groups find themselves facing housewives who angrily defend the inferior status of women. Reformers have more sympathy for such

Interpersonal Attraction and Social Influence

"Uncle Toms" and "Doris Days" when they understand the psychological underpinnings of such reactions. When one is treated inequitably, but has no hope of altering his situation, it is often less degrading to deny reality than to face up to one's humiliating position.

In summary, we can stand by our earlier statement that individuals like those who reward them and dislike those who punish them. However, the preceding section alerts us to the fact that a man often finds that what is materially rewarding is not always spiritually satisfying. One way he can handle his dilemma is to decrease his liking for the man he has exploited. Similarly, the man who is exploited is not merely deprived of material benefits—his confidence in the fairness of the world is shaken. He may choose to maintain his illusions by denying he is exploited. A knowledge of the material benefits conferred on an individual is not, in itself, enough to enable us to predict how he will respond. A knowledge of the symbolic meaning of these benefits is also necessary.

The Balance Theories

Balance theorists would certainly agree that reinforcement is an important determinant of interpersonal attraction. They would point out, however, that one can best predict human behavior if he supplements his knowledge of reinforcement principles with an understanding of the way that information is organized and stored in the mind. Individuals do not separately evaluate and store each of their experiences, they generalize or develop a consistent picture, of others that enables them to react to others in reliable ways.

Two balance theories—the balance theory of Heider and cognitive dissonance theory of Festinger—have most intrigued researchers.

HEIDER'S BALANCE THEORY

Heider's (1958) balance theory deals with the kinds of relationships that exist between a person, P, another, O, and an object of mutual concern, X. Two kinds of relations—sentiment relations and unit relations—are emphasized.

Sentiment relations may be either positive or negative. When P likes, loves, or values another, he has a positive sentiment toward O, which we have labeled +L. When P dislikes O, he has a negative sentiment, or -L.

Unit relations may also be of two types: separate entities comprise a unit when one perceives them as either belonging together (+U) or segregated (-U). According to Heider, the Gestalt principles of perceptual organization provide a reliable guide as to whether or not P will perceive separate entities as units. Similarity, proximity, common fate, good continuation, set, and past experience are all factors which are said to induce unit formation.

Heider argues it is intuitively obvious which kinds of sentiment and unit relationships are balanced and which are not. In discussing imbalanced relationships, for example, he says:

> In some ways we sense that the factors in the situation "do not add up;" they seem to pull in different directions. They leave us with a feeling of disturbance that becomes relieved only when change within the situation takes place in such a way that a state of balance is achieved (p. 180).

Scientists prefer precise rules to intuitions, however. Thus Heider specifies the following rules for determining if a dyadic relationship is balanced or imbalanced: "A dyad is balanced if the relations between the two entities are all positive (+L and +U) or all negative (-L and -U). Disharmony results when relations of different sign character exist" (p. 202).

According to Heider's formulation, sentiment and unit relations tend toward a balanced state. This means, then, that if we can vary the unit relations between people, we should be able to effect their liking for one another. Darley and Berscheid (1967) tested this notion in an ingenious experiment. If one knows he is going to be required to interact intimately with another (thus forming a + unit relationship with him), he will come to like the other.

The authors led college girls to expect that they would soon be discussing their sexual standards with another girl. The students were

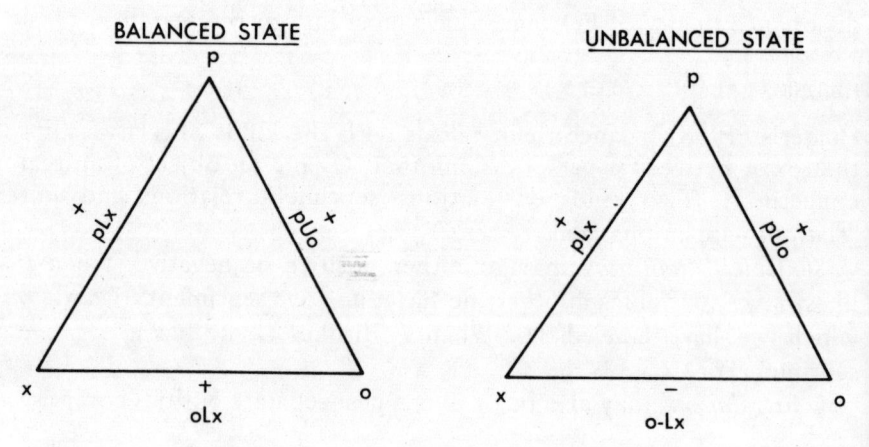

Figure 5.1. Graphic Representation of Balanced and Unbalanced States

then given ambiguous information about the personalities of two girls—their future discussion partner and a stranger with whom they knew they would have no further contact. The girls' impressions of both girls were recorded. It is evident that students develop marked biases in favor of their discussion partners. Whichever girl is introduced as the future partner is seen as being the more likable girl. Girls also claim that had they been allowed to choose their own partner, they would certainly have chosen the girl who had been randomly assigned to be their partner.

An even more striking demonstration that we like those with whom we expect to interact comes from a study by Berscheid, Boye, and Darley (1968). Students were led to believe that they would soon be forced to associate with an undesirable character. Even under such unpromising circumstances students were able to find some good in their partner. They generally stood by their undesirable partner even when they were subsequently allowed to choose any partner they wished.

The finding that forced association breeds acceptance was a source of rare encouragement to community relations experts. Reformers often spend a lifetime trying to change discriminatory policies, only to conclude that their dedicated efforts have changed little. Perhaps they have managed to integrate a few token minority members into new communities or into new occupations. Such realizations are devastating. The preceding research suggests that the modest accomplishments of reformers may not be as limited as they seem. Token integration may do a great deal more than provide improved working conditions for a few minority members. Opponents of reform are fond of arguing that legislation can't change men's hearts. To the extent that legislation forces men to interact, legislation might well have a dramatic impact on their hearts.

Heider's theory also applies to triadic relations: "A triad is balanced when all three of the relations are positive or when two of the relations are negative and one is positive. Imbalance occurs when two of the relations are positive and one is negative" (p. 202).

According to Heider, balanced states are stable states; unbalanced states generally evolve into more balanced states. Thus, from a knowledge of the unit and sentiment relationships existent between people, and a knowledge of whether or not the relationships are balanced, we can predict what kinds of relationships are likely to evolve between individuals. Let us see how this theory operates: Imagine that I like Mae West movies. If my roommate reveals that she shares my enthusiasm for Mae West movies, our relationship is balanced. Someone close to me (+U) likes (+L) the same things that I like (+L). Intuitively, this situation seems psychologically comfortable, and, according to Heider's definition the relationship is balanced.

Now imagine that I discover that my roommate (+U) disdains (-L) the Mae West movies I so much admire (+L). My discovery places me in an unpleasant, unbalanced state. The relationship can be restored to balance only if appropriate change are made in our sentiment or our unit relations. Several balance restoring changes are possible: (1) I can decide that anyone who has the poor taste to dislike Mae West movies is not going to be my roommate any longer *(P–UO)*; (2) I can decide I don't approve of Mae West after all *(P–LX)*; or (3) I can conveniently conclude that my roommate was only teasing, that deep in her heart she really loves Mae West *(O+LX)*. Any one of the preceding changes would restore balance to our relationship.

Data exist to support the notion that individuals prefer psychologically balanced states to unbalanced ones, and that unbalanced states are more unstable than balanced ones (Heider, 1958).

Several conclusions follow from the proposition that we will like those who share positive sentiment and unit relations with us: (1) We should generally prefer those who are similar to us to those who are dissimilar. Support for this proposition comes from Byrne and his associates (1961). (2) We should like those who share our own high opinion of ourselves. Support for this plausible conclusion comes from Newcomb (1961) and Backman and Secord (1959). (3) We should like those who live and work in close proximity to ourselves. Evidence for this proposition comes from a variety of sources. For example, students are known to develop stronger friendships with those students who share their classes, reside in their dormitory or apartment building, or who sit near them in class, than with students who are geographically located only slightly further away (Maisonneuve, Palmade, & Fourment, 1952; Willerman & Swanson, 1952; Festinger, 1951; and Byrne & Buehler, 1955).

Propinquity is also an important factor in mate selection. The greater the distance between potential marriage partners the less likely they are to marry (Kennedy, 1943; Katz & Hill, 1958). In a perhaps tongue-in-cheek observation, Bossard (1932) notes that individuals already living together are most likely to marry.

FESTINGER'S THEORY OF COGNITIVE DISSONANCE

The balance theory which has generated the most research is Festinger's theory of cognitive dissonance (1957). The basic unit which the theory utilizes is the "cognition." "Cognition" is any knowledge, opinion, or belief about the environment, about oneself, or about one's behavior that a person might hold.

Dissonance theory is concerned with the relationship that an individual's ideas have with one another. The theory states that three types of cognitive relationships are possible: dissonant, consonant, or irrelevant relations. Cognitions are said to be in a *dissonant* relationship if they are incompatible. Cognitions can be incompatible for several reasons. They may logically contradict one another, in the individual's own thinking. For example, if a person believes that marihuana rots the mind, and at the same time he believes marihuana is harmless, he would experience dissonance. Cognitions can also be dissonant because they contradict one's past experience. For example, if one discovered that the longer he sunbathed, the whiter his skin became, he would experience dissonance. Cognitive elements are in a *consonant* relationship if one element follows from another on logical or experiential grounds. Finally, cognitions can be in a totally *irrelevant* relationship to one another. For example, the cognitions "letters Q and Z are omitted from the telephone dial" and "very few men wear wool bathing suits" would probably be judged by nearly everyone to be totally irrelevant to one another.

Once we classify cognitions as dissonant, consonant, or irrelevant, we can calculate the total amount of dissonance existing between two clusters of cognitive elements. The magnitude of dissonance may be assessed utilizing the following formula:

$$\text{Dissonance} = \frac{\text{Importance} \times \text{number of dissonant elements}}{(\text{Importance} \times \text{number of dissonant elements}) + (\text{Importance} \times \text{number of consonant elements})}$$

According to Festinger, the existence of dissonance is psychologically uncomfortable and motivates one to try to reduce the dissonance and achieve consonance. The more dissonance one is experiencing, the more eager he will be to reduce his existing dissonance.

There are several ways an individual can eliminate dissonance. He can change his attitude, change his behaviors, or change the relative importance or number of cognitions which support his position. Let us illustrate some of these techniques by example: Imagine that an unmarried Catholic girl is taking birth control pills to prevent pregnancy. She may well experience dissonance, since her behavior is inconsistent with her attitudes. On the one hand, she classifies herself as a good Catholic who rigorously obeys all Church laws. On the other hand, she is aware that by taking the pill she is violating Church law, which proscribes both birth control and sexual dalliance. How can this girl reduce her dissonance? (1) She can abandon her dissonant behavior. She can bring her behavior into conformity with her religious values. (2) She can abandon her dissonance-producing attitudes. She can accept the fact that she is not a good Catholic and fall away from the Church. (3) She can add additional cognitive elements to buttress her behavior. For example, she can seek out friends who will persuade her that it is a good idea for her to have sexual relations with her boyfriend, that sexual relations should be separated from procreation, and that she should take the pill to prevent conception. (4) She can reduce the importance of her "un-Catholic" behavior. She can catalog all the Church laws and convince herself that to break only one out of 8,764 laws is really only a minor deviation—especially considering how conscientiously she has avoided "coveting her neighbor's wife," "striking out the eye" of her enemy, and milling corn on the Sabbath.

Researchers interested in interpersonal relations quickly saw and tested the implications of dissonance theory for interpersonal relations. On the basis of the theory, they hypothesized that if an individual is led to treat a neutral stranger in a cruel way or in an uncommonly generous way, his attitudes should soon become consistent with his cruel or generous behavior. If a person harms another, he would be expected to come to dislike the person he has harmed. If he does a favor for another, he would be expected to come to like his beneficiary. Evidence supporting these predictions was discussed in the section on exchange theories.

Researchers also hypothesized that the more perceived choice an individual has about whether to exploit or befriend another person, the more dissonance he should experience, and the more he should reduce his dissonance by denigrating a victim or aggrandizing a beneficiary. These hypotheses were confirmed by Davis and Jones (1960) and Davidson (1964).

Glass (1964) pointed out that the higher an individual's self-esteem is the more it disturbs him to harm another. If one believes that he has a preponderance of unfavorable characteristics, and is just the kind of vile person who would harm others without cause, he should not experience dissonance when he realizes he has injured another. He may well realize that he has behaved in a socially disapproved way. However, his cruel, socially disapproved act is actually consonant with his general low self-regard. When one believes he is a fine, kind, intelligent person, however, the discovery that he has behaved reprehensibly should be much more upsetting. His cruel behavior conflicts both with social norms and with his self-image. Thus, Glass concludes, the higher a harmdoer's self-esteem, the more he should be motivated to explain away his cruel behavior by denigrating his victim.

Data support Glass' derivations. Glass led students to shock a fellow student. Some students were given a choice about whether or not to shock their comrade; some were simply told they must shock him. The students' liking for their comrade was then assessed. The result indicated that Glass was correct. When students had a choice about whether or not to harm the victim, the harmdoers with high self-esteem defended their actions by denigrating the victim; harmdoers with low self-esteem did not. When subjects were forced to harm the victim, subjects apparently did not experience dissonance. No denigration occurred in either self-esteem condition.

In summary, we can conclude that the balance theories supplement reinforcement theory. Balance theorists point out that the rewarding and punishing experiences we have with others must be organized in meaningful and consistent ways. The balance theory notion that one's behavior and attitudes are generally consistent, and the supporting research lead us to several conclusions: (1) We generally come to like those we help, those who are in close proximity to us, are similar to us, or who like us. (2) We generally come to dislike those who we injure, who are segregated from us, dissimilar to us, or dislike us.

Physiological and Cognitive Determinants of Emotional States

On the basis of an ingenious series of experiments, Schachter (1964) proposed a paradigm for understanding human emotional response. He argued that in order for a person to experience true emotion, two factors must coexist: (1) The individual must be physiologically aroused, and (2) He must label his stirred-up state in emotional terms. Schachter argued that neither physiological arousal nor appropriate labeling *alone* is sufficient to produce an emotional experience.

A drug, Adrenalin, exists whose effects mimic the discharge of the sympathetic nervous system. Shortly after one receives an injection of Adrenalin, systolic blood pressure increases markedly, heart rate increases somewhat, cutaneous blood flow decreases, muscle and cerebral blood flow increase, blood sugar and lactic acid concentration increase, and respiration rate increases slightly. The individual who has been injected with Adrenalin experiences palpitation, tremor, and sometimes flushing and accelerated breathing. These reactions are identical to the pysiological reactions which accompany a variety of natural emotional states.

An injection of Adrenalin will not, by itself, engender an emotional response in a person. When an individual is injected with

Adrenalin and asked about his feelings, he will report either no emotional response or, at most, report feeling "as if" he might be experiencing some emotion (Marañon, 1924). The person who has been injected with Adrenalin perceives that something is not quite authentic about his reactions. Schachter argued that what is missing is an appropriate label for the physiological reactions he is experiencing. If Marañon's drugged individuals had been led to attribute their stirred-up state to some emotion-arousing event (rather than attributing it to their shot), Schachter would argue that they would experience a "true" emotion.

In order to test his notion that both physiological arousal and appropriate cognitions are indispensable components of true emotional experiences, Schachter manipulated these two components separately in an experiment. Schachter and Singer (1962) recruited volunteers for an experiment ostensibly investigating the effects on vision of a new vitamin compound, Suproxin. Volunteers were injected with a substance which was identified as Suproxin. Actually, one half of the students were injected with Adrenalin and one half with a placebo. By manipulating an appropriate explanation Schachter wished to lead some of the volunteers to attribute their physiological state to a nonemotional cause (the injection) and others to attribute it to an emotional cause.

In the *nonemotional attribution* condition, individuals were given a complete explanation of how the shot would affect them. They were warned that in 15 to 20 minutes the injection of "Suproxin" would cause palpitation, tremor, etc. Presumably, when students began to experience these symptoms, they could properly attribute their stirred-up state to the shot and would not attribute their excitement to the activities in which they were engaging at the time the Adrenalin began to take effect.

In the *emotional attribution* conditions, things were arranged to discourage students from attributing their stirred-up state to the shot. One group of volunteers was given no information about possible side effects of the shot. Presumably most volunteers would assume that there were no side effects. A second group of volunteers was deliberately misled as to the potential side effects of the shot. They were told the shot might produce an itching sensation all over their body and a slight headache. In both groups it was assumed that volunteers would be unlikely to attribute their tremors and palpitations to the shot (since these symptoms occurred 20 minutes after the shot and were not described as possible consequences of the shot). Instead, it was assumed that they would be likely to attribute their stirred-up state to whatever they happened to be doing when the drug began to take effect 20 minutes after injection. Schachter

Interpersonal Attraction and Social Influence

then arranged things so that "what they happened to be doing" was participating in a social setting conducive to producing elation or to producing anger.

Schachter placed students in one of two different settings, a euphoria setting and an anger setting. Some volunteers were placed with an experimental accomplice who had been trained to act euphorically. Some volunteers were placed with an accomplice who was trained to act angrily. Shortly after the volunteer received his injection, he was introduced to another subject. The experimenter indicated that both of them would soon have their vision tested; the tests however could not begin until the "Suproxin" could get from the injection site into the bloodstream (a process which presumably took 20 minutes). Students were told to wait in a room which was in a state of great disarray. There were scratch pads, rubber bands, pencils, etc., littered about. As soon as the experimenter left, the stooge began his dramatic presentation. Schachter (1964) described the euphoria setting:

> ...the stooge introduced himself again, made a series of standard icebreaker comments, and then went into his routine. He reached first for a piece of paper, doodled briefly, crumpled the paper, aimed for a wastebasket, threw, and missed. This led him to a game of basketball in which he moved around the room crumpling paper and trying out fancy basketball shots. Finished with basketball, he said, "This is one of my good days. I feel like a kid again. I think I'll make a plane." He made a paper plane, spent a few minutes flying it around the room and said, "Even when I was a kid, I was never much good at this." He then tore off the tail of the plane, wadded it up, and making a sling-shot out of a rubber band, began to shoot the paper. While shooting, he noticed a sloppy pile of manila folders. He built a tower of these folders, then went to the opposite end of the room to shoot at the tower. He knocked down the tower and, while picking up the folders, he noticed a pair of hula hoops behind a portable rock board. He took one of these for himself, put the other within reaching distance of the subject, and then began hula-hooping. After a few minutes he replaced the hula hoop and returned to his seat, at which point the experimenter returned to his room (p. 57).

In the anger setting subjects were introduced to the confederate, and asked to fill out a questionnaire while they were waiting for the Suproxin to be absorbed by the bloodstream. This time, however, the confederate's behavior was designed to make the subject angry.

Most people dislike filling out questionnaires, even under the best of circumstances. Multiple-choice questions often force one to choose between several inappropriate or ambiguous answers. Schachter capitalized on this general aversion and attempted to construct a really horrendous questionnaire—one that would offend everyone who read it. This "model" questionnaire asked a series of personal and insulting questions. For example, one question asked: "How many men (other than your father) has your mother had extra-marital relationships with? (a) Four and under. (b) Five through nine. (c) Ten and over." The conference pretended to complete the questionnaire along with the subject. The confederate's complaints about the questionnaire were mild at first, he grew increasingly quarrelsome, and finally he became enraged. He ripped up his questionnaire and slammed it to the floor shouting angrily, "I'm not wasting any more time. I'm getting my books and leaving," and stomped out of the room.

Schachter tested the hypothesis that both a physiological and psychological component were necessary for an emotional experience by assessing the subjects' emotional reactions to the confederates' behavior.

After viewing the euphoric or the angry confederate, two measures of the intensity of the subjects' emotional responses were obtained. First, the behavior of the volunteers in the euphoric and the angry conditions was closely recorded by observers stationed behind a one-way mirror. The raters assessed to what extent the subject caught the stooge's euphoric or angry mood. For example, in the euphoria condition observers recorded whether or not the subject tossed paper wads out the window. In the anger condition they recorded whether or not the subject joined the confederate in complaining about the offensiveness of the questions. On the basis of these ratings, an estimate was made as to how euphoric and how angry each subject seemed to be.

A second type of measure, a self-report questionnaire, was also collected. The subject was asked to describe his present mood, and to estimate how euphoric and angry he felt.

The experimental findings confirmed Schachter's theory. When subjects had been informed about the physiological side effects which accompanied the shot, the confederate's euphoria or anger was not contagious. In this condition, subjects were simply puzzled about why the confederate was getting so worked up over nothing. Obviously, subjects concluded, the reason the confederate felt excited was that he had received a shot. Subjects attributed their own stirred-up state to the same source—the shot.

When subjects were ignorant of how they should feel (or had been misinformed) *and had received a shot of Adrenalin*, they quickly caught the stooge's mood. They were excited and they attributed their stirred-up state not to the shot, but to the "great fun" they were having or to "the insulting questionnaire" they had been asked to answer. They judged themselves to be euphoric or angry. The emotional responses of control subjects (who had received a placebo shot) were muted.

From these findings, Schachter concluded that two components were necessary before an individual could experience a true emotion. (1) He must become emotionally aroused. (2) He must be able to attribute this arousal to some emotional cause.

The Schachterian framework generates a number of intriguing hypotheses concerning romantic attraction. Our reactions to other people are often inconsistent, vague, and difficult to label. In many cases we are unsure of what we feel or why we feel it. Given this state of affairs, it seems plausible that whether or not an aroused individual will conclude he is "in love" will depend to a great extent on how those around him interpret his behavior.

Schachter made several wildly creative and semiserious suggestions as to how one might indirectly implant in a reluctant suitor the notion that he was in love.

For example, in one scenario, a Machiavellian teaching assistant would strategically mount a heat lamp in the ceiling of his office. As soon as an eligible male came to visit, an attractive young coed would casually sit down next to him. The teaching assistant would be in control of the heat lamp. When the visitor turned to speak to the girl, the teaching assistant would turn on the heat lamp. The visitor should soon notice that he was growing warm; perhaps blushing. The instant he turned his attention away from the girl and toward the TA, the heat lamp would be turned off. The visitor would discover that he had become his usual poised, cool self. Again and again, as the visitor shifted his attention from the girl to the TA, he would find his temperature fluctuating. We might expect that the boy would soon begin to wonder why the girl unnerved him to such an extent; possibly he would conclude that he was unusually attracted to her.

Of course, the content of the girl's conversation would be very important in determining whether or not the boy interpreted his blushing as affection. If the girl were cold and sarcastic he might well interpret his "blushing discomfort" as embarrassment or as hostility.

Schachter's reasoning reminds us of an important principle: One should be very careful about the emotional interpretations he supplies to others. When one labels another's reactions, he may well be creating reality, rather than merely interpreting it. The wife, unsure of her husband, who keeps complaining: "You don't love me, you just think you do. If you loved me you wouldn't treat me this way," is voicing a dangerous conclusion. She may turn out to be right. By consistently interpreting her husband's actions in a damaging way, for long enough, she may effect an actual alteration in his feelings for her.

When one re-examines the romantic literature from the Schachterian perspective, one is surprised at how easily previously inexplicable phenomena fit into his framework. (See Walster, 1970.)

Romantic love has always been acknowledged to be a puzzling phenomenon; love often seems to emerge under the most unlikely conditions. Poets and writers chronicle the stories of disastrous affairs in which one loves the one woman who cannot love him. Young lovers sometimes discover they are hopelessly in love, often at the very time when it is most important to inhibit sexual expression. Individuals sometimes find that they love and hate the same person. Superficially, these observations are puzzling. Some of these variables (loneliness, anger, frustration, etc.) seem more likely to predispose individuals to dislike others rather than to love them. Poets have been inclined to attribute these inexplicable choices to the essential illogic of love. But the Schachterian framework offers another explanation. Perhaps it does not really matter how one produces an agitated state in the lover. So long as one can lure the lover into labeling his agitation as passion, one may secure the emotional response he wishes. If this conclusion is true we may have a key to a previously enigmatic phenomenon.

Many writers have noticed that strong emotional arousal breeds love—although not, of course, interpreting this relationship in Schachterian terms. Finck (1891), for example, concludes:

> Love can only be excited by strong and vivid emotions, and it is almost immaterial whether these emotions are agreeable or disagreeable. The Cid wooed the proud heart of Diana Ximene, whose father he had slain, by shooting one after another of her pet pigeons. Such persons as arouse in us only weak emotions or none at all, are obviously least likely to incline us toward them ... Our aversion is most likely to be bestowed on individuals who, as the phrase goes, are neither "warm" nor "cold"; whereas impulsive, choleric people, though they may readily offend us, are just as capable of making us warmly attached to them (p. 240).

Valins (1966) speculated that, in generating emotion, it is probably more important that one believe that he is having a strong physical reaction to another than that he actually have one. Valins tested his hypothesis in an ingenious experiment. Valins recruited male college students for a study of males' physiological reactions to sexual stimuli. The sexual stimuli Valins used were ten seminude *Playboy* photographs. Men were told that while they scrutinized these photographs, their heartbeat rate would be amplified and recorded. Men were led to believe that their heartbeat rate altered markedly to some of the photographs but that they had no reaction at all to others. (Valins assumed that men would interpret an alteration in heart rate as sexual enthusiasm.)

The men's liking for the "arousing" and "nonarousing" photographs was then assessed in three ways. (1) Men were asked to rate how "attractive or appealing" each pin-up was. Men preferred the pin-ups they believed were arousing to all others. (2) Men were offered a pin-up in remuneration for participating in the experiment. They chose the arousing pin-ups more often than the non-arousing ones. (3) Finally, men were interviewed a month later (in a totally different context) and asked to rank the attractiveness of the pin-ups. Several weeks later the men still markedly preferred the arousing pin-ups to the others.

Brehm et al. (1970) found some evidence that the Schachterian framework may be applicable in romantic settings. The authors demonstrated that when males were severely frightened before being introduced to an attractive girl, they liked her better than they would under normal conditions. Presumably, men would rather attribute their beating heart to affection than to cowardice.

The evidence seems to be compelling that two components—physiological arousal and appropriate labeling—must exist before one can experience true emotion. The judgments of those around us as to how we should label our experiences thus become important determinants of what we do experience.

Antecedents of Social Influence

Definitions

"Social influence" refers to the power individuals possess to affect the attitudes and behaviors of others. When one persuades others to change their *attitudes*, or when he forces them to *conform* to his expectations regardless of their attitudes, he is exerting "social influence."

How do the two components of social influence—conformity and attitude change—differ? An *attitude* is defined as a person's readiness to respond toward a particular object, or class of objects in a favorable or unfavorable manner. *Conformity* is defined as a behavioral change that occurs as a result of some real or imagined group of pressures. We can easily demonstrate the difference between these two concepts with a practical example.

A barber, who is determined that the long-haired young men who enter his shop will emerge with wholesome crew cuts, might attempt to influence his client's attitudes by pointing out the advantages of crew cuts, and the numerous liabilities of "curly, fuzzy, snaggy, shaggy, ratty, matty, oily, greasy . . . hair." By his arguments, the barber is hoping to transform the client's neutral or negative attitude toward crew cuts into a positive one. If persuasion fails, however, the barber might resort to forcing his client to *conform* to his dictates.

The barber might warn his patron that if he does not let the barber dictate his hair style, the client might get an "extra-close" shave

Although in the preceding example the distinction between conformity and attitude change seems clear, in practice it is often difficult to distinguish between them. Often men who seem to be acting out of conviction are really only reluctantly acquiescing to social pressure. Sometimes men who have been coerced into conforming end up changing their convictions. This section will focus on the antecedents of both conformity and attitude change. In the few cases when a variable is known to effect *only* conformity or *only* attitude change, we will point out this fact.

In the previous section we reviewed several theories which help us to understand why individuals like or dislike others. These same theories are useful in predicting when individuals will be influenced by others.

Learning Theory

In 1898 Thorndike proposed a simple learning paradigm: "Pleasure stamps in; pain stamps out." Unfortunately learning theorists were not satisfied with this tidy formulation; they soon developed more complicated, and somewhat more accurate theories about the way rewards and punishments affect attitudes and behavior. (See, for example, Doob, 1947; Hovland, Janis, & Kelley, 1953; Scott, 1959; and Staats, 1967.)

If society properly applied reinforcements, it could have an enormous impact on human behavior. However, learning theory principles are seldom utilized in solving important social problems. Why has such useful information been so neglected?

To control another's reinforcements, one must be able to control himself and the environment. To gain such control is often impossible. As McConnell (1970) points out:

> We can train flatworms to do a great many things because we've learned the proper techniques and because we follow instructions exactly . . .
>
> It took years, but we now know enough that we can train the animals very quickly. We have no trouble training worms, but we have one hell of a time trying to train new laboratory assistants. We explain our findings to them, and they nod their heads, but they don't really believe us and they don't really understand.
>
> I have a friend, a distinguished scientist, who visited my lab one day. He was so fascinated by the worms that he wanted to train one himself . . . .
>
> The flatworm crawled along the maze quite nicely, came to the first choice point, and headed into the black alley. Of course, my friend pressed on the wrong button, gave a shock of the wrong polarity and propelled the poor worm into the black alley. "Silly animal," the man muttered; he pressed the wrong button again. The worm went further into the wrong alley. "Get out

of there, you idiot," he shouted at the worm, and held the shock button down for several seconds.

The worm, I regret to say, went into convulsions about this time and simply lay on its back writhing. My friend thrust the control apparatus back into my hands, advised me that the damned worm was obviously too stupid to learn even the simplest task, and stalked out of the lab.

The more that I think about it, the more convinced I am that the mistake was all mine. Why should I let him try to train a worm ... or a rat ... or a human being unless he had been given the proper education first? (p. 14-15)

Perhaps the most explicit theory concerning the impact that rewards and punishments have on attitudes was developed by Doob (1947). According to Doob, an attitude is "an implicit response." It is "evoked by a variety of stimulus patterns, as a result of previous learning or of gradients of generalization and discrimination." That is, attitudes are learned, and are expressed only in appropriate situations. Doob argues that whether an attitude will persist or will change depends on at least three factors. (1) *The reward or punishment associated with the expression of the attitude.* An attitude will persist when it is consistently reinforced; it will change when it is partially or wholly extinguished. (2) *Conflicts with competing drives.* If the drive strength of an attitude is weak in comparison with other attitudes or drives which are aroused simultaneously, the attitude may be suppressed. For example, an individual may possess an extremely unfavorable attitude toward traffic policemen. When he is stopped by a policeman, however, he might carefully avoid expressing his negative attitude because he has an even stronger prejudice against going to jail. He behaves, therefore, in accord with the stronger attitude. (3) *The process of forgetting.* If the stimulus patterns which arouse the attitude do not appear in the environment for a length of time, the attitude may weaken.

One of the first experiments investigating the efficacy of reinforcement in modifying attitudes was reported by Razran (1940). Razran chose social political slogans such as "Down with War and Racism!" and "America for Americans" as his attitudinal stimuli. One set of slogans was presented when his hungry subjects were enjoying a free lunch. The other set of slogans was presented when the subjects were surrounded by disgusting odors. After several such "conditioning" sessions, observers rated the attractiveness of each slogan. Razran found that slogans associated with the lunch (reinforcement) increased in attractiveness; slogans associated with unpleasant odors (punishment) became less attractive. Razran (1940), Staats, Staats, and Briggs (1958), and Janis, Kaye, and Kirschner (1965) also demonstrated the effectiveness of reinforcements in modifying attitudes.

Learning Theory Versus Dissonance Theory

For the most part, reinforcement and cognitive consistency theories supplement one another. In a very few instances the two theories make opposite predictions. One theoretical conflict has generated unusual controversy.

Learning theory predicts that the more reward associated with an act, the more pleasure the actor experiences when contemplating the act and the more inclined he is to repeat the act. Dissonance theory makes an opposite prediction. It predicts that the less incentive a person has to perform an act, the more compelled he is to personally defend his action once he's done it. Thus, they predict the less you offer someone to do something, the more he will come to value doing it for its own sake.

The focal point of the reinforcement-dissonance controversy has been an experiment conducted by Festinger and Carlsmith (1959). In this experiment, the authors asked students to perform a very monotonous task. After a student had completed it, the experimenter implored him to "pinch-hit" for his regular research assistant, who had failed to show up, and to inform the next subject that the task he had just performed was "very interesting." The amount of money the students were offered to lie was varied. Some were offered $1.00 to lie, others were offered $20.00. After a subject had lied to his fellow student, he was asked to evaluate the experiment. The results supported the dissonance theory prediction. The less money the subject was given to praise the boring experiment, the more inclined he was to argue that the experiment was an interesting one. Aronson and Carlsmith (1963) and Freedman (1963) provided further support for the dissonance predictions and further opposition to reinforcement predictions.

Proponents of "incentive theory" soon took up the cudgels. Janis and Gilmore (1965) and Rosenberg (1965) conducted experiments, which they argued explained away the dissonance findings and supported the reinforcement theory. Dissonance theorists such as Linder, Cooper, and Jones (1967) quickly countered with research in which they explained away the reinforcement findings and supported the dissonance point of view.

The results of most recent experiments indicate that both theories are partially correct. In a theoretical discussion of the issues involved in the dissonance-incentive controversy and an accompanying review of the literature, Aronson (1966) concludes that high incentives, taken by themselves, may lead a person to greater attitude change. If, however, a powerful opposing force, due to dissonance, is set into motion, the dissonance-reduction effects may overpower the effects due to incentive. Dissonance effects and reinforcement effects seem *not* to be mutually exclusive; reinforcement effects will emerge when cognitive dissonance has been minimized in the experimental operations. Research by Carlsmith, Collins, and Helmreich (1966) supports this notion.

Essentially, then, human behavior seems to be a compromise between the desire to secure immediate rewards and the desire to appear to be logically consistent.

Conformity Versus Attitude Change

Thus far we have surveyed those factors which effect both conformity and attitude change. However, some authors have focused on the differences in these two forms of social influence, rather than on the similarities.

Festinger (1953) distinguished between compliance (public compliance without private acceptance) and attitude change (public compliance with private acceptance). According to Festinger, threats may make a man conform, but they will not change his attitudes. He argues that a person will change his attitudes only if his relationship with the communicator is valuable to him.

Simply by observing people, it is, of course, difficult to determine whether they are conforming out of fear or conviction. Festinger (1953) proposed two methods for empirically distinguishing between compliance and true attitude change. The two techniques he proposed were: (1) "Observation of public behavior together with the elicitation of a private response" (p. 247). An individual who takes a different position, in private, than he is willing to admit to in public, would seem to be more of a conformer than a "true believer." (2) "Observation of behavior before and after the removal of the source of influence" (p. 246). If the instant the communicator's influence is removed, an individual stops complying, it seems obvious that previously he was merely complying because of social pressures.

Festinger's point can easily be illustrated. Suppose one Sunday afternoon a young woman is observed at a zoo entrance milling around with a large group of people, and carrying a sign which reads "Zoos are Prisons—Free the Animals." The young woman may be picketing the zoo because: (1) Her boyfriend has issued an ultimatum: "No picketing, no dates." (2) Her zoology text has convinced her that zoos are inhumane. (3) She was hired as a shill by the Society for Prevention of Cruelty to Animals.

Festinger would argue that we can determine whether the girl's behavior was conformity or attitude change by observing her behavior at a subsequent zoo demonstration, when the preceding influences have been removed—that is, we can examine the girl's behavior when she has switched to a less domineering boyfriend, she has completed her zoology course, or the SPCA has run out of money. If, in spite of the changed conditions the girl nevertheless was present and waving her sign at the next zoo gathering, we could guess that her crusading actions had become independent of the original influence. We would assume true attitude change had occurred. If, on the other hand, the girl rudely snickered and pointed at the demonstrators while walking her leashed and muzzled dog, it is likely that her former feelings toward animals were transient and depended on external encouragement.

Kelman (1961) distinguishes among *three* different types of social influence—compliance (similar to Festinger's "public compliance without private acceptance"), identification (similar to "public compliance with private acceptance"), and internalization. According to Kelman:

Compliance can be said to occur when an individual accepts influence from another person or from a group because he hopes to achieve a favorable reaction from the other. He may be interested in attaining certain specific rewards or in avoiding certain specific punishments that the influencing agent controls (p. 462).
Identification can be said to occur when an individual adopts behavior derived from another person or a group because this behavior is associated with a satisfying self-defining relationship to this person or group (p. 463)
Internalization can be said to occur when an individual accepts influence because the induced behavior is congruent with his value system (p. 465).

Kelman cautions that these three processes of social influence are not mutually exclusive and would rarely exist in a pure state in nature.

In summary, two general theoretical approaches, learning theory and cognitive consistency theory, are useful guides to improving social influence.

Learning theory posits that if one can control the administration and timing of reinforcements, he can develop and maintain the attitudes he wishes in others. To be effective in changing attitudes, however, one must be precise in his application of learning theory principles. Dissonance theory posits that individuals relentlessly pursue cognitive consistency. Attitudes which are consistent with other cognitions will be stable and difficult to change. If one wishes to change attitudes, he should make the attitude he wishes to establish appear to be consistent with the listener's other cognitions and make the attitudes which he wishes to change appear to be incompatible with the listener's other cognitions.

Interpersonal Attraction and Social Influence

Empirical Evidence

Interpersonal attraction and social influence are so intimately related that if one understands each process, he can probably intuit the relationships between them. Thus, many readers may already feel they can guess at many of the ways in which attraction and influence are related. Nearly all theorists agree that a likable person will be more effective in exerting social influence than will be a less likable person. Some theorists have attempted to specify precisely the relationship between these two variables: they contend that there is a monotonic relationship between attractiveness and the ability to elicit attitude change or conformity (e.g., Festinger, Schachter, & Back, 1950; Moreno, 1934; and Kelley & Shapiro, 1954).

Among the first studies to demonstrate that likable people are influential people were the classic investigations of group cohesiveness. *Group cohesiveness* denotes the attraction of membership in a group for its members.

Cohesiveness theorists argue that the more attractive a group is to its members, the more eager these members will be to prevent the group from disintegrating, and thus the harder they will try to secure agreement on important issues. For example, Festinger, et al. (1952) argue that "... pressures toward uniformity in a group are manifested in at least three ways: by readiness to change (one's own) opinion, by attempts to influence others in the group, and by a tendency to reject disagreers from the group" (p. 327). These three procedures combine to insure that cohesive groups will be more uniform than will be noncohesive groups.

Back (1951) demonstrated that in cohesive groups, members do make unusual efforts to agree with their colleagues or to persuade their colleagues to agree with them.

Back manipulated cohesiveness in an imaginative way. In essence, Back applied Lawrence Durrell's (1961) insight to the laboratory. Durrell said:

> Balthazar claimed once that he could induce love as a control experiment by a simple action: namely telling each of two people who had never met that the other was dying to meet them, had never seen anyone so attractive, and so on. This was, he claimed, infallible as a means of making them fall in love: they always did ...

This insight was translated into an experimental manipulation in the following way: In some groups Back told members that they were likely to get along remarkably well with their discussion partner. In other groups he told individuals that they would probably get along "alright." As Back had hoped, individuals who were assured they would especially like their companions did; individuals who were not given such information did not.

All partners were then subtly, but effectively, led to hold different opinions on a single issue. They were shown photographs of a discussion between a middle-aged man and a youth, and asked to make up a story about the discussion. Although ostensibly both partners had received the same pictures, actually the sets were slightly different. In one set, the middle-aged man appeared to be directing the discussion, in the other, the youth was clearly in command. Each partner then wrote his own story about the pictures. (This undoubtedly crystallized their divergent impressions.) Then the partners discussed their stories. To their consternation, they soon discovered that they had interpreted the same set of pictures in diametrically opposed ways.

Back found that in the cohesive groups, members made a *greater* effort to argue out their differences than did members of less cohesive groups. In less cohesive groups, members tended to withdraw from the discomforting discussion. The intense persuasive efforts made in cohesive groups seem to have been generally successful. By the end of the discussion, compatible groups agreed on an interpretation of the picture sequence more than did less friendly groups.

Festinger et al. (1952) also documented that members of highly cohesive groups are especially receptive to their partners' influence attempts. They manipulated cohesiveness much as Back had done: by leading some people to believe that their group would be unusually congenial and leading others to believe that scheduling problems had made the aggregation of a congenial group difficult. The authors then led some of the members in the various groups to believe that few group members shared their opinions. Upon making the discovery that they deviated from the group, members of highly congenial groups changed their opinions more readily than did members of the uncongenial groups.

Many recent researchers (e.g., Hare, 1962; Lott & Lott, 1961 corroborate the finding that attractive groups demand and secure unusual conformity from their members.

Theoretical Bases for the Attraction-Influence Relationship

Virtually all the theories we have discussed would lead us to expect attractive communicators to be especially effective communicators. The various theories disagree, however, about what particular characteristic of the likable person makes him so effective. Attracted people differ in many ways from others. For example, if all we know about two individuals is that they are "friends," we would be wise to guess that they probably live near to one another, that they have plans to see one another soon, that they hold similar opinions, and that they mediate valuable rewards for one another

Many theories would emphasize these correlated variables in their attempts to explain why likable people will be powerful people, rather than concentrating on the impact of liking itself. Learning and cognitive theories would focus on liking itself in attempting to explain the interpersonal attraction/social influence relationship.

Let us first consider those explanations for the fact that likable people are influential people which focus on variables correlated with liking

LIKING, PROPINQUITY, AND SOCIAL INFLUENCE

One generally spends a great deal of time with his friends, and conscientiously avoids his enemies. Newcomb (1961) shrewdly observes that people rarely have to "fight it out" with their enemies. They simply avoid seeing those they feel are obnoxious long before things ever get to the fighting stage.

The fact that we voluntarily spend most of our time with those we like gives our friends an enormous advantage in influencing us. They have almost unlimited opportunities to present us with the persuasive information they possess. Thus, the fact that a friend is a frequent associate gives him an extra advantage in exerting social influence.

LIKING, COMMITMENT, AND SOCIAL INFLUENCE

During the course of friendship, one commits himself in numerous ways to his friends. He commits himself to seeing his friends at various times in the future, to treating them with kindness and consideration, to helping them out of difficulties (or at least not unduly adding to their problems), etc. Such commitments may seem trivial, but they have been found to be enormously important in shaping behavior (see Brehm & Cohen, 1962).

Several theorists have pointed out how important such commitments can be in crystallizing attitude change. Kelman (1961) distinguished three types of social influence—compliance, identification, and internalization. Presumably, the first two types of social influence—compliance and identification—cannot occur unless the listener is committed to the communicator. According to Kelman, a communicator can elicit compliance or identification only so long as the listener is committed to his relationship with the communicator. The minute the relationship is permanently dissolved, the communicator's message will lose all effectiveness. The importance of commitment in facilitating attitude change has been demonstrated experimentally (cf.Kiesler & Corbin, 1965).

LIKING, THE POWER TO PRAISE OR REJECT OTHERS, AND SOCIAL INFLUENCE

Everyone wants to be liked. Most individuals will markedly alter their behavior in order to win social approval.

The story may be apocryphal, but according to student lore, professors find vague signs of life in their students so rewarding, that if a group of students follow some simple procedures, they can easily condition their professor to perform bizarre behaviors. The following strategy is reputed to be effective: When the professor lectures in his normal voice, the students look blank or bored. However, every time he raises his voice or strikes the lectern to emphasize a point, a marked transformation occurs in the students—they beam with enthusiasm and sudden understanding. According to students and reinforcement theorists, the professor should soon learn to lecture in an ear-shattering shout, accompanied by vigorous pounding.

The approval of strangers is valuable to us, but the approval of our intimates is indispensible. The idea that our friends might cease to like us is very threatening. Thus, when they wish to influence us, friends have an especially valuable resource available to them. A friend can hint that he will continue to like us only if we continue to comply with his wishes. Of course, an acquaintance could make similar threats, but since we are less emotionally dependent on acquaintances than on friends, such threats would be far less potent.

A person's concern that his friends will reject him if he does not conform to their standards is usually a realistic concern. Few groups will tolerate nonconformity. Festinger et al. (1952) point out that on important issues, friends are even less tolerant of deviance than are strangers!

There is abundant evidence that one must conform or face rejection. In a classic study, Newcomb (1943) found that girls who did not conform with the political views that were cherished on their campus were almost always unpopular. Newcomb conducted his research at Bennington College in 1935-1939. At that time the Bennington faculty was uniformly liberal. The arriving students were not. Tuition was high, and entering students usually came from wealthy—and Republican—families. But students were soon socialized into liberal Bennington attitudes. For example, in the 1936 election, 62 percent of the newly-arrived freshmen were for the Republican candidate. Only 14 percent of the juniors and seniors favored the Republicans. As might be anticipated in such a political climate, individual prestige among upperclassmen was related to liberal attitudes.

The liberal political attitudes which were instilled in the Bennington girls were remarkably stable. In 1960, some twenty years after the girls had first been interviewed, Newcomb (1963) again interviewed the original sample. He discovered that very few of the matrons had drifted back into the conservative attitudes of their parents. When compared with a sample of American women of the same socioeconomic class, Bennington women were exceptionally liberal in their political views.

Tightly controlled experimental studies have also demonstrated that the penalty of deviation is rejection. Scientists from seven nations—Belgium, England, France, Germany, Holland, Norway, and Sweden—combined forces to conduct a most unusual experiment. Schachter et al. (1954) planned experiments to determine whether or not children from a wide variety of nations would be as relentless in their rejection of deviants as were American children.

The experiments were conducted in the following way. In each country, boys' aviation clubs were organized. A recruiter explained to boys that the Institute of Aviation was interested in forming clubs for interested boys. The clubs were glamorous organizations. Members would meet pilots, build models, see aviation movies, visit airfields, fly, etc. Needless to say, boys eagerly joined these clubs.

The experiment was conducted during each club's organizational meeting. At the start of the first meeting a model-building competition was announced. The experimenter described five different model airplane kits to the boys. Four of the models were extremely attractive motor-driven airplanes; the fifth was a plain glider. The boys were asked to choose a model and work on it together. Almost all of the boys preferred to work on the motor-driven model. One boy, however, was a confederate of the experimenters, and he always chose the glider. A discussion about the merits of the various planes then ensued. Throughout the discussion the confederate defended his deviant position in an objective and nonaggressive manner. Eventually, the experimenter terminated the discussion and then asked the boys to vote on the airplane they wished to build.

The experimenter was able to ascertain how much the deviate was liked compared to the other boys under the pretext of getting the club organized. Boys were told they would work together in small groups and were asked for their preferences in work partners. In addition, boys were asked to vote for a club president. The data made it clear that rejection is virtually a universal reaction to a deviate. In all countries the boy who stuck to his own deviate opinion was considered undesirable as either a working partner or as a club president. People are acutely aware that if they are deviant they will be estranged. Thus, when another's regard is important to them they are generally willing to conform to his standards—or at least pretend to do so. (See Jones, 1963.)

Often our loved ones control our attitudes and behavior so subtly and so persuasively that we do not even notice we are systematically conforming to their demands. Many of us do not even recognize the restraints that have been imposed on us until a sudden opportunity for liberation occurs and we experience an exhilarating rush of freedom.

Durrell (1961) discusses such a phenomenon when he reports the liberation one feels when wearing a mask:

> But what stamps the carnival with its spirit of pure mischief is the velvet domino—conferring upon its wearers the disguise which each man in his secret heart desires above all. To become anonymous in an anonymous crowd, revealing neither sex nor relationship nor even facial expression ... Nothing else to distinguish one by; the thick folds of the blackness conceal even the contours of the body. Everyone becomes hipless, breastless, faceless. And concealed beneath the carnival habit (like a criminal desire in the heart, a temptation impossible to resist, an impulse which seems preordained) lie the germs of something; of a freedom which man has seldom dared to imagine for himself. One feels free in this disguise to do whatever one likes without prohibition. All the best murders in the city, all the most tragic cases of mistaken identity, are the fruit of the yearly carnival; while most love affairs begin or end during these three days and nights during which we are delivered from the thrall of personality, from the bondage of ourselves (p. 191).

For Americans, conventions provide a ritualized opportunity to escape from usual inhibitions and restraints. The sudden attainment of anonymity produces unusual liberation for the convention delegate, and as a result he feels free to revel in most uncharacteristic behavior. As Festinger et al. (1952) observed, "The delegates to an American Legion convention, all dressed in the same uniform manner, will sometimes exhibit an almost overwhelming lack of restraint." Their research, and subsequent research by Singer, Brush, and Lubin (1965) and Zimbardo et al. (1967) confirm the hypothesis that when individuals feel anonymous (or "deindividuated") they are most likely to engage in socially disapproved behavior.

Likable people, then, have an advantage in controlling our attitudes and behavior because their regard is unusually important to us. We soon learn how readily our friends will reject us if we behave "peculiarly," and learn to acquiesce—almost automatically—to the standards of those whose good opinion we value.

Interpersonal Attraction and Social Influence

LIKING, BALANCE, AND SOCIAL INFLUENCE

The prediction that likable people will be persuasive people flows most directly from Heider's (1958) balance theory. When we agree with a friend—or disagree with an enemy—about some issue, we are in a comfortable, balanced state. If we disagree with a friend or agree with an enemy on some issue, however, we are in an imbalanced, unstable state.

An individual in an unbalanced state can reestablish balance in several ways: He can repudiate his friendship. He can change his opinion on the single issue in question. Usually, friends are seen as being less expendable than one's convictions.

According to the balance formulation, then, friends are much more effective communicators than neutral acquaintances or enemies. An enemy is not only an ineffective communicator—he is a disastrous one. The minute a disliked communicator upholds a cause, his listeners are likely to unite to defeat it

Several generations of cunning, devious, and slippery researchers have been fascinated by the notion that one could recruit individuals to a cause by arguing against it. A typical fantasy runs something like this: An advertising agency would be hired to promote the election of Candidate Charlatan. The agency would immediately issue an announcement that they were donating their servies to help elect his rival, Candidate Smith. With an unfailing eye, the ad agency would then round up a collection of Smith supporters, so repulsive in appearance and so obnoxious in manner, that they would unfailingly engender hatred in any voter. These offensive backers would then deliver their endorsements. One would expect these endorsements to be totally effective—in motivating voters to support our Charlatan.

Just what it takes to design a speech so poor that it drives people in the opposite direction has been the subject of much speculation. Hovland, Janis, and Kelley (1953) suggested several rules to guide one in producing boomerang effects. They suggest that a boomerang communication: (1) be delivered by a noncredible source; (2) contain no arguments favorable to the position taken in the communication, since even ridiculous arguments are taken seriously by many people; (3) lead audience members to anticipate that the communicator's conclusions will consistently oppose their own best interests; (4) arouse anger or resentment, by making offensive statements; (5) cause the communicatee to experience guilt and anxiety from the realization that he was in the process of accepting a position that is contrary to beliefs and standards of a group he values; and (6) take a position so outrageously far from the initial position of the audience that a "contrast" effect occurs (cf. Sherif, Sherif, & Nebergall, 1965.

In spite of the plausibility of these recommendations, researchers have found it extremely difficult to produce boomerang effects in either laboratory or field settings. Thus far, only Cohen (1962), Berscheid (1966), and Abelson and Miller (1967) have been successful in devising successful boomerang effects.

Abelson and Miller produced boomerangs by utilizing the services of an insulting communicator. The experimenter posed as a roving reporter, interviewing individuals seated on park benches in Washington Square Park in New York City. After a person had been asked what he thought about Negro protest against job discrimination, a confederate seated nearby took exception to the speaker's statements. In one condition, the confederate simply stated his opposition to the subject. In the insult condition, the confederate also expressed his opposition, but this time he prefaced each of *his* opinion statements with an insult. He made such comments as: "That's ridiculous"; "That's the sort of thing you'd expect to hear in this part"; "That's obviously wrong"; "That's terribly confused"; or "No one really believes that." As was expected, the insulted individual became a more extreme advocate of his initial position than he had been before the gratuitous attack. Shouting wins enemies, not votes.

In summary, the evidence is abundant that likable people are unusually persuasive in a wide variety of situations. The communicator who is liked by his listeners is likely to possess a panoply of assets. He is likely to have easy access to the desired audience, to be perceived as a credible person, and to control important rewards for the listeners. These assets augment the advantage that likability itself gives one in persuading others.

The advice that when one wishes to persuade he should choose a communicator who is attractive to the audience may sound obvious. However, it is advice that is most difficult to follow. Those who plan attitude-change campaigns are subject to the same psychological laws as are those they are trying to persuade. Thus, public relations men often end up choosing a communicator who is attractive to *them* rather than a communicator who is attractive to their intended audience. The middle class, WASP, clean-shaven ad man who designs a campaign to convince drug users that speed is dangerous knows intellectually that he should get a communicator that is attractive to the drug culture. In his heart, however, he cannot really believe that a long-haired, disheveled inidvidual is an "attractive" communicator, even though group members tell him so. "Perhaps if the model just

Interpersonal Attraction and Social Influence

combed his hair *a little*, or clipped his sideburns." "Perhaps if he just wore a tie—a mod tie, of course." It is difficult for anyone to recognize that attractiveness does not reside in the object, but only in the eye of the beholder.

Usually it is only when an individual designs an appeal for his colleagues that he can select a truly "attractive," and effective, communicator. One of the most cunning and successful advertisements arguing that "Speed Kills" was designed by Frank Zappa of the Mothers of Invention. In a low-key appeal, Zappa said, "I would like to suggest that you do not use speed and here is why: It's going to mess up your heart, mess up your liver, kidneys and rot out your mind. In general, this drug will make you just like your father and mother." To the student group, this ad had great appeal. It is unlikely that parents, trying to convince their children of the same point, could have designed such a message, or would have had the ability to spot Zappa as an "attractive" communicator.

Exceptions to the Rule that Attraction Facilitates Social Influence

Assessing the Bases of Our Opinions

In only a few very special circumstances would one hesitate to employ the most likable person available as his communicator. Most of the time individuals respond in a semiautomatic way to influence attempts. After a communication is over, they certainly do not usually spend much time assessing how much their attitudes have changed, and trying to disentangle how much of the change in attitudes should be attributed to the communicator's likability and how much should be attributed to the compelling content of the message. In fact, people are probably generally reluctant to admit that the noncontent aspects of the message had *any* effect on their attitudes. On rare occasions, however, individuals do engage in such introspection. On occasion it becomes very important for one to be as objective as possible. At such times, individuals often try to identify and eliminate any nonrational pressures that might be effecting their behavior or attitudes. For example, imagine that a student is faced with the necessity of choosing a major. He may well make unusual efforts to analyze to what extent his inclination to become a brain surgeon is due to parental pressure, or to what extent his inclination to become a revolutionary is due to his girlfriend's enthusiasms. He hopes that by pinpointing such influences, he may be able to discount them somehow, and thereby, discover what *he* really wants to do. Usually when one tries to disentangle "illegitimate" influences from "rational" influences, he succeeds only in getting very confused.

On those rare occasions when a listener is trying very hard to assess and discount any such illegitimate influences on his attitudes, the attractive communicator might well lose the advantage he normally possesses. In a dissonance experiment, Zimbardo (1969) demonstrated that under certain very special conditions an attractive communicator may be a liability. The rationale for the experiment was as follows: The person who finds himself responding to an enemy's argument should experience dissonance; the person who finds himself agreeing with a friend should not.

When the person tries to analyze his reason for accepting the friend's or enemy's message, he has only two alternatives: (1) He can conclude that his change of heart was due to the obvious correctness of the message. (2) He can conclude that his conversion is due to the skill of the communicator. When one hates the communicator, it is undoubtedly more satisfying to attribute one's change of heart to the validity of the arguments than to attribute one's conversion to the charm of the obnoxious communicator The person who was swayed by the attractive communicator, on the other hand, should be more willing to admit that his conversion could have been partially due to the persuasive skill of the communicator. Zimbardo argues that if one has a good enough communication to completely change everyone's attitudes, he is better off having an unattractive communicator deliver it.

The details of Zimbardo et al.'s (1967) somewhat flamboyant experiment are interesting. The experiment was billed as a study of soldiers' and students' preferences for various survival foods. The authors chose as their communicator the brigade commander of NYU-ROTC. Zimbardo's first step was to teach the commander to be attractive or obnoxious at will. When the commander wanted to be an attractive person, he was unfailingly considerate and pleasant to an "assistant" helping with the experiment. He politely phrased his requests, called the assistant by his first name, and responded to a mistake by the assistant with equanimity and good humor. When the commander was posing as an obnoxious person, however, his behavior was quite different. He was cold and formal with his assistant. He referred to him by his last name and ordered him about in an annoyed and irritated way. When the assistant mistakenly brought in the wrong experimental food, the commander lost his temper and berated him. That the commander was insincere as well as offensive was also made evident when immediately after shouting at the assistant, he returned to the group, flashed a pasteboard smile, and continued speaking in the same agreeable tones that he had used before losing his temper.

After the commander was established as a "good guy" or a "bad guy," he delivered his persuasive communication. He attempted to persuade individuals to try a revolting survival food—fried grasshoppers. It is clear that fried grasshoppers were unattractive to participants. When they were asked to list their associations to fried grasshoppers, the following associations emerged: ugly, greasy appearance, slimy, shiny, charred, repulsive, squirming, eyes, wing, dirty, rat faces, might hurt me, burned them as a child, biology laboratory, graveyard, and not kosher. Nevertheless, about half of the participants (in both conditions) acquiesced to the commander's request to try grasshoppers.

The pattern of Zimbardo et al.'s results is clear and it supports the author's hypothesis. The individuals who tried the grasshoppers exaggerated their palatability. Those who refused to try grasshoppers showed boomerang effect; they convinced themselves that grasshoppers were even more disgusting than they had thought initially. In addition, the more dissonance the subjects had about trying or not trying the grasshoppers, the more they justified their behavior. Those who ate grasshoppers in response to the obnoxious commander's plea had great dissonance. As was expected, those who helped the negative communicator were much more likely to attribute their eating to the fact that grasshoppers were "not too bad," than were those who had helped the attractive communicator. On the other hand, of the men who refused to eat the grasshoppers, those who had refused to do a favor for a "good guy" had more need to justify their refusal than did men who refused to help the obnoxious commander. And, as dissonance theory predicted, the former group of men were more likely to exaggerate the repulsiveness of the grasshoppers than were the latter group.

When one has a totally effective message, one may be better off having it delivered by a communicator who is *not* extremely attractive. Then, should individuals subsequently question their own motives in accepting such a message, they will *not* be tempted to attribute their conversion to "the smooth-talking charm" of the communicator. It will be obvious to them that, if anything, the unattractive communicator must have been a liability.

Ambivalent Emotions

In virtually all texts, attraction is considered to be a unidimensional variable. It is assumed that attraction and hostility are mirror images of one another, and that the more we dislike someone, the less we like him. In most cases, such a conception of liking seems to accurately reflect reality. There is a good possibility, however, that in a few associations, attraction and hostility may be relatively independent: one might feel both extreme attraction and extreme hostility toward the same individual. Such mixtures of feelings probably exist more commonly in intimate relationships. For example, we may love *and* hate our best friend more intensely than we could ever love or hate a brief acquaintance. La Rochefoucauld claims that the more one loves a mistress, the more one is ready to hate her.

When we discussed romantic love, we suggested that a mixture of emotions might be a common prelude and accompaniment to romantic love. Schachter's (1964) research suggested all that was necessary to produce "love" was strong physiological arousal accompanied by the cognitive label "love." The physiological arousal so necessary to a romantic experience could presumably come from a wide variety of sources. Anxiety, anger, desperation, loneliness, and sexual arousal may all be potential sources of emotional arousal, which under the right circumstances, one might label as love.

If, in intimate relationships, liking and hostility do tend to go hand in hand, one's feelings for his loved ones might be expected to fluctuate dramatically. Generally, he would feel great love for his friend. When they argued, however, he might hate his friend more intensely than he could ever hate a stranger. Depending on the state of their friendship, then, the friend's communication effectiveness should alter. In choosing a communicator then, we are probably better off choosing a person that the listener holds in constant high regard, rather than choosing his loved ones, whom he may find to be extremely attractive—at times.

In summary, we have been able to discern two exceptions to the general principle that the more attractive a communicator is, the more effective he will be: (1) When one has a *completely effective* message, he should utilize a neutral or negative communicator. (2) One should avoid choosing a communicator who is *generally* attractive, but who, on rare occasions, is capable of arousing violent hatred or jealousy.

References

Abelson, R. P., & Miller, J. C. Negative persuasion via personal insult. *Journal of Experimental Social Psychology*, 1967, 3, 321-333.

Adams, J. S. Inequity in social exchange. In L. Berkowitz (Ed.), *Advances in experimental social psychology*. Vol. 2. New York: Academic Press, 1965. Pp. 267-300.

Aronson, E. Psychology of insufficient justification: an analysis of some conflicting data. In S. Feldman (Ed.), *Cognitive consistency*. New York: Academic Press, 1966. Pp. 116-133.

Aronson, E., & Carlsmith, J. M. Effect of the severity of threat on the devaluation of forbidden behavior. *Journal of Abnormal and Social Psychology*, 1963, 66, 584-588.

Back, K. The exertion of influence through social communication. *Journal of Abnormal Social Psychology*, 1951, 46, 9-24.

Backman, C. W., & Secord, P. F. The effect of perceived liking on interpersonal attraction. *Human Relations*, 1959, 12, 379-384.

Berkowitz, L. *Aggression: a social psychological analysis*. New York: McGraw-Hill, 1962.

Berscheid, E. Opinion change and communicator-communicatee similarity and dissimilarity. *Journal of Personality and Social Psychology*, 1966, 4, 670-680.

Berscheid, E., Boye, D., & Darley, J. M. Effects of forced association upon voluntary choice to associate. *Journal of Personality and Social Psychology*, 1968, 8, 13-19.

Berscheid, E., & Walster, E. *Interpersonal attraction*. Reading, Mass.: Addison-Wesley, 1969.

Blau, P. N. *Exchange and power in social life*. New York: Wiley, 1967.

Bossard, J. H. S. Residential propinquity as a factor in mate selection. *American Journal of Sociology*, 1932, 38, 219-224.

Bovard, E. W. The effects of social stimuli on the response to stress. *Psychological Review*, 1959, 66, 267-277.

Brehm, J. W., & Cohen, A. R. *Explorations in cognitive dissonance*. New York: Wiley, 1962.

Brehm, J. W., Gatz, M., Goethals, G., McCrimmon, J., & Ward, L. Psychological arousal and interpersonal attraction. Mimeographed paper, available from authors, 1970.

Brock, T. C., & Buss, A. H. Dissonance, aggression and evaluation of pain. *Journal of Abnormal and Social Psychology*, 1962, 65, 192-202.

Brock, T. C., & Buss, A. H. Effects of justification for aggression in communication with the victim on post-aggression dissonance. *Journal of Abnormal and Social Psychology*, 1964, 68, 403-412.

Byrne, D. Interpersonal attraction and attitude similarity. *Journal of Abnormal and Social Psychology*, 1961, 62, 713-715.

Byrne, D., & Buehler, J. A. A note on the influence of propinquity upon acquaintanceships. *Journal of Abnormal and Social Psychology*, 1955, 51, 147-148.

Byrne, D., London, A., & Reeves, K. The effect of physical attractiveness, sex and attitude similarity on interpersonal attraction. *Journal of Personality*, 1968, 36, 269-271.

Byrne, D., Ervin, C. R. & Lamberth, J. A continuity between the experimental study of attraction and real-life computer dating. Mimeographed paper, available from authors, 1970.

Carlsmith, J. M., Collins, B. E., & Helmreich, R. L. Studies in forced compliance: I. The effect of pressure for compliance on attitude change produced by face-to-face role playing and anonymous essay writing. *Journal of Personality and Social Psychology*, 1966, 4, 1-13.

Cohen, A. R. A dissonance analysis of the boomerang effect. *Journal of Personality*, 1962, 30, 75-88.

Darley, J. M., & Aronson, E. Self-evaluation vs. direct anxiety reduction as determinants of the fear-affliction relationship. *Journal of Experimental Social Psychology Supplement*, 1966, 1, 66-79.

Darley, J. M., & Berscheid, E. Increased liking as the result of the anticipation of personal contact. *Human Relations*, 1967, 20, 29-40.

Davidson, J. Cognitive familiarity and dissonance reduction. In L. Festinger (Ed.), *Conflict, decision and dissonance*. Stanford, Cal.: Stanford University Press, 1964. Pp. 45-60.

Davis, K. E., & Jones, E. E. Changes in interpersonal perception as a means of reducing cognitive dissonace. *Journal of Abnormal and Social Psychology*, 1960, 61, 402-410.

de Josselin, & DeJong, J. P. B. *Levi-Strauss's theory on kinship and marriage*. Leiden, Holland: Brill, 1952.

Dittes, J. E. Attractiveness of group as function of self-esteem and acceptance by group. *Journal of Abnormal and Social Psychology*, 1959, 59, 77-82.

Dollard, J., Doob, L., Miller, N., Mowrer, O., & Sears, R. *Frustration and aggression*. New Haven, Conn.: Yale University Press, 1939.

Doob, L. W. The behavior of attitudes. *Psychological Review*, 1947, 54, 135-156.

Durrell, L. *Balthazar*. New York: Dutton, 1961. P. 240.

Festinger, L. An analysis of compliant behavior. In M. Sherif and M. O. Wilson (Eds.) *Group relations at the crossroads*. New York: Harper, 1953. Pp. 232-256.

Festinger, L. Architecture and group membership. *Journal of Sociology Issues*, 1951, 1, 152-163.

Festinger, L. *A theory of cognitive dissonance*. Evanston, Ill.: Row Peterson, 1957.

Festinger, L. A theory of social comparison processes. *Human Relations*, 1954, 7, 117-140.

Festinger, L., and Carlsmith, J. M. Cognitive consequences of forced compliance. *Journal of Abnormal and Social Psychology*, 1959, 58, 203-210.

Festinger, L., Gerard, H., Hymovitch, B., Kelley, H., & Raven, B. The influence process in the presence of extreme deviates. *Human Relations*, 1952, 5, 327-346.

Festinger, L., Schachter, S., & Back, K. *Social pressures in informal groups: a study of human factors in housing*. New York: Harper, 1950.

Finck, H. T. *Romantic love and personal beauty: their development, causal relations, historic and national pecularities*. London: Macmillan, 1891.

Freedman, J. L. Attitudinal effects of inadequate justification. *Journal of Personality*, 1963, 31, 371-383.

Gerard, H. B., & Rabbie, J. M. Fear and social comparison. *Journal of Abnormal and Social Psychology*, 1961, 62, 586-592.

Glass, D. C. Changes in liking as a means of reducing cognitive discrepancies between self-esteem and aggression. *Journal of Personality*, 1964, 32, 520-549.

Hare, A. P. *Handbook of small group research*. New York: Free Press, 1962.

Heider, F. *The psychology of interpersonal relations*. New York: Wiley, 1958.

Homans, G. C. *The human group*. New York: Harcourt, Brace, 1950.

Homans, G. C. *Social behavior: its elementary forms*. New York: Harcourt, Brace, 1961.

Hovland, C. I., Janis, I. L., & Kelley, H. H. *Communication and persuasion*. New Haven, Conn.: Yale University Press, 1953.

Jacobs, L., Walster, E., & Berscheid, E. Self-esteem and attraction. Mimeographed paper, available from authors, 1970.

Janis, I. L., & Gilmore, J. B. The influence of incentive conditions on the success of role playing in modifying attitudes. *Journal of Personality and Social Psychology*, 1965, 1, 17-27.
Janis, I. L., Kaye, D., & Kirschner, P. Facilitating effects of eating-while-reading on response to persuasive communications. *Journal of Personality and Social Psychology*, 1965, 1, 181-185.
Jecker, J., & Landy, D. Liking a person as a function of doing him a favor. *Human Relations*, 1969, 22, 371-378.
Jones, E. E. *Ingratiation*. New York: Appleton-Century-Crofts, 1963.
Judges, *Holy Bible, King James Version*. Nashville: The Methodist Publishing House, 1911, 333-334.
Katz, A. M., & Hill, R. Residential propinquity and marital selection: a review of theory, method and fact. *Marriage and Family Living*, 1958, 20, 327-335.
Kelley, H. H., & Shapiro, M. M. An experiment on conformity to group norms where conformity is detrimental to group achievement. *American Sociology Review*, 1954, 19, 667-677.
Kelman, H. C. Process of opinion change. *Public Opinion Quarterly*, 1961, 25, 57-78.
Kennedy, R. Premarital residential propinquity. *American Journal of Sociology*, 1943, 48, 580-584.
Kiesler, C. A., & Corbin, L. H. Commitment, attraction and conformity. *Journal of Personality and Social Psychology*, 1965, 2, 890-895.
Lerner, M. J., & Matthew, C. Reactions to the suffering of others under conditions of indirect responsibility. *Journal of Personality and Social Psychology*, 1967, 5, 319-325.
Linder, D. E., Cooper, J., & Jones, E. E. Decision freedom as a determinant of the role of incentive magnitude in attitude change. *Journal of Personality and Social Psychology*, 1967, 6, 245-254
Lott, A. J., & Lott, B. E. Group cohesiveness, communication level, and conformity. *Journal of Abnormal and Social Psychology*, 1961, 62, 408-412.
Maisonneuve, J., Palmade, G., & Fourment, C. Selective choices and propinquity. *Sociometry*, 1952, 15, 135-140.
Maronon, G. *Rev. Franc. Endocrinal*. 1924, 2, 301-325.
Massie, R. K. *Nicholas and Alexandra*. New York: Atheneum, 1967.
McConnell, J. V. Stimulus/response: criminals can be brainwashed—now. *Psychology Today*, 1970, 3, 14-18.
Moreno, J. L. *Who shall survive? A new approach to the problem of human interrelation*. Washington, D. C.: Nervous and Mental Disease Publication Company, 1934.
Newcomb, T. M. Persistence and regression of changed attitudes: long range studies. *Journal of Social Issues*, 1963, 19, 3-14.
Newcomb, T. M. *Personality and social change*. New York: Holt, Rinehart & Winston, 1943.
Newcomb, T. M. *The acquaintance process*. Holt, Rinehart & Winston, 1961.
Razran, G. H. S. Conditioned response changes in rating and appraising sociopolitical slogans. *Psychological Bulletin*, 1940, 37, 481.
Rosenberg, M. J. When dissonance fails: on eliminating evaluation apprehension from attitude measurement. *Journal of Personality and Social Psychology*, 1965, 1, 28-42.
Sarnoff, I., & Zimbardo, P. G. Anxiety, fear, and social affiliation. *Journal of Abnormal and Social Psychology*, 1961, 62, 356-363.
Schachter, S., Nuttin, J., DeMonchaux, C., Maucorps, P. H., Osmer, D., Duijker, H., Rommetveit, R., & Israel, J. Cross-cultural experiments on

threat and rejection. *Human Relations*, 1954, 7, 403-440.

Schachter, S. The interaction of cognitive and physiological determinants of emotional state. In L. Berkowitz (Ed.), *Advances in experimental social psychology*. Vol. 1. New York: Academic Press, 1964.

Schachter, S. *The psychology of affiliation*. Stanford, Cal.: Stanford University Press, 1959.

Schachter, S., & Singer, J. Cognitive, social and physiological determinants of emotional state. *Psychological Review*, 1962, 69, 379-399.

Scott, W. A. Cognitive consistency, response, reinforcement and attitude change. *Sociometry*, 1959, 22, 219-229.

Sherif, C. W., Sherif, M., & Nebergall, R. E. *Attitude and attitude change*. Philadelphia: W. B. Saunders, 1965.

Singer, J. E., Brush, C. A., & Lubin, S. C. Some aspects of deindividuation: identification and conformity. *Journal of Experimental Social Psychology*, 1965, 1, 356-378.

Staats, A. W. An outline of an integrated learning theory of attitude formation and function. In M. Fishbein (Ed.), *Readings in attitude theory and measurement*. New York: Wiley, 1967.

Staats, C. K., Staats, A. W., & Briggs, D. W. Meaning of verbal stimuli changed by conditioning. *American Journal of Psychology*, 1958, 71, 429-431.

Stevenson, H. W., & Odom, R. D. The effectiveness of social reinforcement following two conditions of social deprivation. *Journal of Abnormal and Social Psychology*, 1962, 65, 429-431.

Sykes, G. M., & Matza, D. Techniques of neutralization: a theory of delinquency. *American Sociological Review*, 1957, 22, 664-670.

Valins, S. Cognitive effects of false heart-rate feedback. *Journal of Personality and Social Psychology*, 1966, 4, 400-408.

Walster, E. The effect of self-esteem on romantic liking. *Journal of Experimental Social Psychology*, 1965, 1, 184-197.

Walster, E. Passionate love. Paper delivered at Conference on "Theories of Interpersonal Attraction in the Dyad," Connecticut College, October 15-16, 1970.

Walster, E., Berscheid, E., & Walster, G. W. Reactions of an exploiter to the exploited: compensation, justification or self-punishment? In J. R. Macaulay and L. Berkowitz (Eds.), *Altruism and helping behavior*. New York: Academic Press, 1970.

Walster, E., & Prestholdt, P. The effect of misjudging another: overcompensation or dissonance reduction? *Journal of Experimental Social Psychology*, 1966, 2, 85-97.

Webb, E. J. Campbell, D. T., Schwartz, R. D., & Sechrest, L. *Unobtrusive measures: non-reactive research in the social sciences*. Chicago: Rand McNally, 1966.

Willerman, B., & Swanson, L. An ecological determinant of differential amounts of sociometric choices within college sororities. *Sociometry*, 1952, 15, 326-329.

Zimbardo, P. G. *The cognitive control of motivation: the consequences of choice and dissonance*. Glenview, Ill.: Scott, Foresman, 1969.

Zimbardo, P. G., Abric, J. C., Lange, F., Rijsman, J., Bokorova, V., Potocka-Hoser, A., & Honai, R. The aggressive consequences of loss of personal identity. Mimeographed technical report, European Research Training Seminar in Experimental Social Psychology, 1967.

Zimbardo, P. G., & Formica, R. Emotional comparison and self-esteem as determinants of affiliation. *Journal of Personality*, 1963, 31, 141-162.

VI

H. Andrew Michener and Robert W. Suchner

The Tactical Use of Social Power

Many valued outcomes are socially mediated. A politician, for example, who seeks election to office, a student who desires admission to graduate school, a landlord who wants to rent an apartment, a young man who aspires to marry his girlfriend are all examples of those who seek outcomes that must be socially mediated. Typically, such outcomes are attainable only if other persons can be induced or persuaded or forced to provide them. Controlling the behavior of others, therefore, constitutes an important aspect of relations among people. Social power involves both the *capacity to influence* the behavior of others, which enables a person to obtain valued outcomes, and the *capacity to resist* the influence of others, which permits him to deny others the outcomes they want from him. Viewed in this manner, "social power" stands as a general concept, applicable to a wide variety of social encounters.

Theorists have treated social power in different ways and with a diversity of perspectives. Central among these orientations are the bases of social power, the interpersonal comparisons of power, and field theory. (See the excellent reviews by Schopler, 1965, and by Collins & Raven, 1969, for a discussion of these approaches to power.) In contrast with other perspectives, the present chapter conceptualizes interactions among persons as *exchange processes*. In discussing the determinants and consequences of power, it treats social relations as transactions where individuals reciprocally reward and punish one another.

While many interpersonal exchanges become stable and routine, even established relationships may undergo radical transformation.

The authors extend their appreciation to Richard T. Campbell, Sharon M. Guten, Thomas Heberlein, Shelley Kolton, Mark B. Tausig, Richard Tessler, and Richard A. Zeller, all of whom offered helpful comments on earlier versions of this chapter.

Frequently, changes occur through the use of social power, as when participants in an exchange utilize various tactical behaviors to modify the prevailing terms of the relationship. Employing such tactics, an individual may attain valued outcomes from another person or remain independent of the other's demands. This chapter's fundamental concern lies with these strategic behaviors, which are termed *power tactics*, and with the determinants of their use and effectiveness.

This chapter, therefore, has two objectives: to present an exchange model of power tactics and to review recent experimental research treating issues raised by the model. To begin the chapter, we explicate the model of power relationships and demonstrate how it systematizes a perplexing array of power tactics discussed by various writers. A subsequent discussion of research questions applicable to the model substantiates its merit as a conceptual framework. Next, we review some of the recent experimental studies bearing on these research questions, thereby indicating which questions have been (partially) answered and which have not. Finally, this chapter explores some relations between power tactics and the emergence of norms and status in groups.

Our goal is the understanding of power tactics in social interaction. Our route toward that goal takes us through a discussion of social interaction as an exchange process.

Social Relationships as Exchanges

People in interaction often control the flow of valued outcomes to one another. These valued outcomes may be tangible, as in an exchange of money for food or clothing, or they may be intangible, as in the requital of conformity to group expectations for expressions of approval from other group members. Social exchange theory, as explicated by Homans (1961) and Gergen (1969), specifies conditions under which persons will reciprocate valued outcomes. In general terms, the *value* of a behavioral outcome to others and the *scarcity* of the outcome are the primary determinants of its exchangeability. If a behavior is not valued by others, or if the behavior is valued but readily available from other sources at a cheaper "price," it will not be exchangeable. That is, the behavior will not impel others to furnish valued outcomes in return. An exchange, then, takes place when the holder of one set of valued outcomes encounters the holder of another set and an exchange rate is agreed upon by both persons.

The economic transaction provides the most familiar example of an exchange. When a person walks into a store to buy clothing, he enters a potential exchange relationship with the retailer. The retailer is in business to sell clothes—that is, to trade the garments he controls for the money controlled by his customers. Theoretically, the price established by the seller and accepted by the buyer depends both on the value and scarcity of clothing to the customer and on the value and scarcity of dollars to the retailer. A sale will occur when the buyer and seller agree on the rate at which to trade money for specified articles of clothing.

The economic transaction constitutes a special case of behavioral exchange. People frequently participate in noneconomic exchanges. A politician and a political interest group may conduct such a noneconomic exchange. When, for example, a particular congressman, running for reelection, approaches a conservation group whose members want the government to enact land-use legislation and to establish a number of new parks in their state, the basis for an exchange exists. The politician approaches the interest group because its members control something of value to him: campaign workers and money he needs to achieve reelection. The conservation group is receptive to the politician because he mediates something of value to them: a means for them to influence governmental decisions on land use and natural resources. Both the congressman and interest group will find it advantageous to enter the transaction, and the rate of exchange of political representation for electoral support will reflect how much each party desires what the other has to offer and how readily the desired outcomes can be attained from other sources.

The Demand Curve

How much an individual desires, or values, a behavioral product is represented in exchange theory by a *demand curve* for that product. The reader probably remembers the concept of "demand" from elementary economics. An individual's demand curve describes the quantities of a (behavioral) product that he will take off the market at various rates of exchange, or prices. Typically, a person will accept different quantities of a behavioral product at different prices. Such prices specify the number of units of one (behavioral) product that will be exchanged *per unit* of another product. The demand curve, then, represents the value of the desired behavioral product in terms of some other product, for each specified quantity of the demanded product.

The demand curve portrayed by the solid line in Figure 6.1 describes the exchange rates, in terms of units of political representation *per unit* of electoral support, that the congressman is willing to "pay" for the support of the interest group. Units of political representation provided by the politician might be measured in terms of the number of legislative bills he submits for creating new parks or, alternatively, the amount of time he spends convincing other politicians to support conservation bills. Units of electoral support might be the number of campaign workers supplied by the pressure group or the quantity of funds donated to the politician's reelection efforts. The congressman exchanges political representation (in the present congress) for electoral support, and the demand curve expresses the "prices" in terms of representation he is willing to pay for different amounts of electoral support from the interest group.

Note several features of the demand curve. First, the demand curve typically has a downward or *negative slope*. That is, a person customarily accepts a greater quantity of the same (behavioral) product only at decreasing prices. The congressman, for example, will provide seven units of representation (e.g., spend seven hours trying to persuade fellow congressmen to support a land-use bill in the state legislature) for the first unit of support from the conservation group, but he will provide only four units of represen-

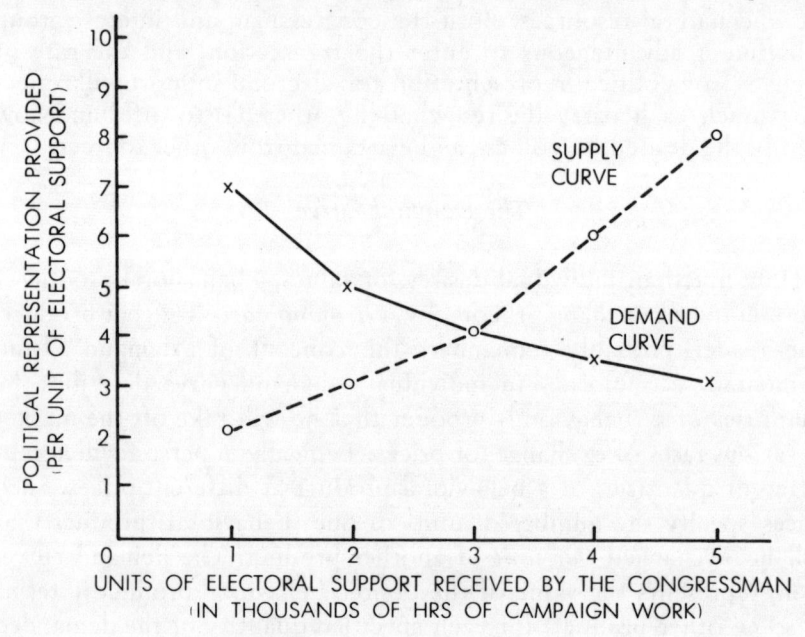

Figure 6.1. *Demand and Supply Curves Describing an Exchange Relationship Between a Congressman and a Political Interest Group*

tation (e.g., work four hours for the bills) for *each* of three units of support. This negative slope reflects the principle of "satiation" presented in psychology (Homans, 1961) and the principle of "decreasing marginal utility" presented in economics (Leftwich, 1961). Both principles suggest that, as a person consumes more and more of a single commodity or behavioral outcome, each additional unit of that commodity becomes less and less valuable to him, and the person will consume additional units only at lower and lower prices. In our example, the politician would be very eager to obtain the first thousand hours of campaign work from the conservation group, but he will accept more support only if the "price" in terms of representation is less for each additional thousand hours of electioneering by campaign workers.

Second, the demand curve describes the *maximum* rates of exchange at which a consumer will accept specific quantities. Obviously, if the congressman could obtain the same amount of campaign funds without having to promise as much attention to the interests of the conservation group, he would accept the campaign funds at this lower rate. In representing the maximum rate the demander will pay for specific quantities of a given (behavioral) product, the position of the demand curve suggests that he will accept an offer at any price *up to and including* the rate of exchange specified by the demand curve itself.

Finally, the rates of exchange expressed in the demand curve can *fluctuate* over time. That is, a demand curve can shift, depending on the consumer's values regarding the outcomes exchanged. If a shift occurs in the conditions underlying the congressman's values regarding political support—if, for example, his opponent in the election appears to be gaining unanticipated strength—the incumbent congressman may begin to value electoral support more highly, and this change will be reflected in an upward shift in his demand curve. On the other hand, if the opponent appears to be weakening, the congressman's demand for electoral support from the political interest group might shift downward. Changes in demand, then, are represented by upward or downward shifts in the entire demand curve. As we shall see, these fluctuations in the demand curve are of cardinal importance in any discussion of social power, for power tactics can impel such upward or downward shifts in demand.

Supply Curve

With the addition of a *supply curve*, the description of a simple exchange relationship is complete. A supply curve denotes the quantities of a (behavioral) product that suppliers in a market will provide at various rates of exchange. Note that this curve reflects what is available from all potential suppliers, not just a single given supplier. In the context of the negotiations between the congressman and the conservation group, the supply curve represents the amount of electoral support that diverse sources of supply (i.e., the conservation group as well as other competing political interest groups) are willing to provide at various rates of exchange.

The supply curve confronting the congressman is represented by the dashed line in Figure 6.1. This curve is upward sloping to the right, which is typical of supply curves, indicating that suppliers will provide additonal quantities of their (behavioral) product only at an increasing rate of exchange. Thus, various political interest groups will supply two thousand hours of campaign work at the rate of three units of representation (e.g., hours spent in behalf of a bill by a congressman) per thousand hours, but they will supply as much as five thousand hours of campaign work only at the higher rate of eight units of representation per thousand. Supply curves evince this upward or *positive slope* because to provide additional units of a product usually proves costly, and suppliers will do so only when induced by an increasing rate of exchange. The supply curve, then, represents the availability, or obversely, the relative *scarcity* of the suppliers' (behavioral) product in the market. In our example, the supply curve facing the congressman portrays the rates of exchange (in terms of representation) acceptable to at least one of the political groups that can provide campaign workers for the congressman. As such, the curve indicates the *minimum* the congressman must provide to obtain campaign workers.

The supply curve, like the demand curve, can *shift* position. Any shift reflects a change in the suppliers' values regarding the behavioral outcomes being reciprocated. If, for example, propitious circumstances increase the availability of election workers, this change will be mirrored in a downward shift in the supply curve, indicating that the conservationists (or other interest groups) are willing to supply more electoral support for the same amount of political representation. Upward shifts in the supply curve are also possible, under the appropriate circumstances. As with demand, shifts in supply are central to any discussion of social power, and the use of power tactics can cause upward or downward fluctuations in this demand.

The Actual Rate of Exchange

Assuming that everyone involved has complete knowledge of the situation—and this is an important (although sometimes unrealistic) assumption that we will consider again in discussing the "deceptive"

Tactical Use of Social Power

use of power tactics—the point at which the supply and demand curves intersect indicates the terms under which an exchange will actually occur. Since the supply curve states the *minimum* the congressman must pay in representation to obtain campaign work from the political interest groups, and since the demand curve indicates the *maximum* he is willing to requite for various amounts of campaign work, the point of intersection defines the "actual rate of exchange." Referring to Figure 6.1, the actual rate of exchange between the congressman and that interest group with which he strikes a deal will be three thousand hours of campaign work (i.e., electoral support) at the rate of four units of political representation per thousand hours of support. At this point of intersection, both parties are maximizing their outcomes within the range of possibilities defined by the other's preferences.

The Use of Power Tactics

We have seen that a set of supply and demand curves represents an exchange relationship and that, when all participants have full knowledge, the intersection of these curves designates the actual rate of exchange. But such a representation fails to reflect the *dynamic* character of social relations, for it treats only those interactions where all parties accept the terms of the exchange relationship. In other words, this model epitomizes a "compliant" system of interaction—a system where the terms of the exchange are specified and where the participants simply comply with the (minimally acceptable) demands of others. But many interactions involve efforts to *change the terms of exchange*. That is, persons frequently attempt to alter the conditions underlying the supply and demand curves that delineate the relationship. *Power tactics*, such as those discussed by various theorists (Blau, 1964; Emerson, 1962; Gergen, 1969; Homans, 1961; Jones & Gerard, 1967; Thibaut & Kelley, 1959) constitute attempts to modify the terms of a relationship. Thus, power tactics can be seen as alternatives to compliance.

In this section, we will explicate how power tactics change the conditions underlying an existing exchange relationship; that is, we will show how they shift the positions of the supply and demand curves that describe such a relationship.

Blocking Outcomes

One power tactic consists of blocking another person's access to valued outcomes. By reducing his rate of productivity, for example, an employee may impair his supervisor's capacity to achieve departmental goals. Similarly, by mobilizing opposition, a political coalition might block a political candidate from attaining his party's nomination at the national convention. Theorists have treated this tactic of blocking outcomes under a diversity of rubrics. Blau (1964) termed it "barring access to alternatives." Emerson (1962) described a variant of this tactic as "coalition formation," which is a joint effort by two or more persons to block another from attaining commodities or services that he values.

The central feature of this tactic is precisely what its name implies—obstructing another's attainment of valued outcomes or goals. If one has sole control over outcomes that another values, then outcome blockage simply involves refusal to provide those outcomes. More commonly, however, similar (or at least substitutable) outcomes will be available from other sources and, in this case, outcome blockage entails cutting off outcomes originating from these other suppliers. To prevent another person from attaining outcomes from other sources—especially when the person using this tactic can provide the same outcome—makes the (behavioral) product less available to the other, and in consequence the other becomes more dependent upon the person using this tactic.

Examples of outcome blockage abound, but perhaps the most dramatic involve the maneuvers of political coalitions and labor unions. If a labor union, for example, calls a strike, it is moving to block an employer's access to labor resources needed for profitable industrial operations. By walking off the job, the union restricts the availability of labor, an act that fortifies their verbal demands for higher pay and greater benefits from the employer. If successful, the union's tactical action to block outcomes from the employer will modify the terms of the exchange relationship between the union and the employer.

Demand Creation

A second power tactic suggested by numerous writers is demand creation. This entails any action that increases the value of behavioral products exchanged in a relationship. Using other descriptive labels, Thibaut and Kelley (1959) have referred to this tactic as "building up the value" of one's product, and Jones and Gerard (1967) have described it as "creating a need for behavior products." In contrast to the tactic of blocking outcomes, demand creation does not affect the scarcity of outcomes. Instead, it modifies the extent to which another person values the outcomes being supplied.

Consider an example. That butt of many jokes, the used-car

salesman, frequently attempts demand creation. Using an elaborate spiel, he may inundate his customer with information about his cars' "finer points." This, of course, is an attempt to increase the automobiles' value in the eyes of the customer, the object of which is to get a higher price for the used merchandise. This tactic in no way changes the actual product being sold. To tell the customer that a car was "driven only on Sunday by a little old lady" does not change the product, but it may increase the product's attractiveness to the customer. If such tactics prove effective (and, of course, they may not), they cause a shift in the customer's demand and consequently modify the rate of exchange at which a transaction occurs.

Extension of the Power Network (Utilizing Alternatives)

The first two tactics—blocking outcomes and demand creation—involve actions that will affect the availability and the value of the behavioral product supplied to the *other* person in the relationship. The third tactic, extension of the power network, affects the availability of outcomes to the *person using the tactic*. By extending the power network, a person expands the sources of supply for the product he desires. Typically, he would find a new supplier who is willing to exchange at a more favorable rate.

This tactic was labeled "extension of the power network" by Emerson (1962), who used it to characterize situations where a person literally extends the number of relationships in which he is involved and thereby shifts the balance of power within the original exchange relationship. Thibaut and Kelley (1959) referred to this tactic as "developing better alternatives," and Jones and Gerard (1967) termed it "raising the attractiveness of alternative relationships." Blau (1964) expressed a similar notion by describing the tactical aspects of "attaining the needed services elsewhere."

Extension of the power network may be the most frequently used of the power tactics. In many situations, it emerges as the tactic that is not only the least costly, but also the most likely to succeed. Consider a typical example. Assume that a young engineer, working for a large corporation, has become dissatisfied with his rate of advancement in the company. His work is pleasant, but promotions are slow. To cope with this frustrating situation, he may promote contacts outside his company and seek a new job. Friends working at other engineering firms, contacts at annual professional conventions, newpaper want-ads—all constitute channels through which he may operate. If he succeeds in attaining one (or several) attractive job offers involving more responsibility with other engineering companies, he may augment his power positon where he presently works.

His dependence on his present employer is lessened—he has attractive offers elsewhere—and he can either leave his present job for another or try to play off the various potential employers against one another. That is, he may indicate to his present supervisor that nothing short of a promotion (with added responsibility and perquisites) will command his continued loyalty. Whatever his supervisor's response, the engineer will shortly attain a better position. By using extension of the power network (that is, by finding alternative sources of supply for a valued outcome, the better job), the engineer augments his power by reducing his dependency.

Withdrawal

Withdrawal is the fourth tactic considered here. Emerson (1962) used the term "motivational withdrawal" to designate the tactic where one person reduces the extent that he values the behavioral product supplied by another. Thibaut and Kelley (1959) have alluded to the same tactic as "devaluating (another's) product," and Jones and Gerard (1967) have referred to it as "outcome devaluation."

Whatever its label, this tactic involves a devaluation of the behavioral product supplied by another person, with the consequence that the individual using the tactic becomes less dependent on the supplier and less constrained to provide something in return. Romantic relationships, interpreted in exchange terms, occasionally provide a setting for the tactical use of withdrawal. If a girl, for example, is not getting what she wants from her relationships with the opposite sex, she might withdraw from romantic involvement. That is, she might decide the companionship provided by males is really not all it is touted to be. If such devaluation is genuine and not just ephemeral, the girl using the tactic gains independence from the demands of importunate young gallants. The terms of the romantic exchange have shifted, and her boyfriends will have to work harder to again interest her in what they have to offer and to achieve her compliance with their demands.

Power Tactics as Shifting Supply and Demand Curves

As adumbrated by the foregoing discussion, the theoretic and empirical literature on power tactics can be organized, for the most part, into four general tactics: blocking outcomes, demand creation, extension of the power network, and withdrawal. This does not imply that these four tactics exhaust the techniques that one can

Tactical Use of Social Power

employ to alter exchange relationships. It does suggest, however, that these tactics provide a basic structure for the study of social power, as well as for the study of the mutation and transformation of social exchanges.

Throughout our discussion of power tactics, we have noted that each tactic causes shifts either in the *valuation* of behavioral products or in the *scarcity* of such products. Demand creation and withdrawal affect valuation: blocking outcomes and extension of the power network affect scarcity. Note that valuation and scarcity are exactly the same concepts used earlier in defining the conditions that underlie the supply and demand curves characterizing an exchange relationship. Any change in valuation will shift the position of the supply curve. It should come as no surprise, therefore, that we can represent the four power tactics as shifts in the demand and supply curves that define a social exchange.

Figures 6.2 and 6.3 illustrate this point. These figures, considered jointly, represent the exchange relationship between the congressman running for reelection and the conservation group pressing for land-use legislation. Figure 6.2 portrays the relationship from the perspective of the congressman, while Figure 6.3 depicts the same relationship from the viewpoint of the political interest group.

Figure 6.2 indicates the shifts in the demand and supply curves that will occur if the congressman used the power tactics of withdrawal and extension of the power network. The congressman's demand curve before the use of withdrawal (designated curve D_1 in Fig. 6.2) is the same as the demand curve shown earlier in Figure 6.1. The use of withdrawal by the congressman is represented as a shift in his demand curve from D_1 to D_2. This downward shift in the demand curve represents a reduction in the congressman's desire for electoral support from political interest groups. This might happen, for example, if the congressman suddenly decides that reelection is not so important and that defeat at the polls would still enable him to be an effective political force. Following withdrawal, the congressman is willing only to pay lower "prices" (shown by curve D_2) for the same amounts of electoral support that he would have earlier accepted at higher prices (shown by curve D_1). The congressman now values campaign workers less and his demand drops.

But suppose, instead, that the congressman does not use withdrawal and that he still greatly desires reelection. In this case, he might attempt to extend the power network. Figure 6.2 portrays the congressman's use of this tactic by a shift in his supply curve from S_1 to S_2. Just as a downward shift in his demand curve represents withdrawal, a downward shift in his supply curve represents

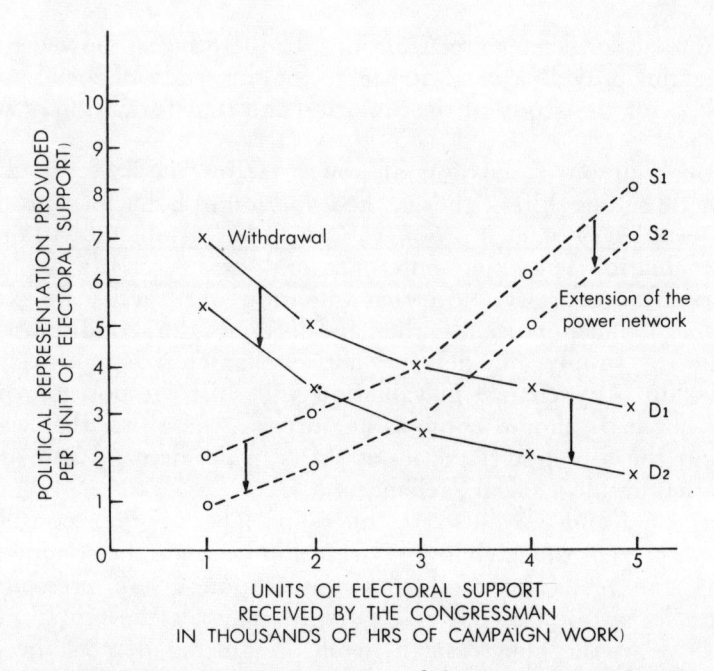

Figure 6.2. "Withdrawal" and "Extension of the Power Network" Represented as Shifts in the Demand and Supply Curves Facing the Interest Group.

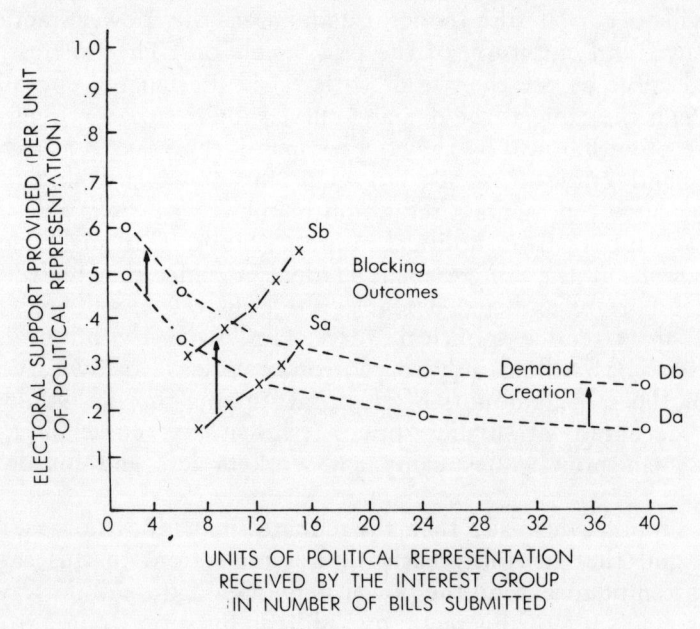

Figure 6.3. "Demand Creation" and "Blocking Outcomes" Represented as Shifts in the Demand and Supply Curves Facing the Interest Group.

Tactical Use of Social Power

extension of the power network. In using this tactic, the politician establishes alternative sources of supply of electoral support, the product he values. He might, for example, approach various interest groups with which he has previously had little contact. If one of these alternative sources is willing to provide electoral support at a lower price (in terms of political representation) than the conservation group, this constitutes a downward shift in the supply curve facing the congressman.

But just as the congressman can use withdrawal and extension of the power network to affect the demand and supply of electoral support, he can also tip the balance of power in the exchange relationship by using tactics that affect the demand and supply of political representation. Figure 6.3 represents the exchange relationship from the perspective of the interest group. Curve D_a indicates the interest group's initial demand for political representation and curve S_a indicates the initial supply of such representation available to the group. By using the tactics of blocking outcomes and demand creation, the congressman can cause shifts in these supply and demand curves, respectively.

Suppose that the congressman, running for reelection, feels that he needs all the electoral support he can get—and at the lowest price. He is willing to represent the conservation group, but only for a substantial quantity of electoral support. To bolster his position, he approaches other congressmen (who might potentially represent the conservation group) and reaches an agreement whereby they won't undercut his actions. The effect of this coalition is to restrict the supply of political representation potentially available to the conservation group. Such restriction constitutes an upward shift (from S_a to S_b) of the supply curve facing the interest group. In other words, by using the tactic of blocking outcomes the congressman raises the rate of exchange, so that each unit of political representation that he provides will now command higher rates of electoral support from the interest group.

Finally, the tactic of demand creation, through which the congressman increases the interest group's desire for political representation, is represented by an upward shift in the interest group's demand curve (from D_a to D_b). The incumbent might, for instance, persuade the conservationists that they need land-use legislation even more desperately than they had imagined and that such legislation can be attained only through his great influence in legislative circles. With a heightened demand for this behavioral product, the conservationists will provide more electoral support for each unit of representation from the congressman.

Research Questions Concerning Power Tactics

Thus far, we have shown that by adopting the perspective of exchange theory and characterizing social interaction as transactions involving behavioral products, one can evolve an analytic framework describing power tactics. Behavioral exchanges entail the traditional supply and demand functions discussed in elementary economics. And power tactics, by shifting these supply and demand curves, are actions that modify the relative dependencies of participants in such an exchange.

But now that the model has been presented, of what use is it? That is, what do we get from an exchange model of social power tactics? One can assess the utility of a theoretic model in terms of the important questions it provokes as well as of the organization it provides for extant research findings. The exchange model satisfies these criteria, for it engenders several interesting and pivotal questions regarding power tactics. Four of these are elaborated below. The remainder of this chapter, which selectively reviews empirical findings on power tactics, endeavors to answer these questions.

1. Under what conditions will people use power tactics to alter the relative dependencies in a relationship? That is, under what conditions will people attempt to change the demand and supply functions that define the balance of power in the behavioral exchanges they transact?

As mentioned earlier, the use of power tactics constitutes an alternative to compliance in social interactions. Persons do not use power tactics all the time. Some writers (e.g., Gamsón, 1968; Heslin & Dunphy, 1964; Homans, 1961) have theorized that such attitudinal states as "dissatisfaction," "inequity," and "distrust" activate power tactics. Nevertheless, persons may decide not to use power tactics even when they are dissatisfied. Question 1 poses the general issue of the conditions under which such tactics will be used.

When power tactics are actually used, a question arises concerning their effectiveness.

2. Under what conditions will the various power tactics be effective in changing the terms underlying an exchange relationship? That is, what conditions determine whether the demand or supply functions underlying a relationship actually shift in response to an attempted use of various power tactics?

Attempts to use power tactics are not always successful. For example, when an individual tries to create demand for his behavioral products, he may be more or less successful in shifting the values of other persons. Similarly, when he strives to form a coalition, he may be more or less successful in getting the coalition to form, and the coalition, once formed, may be more or less successful in its efforts to block outcomes. Other power tactics, as well, vary in their success. Question 2 poses the general issue of when tactics will succeed and when they will fail.

A third question deals with the morphology of those behaviors functioning as power tactics. The exchange model assumes that all parties in an exchange relationship have *full knowledge* of the relevant demand and supply curves. In everyday life, of course, this stringent assumption is rarely met. Information is frequently imperfect. Interestingly, this suggests that certain behaviors that *intentionally misrepresent* the value and availability of behavioral products might be effective substitutes for the standard power tactics.

3. What kinds of deceptive behaviors can modify the terms of an exchange relationship by causing persons to misperceive the actual dependencies in the relationship? Under what conditions will such deceptions be used, and under what conditions will they be successful in changing the terms of the exchange relationship?

Behaviors that deceptively shift power relationships include "playing hard to get," feigning disinterest, "ingratiating" others, and threatening to use a coalition that does not really exist. A person can employ deceptive tactics when others are uncertain about the true conditions of supply and demand underlying the relationship. Various researchers (e.g., Fischer, 1969; Jones, 1964) have looked at deceptive tactics, and Question 3 inquires about the form, use, and effectiveness of such deceptions.

Finally, consequences result from the use of power tactics, and such tactics often have important effects upon continuing relationships. Some writers (Harsanyi, 1966; Thibaut & Kelley, 1959) have suggested that norms and rules arise from the use of power tactics. These theorists view norms as substitutes for the overt use of power. A final question, then, is:

4. What are some of the consequences of the use of power tactics in continuing relationships? Specifically with reference to interpersonal expectations, how does the use of power tactics affect the formation of norms and the emergence of social status in social interaction?

In the remainder of this chapter, we will review recent empirical research addressing these questions. In most cases, a complete answer still eludes investigators, but progress has been made and some consistent, interpretable results have emerged. We will survey these research results from the vantage afforded by the exchange model of power tactics.

Some Determinants of the Use and Effectiveness of Power Tactics

Blocking Outcomes

The tactic of blocking outcomes constricts the availability of valued outcomes to other persons, causing a downward shift in the supply curve confronting them. Such a shift magnifies the dependence of others on the individual using the tactic and thereby extends his power over them. Blocking outcomes can be used by groups as well as by individuals. In describing this tactic, we considered the striking labor union, which created a scarcity of labor resources needed by employers for profitable industrial operations. Political coalitions also exemplify the collective use of this tactic. Analytically, the important characteristic of blocking outcomes is that, whether undertaken individually or in concert with others, it limits the supply of valued outcomes. Used by individuals, this tactic typically involves threats; used by collectivities, it involves coalition formation. In this section, we will consider research on both topics. The central questions are: under what conditions will the tactic of blocking outcomes be used, and under what conditions will it be effective?

Blocking Another's Outcomes by Individual Action

An important line of research has investigated the effectiveness of *threats* to block another's outcomes. Typically, the use of threats is less costly than efforts to actually block another's outcomes, which involves depletion of resources. Therefore, if an individual can gain compliance by merely using threats, he may prefer this to direct obstruction.

Horai and Tedeschi (1969) observed some conditions under which threats to block another's access to his goal proved effective in gaining compliance. Using a competitive game situation, Horai and Tedeschi varied two facets of threat potential. One was the size of the penalty imposed for noncompliance, the other was the credibility of the threat. Subjects faced an antagonist who could penalize them to a large or small extent. This opponent, working as a confederate of the experimenter, varied the credibility of his threats by manipulating the proportion of times (either 10, 50, or 90 percent) he actually carried out his threats over a series of trials. Results indicate that both factors affect the level of compliance gained from subjects. Compliance with the demands of the threatener increased as the credibility of the threats and the size of the forfeiture increased. Thus, in situations where *only one* participant has the capacity to

Tactical Use of Social Power

threaten, the most effective threat is one that is highly credible and that, if carried out, would prove very damaging.

But what happens when *both* parties in a conflict can threaten one another? A study by Deutsch and Krauss (1960) addressed this question. This laboratory experiment, which used a trucking game that involved two subjects, varied the subjects' capacity to block each other's attainment of his goal. Each subject attempted to move a "truck" from one point to another in a minimum amount of time. The shortest distance between the starting point and the destination, however, involved crossing a stretch of "highway" that only one truck could traverse at a time. Since the two trucks were going in opposite directions, this stretch of highway constituted a conflict situation. If one person tried to cross this highway and met the other person coming the other way, he would lose precious time in convincing the other to back up or in backing his own truck to let the other pass. To avoid such a confrontation, each person could take an alternative route, but the time required to follow this longer bypass would greatly reduce the winnings.

Deutsch and Krauss varied the capacity to block outcomes in the following way. In some of the experimental sessions, subjects could lower a gate across their end of the common highway, thereby blocking the other person's most direct route to the destination. In one condition (bilateral threat), both subjects had such gates; in another condition (unilateral threat), only one subject had a gate; and in a third condition (no threat), neither subject had a gate.

The results indicate that different capacities to block outcomes determine the rewards attained in the situation. Deutsch and Krauss found that subjects won the most in the condition with no threats, won less in the unilateral threat condition, and won the least in the bilateral threat condition. Subjects fared best when *no one* had the capacity to block outcomes. In this situation, the potential to block another's outcomes produced a decrease in the total points attained by both persons. As might be expected, when only one person had the capacity to levy threats (unilateral threat condition), the person with the threat capacity received considerably more points than the other. But, surprisingly, even the person with threat capacity achieved poorer outcomes than did individuals in the situation where no one could make threats.

A study by Hornstein (1965) replicated these results under different circumstances. Subjects played the roles of realtors and bargained over the value of a piece of land. Each realtor's goal was to make the greatest profit he could on the sale of the land. Hornstein varied the size of the threat potential by allowing each subject to diminish the other's profits by some specified amount, either 90, 50,

20, or 10 percent. In some bargaining sessions subjects had equal threat potential, while in other sessions subjects had various combinations of unequal threat potential. Again, as in Deutsch and Krauss' experiment, Hornstein found that the greater the use of threats, the less the agreement on a solution. Hornstein also replicated the finding that when one person has substantial threat capacity but the other has little or none (i.e., Deutsch and Krauss' unilateral threat), the person having the threat capability fares better than the other. The results further indicate that similarity or equality of threat potential intensifies conflict. The more nearly equal the threat potentials of the two parties, the less the agreement and the poorer the outcomes.

The experiments by Deutsch and Krauss and by Hornstein, then, indicate that threatening to block another's outcomes is not an effective power tactic when the other person has the capacity to retaliate. But does this finding hold true under all conditions, or does it require qualification?

Research by Shomer, Davis, and Kelley (1966) suggests that bilateral threat potential will not cause internecine conflict if both parties are compelled to remain in the threatening situation. Using a variant of the Deutsch and Krauss trucking game, Shomer et al. eliminated the alternative route and installed a threat capability that not only inflicted punishment but also served as a signal. The experimental results indicate that when no alternative route is available (i.e., when persons cannot attain valued outcomes from an alternative source), the presence of bilateral threat potential does *not* negatively affect the winnings of the bargainers. Unable to exercise an alternative, subjects sought an accommodation within the minatory situation. The results further indicate that if subjects can use the threats as a signalling device when no alternative routes are available, threat potentials actually enhance cooperation in the short run. A study by Geiwitz (1967) also found this enhancement effect of threat potential in a different game situation.

In sum, research suggests that, although threats to block others' outcomes will gain compliance under some circumstances, they must be used with care. When the other person has counterthreat capabilities or when he can utilize a different power tactic, the situation may deteriorate and become unprofitable to everyone, unless some other pressures force the individuals to remain in the situation and resolve the conflict.

Blocking Another's Outcomes by Coalition Formation

In blocking outcomes, one does not always operate alone. Often an individual must form a *coalition* with others to block the outcomes of a third party. As indicated by the exchange model of power tactics, coalitions constrict the supply of available outcomes.

An important research issue concerns the *formation* of coalitions. Some situations impel the emergence of outcome-blocking alliances. One such case is a political convention, where any of several possible coalitions can flourish. In this instance, the important question is not whether a coalition will form, but rather which coalition will form. Exactly this question has been the basis of much research. Numerous studies have investigated the factors that determine which coalition an individual will join when he chooses among available possibilities.

Research on this issue has stressed the *properties* of the potential, alternative coalitions. For instance, Caplow (1956) proposed that the distribution of power within alternative coalitions would determine how an individual chooses among them. Caplow postulated that persons strive to dominate others and, consequently, that they would join the coalition which affords control over the largest number of people, both inside and outside the coalition. Gamson (1961a) reformulated Caplow's theory and suggested that, instead of seeking control over others as an end in itself, people form coalitions with others primarily to maximize their personal gain. Viewed in this perspective, coalitions do not merely block others' outcomes, but also provide rewards for their members. Gamson argued that a coalition's resources—that is, the power base contributed to a coalition by its members—determine which coalition a person would prefer to join. He hypothesized that a person would choose the coalition with the *smallest* amount of resources sufficient to block others and obtain the valued outcomes for itself.

Gamson's theory truly differs from Caplow's, for it yields different empirical predictions. Data from a study conducted prior to the formulation of Gamson's theory (Vinacke & Arkoff, 1957) afford a comparison between Caplow's predictions and Gamson's. Vinacke and Arkoff varied the resources held by three subjects and observed which two-person coalition emerged under conditions where formulation of a coalition blocked the third person's access to a valued outcome. Consistent with Gamson's predictions, Vinacke and Arkoff found that coalitions with minimum resources sufficient to block the other formed most frequently.

An empirical study by Gamson (1961b) further supports his theory. In a five-person experimental situation, subjects simulated a political convention where the formation of coalitions simultaneously led to control of political patronage and prevented others from attaining this valued outcome. The study varied the distribution of resources (e.g., votes) controlled by different persons. Results showed that the most frequently preferred coalition in this situation included the three persons who individually controlled the fewest votes.

Several empirical studies, then, substantiate Gamson's theory. But why do individuals prefer the coalition with the fewest resources sufficient to block others and obtain the valued outcomes for itself? Gamson postulated that a norm of equity would govern the distribution of rewards among coalitional members, so that each member would receive rewards proportional to the resources he contributed to the coalition. Under these conditions, and assuming that a fixed quantity of rewards are available, the coalition offering each of its members the largest individual winnings is the successful coalition with the fewest resources.

But variables other than the pattern of resources affect which coalition a person will join when he confronts a choice among potential alliances. In the studies just discussed, the mere formation of a coalition assured that it would win, that is, that it would attain its goal and block others from attaining theirs. Coalitions, however, are not always successful. That is, depending on the situation, coalitions differ in the probability that they will be effective in blocking others' outcomes.

A study by Chertkoff (1966) indicates that a coalition's probability of success affects a person's choice to join. Chertkoff varied both the resources available to different subjects in the situation and the probability that any particular coalition would be successful in winning. The results indicated that when all coalitions had the same probability of success in attaining the goal, the coalition with the minimum resources sufficient to win formed most frequently. However, when the inclusion of a larger quantity of resources increased the probability of the coalition winning, the minimum resource coalition did not form; instead, coalitions with greater resources formed more frequently.

The evidence, then, suggests that when a person faces a choice among alternative coalitions, he will prefer the coalition that seems most profitable. Under conditions where the mere formation of a coalition assures victory, he will join the coalition with minimum resources sufficient to win. But under conditions of uncertainty, he will join coalitions with higher levels of resources, especially when the amount of resources affects the probability that the coalition will win. The principle that a person will attempt to maximize his utility when choosing among alternative coalitions has been stated formally by Ofshe and Ofshe (1969), who argue that the same factors considered by Gamson and Chertkoff—the rewards associated with each alternative, the probability of success, and equity considerations

—determine a person's choice of coalition.

To this point, we have looked at determinants of a person's action when he faces a choice among alternative coalitions. In many situations, however, the issue confronting an individual is not which of several possible coalitions to join, but whether to join any coalition. That is, the question facing him is whether or not to block someone's outcomes by means of a coalition with others. Behavior of individuals in such circumstances has been studied by various researchers, including Kelley and Arrowood (1960), Uesugi and Vinacke (1963), and Michener and Lyons (1970).

Kelley and Arrowood's (1960) study, using triads, varied the extent to which individuals had attractive and valued alternatives leading to their goal outside the coalition. Results suggest that the more attractive a person's independent action, the greater his reluctance to join a coalition. In this situation, weaker persons (i.e., those with less attractive outside alternatives) are more likely to be included in any alliance that emerges.

Uesugi and Vinacke (1963) report data suggesting a sex difference in the propensity to form coalitions in experimental situations. Generally, in triadic situations, female subjects form two-person coalitions against a third female less frequently than do males in situations involving other males. This apparently occurs because females, when under surveillance by others, are particularly prone to cooperate, thereby avoiding coalitions against anyone.

Michener and Lyons (1970) studied the formation of "revolutionary coalitions," i.e., coalitions established by lower-status persons to restrain the actions of higher-status persons. Such coalitions are revolutionary in the sense that they violate the prescribed status ordering and force a redistribution of rewards among group members. A low-status person's propensity to form revolutionary coalitions depends on the extent to which other low-status members are perceived as supporting the legitimate high-status member of the group. A high level of perceived support for the high-status member reduces the number of attempts to form revolutionary coalitions. This apparently occurs not only because a high level of perceived support diminishes a person's subjective probability of successfully forming a coalition, but also because it palliates his dissatisfaction with the existing status arrangements.

In sum, the results demonstrate that, in addition to winning rewards as suggested by Gamson, other factors—such as the availability of alternatives outside the coalition, the sex of participants, and the perceived support for status arrangements—operate as determinants of coalition formation

Demand Creation

Blocking outcomes, the power tactic just discussed, restricts the *supply* of outcomes to others. Demand creation, in contrast, affects the *value* of outcomes to others. The preponderance of research on demand creation has investigated the prerequisites for *effectiveness* of various strategies to modify value; the conditions impelling *use* of such strategies have received less attention.

Remember how demand creation operates. In our example, the congressman running for reelection may try to persuade members of the conservation group that through his influence in legislative circles, and only through his influence, can they attain their ultimate goals. If the conservationists can be convinced, their demand for the congressman's behavioral product (i.e., political representation) will shift, and they may be willing to reciprocate a higher price (in terms of electoral support).

In what ways might the politician increase the conservationists' demand for his political representation? Expressed more generally, how does someone increase others' demand for his behavioral product? The literature addressing this issue is extensive and, making no attempt to cover it exhaustively, we will consider only a sampling of studies. We organize our review in terms of *what an influencing agent can do* to increase another's demand for the outcomes he mediates. Two such strategies involve *persuading others* that the outcomes he controls are of greater value and *manipulating another's situation* (through the use of rewards and punishments) so that, as a secondary effect, the other comes to view these outcomes as having greater value than before. Our review will look at both strategies, but even here it will be only illustrative, not comprehensive. The interested reader can find more extensive presentations in several articles specifically intended as reviews of research on value and attitude change (see Berscheid & Walster, 1969; McGuire, 1969; Zimbardo & Ebbesen, 1969).

Demand Creation Through Persuasion

What are some characteristics of an influencing agent that make him a persuasive communicator? In seeking to answer this question, many researchers have discussed the *credibility* of the communicator, treating the extent to which the communicator appears expert and trustworthy as facets of his credibility.

Bergin (1962) reports a study that varied the "expertise" of the communicator. Bergin obtained college students' perceptions of themselves on a number of personality dimensions, including their "masculinity-femininity" characteristics. Subjects were subsequently exposed to varying sources of information regarding their standing on this personality dimension. In the "high expertise" condition, subjects took a battery of objective personality tests as part of a personality assessment project supposedly run by the university medical school. In the "low expertise" condition, subjects were introduced to a "high school student" (actually an experimental confederate) who rated them individually on a series of personality traits. In both conditions, the communicator (either the high-expertise project director or the low-expertise high school student) told each subject that a discrepancy existed between his measures of the subject's masculinity-femininity and the subject's self-rating on this trait. The results indicate a significant effect of communicator expertise on changes in the subjects' beliefs regarding their "masculinity-femininity." More change in self-perception resulted when the communicator was of high-expertise than when he was of low-expertise, even though the information given by the different communicators was identical. This same result—greater attitude change produced by more expert communicative sources—has also been reported in studies by Aronson and Golden (1962) and Aronson, Turner, and Carlsmith (1963).

A second aspect of communicator credibility—"trustworthiness"—has been investigated in numerous studies. One of these, conducted by Walster, Aronson, and Abrahams (1966), manipulated the perceived trustworthiness of a communicator by varying whether the position advocated in a communication reflected or contravened the self-interest of the communicator. The researchers hypothesized that a communicator who argued against his own best interests would be more persuasive than a communicator who argued in favor of a position benefitting him. Subjects received a persuasive communication from a source who was identified either as a successful prosecuting attorney or as a criminal ("Joe the Shoulder"). The communications argued either for the position that courts should have more power (a position favoring the interests of the prosecutor) or for the view that courts should have less power (a position favoring the criminal). The results indicate that the persuasiveness of a communicator was greater when he was seen as arguing against his self-interest, presumably because the communicator had no incentive to bias his arguments.

Earlier studies by Hovland and Weiss (1951) and Kelman and Hovland (1953) also indicate that the trustworthiness of the communicator affects the persuasiveness of his communication. The difference in effectiveness between high-credibility and low-credibility communicators, however, is relatively short-lived. Several studies (Hovland, Lumsdaine, & Sheffield, 1949; Hovland & Weiss, 1951; Kelman & Hovland, 1953) find that with the passage of time, the amount of attitude change generated by the high-credibility source decreases while that generated by the low-credibility source increases. Hovland, Lumsdaine, and Sheffield have suggested that this occurs because message recipients dissociate *what* was said from *who* said it. Kelman and Hovland supported this interpretation by showing that when subjects are reminded of the source of the communication after a period of several weeks, the original effect of credibility recurs.

Although differences in communicator credibility do affect the persuasiveness of a communication, one might argue that this effect has little practical utility to a person wanting to use demand creation to increase his power in a real situation. As Zimbardo and Ebbesen (1969) point out, variations in communicator credibility manipulated in the experimental laboratory are much larger than what a person can usually accomplish in natural settings.

Nevertheless, an individual can frequently manipulate his apparent expertise and/or trustworthiness enough to produce differences of practical importance, especially if he simultaneously considers the discrepancy between the position he is advocating and that of the person he is trying to persuade. Koslin, Stoops, and Loh (1967), for instance, report a curvilinear relationship between a communication's discrepancy (from the recipient's beliefs) and the amount of resulting attitude change. Larger discrepancies lead to greater attitude change until the discrepancy becomes quite large, at which point the person receiving the message grows skeptical and consequently does not change his beliefs. This study also indicates that the combination of a high level of discrepancy and a high-prestige communicator (i.e., a high-credibility communicator) produces the greatest amount of attitude change. Aronson, Turner, and Carlsmith (1963) corroborate this finding, similarly reporting that a combination of high discrepancy with high credibility is most effective in producing attitude change. If a highly credible or prestigious person attempts to increase his power by persuading others to value more highly the outcomes he controls, he should use a discrepant message (such as grossly exaggerating the worth of his products) to achieve maximum effect.

Demand Creation Through Manipulation of the Situation

Manipulating the perceived characteristics of the communicator, or manipulating the content of the communication, are not the only mechanisms for shifting the values held by other persons. Individuals do not always act consistently with their values, especially if the situation forces or induces them to do otherwise. Interestingly, research indicates that a person can cause changes in the values held by others by forcing or inducing them to act contrary to these values. If a person behaves contrary to the values he holds—if, for instance, he works strenuously to attain outcomes he did not think he valued highly—then under some conditions he will change his values, rendering them consistent with his contravalent act. Since this effect depends upon the *amount* of threat or inducement used in compelling another to act contrary to his values, an influencer can create demand for the outcomes he controls by applying threats or inducements of the appropriate magnitude.

An early study by Festinger and Carlsmith (1959) investigated the effects of various levels of reward (i.e., money) on changes in values after performing an act that contravened one's original values. In this experiment, each subject performed an extremely dull task—putting spools on trays and turning pegs for an hour. Afterward, the subject was told that the experiment was investigating the effects of expectancies on performance, and he learned that, unlike himself, the next subject was supposed to believe at the start of the experiment that the impending task would prove very interesting. The experimenter mentioned that, unfortunately, the assistant who normally would tell the next subject about the "interesting" task was sick. The experimenter, therefore, requested the subject to take the place of the assistant and tell the next subject in the waiting room that the dull task was in fact interesting. The experimenter offered to pay the subject for telling this lie; the subject received either $1 or $20 for acting as the assistant, depending on the experimental treatment. Measures of the subjects' attitudes toward the task after telling the lie indicated that subjects who were paid $1 for lying liked the task more than those who were paid $20. In other words, the subjects receiving *less* inducement for performing a contravalent act changed their values *more*.

In addition to inducements, one can also use coercion to gain compliance, and research shows that the magnitude of the threat bears an *inverse* relation to the amount of value change. Brehm (see Brehm & Cohen, 1962) reports a study in which fraternity pledges were forced to perform a dull task (copying random numbers for three hours). The experimenter varied the magnitude of threat by telling half of the pledges that they would be paddled if they did not "volunteer" (low coercion), while telling the other half that they would appear before a tribunal and possibly be barred from membership in the fraternity if they did not participate (high coercion). The results indicated that, after completing the task, pledges in the low-coercion condition expressed greater liking for the dull task than pledges in the high-coercion condition. That is, the *less* the severity of the threat, the *greater* the value change following compliance.

The studies by Festinger and Carlsmith (1959) and by Brehm (1966) suggest that the greatest value change results when *small* threats and *small* inducements are used to obtain compliance. Under these circumstances, a person connot view his behavior as compelled by irresistible inducements or threats. Therefore he will see his behavior as stemming from the positive attributes of the activity or object in question (i.e., he will not see himself as lying, but rather as describing a task that is truly interesting), and he will distort the value of these attributes, rendering them consistent with his action in the situation. Presumably, in future behavioral exchanges, these modified values will determine his demand for the products being exchanged.

Note, however, that value change does not always bear an inverse relation to the magnitude of the inducement or threat used to gain compliance. For instance, a study by Carlsmith, Collins, and Helmreich (1966) suggests that the degree of a person's *public commitment* to a counterattitudinal act affects his change of values. In that experiment, subjects received varying amounts of inducement ($.50, $1.50, or $5) to tell a lie, and they told these lies in either a face-to-face situation (high public commitment) or an anonymous situation (low public commitment). The results show an *inverse* relationship between size of inducement and amount of value change only under the high commitment condition; in contrast the results show a *direct* relationship under low commitment. A person must feel publicly committed to, or identified with, his actions before a low level of inducement produces large changes in value consistent with the actions.

Studies by Linder, Cooper, and Jones (1967) and by Holmes and Strickland (1970) indicate that a second factor—*freedom of choice*— is a necessary condition for small inducements to produce large changes in value. Linder et al. report two studies that varied the degree to which subjects felt free *not to comply* with the request for counterattitudinal behavior. When subjects felt free to refuse taking a counterattitudinal position but went ahead and did so anyway, the inverse relationship between size of inducement and amount of attitude change appeared: small inducements effected large attitude change. But when subjects had no free choice to refuse the request for counterattitudinal behavior, size of inducement showed a positive relation with attitude change. Under this condition, small inducements produced little attitude change, and large inducements produced more attitude change. Results reported by Holmes and Strickland (1970) substantiate these findings.

In sum, various studies suggest that, by using threats or inducements to compel counterattitudinal behavior, an individual can induce changes in another's values. A person might especially do this to increase another's desire for the outcomes he supplies. Small inducements or small threats are effective in producing changes in values, but this necessitates public commitment and high freedom of choice. Under low commitment and little freedom of choice, large inducements are required to engender greater value changes.

Extension of the Power Network (Utilizing Alternatives)

Just as blocking outcomes and demand creation affect the availability and the value of outcomes to other persons, still other tactics modify the availability and the value of *one's own outcomes*. The tactics of withdrawal and extension of the power network shift the value and scarcity, respectively, of the outcomes obtained by the use of the tactic, and in consequence they, too, realign the balance of power.

If the congressman, mentioned in earlier examples, seeks (and subsequently attains) electoral support from sources other than the conservation group, he extends the power network. By increasing his availability of valued outcomes (electoral support), he improves his negotiating position vis-à-vis the conservationists. If they refuse to provide electoral support at a reasonable price (in terms of political representation), the congressman can terminate the relationship and go elsewhere for support.

In using extension of the power network, then, a person attains (or creates the possibility of attaining) valued outcomes from alternative suppliers outside a given relationship. The extent to which he will use this tactic depends, in part, on the attractiveness of the external alternatives. Thibaut and Kelley (1959) have argued that dependency (and conversely, power) rests on the value of outcomes available outside a relationship relative to the value of those available within it. They postulate that a person will leave a (voluntary) exchange, even though he may be dissatisfied, only when the rewards outside the relationship exceed those available within it. Research by Schellenberg (1965) and by Thibaut and Faucheux (1965) lends credence to this proposition. In these experiments, subjects had access to valued alternatives outside a situation in which they depended on another person for rewards. A subject either could cooperate with the other person or could opt for an alternative reward outside the relationship. Both studies demonstrated that the greater the value of the available alternatives, the greater the subjects' proclivity to "defect" from the dependency situation and choose the external alternative.

But rewards outside the relationship are not always certain. To defect from a stable relationship may involve some risk, for the alternative outcomes might not be assured. People often remain in relationships that provide poorer outcomes than might be obtained elsewhere, because they eschew the risk that may accompany pursuit of the better outcomes. A person's decision to opt for an outside relationship depends on the probability of actually obtaining the better outcome as well as on the value of the outcome itself. In other words, the expected value (or, as Ofshe & Ofshe, 1969, term it, the "expected utility") of outside alternatives determines the use of extension of the power network. Using a gaming situation, Vinacke, Lichtman, and Cherulnik (1967) varied subjects' perceived probability of winning if they played independently of other participants. In some instances, success outside the relationship with others appeared relatively likely; in other instances, it appeared relatively unlikely. Results indicate that use of extension of the power network depends both on the attractiveness (value) of alternatives and on the certainty of attaining the alternative rewards.

Given that a person's propensity to *use* this tactic depends on attractiveness and certainty of the alternative, we may ask what determines the *effectiveness* of extension of the power network in modifying the terms of an existing relationship. In other words, when will this tactic successfully alter the rate of exchange within the relationship that one threatens to leave?

Several studies have investigated the determinants of this tactic's effectiveness. Research reported by Kelley and Arrowood (1960) indicates that the value of alternatives available to a person outside a given relationship affects the amount of rewards he receives inside that relationship. In this study, which used three-person groups, subjects could establish cooperative subgroups (dyads) to foster attainment of their goals in a game situation. Such groups formed when two subjects made mutual choices of each other as partners *and* agreed upon the division of rewards if their subgroup should win. Each subject also had access to alternative rewards outside the dyad; these alternative rewards varied in value. The results indicated that subjects having the more valuable alternatives received a larger share of winnings *within* the dyads than did subjects having the less valuable alternatives. Access to attractive external alternatives afforded greater influence and enabled subjects to secure greater rewards within the dyadic relationship.

Another study, reported by Kiesler and Corbin (1965), demonstrates that attractive alternatives increase the degree to which individuals act independently and resist influence from other members of the group. As the reader will remember, power was defined earlier in this chapter as the capacity both to influence others and to remain independent of the influence of others. Kiesler and Corbin manipulated the extent to which subjects liked the other members of a group as well as the degree to which they felt they could leave the group and join another group during subsequent sessions of the experiment. Subjects then received (bogus) information indicating that their individual aesthetic judgments about paintings differed from the group's consensus. The experiment's results indicate that, for those subjects who did not like the other members of the group, the availability of ready alternatives outside the group resulted in a low level of conformity to the group's apparent standards; in contrast, subjects not liking the group but having only a poor outside alternative conformed more highly. The group could not attain conformity from an unattracted subject if he had access to alternatives.

These studies by Kelley and Arrowood and by Kiesler and Corbin, then, suggest that the availability of attractive alternatives outside a relationship increases a person's influence within that relationship (as indexed by the level of rewards received) as well as his capacity to resist influence from other group members. In both senses, extension of the power network can effectively change the terms of an ongoing relationship.

Withdrawal

Extension of the power network, as just discussed, affects one's outcomes by increasing alternative sources of supply. In contrast, the fourth tactic, withdrawal, changes the balance of power by reducing the extent to which one *values* outcomes provided by others. Such a devaluation constitutes a downward shift in the demand curve for those outcomes. In the politician-conservationist example, if the congressman decides he does not care about winning the election as much as he once did, he "withdraws" valuation from electoral support. All other things remaining the same, this renders the politician more independent of the conservationists' demands for political representation, because he no longer desires what they offer in exchange.

Under what conditions will people use the tactic of withdrawal? Leventhal and Bergman (1969) have demonstrated that withdrawal may occur when an exchange creates extreme inequity. Subjects participated in a mathematical problem solving task with an experimenter's confederate who posed as another subject. The confederate had discretion over the division of the money won by the two persons acting as a team. In one condition (mild inequity), the confederate allotted the subject slightly less money than he kept for himself, even though both persons did the same amount of work. In the other condition (extreme inequity), the confederate retained almost all the money for himself. Leventhal and Bergman reasoned that only under extreme inequity would subjects devalue the monetary reward. To test this, they afforded each subject an opportunity to redistribute the rewards to a limited degree, taking a little bit more for himself if he desired. Most subjects gave themselves more money when allowed to do so, but a few used this opportunity to give away the small amount of money they had received. As predicted, more subjects experiencing extreme inequity gave away their money than did subjects experiencing mild inequity, suggesting that extreme inequity can produce withdrawal from valued outcomes.

Another study, Schachter's (1951) classic research on reactions to deviance in groups, can be interpreted as demonstrating another factor that influences withdrawal—the extent of deviant behavior. Schachter created a situation where several confederates intentionally deviated from the standards prevailing within the group. Schachter varied the length of time that confederates adamantly repudiated the wishes of the group. One confederate (the "deviate") adopted a stance distant from the group's consensus and maintained this position throughout the interaction, another confederate (the "slider") initially assumed a deviant stance but subsequently changed his position to conform to the group's, and a third (the "mode") always assumed the average position prevailing within the group. The duration of deviance represented a person's intransigence, and the group members seemed to realize that they were less likely to gain valuable compliance from the more obstinate deviate. The experiment's results suggest that members eventually devalued the outcomes that the deviate potentially mediated for them. One indication stems from the patterns of communication within the group. Members directed intensive pressure toward the deviate early in the session, but they subsequently stopped talking to him when they discerned that he couldn't be persuaded. Apparently, they no longer valued the deviate's compliance, and they ostracized him. A second indication of withdrawal is found in the committee assignments made by the members. When asked to specify which persons they would assign to several committees established by the group, members placed the deviate on the least important committee. In contrast, they placed the conforming confederate (the "mode") on the more important committees. Persons seen as less likely to comply were assigned roles on which the other members did not depend highly. In sum, Schachter's findings suggest that the duration of deviance (or the perceived likelihood that valuable outcomes will not eventually be attained) determines the degree of withdrawal

Several factors in addition to those mentioned by Leventhal and Bergman and by Schachter can induce withdrawal. Our earlier discussion of demand creation suggested that the judicious use of force (coercion and inducements) by one person could produce changes in another's values, as a secondary effect. A person, forced to engage in contravalent behavior, would bring his values in line with his behavior. Since both demand creation and withdrawal involve changes in value, the logic applying to demand creation also applies to withdrawal. Research, for instance, demonstrates that a person forced to forego a valuable outcome may change the extent to which he values that outcome.

Aronson and Carlsmith (1963), using a forced compliance situation, showed that the magnitude of the threat used to gain compliance determines the extent of devaluation. Using children as subjects, this study varied the level of coercion associated with the demand not to play with an attractive toy, and looked at changes in the value of the toy. Subjects received either a severe threat or a mild threat not to play with the toy. The results indicate that children who received the mild threat (and who subsequently renounced playing with the toy) devalued the toy more than those who refrained from playing because of a severe threat. In other words, when required to abjure a value outcome (as in Schachter's study mentioned above), subjects lessened their value for that outcome; and they lessened it more, the smaller the threat used in forcing them to give it up. Pepitone, McCauley, and Hammond (1967), in replicating these results, also found a reduction in value under mild threat.

Still another determinant of withdrawal—perceived freedom of choice—has been investigated by Brehm and his associates. In presenting a theory of "psychological reactance." Brehm posits that people may either increase or decrease their valuation of rewards whenever their freedom to choose or judge those rewards becomes constricted by other persons.

A study by Hammock and Brehm (1966) demonstrates this effect clearly. In this experiment, Hammock and Brehm led one group of children to expect they would have a choice among various candy bars (expected choice condition); another group of children were led to believe that the choice among candy bars would be made for them (no expected choice). In all cases, each child subsequently received a candy bar that the experimenter chose for him. No child chose for himself. The results indicated that the children who expected to have a choice decreased their valuation of the candy bar they received more than the children who expected no choice, suggesting that the usurpation of an individual's right to choose may lead to withdrawal.

In sum, research indicates that various factors—extreme inequity, deviance, magnitude of threat, and usurpation of free choice—may lead to a withdrawal response in power relations.

The Use of Deception in Power Tactics

We have viewed power tactics as behaviors that cause shifts in dependency relationships by modifying the value and scarcity of behavioral outcomes exchanged between people. Our review of the four general tactics—blocking outcomes, demand creation, extension of the power network, and withdrawal—was limited exclusively to strategies that caused *actual* shifts in these bases of dependency. But our model reveals that all power does not rest upon the *actual* state of the relationships, because the demand and supply curves defining the power relationship describe the *perceived*, not the actual, dependencies between people.

The original statement of the exchange model made the simplifying assumption that all participants had full knowledge of the actual demand and supply curves confronting the parties in the relationship. By making this assumption we were able to talk about the "actual rate of exchange." But, palpably, this stringent assumption does not accurately describe normal, everyday affairs.

In this section we will relax this assumption of "full knowledge." A number of behaviors can change the *perceived* relationships between people—the perceived demand and supply curves—without causing *actual* shifts in the real value or scarcity of outcomes. Such behaviors involve *deception*. If a person can be deceived regarding the true positions of the demand and supply curves defining the exchange, the effect on his behavior will simulate the usage of actual power tactics against him. Interestingly, there seems to be a deceptive counterpart to each of the four power tactics already described.

Some illustrations can make this point clear. A person can feign withdrawal from outcomes mediated by others, even though he actually is still interested. A customer, for example, might play down his interest in a particular used car, thereby misleading the salesman in the hope of getting a low price. Similarly, "playing hard to get" is a deceptive variant of withdrawal frequently used in romantic relationships. Delusive use of withdrawal is commonplace, but other tactics can be used deceptively, as well. Exaggerating the attractiveness or availability of alternatives may prove especially useful in gaining added independence within a relationship. Potter (1951) describes such a delusory version of extension of the power network as "clubmanship." He suggests that to raise one's power within a given relationship (or "club"), one should be at pains to let others know he has attractive alternatives available, even if he actually does not. Such tactics diminish the demands that other persons ("club members") would dare to levy, lest one of the ostensive alternatives be exercised. In similar fashion, a person may use a deceptive variant of blocking outcomes. Threats that appear plausible, even though they cannot actually be carried out, may effectively deter certain actions and change the terms of a relationship. Politicians, for instance, may threaten to block outcomes by forming coalitions, even though they lack control over the alleged coalition partners. If a person can be convinced of the veracity of such a coalition, he may respond as if it really exists. It is exactly the lack of information that makes deception possible, especially when a person finds it costly or impossible to test the deceiver's claims.

Fischer (1969) reports an experiment where the deceptive use of withdrawal enabled one person to gain an advantageous agreement from another. Fischer had two subjects bargain over the division of ninety points in ten point units (80-10, 70-20, 60-30, etc.). Each subject's goal was to gain as many points as possible. The situation was complicated by time pressure, for the subjects lost points for each second they took in reaching an agreement. Moreover, subjects were constrained with regard to what they could accept in the bargain. Before each bargaining session, each subject received a slip of paper indicating his "minimum necessary share" (MNS). The MNS constituted a number that would be subtracted from the subject's winnings after each bargain; thus, for the subject to make a profit, he had to receive more than his MNS for that trial. For each trial, one subject's MNS differed from the other's, and neither subject knew the MNS of the other.

Fischer's study manipulated the "threat potential" of the players. "Low threat" involved the ability to fine the other an insignificant three points per trial, while "high threat" involved the ability to fine the other thirty points per trial. During the experiment, the subjects bargained verbally over the distribution of the ninety points, using any tactics they chose. The results indicate that deceptive power tactics can substitute effectively for actual power tactics under conditions of incomplete information. One of the ploys used by subjects was to misrepresent the size of their MNS, that is, to misrepresent the outside constraints that they must meet while striking a bargain. Such pervarication, which constituted the deceptive use of withdrawal because subjects mendaciously represented low outcomes as useless and therefore valueless, was more prevalent among subjects with low threat potential than among those with high threat potential. Results showed that, in those groups where members held unequal threat potentials, the subjects with high threat potential preferred to use threats, while the subjects with low threat potential used the deceptive tactic of lying about their MNS. Feigned withdrawal was substituted for the actual manipulation of outcomes when the latter was impossible. Moreover, results show that, in terms of gaining points in the bargaining, lying proved as efficacious as making threats: the effects of the deceptive tactics equalled the effects of the actual power tactic.

Thus far, we have suggested that an individual can use duplicity and deception as a direct substitute for power tactics. By capitalizing on uncertainty and misrepresenting the conditions of supply and demand that characterize an interpersonal exchange, he may simulate the actual power tactics and attain a more favorable rate of exchange. But if there exist delusory counterparts of the four power tactics, still other forms of deception occur in social interaction. Specifically, one person can deceive another regarding the behavioral *product* involved in an exchange. Misrepresentation of a product's true properties must be distinguished from misrepresentation of the supply and demand conditions governing the product's availability. A blatant example of product misrepresentation occurs in the case of the fly-by-night salesman. If he can dupe his customers into thinking his shoddy wares are actually well made, durable, highly serviceable, and fully guaranteed, then he can command a high price for his merchandise. This technique works not because the salesman is using deceptive variants of the power tactics themselves, but because the customer has no means to test the truth of the claims regarding the nature of the merchandise. Certainly if the customer realized the merchandise was inferior, he would pay a low price or perhaps not purchase the items at all. But deception involving product misrepresentation is not limited to material items, for behavioral products can also be misrepresented, as in the case of false friendship. A person may intentionally misrepresent himself as a friend, especially when friendship is an expedient route to personal gain. Such behavior is commonly branded "ingratiation."

This intriguing form of deception has been studied by Jones (1964) and his associates. Jones conceptualizes ingratiation as the attempt to increase one's personal attractiveness (i.e., value) to another in the hope of gaining something of value in return. He proposes that three basic modes of ingratiation may be used to increase one's personal value: self-presentation (i.e., selective overemphasis and exaggeration of one's valued attributes), conformity to the opinions of another even when one does not actually share these opinions, and other-enchancement (i.e., flattering the other person). Each mode of ingratiation has received some attention from investigators.

Use of ingratiation tactics is most probable when one person depends upon another for important outcomes (Davis & Florquist, 1965; Jones & Jones, 1964; Kaufman & Steiner, 1968). However, a study by Jones, Gergen, Gumpert, and Thibaut (1965) has demonstrated that the "target person" (i.e., the person to whom the ingratiation attempts are directed) must also have some palpable choice in the use of his power for ingratiation to occur. In other words, ingratiation is more likely when the target person has the discretionary power either to provide or to withhold something of value for the ingratiator.

The choice of ingratiation tactic (self-presentation, opinion conformity, or other-enhancement) depends on the situation. Jones, Gergen, Gumpert, and Thibaut (1965) hypothesized that the "supervisor" who can mediate benefits to his "workers" only when they meet preestablished criteria in solving problems will not be ingratiated as much as the supervisor who manifestly exercises discretion in judging the correctnesss of solutions. The experimental results supported this notion. When subjects were afforded a chance to express their position on various opinion items to their supervisor (opinion conformity ingratiation), they conformed more to the supervisor's opinion when he had some discretion than when he had none. The results did not indicate, however, that this held true for other forms of ingratiation. For instance, the subjects did *not* flatter the supervisor having discretion more extensively than the supervisor having no discretion.

The lack of any difference in use of flattery (i.e., ingratiation through other-enhancement) between the "discretion" and "no discretion" conditions in the Jones et al. (1965) study might result from the subjects' feeling that flattery in the discretion situation would be detected as ingratiation, which would cause the attempt to fail. Research by Jones and Jones (1964), Kaufman and Steiner (1968), and Stires and Jones (1969) suggests that the possibility of detection enters the deliberations of would-be ingratiators. Jones and Jones found that ingratiators preferred moderate levels of opinion conformity, presumably because extremes in conformity make the target person suspicious. Kaufman and Steiner found that the use of ingratiation declined as the transparency of ingratiation-inducing conditions became greater, again indicating that ingratiators seek an "optimal" level of ingratiation that will escape detection. Stires and Jones found that ingratiators using self-presentation portray themselves favorably only on those dimensions not limited to the subjective judgments of others (e.g., they would not represent themselves as highly popular), and this also supports the notion that ingratiators structure their techniques to avoid detection. Presumably, the target evaluator would find it suspect that another makes favorable remarks about himself in areas that are the province only of other persons' subjective judgments.

Finally, some research has dealt with the costs of ingratiation. A study of Jones, Gergen, and Jones (1963) suggests that persons use ingratiation more frequently when it involves low cost to the ingratiator, where cost is expressed in terms of maintaining his status in the situation. In this study, ROTC cadets were placed in a situation where they could use opinion conformity to ingratiate. Higher-status cadets avoided opinion conformity with lower status cadets on issues associated with rank in the corps. Interestingly, these same higher-status cadets were *more* willing than their lower-ranking counterparts to use opinion conformity on issues not related to their differences in rank. The higher-status cadets avoided conforming on status-relevant issues because conformity would bring into question their independence from influence on these issues.

Norm Formation and Status Emergence

To this point, we have shown how a model of power tactics devolves from the exchange framework and how this model organizes many theoretical and empirical studies on the use and efficacy of the tactics.

Let us now consider one of the *consequences* resulting from the use of power tactics. While power tactics can lead to many different consequences—such as changes in liking among persons, provocation of countertactics, and variations in group effectiveness—we shall limit our present discussion to the emergence of status and the formation of norms resulting from tactical power capabilities.

We choose to discuss status emergence and norm formation because such normative arrangements can function, in considerable degree, as *direct substitutes* for raw power. Persons do not use power tactics all the time, since they can be very costly as well as disruptive in ongoing relations. Instead, as Thibaut and Kelley (1959) have argued, people prefer to invoke norms to gain compliance to their wishes. Of course, for someone to use norms as a means of influence to attain outcomes he desires, the norms must prescribe behaviors that facilitate attainment of these outcomes. While norms can serve as substitutes for power in selectively limiting behavior, the content of norms—the behaviors prescribed or proscribed—becomes problematic.

The content of norms reflects, at least in some degree, the raw power capabilities that persons have and could use if needed. In the present section we shall review a panoply of studies demonstrating that such power capabilities underlie normative arrangements in ongoing groups.

Norms and Status

Norms are rules governing behavior. They express the expectations or agreements prevailing among group members, thereby demarcating the rights and obligations of members vis-à-vis one another. "Norm" and "status" are parallel concepts in the sense that both specify *rights* and *obligations*. But rights and obligations need not apply equally to all members of the group: sometimes they are distributed differentially among group members. Where we find such differentiation, we speak not merely of rules or norms, but of status. That is, persons of high status hold more rights to highly valued outcomes (such as greater access to group resources, including greater individual rewards and perquisites) as well as different obligations from those applying to lower status persons.

How do persons gain high status within groups? Several theorists, operating from the exchange perspective, have proposed answers to this question. Fundamentally, they argue that *differential obligations (i.e., status) arise from unreciprocated exchange relationships*.

Homans (1961) views the emergence of status as the creation of "debt." When a person provides others with valued outcomes that they cannot immediately reciprocate, obligations emerge within exchange relationships. These debts typically are *generalized* obligations: when subsequently invoked at the discretion of the higher-status person, their repayment can assume a variety of forms. But in every case, repayment of the obligations occurs by compliance to the requests of the high-status person.

Blau (1964) and Harsanyi (1966) similarly view the emergence of status as a function of differential contributions in an exchange relationship. Blau suggests that people incur obligations by accepting rewards from others under circumstances where immediate reciprocation is impossible. Harsanyi, looking at social exchange in terms of bargaining relationships, sees status arising from a "bargain" in which status differences emerge from the differential "rewards and punishments" members can deliver to one another. Harsanyi argues that higher status gives an individual more influence over the actions of other members and greater access to resources controlled by the group.

If these arguments concerning the sources and consequences of status are correct—that is, if status emerges from unreciprocated exchange as Homans suggests and if status functions as a substitute for power as suggested by Thibaut and Kelley and by Harsanyi—we would expect research on status and power to demonstrate two things: first, that status differences emerge in groups where members make unequal contributions and, second, that once status differences emerge from unreciprocated exchange, they engender consequences similar to those resulting from differences in power. Moreover, since the *power tactics* can augment or diminish one's capacity to provide unreciprocable outcomes in an exchange, research should demonstrate that these tactics influence the emergence of status differences in groups. As we shall see below, some research supports these expectations. Power can lead to status, and status differences can, under certain circumstances, serve as substitutes for power.

Normative Arrangements Resulting From Power Capabilities

We shall review some empirical research that lends support to this argument about the relationships between power and status. To begin, we look at some determinants of norm formation and status emergence.

Several studies have demonstrated that differential power capabilities give rise to contractual norms. An important study by Thibaut and Faucheux (1965) demonstrates that when both persons in a competitive situation have access to power tactics which can lower the outcomes of the other, a norm restricting the user of power by both persons probably will emerge. In comparison, when only one party has access to a power tactic, such a contractual norm is less likely to form.

In their study, Thibaut and Faucheux established a situation where two subjects made choices that involved conflicting interests. One subject had the prerogative of distributing the rewards from whatever outcome the two persons chose jointly. Depending upon the experimental treatment, he had a very wide or very narrow range of discretion. In our terms, he could use the tactic of blocking the other subject's outcomes, and his capacity to block outcomes was greater when he had a wide range of discretion. The other subject also had power, which he could exercise by choosing an alternative outside the immediate situation. In some cases, this external alternative was valuable to him; in other cases, less so. If this subject chose the external alternative, his opponent received nothing. This subject, then, could use the tactic of extending the power network, coupled with blocking outcomes.

These distributions of power created the following possibilities. When the first subject could distribute rewards within a wide range, he could threaten the other with a sharp inequality in outcomes. However, if the other person had access to an external alternative that was very valuable, he could threaten to leave the first person with no winnings whatever. The results indicated that when both persons held a high level of power, they typically established contractual agreements (i.e., norms) controlling one another's behaviors and restricting the use of power. Subjects established contractual norms less frequently when their tactical power capabilities were less strong. Further, the norms established under high mutual threat carried large penalties for violation; penalties declined when threats were less severe.

In a study paralleling that by Thibaut and Facheux, Murdoch (1967) manipulated subjects' perceptions of the likelihood that others would use their power. Murdoch's results indicate that variations in these probabilities lead to differences in the frequency of norm formation. Where both persons in a dyad are perceived as prone to use the power they hold, contractual norms are most likely to form and the penalties imposed for violation of the norms are most severe.

In a third study demonstrating the connection between power tactics and norm formation, Michener and Zeller (1970) used a situation involving a different power tactic—coalition formation—and studied the extent to which strength of a coalition affects the emergence of contractual norms. This study varied the strength of the coalition that two persons could form to block the outcomes of a third (i.e., the magnitude of the damage that a coalition could wreak). The results show that, when subjects formed contracts limiting the use of power, they attached greater fines for violation under high coalition strength than under low coalition strength.

In sum, these three studies suggest that differences in the access to various power tactics—extension of the power network, blocking outcomes individually, and coalition formation—can lead to differences in emerging contractual norms. In a parallel fashion, other experimental research has shown that power discrepancies can lead to differences in *status*. Both contractual norms and status norms specify rights and obligations among group members. The concept "status" merely emphasizes that rights and obligations are distributed *differentially* among members.

A study by Burnstein and Wolosin (1968) demonstrated that differences between group members in performance lead to disparities in status within the group. Burnstein and Wolosin set up two-person groups, whose goal was to win money on a reaction-time task. The faster the reaction-time of group members, the more money the group won. Subjects received false feedback concerning their relative abilities on the task, which created the perception of differences in performance capabilities. Since the subjects could enhance their chances of winning a large reward by distributing "control status" among themselves in a pattern corresponding to their performance differences, group members had to decide how they would weight their responses, that is, who, if either, would have more control over the activities of the group.

One can see that, under this arrangement, performance becomes equivalent to the capacity to provide rewarding and valued services to other group members. For this reason, performance becomes a resource base, and the capacity to withhold valued performance serves as the power to block outcomes. Differences in performance, then, imply differences in the magnitudes of valued outcomes that persons can withhold, or equivalently, differences in access to power tactics.

The results of Burnstein and Wolosin's study indicate that the greater the superiority of a member's performance (i.e., the greater his capacity to block outcomes), the greater the level of control status given to him. Moreover, the amount of control status given to a person depended on the extent to which the status represented valued attributes. When subjects believed that the reaction-time task reflected such highly valued attributes as intelligence, creativity, and adaptibility, members gave status to others less reluctantly than when they believed that the task reflected no important personal skills. When the value of a unit of status was greater, members granted it to others less willingly.

The study by Burnstein and Wolosin, then, indicates that status differences can emerge from, and reflect, differences in the tactical power capabilities of group members.

A related study by Michener and Lawler (1970) provides another demonstration that power is convertible into status. In this study, lower-status members of a group could form a coalition to confiscate rewards from a higher-status leader. The strength of such coalitions varied. Depending on the experimental treatment, they could inflict either substantial damage or only minor damage. Results indicate that coalitional members utilized their threat potential to compel a reallocation of status prerogatives and responsibilities among group members. Reallocation was particularly likely when the group, under the leadership of the high-status member, appeared to fail repeatedly at its collective task. When mobilized under such conditions of failure, the highly potent coalitions proved especially successful in stripping the leader of status and responsibility. Their greater threat capability enabled the members of the strong coalitions to arrogate more status to themselves.

Influence and Independence Resulting from Status

The studies of contractual norms and status emergence suggest that differences in power cause normative and status differences. But just as power can lead to status, status can lead to power. At least, status can be substituted for the overt use of power, because it can provide the same outcomes attainable through the use of overt power—the ability to influence others and the capacity to remain independent of the influence of others.

Several theorists provide a conceptual base indicating why status is convertible into influence. Both Homans (1961) and Blau (1964) conceptualize status as a sort of "debt" or "expendable capital." People accord status to others who supply valuable, scarce outcomes that cannot be reciprocated immediately. Status thus signifies the debt and becomes a sort of "promissory note" that the higher-status person can redeem at some future occasion of his own choosing, within limitations. One way a higher-status person may redeem such a "note" is in the form of influence, that is, having the other comply with his wishes under the appropriate circumstances.

Status, then, should afford influence, and some experimental research demonstrates clearly that it does.

A number of studies show that *performance status* leads to influence. Performance status means simply that group members have differential ability to provide valued outcomes for the group. A study by Hollander, Julian, and Perry (1966) manipulated performance status by giving subjects false feedback concerning their performances on a group task. Some subjects were led to believe they had performed poorly on the task, while other subjects thought they had performed well. Within each group, subjects knew how all of the other members had done. The situation required each group to make a number of decisions. The group designated a leader, but the experiment manipulated the group's perception of how well the leader performed on the group task. The role of the leader was to offer initial suggestions concerning the group's decision on its task.

The group then discussed the leader's suggestions, although the leader made the final determination regarding the group's action. The results of the study indicated that when the members perceived the leader as having high-performance status, they agreed with and accepted the leader's suggestions more than when they perceived the leader as having low-performance status. In other words, high status afforded the leader more influence over others. Studies by Mausner (1954) and Cohen, Mayer, Schulman, and Terry (1961) similarly report that differences in performance status lead to differences in influence over others.

Pruitt (1968) extends the argument that status confers influence. In his study, Pruitt manipulated the status of his subjects by varying the resources available to them. He found that influence, measured in terms of the money distributed willingly to the high-status person by people of lower-status, depended both upon the amount of resources the high-status person had controlled at an earlier time (when he provided unreciprocated outcomes) and upon the resources that others expected he would hold in the future. In other words, influence depends not only on a person's present contributions to the group (as reflected in performance differences), but also on his past contributions and his expected future contributions.

These studies (Hollander, Julian, & Perry, 1966; Mausner, 1954; Pruitt, 1968) have dealt with influences resulting from differences in the capacity to reward others through performance within the group. Other studies have indicated that performance differences in external settings, outside the group, also constitute a basis for influencing others, possibly because they engender expectations regarding performance within the group setting. Studies by Strodtback, Simon and Hawkins (1958) and Moore (1968) have demonstrated this effect.

Strodtbeck and his associates conducted a number of studies involving simulated juries. These studies consistently showed that persons of higher (occupational) prestige, or status, outside the jury setting had proportionately greater influence over decisions within the jury setting. Moore (1968) has substantiated and extended this general finding by experimentally manipulating subjects' perceptions of external status characteristics. Moore used pairs of subjects recruited from the same junior college. He manipulated the perceived external status of the subjects by creating the impression that one of the persons present attended either a prestigious college (high external status) or a local high school (low external status). Moore observed the influence in the situation by counting the number of times a subject yielded to the conflicting judgments of the other subject during a perceptual recognition task. The results indicate that when the subjects thought the other subject had high external status (prestigious college), they yielded to his judgments more than when they thought he had low external status (local high school).

To this point, we have argued that status is transformed into influence, with high-status persons exercising more influence. But power, as we noted in the beginning of the chapter, includes the capacity to *resist influence*, as well as the capacity to *exercise influence*. It follows, then, that if status substitutes for power, we would expect to see high status afford not only influence but also immunity from influence by others.

Hollander (1958) propounds a theory of the acquisition and use of status that suggests why status might enable one to resist influence. Hollander coined the term "idiosyncrasy credit" to refer to this capacity to flout the demands of others. He suggests that a person acquires idiosyncrasy credits by demonstrating competence on the group task and by conforming to group norms. The greater the number of idiosyncrasy credits accumulated, the greater one's capacity to deviate from group norms with impunity. In essense, Hollander suggests that one has to demonstrate he is a "good" member of the group—in terms of contributions and conformity— before he can deviate from the group's norms without incurring punishment.

Hollander's theory, then, maintains that a person with accumulated idiosyncrasy credits (i.e., a high-status person) has the prerogative to deviate, which is tantamount to the capacity to remain independent of group norms and pressures from other members. Given this argument, we would expect empirical data to show that high-status members act more independently than lower-status members—i.e., that differences in status lead to differences in independent behavior. Several studies do, in fact, provide such evidence.

Dittes and Kelley (1956) and Harvey and Consalvi (1960), using acceptance by other group members as an index of status, found a curvilinear relationship between status and conformity in groups facing perceptual judgment tasks. Conformity was greatest for middle-status members; nonconforming, independent behavior was exhibited most by low-status and high-status members. These findings, however, do not show unequivocally that this curvilinear relationship represents the true relationship between status and conformity, because differences in attraction to the group confound the results. Apparently, lower status members (i.e., those least accepted by others) found the group less attractive, which might explain why they conformed relatively less. Since Dittes and Kelley, however, provide evidence of no differences in attraction between their high-status and middle-status members, the data seem to indicate that high-status members, as against middle-status members, conform less to the norms of the group, at least as they apply to the measures used in these experiments.

Hollander, Julian, and Sorrentino (1969) report a third study demonstrating that higher status leads to greater independence of action. In their study, Hollander et al. varied status by imparting false feedback to a group regarding the strength of endorsement of their leader. In some groups the leader was represented as strongly endorsed by the members while in other groups he ostensibly received a weaker endorsement. Following the endorsement, the groups discussed a number of issues, with the other members separated physically from their leader. Following the discussions, the group recommended a course of action to their leader. The leader could either endorse the group judgment or veto it and substitute his own judgment. In all cases the group was informed of the leader's decision, and the leader was allowed to justify his action to the group. The results indicate that strength of endorsement—or security about one's status—leads to a greater number of vetoes over decisions proposed by the group. In other words, the high-status leaders who felt more secure about their status behaved more independently of group influence than those who felt less secure about their status.

Various studies, then, substantiate the proposition that higher-status persons are not only more able to influence the behavior of others, but also more able to resist others' efforts to dominate. Just as power tactics can impel the emergence of status differences, status itself can lead to capabilities similar to those conferred by power.

Summary

In this chapter we have shown that the basic power tactics—blocking outcomes (threats and coalitions), demand creation, extension of the power network, and withdrawal—derive from the elementary concepts of social exchange theory. These tactics are interesting because they constitute a fundamental means by which individuals modify relationships with other people. Using the exchange framework as a theoretical base, we have reviewed various empirical studies on the conditions determining the use and the effectiveness of each power tactic. Further, we have noted that one can use deceptive variants of these tactics (such as ingratiation) to change the terms of a relationship when uncertainty shrouds activity.

The value of proposing a model of power tactics rests not so much in the answers it provides but in the questions it raises. We have treated only a few of the questions implied by the model, and the literature we have reviewed yields only partial answers to those we did treat. The last section of this chapter, in providing an example of the issues that the model raises, proposes that contractual norms and status distinctions emerge from the use of power tactics. But many other consequences (e.g., the escalation of conflict, changes in affective relations) could be considered as well, and the exchange model of power tactics should prove useful in the search for answers to these further questions.

References

Aronson, E., & Carlsmith, J. M. Effect of the severity of threat on the devaluation of forbidden behavior. *Journal of Abnormal and Social Psychology*, 1963, 66, 584-588.

Aronson, E., & Golden, B. W. The effect of relevant and irrelevant aspects of communicator credibility on opinion change. *Journal of Personality*, 1962, 30, 135-146.

Aronson, E., Turner, J. A., & Carlsmith, J. M. Communicator credibility and communication discrepancy as determinants of opinion change. *Journal of Abnormal and Social Psychology*, 1963, 67, 31-36.

Bergin, A. E. The effect of dissonant persuasive communications upon changes in self-referring attitudes. *Journal of Personality*, 1962, 30, 423-438.

Berscheid, E., & Walster, E. Attitude change. In J. Mills (Ed.), *Experimental social psychology*. London: Macmillan, 1969.

Blau, P. M. *Exchange and power in social life*. New York: Wiley, 1964.

Brehm, J. W. *A theory of psychological reactance*. New York: Academic Press, 1966.

Brehm, J. W., & Cohen, A. R. *Explorations in cognitive dissonance*. New York: Wiley, 1962.

Burnstein, E., & Wolosin, R. J. The development of status distinctions under conditions of inequity. *Journal of Experimental Social Psychology*, 1968, 4, 415-430.

Caplow, T. A. A theory of coalitions in the triad. *American Sociological Review*, 1956, 21, 489-493.

Carlsmith, J. M., Collins, B. E. & Helmreich, R. L. Studies in forced compliance: I. The effect of pressure for compliance on attitude change produced by face-to-face role playing and anonymous essay writing. *Journal of Personality and Social Psychology*, 1966, 4, 1-13.

Chertkoff, J. N. The effect of probability of future success on coalition formation. *Journal of Experimental Social Psychology*, 1966, 2, 265-277.

Cohen, B. P., Mayer, T. F., Schulman, G. I., & Terry, C. Relative competence and Conformity. Mimeographed paper, Sociology Department, Stanford University, 1961.

Collins, B. E., & Raven, B. H. Group structure: attraction, coalitions, communication, and power. In G. Lindzey & E. Aronson (Eds.), *The handbook of social psychology*. Vol. 4. Reading, Mass.: Addison-Wesley, 1969.

Davis, K. E., & Florquist, C. C. Perceived threat and dependence as determinants of the tactical usage of opinion conformity. *Journal of Experimental Social Psychology*, 1965, 1, 219-236.

Deutsch, M., & Krauss, R. M. The effect of threat on interpersonal bargaining. *Journal of Abnormal and Social Psychology*, 1960, 61, 181-189.

Dittes, J. E., & Kelley, H. H. Effects of different conditions of acceptance upon conformity to group norms. *Journal of Abnormal and Social Psychology*, 1956, 53, 100-107.

Emerson, R. M. Power-dependence relations. *American Sociological Review*, 1962, 27, 31-40.

Festinger, L., & Carlsmith, J. M. Cognitive consequences of forced compliance. *Journal of Abnormal and Social Psychology*, 1959, 58, 203-210.

Fischer, C. S. The effects of threats in an incomplete information game. *Sociometry*, 1969, 32, 301-314.

Gamson, W. A. A theory of coalition formation. *American Sociological Review*, 1961, 26, 373-382. (a)

Gamson, W. A. An experimental test of a theory of coalition formation. *American Sociological Review*, 1961, 26, 565-573. (b)

Gamson, W. A. *Power and discontent*. Homewood, Ill.: Dorsey Press, 1968.

Geiwitz, J. P. The effects of threats on prisoner's dilemma. *Behavioral Science*, 1967, 12, 232-233.

Gergen, K. J. *The psychology of behavior exchange*. Reading, Mass.: Addison-Wesley, 1969.

Hammock, T., & Brehm, J. W. The attractiveness of choice alternatives when freedom to choose is eliminated by a social agent. Reported in J. W. Brehm, *A theory of psychological reactance*. New York: Academic Press, 1966.

Harsanyi, J. C. A bargaining model for social status in informal groups and formal organizations. *Behavioral Science*, 1966, 11, 357-369.

Harvey, O. J., & Consalvi, C. Status and conformity to pressure in informal groups. *Journal of Abnormal and Social Psychology*, 1960, 60, 182-187.

Heslin, R., & Dunphy, D. Three dimensions of member satisfaction in small groups. *Human Relations*, 1964, 17, 99-112.

Hollander, E. P. Conformity, status, and idiosyncrasy credit. *Psychological Review*, 1958, 65, 117-127.

Hollander, E. P., Julian, J. W., & Perry, F. A. Leader style, competence, and source of authority as determinants of actual and perceived influence. *Technical Report No. 5*, State University of New York at Buffalo, 1966.

Hollander, E. P., Julian, J. W., & Sorrentino, R. M. The leader's sense of legitimacy as a source of his constructive deviance. *Technical Report No. 12*, State University of New York at Buffalo, 1969.

Holmes, J. G., & Strickland, L. H. Choice freedom and confirmation of incentive expectancy as determinants of attitude change. *Journal of Personality and Social Psychology*, 1970, 14, 39-45.

Homans, G. C. *Social behavior: its elementary forms*. New York: Harcourt, Brace, 1961.

Horai, J., & Tedeschi, J. T. Effects of credibility and magnitude of punishment on compliance to threats. *Journal of Personality and Social Psychology*, 1969, 12, 164-169.

Hornstein, H. The effects of different magnitudes of threat upon interpersonal bargaining. *Journal of Experimental Social Psychology*, 1965, 1, 282-294.

Hovland, C. I., Lumsdaine, A. A., & Sheffield, F. D. *Experiments on mass communication*. Princeton, N. J.: Princeton University Press, 1949.

Hovland, C. I., & Weiss, W. The influence of source credibility on communication effectiveness. *Public Opinion Quarterly*, 1951, 15, 635-650.

Jones, E. E. *Ingratiation: a social psychological analysis*. New York: Appleton-Century-Crofts, 1964.

Jones, E. E., & Gerard, H. B. *Foundations of social psychology*. New York: Wiley, 1967.

Jones, E. E., Gergen, K. J., Gumpert, P., & Thibaut, J. W. Some conditions affecting the use of ingratiation to influence personal evaluation. *Journal of Personality and Social Psychology*, 1965, 1, 613-626.

Jones, E. E., Gergen, K. J., & Jones, R. G. Tactics of ingratiation among leaders and subordinates in a status hierarchy. *Psychological Monographs*, 1963, 77, (Whole No. 566).

Jones, E. E., & Jones, R. G. Optimum conformity as an ingratiation tactic. *Journal of Personality*, 1964, 32, 436-458.

Kaufman, D. R., & Steiner, I. D. Some variables affecting the use of conformity as an ingratiation technique. *Journal of Experimental Social Psychology*, 1968, 4, 400-414.

Kelley, H. H., & Arrowood, A. J. Coalitions in a triad: critique and experiment. *Sociometry*, 1960, 23, 231-244.

Kelman, H. C., & Hovland, C. I. Reinstatement of the communicator in delayed measurement of opinion change. *Journal of Abnormal and Social Psychology*, 1953, 48, 327-335.

Kiesler, C. A., & Corbin, L. H. Commitment, attraction, and conformity. *Journal of Personality and Social Psychology*, 1965, 2, 890-895.

Koslin, B. L., Stoops, J. W., & Loh, W. D. Source characteristics and communication discrepancy as determinants of attitude change and conformity. *Journal of Experimental Social Psychology*, 1967, 3, 230-242.

Leftwich, R. H. *The price system and resource allocation*. New York: Holt, Rinehart & Winston, 1961.

Leventhal, G. S., & Bergman, J. T. Self-depriving behavior as a response to unprofitable inequity. *Journal of Experimental Social Psychology*, 1969, 5, 115-126.

Linder, D. E., Cooper, J., & Jones, E. E. Decision freedom as a determinant of the role of incentive magnitude in attitude change. *Journal of Personality and Social Psychology*, 1967, 6, 245-254.

Mausner, B. Prestige and social interaction: the effect of one partners's success in a relevant task on the interaction of observer pairs. *Journal of Abnormal and Social Psychology*, 1954, 49, 557-560.

McGuire, W. J. The nature of attitudes and attitude change. In G. Lindsey & E. Aronson (Eds.), *The handbook of social psychology*. Vol. 3. Reading, Mass.: Addison-Wesley, 1969.

Michener, H. A., & Lawler, E. J. Revolutionary coalition strength and collective performance as determinants of status reallocation. Unpublished manuscript, University of Wisconsin, 1970.

Michener, H. A., & Lyons, M. Perceived support, mobility, and equity as determinants of revolutionary coalitional behavior. Unpublished manuscript, University of Wisconsin, 1970.

Michener, H. A., & Zeller, R. A. The effects of coalition strength on the formation of contractual norms. Unpublished manuscript, University of Wisconsin, 1970.

Moore, J. C. Status and influence in small group interaction. *Sociometry*, 1968, 31, 47-63.

Murdoch, P. The development of contractual norms in a dyad. *Journal of Personality and Social Psychology*, 1967, 6, 206-211.

Ofshe, R., & Ofshe, L. Social choice and utility in coalition formation. *Sociometry*, 1969, 32, 330-347.

Pepitone, A., McCauley, C., & Hammond, P. Change in attractiveness of forbidden toys as a function of severity of threat. *Journal of Experimental Social Psychology*, 1967, 3, 221-229.

Potter, S. *One-upmanship.* New York: Holt, 1951.

Pruitt, D. G. Reciprocity and credit building in a laboratory dyad. *Journal of Personality and Social Psychology*, 1968, 8, 143-147.

Schachter, S. Deviation, rejection, and communication. *Journal of Abnormal and Social Psychology*, 1951, 46, 190-207.

Schellenberg, J. A. Dependence and cooperation. *Sociometry*, 1965, 28, 158-172.

Schopler, J. Social power. In L. Berkowitz (Ed.), *Advances in experimental social psychology.* Vol. 2. New York: Academic Press, 1965.

Shomer, R. W., Davis, A. H., & Kelley, H. H. Threats and the development of coordination: further studies of the Deutsch and Krauss trucking game. *Journal of Personaltiy and Social Psychology*, 1966, 4, 119-126.

Stires, L. K., & Jones, E. E. Modesty versus self-enhancement as alternative forms of ingratiation. *Journal of Experimental Social Psychology*, 1969, 5, 172-188.

Strodtbeck, F. L., Simon (James), R. M., & Hawkins, C. Social status in jury deliberations. In E. E. Maccoby, T. M. Newcomb, & E. L. Hartley (Eds.), *Readings in social psychology.* New York: Holt, Rinehart & Winston, 1958.

Thibaut, J., & Faucheux, C. The development of contractual norms in a bargaining situation under two types of stress. *Journal of Experimental Social Psychology*, 1965, 1, 89-102.

Thibaut, J. W., & Kelley, H. H. *The social psychology of groups.* New York: Wiley, 1959.

Uesugi, T. K., & Vinacke, W. E. Strategy in a feminine game. *Sociometry*, 1963, 26, 75-88.

Vinacke, W. E., & Arkoff, A. An experimental study of coalitions in a triad. *American Sociological Review*, 1957, 22, 406-414.

Vinacke, W. E., Lichtman, C. M., & Cherulnik, P. K. Coalition formation under four different conditions of play in a three-person competitive game. *Journal of General Psychology*, 1967, 77, 165-176.

Walster, E., Aronson, E., & Abrahams, D. On increasing the persuasiveness of a low prestige communicator. *Journal of Experimental Social Psychology*, 1966, 2, 325-342.

Zimbardo, P., & Ebbesen, E. B. *Influencing attitudes and changing behavior.* Reading, Mass.: Addison-Wesley, 1969.

VII

James T. Tedeschi, Barry R. Schlenker and
Svenn Lindskold

The Exercise of Power and Influence: The Source of Influence

Entire books concerned with attitude change, persuasion, indeed, social psychology are devoted to the study of the target of influence, with subsections or chapters given over to the various topics of perception, attraction, group pressure and conformity, and so forth. Yet, one must sift and strain through the entire social psychology literature to find stray bits and pieces that pertain to the factors which contribute to the source's use of influence. The reasons for the almost exclusive contemporary focus upon the target of influence are complex but they must include the principle of least effort. It is simply easier to place a target in a binary situation in which he either complies with or defies an influence attempt. It is much more difficult to observe the conditions which lead to the source's choice of a target and to his choice of tactics in gaining compliance from his target. In studying a target we can simulate the source and present stimuli and messages to the subject and ask him to respond "yes" or "no." But with the source, we must provide response alternatives of a more complex nature, which creates problems of verisimilitude, experimental control, and expense. Also, during the Second World War social scientists served their nation by focusing their expertise on gaining public compliance to government policy. Relevance-minded social psychologists explored the factors which affect attitude change, social conformity, and obedience in their attempts to bolster morale, increase productivity, and sell war bonds. The precedents arising from these early experimental studies have carried over to the

The present chapter was written with support of Grant #GS-27059 from the National Science Foundation to the senior author and by a predoctoral fellowship from the National Science Foundation to the second author.

present. Whatever the reasons for the lack of effort and the theoretical vacuum regarding the study of the source of influence, the present chapter is an attempt to assemble what we seem to know about him at the moment.

A subjective expected utility (SEU) model will be employed as a heuristic device to generate hypotheses and to integrate the existing experimental evidence concerning the behavior of the source of influence. The authors have chosen not to develop the mathematical aspects of the model, though such a development is both possible and desirable. Rather, the language of decision theory is employed to loosely integrate a rather disparate set of empirical findings with the hope of providing the basis for subsequent mathematical treatment. Ordinarily, the use of such a model formally requires that assumptions concerning perfect information and rationality of the decision maker be fulfilled (see Edwards, 1954). For a person to be rational, he must display transitivity of preferences and be able to select that preference which "maximizes something" (Edwards, 1954). Transitivity of preferences occurs when an individual can state that he prefers commodity (or outcome or consequence) A to B; B to C; and therefore, A to C. Where commodities differ qualitatively, transitivity assumptions are frequently violated. This problem can be bypassed in experimental situations by giving subjects a choice between more or less of the same commodity. It is generally safe to assume that the subject will want more of a positive commodity and less of a negative commodity. The rational individual behaves to maximize something. The "something" that we will assume to be maximized is subjective expected utility.

SEU theory deals with two conceptual components: (1) probabilities of obtaining outcomes, and (2) the worth of these outcomes to the individual (see Edwards, 1954; Lee, 1971). The subjective worth or attractiveness of an outcome is referred to as its utility. The utility of an outcome is determined by at least two factors: (1) the general reinforcement value of an outcome to the person, and (2) the amount of reinforcement which he has been receiving in recent interactions. The latter refers to the law of marginal utility, which states that each succeeding unit of any commodity is worth somewhat less than the preceding one (Homans, 1961). Hence, one dollar is worth more to a beggar than to a millionaire, and a supervisor who is too critical will have less influence than one who criticizes more sparingly. Any behavior usually has several consequences, each of these consequences having a particular utility to the person and being estimated by him to have a particular subjective probability of occurrence. Naturally, the consequences of behaviors may contain both positive and negative aspects which combine to form their overall utility. The positive or desirable outcomes are referred to as rewards, while the negative or undesirable aspects are called costs. *Formally, the subjective expected utility of a behavior is the sum of the products of the utilities of each of the outcomes associated with the behavior and the subjective probability of occurrence of each of the outcomes.* The SEU for the behavior of initiating influence in a simplified influence situation might be calculated as follows. A father decides that it is late and wants his son to go to bed, an outcome which would be worth 100 units of satisfaction to the father. If he tries to persuade his son to go to bed, he estimates that there is an 80 percent chance that the son will comply with the request (the influence will be successful with a subjective probability of .8). Assuming this was the only consequence associated with a successful influence attempt, the subjective expected gains for the father would be 80 units (100 x .8). However, there is a 20 percent probability that the son will noncomply to the influence, causing a terrible scene which otherwise would not have occurred and gaining the father -100 units of satisfaction. Assuming this to be the only outcome associated with noncompliance, the subjective expected costs of unsuccessful influence would be -20 units (-100 x .2). The sum of the products of the utilities and probabilities of these consequences is 60 units (60 = 80 + [-20]), and this figure is the SEU for the initiation of influence. In a similar fashion, the father would calculate the SEU for not attempting to influence his son, and then compare the two. According to SEU theory, an individual will compute the SEU for each of his several behavioral alternatives and then choose that alternative which has the greatest SEU. It should be noted that in the above example, only one outcome was associated with each of the two states (compliance or noncompliance) following the use of influence. In most situations, numerous outcomes would accompany each of the possible states following a behavior, some being rewards and some being costs. Even though the influence attempt had succeeded, the son still might have caused a scene before going to bed. All of these outcomes and their respective subjective probabilities of occurrence must be taken into account when calculating SEU. Without extensive information about the target individual or prior interaction experience with him, the source's subjective probability estimations of compliance, noncompliance, retaliation from the target, etc., are likely to be highly biased by other factors in the situation, such as his own propensity to take risks, his self-confidence, optimism, resources, and his liking for the target. Similarly, the source's calculation of the utilities (both rewards and costs) associated with particular behaviors is likely to be biased by the same factors, which will receive attention in the remainder of the chapter. A few general predictions from the model can be made at the outset. Holding each of the other factors constant, the greater the rewards or the probability of receiving rewards from exercising influence, the greater the SEU for influence and the more influence will be attempted. Had the father thought that there was a greater probability his son would comply to the influence attempt or had the satisfaction (and other rewards) to be gained from influence been higher, the SEU for influence would have been higher. Conversely, the greater the costs or the probability of incurring costs through influence, the smaller the SEU for influence and the less influence will be attempted. Had the father estimated that there was a greater probability of noncompliance or had the costs of unsuccessful influence been greater, the SEU for influence would have been lower.

A number of theorists (Gamson, 1968; Harsanyi, 1962; Homans, 1961) have pointed out that a source will usually incur costs for attempting and/or succeeding in exercising influence. Two basic types of costs are associated with any particular influence attempt: (1) source-based costs, which the source voluntarily incurs (e.g., taking out an advertisement in the newspaper or making an expenditure of resources to enforce threats), and (2) target-based costs, which the target imposes upon the source either through resistance, counterinfluence, or retaliation. Costs which are source-based require a decision by the source whether or not to allocate resources for the purposes of gaining access to the target, whether or not to fulfill promises by giving compliance-dependent rewards, to make threats credible by punishing noncompliance with demands, and to monitor the behavior of the target to ascertain whether compliance occurs. Some source-based costs are dependent upon the target's behavior, while others, such as monitoring, are not. For example, if the target complies to a promise of reward which is contingent upon the target's behavior, the source must decide whether or not to mediate the reward; however, if the target does not comply, the source is no longer in the position of deciding whether or not to mediate the reward. Thus, incurring the expense of mediating a promised reward is a source-based cost which is dependent upon the target's compliance. Source-based costs which are dependent upon the behavior of the target (e.g., fulfilling a promise or carrying out a threatened punishment) have been referred to as opportunity costs (Harsanyi, 1962). The distinction between source-based costs and target-based costs centers upon the origin of the costs. In the former case, the source decides to make the expenditure and, in the latter case, the target imposes costs upon the source. The total cost to the source for any influence attempt is the sum of both source- and target-based costs. A distinction between the possible origins of the costs of influence may have important ramifications because the less control the source has over the probability of incurring costs, the greater may be the likelihood that the actual probabilities associated with the occurrence of costs will be biased by source, target, and situational factors.

In many cases, a person does not have much choice in picking a target of influence—he either influences or does not influence the person who has the commodity he desires. However, in some cases several targets might possess identical desirable commodities. The only determinant of the choice, given that each target is seen as equally likely to comply, will be the utility and subjective probability of incurring costs (i.e., subjective costs). The choice will be the target that maximizes SEU.

Decisions regarding the use of influence, the choice of a target, and the choice of a mode or technique of influence are not separable from each other, from the characteristics of the source and target, or from the situational context of the interaction. Different targets and modes of influence produce different SEUs for exercising influence, and hence, in practice, all of these factors must be considered as a whole. Different modes of influence are more appropriate in particular situations and with particular targets. Also, different modes of influence result in different costs to the source and require possession of different types of resources. For analytical purposes, however, we are going to consider separately the modes of influence, who employs them and when, the choice of a target of influence, and the effects of situational factors on the use of influence.

The Modes of Influence

The failure to analytically examine the modes of influence has led social scientists to conceptual ambiguities which are particularly evident in the research literature (see Schlenker & Tedeschi, 1971). The categorization of influence modes that will be adopted here derives from several considerations. First, influence is conceived as a causal relationship between a source's behavior and a target's behavior. Hence, only the modes of influence which can be utilized in rather direct interactions are considered. Second, a distinction is maintained between those modes in which the source directly mediates or offers to mediate reinforcements for the target and those modes in which the source does not directly mediate them. Third, a distinction is drawn between influence attempts which are manipulatory and influence attempts which are overt statements to the target of the intentions of the source. Fourth, instances in which the source intends to control the behavior of the target are distinguished from situations in which the target imitates the behavior of the source or anticipates the source's unexpressed wishes. In the latter situation, it is the target's behavior rather than the source's which defines influence and hence cannot be considered as an example of the *exercise of influence*.

Figure 7.1 presents a 2 x 2 matrix which maintains the distinctions offered above and which does not attempt to categorize modeling effects or social contagion; it focuses instead upon intentional influence attempts of a source. The first dimension of the matrix refers to whether the source does or does not control the reinforcements which guide the target's behavior. This distinction may be first understood with respect to the difference between threats and warnings. A threat refers to punishments controlled by the source that can be administered to the target for failing to comply with the source's demands. A warning, on the other hand, refers to environmental contingencies involving probable punishments for the target, which the source communicates to the target in an attempt to influence him. The important distinction between a threat and a warning is that the source controls the punishment in the first instance but not in the second. Similarly, a promise refers to

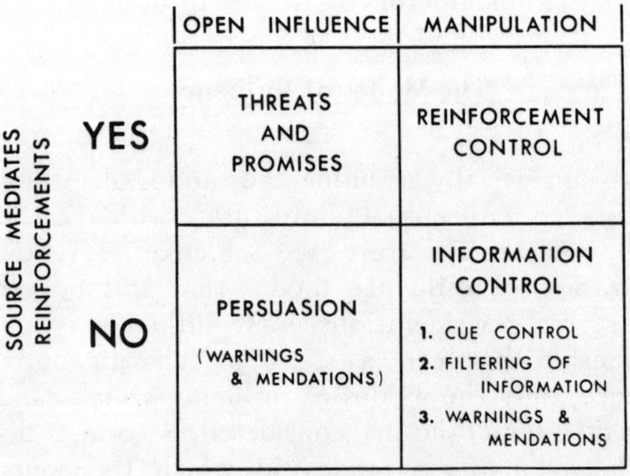

	OPEN INFLUENCE	MANIPULATION
SOURCE MEDIATES REINFORCEMENTS — YES	THREATS AND PROMISES	REINFORCEMENT CONTROL
SOURCE MEDIATES REINFORCEMENTS — NO	PERSUASION (WARNINGS & MENDATIONS)	INFORMATION CONTROL 1. CUE CONTROL 2. FILTERING OF INFORMATION 3. WARNINGS & MENDATIONS

Figure 7.1. The Modes of Influence

rewards controlled by the source; a mendation refers to environmental contingencies involving rewards for the target which are not controlled by the source.

The second dimension in the matrix presented in Figure 7.1 concerns whether or not the source tries to keep the target unaware of the influence attempt. The deliberate attempt of the source to prevent the target from discovering the source's intentions is generally referred to as manipulation. No assumption is made as to whether the source actually succeeds in keeping the influence attempt undiscovered. What is crucial to the distinction is that the source behaves *as if* the target were unaware of such manipulation. Open influence, on the other hand, is an attempt by the source to structure the rewards or punishments (values) of the target's decision matrix (or the target's perception of those rewards or punishments) so that the target will decide upon a course of action desired by the source.

Threats and Promises

Contingent threats and promises involve some form of communication between the source and target about something that the source would like the target to do, or refrain from doing. A threat offers punishment for noncompliance; a promise offers a reward for compliance. Oftentimes, a communication offers both the carrot and the stick in an attempt to place the target in an approach-avoidance conflict situation and hence produce behavior that is rewarding to both the target and the source.

The communication of threats and promises may be tacit or explicit. A tacit influence attempt is one which merely implies, either verbally or nonverbally, but does not state specifically what the source wants the target to do, or what the value consequences to the target would be for the various reactions of the target to the source's influence attempt. An explicit influence attempt depends upon the use of clear statements of the behaviors desired by the source and the consequences for the target of doing or not doing as recommended, requested, or demanded. The tacit-explicit dimension of influence attempts can also be applied to other types of influence communications, such as warnings and mendations.

The ambiguity of a tacit communication may be used to advantage by the source. The source, for example, might not have clearly formulated his own objectives. Lack of clear objectives often occurs in complex decision making, such as in determining foreign policy (Fisher, 1969). In such cases, the source has decided that he will attempt to modify the target's behavior toward a particular class of responses, but has not decided upon a particular response. An ambiguous influence attempt also leaves open the possibility that the target will overreact and yield more to the source than the latter could have reasonably expected on the basis of SEU considerations. Then, too, a tacit communication leaves the source room for rationalization and reinterpretation after the influence attempt has been made. A tacit threat to exploit the target may remain unenforced with the rationalization that it was a benevolent warning, and a tacit promise to which the target responds may remain unfulfilled with the rationalization that in fact no promise had been offered.

In many situations, the disadvantages of tacit communication far outweigh the advantages. For example, R. Fisher (1969) has postulated that explicit communications give the source an advantage by placing the target in the position of receiving a "yesable" proposition. The target will know precisely what the source desires and cannot refuse to comply on the grounds of misunderstanding. Fisher implies that explicit influence attempts will gain far more compliance than tacit or ambiguous influence attempts. Goldberg (1970) has verified that an unequivocal, explicit communication (warnings were used in the study) does gain greater compliance than an equivocal message. Schelling (1966) has pointed out two disadvantages of tacit communications: (1) veridical attributions of intentions are difficult and therefore the probable effects of each actor's actions are uncertain; and (2) at high conflict levels, tacit communications are apt to result in heightened hostility and distrust since they can be easily interpreted according to the suspicions and fears of the target rather than to the real content of the communications. Shared symbols and low levels of conflict seem to provide the minimum bases for the advantageous use of tacit communications.

Warnings and Mendations

The open use of warnings and mendations ordinarily makes clear, either implicitly or explicitly, the source's recommended actions and are not associated with any attempt on the part of the source to hide his self-interests. If the target is persuaded to believe the source's versions of the relevant aspects of a situation, then he presumably will act in a manner preferred by the source. The traditional approach to persuasion does not specifically refer to warnings and mendations, but the attitude change literature can be reconceptualized in these terms. Concepts of probability and value can be applied to warnings and mendations as well as to threats and promises. With regard to warnings and mendations, it may be asked how probable to the target the source's description of the causal structure of the environment is, what the target's costs of doing nothing would be, and what advantages he would have in acting in various alternative ways. Such a model in fact has been devised for the target (Chu, 1966). Building a theory of source expertise, apart from consensual bases for validation, requires that the source's version of the world be matched with the actual state of the world. Such subjective-objective comparisons are possible only in respect to rather sophisticated scientific areas of knowledge. The task is much simpler with respect to threats and promises because the question revolves around the probability that the source's words will be followed by deeds. It is more difficult to determine the utility of the deeds, than to ascertain their occurrence.

Considerations of the truthfulness of threats, promises, warnings, and mendations are pertinent to the source's choice of a mode of influence. The choice of threats raises questions of reputation and creates pressures to maintain credibility irrespective of costs, since credibility is a requirement for the success of future influence attempts. Promises bring about ethical obligations and responsibilities which the source would have difficulty avoiding. Warnings and mendations may not involve these consequences. The target who does as recommended but does not receive the rewards or punishments he was told to expect can always be told that conditions changed after the warning or mendation was issued. Thus, the reputation of the source is more secure when persuasion rather than threats and promises is used, and the cost of persuasion is less than the costs associated with threats and promises.

If it is assumed that the target's reaction to influence attempts will be determined by the decision with the highest SEU, warnings and mendations may be used by the source for any or all of six purposes: (1) to change the target's perception of the probability of his achieving a desired outcome; (2) to restructure the value of a particular outcome for the target; (3) to change the target's perception of the probability of incurring various costs; (4) to restructure the value of various costs to the target; (5) to change the target's perception of his own characteristics or source characteristics to invoke desired deference or compliance patterns; and (6) to restructure the target's view of the situation, calling forth norms which the target might not have perceived as applicable to the interaction.

Manipulatory Modes

Subtle forms of social reinforcements or punishments may be used as means of manipulating a target. In the category of *reinforcement control*, the source controls rewards and punishments which are used to directly manipulate the target's behavior. The prime example of such direct manipulation of behavior is the use of verbal reinforcement techniques (Greenspoon, 1955; Verplanck, 1962). The rationale behind the use of social reinforcements is that verbal approval (e.g., "good," or "uh-huh") will increase the probability of the emission of behaviors upon which the reinforcement was made contingent. Whether or not the target must be aware of the contingencies for influence to occur is a moot point (cf. Bandura, 1969). Thus, although the source may be attempting to manipulate the target, the latter may be responding to such verbal reinforcement as if it were the open influence mode of promises (i.e., "If you make response X, I will give you reward Y"). Nonetheless, the source of influence, who in verbal conditioning studies is the experimenter, behaves *as if the subject were not aware of the attempted manipulatory control.*

Control over the environment may be used to gain influence over a target individual. The manipulation category which we refer to as *information control* includes: (1) cue control; (2) the filtering of information; (3) impression management communications; and (4) warnings and mendations. The latter category differs from open persuasion in that the source attempts to disguise his desire to influence and hence to be perceived as disinterested, truthful, informed, and trustworthy.

Jones and Gerard (1967) have emphasized the importance of cue control as an influence mode. When a target individual has developed a habit such that responses can be elicited by discriminative stimuli (cues), and the source is aware of the habit, the latter can produce the cue and bring about the desired response. Cue control is a very inexpensive means of influence since no resources other than those necessary to bring about the cue need be expended, and as long as the target does not find out about the source's actions and intentions, the source has no need to use resources for purposes of rewards or punishments. However, cue control does require that the source have sufficient knowledge about the target so that he can reliably predict the target's behavior. Naturally, cue control is subject to extinction.

Information filtering includes both the source's censoring capability and his control over the gatekeepers of mediated information. When used for purposes of indirect influence, this method of manipulation is very expensive because of the need to acquire control over both the channels of communication and other communicators. The expense of information filtering explains why it is usually the established elites or authorities who gain control over information. Censorship, of course, ultimately requires the use of the legal apparatus and legitimate coercion for its exercise.

Another manipulatory tactic in the use of information is to establish the target's perception of the source's trustworthiness (disinterestedness) and credibility in relation to third parties. Arguments for the individual's need for cognitive balance or consistency by Festinger (1957), Heider (1958), Newcomb (1953), and Osgood and Tannenbaum (1955) have been re-interpreted as ultimately resting upon the idea that the source attempts to build a basis for influence (Tedeschi, Schlenker. & Bonoma, 1971). If the source were not perceived by the target as consistent both over time and in his actions and attitudes, the source's open influence attempts would fall upon deaf ears and he would be restricted in his ability to utilize manipulatory techniques. An inconsistent source would not be trusted and his every action would be suspect, making it difficult for him to hide selfish intentions.

Conclusion

In summary, a source may use open modes of influence or he can operate clandestinely and disguise his intentions from the target in his attempts to manipulate the latter. Open influence modes include the coercive use of threats of punishment and promises of rewards, and the dissuasive or persuasive use of warnings or mendations. Manipulatory modes of influence include the direct control of reinforcements or information in a manner contrived to gain compliance from the target without the target's awareness of the source's control. Information control techniques include the introduction of cues to elicit predictable habits, the filtering of information to constrain perception of alternative actions, to affect probability estimates of response-outcome contingencies, and to modify the expected utility associated with outcomes. Warnings and mendations may be used as forms of persuasion, in which case the source may either manipulate the target or make no attempt to hide his preferences. When used as manipulation, warnings and mendations may relate not only to the target but to other parties, and they may be used either to incur obligations from the target or to affect the perceived trustworthiness or credibility of the source.

A mode of influence may be used offensively or defensively. Although it is not always possible to distinguish between offensive and defensive influence, the source's intentions are clearly different in the two cases. In offensive influence, the source wants the target to do something that will mediate positive outcomes for the source, while in defensive influence the source wishes the other person to leave him alone. Defensive influence has the goal of deterring the other party and of protecting the source's own resources and prerogatives. Defensive influence should be more successful than offensive influence for the reason that much less is usually sought. Furthermore, norms tend to support the defensive person. The focus through the next sections is on the source who initiates influence for offensive purposes.

Who Influences

Factors which affect the source's exercise of influence include the enduring response dispositions of the source (i.e., personality factors), the status derived from the source's role position, the resources which are at the disposal of the source (prestige), and the expertise which the source possesses relevant to a particular task or group goal. It is hypothesized that each of these factors has a bearing on the source's estimation of the probability of success of his contemplated influence attempt and hence that each factor affects the probability that the source will make the attempt, *ceteris paribus*.

Self-Confidence

Chronic self-confidence is a generalized expectancy of success derived from the individual's history of success in a variety of problem situations. Expertise is a more narrow concept of what a person "knows" about a formal area of knowledge and is based upon a proven capacity in a skill or discipline. As such, expertise can be more readily viewed as a resource of the influencer. Self-confidence as used here is similar to familiar concepts in psychology, including need-achievement motivation (Atkinson, 1964; Moulton, 1965), self-esteem (Coopersmith, 1967), and internal control orientation

(Lefcourt, 1966; Rotter, 1966). Need achievement, in turn, is closely related to the notion of level of aspiration (Lewin et al., 1944) and to the concept of comparison level offered by Thibaut and Kelley (1959). Each of these concepts imply that the individual who is a high scorer on some test of self-confidence, or similar factor, believes that he is competent and will succeed at tasks he undertakes. They imply that such an individual sets his goals at a rather high but realistic level, feels he controls his own reinforcements through his own actions and believes that he deserves the success and approval he receives. A person who more or less fits this description is considered self-confident.

High self-confidence is tantamount to an upward bias in subjective probabilities concerning success. If the source is self-confident, he should initiate more influence attempts because he anticipates success and perhaps lower costs; if the source lacks confidence in himself and perceives the target as self-confident, he would consider resistance by the target as highly probable and have a correspondingly low general expectancy of success. In the latter case, the source will make few influence attempts—the subjective expected costs are perceived to be high and the subjective expected gains low.

A number of studies have demonstrated a positive relationship between self-confidence and initiation of influence attempts. Bass (1961) noted that frequency of attempts at leadership are related to self-esteem and self-accorded status as well as with the ability to cope with the group problem. Fouriezos, Hutt, and Guetzkow (1950) found greater participation in goal achievement by those who are confident of their own views. The complementary relationship of low self-esteem with greater influenceability is quite well established, especially for males (Janis & Field, 1959; Marlowe & Gergen, 1969). It is interesting to note that those with high self-esteem as compared to those with low self-esteem are more responsive to warnings (cf. Higbee, 1969). This implies that when it comes to taking actions in the environment to control their own fate, high self-esteem people take such actions while when it comes to a passive change in attitudes as a function of persuasion, low self-esteem individuals are more easily changed. Lindskold and Tedeschi (1971a) found that children with high self-esteem are more compliant to both threats and promises and hence avoid more punishments and attain more rewards than do children with low self-esteem.

Feelings of power also affect the frequency with which influence attempts will be made. Guetzkow (1968), in a study of the differentiation of roles in various communication networks, found that persons who take on the key role are those who obtain high scores on the Guilford-Zimmerman Ascendency scale. Veroff (1957) measured motivation for power and recognition on a projective test and found that high scorers are rated by their instructors as being high in argumentation and attempts to control others. Carter, Haythorn, Shriver, and Lanzetta (1950) observed that those persons who emerged as leaders in groups and those who are forceful and domineering. Gore and Rotter (1963) and Strickland (1965) found that persons who are internal control oriented are more likely to commit themselves to civil rights actions than are persons who are external control oriented.

There is some evidence that high or low confidence can be temporarily induced by various laboratory manipulations, and that such inducements under some conditions will produce the same kinds of effects as do chronic states of confidence. Induced competence is closely related to felt expertness, though the latter concept is probably more general in implications for demonstrated skill or knowledge. In effect, induced competence manipulations increase the perceived probability of the success of an influence attempt—that is, they set SEU at a higher level—and encourage the individual to attempt influence. Levinger (1959) brought together pairs of people who were previously unacquainted to engage in a task requiring a series of joint decisions. Prior to the decision-making, one of each pair of subjects was led to believe that his knowledge about the task was either superior or inferior to that of his partner. Those subjects with the impression of superior knowledge made more influence attempts, were more assertive, and concluded that they had greater impact upon decisions made.

Bavelas, Hastorf, Gross, and Kite (1965), in a study that manipulated the feedback regarding the effectiveness of contribution of subjects in group discussions of case problems, found that positive feedback increased self-ratings concerning the quality of ideas, effectiveness in guiding the discussion, and general leadership ability. Behavioral measures showed increases in talking time and frequency of talking. Hastorf (1961) and Aiken (1965) have also shown that induced competence mediates increased frequency of influence attempts.

Marak (1964) found a positive relationship between induced task competence and frequency of leadership attempts. When groups were offered a monetary bonus, the relationship was much stronger. Thus, consistent with an SEU interpretation, highly competent individuals attempted influence more frequently than did less competent members, and the effect was heightened when the monetary value to be gained was greater.

Unlike the above studies which focused on group problem-solving tasks Lindskold and Tedeschi (1970) carried out a study which examined both induced competence and chronic self-confidence in a mixed-motive situation. The success and failure experiences were manipulated by having a confederate of the experimenter follow a set of strategy selections which resulted in the subject succeeding or failing in his goal of winning points no matter what choices the subject made. Thereafter subjects could utilize options to send messages. In one condition of the experiment, the subjects could send promises of their intentions to cooperate with the simulated player on the next trial of the game. These self-committing promises of cooperation were not contingent upon the behavior of the target. In a second condition, subjects could send threats to penalize the simulated target *if* the latter did not cooperate on the next trial of the game. A third condition gave subjects their choice of sending either the noncontingent promises or the contingent threats. The simulated target was either 50 percent or 100 percent accommodative on trials when subjects sent the influence communications. Lindskold and Tedeschi obtained pre-interaction ratings of the subjects' chronic self-confidence. The results were analyzed for effects of both induced competence and chronic confidence.

Subjects high in chronic self-confidence sent more influence messages than did subjects low in self-confidence, supporting SEU predictions. A similar effect was not found when induced competence was analyzed. The only effect of the induced competence manipulation was in interaction with message availability and target accommodativeness. When the target was 100 percent accommodative subjects in the high induced competence condition sent promises frequently and mixed their use of threats and promises when they had the opportunity; subjects in the low induced competence condition sent few promises and relied heavily upon threats against the totally accommodative target. A similar pattern of results was found with respect to chronic confidence and the choice of influence modes. Subjects high in self-confidence were particularly willing to make a self-committing promise when the target was 50 percent accommodative. The pattern of these interactions indicates that high chronic self-confidence, and to some degree high induced competence, predisposes an individual to take risks not taken by persons low in these qualities. Apparently, confidence and competence generate perceptions of high probabilities of success.

There is also indirect evidence that actual success in influencing others encourages individuals to make frequent attempts at influence. Lippitt, Polansky, Redl, and Rosen (1952) observed the free operants of boys at a fresh-air camp. The most successful or influential of the boys were indentified on the basis of sociometric ratings made by the boys themselves. These boys were found to be those who subsequently made more frequent influence attempts, were more successful in their attempts, and were more self-assertive in making them than were control individuals.

The evidence, then, is supportive of the hypotheses that self-confidence is related or equivalent to heightened subjective probabilities of success in social interaction and is positively related to the frequency of influence attempts. Closely associated with and perhaps generative of self-confidence are other sources characteristics, such as status, prestige, and expertise, which, accordingly, should be positively related to initiatives taken in social interactions.

Status of the Source

Status, because it is fundamentally a concept implying ranking along some dimension, is not a very precise term. Brown (1965) has indicated the multidimensionality of the concept of status. He suggests that status is any sort of social value, usually agreed upon by most members of a society. The social value is reflected in the characteristics of those who form the social hierachy. Such characteristics may include "seniority, maleness, noble lineage, higher education, larger income, and positions of formal authority" (p. 74). Status, as defined herein, will refer to the degree of deference which others believe a person should receive *by virtue of his role position*. Hence, status is largely inseparable from legitimate authority and leadership.[1]

A formal role position usually carries with it the capacity to mediate rewards and punishments for other people. Various roles possess the authority or provide access to the resources or the control over resources that gives the person holding the position the ability to successfully influence others. Thus, Whiting (1960) defines status as the degree of an individual's control over rewarding or punishing resources. Similarly, Hollander (1964) considers status to derive from the competence which an individual shows in group-related activities; in other words, the person can reward the group because of his superior knowledge or ability. Most such definitions of status include various combinations of the individual's resource control (i.e., prestige), competence, or expertise, and the legitimacy or authority associated with his role position. These composite definitions of status appear to confound orthogonal factors. For the

---

[1]. See Chapter 1 for a more thorough discussion of the concepts of authority, legitmacy, and leadership.

sake of future operational clarity, the definition of status will be simplified herein and restricted to the privileges which come with the occupation of a particular role position, apart from the control over resources, expertise, or other factors which may also be associated with either the person or the role position.

The higher the status of an individual, the more deference he believes he deserves, and hence he perceives himself as likely to be more successful in his influence attempts. Hollander and Julian (1970) have similarly reasoned that a leader fulfills group expectations in exchange for status and subsequent greater influence over the behavior of the group members. High status also seems to be associated with self-confidence. Thus, the probability of success as subjectively estimated by the source is presumed to be directly related to status and should lead the high-status individual to make more influence attempts than the low-status person; status increases the source's expectations that his influence attempts will succeed.

Hollander (1964) has proposed that a high-status individual has greater behavioral latitude than a low-status individual by virtue of "idiosyncrasy credits" which he has accumulated through conformity to group standards and contributions to group goals. A high-status person can afford to spend his extra credits for innovative or deviant behaviors. It follows that a high-status individual can better afford to fail in attempting influence than can a low-status person. If idiosyncrasy credits are considered as a commodity, and if the law of marginal utility is applied, it may be concluded that those who control a larger supply will value each unit less than will those who control a smaller supply. Thus, if a person of high status and a person of low status incur the same costs in idiosyncrasy credits for an influence attempt, the costs are actually of less value to the high- than to the low-status person. Holding self-confidence constant, Hollander's formulation when combined with the SEU model leads to the prediction that a source will attempt more influence as his status increases because the costs of failure lessen as status increases. High status, then, increases the individual's perceived probability of success and decreases the perceived costs of failure. The expected net profit associated with a contemplated influence option is therefore directly related to status, when expected value of success and probability of costs are held constant.

The avilable evidence supports the above hypotheses, although more data is desirable due to frequent confounding of role position with prestige and expertise. Communication frequency is positively related to status and to the degree of security the person feels in that status (Cohen, 1958; Heinicke & Bales, 1953; Kelley, 1951).

Hurwitz, Zander, and Hymovitch (1968) found that high-status persons communicated more frequently in a group discussion (the type of communication was not analyzed) than did low-status persons. Low-status persons seemed to act in an ego-defensive manner designed to reduce the tension associated with interacting with persons of high status. Torrance (1954) found that Air Force crew members, whether or not the members had previous experience together, exerted influence on others in a projective story-construction task in direct relationship to their ranks. Strodtbeck and his associates (Strodtbeck, James, & Hawkins, 1957; Strodtbeck & Mann, 1956) found that both occupational status and sex determine the frequency of influence attempts, the frequency of success, and the group choice of leaders. Berger, Cohen, and Zeldditch (1966) concluded that status differentiations determine the observable patterns of group influence whether or not status is relevant to the group task.

In summary, status, defined as the perceived deference to an individual because of his occupation of a role position, is positively related to self-confidence and security, communication frequency, frequency of influence attempts, and success of influence attempts. These results support an SEU model of influence which interprets status as a factor which affects subjective probability of success and perceived reduction in costs. None of the available research so far done on status and influence has investigated target or mode preferences of persons who hold various statuses. Status, of course, is not easily separable (practically) from the degree of an individual's knowledge or skills or from the amount of his resources. Expertise is a means of achieving status, while the control of resources is often conferred by role position.

Source Expertise

Expertise has been customarily considered as the amount of relevant information or knowledge possessed by one person which is useful to another's goal achievement. A person's expertise is directly proportional to his informational resources. The greater the expertise of the person, the more self-confident he would be and the more often his help would be sought by others (Homans, 1961). The expert's knowledge is a positive resource which can be exchanged for values mediated by others. The possession of knowledge resources should increase the probability that an expert source will be successful in his influence attempts, a result that could be expected to enhance his self-confidence and increase the subjective probability of success of his contemplated influence attempts. Hence an SEU model of influence would predict that the more expert the individual, the more often he would initiate influence attempts.

Lippitt et al. (1952) found the more influencial boys at a camp were those who were superior in such situationally important skills as fighting and campcraft. In field studies of the interaction of persons in the mental-health professions, the more influential persons were those in the more highly trained prefessions (Hurwitz, Zander, & Hymovitz, 1968; Zander, Cohen, & Stotland, 1957). Unfortunately, these latter studies probably confounded the effects of status and expertise.

A factor related to the effectiveness of expertise as a basis of influence is the difficulty, complexity, or ambiguity of the task (Coleman, Blake, & Mouton, 1958; Luchins, 1945). That is, information dependence leads to the seeking and acceptance of information. The nonexpert may be assumed to withdraw from efforts to influence in favor of efforts to secure information, which gives the expert a free rein in exerting influence in the areas of his expertise. Shevitz (in Hemphill, 1961) found that group members who were given task-relevant information by the experimenter initiated changes in group problem-solving activities more often than members who had possession of irrelevant information.

Jaffee (1968), in an analysis of factors which affect the frequency of leadership attempts, listed three expertise factors as important: (1) the amount of task-relevant information possessed by the individual (Hemphill, 1961; Levinger, 1959; Lippitt et al., 1952); (2) the previous experience of the individual in the same or similar group (Hemphill, 1961); and (3) the competence which both the individual and group members believe he has as a result of his purported contributions to group tasks (Aiken, 1965; Bavelas et al., 1965; French & Snyder, 1959). Each of these factors has similar effects, though whether they are cumulative remains for future research to ascertain. As with status, the research on the source expertise has focused primarily upon the effectiveness of persuasion attempts on the target. Although the existing evidence on source behavior is clearly consistent with the SEU model's prediction of a positive relationship between the expertise of the sources and the frequency and success of his influence attempts, a finer-grained approach seems desirable. It could be expected that since the expertise of the source refers to special information he possesses, the expert source would prefer the influence mode of persuasion or the informational modes of manipulation to coercive modes. Expertise does not provide the source with the kinds of resources that would be required to manipulate reinforcements or to make threats or promises.

Source Prestige

A number of political scientists have defined prestige in terms of perceived power (Dahl, 1961; K. Deutsch, 1966; Gamson, 1968; Morgenthau, 1961). A similar definition is offered here. The quantity of disposable resources possessed by an individual which can be used to directly reward or punish another individual is presumed to be the primary factor for generating the perception of power. Resources which an individual has invested in relatively permanent assets and which can't be quickly liquidated for purposes of influence (or retaliation) are not relevant for determining prestige, though they may be cues to the person's status. From the point of view of an SEU theory of social influence, high prestige should be positively related to both the frequency and the success of influence attempts for several reasons. First, the possession of great disposable resources should produce high self-confidence and frequent influence attempts. Second, the law of marginal utility should operate to reduce the relative costs of influence as disposable resources increase.

The relative costs of influence, given that the needed resources for successful influence are about the same for two persons, are subjectively less for the one who has the greater disposable resources. Finally, the target individual should give less resistance to a source who has vast resources and who cannot be resisted without incurring great costs. Thus, the high-prestige source should perceive the probability of costs associated with target resistance as rather low.

Disposable resources, then, are directly related to the source's self-confidence and to subjective estimations of the probable success of influence. Disposable resources should be inversely related to the source's estimation of the probability of incurring target-based costs associated with resistance and with the subjective utility assigned to each unit of cost. Since prestige affects three of the four factors determining expected net gains associated with influence options (i.e., decreases probability and value of costs and increases probability of successful influence), it could be argued that as compared with status and expertise, prestige is a more potent base of influence. Whereas the possession of status or expertise encourages a source to attempt the use of informational forms of influence, the possession of prestige should lead the source to use those forms of influence that rely upon the mediation of rewards and punishments. In any case, the SEU model of influence predicts that as an individual's prestige increases, so will the frequency and effectiveness of his influence attempts.

Although the authors could not find any study in which the disposable resources available to a source were varied, a few studies have varied the punishment magnitude given to the source. Punishment magnitude manipulations do not place a limitation on the number of attempts which a source can make to influence the behavior of the target, but they do provide a manipulation of the degree or amount of power given to the source. Thus, subjects who are given the ability to impose a severe punishment on the target may be conceptualized as high in prestige, while subjects with a low punishment capability might be considered low in prestige.

Fischer (1960) attempted to replicate an experiment by Deutsch and Krauss (1960) which was interpreted as showing that the possession of bilateral threats was detrimental to interpersonal bargaining. Fischer used a two-person negotiation game in which both subjects were given either a low punishment capability of three points (and a source-based cost of two points for use) or a high punishment capability of thirty points (and a source-based cost of fifteen points). In a third condition, one subject was provided with a low punishment capability and the other with a high punishment capability. It should be noticed that the proportional cost of using each level of punishment was roughly consistent with the notion of marginal utility; the low punishment capability cost its user two-thirds of the punishment delivered to the opponent, the high punishment capability cost its user only one-half. Fischer found that subjects who possessed a high punishment capability threatened to use the punishment more often than did subjects who possessed a low punishment capability. The same effect was obtained whether the parties were equal or unequal in power but was most pronounced when a high-prestige subject interacted with a low-prestige subject. It is interesting to note, however, that in the unequal power conditions, the low-prestige subjects attempted to influence the course of negotiations by manipulating information about the nature of the situation by lying, and by initially bidding higher than the high-power subjects. These tactics were successful and gained the low-prestige subjects an even greater gross profit than the high-prestige subjects, although the differences tended to disappear after the punishments were subtracted from the scores. Viewing the results as a whole, it seems clear that prestige did increase the frequency of those modes of influence associated with the relative level of disposable resources possessed by the source. But when the actor lacks the resources for effective use of coercive power, rather than capitulate to an opponent, he will switch to an alternative mode of influence.

Smith and Leginski (1970) suggested and received support for the proposition that the greater the punishment which a source can administer to a target—a direct manifestation of disposable resources—the greater is the source's confidence that he can control the behavior of the target and the more frequently he threatens to use his power. Subjects were given the capability of threatening and fining a bargaining opponent (a confederate of the experimenter). The maximum fine he could impose was 20, 50, 90, or 140 points. Half the subjects in each of the four punishment magnitude conditions had to use the gross amount of the fine available to them (i.e., imprecise power), while the others were told that they could use any punishment magnitude up to the amount provided (i.e., precise power). It was found that the frequency with which threats and fines were used was directly related to punishment capability, but only for the precise power conditions. Thus, an interesting limitation must be placed on the hypothesis that prestige is directly related to the frequency of influence attempts. When a high-prestige source uses his resources in an all-or-none fashion, the quantity of resources seems not to affect his use of resource-relevant threats.

When individuals were unequal in prestige, the one with the greater resources attempts the most resource-relevant influence. However, when individuals are prestige equals, should the absolute amount of potential resource utilization make a difference in the use of influence? Would two high-prestige individuals, capable of inflicting severe harm on one another, refrain from influence more than two low prestige individuals? Or would the former pair use their power to the hilt, impervious to the potential dangers? Hornstein (1965) investigated the use of threats in a real estate game which required bargaining between two equal or unequal power players. Over different conditions of the experiment, players were given the capability of reducing the other player's profits by 10, 20, 50, or 90 percent and were placed in strong, weak, or equal power relationships with their opponent. As predicted from the SEU model, strong bargainers did initiate more threats to a weak opponent than vice versa. Similarly, the closer the weak bargainer was in strength to the strong bargainer, the more influence the weaker bargainer attempted. When the bargainers were power equals, pairs with high punishment potential used fewer threats than the weaker pairs. As the size of possible retaliation increased for the equal-power pairs, SEU for influence decreased, and the number of influence attempts likewise decreased.

Although studies should be carried out which vary the amount of disposable resources provided to a source of influence, who should be able to choose among modes of influence, the available evidence pertaining to prestige is clearly supportive of SEU predicitons. The greater the disposable resources possessed by a source, relative to the prospective target, the more frequently will resource-relevant influence be attempted. And, the greater the threatening resources of prestige equals, at least beyond some threshold, the less influence will be attempted due to the dangers of costly retaliation.

Conclusion

In summary, and despite the chaos in personality research noted by Marlowe and Gergen (1969), rather commonplace conclusions regarding the effects of such dispositional variables as self-confidence, dominance, need-achievement motivation, self-esteem, and internal control orientation upon the source's exercise of influence are justified and are interpretable by an SEU model of social influence. High self-confidence apparently biases the estimated probability of success upwards and hence encourages the source to attempt more influence.

The status, expertise, and prestige of the source can also be used to predict the degree of influence he will attempt, but with the caveat *ceteris paribus*. High status leads the source to expect deference from those below him in the status hierachy and hence encourages him to use persuasive means of influence. High expertise similarly encourages the person to employ information for the purposes of influence. High prestige encourages the source to employ those modes of influence which require the mediation of rewards and/or punishments, but only when the target is lower in prestige than the source, and where the resources possessed can be utilized in a precise manner.

It is not enough to be able to predict who will influence, it is also important to know who the source will choose as the target of influence. Who the target is will often be a determinant of the influence mode chosen by the source.

Choosing a Target

The major consideration determining the choice of a target is the expectation by the source that the target possesses or controls access to important values that the source wants for himself. The source will choose his targets in a manner expected to maximize net profits.

What a source wants or expects to receive from any interaction is primarily determined by his previous social experiences and by the current allocations of resources in the group of which he is a part. An individual's level of aspiration (or comparison level) defines what will satisfy him and what will not. The level of aspiration is generally a function of past successes and failures and is higher in persons who are self-confident and achievement-oriented (Aktinson, 1964). Aside from the individual's level of aspiration, the current distribution of resources within the individual's group is important in determining his expectancies of reward. Individuals generally expect to receive from a group rewards commensurate with the investments they have made relative to other group members (Adams, 1965; Homans, 1961). The individual expects the ratio of his work input to his reward outcome to be proportional to the input-outcome ratios of other group members, and will go to great lengths to influence the allocation of resources so that distributive justice is established (e.g. Adams & Rosenbaum, 1962; Jaques, 1961; Lerner & Becker, 1962; Leventhal & Bergman, 1969; Levanthal, Allen & Kemelgor, 1969; Sayles, 1958). Within the context of his aspirations and the group situation, the source will attempt to influence those who maximize his SEU.

In exerting influence upon a target, a source will usually need to have direct access to the target. In Dahl's (1957) terms, a "connection" must exist between the parties. Of course, the source can influence indirectly by virtue of his position in an influence network, the prerogatives of high status, and the possession of great resources (prestige). He can have his wishes carried out by directly influencing person A to influence person B, the source's primary but indirect target. However, as Homans (1961) and Thibaut and Kelley (1959) have pointed out, the costs of influencing probably increase with the distance from the target. When targets are not nearby, the source is likely to have communication difficulties, which create problems of transmission of expectancies and contingencies, make surveillance of target responses costly and difficult, and impose problems of timing and delivery of either rewards or punishments.

According to the SEU model, the greater the costs of exercising influence, the less influence should be attempted. Confirmation of this hypothesis was obtained by Tedeschi, Horai, Lindskold, and Faley (1970), who allowed subjects to threaten an "opponent" during the course of a message-modified Prisoner's Dilemma game. The costs to the source for punishing the other person after noncompliance to threats were varied by charging the subjects fixed amounts for each use of the punishment mechanism. The focus was thus upon those source-based costs which were contingent upon target behaviors (or opportunity costs). It was found that subjects *sent fewer threats* when costs were high than when costs were low, but no differences were found on the number of punishments mediated. If it is remembered that it did cost subjects to punish the target but that it did not cost anything to send a threat, the results are clearly interpretable as indicating that a source will take the costs of exercising influence into account *before* making an influence attempt.

If accessibility of the target and the costs of influence are inversely related (Thibaut & Kelley, 1959), it might be expected that propinquity and interpersonal attraction would be significant factors in determining the choice of a target. Given that a number of potential targets are nearby and possess equivalent values that could be mediated to the source, the amount of resistance by the target and the probability and utility of target-based costs will determine which target will in fact be chosen. Friends are likely to give less resistance and are unlikely to impose direct costs upon the source. More often than not, however, the source will find that his potential targets are rather powerful persons, who hold high status, possess scarce expertise, or control large amounts of resources. Powerful persons are those who possess most of the values that weaker people desire. Hence, it should not be surprising that powerful persons are often chosen as targets, despite the fact that their resistance levels are probably high and the sum of source-based and target-based costs could be expected to be high. A small probability of getting something of value is better than a certainty of getting nothing, and nothing ventured is nothing gained. The remainder of this section will concentrate on interpersonal attraction and the relative power of the source and target as factors determining the exercise of influence.

Interpersonal Attraction

Homans (1950; 1961) suggested that, holding all else constant, the greater the frequency of interaction with another person, the greater will be the liking for the other, and vice versa. Barring the imposition of situational restraints which prohibit the termination of an interaction, the failure of liking to develop will result in the cessation of interaction with the nonrewarding, disliked person. Homans proposes, furthermore, that liking develops from the mutual mediation of rewards. Experimental evidence yields generalizations in support of Homans' theory. Persons who willingly reward or otherwise facilitate the goal attainment of others, regardless of the nature of the relationship (i.e., competitive or cooperative), are liked (Berkowitz & Daniels, 1963; Berkowitz & Levy, 1956; Goranson & Berkowitz, 1966; Kleiner, 1960; Lerner & Matthews, 1967; McDonald, 1962; Myers, 1962; Solomon, 1960; Wilson & Miller, 1961; Zajonc & Marin, 1967). Conversely, persons, who willingly impede goal attainment or otherwise punish other persons, and irrespective of the nature of the relationship, are disliked (Burnstein

& Worchel, 1962; French, Morrison, & Levinger, 1960; Kipnis, 1958; Lerner, 1965; Rosenthal & Cofer, 1948; Zajonc & Marin, 1967). Liking produces expectations of cooperative and rewarding interactions (Kaufmann, 1967), and hence encourages frequent interactions and ample opportunities for influence.

Lott and Lott (1968, p. 68) have stated that "learning to like a particular stimulus person is essentially learning to anticipate reward when that person is present...." It should be expected that persons who like one another would be more cooperative in their social interactions than individuals who dislike one another, a hypothesis which has received considerable empirical support (Kaufmann, 1967; Krauss, 1966; Oskamp & Perlman, 1965; Scodel, 1962; Tornatzky & Geiwitz, 1968; Wallace & Rothaus, 1969). It has also been found that subjects prefer to interact with friends rather than strangers or dissimilar others (cf. Secord & Backman, 1964). Lerner and Becker (1962) found that subjects preferred to interact with similar individuals in a cooperative setting where both could win, while dissimilar persons were preferred as partners in a competitive setting where the subjects could win only at the partner's expense. Lerner, Dillehay, and Sherer (1967) found that attraction arises from the anticipation of cooperation, and that in a competitive situation, the subject will prefer a certain amount of dissimilarity to his opponent. Henry Adams was not far wrong when he stated that "to reduce friction is the chief use of friendship" (1931, p. 436).

Given the above relationship of liking to expectations of rewarding interactions, SEU theory may be used to interpret the effects of liking on interpersonal influence. A source's perception that another person likes him increases the subjective probability that the other person will be compliant to influence attempts, especially to such modes as promises and persuasion. Attraction should therefore be directly related to the frequency of such influence attempts. In confirmation of this hypothesis, French and Snyder (1959) found that subjects attempted more persuasive influence attempts when the other members of the group rated the source as better liked. They also found that "almost twice as much influence was attempted toward high- as toward low-accepting opponents" (p. 135). Back (1951) also found that the higher the attraction between parties, the more frequently persuasive influence was attempted.

Interpersonal attraction should not only affect the frequency of influence but should also affect the mode chosen by the source. Bramel (1969) has stated that a person should want to give those he likes what he believes they want and those he dislikes what he believes they don't want. Consistent with this reasoning, Walster and Prestholdt (1966) found that social work trainees' offer to help fictitious clients were consistent with the liking expressed for them. On the other hand, it could be hypothesized that as interpersonal attraction increases, the frequency with which threats are used should decrease. Krauss (1966) induced attraction between subjects by manipulating attitude similarity and then either legitimated the validity of the scale (strong anchoring) or denied its validity (weak anchoring). The subjects played the trucking game and were given the power to use gates to block their opponent's access to the most profitable route. When attitude anchoring was strong, low-attraction subjects used the gates more often than did high-attraction subjects. The weak anchoring did not produce any difference between conditions of the experiment, probably because subjects could not validly infer similarity or dissimilarity; hence, attraction differences were not induced in the first place. It may be concluded from the evidence that high attraction does result in an increased use of positive modes of influence and decreased use of negative forms of influence. The expectations that high-attraction persons have toward one another reflect their interaction history and may explain why people like to be liked. Those who like you are not likely to use threats to coerce compliance from you. The least that can be expected from a liked person is some form of *quid pro quo*.

Unlike the above experiments, Schlenker and Tedeschi (in press) gave subjects a choice between modes of influence. Across conditions of the experiment, subjects were given reward power in the form of promises and rewards, coercive power in the form of threats and punishments, or both, which could be used to attempt influence over a "peer" in a modified Prisoner's Dilemma game. Prior to the interaction, subjects were induced to have either high or low attraction for the relatively weak opponent. It was found that the type of power available to the subjects affected their exercise of power. Subjects who had only coercive power or both reward and coercive power made more influence attempts and established higher credibility for them than did subjects who possessed only reward power. Subjects gave the promised rewards only when they also had coercive power at their disposal. It was concluded that subjects prefer coercive power because it is perceived to give them greater control over the target's behaviors.

The attraction manipulation did not affect the choice of influence mode in the Schlenker and Tedeschi study but attraction did affect how the chosen modes were used. While high-attraction persons were more cooperative themselves when issuing promises, low-attraction persons more often gave the reward to the target when the latter complied to promises. Since joint cooperation meant mutual rewards without giving additonal rewards, high attraction persons may have found the rewards to be excessive and inappropriate, while the low-attraction persons needed to use the reward in order to compensate the target for the fact that the source was exploitative in the use of reward power. Contrary to the findings of Krauss, no effects of attraction on the use of coercive power were found. The differences between experiments, both of which employed experimental games, may be attributed to the distribution of power. In Krauss' study subjects were equals in power but in the Schlenker and Tedeschi study only the source of influence possessed power. It may be hypothesized that when an individual has less than or about the same amount of power as his opponent, he will take interpersonal relationships into account when responding to or exercising social influence; however, when the source has a unilateral advantage in coercive power, he disregards personal relationships in determining the frequency, manner, and resoluteness with which he exercises his power. Henry Adams (1931) was again correct when he asserted that "a friend in power is a friend lost" (p. 108).

In summary, interpersonal attraction develops from and results in expectations of reward from another person. A source of influence therefore anticipates a cooperative, helpful, and compliant interaction with the target. When the source and the target are equal in power, influence attempts will increase toward liked others and take the form of promises and persuasion. When a competitive situation exists and the source has greater power than the target, interpersonal attraction for the target seems to make little difference in the frequency and type of influence employed.

Relative Power

A prime category of prospective targets are those who are relatively more powerful than the source by virtue of expertise, status, or prestige. Such persons generally are the most likely to possess things of value which are desirable to the source. But powerful individuals also can exact more in an exchange, thereby increasing the cost of influence and reducing the subjective expected gains of an influence attempt. Often, weak sources do not possess or control the necessary resources to successfully influence powerful targets. The SEU theory predicts that a source will choose as a target the weakest person who possesses the resources he wants. With regard to behavior in organizations, this hypothesis suggests that people have a "natural" tendency to go through the channels of authority.

Evidence indicates that relatively powerful sources will indeed be the most frequent targets of influence attempts. Hurwitz, Zander, and Hymovitch (1968) found that high-status mental health workers were the targets of communications by both high- and low-status others, while low-status individuals were infrequently addressed by other group members. Watson (1965) had either one or two members of a group act as coordinators to facilitate group problem-solving activities. The coordinators were given the authority to command the other subjects and make all final decisions, and the group members were informed by the experimenter that they were required to comply to any and all directives issued by the coordinator. Low-power group members sent fewer messages than did the coordinators and sent most of their communications to high status coordinators. Similar results have been reported by Cohen (1958) and Kelley (1951).

There is little question that the relative power of source and target greatly affects the mode of influence chosen by the source. It was previously seen in the study by Schlenker and Tedeschi (in press) that a source with a unilateral power advantage in a conflict situation generally prefers the use of threats to the use of promises, a preference also demonstrated in studies by Lindskold and Tedeschi (1970) and MacLean and Tedeschi (1970). In the Schlenker and Tedeschi study, it was found that the credibility of contingent promises (i.e., the proportion of times that the source actually gave the promised reward to the number of opportunities for giving them) was greater in the conditions of reward and coercive power than in the conditions of reward power only. The number of promises sent did not differ between the two conditions. Therefore, the carrot will be *offered* whether or not one possesses the stick, but the carrot will be *given* only when one possesses the stick. The indications that a source prefers to be in the driver's seat in a mutual dependence situation is symptomatic of the reluctance shown to Osgood's (1962) idea of a strategy for Graduated Reduction in International Tensions (GRIT). GRIT requires that one party make a conciliatory act which *can* be exploited by the second party. Osgood believes that a series of such noncontingent conciliatory initiatives will eventually be reciprocated and that both parties will then partake in a benign, tension-reducing spiral. Tedeschi, Lindskold, Horai, and Gahagan (1969) found, however, that unilateral benevolent initiatives in the form of noncontingent promises induced reciprocation and conflict amelioration only when the parties were equals in power. Findings obtained by Tedeschi, Bonoma, and Lindskold (1970) suggest that honest verbal announcements by a target of his intentions to comply to a source's threats has the effect of converting the threatener into a mutual cooperator, while the firm and honest verbal commitment to defy a source somewhat deters the use of threats (probably because of the decrease in the subjective probability of success as perceived by the source).

When a source has less power than a target, it is unlikely that the source would choose negative modes of influence for use against the relatively powerful target, unless, of course, his intent was a defensive one. The use of coercion encourages retaliation and elicits negative reciprocity norms, increasing costs while decreasing the probability of successful influence. Indirect support for this hypothesis is the evidence that verbal aggression against a high-power source decreases as his power increases (Graham et al., 1951; Reiser et al., 1955; Worchel, 1957). Similarly, Lippitt, Polansky, Redl, and Rosen (1952) found that nondirective persuasive influence attempts were more often used by low- than by high-power children.

Jones (1964) has conducted a series of experiments which explore the ways in which dependent individuals ingratiate themselves with high-power persons. The major tactics of the ingratiator are opinion conformity, flattery, and the pronouncement of one's own strengths and weaknesses (Jones & Gerard, 1967). According to the previously presented categorization scheme for the modes of influence, ingratiation is a manipulatory form of influence which can involve both reinforcement control (e.g., the use of the secondary reinforcer of social approval) and information control (e.g., the use of a mendation to enhance one's own image in the eyes of the target). When ingratiation involves the use of opinion conformity, both types of manipulatory control may be involved. For example, Byrne (1969) provides evidence which indicates that similarity of opinions acts as a secondary reinforcer (hence involving reinforcement control); while other studies (cf. Jones & Gerard, 1967) indicate that opinion conformity can result in an increase of the perceived expertise of the source (hence involving information control). The ultimate goal of the ingratiator is not only to affect the success of his own offensive influence attempts but also to defend himself from the other's power. In his attempts to manipulate the target, the ingratiator seems to assume that the establishment of high attraction will not only deter the high-power person from using coercive influence modes against him but will also improve the terms of subsequent exchanges. However, evidence reviewed above indicates that the ingratiator's assumptions may be partially in error. The use of coercive power is not affected by attraction when the wielder is more powerful than the target. On the other hand, Kipnis and Vanderveer (1971) have demonstrated the success of ingratiation tactics in gaining pay raises from a subject acting as a supervisor in a simulated industry experiment.

Ingratiation could be expected to be used most frequently by persons who are relatively weak and to be directed towards those targets who are relatively powerful. Jones, Gergen, and Jones (1963) found that opinion conformity was greater among low-status ROTC cadets than among high-status ROTC members.

Ingratiation, however, does have its drawbacks. Jones (1965) described the "ingratiator's dilemma" as arising from the fact that the greater the source's stake in making himself attractive to the target, the more the target is likely to be sensitized to attempts at ingratiation. In general terms, Hovland, Janis, and Kelley (1953) have observed that the person who is too obvious in his use of flattery is relatively ineffective. In other words, as the value of ingratiation goes up, the probability of success goes down. Jones, Gergen, and Jones (1963) had subjects evaluate a stimulus person who was either dependent or not dependent upon another and who either agreed closely with the other's expressed opinions or did not agree closely. The dependent stimulus person was evaluated negatively if he agreed closely, while the degree of agreement did not affect ratings when dependence was low. The ingratiator must be very careful, then, since not only does the need for guile become more essential the more powerful the target (and the more dependent the source) but also the target is apt to be more wary as the need increases.

The use of ingratiation, therefore, has its risks, though discovery and unmasking are not likely to invite immediate retaliation from the target as would be the case should the ingratiator use some other form of deceit, such as not keeping his promises, bluffing through the use of threats, or issuing deliberately false warnings and mendations. Unmasking will cause the powerful individual to dislike and distrust the ingratiator, factors that will affect the powerful person's choice of influence modes in the future and will affect the believability of the ingratiator's future influence attempts. Discovery, then, produces exactly the opposite short-term and long-term results as are sought through the use of ingratiation.

Jones and Jones (1964) have shown that one way in which the ingratiator attempts to deal with his dilemma is to disagree to some extent with the target's opinions but, at the same time, to express little public confidence in his own opinions. When not dependent upon the target, the ingratiator did not employ the low-confidence expression technique.

Another way of attempting conformity ingratiation without being too obvious about it was demonstrated in a study by Davis and Florquist (1965). Subjects who were dependent upon an obnoxious supervisor differed from subjects who were dependent upon a sympathetic supervisor in the degree to which they agreed with the supervisors' implied views. When dependence was low there was more agreement with the sympathetic supervisor than with the obnoxious one, but there was no difference in agreement with direct statements of opinion made by the supervisors. The tactic again was to avoid the obvious conformity of parroting stated opinions; ingratiation was attempted by agreement with supporting statements rather than with explicitly endorsed opinions. Davis and Florquist point out that an ingratiator's use of opinion conformity seemed to result in a cost in terms of the loss of self-esteem and respect. The use of opinion conformity, especially if such conformity is contrary to the subjects' own publicly-known beliefs, might therefore be expected to be used less than other ingratiation tactics which do not cause the ingratiator to suffer comparable losses (e.g., self-enhancement and other-enhancement). However, a comparison of the ingratiation modes has yet to be done.

Cooper and Jones (1969) have reported results related to the judicious use of information control in the form of the self-legitimizing kind of ingratiation tactic. Several days before the experiment, subjects' attitudes were obtained from a mass testing of introductory psychology students. In the experiment, subjects were led to believe that they were either similar or dissimilar to a confederate in background, attitudes, and dress. The confederate then acted either obnoxiously or sympathetically toward the experimenter. After the subjects had seen the confederate's attitudes, their own attitudes were tested again. The results indicated that opinions changed most when the confederate was similar and obnoxious. The authors interpreted these results as showing opinion divergence as a strategy to avoid being miscast as obnoxious by the experimenter. When the confederate was dissimilar, but obnoxious, the subjects' opinions were not modified to the same degree.

It might be expected that self-legitimizing forms of ingratiation would extend to actions intended to establish the source as an expert or as possessing high status. Such actions may result in the production of false and exaggerated perceptions of his prestige. The objective, in any case, is to present oneself as having desirable qualities, which increases the effectiveness of other modes of influence. Thus, self-legitimizing ingratiation may be used to enhance source characteristics as perceived by a powerful target. For example, Aronson, Willerman, and Floyd (1966) found that subjects liked an expert more when he committed a minor faux pas (by spilling coffee over himself) after a scholarly discussion than when he did not. Jones, Gergen, and Jones (1963) found that when high-status subjects were told to make themselves liked by their subordinates, they tended to advertise their minor faults. Similar experiments dealing with status or prestige would be instructive.

Thibaut and Kelley (1959) have suggested that "creating a need" or "setting the stage" are strategies related to building up the value of one's own product and devaluing the other person's product. Blau (1964) suggested that remaining indifferent to the benefits others can offer is a means of devaluing the other's resources. Through such strategies, the source can attempt to reverse the perception of the relative power existing between himself and the other, and if he is successful, he will be more likely to gain compliance to his other influence modes (say, threats).

Emerson (1962) has suggested that a relatively weak person may attempt to establish equality or superiority over another by the tactic of increasing the size of the group, bringing in nth parties, and then forming coalitions against the powerful individual. This form of behavior involves deceit and forms a basis of future offensive or defensive influence attempts. The relevant point in the present context is that the study of coalition does provide information about the source's selection of a target. Gamson's (1964) analysis suggests that in a triad the two weak individuals will join to form a coalition against a third party who is the strongest of the three. The third party may then be shut out while the two "weak" persons divide the pie according to the principle that each take a share proportional to his strength. When more than three parties are involved, the parity principle guides the selection of members in the coalition as well as the agreement regarding reward allocation. Although other formulations and a number of experiments indicate that coalition formation is a more complicated process than is indicated here, there is little doubt that relative power is an important factor in the forming of coalitions.

Norms are shared understandings of the forms that social interactions may take under given circumstances and the manner in which rewards and punishments may legitimately be utilized or allocated; norms specify (usually implicitly) the rights and responsibilities of the individual according to his role and the situation. A norm may be utilized to dampen or change the behavior of another person (defensive counterinfluence) or to induce a target individual to bestow benefits (offensive influence). Responsibility norms have most often been studied in terms of providing help to a dependent person, while reciprocity norms assume that help is exchanged for help and harm for harm.

There are situations in which it is productive (from the point of view of short-range and effective influence) to present the aura of helplessness, impotence, or dependency. The power of dependency is a form of manipulation used by the weak which, unlike ingratiation, is strongly and powerfully sanctioned by society. Schopler and

Bateson (1965) suggest that invoking the norm of social responsibility is a strategy of influence especially utilized by American females, who learn to play the helpless role. Failure of the male target to respond to the signal that assistance is required is generally viewed as displaying socially reprehensible conduct. Likewise, society, recognizing the obligation to the needy, established governmental welfare programs. Recently, for example, the Supreme Court has held that welfare recipients have the *right* to demand review of any effort to reduce their welfare benefits. Additionally, the pacifist strategy of nonviolence or passive resistance is an attempt by the weak to demonstrate an injustice perpetrated by the strong. While violations of norms and standards can be ignored by the powerful as long as they only affect the weak and the violations are hidden from an articulate and responsible public, once such violations are made salient, two possibilities arise. Either the activators will be suppressed or, failing that, corrective measures are likely to be adopted.

Berkowitz (1957) and Berkowitz and Daniels (1963) have shown that subjects will work harder if their efforts materially affect the profits to be gained by their partner than if their efforts are not consequential to the partner's outcomes. Schopler and Bateson (1965) found that, at least in some circumstances, females are more responsive to dependent others; the nurturing role is well drawn for females in this culture, while males often fill a more aggressive nonnurturing, and competitive role. These investigators also found that the powerful person gave more help as his costs decreased; hence, the powerless source should apparently address his influence attempts to the target who is most different from himself in terms of possession of the critical resource. In additon, Schopler and Matthews (1965) have presented evidence that the powerful person will give more help to one whose dependence is caused by external rather than personal factors; voluntary dependence weakens the effect of the social responsibility norm. This result is reminiscent of the finding by Jones and deCharms (1957) that an accomplice was negatively evaluated if he caused the group to fail and his failure resulted from lack of motivation; subjects were kinder in their evaluations if the failure derived from a lack of ability. Apparently, the dependent source would be wise to attempt to link the norm of social responsibility to the norm of reciprocity. Berkowitz and Daniels (1964) and Goranson and Berkowitz (1966) have found that greater assistance will be given by the the powerful person if the dependent source has helped the target in the past. Thus, the dependent person with manipulative designs ought to address his influence attempts to a target he has previously helped, and he ought to present himself as being the unwitting victim of a cruel environment.

The norms of equity (Adams, 1965) and distributive justice (Homans, 1961) are concerned with the allocation of reinforcements. Simply stated these norms assert that one's outcomes ought to be proportionate to his inputs, relative to other inputs and outcomes in the group. Thus, in work situations, salaries ought to be commensurate with duties and responsibilites, with training and experience, and with the salaries received by other employees. When the norm is not satisfied by actual allocation procedures, the person suffering from injustice or inequity is presumed to experience anger and dissatisfaction and is motivated to do something about it. Another employee might become the target of influence if he is "rate-buster," but in most instances the target will be management rather than the employee receiving disproportionate pay, having less education, or performing less responsible or difficult work. Dissatisfaction may lead to quitting the job and leaving the field, submitting a complaint, or setting up a grievance organization. The objective of organizing is similar to other coalitions that are formed and may be analogized to passive resistance movements (e.g., sit-down strikes). Greater numbers not only serve as self-protection but also call attention to the normative features of the situation through consensual validation. Hence, the existence and violation of the norm is made salient. Success of organized labor of course is not only a matter of business ethics and standards (despite Berle, 1963) but involves real economic and political power.

Clark (reported in Adams, 1965) has shown that cashier-bagboy pairs with discrepant input-outcome ratios are less productive than pairs with "fair" allocations. This result may be taken as evidence that work slowdowns may result from inequitable allocations and constitute both retaliation and a threat that if the injustice is not remedied the work slowdown will continue. On the other hand, a number of studies (Adams & Jacobson, 1964; Arrowood, reported in Adams, 1965; Leventhal, Reilly, & Lehrer, 1964) have demonstrated that overpaid subjects attempt to restore equity by overworking. Thus, when a person senses inequity, he will attempt to ameliorate it. A source of influence who seeks to manipulate by use of information control may attempt to impress others that he has contributed more than anyone thinks and that he has received far less than he deserves. In this manner, if the source is successful, he may receive extra benefits with no more effort other than that which occurred through the influence attempt.

It has been seen that relatively weak individuals must often take actions that are considered less "moral" than the actions taken by strong persons, even apart from the greater ability of the strong persons to impose their morality on the society at large. Hypocrisy in the form of deliberate ingratiation (Jones, 1964), behind-the-scenes plotting to form coalitions (Gamson, 1964), and dishonesty (Fischer, 1969; Tedeschi, 1970), often characterize the influence attempts of weak individuals. It would be awkward for a weak person to threaten a powerful person, and the former seldom possesses rewards which could be promised to the latter. Then, too, the powerful individual has so many resources at his disposal (and has special access to information) that it would be unusual for the weak individual to possess the kinds of information that could be used in trustworthy and persuasive arguments. Most of the weak individual's influence attempts, therefore, must take the form of manipulation. To the extent that open influence is morally better than manipulation, which implies stealth, sneakiness, and dishonesty, to possess power makes virtuous behavior much easier.

Conclusion

In summary, a source will choose a target among all those persons available based on SEU considerations. Propinquity is an important factor because it is less expensive to attempt influence of those who are nearby than those who are far away. Friendship and attraction are important because those who like one another are usually near to one another and because friends are more likely to be compliant to influence attempts. Individuals who are high in status and prestige are also likely to be chosen as targets because they more often possess or control the resources or values sought by the source. Persuasion and promises will be the primary modes of influence directed toward friends. Manipulation will be primarily used by low-power sources toward high-power targets. Although a high-power person may be restrained by normative obligations, unilateral power in a conflict situation is likely to result in a confirmation of Lord Acton's dictum that power corrupts and absolute power corrupts absolutely.

Relatively powerful persons are likely to be chosen as targets of influence attempts and are also most likely to initiate such attempts themselves. Presumably, powerful persons have had histories of success and develop high levels of aspiration. Hence, powerful persons are likely to be more confident and having "champagne" tastes, seek influence more often than do less confident and less powerful persons; the latters' "beer" tastes provide a measure of safety and caution in their approach to others. On the other hand, persons who have relatively great power are constantly bombarded with the influence attempts of persons who wish to gain their approval, status, or resources. The result is that the more status and prestige an individual acquires, the more he seeks influence and the more successful he is. This is what is meant by getting caught up in the rat race and may help to explain what makes Sammy run.

Situational Factors

Individuals often find themselves enmeshed in situations over which they have no control. The situational context may be controlled by others or by forces free from human contrivance which they do not understand. Whatever the cause of the situation, the context of social interaction does have important implications for the exercise of social influence. Among the most important situational factors are the intensity of interpersonal conflict, the opportunities for and restrictions upon communications, and the physical and social arrangements of the actors. These structural factors are particularly well illustrated in studies of bargaining behavior, in which communication availability, time pressures, group size, and the presence or absence of third parties affect concession rates and bargaining outcomes. The present section will explore the effects of each of these situational factors on the exercise of influence within the context of SEU considerations.

Conflict Intensity

The exercise of control over others seems to be satisfying in itself (Mulder, 1960; Trow, 1957; Watson, 1965; Watson & Bromberg, 1965), a fact that has led to visions of Mephistopheles laughing as he took Faust's soul. Yet, aside from whatever intrinsic satisfactions derive from the exercise of power and influence, rational considerations require that persons use each other as mediators of rewards, particularly as roles in society become highly specialized and articulated. People in all societies are highly interdependent and rewards and punishments accrue to them as a result of their coordinated (or uncoordinated) mutual decisons and behaviors.

The outcomes that different parties achieve as a function of their interactions are rarely identical. If such outcome congruence did occur, the individuals could easily maximize their gains and each interaction would be cooperative and harmonious. Instances of such pure cooperation are exceedingly rare, if indeed they exist at all. On the other hand, cases of pure competition, in which one party can profit only at the expense of the other, do exist, although they are probably quite rare. When such (zero-sum) situations are found, as in parlor games, sporting events, and wars (perhaps), they are usually regulated by a complex of rules and norms. Thus, most real-world interactions are mixed-motive or non-zero-sum in which each person is able to achieve something through cooperation but a temptation exists to gain even more by exploiting the other person. The element of conflict, then, is always present in social interactions, although it may often be veiled by social amenities. As Kuhn (1963) has noted, the phenomenology of conflict is muted or absent in many interpersonal interactions because "custom or habit has decreed the terms, the costs are too small to argue about, or sympathy has transformed the motives" (p. 340). The presence of interdependent outcomes, whether admitted by the parties or concealed by social norms, gives the individual a rational motive to attempt influence and to maximize his own long-term gains. Even the person who wants nothing from others and desires to stay above the fray is not likely to succeed. As long as one stays in society, he must vie for power in order to counter the attempts of others to gain what he has or may be expected to attain. The exercise of influence, offensively or defensively, is not so much a matter of morality as it is necessity.

Interpersonal conflict results from a failure to coordinate goals and values, or more formally, from the fact that what increases one person's subjective expected gains decreases the other person's subjective expected gains. A continuum exists, in dyadic interaction, between those situations in which persons find little or no conflict between them to those in which life itself hangs in the balance. Intense levels of conflict, by definition, imply that important values are at stake and that any type of conflict resolution or mitigation most often will require a value compromise. However, intense conflict undermines the legitimacy of a source's status and the trustworthiness of the expert, and produces enough distrust to discourage the utilization of positive norms such as reciprocity to unilateral promises of cooperation. Parsons (1963) has stated that all modes of influence require trust (by which Parsons seems to mean the belief in the credibility of the source's communications) for their effectiveness. When conflict is intense, it is much easier to believe that the other person will fulfill his threats rather than make good his promises. Additionally, Kite (1964) has found that subjects view coercion as a more controlling mode of influence than inducements (rewards). Thus, coercive influence modes would tend to be perceived as the only modes which would be effective in controlling the behavior of the target when a high degree of conflict exists in a relationship. Kelley and Thibaut (1969) have similarly suggested that when convergent interests dominate a relationship, influence will be achieved through information control and behavior control; but when divergent interests characterize a relationship, influence will be based on outcome control and fate control.

Given a choice between influence modes, subjects do prefer the use of coercion at high levels of conflict intensity (Goodstadt & Kipnis, 1970; Lindskold & Tedeschi, 1970; MacLean & Tedeschi, 1970; Rothbart, 1968; Schlenker & Tedeschi, in press). However, conflict intensity not only affects the choice of a mode of influence, but also the frequency with which threats and coercion are used. Fischer (1969) operationally defined conflict intensity as the scarcity of resources available to subjects in a bargaining game. The greater the quantity of resources which could be divided by the bargainers, the less intense the conflict was presumed to be. A direct linear relationship was found between conflict intensity and the frequency with which threats were used by the bargainers.

Just as high levels of conflict result in the use of coercive modes of influence, the use of coercive modes of influence appears to increase the perception of conflict by the interacting parties. In their classic trucking game studies, Deutsch and Krauss (1960, 1962) found that the possession of threat capability not only proved detrimental to bargaining outcomes, but that the detrimental effects were heightened if both parties (as opposed to only one party) were armed. Their interpretation was that bilateral threat availability resulted in a conflict spiral, intensified the conflict, fostered mutual hostility, and reduced bargaining outcomes. Similar findings have been obtained by Froman and Cohen (1969), Harford, Solomon, and Cheney (1969), and Tedeschi, Bonoma, and Novinson (1970).

Given the damaging and escalatory consequences that the use of threats portend for dyadic interactions, it would seem especially rational for parties of equal power to attempt to ameliorate the conflict through the establishment of normative contracts. A number of studies have shown that formal agreements arise most frequently between bargainers when a high degree of conflict exists and attractive alternatives to the relationship are present as disruptive factors to any type of high mutual profit (Murdoch, 1967; Thibaut, 1968; Thibaut & Faucheux, 1965).[2] When one of the bargainers has greater control over the other because the latter has a poor

---

2. A contract is composed of mutual contingent promises between pairs of individuals for which legal penalties accrue for the failure to maintain credibility. Although high conflict levels thus produce an exchange of contingent promises between powerful individuals, the higher the conflict and the more powerful the bargainers, the greater will be the mutually agreed upon penalties for failure to uphold the contract (Murdoch, 1967; Thibaut & Faucheux, 1965).

alternative relationship, contract formation is impeded. Murdoch and Rosen (1971) found that in an informal work task, a high conflict of interest and the existence of attractive alternative relationships caused subjects to send more verbal threats to one another, but also fostered more informal agreements and a higher final level of accommodation. Thus, the instability of high levels of conflict can result in the formation of normative agreements.

It was observed earlier that norms tend to be invoked by low-power individuals as an influence tactic to gain rewards and avoid punishments mediated by those who are powerful. Such phenomena caused Nietzsche (1956) to remark that the propagation of morals is a tactic of the weak and powerless to undermine the power of the strong. However, as has been seen from studies concerned with the formation of contractual agreements and normative obligations (e.g., Murdoch, 1967; Thibaut, 1968; Thibaut & Faucheux, 1965), norms are not *formed* by the weak, but by the strong to protect the resources which they have or hope to attain. Norms tend not to be formed between weak and strong parties unless the weaker party can contrive some method for compensating the more powerful party for limiting his own power (Thibaut & Gruder, 1969). Thus, norms are originally formed by the strong to protect themselves from the coercive attempts of other powerful individuals. Once formed, however, low-power individuals can evoke established norms to gain leverage in their attempts to influence the behavior of high-power parties.

Under conditions of low or intermediate conflict, rewards seem to be the basis of social interaction (Blau, 1964; Homans, 1958, 1961; Nord, 1969). Exchange theorists suggest that the use of promises and rewards in social interactions allow the source an advantage over coercion because of reciprocity norms invoked by the use of rewards. Gouldner (1960) has posited that the norm that one should help those who help him is universal. Lindskold and Tedeschi (1971b) and Lindskold, Bonoma, Schlenker, and Tedeschi (1970) have found that neither reward magnitude nor the credibility of promises affect compliance when the source is totally accommodative; apparently promises arouse a reciprocity norm which overrides the utility of the promise. The reciprocation of cooperative and rewarding gestures thus will tend to have ameliorative effects on social conflicts (Schlenker et al., 1971). Additionally, the use of promises and rewards results in an increase in other potential resources which may be used for influence purposes, while the use of threats and punishments results in a decrease. For example, French, Morrison, and Levinger (1960) found that sociometrically measured attraction decreased in an interaction during which fines were used as punishments, while Kipnis (1958) found that subjects liked a rewarding figure more than a punishing figure. Given the above considerations, promises should be most effective and therefore used more frequently at low and intermediate levels of conflict. A series of studies (Butler & Miller, 1965; Miller & Butler, 1969; Miller, Butler, & McMartin, 1969) have shown that when a source could choose between reward and coercive power and the cooperative nature of the situation was stressed, the source preferred reward power.

Persuasion is probably the most preferred mode of influence. It is also the least likely to be successful when conflict intensity is high. The use of influence modes which require the mediation of rewards or punishments cause the target to perceive any control of his behavior as due to external causes (Bem, 1967). Persuasive modes of influence, on the other hand, allow the target to attribute his compliance to internal causes (Fotheringham, 1966). For example, the target is likely to rationalize compliance to persuasive attempts by viewing his behavior as predicated by the logic or reason of the source's communication rather than to any extrinsic reinforcement which is immediately attainable. Such self-attributions yield the illusion of freedom from outside influence and control, and minimize the perception of conflict by the target. The derivation of the word "persuasion"—from the Latin per suasio—indicates influence through sweetness (Fotheringham, 1966, p. 80). Persuasion costs less to use than other forms of influence not only because of low initial investments by the source but because even staunch resistance by the target imposes little opportunity costs on the source. Resistance may merely mean that the target will not change his world view or that the target may attempt counterpersuasion. However, at intense conflict levels, the target would be likely to perceive the source's warnings as threats; while mendations would appear as ploys to trick, deceive, or blatantly bribe the target.

Availability of Communications

In a discussion of the communication processes involved in negotiation, Smith (1968a, 1968b) has pointed out three facilitative functions of communication for the settlement of conflicts: (1) to probe the other for information about his minimum disposition (i.e., the least he will take in settlement; Ilké & Leites, 1962) and to conceal from the other one's own minimum disposition; (2) to influence by persuasion or threats of punishment and to be similarly influenced by one's opponent; and (3) to offer or seek rationalizations for a settlement which was not previously thought to be acceptable. If communication restrictions are placed on negotiations, a full range of influence techniques are removed from possible use by the interacting parties, and it could be expected that such restrictions would increase the use of the modes which were available. For example, tacit communications would become more prevalent, but since their interpretation is quite ambiguous, especially under conflict conditions, settlements would become more difficult. Smith notes that communication restrictions do affect negotiation outcomes by allowing parties to reach fewer agreements and by narrowing the range of settlements which do occur. The wider range of settlements when communication is unrestricted indicates that some bargainers are more effective at influence than others.

Just as increasing the availability of communication channels increases a source's use of influence, increasing the number of modes of influence available to a person should encourage attempts at influence. Kipnis and his colleagues (Goodstadt & Kipnis, 1970; Kipnis & Vanderveer, 1971; Kipnis & Cosentino, 1969; Kipnis & Lane, 1962) have found that many different types of corrective powers (i.e., control of sanctions, rewards, communication channels, direction of task performance) were used to cope with subordinate problems. It can be hypothesized that as limitations are placed upon the number of modes of influence available to the source, situational constraints (including the characteristics of the source and target) will limit the overall usefulness of any particular mode. The greater the number of influence modes available to the source, the greater will be the source's range of applicable power, and hence the more frequently influence will be attempted.

Another aspect of limitations on communication has been pointed out by Moscovici (1967), who, in contrasting written and spoken language, notes the importance of gestures and mimetic signals in the latter. Spoken language is rapid, familiar, and automatic. Since the influence process is dynamic and requires mutual involvement and reciprocal influence, the relative disadvantage of written communication is quite evident. However, in situations in which the source wants to reduce emotional and personal involvement and to make his statements precise, he will choose writing. Thus, most lawyers and scientists choose written communication to achieve just the right coloration of statement, one that would hold up under careful logical or judicial scrutiny. On the other hand, politicians and trial lawyers prefer the use of oral communications for propagandistic eloquence and generally wish to avoid logical analysis.

There are many social situations in which the individuals involved cannot explicitly communicate with one another but must coordinate their behaviors in order to avoid conflict and to maximize mutual gains (e.g., approaching each other in automobiles at high speeds on a narrow road). Kelley, Thibaut, Radloff, and Mundy (1962) have shown that consistent behaviors which tacitly communicated the rule of "win-stick, lose-shift" were efficient in coordinating beneficent actions when simultaneous (as opposed to alternating) responding was permitted. The signal or response utilized may be interpreted as either conciliatory or hostile by the target individual depending upon the entire sequence or pattern of behaviors performed by the source. For example, Shomer, Davis, and Kelley (1966) found that the gates which are otherwise interpretable in a trucking game as threats or punishments could be used as signals to coordinate cooperation. Similarly, Schlenker, Bonoma, Tedeschi and Pivnick, (1970) and Bonoma and Tedeschi (1970) found that even explicit threats of punishment could be interpreted by targets as coordinating signals if only threats were available to the source and the latter used the threats in an accommodative manner. Anderson and Smith (1970) found that threats of fines actually promoted cooperation when no other channels of communications were available between bargainers, but were detrimental to bargaining success when subjects were allowed to communicate with each other in other ways. When no communication was allowed, subjects were likely to view the threat as a signalling device; when other communications were allowed, such threats could not be interpreted in that way. Apparently, a restriction must be placed on the belief of the caterpillar in *Alice in Wonderland* that words can mean anything at all. When a limited mode of communication is allowed to a source and the target is aware of the limitation, then the source can communicate accommodative or exploitative intentions with the same mode; what he does becomes more important than what he says.

Communication structure will also have important effects on the frequency of influence attempts. Centrally located members of communication networks have more opportunity to influence others because they have access to more people (propinquity) and they often possess the most important and relevant information for solution of a group problem. Centrality also induces self-confidence that influence attempts will be successful. Thus, centrality biases the person's estimation of the probability of exercising successful influence, provides him with a valuable commodity (information) for exchange purposes, and decreases the source-based costs associated with information control and persuasive modes of influence.

Leavitt (1951) has noted that centrality in certain networks, which allows the individual to interact with anyone of his choice, increases that person's perception of autonomy, independence, and freedom of action. Shaw (1964) adds that the degree of centrality within communication networks is positively related to the person's willingness to perform at an optimum level on group tasks. It is not surprising that centrality is associated with personal satisfaction in the group (Leavitt, 1951; Mulder, 1959; Watson, 1965; Watson & Bromberg, 1965). Also, persons occupying a central position perceive that they are in a better position to influence others (Watson & Bromberg, 1965).

Centrally located members of communication networks do send more communications than peripherally located persons. Research indicates that individuals who communicate the most have the best chance of being perceived and selected as leaders (Bales, 1953; Bass, 1949; Kirscht et al., 1959; Mann, 1961; Morris & Hackman, 1969; Norfleet, 1948; Riecken, 1958; Shaw & Gilchrist, 1956), are more likely to be perceived as having the highest status (Bass et al., 1958), and are most successful in influencing others (Hoffmann & Maier, 1964; Riecken, 1958; Strodtbeck, 1951). Centrality permits the reception of more communications from others and increases the number of communications sent to others (Watson & Bromberg, 1965). Those who control the means of communication (i.e., those who are centrally located) either have or acquire high status and a cycle is created in which high-status individuals influence more because they have the means to do so. Since high-status persons have more opportunity to influence, they retain and probably enhance their status more easily than do those of lower status.

Physical and Social Arrangements

Another set of situational influences upon the source has to do with physical variables such as seating arrangements and proximity. Moscovici (1967) described an experiment which analyzed the use of language of two persons in various seating arrangements. Those persons who faced each other, even when separated by a screen, used typical spoken language; those seated side by side or back to back used language resembling written communications—indicating the sense of loss of gestural and postural signal capacity. Argyle and Kendon (1967) have discussed similar factors in social performance relating to distance, orientation, posture, contact, etc. For example, a more conversational and cooperative atmosphere prevails in a discussion over the corner of a table; a more competitive atmosphere is generated when two people sit across from each other. Thus, heads of state meet across the table when a treaty or trade is negotiated, but they pose side by side to suggest informal good will.

In addition to the restrictions on communications and effects on social atmosphere, seating arrangements also have the effect of determining group leadership and the frequency and success of influence attempts. Strodtbeck and Hook (1961) analyzed the social dimensions of a twelve-man jury table. They found that those persons who were at end and corner positions did the most talking. Ward (1968) used a round table at which several chairs were kept empty. He found that the person or persons who were opposite to the largest number of others tended to do the most talking and were perceived as leaders on sociometric measures. Similar results have been obtained by Howells and Becker (1962), who placed two persons on one side of a table and three persons opposite them. These seating arrangement studies are clearly related to communication network studies; the location of a person in space is related to norms about who can speak to whom in given circumstances; a person occupying a central position has advantages which can be used for the purposes of influence. Thus, the protracted discussion about the seating arrangements and the shape of the table preceding the American-North Vietnamese talks in Paris was not a trivial matter.

Intense conflicts have the effect of vitiating norms of proper conduct (depersonalization) and encourage the perpetration of destructive acts (Coser, 1956; Frank, 1967). When physical contact through proximity is absent, the opponent can be further dehumanized, a process that has been referred to as deindividuation (Festinger, Pepiton, & Newcomb, 1952). Thus, it is easier to kill thousands of people by dropping a bomb from an airplane at high altitude on a target seen through a bombsite than it is to strangle men, women, and children one by one. Milgram (1965) found support for the notion that as proximity decreases, the use of punishments increases. He found that subjects more often refused requests from a legitimate authority (the experimenter scientist) to shock a helpless confederate when the latter was nearby than when he was far away. Marlowe, Gergen, and Doob (1966) found that subjects would exploit a self-effacing opponent more often when they did not expect to meet him personally then when they did anticipate future physical proximity and interaction. It may be that the target-dependent costs associated with threats are perceived as more probable the nearer the target is. Thus, Russian missiles in Cuba produce more fear than do those on Russian soil, though of course the real scale of danger was just the reverse. Finally, Gahagan and Tedeschi (1970) found that target individuals were more responsive to unilateral conciliatory gestures from a source when they were placed in the same room to interact than when they were kept in separate rooms and anonymity was maintained.

Although proximity might decrease the use of threats, a certain degree of proximity or at least information about the target's behavior is essential to the threatener. Threats have little utility to a source if he cannot monitor the target's behavior and determine whether compliance has been gained or whether punishment is required to maintain credibility for future influence attempts.

Group size, audience effects, and social facilitation affect the behavior of a source of influence. More demands are placed upon a leader in large groups, his participation rate is greater, and his style is more autocratic (Bales, 1953; Hemphill, 1950). Verifying conclusions from field studies, Hamblin (1958) has shown that the leader in emergency, stressful, or high-stake situations is more autocratic. Cartwright and Zander (1968) similarly observe that as the size of a group increases, group cohesiveness, satisfaction and pressures toward uniformity decrease. It might therefore be expected that the larger the size of the group, the less time a leader has to devote to individuals and the more likely he is to use aversive influence modes to accomplish group goals. Kipnis and Lane (1962) and Kipnis and Cosentino (1969) found in field studies that as the number of subordinates increased, supervisors relied more upon threats and less upon the use of persuasion.

Wells (in Thibaut, 1968) has suggested that the presence of a third party in bargaining situatons may contribute to the establishment of contractual agreements. A neutral third party could encourage the bargainers to reach an agreement, circumvent early pessimism on the part of the competing bargainers which might cause a conflict escalation, and enforce any violations of contracts which were formed. On the other hand, Ziller et al. (1969) have indicated that a neutral third party can prolong an opinion conflict when the mode of influence used was persuasion. Ziller et al. indicated that subjects viewed the neutral as the embodiment of social norms. Thus, as long as the third party remained uncommitted, each party could assure himself of the correctness of his own position. No inducements were offered to subjects for reaching agreements. It is plausible to assume that subjects were more concerned about the costs of losing face in front of the neutral than about any benefits of reaching an agreement. With greater benefits of reaching an agreement or with greater costs associated with the failure to form an agreement, Wells' positive expectations regarding the neutral's effects on bargaining agreements may be confirmed. In any event, it seems likely that the presence of a neutral discourages the use of coercive modes of influence, especially if such use is illegitimate.

Normative standards regulating social interactions may be considered part of the structure of the situation. Although we have not always made salient the normative aspects of the source's use of influence, most of the factors discussed involve the use of normative appeals. Status of the source, for example, has little effect in producing deference when he is not operating in a situation in which his legitimacy has been cultivated. Hollander's (1958, 1960, 1964) theory of idiosyncrasy credits is based upon prior self-legitimizing, while the frequency of influence attempts by leaders and aspiring leaders is a function of the security of their position and the mobility of status. Defiance of a source who has high formal status is one of the ways that children earn peer acceptance, particularly if the defiance is in defense of peer norms (Berenda, 1950; Harari & McDavid, 1969). The influence base of the expert is also founded on the information dependency of the target. Here again, the acceptability of the expert in terms of the norms and standards of the target is consequential.

Conclusion

Situational factors are important for determining both the frequency with which the source will attempt influence and the mode of influence he will choose to use. Conflict intensity, availability of communication modes, and physical and social arrangements are among the more important situational determinants of how influence will be wielded. At low levels of conflict, the open influence modes of persuasion and promises are most likely to be used; at high levels of conflict, threats are more likely to be used. However, since high levels of conflict encourage the use of threats, vicious cycles develop and high costs are imposed on the parties unless some compromise is achieved. Thus, contracts are paradoxically encouraged when conflicts are intense.

The wide availability of various modes of influence requires that the source be quite explicit in his attempts to influence. When communications are restricted to a single mode, the source can communicate either conciliatory or exploitative intentions by the context of his deeds. A person who is centrally located in a communication network is in possession of scarce information resources in a problem-solving group; his position also develops the dependency of other group members, raises his status, and provides access to a greater number of potential targets. Thus, centrality facilitates the frequency of influence attempts and probably encourages the use of those modes of influence which depend upon information.

Physical proximity has the effect of providing access for purposes of communication and surveillance of results, as well as to make normative factors involved in the influence process more salient and effective. Group size and the physical positioning of persons relative to one another have important effects in determining who will seek influence and who will be chosen as a target, as well as which influence mode will be chosen.

In summary, situational factors may increase the opportunities that an individual has to influence others by giving him access to others who have what he wants, by placing him in a strategic position that will enhance the probability of his succeeding at influence, or by reducing the resistance by the target of influence because of either increased clarity of communication or the normative requirements of the situation. Hence, situational factors contribute to the subjective expected gains associated with potential influence attempts.

Conclusions

The theoretical notion of SEU has been applied to the available research on a source's exercise of social influence. By attaching lower level concepts to those of subjective probability and utility, a integration of the literature has been attempted and many hypotheses generated for future tests. It is rather clear that more frequent and more successful influence is directly related to the source's estimates of his own capacities and resources, as well as his motivation for achieving, his propensity to take risks, and his competence or expertise. These factors plug into the "probability of success" factor of SEU as do such outside-of-self determinants as interpersonal attraction between the source and the target, the relative status of target and source, the relative prestige of target and source, the centrality or other positioning of the source, and the availability and variety of modes of influence existent in the situation.

Self-confidence and other related factors directly bias subjective expected probabilities of success for a potential influence attempt, as do most of the outside-of-self variables, such as status, prestige, and attraction. The choice of a target rests, of course, upon whether the target possesses the sought value and how freely he may be disposed to bestow it upon any influencer. What is valuable to a source will depend upon his level of aspiration, which in turn depends upon how much status and prestige he already possesses (notion of marginal utility). A source may usually assume that the probability of accumulating target-dependent (opportunity) costs is lower when the difference in status and prestige between himself and target individuals is greater. Also, high status and prestige may mean that costs are subjectively less for the source, when in fact target-based costs are imposed on the source (again, marginal utility).

The prediction of source behavior is always predicated upon SEU, which takes into account both the gains and costs associated with an influence attempt. Cost considerations are quite complex. They include the initial expenditure on media or channels of communication, the requirements for surveillance of target, the resources needed to enforce threats or make good promises, the vulnerability to exploitation if benign influence is attempted, and the lower interpersonal attraction that results if threats are used, if bribes are offered to friends, or if flattery used to ingratiate oneself with powerful sources is unmasked for what it is.

Although throughout we have made predictions based on the estimations subjectively made by the prospective source of influence, the determination of SEU is made on the basis of observables. No claim is made that rigorous treatment has been given to the theory advanced herein but it is hoped that a heuristic outcome has been achieved which may be the basis of more rigorous and mathematical treatment of the social influence processes.

References

Adams, H. *The education of Henry Adams*. New York: Random House, 1931.
Adams, J. S. Inequity in social exchange. In L. Berkowitz (Ed.), *Advances in experimental social psychology*. Vol. 2. New York: Academic Press, 1965. Pp. 267-299.
Adams, J. S., & Jacobson, P. R. Effects of wage inequities on work quality. *Journal of Abnormal and Social Psychology*, 1964, 69, 19-25.
Adams, J. S., & Rosembaum, W. B. The relationship of worker productivity to cognitive dissonance about wage inequities. *Journal of Applied Psychology*, 1962, 46, 161-164.
Aiken, E. G. Changes in interpersonal descriptions accompanying the operant conditioning of verbal frequency in groups. *Journal of Verbal Learning and Verbal Behavior*, 1965, 4, 243-247.
Anderson, A. J., & Smith, W. P. Threat, communication, and bargaining. Paper presented at the Eastern Psychological Association meeting, Atlantic City, N. J., April, 1970.
Argyle, M.,& Kendon, A. The experimental analysis of social performance. In L. Berkowitz (Ed.), *Advances in experimental social psychology*. Vol. 3. New York: Academic Press, 1967. Pp. 55-98.
Aronson, E., Willerman, B., & Floyd, J. The effect of a pratfall on increasing interpersonal attractiveness. *Psychonomic Science*, 1966, 4, 157-158.
Atkinson, J. W. *An introduction to motivation*. New York: Van Nostrand, 1964.
Back, K. W. Influence through social communication. *Journal of Abnormal and Social Psychology*, 1951, 46, 9-23.
Bales, R. F. The equilibrium problem in small groups. In T. Parson, R. F. Bales,

& E. A. Shils (Eds.), *Working papers in the theory of action.* Glencoe, Ill.: Free Press, 1953. Pp. 111-161.

Bandura, A. *Principles of behavior modification.* New York: Holt, Rinehart & Winston, 1969.

Bass, B. M. An analysis of the leaderless group discussion. *Journal of Applied Psychology,* 1949, 33, 527-533.

Bass, B. M. Some observations about a general theory of leadership and interpersonal behavior. In L. Petrullo & B. M. Bass (Eds.), *Leadership and interpersonal behavior.* New York: Holt, Rinehart & Winston, 1961. Pp. 3-9.

Bass, B. M., Pryer, M. W., Gaier, E. L., & Flint A. W. Interacting effects of control, motivation, group practice and problem difficulty on attempted leadership. *Journal of Abnormal and Social Psychology,* 1958, 56, 352-258.

Bavelas, A., Hastorf, R. H., Gross, A. E., & Kite W. R. Experiments on the alteration of group structure. *Journal of Experimental Social Psychology,* 1965, 1, 55-71.

Bem, D. J. Self-perception: an alternative interpretation of cognitive dissonance phenomena. *Psychological Review,* 1967, 74, 183-200.

Berenda, R. W. *The influence of the group on judgments of children.* New York: Columbia University Press, 1950.

Berger, J., Cohen, B. P., & Zelditch, M., Jr. Status characteristics and expectation states. In J. Berger, M. Zelditch, Jr., & B. Anderson (Eds.), *Sociological theories in progress.* Vol. 1. Boston: Houghton Mifflin, 1966. Pp. 29-46.

Berkowitz, L. Liking for the group and the perceived merit of the group's behavior. *Journal of Abnormal and Social Psychology,* 1957, 54, 353-357.

Berkowitz, L., & Daniels, L. R. Responisbility and dependency. *Journal of Abnormal and Social Psychology,* 1963, 66, 429-437.

Berkowitz, L., & Daniels, L. R. Affecting the salience of the social responsibility norm: Effects of past help on the response to dependency relationships. *Journal of Abnormal and Social Psychology,* 1964, 68, 275-281.

Berkowitz, L., & Levy, B. I. Pride in group performance and group-task motivation. *Journal of Abnormal and Social Psychology,* 1956, 53, 300-306.

Berle, A. A. *The American economic republic.* New York: Harcourt, Brace, 1963.

Blau, P. M. *Exchange and power in social life.* New York: Wiley, 1964.

Bonoma, T. V., & Tedeschi, J. T. The effects of source behavior on target's compliance to threats. Mimeographed manuscript. State University of New York at Albany, 1970.

Bramel, D. Interpersonal attraction, hostility, and perception. In J. Mills (Ed.), *Experimental social psychology.* New York: Macmillan, 1969. Pp. 1-120.

Brown, R. *Social psychology.* New York: Free Press, 1965.

Burnstein, E., & Worchel, P. Arbitrariness of frustration and its consequences for aggression in a social situation. *Journal of Personality,* 1962, 30, 528-540.

Butler, D. C., & Miller, N. Power to reward and punish in social interaction. *Journal of Experimental Social Psychology,* 1965, 1, 311-322.

Byrne, D. Attitudes and attraction. In L. Berkowitz (Ed.), *Advances in experimental social psychology.* Vol. 4. New York: Academic Press, 1969. Pp. 35-89.

Carter, L., Haythorne, W., Shriver, B., & Lanzetta, J. The behavior of leaders and other group members. *Journal of Abnormal and Social Psychology,* 1950, 46, 589-595.

Cartwright, D., & Zander, A. The structural properties of groups: introduction.

In D. Cartwright & A. Zander (Eds.), *Group dynamics: research and theory,* 3rd ed. New York: Harper & Row, 1968. Pp. 485-502.
Chu, G. C. Fear arousal, efficacy, and imminency. *Journal of Personality and Social Psychology,* 1966, 4, 517-524.
Cohen, A. R. Upward communication in experimental hierarchies. *Human Relations,* 1958, 11, 41-53.
Coleman, J. F., Blake, R. R., & Mouton, J. S. Task difficulty and conformity pressures. *Journal of Abnormal and Social Psychology,* 1958, 57, 120-122.
Cooper, J., & Jones, E. E. Opinion divergence as a strategy to avoid being miscast. *Journal of Personality and Social Psychology,* 1969, 13, 23-30.
Coopersmith, S. *The antecedents of self-esteem.* San Francisco: W. H. Freeman, 1967.
Coser, L. *The function of social conflict.* New York: Free Press, 1956.
Dahl, R. A. The concept of power. *Behavioral Science,* 1957, 2, 201-218.
Dahl, R. A. *Who governs?* New Haven, Conn.: Yale University Press, 1961.
Davis, K. E., & Florquist, C. C. Perceived threat and dependence as determinants of the tactical usage of opinion conformity. *Journal of Experimental Social Psychology,* 1965, 1, 219-236.
Deutsch, K. W. *The nerves of government.* New York: Free Press, 1966.
Deutsch, M., & Krauss, R. M. The effect of threat upon interpersonal bargaining. *Journal of Abnormal and Social Psychology,* 1960, 61, 181-189.
Deutsch, M., & Krauss, R. M. Studies of interpersonal bargaining. *Journal of Conflict Resolution,* 1962, 6, 52-76.
Edwards, W. The theory of decision making. *Psychological Bulletin* 1954, 51 380-417.
Emerson, R. M. Power-dependence relations. *American Sociological Review,* 1962, 27, 31-41.
Festinger, L. *A theory of cognitive dissonance.* Evanston, Ill.: Row, Peterson, 1957.
Festinger, L., Pepitone, A., & Newcomb, T. Some consequences of de-individuation in a group. *Journal of Abnormal and Social Psychology,* 1952, 47, 382-389.
Fischer, C. S. The effect of threats in an incomplete information game. *Sociometry* 1969, 32, 301-314.
Fisher, R. *International conflict for beginners.* New York: Harper & Row, 1969.
Fotheringham, W. C. *Perspectives on persuasion.* Boston: Allyn and Bacon, 1966.
Fouriezos, N. T., Hutt, M. L., & Guetzkow, H. Measurement of self-oriented needs in discussion groups. *Journal of Abnormal and Social Psychology,* 1950, 45, 682-690.
Frank, J. *Sanity and survival.* New York: Random House, 1967.
French, J. R. P., Jr., Morrison, H.W., & Levinger, G. Coercive power and forces affecting conformity. *Journal of Abnormal and Social Psychology,* 1960, 61, 93-101.
French, J. R. P., Jr., & Snyder, R. Leadership and interpersonal power. In D. Cartwright (Ed.), *Studies in social power,* Ann Arbor: University of Michigan, 1959. Pp. 150-165.
Froman, L. A., & Cohen, M. D. Threats and bargaining efficiency. *Behavioral Science,* 1969, 14, 147-153.
Gahagan, J. P., & Tedeschi, J. T. Effects of promise credibility, outside options and social contact on interpersonal conflict. Mimeographed manuscript, State University of New York at Albany, 1970.

Gamson, W. A. Experimental studies of coalition formation. In L. Berkowitz (Ed.), *Advances in experimental social psychology*. Vol. 1. New York: Academic Press, 1964. Pp. 81-110.

Gamson, W. A. *Power and discontent*. Homewood, Ill.: Dorsey Press, 1968.

Goldberg, C. Attitude change as a function of source credibility, authoritarianism, and message ambiguity. *Proceedings* of the 78th annual convention of the American Psychological Association, Miami Beach, 1970.

Goodstadt, B., & Kipnis, D. Situational influences on the use of power. *Journal of Applied Psychology*, 1970, 54, 201-207.

Goranson, R. E., & Berkowitz, L. Reciprocity and responsibility reactions to prior help. *Journal of Personality and Social Psychology*, 1966, 3, 227-232.

Gore, P.M., & Rotter, J. B. A personality correlate of social action. *Journal of Personality*, 1963, 31, 58-64.

Gouldner, A. W. The norm of reciprocity: a preliminary statement. *American Sociological Review*, 1960, 25, 161-179.

Graham, F. K., Charwat, W. A., Honig, A. S., & Weltz, P. C. Aggression as a function of the attack and the attacker. *Journal of Abnormal and Social Psychology*, 1951, 46, 512-520.

Greenspoon, J. The reinforcing effect of two spoken sounds on the frequency of two responses. *American Journal of Psychology*, 1955, 68, 409-416.

Guetzkow, H. Differentiation of roles in task-oriented groups. In D. Cartwright & A. Zander (Eds.), *Group dynamics: research and theory*, 3rd ed. New York: Harper & Row, 1968.

Hamblin, R. L. Group integration during a crisis. *Human Relations*, 1958, 11, 67-76.

Harari, H., & McDavid, J. W. Situational influence on moral justice: a study of finking. *Journal of Personality and Social Psychology*, 1969, 11, 240-244.

Harford, T., Solomon, L., & Cheney, J. Effects of proliferating punitive power upon cooperation and competition in the triad. *Psychological Reports*, 1969, 24, 355-360.

Harsanyi, J. C. Measurement of social power, opportunity costs, and the theory of two-person bargaining games. *Behavioral Science*, 1962, 7, 67-80.

Hastorf, A. H. The "reinforcement" of individual actions in a group situation. In L. Krasner & L. P. Ullman (Eds.), *Research in behavior modification: new developments and implications*. New York: Holt, Rinehart & Winston, 1961. Pp. 268-284.

Heider, F. *The psychology of interpersonal relations*. New York: Wiley, 1958.

Heinicke, C., & Bales, R. Developmental trends in the structure of small groups. *Sociometry*, 1953, 16, 7-38.

Hemphill, J. K. Relations between the size of the group and the behavior of "superior" leaders. *Journal of Social Psychology* 1950, 32, 11-22.

Hemphill, J. K. Why people attempt to lead. In B. Bass & L. Petrullo (Eds.), *Leadership and interpersonal behavior*. New York: Holt, Rinehart & Winston, 1961. Pp. 201-215.

Higbee, K. L. Fifteen years of fear arousal: research on threat appeals: 1953-1968. *Psychological Bulletin*, 1969, 72, 426-444.

Hoffman, L. R., & Maier, N. R. F. Valence in the adoption of solutions by problem-solving groups: concept, method, and results. *Journal of Abnormal and Social Psychology*, 1964, 69, 264-271.

Hollander, E. P. Conformity, status, and idiosyncrasy credit. *Psychological Review*, 1958, 65, 117-127.

Hollander, E. P. E. P. Competence and conformity in the acceptance of influence. *Journal of Abnormal and Social Psychology*, 1960, 61, 365-369.
Hollander, E. P. *Leaders, groups, and influence.* New York: Oxford, 1964.
Hollander, E. P., & Julian, J. W. Studies in leader legitimacy, influence, and innovation. In L. Berkowitz (Ed.), *Advances in experimental social psychology.* Vol. 5. New York: Academic Press, 1970. Pp. 33-69.
Homans, G. C. *The human group.* New York: Harcourt, Brace, 1950.
Homans, G. C. Social behavior as exchange. *American Journal of Sociology*, 1958, 63, 597-606.
Homans, G. C. *Social behavior: its elementary forms.* New York: Harcourt, Brace, 1961.
Hornstein, H. A. The effects of different magnitudes of threat upon interpersonal bargaining. *Journal of Experimental Social Psychology*, 1965, 1, 282-293.
Hovland, C. I., Janis, I. L., & Kelley, H. H. *Communication and persuasion.* New Haven, Conn.: Yale University Press, 1953.
Howells, L. T., & Becker, S. W. Seating arrangement and leadership emergence. *Journal of Abnormal and Social Psychology*, 1962, 64, 148-150.
Hurwitz, J. I., Zander A. F., & Hymovitch, B. Some effects of power on the relations among group members. In D. Cartwright & A. Zander (Eds.), *Group dynamics: research and theory*, 3rd ed. New York: Harper & Row, 1968. Pp 291-297.
Ilké, F. C.. & Leites, N. Political negotiation as a process of modifying utilities. *Journal of Conflict Resolution,* 1962, 6, 19-28.
Jaffee, C. L. Leadership attempting: why and when? *Psychological Reports,* 1968 23, 939-946.
Janis, I. L., & Field, P. B. Sex differences and personality factors related to persuasibility. In C. I. Hovland & I. L. Janis (Eds.), *Personality and Persuasibility.* New Haven, Conn.: Yale University Press, 1959. Pp. 55-68.
Jaques, E. An objective approach to pay differentials. *Time Motion Study*, 1961, 10, 25-28.
Jones, E. E. *Ingratiation: a social psychological analysis.* New York: Appleton-Century-Crofts, 1964.
Jones, E. E. Conformity as a tactic of ingratiation. *Science*, 1965, 149, 144-150.
Jones, E. E., & de Charms, R. Changes in social perception as a function of the personal relevance of behavior. *Sociometry*, 1957, 20, 75-85.
Jones, E. E., & Gerard, H. B. *Foundations of social psychology.* New York: Wiley, 1967.
Jones E. E., Gergen, K. J., & Jones, R. G. Tactics of ingratiation among leaders and subordinates in a status hierarchy.*Psychological Monographs*, 1963, 77 (Whole No. 566).
Jones, R. G., & Jones, E. E. Opinion conformity as an ingratiation tactic. *Journal of Personality*, 1964, 32, 436-458.
Kaufmann, H. Similarity and cooperation received as determinants of cooperation rendered. *Psychonomic Science*, 1967, 9, 73-74.
Kelley, H. H. Communication in experimentally created hierarchies. *Human Relations*, 1951, 4, 39-56.
Kelley, H. H., & Thibaut, J. W. Group problem solving. In G. Lindzey & E. Aronson (Eds.), *The handbook of social psychology*, 2nd ed. Vol 4. Reading, Mass.: Addison-Wesley, 1969. Pp. 1-101.
Kelley, H.H., Thibaut, J. W., Radloff, R., & Mandy, D. The development of

"cooperation" in the "minimal social situation." *Psychological Monographs*, 1962, 76 (Whole No. 19).

Kipnis, D. The effects of leadership style and leadership power upon the inducement of an attitude change. *Journal of Abnormal and Social Psychology*, 1958, 57, 173-180.

Kipnis, D., & Cosentino, J. Use of leadership powers in industry. *Journal of Applied Psychology*, 1969, 53, 460-466.

Kipnis, D., & Lane, W. P. Self-confidence and leadership. *Journal of Applied Psychology* 1962, 46, 291-295.

Kipnis, D. & Vanderveer, R. Ingratiation and the use of power. *Journal of Personality and Social Psychology*, 1971, 17, 280-286.

Kirscht, J. P., Lodahl, T. M., & Haire, M. Some factors in the selection of leaders by members of small groups. *Journal of Abnormal and Social Psychology*, 1959, 58, 406-408.

Kite, W. R. Attributions of causality as a function of the use of reward and punishment. Unpublished doctoral dissertation, Stanford University, 1964.

Kleiner, R. The effects of threat reduction upon interpersonal attraction. *Journal of Personality*, 1960, 28, 145-155.

Krauss, R. M. Structural and attitudinal factors in interpersonal bargaining. *Journal of Experimental Social Psychology*, 1966, 2, 42-55.

Kuhn, A. *The study of society; a unified approach*. Homewood, Ill.: Dorsey Press, 1963.

Leavitt, H. J. Some effects of certain communication patterns on group performance. *Journal of Abnormal and Social Psychology*, 1951, 46, 38-50.

Lee, W. *Decision theory and human behavior*. New York: Wiley, 1971.

Lefcourt, H. M. Internal versus external control of reinforcement: a review. *Psychological Bulletin*, 1965, 65, 206-220.

Lerner, M. J. The effect of responsibility and choice on a partners' attractiveness following failure. *Journal of Personality*, 1965, 33, 178-187.

Lerner, M. J. & Becker, S. Interpersonal choice as a function of ascribed similarity and definition of the situation. *Human Relations*, 1962, 15, 27-34.

Lerner, M. J., Dillehay, R. C., & Sherer, W. C. Similarity and attraction in social contexts. *Journal of Personality and Social Psychology*, 1967, 5, 481-486.

Lerner, M. J., & Matthews, G. Reaction to suffering of others under conditions of indirect responsibility. *Journal of Personality and Social Psychology*, 1967, 5, 319-325.

Leventhal, G. S., Allen, J., & Kemelgor, B. Reducing inequity by reallocating rewards. *Psychonomic Science*, 1969, 14, 295-296.

Leventhal, G. S., & Bergman, J. T. Self-depriving behavior as a response to unprofitable inequity. *Journal of Experimental Social Psychology*, 1969, 5, 153-171.

Levanthal, G., Reilly, E., & Lehrer, P. Change in reward as a determinant of satisfaction and reward expectancy. Paper presented at the annual meeting of the Western Psychological Association, Portland, Oregon, 1964.

Levinger, G. The development of perceptions and behavior in newly formed social power relationships. In D. Cartwright (Ed.), *Studies in social power*. Ann Arbor: University of Michigan, 1959. Pp. 83-98.

Lewin, K., Dembo, T., Festinger, L., & Sears, P. S. Level of aspiration. In J. McV. Hunt (Ed.), *Personality and the behavior disorders*. New York: Ronald Press, 1944. Pp. 333-378.

Lindskold, S., Bonoma, T., Schlenker, B. R., & Tedeschi, J. T. Factors affecting the effectiveness of reward power. *Psychonomic Science*, 1972, 26, 68-70.
Lindskold, S., & Tedeschi, J. T. Threatening and conciliatory influence attempts as a function of source's perception of own competence in a conflict situation. Mimeographed manuscript, State University of New York at Albany, 1970.
Lindskold, S., & Tedeschi, J. T. Self-esteem and sex as factors affecting influencibility. *British Journal of Clinical and Social Psychology*, 1971, 10, 114-122. (a)
Lindskold, S., & Tedeschi, J. T. Reward power and attraction in interpersonal conflict. *Psychonomic Science*, 1971, 22, 211-213. (b)
Lippitt, R., Polansky, N., Redl, F., & Rosen, S. The dynamics of power. *Human Relations*, 1952, 5, 37-64.
Lott, A. J., & Lott, B. E. A learning theory approach to interpersonal attitudes. In A. G. Greenwald, T. C. Brock, & T. M. Ostrom (Eds.), *Psychological foundations of attitudes*. New York: Academic Press, 1968. Pp. 67-88.
Luchins, A. S. Social influence on perception of complex drawings. *Journal of Social Psychology*, 1945, 21, 257-273.
MacLean, G., & Tedeschi, J. T. The use of social influence by children of entrepreneurial and bureaucratic parents. Mimeographed manuscript, State University of New York at Albany, 1970.
Mann, R. D. Dimensions of individual performance in small groups under task and social-emotional conditions. *Journal of Abnormal and Social Psychology*, 1961, 62, 674-682.
Marak, G. E., Jr. The evolution of leadership structure. *Sociometry*, 1964, 27, 174-182.
Marlowe, D., & Gergen, K. J. Personality and social interaction. In G. Lindzey & E. Aronson (Eds.), *The handbook of social psychology*, 2nd ed. Vol. 3. Reading, Mass.: Addison-Wesley, 1969. Pp. 590-665.
Marlowe, D., Gergen, K. J., & Doob, A. N. Opponent's personality, expectation of social interaction, and interpersonal bargaining. *Journal of Personality and Social Psychology*, 1966, 3, 206-213.
McDonald, R. D. The effect of reward-punishment and affiliation need on interpersonal attraction. Unpublished doctoral dissertation. University of Texas, 1962.
Milgram, B. Some conditions of obedience and disobedience to authority. *Human Relations*, 1965, 18, 57-75.
Miller, N., & Butler, D. Social power and communication in small groups. *Behavioral Science*, 1969, 14, 11-18.
Miller, N., Butler, D. C., & McMartin, J. A. The ineffectiveness of punishment power in group interaction. *Sociometry*, 1969, 32, 24-42.
Morgenthau, H. J. *Politics among nations: the struggle for power and peace*, 4th ed. New York: Knopf, 1966.
Morris, C. G., & Hackman, J. R. Behavioral correlates of perceived leadership. *Journal of Personality and Social Psychology*, 1969, 13, 350-361.
Moscovici, S. Communication processes and the properties of language. In L. Berkowitz (Ed.), *Advances in experimental social psychology*. Vol. 3. New York: Academic Press, 1967. Pp. 225-270.

Moulton, R. W. Motivational implications of individual differences in competence. Paper presented at meeting of the American Psychological Association. September, 1967, Washington, D. C.

Mowrer, O. H. *Learning theory and behavior.* New York: Wiley, 1960.

Mulder, M. Power and satisfaction in task-oriented groups. *Acta Psychologica,* 1959, 16, 178-225.

Mulder, M. The power variable in communication experiments. *Human Relations,* 1960, 13, 241-256.

Murdoch, P. Development of contractual norms in a dyad. *Journal of Personality and Social Psychology,* 1967, 6, 206-211.

Murdoch, P., & Rosen, D. Norm formation in an interdependent dyad. *Sociometry,* 1970, 33, 264-275.

Myers, A. Team competition, success, and the adjustment of group members. *Journal of Abnormal and Social Psychology,* 1962, 65, 325-332.

Newcomb, T. M. An approach to the study of communicative acts. *Psychological Review,* 1953, 60, 394-404.

Nietzsche, F. *The genealogy of morals.* Garden City, N. Y.: Doubleday, 1956.

Nord, W. R. Social exchange theory: an integrative approach to social conformity. *Psychological Bulletin,* 1969, 71, 174-208.

Norfleet, B. Interpersonal relations and group productivity. *Journal of Social Issues,* 1948, 4, 66-69.

Osgood, C. E. *An alternative to war or surrender.* Urbana: University of Illinois Press, 1962.

Osgood, C. E., & Tannenbaum, P. H. The principle of congruity in the prediction of attitude change. *Psychological Review,* 1955, 62, 42-55.

Oskamp, S., & Perlman, D. Effects of friendship and disliking on cooperation in a mixed-motive game. *Journal of Conflict Resolution,* 1965, 10, 221-226.

Parsons, T. On the concept of influence. *Public Opinion Quarterly,* 1963, 27, 37-62.

Reiser, M., Reeves, R., & Armington, J. Effect of variations in laboratory procedure and experiments upon ballistocardiogram, blood pressure, and heart rate in healthy young men. *Psychosomatic Medicine,* 1955, 17, 185-189.

Riecken, H. W. The effect of talkativeness on ability to influence group solutions or problems. *Sociometry,* 1958, 21, 309-321.

Rosenthal, D., & Cofer, C. N. The effect on group performance of an indifferent and neglectful attitude shown by one group member. *Journal of Experimental Psychology,* 1948, 38, 568-577.

Rothbart, M. Effects of motivation, equity, and compliance on the use of reward and punishment. *Journal of Personality and Social Psychology,* 1968, 9, 353-362.

Rotter, J. B. Generalized expectancies for internal versus external control of reinforcement. *Psychological Monographs,* 1966, 80 (1, Whole No. 609).

Sayles, L. R. *Behavior of industrial work groups: prediction and control.* New York: Wiley, 1958.

Schelling, T. C. *Arms and influence.* New Haven, Conn.: Yale University Press, 1966.

Schlenker, B. R., Bonoma, T. V., Tedeschi, J. T., & Pivnick, W. P. Compliance to threats as a function of the wording of the threat and the exploitativeness of the threatener.*Sociometry,* 1970, 33, 394-408.

Schlenker, B. R., Bonoma, T. V., Tedeschi, J. T., Lindskold, S., & Horai, J. Effects of referent and reward power on social conflict. *Psychonomic Science*, 1971, 24, 268-270.

Schlenker, B. R. & Tedeschi, J. T. The exercise of social influence. Paper presented at the 17th International Congress of Applied Psychology, Liege, Belgium, July, 1971.

Schlenker, B. R., & Tedeschi, J. T. Interpersonal attraction and the exercise of coercive and reward power. *Human Relations* (in press)

Schopler, J., & Bateson, N. The power of dependence. *Journal of Personality and Social Psychology*, 1965, 2, 247-254.

Schopler, J., & Matthews, J. W. The influence of the perceived causal locus of partner's dependence on the use of interpersonal power. *Journal of Personality and Social Psychology*, 1965, 2, 609-612.

Scodel, A. Induced collaboration in some non-zero-sum games. *Journal of Conflict Resolution*, 1962, 6, 335-340.

Secord, P. F., & Backman, C. W. *Social psychology*. New York: McGraw-Hill, 1964.

Shaw, M. E. Communication networks. In L. Berkowitz (Ed.), *Advances in experimental social psychology*. Vol. 1. New York: Academic Press, 1964. Pp. 111-147.

Shaw, M. E., & Gilchrist, J. C. Intra-group communication and leader choice. *Journal of Social Psychology*, 1956, 43, 133-138.

Shomer, R. W., Davis, A. H., & Keiley, H. H. Threats and the development of coordination: further studies of the Deutsch and Krauss trucking game. *Journal of Personality and Social Psychology*, 1966, 4, 119-126.

Smith, D. H. The classification of communication: problems and a proposal. *Pacific Speech*, 1968, 2, 15-24. (a)

Smith, D. H. Communication and negotiation. In L. O. Thayer (Ed.), *Communication spectrum 7*. Flint, Mich.: National Society for the Study of Communications, 1968, Pp. 52-63. (b)

Smith, W. P., & Leginski, W. A. Magnitude and precision of punitive power in bargaining strategy. *Journal of Experimental Social Psychology*, 1970, 6, 57-76.

Solomon, L. The influence of some types of power relationships and game strategies upon the development of interpersonal trust. *Journal of Abnormal and Social Psychology*, 1960, 61, 223-230.

Strickland, B. The prediction of social action from a dimension of internal-external control. *Journal of Social Psychology*, 1965, 66, 353-358.

Strodtbeck, F. L. Husband-wife interaction over revealed differences. *American Sociological Review*, 1951, 16, 468-473.

Strodtbeck, F. L., & Hook, L. H. The social dimensions of a twelve-man jury table. *Sociometry*, 1961, 24, 397-415.

Strodtbeck, F. L., James, R. M., & Hawkins, C. Social status in jury deliberations. *American Sociological Review*, 1957, 22, 713-719.

Strodtbeck, F. L., & Mann, R. D. Sex role differentiation in jury deliberations. *Sociometry*, 1956, 19, 3-11.

Tedeschi, J. T. Threats and promises. In P. Swingle (Ed.), *The structure of conflict*. New York: Academic Press, 1970. Pp. 155-191.

Tedeschi, J. T., Bonoma, T., & Lindskold, S. Threatener's reaction to prior announcement of behavioral compliance or defiance. *Behavioral Science*, 1970, 15, 171-179.

Tedeschi, J. T., Bonoma, T., & Novinson, N. Behavior of a threatener: retaliation vs. fixed opportunity costs. *Journal of Conflict Resolution*, 1970, 14, 69-76.

Tedeschi, J. T., Horai, J., Lindskold, S., & Faley, T. The effects of opportunity costs and target compliance on the behavior of a threatening source. *Journal of Experimental Social Psychology*, 1970, 6, 205-213.

Tedeschi, J. T., Lindskold, S., Horai, J., & Gahagan, J. P. Social power and the credibility of promises. *Journal of Personality and Social Psychology*, 1969, 13, 253-261.

Tedeschi, J. T., Schlenker, B. R. & Bonoma, T. V. Cognitive dissonance: private ratiocination or public spectacle? *American Psychologist*, 1971, 26, 685-695.

Thibaut, J. The development of contractual norms in bargaining: replication and variation. *Journal of Conflict Resolution*, 1968, 12, 102-112.

Thibaut, J., & Faucheux, C. The development of contractual norms in a bargaining situation under two types of stress. *Journal of Experimental Social Psychology*, 1965, 1, 89-102.

Thibaut, J., & Gruder, C. L. Formation of contractual agreements between parties of unequal power. *Journal of Personality and Social Psychology*, 1969, 11, 59-65.

Thibaut, J. W., & Kelley, H. H. *The social psychology of groups.* New York: Wiley, 1959.

Tornatzky, L., & Geiwitz, P. J. The effects of threat and attraction on interpersonal bargaining. *Psychonomic Science*, 1968, 13, 125-126.

Torrance, E. P. Some consequences of power differences on decision making in permanent and temporary three-man groups. *Research studies*, State College of Washington, 1954, 22, 130-140.

Trow, D. B. Autonomy and job satisfaction in task-oriented groups. *Journal of Abnormal and Social Psychology*, 1957, 54, 204-210.

Veroff, J. Development and validation of a projective measure of power motivation. *Journal of Abnormal and Social Psychology*, 1957, 54, 1-8.

Verplanck, W. S. Unaware of where's awareness: some verbal operants—notates, monents, and notants. In C. W. Eriksen (Ed.), *Behavior and awareness.* Durham, N. C.: Duke University Press, 1962. Pp. 130-158.

Wallace, D., & Rothaus, P. Communication, group loyalty, and trust in the PD game. *Journal of Conflict Resolution*, 1969, 13, 370-380.

Walster, E., & Prestholdt, P. Effect of misjudging another: over-compensation or dissonance reduction? *Journal of Personality and Social Psychology*, 1966, 2, 85-97.

Ward, C. D. Seating arrangement and leadership emergence in small discussion groups. *Journal of Social Psychology*, 1968, 74, 83-90.

Watson, D. L. Effects of certain social power structures on communication in task-oriented groups. *Sociometry*, 1965, 28, 322-336.

Watson, D., & Bromberg, B. Power, communication, and position satisfaction in task-oriented groups. *Journal of Personality and Social Psychology*, 1965, 2, 859-864.

Whiting, J. W. M. Resource mediation and learning by identification. In I. Iscoe & H. W. Stevenson (Eds.), *Personality development in children.* Austin: University of Texas Press, 1960. Pp. 112-126.

Wilson, W., & Miller, N. Shifts in evaluations of participants following intergroup competition. *Journal of Abnormal and Social Psychology*, 1961, 63, 428-431.

Worchel, P. Catharsis and the relief of hostility. *Journal of Abnormal and Social Psychology*, 1957, 55, 238-243.

Zajonc, R. B., & Marin, I. C. Cooperation, competition, and interpersonal attitudes in small groups. *Psychonomic Science*, 1967, 7, 271-272.

Zander, A., Cohen, A. R., &Stotland, E. *Role relations in the mental health professions*. Ann Arbor, Mich.: Institute for Social Research, 1957.

Ziller, R. C., Zeigler, H., Gregor, G. L., Styskal, R. A., & Peak, W. The neutral in a communication network under conditions of conflict. *American Behavioral Scientist*, 1969, 13, 265-282.

VIII

James T. Tedeschi, Thomas V. Bonoma and
Barry R. Schlenker

Influence, Decision, and Compliance

Seldom have social psychologists viewed the myriad social influence processes from the vantage point of a single coherent perspective. Rather the predominant tendency has been to focus attention upon a particular influence process (e.g., persuasion or threats) and to develop "local" theories and narrow research interests. The present chapter is an attempt to develop a theory which will generally apply to seven basic influence processes. The focus of the theory will be upon the characteristics and behaviors of the source of influence as these factors affect the compliant behavior of the target of influence. The theory is relevant to dyadic interactions only. However, certain influence situations such as social conformity can be considered as the dyadic product of the interaction of a group and the individual. The language of decision theory will be employed as the basis of integration.

Anyone attempting a comparison and integration of what have been almost completely separate research areas must come to grips with the attendant language problems. It is well recognized that the label which one investigator uses to designate an experimental manipulation of some source attribute (e.g., status) may or may not correspond to the labels employed by other investigators working in the same problem area. For example, Hurwitz, Zander, and Hymovitch (1968) operationally define source prestige as a third party's perception of co-workers' opinions regarding the target person's skill

---

This chapter was written with the support of Grant #GS-27059 from the National Science Foundation to the senior author, by Grant #ACDA-0331 from the U. S. Arms Control and Disarmament Agency (National Research Council) to the second author, and by a predoctoral fellowship from the National Science Foundation to the last author.

and reputation. French and Raven (1959) use the term "expertise" while Homans (1961) uses the concept of "esteem" to refer to the same operational definition. It is not surprising, therefore, that there is even less agreement in the definition of concepts across the subdisciplines of social influence.

Janda (1960) has pointed out two common difficulties that result from the employment of an overabundance of psychological concepts. The *delusion of sufficiency* refers to a premature satisfaction with a concept which incorporates a wealth of denotations and connotations associated with the layman's use of the word. The *confusion by similarity* refers to the entanglement of a carefully formulated concept with one or more other analytically distinct concepts that share the same label. Both of these conceptual pitfalls present obstacles to the development of a cumulative body of scientific knowledge. Our concern for these conceptual problems requires that we somewhat tediously differentiate the concepts employed in the present theory and that empirical evaluations be drawn only from experiments which appear to clearly operationalize the concepts in question.

Our task, then, is to establish a minimum set of concepts which exclude dissimilar events and include those classes of events which yield generalizations of functional relationships between independent manipulations and resultant target behaviors. Obviously, there are no "good" or "bad" concepts, and arguments that one concept is better than another on a priori grounds are futile. If the present theory succeeds in providing even a partial integration of the influence literature and yields a bonus of testable (but as yet untested) hypotheses, then the effort will have been worth the doing.

A Theory of Influenceability

Basic to all influence situations are a source of influence, a signal system, and an intended target. Source characteristics are important factors in determining the reactions of a target of influence and will be the major focus of the present theory. Target dispositions and attributes also have implications for determining his susceptibility to influence, but we will not consider them here.[1] Probably the most significant aspect of the present approach is the attempt to reinterpret the processes of coercive and reward power, persuasion, modeling, social conformity, and social reinforcement as based on explicit and tacit forms of four kinds of communications: threats,

1. See Chapter 3.

promises, warnings, and mendations. The adequacy of the theory largely depends upon the plausibility of these reinterpretations.

Threats are communications from source to target of the form "If you don't do X, I will do Y," where Y is an action, the withholding of an action, the production of a noxious stimulus, or the removal of a positive reinforcement, any of which can be perceived by the target as detrimental or punishing. A promise offers rewards contingent upon the target's compliance to the source's request. When the source merely describes to the target contingencies which are beyond the source's control, and where the outcomes are predicted to be punishing to the target, the message constitutes a warning to the target. A positive prediction of a contingency between a target's behavior and a favorable outcome not controlled by the source is a mendation.[2]

Warnings and mendations are psychologically more complicated for a target than are threats and promises. The target must take into account not only the motives of the source but also whether in fact the source does have any control over the events described or predicted and what the magnitude of the consequences are. In addition, the target must consider the motives and capability of a possible third party who controls the reward or punishment contingencies.

Influence attempts are often conglomerate forms of communications and may involve simultaneously all four message types. Oftentimes one message form will be made explicit, while another message lurks tacitly behind the scenes. An explicit influence attempt depends upon the use of clear statements of the behaviors desired by the source, descriptions of the causal texture of the environment or of the consequences for the target of doing or not doing as recommended, requested, or demanded. Tacit communications may be verbal or nonverbal and may be attached to the source's behavior or to the situation contrived by the source. Much behavior can be "codified" and reduced to rules resembling language. A type of "grammar of behavior" can be developed (Goodenough, 1969). If a person discovers the rule or contingency connecting a source's behaviors to his own, the relationship may be described as a tacit threat or a tacit promise. If a person can extract a rule relating an observed model's behaviors and outcomes to his own behavior–outcome contingencies, then we may speak of either a tacit warning or a tacit mendation, since the model's behaviors communicate a prediction about the future.

We will restrict the present treatment to influence interactions

---

2. A full discussion of mendations is presented in Chapter 1.

which use one identifiable type of message. The consideration of explicit threats and promises is straightforward. Explicit warnings and explicit mendations may be used as persuasive communications. The source may offer his own recommendations to the target individual. The reinterpretation of persuasive influence attempts as involving the communication of warnings and mendations is still rather straightforward, though somewhat novel. It is when we consider modeling, social conformity, and social reinforcement studies that our approach represents a clear departure from current conceptual schemes.

The first step in redefining imitation of a social model in terms of tacit communications was taken by Bandura and Harris (1966). They found that seven- to nine-year-old children, after hearing a model rewarded for producing sentences which exemplified a familiar grammatical rule, produced their own sentences which reflected the same rule. Thus, as Krebs (1970) has recently suggested, the function of a social model is to draw the attention of the observer to particular courses of action, supply information about what is appropriate in various situations by setting an example, and to supply information about the consequences of various courses of action. Similarly, Walters (1967) has hypothesized that in many cases the rewards which accrue to a model serve as cues delineating particular environmental demands.

The second step in understanding the conditions under which a model's behaviors will lead to imitation by an observer requires that the rules of the unwritten behavioral language be codified. This essentially linguistic task requires the construction of a grammar and the explication of the principles of morphological and syntactical ordering. We suggest that a model's messages take the form of tacit warnings or tacit mendations. Oftentimes, in a laboratory situation in which the observer is quite aware that his own behavior is under observation, the subject actively interprets the model's behavior as indicating the expectancies of the experimenter, and as indicating which responses will be rewarded, punished, approved, or disapproved by the experimenter (cf. Orne, 1962). In a sense, the experimenter has contrived a situation in which a third person mediates influence over the subject, and thus, from the experimenter's point of view, modeling is a form of indirect power. Kiesler and Kiesler (1969, p. 34) were so convinced that the subjects in modeling studies were merely complying with the experimenter's indirect power manipulations that they treated modeling as an aspect of social conformity.

A problem arises for the target in determining if the tacit communications of a model are directed at him since anyone could apparently "tune in." The *relevance* of a nondirected communication will be defined as the target's perception that the communication is useful to him. For example, the greater the difference between the environment of the observer and the environment of the model, the less relevant the tacit communications should be perceived. Hence, Harris (1968) failed to find a difference between the altruistic behavior of children who were exposed to models who were praised for their altruism and to models who were not. This failure to find a modeling effect may be attributed to the fact that the praising agent was present for the model but absent when the observer children performed. The children therefore, had no reason to expect similar consequences. The message communicated by the model was irrelevant (i.e., not perceived as useful) to the children. Other criteria of relevance include the similarity of model and observer, and the observer's social position relative to that of the source. When the observer and source have similar social positions, the observer has the same opportunities or obligations as the model and thus should interpret the model's tacit communications as relevant. It is proposed, then, that a model's tacit communications will be decoded and perceived as relevant if (1) the cues and general problem structure of the model's and observer's environments are similar; (2) the target perceives the model as similar and thus likes the model; or (3) the model has high status and implies by his behavior that the target "ought" to imitate him.

The typical social conformity experiment may also be interpreted in terms of explicit or tacit communications. Compliance in a conformity situation has been postulated to fall into one of two categories: *private acceptance*, where the target privately as well as publicly accepts the group's judgments as correct; and *public conformity*, where the target maintains a private belief that the group is in error, but publicly acquiesces to the group's pressures (Allen, 1965; Festinger, 1953; Kiesler, 1969; Kiesler & Kiesler, 1969). It is generally assumed that private acceptance depends upon some form of persuasive communication. Hence, conformity based on private acceptance can be interpreted to result from the communication of explicit warnings and mendations by the group to the target which serve to restructure the latter's perception of situational contingencies *without* group-mediated rewards or punishments. Public conformity, however, depends for its efficacy upon the target's belief that he will either be rewarded for conformity or punished for nonconformity. Group mediation of future outcomes is usually tacitly communicated. Thus, public conformity may be interpreted in terms of tacit promises or tacit threats.

The failure of experimenters to distinguish between message types has generated some confusion in public conformity experiments, and has blurred the conceptual distinction between private acceptance and public conformity. Private acceptance can clearly be related to unambiguous statements of fact (e.g., the length of a set of lines) provided by the group during interaction. These statements of fact can be retranslated into implicit warnings and mendations, for example, "If you judge the line to be x inches long, you will be correct and the experimenter will approve of you." Presumably, the need for social comparison (Festinger, 1954) promotes the "objective" exchange of information between group members, leading to the kind of lasting change predicted by an independent acceptance of the group's judgments. However, a more potent and less noted form of influence in conformity experiments may be the tacit threats of disapproval or promises of approval by group members for "right-thinking" behavior in general. The presence of the latter influence mode mediates public conformity to the wishes of the group without the subjects' private acceptance of the group's judgments as representing the state of the environment (cf. Shulman, 1967).

The verbal conditioning literature can be redefined in terms of tacit threats or tacit promises. The repetition of a reinforcement directly after a reiterated response provides a basis for a recipient to extract the "rule" governing the causal texture of his relationship to the experimenter. There is evidence that the individual must be fully aware of the contingency rule if significant conditioning is to occur to verbal reinforcers (Spielberger & DeNike, 1966; Volger, 1968). A promise, after all, is a communication meant to invoke a positive expectancy in the target individual, while a threat arouses a negative expectancy. The consistent use of reinforcements arouses such expectancies. Bandura (1962) has contended that the typical verbal conditioning experiment can be interpreted as a problem-solving situation in which the cues to problem solution are provided by the experimenter. He therefore suggested that if the experimenter would just tell the subject to emit a verbal operant, superior conditioning would be manifested. In any case, the bulk of the verbal conditioning research supports the conclusion that subjects must be aware of the contingency before significant conditioning occurs (cf. Bandura, 1969).

Interpretations of events which are descriptive or couched in observational language do not constitute a theory. To formulate a theory, we shall now apply the concepts of decision theory to the influence processes. The effects of source characteristics and behaviors upon the decision criteria and ultimately the influenceability of the target will be placed within the context of a theory of subjective expected value (SEV).

A SEV Theory of Social Influence

If the prime dependent variable of interest in social influence research is limited to a choice between the alternatives of compliance and noncompliance on the part of the target individual, decision theory suggests itself as a possible vehicle of analysis. Decision theory is concerned with the individual who *must* decide between two states, X and Y, and has no other possible choices (Edwards, 1954). It is not surprising that psychologists have long been flirting with the idea of applying decision theory to processes of learning (Tolman, 1952), motivation (Atkinson, 1964; Lewin, 1951), attitude change (Fishbein, 1966), and perception (Bruner & Postman, 1949). Cantril (1967) strongly emphasized the applicability of a SEV model to the understanding of judgmental processes: "... since change seems to be the rule of nature and of life, our perception is largely a matter of weighing the probabilities, of guessing, of making hunches concerning the probable significance of the meaning of 'what is out there,' and of what our reaction should be toward it, in order to protect ourselves and our satisfactions, or to enhance our satisfactions" (p. 284). A number of psychologists have indicated that decision theory could be applied to the social influence processes (Berkowitz, 1969; Cartwright, 1959; March, 1955, 1968), and in a small number of cases, restricted application has been attempted (Gerard, 1965; Lanzetta & Kanareff, 1959). The present effort simply represents an extended attempt to "try out" the SEV language (as redefined) as a general theory of social influence.

Decision theory is derived from classical economics. The "economic man" of classical economic theory was presumed to be perfectly informed about the choices available to him and the exact outcomes of each of his choices. He was further presumed to make his decisions so as to consistently maximize something. The theory assumes that a "weak ordering" of preferences can be made by the individual.[3] Given such simplifying assumptions, the individual's behavior should be perfectly consistent and easily predicted. However, most decisions that an actor must make lead only to probable (risky) outcomes, rather than certain ones, or his choices may be connected with outcomes of unknown probabilities (uncertainty). Contemporary decision theory has been forced to change its assumptions to fit men who are not omniscient.

Under conditions of imperfect information, the decision maker must hazard a guess about the probability that a particular choice

---

3. A "weak ordering" means that the decision maker is able to rank his preferences so that if he prefers A to B and B to C, then he will rank A before C.

will lead to a particular outcome. Each decision alternative considered by a target individual has consequences which have positive or negative value for him. But, these outcomes are not certain, and the target must estimate the probabilities with which gains and costs will accrue to him as a result of choosing a particular alternative. An expected value theory of decision-making postulates that the sum of the product of the probability of gains and their value and the product of the probability of costs and their value will be determined by the individual, who chooses the decision alternative that yields the highest value according to this formula. For example, if a target person is threatened, he must decide whether to comply to the threatener's demands or to defy the threatener. The probabilities and values (negative and positive) associated with compliance must be compared to the probabilities and values associated with defiance. According to expected value theory, the target will choose that alternative which will yield him the highest expected value. The present adaptation of SEV theory attempts specification of the social factors that cause the individual to subjectively bias his estimations of objective probabilities. Source characteristics and behaviors are functionally related to the direction of bias, and predictions about compliance or noncompliance to influence attempts are generated from subjective expected value comparisons.

Before presenting the theory in detail, a word should be said about the assumption of "weak ordering." This assumption can usually be avoided empirically by varying the magnitude but not the quality of outcomes available to the decision makers. Thus, it is assumed that more points, praise, candy, or money will be preferred to less of any of these commodities or sentiments. Of course, one person will subjectively evaluate the same amount of a given commodity as worth more or less than another person, a problem squarely faced by the economic concept of utility.[4] We will skirt this problem by assuming that the traditional procedure of randomizing subjects across treatment conditions ensures that *for each treatment group*, the different utilities possessed by its constituent members cancel each other out. Thus, the net effect is to randomize individual differences and provide the basis for using objective rather than subjective value notions to generate tests of SEV theory. It is recognized, however, that with the development of an adequate theory of motivation, something like the current concept of utility must be used to expand the present first approximation to a subjective expected *utility* theory. For the present, we will assume the single motivation of the individual to maximize his gains and to minimize his losses.

4. For an explication of the concept of utility see Edwards and Tversky (1967).

The SEV theory of influence proffered here postulates that the message sent to the target individual has an expected value.[5] Table 8.1 presents an overview of the relations between message types and expected value calculations. It can be seen from the Table that the determination of the expected value of a message will depend upon which type of message is at issue. The calculation of expected value of a threat or a promise is relatively simple in experimental situations. If a threat is reiterated, the target is likely to comply at some times and not comply at other times. If the target does as requested, the source, naturally, has no occasion to administer the threatened punishment. Hence, it is only on unsuccessful (i.e., noncompliant) threat occasions that opportunities for punishing the target are presented to the source. Tedeschi (1968) has referred to the probability that punishment will be administered on unsuccessful threat occasions as the credibility of a threat. The expected value of a threat message is a product of its credibility (determined over prior interactions between the particular source and target involved) and the magnitude of punishment specified in the contemporary threat message. Similarly, the expected value of a promise is a product of promise credibility and the magnitude of reward offered in the message under active consideration. Promise credibility represents the cumulated probability that when the source has made promises to the target and the target had complied (successful promises), the source gave the promised reward.

It may be recalled that a warning is a communication from a source to a target which predicts that harm will befall the target unless some remedial action is taken to avert the negative outcome, where the harm is not mediated by the source. Table 8.1 indicates that the expected value of a warning is the product of the probability that the harm will occur, given that the target does nothing, and the

---

5. The present use of the term "expected value of the message" represents a shorthand notation to describe *only those outcomes associated with the message*. Technically, however, decision theory (Edwards, 1954; Lee, 1971) reserves the term "expected value" for the sum of the products of all of the consequences and their respective probabilities of occurrence accumulating to an individual as a result of his choice of a particular *behavioral alternative*. Thus, for example, if a target noncomplies to a threat, consequences other than just the potential punishment from the source occur. The target receives the material outcome associated with that behavior, the target might suffer losses in self-esteem due to giving in to the demands of the threatener, etc. Conversely, when a target complies to a threat, certain consequences accrue to him as a function of his choice of that behavioral alternative. The expected value of compliance and noncompliance must take into account all of these consequences. However, outcomes other than those directly associated with the choice of the behavioral alternatives of compliance and noncompliance are assumed to be held constant across the various conditions of the experiment, an assumption fulfilled in most cases. Subsequent extensions of the present framework must incorporate the other consequences of the choice of compliance or noncompliance by a target and systematically relate independent variable manipulations to effects on these other consequences.

negative value of the harm. Chu (1966) has proposed a theory of warnings that is similar to the one proposed here. He suggested that defensive action would be taken by the target as a function of

$$Pa = M \times L \times 1/T \times E,$$

where Pa is the probability that defensive action will be taken, M is the negative value of the harmful outcome, L is the likelihood of the negative outcome occurring, $1/T$ is the imminency of the potential loss (reciprocal of time interval between warning and the occurrence of the potential loss), and E is the efficacy of the preventive action as measured by the amount of harm averted minus the costs of the preventive action.

The expected value of a warning in the present theory is

Table 8.1. The determination of expected value for each message type

Message Type	Determination of Probability (P)	Value (V)	Expected Value (EV)
Threat	cumulative probability of punishment on unsuccessful threat occasions over all past interactions (threat credibility)	magnitude of punishment	P x V
Promise	cumulative probability of reward on successful promise occasions over all past interactions (promise credibility)	magnitude of reward	P x V
Warnings	probability of harm given that the target does nothing as determined by knowledge of the causal texture of the environment or from past warning-outcome sequences	magnitude of harm	P x V
Mendations	probability of benefits given that the target does as the source recommends based on knowledge of the causal texture of the environment or from past mendation-outcome sequences	magnitude of benefits	P x V

equivalent to Chu's term $(M \times L)$. However, Chu fails to consider the probability that the preventive action will actually succeed in circumventing the harm predicted in the warning message. The present theory assumes the constancy of the efficacy and imminency terms. Chu's theory treats expected value as a model which can be derived from a more general theory of SEV.

The expected value of a mendation is a product of the probability that the individual will receive the benefits predicted, provided he does as the source suggests, and the value of those benefits. It is presumed that the alternative decision (that of doing something other than the behavior recommended) will also be considered by the target and that the resultant decision will be determined by expected value considerations.

If the target individual could make his decisions in a social vacuum, he would comply or not comply to influence attempts as a function of expected value considerations. However, the individual is imbedded in a social situation. The social relationship between the source and the target may *authenticate* or *de-authenticate* the probability estimations made by the target. Authentication refers to an upward subjective biasing or exaggeration of the objective probability of an event, while de-authentication refers to a downward subjective biasing of an objective probability. The direction of bias involved in subjective estimates of probabilities will depend upon source characteristics and behaviors and the type of influence message used.

Figure 8.1 presents an overview of the SEV theory of social influence. Source characteristics and message factors constitute the independent variables of the theory. Each of these factors is separately perceived by the target and they combine to produce a subjective expected value estimation, the predictor variable of the theory. The laws of combination are not postulated by the theory, rather they are left to empirical determination. Each factor is treated independently of the others and predictions are made for each type of influence message. The SEV for decision alternatives may be considered the subjective expected value of the nonadvocated alternative in the binary choice presented to the target of influence. If the target is presented with a threat, for example, SEV refers to what happens if the target does not comply with the threatener's demand, while SEV for decision alternatives refers to the SEV attached to compliant behavior. Each type of influence message presents the target with a similar choice. The predictive problem centers on our ability to estimate the SEVs relevant to a particular influence attempt. Of course, the target may choose to leave the

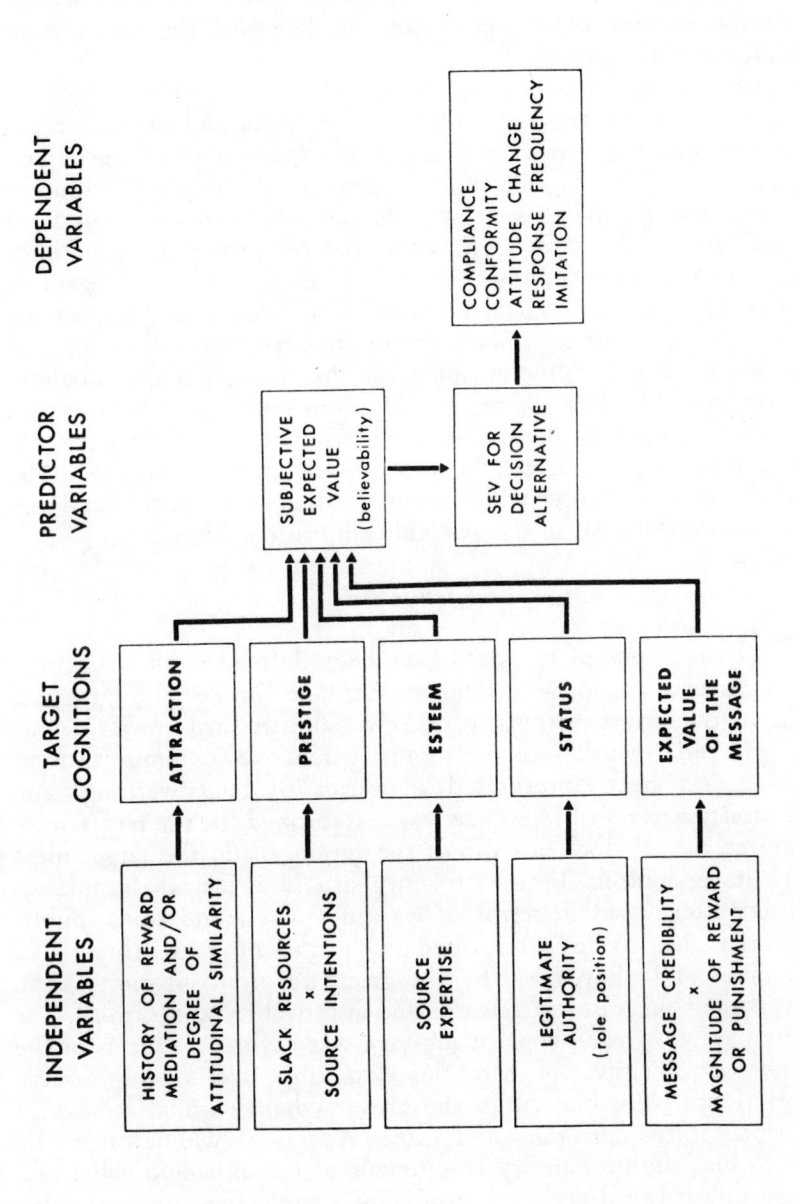

INDEPENDENT VARIABLES	TARGET COGNITIONS	PREDICTOR VARIABLES	DEPENDENT VARIABLES
HISTORY OF REWARD MEDIATION AND/OR DEGREE OF ATTITUDINAL SIMILARITY →	ATTRACTION		
SLACK RESOURCES × SOURCE INTENTIONS →	PRESTIGE		
SOURCE EXPERTISE →	ESTEEM	→ SUBJECTIVE EXPECTED VALUE (believability) → SEV FOR DECISION ALTERNATIVE →	COMPLIANCE CONFORMITY ATTITUDE CHANGE RESPONSE FREQUENCY IMITATION
LEGITIMATE AUTHORITY (role position) →	STATUS		
MESSAGE CREDIBILITY × MAGNITUDE OF REWARD OR PUNISHMENT →	EXPECTED VALUE OF THE MESSAGE		

Figure 8.1. Overview of the SEV Theory of Social Influence

situation altogether, but by so doing he chooses to defy the threat, ignore the request of the promisor, or disregard the warnings or mendations of the source.

Status, prestige, and esteem are postulated as having authentication effects on all types of influence messages and hence serve a facilitative function by increasing the influenceability of the target. Attraction for the source should authenticate explicit promises, warnings, and mendations as well as the tacit communications of promises in social conformity and verbal reinforcement situations. High positive attraction, however, should de-authenticate threats and those comformity and social reinforcement situations interpretable in terms of tacit threats. These predictions regarding the effects of attraction are based on the presumption that a target is apt to believe that someone he likes will benefit him and tends to disbelieve that someone he likes will harm him. Similarly, harm may be expected from a disliked source, but benefits should not be expected. The remainder of the chapter will present the theory in more detail and evaluate it on the basis of the available empirical evidence.

Conclusion

Four basic types of messages have been defined as the basis of a general theory of social influence. Explicit threats and promises represent the overt forms of coercive and reward power, while warnings and mendations represent persuasive communications. Modeling has been interpreted in terms of tacit warnings and mendations; criteria of relevance were established for the target since the source model does not direct the message and the target must discern it for himself. In a conformity situation, private acceptance has been interpreted in terms of warnings and mendations; public conformity has been interpreted in terms of tacit threats of punishment and disapproval by the group for nonconformity or in terms of tacit promises of rewards and approval for conformity. The expected value of each type of message was defined in terms of the product of objective probabilities and objective values. Source characteristics were limited to the presumed orthogonal factors of attraction, status, prestige, and esteem, each of which cause the target to bias the probability component of the expected value of a message upward or downward, producing a subjective expected value estimation by the target. The target then compares the relative gains and costs of compliance and noncompliance and chooses on the basis of maximizing his gains and minimizing his losses.

Expected Value of the Message

Very little research in the area of social influence has been so specifically conceptualized as to provide clear tests of the postulated relationships of the expected values of messages to the influenceability of targets. In fact, the reinterpretation of modeling, public conformity, and social reinforcement experiments as studies of tacit communications is itself a novel approach. Nevertheless, an impressive array of evidence can be culled from the literature to evaluate the hypotheses in question.

Expected Value of Threats

Tedeschi and his colleagues (e.g., Tedeschi, Bonoma, & Brown, 1971) have provided the clearest tests of the effects of the expected value of contingent threats on the frequency of compliance by target individuals. Horai and Tedeschi (1969) used a two-choice mixed-motive game and varied both the probability and magnitude of punishment for noncompliance to a source's specific demand ("If you don't make choice 1, I will take n points away from your counter"). The target subjects could not retaliate and were faced with a least-of-evils choice. If they complied, the threatener exploited them, and if they did not comply, the simulated threatener was provided with an option to punish them. The results indicated a positive linear relationship between threat credibility and punishment magnitude on the frequency with which subjects did as the source demanded. Threat credibility and punishment magnitude were clearly orthogonal factors, and when multiplied to obtain the expected values for the various conditions of the experiment, the model predicted correctly the rank of 7 out of the 9 means obtained.

The generality of the above finding may be determined by a summary of other studies (see Table 8.2) which have used the same basic paradigm. The subject populations have been heterogeneous, and included ROTC cadets, white middle-class college students at two universities (East and West Coast), black children from a ghetto in a large Southern city, and children of white middle-class parents. Procedures have also been widely varied. For example, the response modes provided the subjects and demanded by the threatener included gross bodily movements (turning 180 degrees), verbal choices between colored stimuli (red and green), and pushing buttons (left and right). Punishments have consisted of the loss of points or the loss of play money which could later by exchanged for M&M

candies. The result has been a rather strong confirmation of the expected value hypothesis, with a total of 37 out of 56 means correctly ranked over twelve experiments. The results are even more impressive when the one study that used Negro preadolescents is dropped from consideration (Gahagan, Long, & Horai, 1969). The correctly ranked means would then be 36 out of 47 with one tied rank.

In a complex study of status congruence, Sampson and Bunker (1966) found an effect of punishment magnitude on compliance to

Table 8.2. Evaluation of studies in which the expected values of threats were manipulated*

Study	Probability of Punishment (percentage)	Punishment Magnitude[A]	Number of Means Ranked	Number Correctly Ranked
Bonoma, Schlenker et al. (1970)	50	5, 20	2	2
Bonoma & Tedeschi, (1970)	10, 50, 90	5, 20	6	2
Bonoma, Tedeschi, & Lindskold (1970)	10, 90	5, 20	4	4
Faley & Tedeschi (1971)	10, 50, 90	5, 20	6	6
Gahagan et al. (1969)[B]	10, 50, 90	5, 10, 20	9	1
Gahagan et al. (1970)	50	5, 20	2	2
Horai & Tedeschi (1969)	10, 50, 90	5, 10, 20	9	7
Lindskold et al. (1969)	10, 90	5, 10, 20	6	2
Pivnick & Tedeschi (1972)	0, 100	10	2	2
Schlenker et al. (1970)	10, 90	10	2	2
Tedeschi (1970)	0, 100	10	2	2
Tedeschi et al. (1968)[C]	10, 50, 90	10, 20	6	5
Totals			56	37

*Other experimental factors are collapsed to compute expected values.
[A] In game points or play money.
[B] Subjects were black preadolescents.
[C] The two tied-ranks which occurred in this study were interpreted as a failure of the expected value predictions for one cell.

threats. Pairs of subjects were joined by a confederate of the experimenter, who by deception procedures was placed in the role of evaluator and used explicit threats of monetary fines. Fine magnitudes made available to the evaluator were either high (20 or 40 cents) or low (4 or 8 cents). The high negative value produced a significantly greater increment in performance in accord with the threatener's demands.

French, Morrison, and Levinger (1960) anticipated the present theory by using an expected value model as a predictor of target's compliance to threats. Because their procedures did not reiterate threats and the punishment magnitude manipulation was confused with an "illegitimate power" condition, their evidence is not clearly relevant to the expected value hypothesis. However, threatened individuals sorted more IBM cards, and with fewer errors, than did individuals who were not threatened. Zipf (1960), using a similar paradigm, found that both promises of reward and threats of punishment led to better card-sorting performances than when no influence was exerted. Phenomenological reports gathered after the experimental session indicated that subjective estimations of the degree of own-compliance were direct functions of both subjective probability estimates and the magnitude of reward or punishment associated with the message; however, only the value component reached conventional levels of statistical significance.

Interpretive license is often cheap when one attempts to evaluate the outcome of experiments on the effects of tacit threats. It is perhaps instructive that Vogel-Sprott (1969) demonstrated the "information value" of contingent punishments. She found that once a response is learned under rewarding conditions, the subject can be taught to suppress the response if punishments are made contingent upon the occurrence of the acquired response. Noncontingent punishments did not convey such "information value." Consistent with the interpretation that contingent repetitive punishments are extracted as a "rule" and perceived as tacit threats was the additional finding that the greater the consistency or probability of contingent punishments (tacit threat credibility?), the more efficient was the learning of avoidance responses by human subjects. Thus, punishments serve the function of underscoring tacit demands by the source, especially when the negative consequences are applied in a consistent manner. Parenthetically, such tacit communication between experimenter and subject has received rather vague attention in recent years (Orne, 1962; Rosenthal, 1966). In contrast to the usual recommendation to eliminate such tacit communications from experiments, the present authors suggest their systematic study.

Several other punishment studies may be interpreted as providing evidence relevant to the predicted effect of the expected value of tacit threats. Aronfreed and Leff (1963) employed a complex punisher involving the presentation of a noxious noise, verbal disapproval, and deprivation of candy to teach children not to handle very attractive toys. Both the intensity and quality of the noise was varied to produce two levels of punishment magnitude. Providing that the attractiveness discrimination was relatively easy to make, children learned avoidance responses more readily when the punishment magnitude was greater. Parke and Walters (1967) employed the same paradigm and found the same results.

Finally, a number of nonlaboratory investigations provide some further support for the present theory. Gibbs (1968) examined crime statistics in a number of states and found that the incidence of homocide was inversely related to both the magnitude of legal punishment actually imposed on convicted murderers and the probability that homocides would result in convictions. Although Gibbs concluded that the credibility component was more important than the value component of the legal threats, Gray and Martin (1969) reanalyzed Gibbs' data and concluded that a product of probability and value best accounted for the obtained findings. In a somewhat broader analysis which included several types of crimes, Tittle (1969) reported that certainty of punishment was positively related to the deterrence of all crimes analyzed, whereas severity of punishment contributed only to the deterrence of homocide. Yet, Chambliss (1966) found that the frequency of parking violations on a college campus was inversely related to both the severity and the certainty of punishment.

The preponderance of the available evidence indicates that the expected negative value of both tacit and explicit threats is directly related to the compliant behavior of target individuals.

Expected Value of Warnings

In a rather direct study of the expected value of warnings, Chu (1966) employed persuasive communications which simultaneously varied the probability and magnitude of harm associated with the danger of roundworms to health. Chu also experimentally varied the stated probability that a remedial action could avert the harm (efficacy). He found that children were more willing to take remedial action as expected value became more negative and as efficacy increased. Using a similar fear appeal, Dabbs and Leventhal (1966) found that expected negative values of warnings about tetanus were directly related to the willingness of subjects to take preventive injections. However, as was the case in the Chu study, both probability and value were varied simultaneously, permitting no assessment of their independent contributions to expected value. Berkowitz and Cottingham (1960) found that the stated efficacy of a recommended preventive response to warnings, directly resulted in favorable attitudes toward wearing automobile seat belts.

A controversy currently rages concerning the relationship of magnitude of harm involved in taking no preventive action with respect to a warning and either attitude change or the occurrence of preventive actions. As Higbee (1969) has noted, while a thorough review of the fear arousal literature reveals that the bulk of recent studies do report a positive relationship between the magnitude of punishment contained in the warning and subsequent target attitude change, a significant minority of earlier investigations found the opposite effect (Goldstein, 1959; Haefner, 1956; Janis & Feshbach, 1954; Janis & Terwilliger, 1962).

Janis (1967) has attempted to resolve the apparent contradiction in results between experiments by proposing that the relationship between the degree of fear aroused in the target and the acceptance of the source's recommendations is curvilinear. Janis suggests that when fear is too high, the individual resorts to denial defenses and is motivated to ignore or minimize the importance of the warning (p. 195). Janis' interpretations of the warning literature are based on two basic misconceptions: (1) the equation of independent variable manipulations with arousal of various levels of fear; and (2) the gross generalization of research evidence gained through poorly conceptualized research procedures. These two problems are not unrelated.

Janis chooses to infer the "black box" variable of fear arousal from independent variable manipulations only, a method of inference fraught with perils. Inference is likely to be less tenuous when made to explain a perturbation of an established and known relationship between values of independent and dependent events. Ordinarily, the scientist would wish to be quite clear about his antecedent and consequent conditions and their measurement, for if they are ambiguous and poorly conceived, inferences drawn from them will be worth next to nothing in clarifying problems and issues. A good example of this is the now classic study done by Janis and Feshbach (1953).

Janis and Feshbach presented high school students with an illustrated lecture on dental hygiene. Three warnings with attendant recommended dental care practices were used in an attempt to produce three levels of "fear arousal." The effectiveness of the warnings in producing the intended attitude change was found to be curvilinear with magnitude of "fear." Examination of the independent variable manipulation which is alleged to have aroused the greatest amount of fear shows that a portion of the message warned subjects that failure to brush one's teeth properly produces gangrene of the jaws in old age. As Katz (1960) has noted, this message is quite implausible and could lead subjects to question the sincerity of the communicator, and to assign a low probability to the warning. If the probability component of the expected value of the warning was sufficiently reduced, the target would not believe the warning no matter how high the source said the magnitude of harm was. It could well be the case that the "high fear" condition represented a low expected value and hence produced no more attitude change than did the "low fear" condition, which also represented a low expected value.

Janis (unpublished; cited in Higbee, 1969) has himself provided evidence to support the above interpretation. He presented two versions of communications describing the dangers of excessive cigarette smoking to subjects. The "high fear" communication described the unpleasant consequences in great detail; the "low fear" warning did not provide such detail. The "high fear" condition elicited spontaneous comments from subjects regarding the sincerity of the communicator and suspicion about manipulative intent.

A large number of studies have clearly manipulated the magnitude of harm conveyed in the warning, while holding probability of harm constant, and have found a direct relationship between the expected negative value of warnings and opinion change or frequency of preventive actions. Higbee (1969) has recently reviewed these studies, which have involved such diverse topics as dental hygiene practices (Leventhal & Singer, 1966; Singer, 1965), tetanus innoculations (Dabbs & Leventhal, 1966; Kornzweig, 1968; Leventhal, Jones, & Trembly, 1966; Leventhal, Singer, & Jones, 1965), safe driving practices (Berkowitz & Cottingham, 1960; Leventhal & Niles, 1965), cigarette smoking (Insko, Arkott, & Insko, 1965; Leventhal & Niles, 1964; Snider, 1962), tuberculosis (DeWolfe & Governale, 1964), viewing of the sun during an eclipse (Kraus, El-Assal, & DeFleur, 1966), fallout shelters (Hewgill & Miller, 1965; Miller and Hewgill, 1966; Powell, 1965), and the use of stairway handrails for safety (Piccolino, 1966). The results of each of these studies support the direct function specified between expected negative value of warnings and the influenceability of the target.

Expected Value of Promises and Mendations

The relationship between the expected value of promises and mendations is the converse of that predicted for threats and warnings. Whereas a direct relationship has been predicted and confirmed between the *negative* expected value of threats and warnings and influenceability, the function between the *positive* expected value of promises and mendations and subsequent compliance is postulated as direct and linear.

In an attempt to evaluate the effects of the expected values assigned to contingent promises, Lindskold, Cullen, Gahagan, and Tedeschi (1970) manipulated both promise credibility and the magnitude of rewards offered the targets. Although each factor separately produced the predicted effects on behavioral compliance, their product (expected value) did not clearly order the compliance means. Horai and Tedeschi (1970) have found that a source who established high credibility for his promises received more compliance from target individuals than did a source whose promises were of low credibility. Somewhat weaker results were obtained by Lindskold, Bonoma, Schlenker, and Tedeschi (1972), who found an effect of value on compliance but no effect of promise credibility. Lindskold and Tedeschi (1970) failed to find an effect of either component on the expected value of promises. However, Zipf (1960), using different procedures, did find a direct relationship between the reward magnitude offered and subjects' reports of expected value and consequent behavioral compliance. Finally, Sampson and Kardush (1966) found that an evaluator's promises of rewards were more effective in improving group performance when the values of rewards were higher.

These somewhat inconsistent results do not provide substantial support for the expected value hypothesis and have been interpreted as indicating that normative factors are aroused by the use of promises (Lindskold & Tedeschi, 1971). An obligation is incurred by the promisor—he "ought" to provide the benefits promised when the target does as requested. The same requirement does not obtain in the case of threats; that is, the threatener is not obligated to punish noncompliance, though for many reasons he may wish to maintain high credibility. Problems of interpretation also arise because a number of conditions have differed across experiments: the target was or was not constrained to reply to the promise; subjects were preadolescents or college students; rewards offered were candies, abstract points, and money; etc. More research will be required before we understand why the direct function of the expected value of promises and behavioral compliance does not always obtain.

Conformity, Modeling, and Social Reinforcement

Public conformity, imitation of a model, and responsiveness to another's verbal reinforcements have earlier been interpreted in terms of tacit forms of communication and influence. The tacit form of threats, warnings, promises, and mendations does not change the predicted relationship between their expected value and the effectiveness of the source's influence attempts.

Public conformity is presumed to result from group pressures communicated in the form of tacit threats of punishment for nonconformity or tacit promises of rewards for conformity. A number of experiments have manipulated factors which may be interpreted as credibility and value components of the expected values of the tacit threats or promises involved in gaining public conformity from a critical subject.

Endler (1966) found that the extent of conforming behavior was a function of the amount of reinforcement. Studies by Deutsch and Gerard (1955) and Jones, Wells, and Torrey (1958) also provide evidence that magnitude of reward for conformity directly mediates increases in conformity.

Endler and Hoy (1967) employed a Crutchfield (1955) conformity apparatus, in which subjects sat alone in isolated booths and were given electronic signals indicating the responses of a simulated majority. Subjects were provided with feedback concerning the truth or falsity of their own judgments. Subjects were divided into six groups. The first was positively reinforced 100 percent of the time for conforming and negatively reinforced 100 percent of the time for disagreeing with the majority. The second was treated the same as the first group except that feedback about their own judgments was provided on only half the trials. The third was exposed to majority judgments but not provided with feedback about their own judgments. The fourth was negatively reinforced 100 percent of the time for conforming and positively reinforced 100 percent of the time for disagreeing with the majority. The fifth was treated the same as the fourth group except that feedback about their own judgments was provided on only half the trials. The sixth was a control group, in which subjects made individual judgments without either reinforcements or group pressures. If consistent reinforcements, like consistent punishments (Vogel-Sprott, 1969), underscore the tacit requests of a source, then the expected values of the tacit promises communicated to subjects in the Endler and Hoy experiment should have been found to be ordered from high or low over groups one through six. The conformity means were, in fact, perfectly ordered by the expected values.

Weaker support of the present hypothesis was obtained by Allen and Crutchfield (1963). The experimenter provided partial feedback to critical subjects in one group that "group members" were correct in their judgments. A second group of subjects were not provided with any feedback concerning the accuracy of majority opinions.

Hence, the experimenter was providing subjects with an indication of the probability values associated with the other group members' warnings and mendations. The partial feedback was effective in increasing conformity on items of perception and vocabulary but did not affect judgments related to personal opinions. Thus, only judgments of external referents, judgments which should be most affected by those tacit warnings and mendations which describe how the other group members perceive the situation, were affected by the feedback provided.

A classic study by Asch (1951) can also be reinterpreted according to an expected value hypothesis. The Asch procedure is to place the critical subject face to face with several confederates of the experimenter and then ask for public judgments regarding the length of lines. The confederates publicly provide their unanimous judgments before the subject does. Asch found that by having one other person (another confederate) agree with the minority opinion of the critical subject he could substantially increase the rate of dissent from the majority judgment. If it is assumed that subjects perceive the group as less likely to punish *both* dissenters than a single dissenter, then the results can be taken as support for an expected value hypothesis. The minority "coalition" may also have served as an in-group and as such allowed subjects to devalue the social reinforcements tacitly offered by the majority (cf. Bass & Dunteman, 1963).

A requirement for establishing high credibility for threats is that the source can carry out surveillance of the target's responses. It would therefore seem likely that the more visible a person's behavior is to other group members, the more public conformity he is likely to display. The person would expect that punishment for nonconformity would be less probable under conditions where the group cannot observe his responses. The converse would hold when the group offers rewards for conformity. The person should display more conformity under public than private conditions when the group communicates tacit promises.

Deutsch and Gerard (1955) obtained greater conformity using the face-to-face paradigm of Asch than in using the isolated-subject paradigm of Crutchfield. Similar results were obtained by Argyle (1957) and by Mouton, Blake, and Olmstead (1956), who required that subjects in public response conditions identify themselves by name prior to stating their judgments. Using a somewhat different design, Raven (1959) informed his subjects that they would either pass their essays around for other group members to read (public) or that no one would read their essays (private). More conformity was found in the public than in the private condition. Thus, the evidence is consistent with the interpretation of the effects of surveillance on the expected value of tacit threats presumably communicated in public conformity experiments. Unfortunately, there is no available evidence regarding the effects of public versus private conditions when the group communicates tacit promises of reward to the individual for his conformity.

A model's behavior has been interpreted in terms of the (nondirected) communication of tacit warnings or mendations to an observer. The credibility of the model's tacit message is a function of the cue-response-outcome sequence observed. The greater the probability of problem solutions, the avoidance or escape from harm, or the acquisition of benefits, the higher the credibility of the model's tacit communications.

Lanzetta and Kanareff conducted two studies in which the credibility of the model's tacit mendations was varied. In the first experiment (Kanareff & Lanzetta, 1958), subjects were asked to identify which of two tones had the higher pitch. Actually, the tones were identical 80 percent of the time. Feedback indicated to the subject that a model's judgments were correct 84, 60, or 36 percent of the time. Two sets of instructions were given the subjects. Subjects were asked either to keep their judgments as individual as possible or to keep in mind the group nature of the experiment. These instructions probably served as tacit communications to subjects that the experimenter would disapprove or approve of imitative behavior. When the experimenter tacitly approved of imitative behavior, the subjects imitated the model as a direct function of the probability that the model's judgments were "correct." The credibility of the tacit mendations was not related to the frequency of imitation when the experimenter had tacitly communicated his desire that the subjects not imitate the model.

In their second study, Lanzetta and Kanareff (1959) added monetary rewards for correct answers but otherwise followed the same procedure. When the experimenter tacitly indicated that he condoned imitation by stressing the group nature of the experiment, the direct proportion of the model's correct responses to imitation was replicated. In addition, the inclusion of monetary rewards produced a positive relationship between expected value and imitation in the condition of disapproval of imitation. Apparently, the explicit offer of a reward for "correct" responses was a communication that contradicted the experimenter's tacit communication to the subjects that they should not imitate.

The values of the model's outcomes were more directly varied by Aronfreed and Paskel (1968). Children often imitated the self-sacrificial responses of an adult female model when she emitted expressions of joy and provided hugs than when a model emitted only one of these expressive cues (either joy or hugs) following her own responses. If the observing child interprets the expressive cue as a tacit communication of the form "these kinds of responses are lots of fun," then the more fun the model seems to be having the greater the reward is inferred to be. A clear replication of the direct relationship between the value of the model's outcomes and the imitative behavior of observers was provided by Midlarsky and Bryan (1967).

Allen and Liebert (1967) introduced incentives for not imitating a behavioral model and obtained results consistent with SEV theory. When incentives for not imitating were high, the prior experience or inexperience of the model in the task was irrelevant—observers seldom imitated the model in either case. However, when incentives for not imitating were not present, the prior experience of the model served to define the "appropriate" task responses and hence the behavior which would most likely be approved by the experimenter. As predicted, imitation was positively related to the prior task experience of the model in the latter conditions.

Studies of social reinforcement have been interpreted by the authors as the tacit communication of either threats or promises. In studies which examine the consistent application of contingent verbal reinforcers, the subject's task is to discern the contingency (extract the rule or decode the tacit communication), and then to respond on the basis of the expected values associated with the tacit messages. The credibility of a message tacitly communicated by the use of social reinforcements is related to the apprehension of the "rule" communicated. A very low credibility level would require a great deal of repetition before the subject would learn the rule. But once the rule is learned, expected value considerations would mediate performance.

Only a couple of experiments could be found that varied the value of social reinforcement and none which varied the probability. Littig and Waddell (1967) exposed subjects in a serial learning task to either positively ("You're doing fine"), neutral (silence), or negatively ("You're very slow") reinforcing statements from the experimenter during the intervals between trials. While the differences between the reward and neutral conditions were not significant, learning was significantly more rapid in each of these conditions than under verbal punishment, as would be predicted by expected value calculations. Hetherington and Ross (1963), using a similar paradigm, found no differences in performance for male subjects over reward, neutral, or punishment reinforcement conditions. Female subjects, however, learned the task more rapidly under reward and punishment conditions than under the neutral conditions. Interpretation of these results is unclear because social reinforcements were not contingent upon specific responses and were administered between trials.

After ranking male and female voices according to preferability, Matthews and Dixon (1968) used tape recordings to reinforce subjects in a conditioning task. They found that preferred voices were more effective in conditioning subjects. Similarly, Hemphill (1961) found that the greater the value of the reinforcement for opinion statements, the more frequently the subject attempted leadership behaviors. The evidence permits the tentative conclusion that the expected value of the presumed tacit communication of promises and threats in social reinforcement studies does mediate the frequency of conditioned responses.

Conclusion

The direct function of the expected *negative* value of threats and resultant behavioral compliance has been rather firmly established. Although the evidence is consistent with a postulated similar relationship between expected negative value and the effectiveness of warnings, more evidence is needed to evaluate the multiplicative relationship of the probability and value components of the expected value of warnings. Apparently, the expected value of promises must be understood in terms of the relationship between source and target and the normative obligations of each when promises are used as the influence mode. In any case, the evidence indicates that promise credibility and the amount of reward offered do sometimes mediate compliance. Almost no research is available to evaluate the effects of the expected value of mendations or the expected value associated with the presumed tacit communications of a source of social reinforcements. The research on conformity, though seldom if ever motivated by an expected value hypothesis, can be clearly interpreted to support the mediating effects of expected value. When a group tacitly communicates a promise of reward or a threat of punishment, expected value does seem to mediate public conformity of target individuals. Finally, the interpretation of modeling studies in terms of the tacit communication of warnings and mendations gains plausibility from the evidence supporting expected value hypotheses.

The remainder of this chapter focuses on the postulated effects of source factors on the reactions of target individuals to the four message types under consideration. The source characteristics of attraction, status, prestige, and esteem are postulated as factors which bias the target individual's estimations of the probabilities involved in the expected value of messages. The resultant subjective expected value estimations are then functionally related to the reactions of individuals to social influence attempts.

Attraction

The term "attraction" seems to be useful only as an orienting construct which refers to instances in which an individual responds in an emotionally positive way to another (Marlowe & Gergen, 1969). The term "attraction" does not distinguish between mother love, man-woman love, boy-dog love, or comradeship between adult members of the same sex. Few theoretical attempts have been made to disentangle these forms of attraction; we will refrain from such fine distinctions and will continue the tradition of viewing attraction as a gross emotional orientation between persons.

The antecedents of interpersonal attraction are closely related to mutual expectations that persons have regarding each other's behaviors in an interaction. These mutual expectations in turn provide the bases for the biasing of probabilities involved in the expected values of messages and hence authenticate or de-authenticate SEV considerations of the target relevant to the use of different influence modes chosen by the source.

It has been well documented that those who reward a person or otherwise facilitate his goal attainment, regardless of the cooperative or competitive context of interaction, are liked by the rewarded person (Berkowitz & Daniels, 1963; Berkowitz & Levy, 1956; Goranson & Berkowitz, 1966; Kleiner, 1960; Lerner & Matthews, 1967; McDonald, 1962; Myers, 1962; Solomon, 1960; Wilson & Miller, 1961; Zajonc & Marin, 1967). Conversely, those who punish the subject or impede his goal attainment, irrespective of the nature of the relationship (cooperative or competitive), are disliked (Burnstein & Worchel, 1962; French, Morrison, & Levinger, 1960; Kipnis, 1958; Lerner, 1965; Rosenthal & Cofer, 1948; Zajonc & Marin, 1967). In fact, Griffitt (1968) has found that just the anticipation of rewards from another person increases attraction towards him. The rewards which can be mediated in a social interaction can be materialistic, such as the individual receiving a gift from another or in the presence of another (James & Lott, 1964; Lott & Lott, 1960), in the form of approval mediation (Blau, 1964; Gewirtz & Baer, 1958; Homans, 1961; Nord, 1968), anxiety reduction (Schachter, 1959), or in the form of expressed interpersonal similarities (Bramel, 1969; Byrne, 1969; Simons, Berkowitz, & Moyer, 1970). Additionally, knowing that one is liked by another seems to be rewarding to an individual, presumably as a function of the rewards which can be anticipated from the other person and the confirmation of one's own self-worth. Thus, people tend to like those who like them (Backman & Secord, 1959; Kiesler, 1963; Kiesler & Corbin, 1965; Mills, 1966).

Attraction is directly and linearly related to the proportion of expressed similar attitudes between the parties (cf. Byrne, 1969). Attitudinal similarity apparently serves a facilitative function for cooperative interaction. Lerner and Becker (1962) found that subjects preferred to participate with a similar person in a game where both could win money, but preferred to participate with a dissimilar person in a zero-sum task. Kaufmann (1967) directly assessed the expectations of subjects in a mixed-motive situation and found that subjects expected more cooperation from those they liked than from those they disliked. The expectations deriving from interpersonal attraction seem to be warranted since people who like one another do cooperate more than those who dislike one another (Kaufmann, 1967; Krauss, 1966; Oskamp & Perlman, 1965; Scodel, 1962; Tornatzky & Geiwitz, 1968; Wallace & Rothaus, 1969). Should a person's positive expectations be disconfirmed through the exploitative or competitive actions of the other, his expectations will be corrected and the interaction will take on a competitive character (Swingle, 1966).

In summary, one's liking for another person is based upon a history of rewarding experiences, and implies that positive outcomes will continue to flow from the relationship. As Lott and Lott (1968) have stated, learning to like another person is "essentially learning to anticipate reward when that person is present or, in Mowrer's terms (1960), a liked person is one to whom 'hope'... has been conditioned" (p. 68). From a SEV theory of social influence, it would be predicted that a target would tend to overestimate the probability of receiving rewards and achieving goals when he is interacting with a source whom he likes. Conversely, when a target dislikes the source, he would tend to underestimate the probability of receiving rewards and expect the source to impede his goal attainment. Examination of the authenticating or de-authenticating effects of attraction for the source of influence will be related to the various modes of influence employed.

Attraction, Threats, and Promises

A target should assign a greater credibility to a disliked threatener than the circumstances warrant (as long as that credibility is less than 1.0) and should tend to underestimate the credibility of a liked threatener (as long as that credibility is not 0.0). The exact opposite biasing of probabilities should occur in reaction to a source of promises. These predictions, unfortunately, have been tested by only two experiments. Using a two-person, mixed-motive game, Schlenker, Bonoma, Tedeschi, Lindskold, and Horai (1970a) manipulated the probability that a confederate source would punish noncompliant responses to threats and manipulated the degree of attraction between the target and the source. Subjects in the negative attraction conditions complied frequently, irrespective of the differences in objective threat credibilities, while subjects in the positive attraction conditions complied as a direct function of threat credibilities. Thus, subjects who disliked the source behaved as if all threats were highly credible and subjects who liked the source responded rationally and in direct relationship to the probability of punishment. The SEV theory prediction is confirmed by the negative attraction results but not by those obtained in the positive attraction condition. Further results obtained from postinteraction ratings on a version of the Semantic Differential (Osgood, Suci, & Tannenbaum, 1957) indicated that the subjects' impressions of the source are consistent with the above interpretations. The disliked threatener was perceived as more potent and evaluated less favorably than was the liked source.

An interesting type of power is suggested by these results. If a potential source of influence does not have the resources to maintain high credibility for his threats, his next best strategy is to cause the target to dislike him. The target will then exaggerate the source's power and frequently comply to the threatener's demands. Much of Black Power may derive from this basic process: militant Black Americans seem to be more impressed by the efficacy of fear and hostility than they are by restitutive guilt and norms of justice.

Schlenker et al. (1970b) report a second experiment with the same basic design, but there the focus was upon the target's reactions to contingent promises. The interpretation of the results is clouded by the theoretical consideration that explicit contingent promises, where rewards are offered for cooperative behaviors, may be considered inappropriate to a liking relationship in which the use of unilateral noncontingent promises with tacit understanding of reciprocity is more generally expected. Nevertheless, positive attraction did mediate more cooperativeness, more trust, and more positive postinteraction impressions than did negative attraction. Yet, no compliance differences were obtained. A very weak argument could be made with regard to these generally negative results that the low attraction subjects were not affected by promisor credibilities because they did not believe the promisor in any case, and that high attraction subjects were not affected because they considered the reward as inappropriate to their relationship. The degree of compliance was only about 50 percent across conditions and subjects. The only value of this kind of post hoc reasoning is to suggest future research.

Attraction, Warnings, and Mendations

Almost all social psychological theories of attraction predict that the attractiveness of the source will enhance the efficacy of his persuasive communications (Cartwright & Harary, 1956; Heider, 1958; Newcomb, 1953; Osgood & Tannenbaum, 1955). The contributions of SEV theory are: (1) it more specifically relates attraction to warnings and mendations as two types of persuasive communications; (2) it provides a mechanism which mediates the effects of attraction; and (3) it generalizes the effects of attraction to specific areas of influence research other than persuasion. Hence, the present theory is more specific in predictions and wider in scope than other theories of attraction and influence.

Persuasive communications, composed of tacit or explicit warnings and mendations, describe the causal texture of the environment for a target, and usually include recommended or remedial actions proposed by the source. The causal structure of the environment includes the motives and actions of third parties, who may be represented as the future agents of harm or benefits for the target. Attraction for the source should directly mediate compliance to the recommendations of a persuasive communication because the target should tend to overestimate the probability that the source's descriptions and/or predictions are correct. Such authentication derives from the target's belief that a liked source would desire similar goals and would assess the intentions and capabilities of third parties in much the same way as the target would. Also, a liked source would tend to be perceived as having a concern for the target's best interests and be sincere and honest in his description of reality, considerations not likely to obtain in the case of a disliked source of persuasive communications. Targets are likely to be suspicious about the intentions and objectivity (or accuracy) of a disliked source (cf. Bramel, 1969; Hovland, Janis, & Kelley, 1953; Mills, 1966; Mills & Jellison, 1968).

Substantial evidence has accumulated that the more the target likes a persuasive source of influence, the more effect the latter has on the former's change of attitudes (Abelson & Miller, 1967; Brock, 1965; Burnstein, Stotland, & Zander, 1961; Dabbs, 1964; Mills & Aronson, 1965; Weiss, 1957; Wright, 1966). For example, Weiss

(1957) probably induced perceptions of similarity and dissimilarity by having a confederate first agree or disagree with the subject on a prior question. Targets were then presented with a warning concerning the dangers of fluoridation of public water supplies. Subjects more strongly changed their opinions in the direction of those expressed by the source who was perceived as similar.

Brock (1965) found that perceived similarity (and presumably attraction) mediated compliance to a source's mendations. Salesmen-experimenters, working in the paint section of a department store, attempted to persuade customers to purchase a brand of paint which was either more or less expensive than the kind the customers originally requested. The persuasive communication indicated that the source had used the recommended paint on a similar or dissimilar job with excellent results. More customers purchased the paint recommended by the source with a similar job, irrespective of the price change involved.

The authentication effect of attraction on a target can be generalized and used to interpret the influenceability of third parties. Mills and Jellison (1968) had subjects read a persuasive communication advocating a broad general college education which was ostensibly delivered as a speech by either a musician or an engineer to groups of either music or engineering students. More opinion change in the direction of the persuasive communication was evidenced by third party observers when source and audience were similar than when they were dissimilar. Hence, the source was viewed as more trustworthy and as more concerned with the "welfare" of the targets when their interests appeared to coincide.

Hovland, Janis, and Kelley (1953) have suggested that when a target perceives a source as having clear intentions to change the target's opinions or actions, the target should react suspiciously and hence the source should be less effective than a source who appears to be disinterested. However, revelation of source intentions does not appear to detract from the effectiveness of an attractive source's persuasiveness. Mills and Aronson (1965) found that a physically attractive source was more effective when she announced her intentions to influence the opinions of the male audience than when she did not; an unattractive source was rather ineffective whether she announced her intentions or not. The persuasive communication of the source could be reinterpreted as a tacit promise of the form: "If you agree with me, you will gain my approval." Such a tacit promise would be perceived as more credible coming from an attractive source. Mills (1966), in a follow-up experiment, clarified the issue with respect to mendations and attraction. He found that subjects did agree more with the persuasive communications from a source who liked them and wanted them to follow his advice than they did when the source was known to dislike them and yet desired to influence them.

Jones and Brehm (1967) derived from dissonance theory the hypothesis that an individual who *commits himself to listen* to a persuasive communication should experience dissonance to the extent that the source is unattractive. Since no external basis would exist for the subject to listen to the unattractive communicator, the former would have to interpret his behavior in terms of the "merits" of the communication. It was predicted that the greater the dissonance experienced, the greater should be the subsequent attitude change in the direction advocated by the communication. Hence, the authors expected (contrary to SEV hypotheses) that a disliked source would be more persuasive than a liked source. Their experiment had some subjects directly overhear a communication advocating the abolition of intercollegiate athletics (no choice) and had others listen to the communication (choice) from a source who either expressed liking or disliking for college students. The obtained interaction confirmed the Jones and Brehm hypotheses; however, the only condition of the experiment which produced attitude change significantly different from a control group (which did not hear a persuasive communication) was the no-choice positive communicator condition. Hence, the only significant effects of attraction were found in the direction predicted by SEV theory. It is quite possible that cues provided in the choice condition aroused the suspicions of the subjects about the communicator and consequently, about the experiment, and the typical positive relationship of source attraction and influenceability was disturbed (cf. Elms, 1969).

Dissonance studies provide interesting information concerning the relationship between attraction and the postdecisional consequences of compliant actions. Thus, evidence exists which indicates that *once compliance has taken place* (however accomplished), negative consequences will be more favorably valued if a source is disliked than if he is liked (Kiesler & DeSalvo, 1967; Smith, 1961; Zimbardo et al., 1965). However, consistent with the SEV hypothesis, an attractive communicator *gains* more compliance than does an unattractive communicator (Jones & Brehm, 1967; Smith, 1961).

Attraction, Conformity, Modeling, and Social Reinforcement

Just as liking for a source has been found to increase the influenceability of the target, attraction to a group apparently facilitates conformity to group standards and norms. In fact, Kiesler and Kiesler (1969, p. 66) state that this seems to be "as solid a generalization as one can arrive at in social psychology." In their classic study of informal groups residing at two MIT housing projects, Festinger, Schachter, and Back (1950) found that attraction to a group, as measured by sociometric techniques, was positively correlated with conformity to group norms. Festinger, Gerard, Hymovitch, Kelley, and Raven (1952) replicated the field results in the laboratory. Subjects who were informed by instructions that they would get along well with other members of the group complied to the group requests more frequently than did subjects who were not told that they would get along well with the other persons. Back (1951) found that highly attracted members of groups were more conforming than members of groups with low cohesion. Since these classic studies were performed, the relationship between attraction for the group and conformity has been observed in a number of experiments (Berkowitz, 1954; Darley, 1966; French & Snyder, 1959; Gerard, 1954; Lott & Lott, 1961; McLeod, Harburg, & Price, 1966; Moreno, 1953; Rasmussen & Zander, 1954; Sampson & Insko, 1964; Schachter, Ellertson, McBride, & Gregory, 1951; Stotland & Patchen, 1961; Stotland, Zander, & Natsoulas, 1961; Thrasher, 1954; Wyler, 1966). Greater conformity has also been found in groups composed of friends rather than strangers (Thibaut & Strickland, 1956). Similarly, members of highly cohesive groups show less tolerance of deviant opinions and greater rejection of such deviants than do members of groups of low cohesion (Emerson, 1954; Hewitt & McLaughlin, 1970; Schachter, 1951; Schachter et al., 1954).

Despite the fact that the effects of attraction on public conformity have been strongly confirmed, it would be wise to remember that group cohesiveness has been defined as the sum of all forces acting upon an individual to remain in a group (Festinger, 1953). Attraction may constitute only one of many such forces. In most conformity experiments, group cohesiveness manipulations include some mixture of esteem, status, prestige, and attraction. Consequently, clear interpretations are difficult to make. However, two relatively unambiguous studies strongly confirm the authentication effects of attraction on conformity.

After giving each subject a questionnaire which asked him to rate others with whom he was previously acquainted on the critical item "How well do you like him?", French and Snyder (1959) divided Air Force personnel into groups of four, or tetrads, which were to make perceptual judgments. One pair within each tetrad viewed one set of geometric figures, while a second pair viewed a slightly different pair of figures. The authentication effect of attraction on SEV estimations by target individuals was demonstrated by two major results: (1) in group discussions meant to reconcile differences in judgments, leaders who were most liked were more effective in bringing about changes in judgments; and (2) subjects who complied to a liked leader's persuasive attempts also expressed greater confidence in their "new opinion" than did group members who interacted with less attractive leaders.

The second study could just as well be considered a study of modeling as one of public conformity. Sampson and Insko (1964) induced liking or disliking for a confederate by having the confederate either (1) praise the subject, agree with many of his opinions, and behave cooperatively on two prior tasks, or (2) behave in an insulting and derogatory manner and impede the subject's completion of the prior tasks. After giving independent judgments in an autokinetic situation, subjects made judgments together with the confederate. Subjects agreed more closely with the judgments of the liked confederate than they did with those of the disliked confederate.

Liking for a model should mediate imitation for two reasons: (1) similarity, a basis of attraction, is also a factor in determining the relevance of the model's nondirected tacit communications; and (2) liking for the source authenticates the probabilities of and hence facilitates reactions to warnings and mendations. Rosekrans (1967) and Hartup and Coates (1967) investigated the effects of similarity between a model and observers and found a positive relationship between similarity and imitative behavior.

An experiment by Baron (1970) can be interpreted as a clear demonstration of the effects of both the relevance of a model's tacit communications and their expected value. Baron used an attitude similarity-dissimilarity procedure to induce positive or negative attraction between a model and observers. The model was either highly competent and won on 75 percent of his choices in a "horse race game" or only average, winning on 25 percent of his choices. The observer was reinforced (won) 60 percent of the time for imitation. A dissimilar model's tacit communications should be perceived as irrelevant by the observer, while in the similarity condition, the relevant communications of the more competent model should be perceived as possessing higher probabilities than those of the less competent model. A significant interaction of competence and attraction supported the prediction.

Although very complicated from a social psychological point of view, an experiment by Baron and Kepner (1970) on model-observer similarity and aggressive behavior is interpretable according to the criteria of relevance proposed in the present theory. A situation was contrived in which a confederate was chosen to be a learner and had electrodes attached to his body. Another confederate and the subject were designated as "teachers" and were told to operate the levers and switches on a "shock box" to administer variable intensities and durations of electric shock to the confederate-learner. The degree of similarity-dissimilarity of the confederate-teacher and the subject had been manipulated and the confederate-learner had obnoxiously insulted both of them prior to the "teaching" situation. Since the confederate-teacher *and* the subject were insulted by the same person and then jointly assigned to take turns manipulating the shock, the relevance of the confederate-teacher's responses (as a model) must have been established in the situation of "common fate," and hence would cancel out the tendency of disattraction for a model to cause the observer to interpret the tacit communication as irrelevant. Thus, it should not be surprising that subjects imitated the aggressive or nonaggressive responses of the model, irrespective of attraction for him.

Many modeling studies have investigated the relationship between nurturance and imitative behavior in children. The typical experimental manipulation of nurturance involves the noncontingent conferral of affection and approval by the model to the target (Flanders, 1968), and can be viewed as inducing positive attraction. Bandura and Huston (1961) had children observe a model, who had been previously either nurturant or non-nurturant play a two-choice guessing game. It was found that the children imitated more of the nurturant than the non-nurturant model's behaviors. Grusec and Mischel (1966) and Mischel and Grusec (1966) similarly reported that nurturance was positively related to imitation. Grusec (1966) found that a nurturant experimenter was more effective in eliciting childrens' initial self-critical responses than a non-nurturant experimenter; and that nurturance was particularly effective when combined with the threatened punishment of withdrawal of love in developing subsequent self-critical responses. Hetherington and Frankie (1967) have found that parental warmth is directly related to parental imitation by their children.

Other studies have found either interactions between sex of observer and model and nurturnace (Rosenblith, 1961) or no effects of nurturance (Aronfreed, Cutlick, & Fagan, 1963) on imitative behavior. Procedural variations in the manipulation of nurturance probably account for the failure to find a clear effect of nurturance. For example, Rosenblith (1961) induced nurturance by having the model play with a child for ten minutes prior to the critical modeling situation, while in the non-nurturant condition the model played with the child for the first five minutes of the pre-game period and then read for the last five minutes; only slight differences between the conditions thus existed. Aronfreed et al. (1963) had an experimenter repeatedly take Tootsie Rolls which were in a child's possession away from the child as a purported punishment for transgression. Nurturance was manipulated during the critical trials rather than prior to the experiment by having the experimenter act either in a friendly manner or behave in a formal and authoritarian manner. Nevertheless, since the children's impressions of the experimenter were not reported, it is questionable whether the children viewed the "friendly" experimenter much differently than the "unfriendly" experimenter, particularly since both experimenters deprived the children of rewards.

When a model engages in acts which result in negative payoffs or losses of rewards, his behavior should constitute a tacit warning to the observer. If the tacit communication is perceived as relevant, the observer should *not* imitate the model's behavior. Hence, nurturance does not increase imitation of a model's adoption of stringent criteria for self-reward (Bandura, Grusec, & Menlove, 1967), or imitation of certain types of self-depriving altrustic behaviors (Grusec & Skubiski, 1970; Midlarsky & Bryan, 1967; Rosenhan & White, 1967).

Sapolsky (1960) provided support for the postulated authentication effects of attraction on the effectiveness of social reinforcement. Two experiments were conducted in which attraction was manipulated between the subjects and the experimenter. In a standard verbal-conditioning paradigm, subjects were positively reinforced for the emission of all first person pronouns. Subjects in the high attraction conditions demonstrated considerable "learning" of the correct responses, while subjects in the low attraction conditions did not exhibit "learning." When the original experimenter left the room and another experimenter took over, subjects in the low attraction conditions quickly evidenced a significant "learning" effect. If the social reinforcement paradigm is viewed as involving the transmission of tacit promises of future benefits, and if the promises of the high attraction source were perceived as more credible than the promises of the low attraction source, the results confirm SEV theory.[6]

Conclusion

Attraction serves as a base of power and influence and, as a consequence, most people like to be liked. Since liking is predicated upon a prior history of reward mediation, one learns to expect that those whom he likes will be rewarding, cooperative, and trustworthy

6. Approval from a liked person may also have greater value than approval from a disliked person. However, consideration of this possibility would require a shift from a SEV to a subjective expected utility model.

and that those whom he dislikes will be punishing, competitive, and untrustworthy in social interactions. Thus, the target individual is likely to bias upwards (authenticate) the probability of benefits and bias downwards (de-authenticate) the probability of harm from a liked source of influence. Dislike for the source reverses the direction of bias in estimating SEV. Although the evidence must be drawn from a series of reinterpretations, it may be tentatively concluded that attraction does increase the influenceablility of a target of persuasive communications, increases the tendency to conform to group pressures, enhances the imitative effects of observing a model, and increases the effectiveness of social reinforcements.

Status of the Source

Cartwright and Zander (1968) have aptly noted that "it appears to be almost impossible to describe what happens in groups without using terms which indicate the 'place' of members with respect to one another" (p.486). Numerous definitions of "place" have been offered in an attempt to integrate the notion of a hierarchy of obligations and rights associated with roles in groups. Unfortunately, only diffuse ideas of rights and obligations can be attached to relations between persons other than those based on hierarchical arrangements of roles. For example, one has the "right" to expect benevolent behavior from a friend just as one is "obligated" not to harm one's friends. As a consequence of the focus upon rights and obligations as critical to the definition of source status, a proliferation of conceptualizations has evolved which tend to lump together factors that are analytically separated in the present theory.

On the operational level of analysis, a number of definitions of status have been proffered. Operational definitions have included variations in source competence (Hollander, 1964), the reputation and esteem of the source (Hovland et al., 1953), target estimations of source prestige (Hurwitz et al., 1968) and the degree of source's control over the reinforcing contingencies important to the target (Whiting, 1960). Unfortunately, clear interpretations of most of the research on status cannot be clearly attributable to any *one* source characteristic for the reason that in most experiments two, and often as many as four, different source characteristics have been varied simultaneously.

The definition of status offered here will be restricted to the *authority associated with a role position*. This definition focuses upon the deference patterns required of the target because of the legitimacy of the source's influence attempts (Harsanyi, 1966). The development of legitimacy is, of course, a very complex matter (see Chap. 1), but the concern here is with the effects once status has been acquired. Suffice it to say that status is imbedded in a larger group and, unlike the more direct influence exerted in the form of coercive power, derives its effectiveness from the members of the group who "enforce" compliance to the requests of a high-status source (Blau, 1964). In a sense, status provides the occasion for group conformity pressures to be placed on an individual. An example of such group pressures and how they vary with the legitimacy of the source was shown in a study by Kiesler, Kiesler, and Pallack (1967). Subjects participated in a problem-solving task and interacted either with a neatly dressed and serious experimenter or a sloppily dressed and casual experimenter. In both the high and low legitimacy conditions, a confederate confronted the experimenter in an impolite and disrespectful manner. In subsequent evaluations, subjects in the "legitimate" condition rated the confederate as less attractive than did the subjects in the illegitimate condition. As Aronson and Carlsmith (1968) note, the "presence" and bearing of the experimenter lends legitimacy to the norms governing the importance of subjects' participation in psychological experiments.

Weber (1956) has defined *Herrschaft* (authority) as the probability that a command with a certain content will be met by obedience on the part of certain given persons. The distinction of importance is between the *power* of a man and the *powers* of his role. Wielders of *Herrschaft* tend to claim legitimacy as a means of stabilizing the effectiveness of their influence over others. In his theory of organizations, Weber implied that the professional authority rooted in expert technical knowledge and the bureaucratic authority rooted in a hierarchy of offices were inextricably interrelated, a belief which Parsons has criticized (Introduction to Weber, 1947). As Blau (1968) has pointed out, knowledge is not necessary for the accrual of authority. Expert knowledge is not what authorizes the policeman to direct traffic or what induces us to obey his signals. Gouldner (1954) similarly distinguishes between the expertise of a source and his authority, with the former deriving from technical competence and the latter deriving from potential for imposing punishments. The distinction has been upheld in sociological research, which has shown that authority structures in bureaucracies are not correlated with rational characteristics (specialization, qualifications of personnel, etc.) in the same organizations (Stinchcombe, 1959; Udy, 1959). Similarly, recent research in political anthropology establishes that authority derives from economic factors in a society, while expertise develops through education (Tuden, 1969). To be sure, economic factors are important for the development of professional expertise, but not necessarily for the acquisition of such special skills as plumbing or cooking. Expertise may yield a person status, but it is not the basis of the deference a high-status source receives as a consequence of *having* status. Experimentally, it is difficult to separate status from expertise or other source attributes which may tend to vary with status, such as attraction and prestige (Kiesler, 1969). The present analytic preference for separating these source attributes is based on the desire that the laws of combination be dictated by the data rather than by the intuitive judgment or philosophical bias of the theorist.

High-source status should enhance the effectiveness of each type of influence message. High-source status authenticates the expected value of threats and promises not only because the source is likely to have prestige, and hence the resources to use for purposes of establishing credibility, but also because the source would have a *right* to punish or reward the target. When a policeman hits a person, he is enforcing the law. When a person hits a policeman, he is perpetrating violence.

Just as interpersonal attraction authenticates the source's professed intentions to bestow benefits upon a target because of the normative requirements of friendship, so do the normative requirements associated with status relationships authenticate the use of all types of influence messages. Indirect support for the hypothesized authentication effects of status was provided by Harvey (1953). He obtained ratings of perceived authority from three different sources (i.e., group members, observers of the group, and the experimenter). Not only did high-status members optimistically predict better scores on a dart-throwing task than they actually received, but members of the group tended to overestimate the high-status individual's future performance. Low-status members either pessimistically underestimated their performances or were fairly accurate predictors of their own performance, but other group members consistently underestimated the probable performance of the low-status individual.

High status is also expected to authenticate the expected values of warnings and mendations. Lasswell (1966) has pointed out that one of the functions of those in authority is to "define" the nature of reality for their constituents. In fact, the definition of social reality may be the most important form of power in a group or society.

High status should also be directly related to public conformity, imitation by observers, and the effectiveness of social reinforcements. The higher the status of a person, the more should group members punish noncompliance to his requests and the more consensual validation they should give for his persuasive communications. These group pressures, in turn, should mediate conformity by critical group members. The example of a high-status model produces normative pressures for imitative behavior from the observer. The high-status model might be competent and successful, but the important consequence of status is the tacit communication of "oughtness" of the behavior involved. It is not the profit to be gained so much as it is "right" to imitate the model. In this manner, the status of the source can substitute for similarity between model and observer as a determinant of the relevance of the model's tacit communication. Finally, approval from a high-status source should be "worth" more than similar social reinforcement from a low-status source. Thus, source status should enhance the effectiveness of influence mediated by social reinforcement. [7] We will now examine these hypotheses in more detail.

Status, Threats, and Promises

Few studies have investigated the effects of source status (as defined herein) on compliance to threats and none could be found which relate the status of a source to compliance to his promises. However, the scant evidence which does exist is supportive of a SEV interpretation.

Evan and Zelditch (1961) found more covert disobedience by target subjects to the technical rules and orders administered by a supervisor when the latter was perceived as incompetent. Compliance by targets with the source's commands varied with the extent to which the workers believed that the "supervisor had a right to occupy his office." It might be tentatively concluded that when a particular status is earned by the alleged possession of special knowledge or experience and the person holding the status position is perceived by those beneath him as not possessing expertise commensurate with his status, then the legitimacy of the status is undermined even if the person in question maintains his role position. The fact that role position and expertise could be varied independently and with different effects supports the beliefs of Parsons and Blau (and the present theory) that expertise should be analytically separated from status. The most direct test of the authentication effects of status has been provided by Faley and Tedeschi (1971). They placed low- or high-status ROTC cadets into the position of receiving contingent threats from a simulated source

---

7. The present treatment of status will be restricted to effects on subjective probability. Utility considerations await an adequate theory of human motivation.

who was either high or low in status. The design also included the manipulation of the expected value of the message (three levels of threat credibility and two levels of punishment magnitude). As predicted, low-status targets complied frequently when threatened by a high-status source, while both high- and low-status targets complied infrequently to threats from a low-status source. Somewhat surprising was the finding that a high-status target was very compliant to threats sent by an equally high-status source. Apparently, a strictly hierarchical theory of status will need to be modified. It can be tentatively suggested that the higher the status of source and target, as long as they are peers, the more compliance they will give to each other's verbal demands. Each has more to exchange on a reciprocity basis and, as a consequence, should be willing to give in on something the other strongly desires in exchange for the same kind of deference from the other party. This may be why threatening to resign from a high-status position can be a significant threat to others of high status. As the statuses of peers increase, the saliency of the norm of reciprocity (Gouldner, 1960) appears also to increase. It should be noted that peer status is similar to interpersonal attraction in the sense that when either is highly positive the norm of reciprocity is elicited.

Status, Warnings, and Mendations

A large number of studies have been reported which purport to examine the effects of source status on the efficacy of persuasive communications. This vast literature led Rosnow and Robinson (1967, p. 25) to confidently assert that "the consistent finding thus far is that the more persuasive communicator is the one whose expertise, experience or social role establishes him as a credible source of information presented." Though such a conclusion would add substantial support to SEV theory, it is unfortunately the case that few investigations have managed to examine status defined as legitimate authority.

One of the clearest demonstrations of the direct relationship of source status to the influenceability of target individuals was in a study which focused on an entirely different process (ingratiation). Jones, Gergen, and Jones (1963) explained to pairs of naval ROTC cadets that they should exchange messages (opinions) regarding a number of naval matters. Each dyad was composed of one freshman (low status) and one upperclassman (high status). In one condition, the instructions emphasized that subjects should stress the accuracy of their opinion statements, while in an ingratiation condition subjects were told that the experimenter was looking for compatible commander-subordinate pairs. Standard messages were substituted in all conditions for the messages written by the subjects. The sham statements reflected an unpopular stand on the issues in question. The results showed that low-status subjects more often agreed with the statements from the high-status commander than vice versa. The effect was accentuated in the ingratiation instructions in which the "need to agree" was made salient to the subjects.

A few correlational studies which rely upon phenomenological data indicate the predicted relationship between status and persuasiveness. Bass and Wurster (1953a, 1953b) drew supervisory personnel from various management levels of a large oil refinery and formed small leaderless discussion groups. They found that rank in the organization and observers' ratings of individual effectiveness in the discussion were highly and positively correlated (+.88). When the topic of discussion was relevant to company matters the correlation was higher than when the topic was extraneous to the legitimate business of the corporation. Bass (1954) demonstrated a similar finding with ROTC cadets, and in a more recent investigation Bass (1965) reported the interesting result that this correlation between status and perceived influence was only moderately and temporarily suppressed when the experimenter discussed at length the dysfunctional effects of the phenomenon with the group. Similarly, French and Snyder (1959) found that noncommissioned Air Force officers had more influence than enlisted men, and Crockett (1955) noted that "emergent" leaders held positions of authority in their organizations.

A similar cluster of findings has been reported in the mental-health field. Leff, Raven, and Gunn (1964) found that, while psychologists are equally influenced by either psychiatrists or psychologists in their diagnoses of mental illnesses, psychiatrists discriminate, accepting more influence from their high-status psychiatric colleagues and less from lower-status psychologists. Caudill (1958) noted that the daily exchange of information at administrative conferences among the staff of a mental hospital was asymmetrical in nature. The relative conference participation by the director of the service, the residents, head nurses, nurses, and occupational therapists was ordered positively with their status position in the hospital, even though the low-status participants spent more time with the patients.

Thibaut and Riecken (1955) had a confederate play the role of an Air Force reservist from a unit different from that of subjects and with a rank just above or below the subjects. The confederate then provided verbose, inexact, and self-contradictory instructions over a telephone regarding the placement of military positions on a map. Subjects were then provided with an opportunity to directly criticize the confederate's performance. Analysis of the communications showed that a greater volume of communication and a higher intensity of aggression was directed downward in the status hierarchy than was directed upward against the higher-status confederate. Inhibition of aggressive counterinfluence attempts directed towards a person of high status is contrary to the typical findings of the upward direction of influence attempts in status hierarchies. Thus, although lower-status people will often attempt to influence high-status people, once the high-status person has initiated communications, the low-status person is likely to defer without making a counterinfluence attempt. Horwitz (1963) found a complementary result. Subjects were more hostile to the unilateral action by an authority against the expressed electoral wishes of the majority of the group than they were when the authority's actions were considered to be legitimate.

Rosenbaum and Levin (1968) performed an experiment which considered source status, mendations, and warnings about a third person. Subjects were presented with descriptions of a third person by sources of either high or low status (as determined by occupation level). In two experiments, they found that subjects evaluated the third person as "better" when positive adjectival descriptions had been provided by a high-status communicator than when the mendation was communicated by a low-status source. When negative adjectival descriptions were provided by the high-status source, subjects rated the third person as evaluatively "worse" than did subjects receiving the same warning from a low-status source.

The manipulation of legitimacy in the laboratory is a tricky business. The experimenter can imply that an "illegitimate" action is legitimate because of *his* inaction. For example, in the study by French, Morrison, and Levinger (1960) the experimenter's instructions indicated that a supervisor could legitimately levy a fine of 25 cents, but in one condition of the experiment an "illegitimate" fine of 50 cents was actually levied against subjects by the supervisor. Because the experimenter was present and did nothing, tacit acceptance of a new basis of legitimacy was probably established. A similar problem occurred in studies by Raven and French (1958a, 1958b). As a consequence of the elimination of such experiments from present consideration, the amount of evidence available is sparse and inadequate for any but the most tentative generalizations.

Status, Conformity, Modeling, and Social Reinforcement

The general scarcity of research into the effects of source status is starkly evident when the literature is combed in search of results bearing on the SEV hypotheses concerning public conformity, modeling and social reinforcement. One or two studies in each research area can be clearly interpreted for status effects, but no conclusions can be reached on such a small data base.

Torrance (1954) has provided confirmation that source status does have a direct relationship to public conformity of target individuals. He asked triads of permanently or temporarily assembled Air Force bomber crews to reach unanimous decisions for four ambiguous problems. Each triad was composed of a high-status pilot, an intermediate-status navigator, and a low-status gunner. Crews generally accepted the pilot's suggestions even when his answers to the problems were in the main incorrect. The hierarchical nature of status was indicated by the fact that navigators, although not as effective as pilots, did gain more conformity to their suggestions than did the gunners.

A person's manner of dress may present cues about his status to an observer. Lefkowitz, Blake, and Mouton (1955) have demonstrated that subjects imitated a well-dressed model who violated a clearly marked pedestrian traffic signal more often than they imitated a model who was shabbily dressed. These results are consistent with the SEV hypothesis that high status authenticates the expected value of the model's tacit communication of warnings and mendations and thereby increases the influenceability of the target person.

The same status authentication effect should be expected to mediate the effectiveness of social reinforcement. Efran (1968) asked college freshmen to talk about themselves for five minutes in front of either two seniors (high-status listeners), two freshmen (low-status), or one senior and one freshman (high-low). In each condition one of the confederates consistently reinforced the target subject by smiling and nodding his head, while the other confederate appeared interested but neutral. Instead of measuring the effectiveness of conditioning, Efran measured looking time. The results were: (1) in the high-high and low-low conditions, the dispenser of social reinforcements occupied more of the subjects' looking time; and (2) in the high-low condition, subjects observed the high-status person and the low-status mediator of reinforcements for equal amounts of time. The latter result indicates that reward power (or prestige) may act as the equivalent of status, an hypothesis that will receive ample support in the next section of the chapter.

Conclusion

Status has been defined as the perception by a target individual that an influence attempt originating from another is legitimate by virtue of the latter's role position in the group. Legitimacy may be established and status gained by a variety of means, but those investigated by social psychologists have been rather limited and focus upon group elections and formal position within an existing bureaucracy. SEV theory postulates that high status should authenticate or bias upwards the subjective probability component of a message and hence facilitate the effectiveness of all of the influence modes, as long as the communications are perceived as relevant by the target. The evidence for these hypotheses is spotty and leads to no firm conclusions. However, the evidence is encouraging and indicates that the SEV predictions should be given more adequate tests.

Source Prestige

When a court jester threatens his monarch, the reaction is likely to be robust laughter. The monarch's response stems from the perception that the court jester is completely incapable of actually coercing him. The threat *must* be perceived as humorous or else the jester could literally lose his head. The lesson to be drawn from this example is that the threat of punishment or the promise of reward loses effectiveness if the source is perceived as lacking the resources required to administer the punishment threatened or provide the reward promised. Even if the source is perceived as possessing the capability to credibly employ threats and promises, he will be disbelieved if he is perceived as unwilling to spend his resources in the service of influence. Thus, both the intentions and the capability of the source are important factors in the influence process.

Singer (1958, 1963) has specifically proposed a model of international relations within which he defined prestige as a multiplicative function of source capabilities and intentions. Pruitt (1965) proposed that where great capabilities exist, malevolent intentions are likely to be inferred. Conversely, it could be argued that where strong intentions are perceived, capabilities may be inferred. For example, the United States perceives the Chinese as possessing resolute malevolent intentions and, consequently, infers great capability and reacts to China as if it were a first-rate world power and not a peasant nation struggling to enter the twentieth century. Hence, as one of the factors determining prestige increases, so does the other.

Singer's definition is adopted by the present theory and the impression of prestige is considered to be a multiplicative function of the capability and intentions of the source. Prestige is postulated to produce a direct anthentication of the source's messages. High source prestige, then, increases the influenceability of the target individual. However, these two components of prestige need to be further specified if unambiguous tests of SEV theory are to be made.

Source capability is composed of measureable resources that can be readily used for purposes of influence. Lack of fluid investment capital will lead to perceived weakness or low prestige. Thus, a millionaire may spend a night in jail for want of bail even though he has millions in debentures in his safe in Texas. Capability may take the form of material or economic or political resources (e.g., number of votes controlled) but is not to be confused with other source attributes such as attraction, status, or esteem. Capability and the credibility of messages are assumed to be orthogonal factors. Credibility is established over time and may be quite high, while in the contemporary situation the source may have lost his "wealth" and hence is now perceived as weak (low prestige).

Capability might be considered most important for those forms of influence that require the direct use of resources, such as promises and threats. However, the present theory assumes that high prestige also increases the efficacy of persuasive communications. This assumption derives from several considerations. First, the more power a person has the less sure a target can be that the source does *not* directly or indirectly control the events he describes or predicts. Second, but not clearly different from the first consideration, the recommendations made by a very powerful person are often interpreted as tacit promises or threats, while the same recommendations made by a weak source would not take on the same implicit overtones. Regardless of the form of influence used, then, SEV theory predicts that source capability will directly authenticate the expected value of the source's mesages and as a consequence will increase the influenceability of the target.

The attribution of source intentions will depend upon the past and present behaviors of the source towards the target. Interpersonal interactions can be characterized as varying along a continuum from a total coincidence of interests to the zero-sum situation in which there is a total conflict of interests. It might be expected that attributions of intentions will be made along a continuum reflecting the actual degree of conflict occurring in interactions. Thus, it is proposed that the source will be perceived as motivated to cooperate with or take advantage of the target, along a single accommodative-exploitative dimension.

The strength of the intention attributed to the source will depend upon the type of influence he uses. The very use of a threat by a source should elicit an attribution of exploitativeness by the target. If the threatener takes advantage of the target's compliant responses or clearly indicates that he will or would like to take advantage, then the intensity assigned to the exploitative motive of the threatener would be heightened. On the other hand, the source might utilize the opportunities provided by a target's compliance to be generous in seeking conciliation and conflict resolution. In the latter case, a threatener might be perceived as possessing strong accommodative intentions particularly if threats were the only influence made available to the source (Nardin, 1968). Under conditions of restricted communications evidence to be presented below indicates that either extreme of the accommodative-exploitative dimension represents strong intentions and the middle of the continuum constitutes weak or zero intentions.

Unlike threats, the communication of promises, warnings, and mendations is not likely to be believed if the source is perceived to be exploitative in his intentions. Hence, it is postulated that the strength of the source's intentions when promises or persuasion are the influence modes chosen will be determined on a scale (0-1) of exploitative (weak) to accommodative (strong) intentions. If the source is perceived as totally exploitative, then intentions will take on a value of zero and when multiplied by capability will still yield a prestige score of zero. In this way, intentions can cancel out capability, present an impression of weakness, and increase the resistance of the target to the influence attempts made.

Prestige, Threats, and Promises

Most of the available evidence only tangentially tests the predictions of SEV theory. Once again, when definitions are clearly drawn, source attributes are separated, and predictions are rather rigorously made, the evidence available is no longer abundant and the results are more suggestive than decisive.

Schelling (1966) has provided keen insight into the nature of intentions, commitments, and coercive influence. He suggested that compellent threats, which specify an action the target *must* perform in order to escape punishment, are likely to be perceived as more hostile, coercive, and manipulative than deterrent threats, which specify an action the target must *not* perform in order to escape punishment. If the target of compellent threats does indeed perceive the source as more exploitative, then more prestige would be associated with the source, and more compliance could be expected to his threats than would be the case when the source utilized deterrent threats. The present theory suggests that any unambiguous accommodative or exploitative actions by the source will contribute to prestige.

Schlenker, Bonoma, Tedeschi, and Pivnick (1970) confirmed these hypotheses. Subjects were made targets of explicit threats of punishment for noncompliance to deterrent or compellent threats, which the source used either accommodatively or exploitatively. Targets were more compliant to the compellent threats. Furthermore, subjects rated the source of compellent threats less favorably on the evaluative (good-bad) dimension of the Semantic Differential. Considering the advantages of complying with the totally credible threats of an accommodative source, it should not be surprising that the latter gained more compliance than did the exploitative source.

A more direct test of the predictions of SEV theory was accomplished by Horai and Tedeschi (1970). It may be recalled that the strength of source intentions was assumed to be differently determined for threats and promises. Source accommodativeness contributes to the prestige of a promisor, while both accommodativeness and exploitativeness may contribute to the prestige of a threatener. When a promisor is exploitative, he will be perceived as possessing low prestige. Horai and Tedeschi varied both the credibilities of threats and promises and the accommodativeness or exploitativeness of the source. When the source was accommodative and his threats and promises were credible, the target subjects complied frequently. Thus, when prestige was high and expected value was high, both promises and threats were effective. More crucial for the present theory was the finding that a highly credible exploitative threatener was also effective in gaining compliance, but a highly credible and exploitative promisor was most ineffective. Apparently, exploitativeness of the source's behavior does have different effects on the perceived strength of intentions when the source uses threats and promises. When a threatener is perceived as exploitative, holding capability constant, his prestige is high. When a promisor's behaviors are exploitative, intentions are perceived as weak and prestige is correspondingly low.

Pepitone (1949) also varied both the capability and intentions of a promisor. High school subjects were told that they would be interviewed by three people from a university who were interested in soliciting students' opinions about sports. The panel was said to possess either highly valued tickets to a college basketball game or tickets to "some high school game." The persons judged to have the most worthwhile opinions were to be given free tickets. Aside from the value of their resources, the attitudes of the judges were varied across experimental conditions. In one condition, the panel members were basically either friendly or neutral in affect, while in another condition one member was friendly, a second was neutral, and the third was hostile.[8] Following an actual interview, subjects were asked to estimate the amount of power (prestige) possessed by each interviewer. SEV theory predicts that the promisor with the most valuable resources (capability) and who is most accommodative (friendly) should be perceived as having the greatest prestige. The results strongly confirm the predictions. Subjects interviewed by the panel that could offer the prized basketball ticket perceived the interviewers as more powerful than did subjects interviewed by the panel which possessed the high school ticket. Even more convincing confirmation of SEV theory stems from the finding that the friendly member of the panel was perceived as most powerful in both resource conditions.

Prestige, Warnings, and Mendations

A major concern of research on persuasibility has been the effects of the trustworthiness of the source. Trustworthiness has been defined as a perception by the target individual that the source is accommodatively oriented and desires to communicate valid statements concerning the causal structure of the social or physical environment (Hovland, Janis, & Kelley, 1953). An untrustworthy source is one who is insincere, dishonest, and has exploitative intentions. The present theory would assign strong (accommodative) intentions and hence high prestige to a trustworthy source and weak (exploitative) intentions and hence low prestige to an untrustworthy source. The persuasive communications of the trustworthy source but not the untrustworthy source should be believed, holding all else constant.

Much of the research which attempted to induce perceptions of source intentions has not assessed the success of the manipulation before exposing subjects to persuasive communications. When rating scales have been employed to obtain a target's impressions, the word "credibility" has often been used as descriptive of the source's intentions. In such cases, credibility and believability were typically used as synonymous terms with the present concept of SEV and hence can be seen to be determined by a very complex set of factors. In the following review of the available research an experiment will be considered an adequate test of the present theory if the independent variable manipulation rather clearly varies *only* the perceived intentions and/or capabiliities of the persuader.

Asch (1948) attributed the statement "I hold it that a little rebellion, now and then, is a good thing, and is as necessary in the

---

8. A third treatment condition not relevant to the present discussion was included in the original design.

political world as storms are in the physical" to either Thomas Jefferson (the actual author) or V. I. Lenin. It can be assumed that for American college students, Jefferson would be perceived as accommodative or trustworthy, while Lenin would be perceived as exploitative or untrustworthy. Jefferson, then, presumably because his prestige was higher, produced more attitude change than did the low-prestige source, Lenin. A large number of similar studies have been adequately surveyed by Berscheid and Walster (1969) and consistently replicate Asch's findings. However, there is some evidence that the perceived intentions of the source are not well remembered and that the effects of prestige wear off with time. This so-called "sleeper effect," which indicates that the advantages of high prestige may only be temporary, has been found by Hovland and Weiss (1951), Hovland, Lumsdaine, and Sheffield (1949), Kelman and Hovland (1953), and Weiss (1953).

When a source communicates a message which appears to be contrary to his own best interests or when the source has no intent to persuade the target individual, he should be perceived as trustworthy, since in neither case does he have anything apparently to gain from the target. On the other hand, experiments which forewarn the target of a communicator's exploitative intent to persuade should lead the former to be suspicious of the latter's motives and produce resistance by the target. Thus, a disinterested source should have higher prestige than a source about whom the target has received a warning concerning persuasive intent.

Powell and Miller (1967) provided clear support for the hypothesis that a source would appear less trustworthy when he was perceived as benefiting from the target's compliance. Subjects were exposed to tape-recorded warnings and mendations advocating donating one's blood to the Red Cross without pay rather than selling blood to a private agency. The persuasive communications were attributed to: (1) a chairman of a blood donor recruiting unit of the American Red Cross, who was obviously not a totally disinterested party; (2) a reputable physician, who had no apparent direct interest in the Red Cross; and (3) an anonymous source. Posttest impressions of the source indicated that subjects viewed the disinterested (and hence accommodative) physician as more trustworthy than the somewhat more selfish or exploitative Red Cross chairman. Furthermore, attitude change toward the advocated position was greater the higher the prestige (i.e., perceived accommodativeness) of the source.

Walster, Aronson, and Abrahams (1966) exposed subjects to communications advocating that courts be given more or less power to punish criminals. The attributed source was either a prosecuting attorney or a criminal. Subjects rated the communicator as more honest and influential when he argued against his own interests. However, when opinion change was examined, it was found that the criminal was more effective when arguing against his own interests, but the prosecutor was equally effective whatever position he took. As Collins (1970) has aptly noted, the failure to find the predicted effects with regard to the prosecutor may well have been because such a person is presumed to be objective and disinterested, whatever position he takes. Scientists, philosophers and other experts prefer to be perceived as similarly disinterested—it is an image they cultivate about themselves.

Mills and Jellison (1967) exposed college students to a tape-recorded speech attributed to a political candidate for the state legislature. Subjects were told that the speech advocating the passage of a bill to triple licensing fees of tractor-trailers was delivered either to a local union of railway men or to a truck drivers' union. Subjects shifted their own opinions to agree with the persuasive communication when the source was perceived as making an unpopular speech.

Taking a somewhat different approach, Walster and Festinger (1962) tested the hypothesis that inadvertently overheard communications are more likely to be effective in changing the opinions of the target than are communications that are deliberately addressed to him. An overheard communication is closely related to observing an unaware model. Like the tacit communication presumed to be transmitted by the model, the unaware communicator is not directing his persuasive attempts at passersby. As a consequence, the listener of an overheard communication may find the message relevant or irrelevant according to approximately the same criteria previously outlined above for the relevancy of a model's behavior. Thus, Walster and Festinger found that smokers but not nonsmokers were affected by an overheard persuasive message (warning) connecting cigarette smoking and lung cancer, presumably because the communication was motivationally relevant only to smokers. Although they used completely different procedures, Brock and Becker (1965) replicated these findings. Mills (1966) found that a friendly source gains more influence when he intends it, while an unfriendly source is somewhat more influential when not seeking it. However, a friendly source gained consistently more influence from targets than an unfriendly source, regardless of intent to persuade. Supporting evidence has been found by Mills and Aronson (1965).

Experimental paradigms which have focused upon forewarning subjects of the source's persuasive attempts are generally very complex and do not explicitly vary the accommodativeness—exploitativeness of the source's intentions. However, the very act of forewarning a third person about the source's persuasive intentions implies planning, scheming, or subterfuge, and may lead the target to infer exploitative intent. This is particularly true when the source is a stranger. A series of studies indicate that forewarning does decrease the influenceability of target persons (Freedman & Sears, 1965; Kiesler & Kiesler, 1964; McGinnies & Donelson, 1963). However, this effect must be restricted to issues that are important and relevant to the target or else forewarning does not reduce persuasibility (Allyn & Festinger, 1961; Apsler & Sears, 1968; Greenberg & Miller, 1966). Several experiments fail to support these conclusions (McGuire & Millman, 1965; McGuire & Papageoris, 1962), but were sufficiently complex in procedure to throw doubt on their relevance to the hypotheses presently under consideration (cf. Collins, 1970).

Correlational evidence has been provided by Bennis et al. (1958) confirming a direct effect of source capability upon influence effectiveness. Bennis compiled an index of congruence-incongruence from questionnaire and interview data of nurses' ratings of the resources *possessed* by their supervisor as compared with the resources *desired* by the nurses. In hospitals where desired and obtained resources were most congruent, correlational measures indicated that supervisor effectiveness in gaining compliance to her directives was greatest.

Bass (1963) assigned ROTC cadets, some of whom were and some of whom were not highly motivated towards military service, to five-man groups in which each person was given a weighted value in evaluating other subjects in the group in reference to their candidacy for advanced ROTC. Three distributions of capability were created: (1) all five members of the group were of equal capability; (2) weights were 3-2-1-1-1; and (3) weights were 4-1-1-1-1. Subjects individually ranked five adjectives in terms of judgments about their frequency of usage, held a group discussion concerning the judgments, and then again made individual judgments. It was found that for the high-motivation subjects the greater the capability of the subject, the more influence he attempted and the more influence he successfully exerted over the others. The capability provided to subjects was irrelevant and hence was not effective in mediating influence when subjects were not motivated for military service.

The importance of integrating attribution theory into a more general theory of social influence cannot be exaggerated. The single attribution continuum of accommodation-exploitation may be sufficient to explain the reactions of a target to persuasive influence attempts as long as this variable is imbedded in a more general theory. The evidence available confirms that more opinion change is produced by the source of persuasive influence, the more accommodative or the less exploitative he is perceived to be. However, little

Influence, Decision, and Compliance

or no evidence could be gathered to confirm the relationship of source prestige to the *behavioral* effects of persuasion.

Prestige, Conformity, Modeling, and Social Reinforcement

The effects of source prestige on public conformity and the effectiveness of social reinforcements cannot be assessed since no relevant evidence could be found. However, several studies indicate that the prestige of a model is positively related to imitation by an observer. Grusec and Mischel (1966) and Mischel and Grusec (1966) had children interact with a female adult who was introduced as the new nursery school teacher or as a visiting teacher. The permanent teacher can be viewed as possessing greater future control over resources than the temporary teacher, thus giving the former higher prestige than the latter. As predicted, high-prestige models gained greater compliance than did low-prestige models.

Finally, Mischel and Liebert (1967) found that a model, who had possessed the capability of rewarding children by providing them with a toy, gained higher levels of imitation than a model who did not possess rewarding capability. However, when the children were subsequently informed that the prestigious model had depleted his supply of toys, no differences in imitation were found between conditions.

Conclusion

The present formulation of the direct effects of source prestige on the influenceability of a target individual reveals large gaps in the empirical literature. Virtually no evidence is available concerning source capability and the effectiveness of threats, promises, warnings, or mendations. The evidence with respect to source prestige and persuasion is limited to source intentions and attitude or opinion change, with no available evidence on behavioral change following persuasive communications. However, the evidence with respect to source intentions and compliance to threats and promises or attitude change in response to persuasive communications does support the predictions of SEV theroy. No evidence of any kind could be found relating source prestige to public conformity or to the effectiveness of social reinforcements. Several studies confirm that the prestige of a model does directly mediate the imitative behavior of observers.

Esteem for the Source

Expertise is an informational or skill resource which allows its possessor an increased probability of accurately specifying environmental contingencies. French and Raven (1959) have viewed expertise as an important base of power for a source of influence. Similarly, Lasswell and Kaplan (1950) have included respect and enlightenment as important base values which could be used for purposes of power and influence by those who possess them. Expertise implies the value of, availability of, and ability to provide help or information. Homans (1961) has proposed that a person who has valuable help to give others will receive approval in exchange for help rendered. We will define the concept of *esteem* as the degree of respect granted to the source by the target, and will assume that the major basis for the development of respect is the real ability, native intelligence, or special experience of the referent person. Thus, expertise is the independent variable or source characteristic and esteem is the resultant perception by the target. Blau (1964) has similarly suggested that respect entails unilateral approval of special abilities presumably judged by objective standards. He is careful to point out that the ability of a person to command respect requires either that his abilities be superior to those from whom he desires respect or that he possesses expertise in some area other than that possessed by his audience.

Already we have argued for analytically separating the source characteristics of status and esteem (expertise). A similar argument needs to be made for the provisional belief that esteem and attraction are orthogonal factors. It is not unusual to find psychologists measuring attraction with sociometric scales which include items concerning popularity and friendship and which ask persons to choose someone with whom they would like to live, play, *and* work. Yet, there are no intrinsic reasons to suppose that a person should want to engage in all activities with his friends or that he should choose to work with an incompetent friend over an extremely competent but rather unattractive other person. Blau (1955, p. 159) has observed that the best high school students and the fastest factory workers, persons who are respected for their abilities, are nevertheless usually unpopular with their peers. In a classic study which often has been replicated, Bales (1958) found that persons who are most respected for their group contributions and who are consistently chosen as leaders are not the best-liked members of the group. Hence, we may assume that esteem is orthogonal to attraction.

Expertise has been theorized to be an effective base of influence due to a target's dependence upon the superior task-relevant information or skills possessed by the source (Jones & Gerard, 1967; Kelley & Thibaut, 1969; Thibaut & Kelley, 1959). Bandura (1969) has expressed the rather general consensus: "A competent, ... communicator is generally more influential than a less competent one because the former's behavioral recommendations, if executed, are more likely to result in favorable outcomes" (p. 600). Since experts are more likely to provide accurate predictions regarding the future than are nonexperts, target individuals bias upwards the probability estimates of the truth of an expert's warnings and mendations.

It is quite straightforward to predict that the higher the esteem of the source, the more persuasive his communications will be. But it is not common sense to suggest that an expert's threats and promises will also gain more compliance than those of a nonexpert. Since the expert's reputation is his most important resource, he is likely to avoid telling lies whatever influence mode is chosen. Consistency is an important concern for people in general. However, it is a paramount concern for experts. Presumably, each of us learns that esteemed individuals are concerned about their reputations and hence we authenticate their tacit and explicit communications, including threats and promises.

Esteem, Threats, and Promises

To the authors' knowledge, the only study which has manipulated the esteem of a source of either threats or promises was performed by Tedeschi (1970b). Subjects were exposed to a scenario in which it became apparent that the "surprised" experimenter was acquainted with the future confederate opponent of the subject. In the high-esteem condition, the experimenter asked the confederate if he was still taking karate lessons and if he had yet obtained his black belt. The confederate replied that he had a black belt and in response to a direct question confessed that he had once used karate but only in self-defense. The high-esteem manipulation was thus designed to portray the confederate as an individual who was an expert in controlled violence but who used his expertise defensively. In the low-esteem scenario, the "surprised" experimenter asked the subject if he had really flunked out of a course he had been taking. The confederate answered that he had, and joked about the fact that he was glad he didn't bother to purchase the textbook for the course. The low-esteem manipulation was designed to portray the confederate as a rather incompetent and unmotivated individual who was not taken seriously by others. A postinduction pretest established that differences between the two esteem conditions on judgments of respect and intelligence with regard to the confederate did occur, and that differences in attraction did not.

The confederate was the alleged source of threats of 0 or 100 percent credibility and subjects were targets of the coercive influence attempts. Subjects who were threatened by the low-esteem source complied in direct relation to the credibility of threats, while subjects in the high-esteem conditions complied frequently whatever the credibility of threats. This pattern of results is directly opposite to that found when source attraction was manipulated by Schlenker et al. (1970). Apparently, high esteem, like low attraction, causes an authentication of the source's threats. Contrary to SEV hypotheses, low esteem, like high attraction, frees the target from the biasing effect of a source orientation (McDavid, 1959) so that the expected value of threats remains relatively unbiased by the salient source attribute.

Esteem, Warnings, and Mendations

The literature on persuasion and attitude change abounds with studies of source expertise. Since the classic laboratory studies by Hovland and Weiss (1951) and Kelman and Hovland (1953), it has been generally accepted that expertise of the communicator increases both the probability and the degree of attitude change of the target. Both studies can be reconceptualized as mendations which advise the target to alter his attitudes toward certain issues so that he could thereby enjoy a more veridical picture of environmental contingencies. A direct effect of source expertise on degree of communicatee attitude change was found.

Miller and Hewgill (Hewgill & Miller, 1965; Miller & Hewgill, 1966) presented subjects with communications about the consequences of nuclear war or natural disasters. The source was said to be either a professor of nuclear physics or a high school sophomore and the consequences of the disaster were either briefly mentioned or vividly described in detail. The two experiments presented to the target warnings that were attributed either to an expert or a nonexpert and were either of low or high expected value. The high-esteem source produced greater attitude change than did the low-esteem source. Additionally, the high-esteem source produced more attitude change toward fallout shelters and underground schools when his warning had a high expected value; differences in the expected value of the warnings issued by the low-esteem source did not affect the attitudes of subjects. Apparently if esteem is low enough, the expected value of the source's influence messages will not mediate effective influence.

Johnson and his associates (Johnson & Izzett, 1969; Johnson, Torcivia, & Poprick 1968; Johnson & Scileppi, 1969; Johnson &

Stanicek, 1969) have investigated the effects of source expertise on attitude change toward the position advocated in a warning of the danger of X-rays. In all of the studies, one source was described as a medical authority who was an expert in the area of X-rays, while the other source was portrayed as a quack who had served a term in prison for medical fraud. In all of the above studies, the high-esteem source produced greater attitude change than did the low-esteem source. In a somewhat similar design, Goldberg (1970) had subjects read a message which warned of the dangers of frequent toothbrushing. The message was said to be written by either a dental surgeon (high-esteem), a factory worker (low-esteem), or an anonymous source. It was found that the high-esteem source produced greater attitude change than either of the other two sources.

Tannenbaum (1967) reports two experiments investigating the amount of resistance to subsequent persuasive appeals. In the first experiment, target subjects were exposed to identical communications attributed to a professor of clinical medicine at Johns Hopkins University or *Truth and Health* magazine, distributed through health-food stores. The persuasive communication consisted of an explicit mendation regarding health practices. As predicted, the more expert the source, the greater the subjects' resistance to subsequent counterpersuasive appeals. In the second study, Tannenbaum reversed the procedure and had either the professor or the magazine directly attack the subjects' opinions through the persuasion mode of warnings. Greater attitude change was produced by the more expert source.

Aronson and Golden (1962) exposed sixth-grade children to a mendation extolling the virtues of and benefits accruing from a knowledge of arithmetic. In one treatment condition, the communication was presented from an engineer while in another condition, the source was described as a dishwasher. The children's attitudes toward arithmetic were more favorable in the high-esteem condition.

Aronson, Turner, and Carlsmith (1963) had subjects judge obscure poems and then read an evaluation of one of the judged poems. The poetry was purportedly written by either another student or T. S. Eliot. It was found that the greater the discrepancy of judgments communicated by the high-esteem source the more the subjects changed their initial rating of the critical poem. The same function was not found for the nonexpert's communication. Similar results were obtained by Bergin (1962).

There is little question that source esteem is an important base of influence. However, the "sleeper effect" which has been shown to obscure the long-term effects of source prestige also throws a question upon the permanency of attitude change brought about by source esteem (Hovland, Lumsdaine, & Sheffield, 1949; Hovland & Weiss, 1951). But Kelman and Hovland (1953) discovered that the effects of source expertise typically found immediately following persuasive communications but lost as a function of the "sleeper effect" could be restored by reminding the subjects after a three-week interval that the source indeed was an expert. On the other hand, Johnson, Torcivia, and Poprick (1968) did not find the "sleeper effect" one week after the persuasion attempt was made. Since changes in the topography or probability of a verbal or behavioral response should be a function of reinforcement contingencies, changes produced by persuasive communications, if seldom reinforced, could be expected to be subject to rapid extinction. If the source's recommendations result in real benefits for the target, then the attitude or behavior changes wrought through persuasive messages should be expected to be more permanent.

Weiss and his colleagues have taken the interesting position that, in the absence of dimensional criteria permitting some numerical scaling of source expertise, communicator-consensus may offer an indirect method for measuring the quantitative relation of source esteem to attitude change. In an early study, Weiss, Buchanan, and Pasamanick (1964) exposed subjects to counterbalanced speeches from which the targets could draw the "logical" (advocated) conclusion. The persuasive arguments were said to be either advocated by "all the experts" or by "somewhat less then half the experts." As predicted, the high communicator-consensus condition produced significantly more attitude change than did the low consensus conditions.

In an extension of the basic paradigm, Weiss, Weiss, and Chalupa (1967) presented targets with persuasive arguments advocated by a group of experts of five levels of consensus (0, 25, 50, 75, and 100 percent of the experts). After hearing the persuasive communications, subjects rated on a scale from 0 to 100 percent the probability that "the communication was true." As predicted by Weiss' classical conditioning model of attitude change, the targets' probability of agreement with the persuasive communications bore a direct and linear relationship to the consensus conditions. It would appear that not only the amount of expertise possessed by a single source, but the *number* of (assumedly) equally expert sources who advocate a similar course of action for the target has a direct relation to the amount of target compliance obtained.

Esteem, Conformity, Modeling, and Social Reinforcement

If conformity, imitation, and responsiveness to social reinforcers are consequences of tacit communications, then source expertise should facilitate all three behaviors. In two studies, Mausner (1953, 1954) found that students conformed more to the artistic or geometric judgments of experts than of nonexperts. Other conformity studies have established that confederates who were rated high in intelligence (French & Snyder, 1959), scored high in arithmetic ability, problem-solving ability, and eye-hand coordination (Gelfand, 1962), or demonstrated skill in estimating the area of irregular figures (Croner & Willis, 1961) produced more conformity (or imitation) from critical subjects than did their less-esteemed counterparts. Vidulich and Kaiman (1961) found more conformity in an autokinetic situation when a confederate was introduced as a research professor than when he was introduced as a high school student. The interpretation of some of these studies in terms of modeling is suggested by the sporadic finding that the expertise of the source must be relevant to the problem faced by the target individual (Croner & Willis, 1961; Moore, 1969).

Finally, Oakes (1962) rewarded a group member in an attempt to "shape" his behavior as a group leader. The social reinforcements were delivered either by a professional psychologist, who presumably was perceived as an expert in the context of psychological experimentation, or a layman. The social reinforcements more successfully produced leadership behavior when they were delivered by the expert than when they were delivered by the nonexpert.

Conclusion

In summary, esteem for the source established by the source's general competence or intelligence in solving problems is an informational base of social influence. High esteem for a source causes a target person to bias upwards the probability associated with the expected value of the message used by the source. Consequently, as the expertise of the source increases, so does the effectiveness of his influence attempts. The evidence, where it exists, tentatively confirms the SEV theory prediction that the general competence of the source is directly related to target influenceability.

Conclusions

The present attempt to bring about a general integration of the influence literature was based on the assumptions that people are rational and that all forms of influence involve some form of explicit or tacit communications. The types of messages analysed included threats, promises, mendations, and warnings. Public conformity and social reinforcement experiments were interpreted as studies of tacit threats and promises, while modeling studies were interpreted in terms of tacit mendations and tacit warnings. Criteria of relevance were offered to help organize the literature dealing with nondirected communications. Each message type was interpreted in terms of the probability and value of benefits or harm associated with the communication. The product of the probability and value of a message was considered the expected value of that message. The theory predicts that, all else equal, a target will compare the expected value of the message with the expected values of alternative decisions and will act to maximize his gains or minimize his losses. Support for this prediction was rather strong with respect to threats and warnings but weak with respect to explicit promises and explicit mendations.

A rather uncomplicated theory was built upon the expected value definitions. Source characteristics of attraction, status, prestige, and esteem were defined as orthogonal factors which serve to bias the target's estimations of the probability component of the expected value of the message and hence affect the influenceability of the target. The reader should also be reminded that the present theory concerned a rather passive target in a dyadic influence process in which predictions were of a binary nature. The theory does present, however, a firm framework for a more dynamic conception of human interaction. The evidence, where it exists, is generally encouraging for a subjective expected value theory of influenceability. However, individual difference factors, when considered, may well produce a number of interactions and destroy the simplicity of the present formulation, which has deliberately ignored personality theory.

References

Abelson, R., & Miller, J. Negative persuasion via personal insult. *Journal of Experimental Social Psychology*, 1967, 3, 321-333.

Allen, M. K., & Liebert, R. M. Children's adoption of self-reward patterns: model's prior experience and incentive for non-imitation. *Child Development*, 1969, 40, 921-926.

Allen, V. L. Situational factors in conformity. In L. Berkowitz (Ed.), *Advances in experimental social psychology*. Vol. 2. New York: Academic Press, 1965. Pp. 133-175.

Allen, V. L., & Crutchfield, R. S. Generalization of experimentally reinforced conformity. *Journal of Abnormal and Social Psychology*, 1963, 67, 326-333.

Allyn, J., & Festinger, L. The effectiveness of unanticipated persuasive communications. *Journal of Abnormal and Social Psychology*, 1961, 62, 35-40.

Apsler, R., & Sears, D. O. Warning, personal involvement, and attitude change. *Journal of Personality and Social Psychology*, 1968, 9, 162-166.

Argyle, M. Social pressures in public and private situations. *Journal of Abnormal and Social Psychology*, 1957, 54, 172-175.
Aronfreed, J., Cutlick, R. A., & Fagan, S. A. Cognitive structure, punishment, and nurturance in the experimental induction of self-criticism. *Child Development*, 1963, 34, 281-294.
Aronfreed, J., & Leff, R. The effects of intensity of punishment and complexity of discrimination upon the generalization of an internalized inhibition. Unpublished manuscript, University of Pennsylvania, 1963.
Aronfreed, J., & Paskel, V. Altruism, empathy, and the conditioning of positive affect. Reported in J. Aronfreed, *Conduct and conscience*. New York: Academic Press, 1968.
Aronson, E., & Carlsmith, J. M. Experimentation in social psychology. In G. Lindzey & E. Aronson (Eds.), *Handbook of social psychology*, 2nd ed. Vol. 2. Reading, Mass.: Addison-Wesley, 1968. Pp. 1-79.
Aronson, E., & Golden, B. The effect of relevant and irrelevant aspects of communicator credibility on opinion change. *Journal of Personality*, 1962, 30, 135-146.
Aronson, E., Turner, J., & Carlsmith, J. Communicator credibility and communication discrepancy as determinants of opinion change. *Journal of Abnormal and Social Psychology*, 1963, 67, 31-36.
Asch, S. E. The doctrine of suggestion, prestige and imitation in social psychology. *Psychological Review*, 1948, 55, 250-276.
Asch, S. E. Effects of group pressure upon the modification and distortion of judgment. In H. Guetzkow (Ed.), *Groups, leadership and men*. Pittsburgh: Carnegie Press, 1951. Pp. 177-190.
Atkinson, J. W. *An introduction to motivation*. New York: Van Nostrand, 1964.
Back, K. W. Influence through social communication. *Journal of Abnormal and Social Psychology*, 1951, 46, 9-23.
Backman, C. W., & Secord, P. F. The effect of perceived liking on interpersonal attraction. *Human Relations*, 1959, 12, 379-384.
Bales, R. F. Task roles and social roles in problem solving groups. In E. E. Maccoby, T. M. Newcomb, & E. L. Hartley (Eds.), *Readings in social psychology*, 3rd ed. New York: Holt, Rinehart & Winston, 1958. Pp. 437-447.
Bandura, A. Social learning through imitation. In M. R. Jones (Ed.), *Nebraska symposium on motivation, 1962*. Lincoln: University of Nebraska Press, 1962. Pp. 211-274.
Bandura, A. *Principles of behavior modification*. New York: Holt, Rinehart & Winston, 1969.
Bandura, A., Grusec, J. E., & Menlove, F. L. Some social determinants of self-monitoring reinforcement systems. *Journal of Personality and Social Psychology*, 1967, 5, 449-455.
Bandura, A., & Harris, M. B. Modification of syntactic style. *Journal of Experimental Child Psychology*, 1966, 4, 341-352.
Bandura, A., & Huston, A. C. Identification as a process of incidental learning. *Journal of Abnormal and Social Psychology*, 1961, 63, 311-318.
Bandura, A., Ross, D., & Ross, S. A comparative test of the status envy, social power, and the secondary-reinforcement theories of identificatory learning. *Journal of Abnormal and Social Psychology*, 1963, 67, 527-534.
Baron, R. A. Attraction toward the model and model's competence as determinants of adult imitative behavior. *Journal of Personality and Social Psychology*, 1970, 14, 345-351.

Baron, R. A., & Kepner, C. R. Model's behavior and attraction toward the model as determinants of adult aggressive behavior. *Journal of Personality and Social Psychology,* 1970, 14, 335-344.

Bass, B. M. Amount of participation, coalescense, and profitability of decision making discussions. *Journal of Abnormal and Social Psychology,* 1963, 67, 92-94.

Bass, B. M. *Organizational psychology.* Boston: Allyn & Bacon, 1965.

Bass, B. M. The leaderless group discussion. *Psychological Bulletin,* 1954, 51, 465-492.

Bass, B. M., & Dunteman, G. Biases in the evaluation of one's own group, its allies and opponents. *Journal of Conflict Resolution,* 1963, 7, 16-20.

Bass, B. M., & Wurster, C. R. Effects of company rank on LGD performance of oil refinery supervisors. *Journal of Applied Psychology,* 1953, 37, 96-104.(a)

Bass, B. M., & Wurster, C. R. Effects of the nature of the problem on LGD performance. *Journal of Applied Psychology,* 1953, 37, 96-99. (b)

Bennis, W. G., Berkowitz, M., Affinito, M., & Malone, M. Authority, power and the ability to influence. *Human Relations,* 1958, 11, 143-155.

Bergin, A. The effect of dissonant persuasive communications upon changes in self-referring attitudes. *Journal of Personality,* 1962, 30, 423-438.

Berkowitz, L. Group standard, cohesiveness, and productivity. *Human Relations,* 1954, 7, 509-519.

Berkowitz, L. The frustration-aggression hypothesis revisited. In L. Berkowitz (Ed.), *Roots of aggression: a re-examination of the frustration-aggression hypothesis.* New York: Atherton Press, 1969. Pp. 1-28.

Berkowitz, L., & Cottingham, D. L. The interest value and relevance of fear-arousing communications. *Journal of Abnormal and Social Psychology,* 1960, 60, 37-43.

Berkowitz, L., & Daniels, L. R. Responsibility and dependency. *Journal of Abnormal and Social Psychology,* 1963, 66, 429-437.

Berkowitz, L., & Levy, B. I. Pride in group performance and group-task motivation. *Journal of Abnormal and Social Psychology,* 1956, 53, 300-306.

Berscheid, E., & Walster, E. Attitude change. In J. Mills (Ed.), *Experimental social psychology.* New York: Macmillan, 1969. Pp. 121-231.

Blau, P. M. *The dynamics of bureaucracy.* Chicago: University of Chicago Press, 1955.

Blau, P. M. *Exchange and power in social life.* New York: Wiley, 1964.

Blau, P. M. The hierarchy of authority in organizations. *The American Journal of Sociology,* 1968, 73, 453-467.

Bonoma, T. V., Schlenker, B. R., Smith, R. B., & Tedeschi, J. T. Source prestige and target reactions to threats. *Psychonomic Science,* 1970, 19, 111-113.

Bonoma, T., & Tedeschi, J. T. The effects of source behavior on target's compliance to threats. Mimeographed manuscript, State University of New York at Albany, 1970.

Bonoma, T., Tedeschi, J. T., & Lindskold, S. Reactions to a threatening simulated opponent. Mimeographed manuscript, State University of New York at Albany, 1970.

Bramel, D. Interpersonal attraction, hostility, and perception. In J. Mills (Ed.), *Experimental social psychology.* New York: Macmillan, 1969. Pp. 1-120.

Brock, T. C. Communicator-recipient similarity and decision change. *Journal of Personality and Social Psychology,* 1965, 1, 650-654.

Brock, T. C. & Becker, L. A. Ineffectiveness of "overheard" counterpropaganda. *Journal of Personality and Social Psychology*, 1965, 2, 654-660.
Bruner, J., & Postman, L. Perception, cognition, and behavior. In J. S. Bruner & D. Krech (Eds.), *Perception and personality*. Durham, N. C.: Duke University Press, 1949. Pp. 14-32.
Burnstein, E., Stotland, E., & Zander, A. Similarity to a model and self-evaluation. *Journal of Abnormal and Social Psychology*, 1961, 62, 257-264.
Burnstein, E., & Worchel, P. Arbitrariness of frustration and its consequences for aggression in a social situation. *Journal of Personality*, 1962, 30, 528-540.
Byrne, D. Attitudes and attraction. In L. Berkowitz (Ed.), *Advances in experimental social psychology*. Vol. 4. New York: Academic Press, 1969. Pp. 35-89.
Cantril, H. Perception and interpersonal relations. In E. P. Hollander & R. G. Hunt (Eds.), *Current perspectives in social psychology*, 2nd ed. New York: Oxford University Press, 1967. Pp. 284-291.
Cartwright, D. Power: a neglected variable in social psychology. In D. Cartwright (Ed.), *Studies in social power*. Ann Arbor, Mich.: Institute of Social Research, 1959. Pp. 183-220.
Cartwright, D., & Harary, F. Structural balance: a generalization of Heider's theory. *Psychological Record*, 1956, 63, 277-293.
Cartwright, D., & Zander, A. I. *Group Dynamics*, 3rd ed. New York: Harper & Row, 1968.
Caudill, W. *The psychiatric hospital as a small society*. Cambridge, Mass.: Harvard University Press, 1958.
Chambliss, W. J. The deterrent influence of punishment. *Crime and Delinquency*, 1966, 12, 70-75.
Chu, G. C. Fear arousal, efficacy, and immenency. *Journal of Personality and Social Psychology*, 1966, 4, 517-524.
Collins, B. E. *Social psychology*. Reading, Mass.: Addison-Wesley, 1970.
Crockett, W. H. Emergent leadership in small decision-making groups. *Journal of Abnormal and Social Psychology*, 1955, 51, 378-383.
Croner, M. D., & Willis, R. H. Perceived differences in task competence and asymmetry of dyadic influence. *Journal of Abnormal and Social Psychology*, 1961, 62, 705-708.
Crutchfield, R. S. Conformity and character. *American Psychologist*, 1955, 10, 191-198.
Dabbs, J. M., Jr. Self-esteem, communicator characteristics, and attitude change. *Journal of Abnormal and Social Psychology*, 1964, 69, 173-181.
Dabbs, J. M., Jr., & Leventhal, H. Effects of varying the recommendations in a fear-arousing communication. *Journal of Personality and Social Psychology*, 1966, 4, 525-531.
Darley, J. Fear and social comparison as determinants of conformity behavior. *Journal of Personality and Social Psychology*, 1966, 4, 73-78.
Deutsch, M., & Gerard, H. G. A study of normative and informational influence upon individual judgment. *Journal of Abnormal and Social Psychology*, 1955, 51, 629-636.
DeWolfe, A., & Governale, C. Fear and attitude change. *Journal of Abnormal and Social Psychology*, 1964, 69, 119-123.
Edwards, W. The theory of decision making. *Psychological Bulletin*, 1954, 51, 380-417.

Edwards, W., & Tversky, A. (Eds.), *Decision making.* Baltimore: Penguin Books, 1967.

Efran, J. S. Looking for approval: effects on visual behavior of approbations from persons differing in importance. *Journal of Personality and Social Psychology*, 1968, 10, 21-25.

Elms, A. C. *Role playing, reward, and attitude change.* New York: Van Nostrand, 1969.

Emerson, R. M. Deviation and rejection: an experimental replication. *American Sociological Review*, 1954, 19, 688-694.

Endler, N. S. Conformity as a function of different reinforcement schedules. *Journal of Personality and Social Psychology*, 1966, 4, 175-180.

Endler, N. S., & Hoy, E. Conformity as related to reinforcement and social pressure. *Journal of Personality and Social Psychology*, 1967, 7, 197-201.

Evan, W. M., & Zelditch, M., Jr. A laboratory experiment on bureaucratic authority. *American Sociological Review*, 1961, 26, 883-893.

Faley, T., & Tedeschi, J. T. Status and reactions to threats. *Journal of Personality and Social Psychology*, 1971, 17, 192-199.

Festinger, L. An analysis of compliant behavior. In M. Sherif & M. O. Wilson (Eds.), *Group relations at the crossroads.* New York: Harper, 1953. Pp. 232-256.

Festinger, L., Gerard, H. B., Hymovitch, B., Kelley, H. H., & Raven, B. H. The influence process in the presence of extreme deviates. *Human Relations*, 1952, 5, 327-346.

Festinger, L., Schachter, S., & Back, K. *Social pressures in informal groups: a study of human factors in housing.* New York: Harper & Row, 1950.

Fishbein, M. The relationship between beliefs, attitudes and behavior. In S. Feldman (Ed.), *Cognitive consistency: motivational antecedents and behavioral consequents.* New York: Academic Press, 1966. Pp. 199-223.

Flanders, J. P. A review of research on imitative behavior. *Psychological Bulletin*, 1968, 69, 316-337.

Freedman, J., & Sears, D. Selective exposure. In L. Berkowitz (Ed.), *Advances in experimental social psychology.* Vol. 2. New York: Academic Press, 1965. Pp. 57-97.

French, J. R. P., Jr., Morrison, H. W., & Levinger, G. Coercive power and forces affecting conformity. *Journal of Abnormal and Social Psychology*, 1960, 61, 93-101.

French, J. R. P., Jr., & Raven, B. The bases of social power. In D. Cartwright (Ed.), *Studies in social power.* Ann Arbor, Mich.: Institute of Social Research, 1959. Pp. 150-167.

French, J. R. P., Jr., & Snyder, R. Leadership and interpersonal power. In D. Cartwright (Ed.), *Studies in social power.* Ann Arbor, Mich.: Institute of Social Research, 1959. Pp. 118-149.

Gahagan, J., Long, H., & Horai, J. Race of experimenter and reactions to threats by black preadolescents. *Proceedings of the 77th Meeting of the American Psychological Association*, 1969, 397-398.

Gahagan, J. P., Tedeschi, J. T., Faley, T. E., & Lindskold, S. Patterns of punishment and reactions to threats. *Journal of Social Psychology*, 1970, 80, 115-116.

Gelfand, D. M. The influence of self-esteem on rate of verbal conditioning and social matching behavior. *Journal of Abnormal and Social Psychology*, 1962, 65, 259-265.

Gerard, H. G. The anchorage of opinions in face-to-face groups. *Human Relations*, 1954, 7, 313-325.

Gerard, H. B. Deviation, conformity and commitment. In I. D. Steiner & M. Fishbein (Eds.), *Current studies in social psychology*. New York: Holt, Rinehart & Winston, 1965. Pp. 263-277.

Gewirtz, J. L., & Baer, D. M. Deprivation and satiation of social reinforcers as drive conditions. *Journal of Abnormal and Social Psychology*, 1958, 57, 165-172.

Gibbs, J. P. Crime, punishment, and deterrence. *Southwestern Social Science Quarterly*, 1968, 48, 515-530.

Goldberg, C. Attitude change as a function of source credibility, authoritarianism, and message ambiguity. *Proceedings of the 78th annual convention of the American Psychological Association*, Miami Beach, 1970.

Goldstein, M. J. The relationship between coping and avoiding behavior and response to fear-arousing propaganda. *Journal of Abnormal and Social Psychology*, 1959, 58, 247-252.

Goodenough, W. H. Frontiers of cultural anthropology: social organization. *Proceedings of the American Philosophical Society*, 1969, 113, 329-335.

Goranson, R. E., & Berkowitz, L. Reciprocity and responsibility reactions to prior help. *Journal of Personality and Social Psychology*, 1966, 3, 227-232.

Gouldner, A. W. *Patterns of industrial bureaucracy*. Glencoe, Ill.: Free Press, 1954.

Gouldner, A. W. The norm of reciprocity: a preliminary statement. *American Sociological Review*, 1960, 25, 161-179.

Gray, L. N., & Martin, J. D. Punishments and deterrence: another analysis of Gibbs' data. *Social Science Quarterly*, 1969, 50, 389-395.

Greenberg, B. S., & Miller, G. R. The effect of low credibility sources on message acceptance. *Speech Monographs*, 1966, 33, 127-136.

Griffitt, W. B. Anticipated reinforcement and attraction. *Psychonomic Science*, 1968, 11, 355-356.

Grusec, J. Some antecedents of self-criticism. *Journal of Personality and Social Psychology*, 1966, 4, 244-252.

Grusec, J., & Mischel, W. The model's characteristics as determinants of social learning. *Journal of Personality and Social Psychology*, 1966, 4, 211-215.

Grusec, J. E., & Skubiski, S. L. Model nurturance, demand characteristics of the modeling experiment, and altruism. *Journal of Personality and Social Psychology*, 1970, 14, 352-359.

Haefner, D. P. Some effects of guilt-arousing and fear-arousing persuasive communications on opinion change. *American Psychologist*, 1956, 11, 359. (Abstract)

Harris, M. Some determinants of sharing in children. Unpublished doctoral dissertation, Stanford University, 1968.

Harsanyi, J. A bargaining model for social status in informal groups and formal organizations. *Behavioral Science*, 1966, 11, 357-369.

Hartup, W. W., & Coates, B. Imitation of a peer as a function of reinforcement from the peer group and rewardingness of the model. *Child Development*, 1967, 38, 1003-1016.

Harvey, O. J. An experimental approach to the study of status relations in informal groups. *Sociometry*, 1953, 18, 357-367.

Heider, F. *The psychology of interpersonal relations*. New York: Wiley, 1958.

Hemphill, J. K. Why people attempt to lead. In L. Petrullo & B. M. Bass (Eds.), *Leadership and interpersonal behavior*. New York: Holt, Rinehart & Winston, 1961. Pp. 201-215.

Hetherington, E. M., & Frankie, G. Effects of parental dominance, warmth, and conflict on imitation in children. *Journal of Personality and Social Psychology*, 1967, 6, 119-125.

Hetherington, E. M., & Ross, L. E. Effects of sex of subject, sex of experimenter, and reinforcement condition on serial verbal learning. *Journal of Experimental Psychology*, 1963, 65, 572-575.

Hewgill, M. A., & Miller, G. R. Source credibility and response to fear-arousing communications. *Speech Monographs*, 1965, 32, 95-102.

Hewitt, J., & McLaughlin, D. Intra-group similarity and the rejection of a deviate. *Psychonomic Science*, 1970, 18, 71-72.

Higbee, K. L. Fifteen years of fear arousal: research on threat appeals: 1953-1968. *Psychological Bulletin*, 1969, 72, 426-444.

Hollander, E. P. *Leaders, groups, and influence*. New York: Oxford University Press, 1964.

Homans, G. C. *Social behavior: its elementary forms*. New York: Harcourt, Brace, 1961.

Horai, J., & Tedeschi, J. T. The effects of threat credibility and magnitude of punishment upon compliance. *Journal of Personality and Social Psychology*, 1969, 12, 164-169.

Horai, J., & Tedeschi, J. T. The attribution of intent and the norm of reciprocity under dyadic conflict. Mimeographed manuscript, State University of New York at Albany, 1970.

Horwitz, M. Hostility and its management in classroom groups. In W. W. Charters & N. L. Gage (Eds.), *Readings in the social psychology of education*. Boston: Allyn & Bacon, 1963. Pp. 196-211.

Hovland, C. I., Janis, I. L., & Kelley, H. H. *Communication and persuasion*. New Haven, Conn.: Yale University Press, 1953.

Hovland, C. I., Lumsdaine, A. A., & Sheffield, F. D. *Experiments on mass communication*. Princeton, N. J.: Princeton University Press, 1949.

Hovland, C. I., & Weiss, W. The influence of source credibility on communication effectiveness. *Public Opinion Quarterly*, 1951, 15, 635-650.

Hurwitz, J. I., Zander, A. F., & Hymovitch, B. Some effects of power on the relations among group members. In D. Cartwright & A. Zander (Eds.), *Group dynamics*, 3rd ed. New York: Harper & Row, 1968. Pp. 291-297.

Insko, C. A., Arkoff, A., & Insko, V. M. Effects of high and low fear-arousing communications upon opinions toward smoking. *Journal of Experimental Social Psychology*, 1965, 1, 256-266.

James, G., & Lott, A. J. Reward frequency and the formation of positive attitudes toward group members. *Journal of Social Psychology*, 1964, 62, 111-115.

Janda, K. F. Towards the explication of the concept of leadership in terms of the concept of power. *Human Relations*, 1960, 13, 345-363.

Janis, I. L. Effects of fear arousal on attitude change: recent developments in theory and experimental research. In L. Berkowitz (Ed.), *Advances in experimental social psychology*. Vol. 3. New York: Academic Press, 1967. Pp. 166-224.

Janis, I. L., & Feshbach, S. Effects of fear-arousing communications. *Journal of Abnormal and Social Psychology*, 1953, 48, 78-92.

Janis, I. L., & Feshbach, S. Personality differences associated with responsiveness to fear-arousing communications. *Journal of Personality*, 1954, 23, 154-166.

Janis, I. L., & Terwilliger, R. F. An experimental study of psychological resistances to fear-arousing communications. *Journal of Abnormal and Social Psychology*, 1962, 65, 403-410.

Johnson, H. H., & Izzett, R. R. Relationship between authoritarianism and attitude change as a function of source credibility and type of communication. *Journal of Personality and Social Psychology*, 1969, 13, 317-321.

Johnson, H. H., & Scileppi, J. A. Effects of ego-involvement conditions on attitude change to high and low credibility communicators. *Journal of Personality and Social Psychology*, 1969, 13, 31-36.

Johnson, H. H., & Stanicek, F. F. Relationship between authoritarianism and attitude change as a function of implicit and explicit communications. *Proceedings of the 77th Annual Convention of the American Psychological Association*, 1969, 415-416.

Johnson, H. H., Torcivia, J. M., & Poprick, M. A. Effects of source credibility on the relationship between authoritarianism and attitude change. *Journal of Personality and Social Psychology*, 1968, 9, 179-183.

Jones, E. E., & Gerard, H. B. *Foundations of social psychology*. New York: Wiley, 1967.

Jones, E. E., Gergen, K. J., & Jones, R. G. Tactics of ingratiation among leaders and subordinates in a status hierarchy. *Psychological Monographs*, 1963, 77, (Whole No. 566).

Jones, E. E., Wells, H. H., & Torrey, R. Some effects of feedback from the experimenter on conformity behavior. *Journal of Abnormal and Social Psychology*, 1958, 58, 207-213.

Jones, R. A., & Brehm, J. W. Attitudinal effects of communicator attractiveness when one chooses to listen. *Journal of Personality and Social Psychology*, 1967, 6, 64-70.

Kanareff, V., & Lanzetta, J. T. The acquisition of imitative and opposition responses under two conditions of instruction-induced set. *Journal of Experimental Psychology*, 1958, 56, 516-528.

Katz, D. The functional approach to the study of attitudes. *Public Opinion Quarterly*, 1960, 24, 163-204.

Kaufmann, H. Similarity and cooperation received as determinants of cooperation rendered. *Psychonomic Science*, 1967, 9, 73-74.

Kelley, H. H., & Thibaut, J. W. Group problem solving. In G. Lindzey & E. Aronson (Eds.), *The handbook of social psychology*, 2nd ed. Vol. 4. Reading, Mass.: Addison-Wesley, 1969. Pp. 1-101.

Kelman, H. C., & Hovland, C. I. "Reinstatement" of the communicator in delayed measurement of opinion change. *Journal of Abnormal and Social Psychology*, 1953, 48, 327-335.

Kiesler, C. A. Attraction to the group and conformity to group norms. *Journal of Personality*, 1963, 31, 559-569.

Kiesler, C. A. Group pressure and conformity. In J. Mills (Ed.) *Experimental social psychology*. New York: Macmillan, 1969. Pp. 235-306.

Kiesler, C. A., & Corbin, L. H. Commitment, attraction and conformity. *Journal of Personality and Social Psychology*, 1965, 2, 890-895.

Kiesler, C. A., & DeSalvo, J. The group as an influencing agent in a forced compliance paradigm. *Journal of Experimental Social Psychology*, 1967, 3, 160-171.

Kiesler, C. A., & Kiesler, S. B. Role of forewarning in persuasive communications. *Journal of Abnormal and Social Psychology*, 1964, 68, 547-549.

Kiesler, C. A., Kiesler, S. B., & Pallak, M. S. The effect of commitment to future interaction on reactions to norm violations. *Journal of Personality*, 1967, 35, 585-599.

Kiesler, C. A., & Kiesler, S. B. *Conformity*. Reading, Mass.: Addison-Wesley, 1969.

Kipnis, D. The effects of leadership style and leadership power upon the inducement of an attitude change. *Journal of Abnormal and Social Psychology*, 1958, 57, 173-180.

Kleiner, R. The effects of threat reduction upon interpersonal attraction. *Journal of Personality*, 1960, 28, 145-155.

Kornzweig, N. D. Behavior change as a function of fear-arousal and personality. Unpublished doctoral dissertation, Yale University, 1968.

Kraus, S., El-Assal, E., & DeFleur, M. L. Fear-threat appeals in mass communications: an apparent contradiction. *Speech Monographs*, 1966, 33, 23-29.

Krauss, R. M. Structural and attitudinal factors in interpersonal bargaining. *Journal of Experimental Social Psychology*, 1966, 2, 42-55.

Krebs, D. L. Altruism—an examination of the concept and a review of the literature. *Psychological Bulletin*, 1970, 73, 258-302.

Lanzetta, J. T., & Kanareff, V. T. The effects of a monetary reward on the acquisition of an imitative response. *Journal of Abnormal and Social Psychology*, 1959, 59, 120-127.

Lasswell, H. D. Conflict and leadership: the process of decision and the nature of authority. *Ciba Foundation Symposium on Conflict in Society*, 1966.

Laswell, H. D., & Kaplan, A. *Power and society*. New Haven, Conn.: Yale University Press, 1950.

Lee, W. *Decision theory and human behavior*. New York: Wiley, 1971.

Leff, W. F., Raven, B. H., & Gunn, R. L. A preliminary investigation of social influence in the mental health professions. *American Psychologist*, 1964, 19, 505. (Abstract)

Lefkowitz, M., Blake, R. R., & Mouton, J. S. Status factors in pedestrian violations of traffic signals. *Journal of Abnormal and Social Psychology*, 1955, 51, 704-706.

Lerner, M. J. The effect of responsibility and choice on a partner's attractiveness following failure. *Journal of Personality*, 1965, 33, 178-187.

Lerner, M. J., & Becker, S. Interpersonal choice as a function of ascribed similarity and definition of the situation. *Human Relations*, 1962, 15, 27-34.

Lerner, M. J., & Matthews, G. Reaction to suffering of others under conditions of indirect responsibility. *Journal of Personality and Social Psychology*, 1967, 5, 319-325.

Leventhal, H., Jones, S., & Trembly, G. Sex differences in attitude and behavior change under conditions of fear and specific instructions. *Journal of Experimental Social Psychology*, 1966, 2, 387-399.

Leventhal, H., & Niles, P. A field experiment on fear arousal with data on the validity of questionnaire measures. *Journal of Personality*, 1964, 32, 459-479.

Leventhal, H., & Niles, P. Persistence of influence for varying durations of exposure to threat stimuli. *Psychological Reports*, 1965, 16, 223-233.

Leventhal, H., & Singer, R. P. Affect arousal and positioning of recommendations in persuasive communications. *Journal of Personality and Social Psychology*, 1966, 4, 137-146.

Leventhal, H., Singer, R. P., & Jones, S. Effects of fear and specificity of recommendation upon attitudes and behavior. *Journal of Personality and Social Psychology*, 1965, 2, 20-29.

Lewin, K. *Field theory in social science* ed. by D. Cartwright. New York: Harper, 1951. Pp. 77 ff.

Lindskold, S., Bonoma, T., Schlenker, B. R., & Tedeschi, J. T. Factors affecting the

effectiveness of reward power. *Psychonomic Science,* 1972, 26, 68-70.
Lindskold, S., Bonoma, T., & Tedeschi, J. T. Relative costs and reactions to threats. *Psychonomic Science,* 1969, 15, 205-207.
Lindskold, S., Cullen, P., Gahagan, J. P., & Tedeschi, J. T. Developmental aspects of reactions to positive inducements. *Developmental Psychology,* in press.
Lindskold, S., & Tedeschi, J. T. Reward power and attraction in interpersonal conflict. *Psychonomic Science,* 1971, 22, 211-213.
Littig, L. W., & Waddel, C. M. Sex and experimental interaction in serial learning. *Journal of Verbal Learning and Verbal Behavior,* 1967, 6, 676-678.
Lott, A. J., & Lott, B. E. Group cohesiveness, communication level, and conformity. *Journal of Abnormal and Social Psychology,* 1961, 62, 408-412.
Lott, A. J., & Lott, B. E. A learning theory approach to interpersonal attitudes. In A. G. Greenwald, T. C. Brock, & T. M. Ostrom (Eds.), *Psychological foundations of attitudes.* New York: Academic Press, 1968, 67-88.
Lott, B. E., & Lott, A. J. The formation of positive attitudes toward group members. *Journal of Abnormal and Social Psychology,* 1960, 61, 297-300.
March, J. G. An introduction to the theory and measurement of influence. *American Political Science Review,* 1955, 49, 431-451.
March, J. G. Power. *International encyclopedia of the social sciences,* 1968. Pp. 405-415.
Marlowe, D., & Gergen, K. J. Personality and social interaction. In G. Lindzey & E. Aronson (Eds.), *The handbook of social psychology,* 2nd ed. Vol. 3. Reading, Mass.: Addison-Wesley, 1969. Pp. 590-665.
Matthews, G., & Dixon, T. R. Differential reinforcement in verbal conditioning as a function of preference for the experimenter's voice. *Journal of Experimental Psychology,* 1968, 76, 84-88.
Mausner, B. Studies in social interaction: III. Effect of variation in one partner's prestige on the interaction of observer pairs. *Journal of Applied Psychology,* 1953, 37, 391-393.
Mausner, B. The effect of one partner's success or failure in a relevant task on the interaction of observed pairs. *Journal of Abnormal and Social Psychology,* 1954, 49, 557-560.
McDavid, J., Jr. Personality and situational determinants of conformity. *Journal of Abnormal and Social Psychology,* 1959, 58, 241-246.
McDonald, R. D. The effect of reward-punishment and affiliation need on interpersonal attraction. Unpublished doctoral dissertation, University of Texas, 1962.
McGinnies, E., & Donelson, E. Knowledge of experimenter's intent and attitude change under induced compliance. Mimeographed manuscript, University of Maryland, 1963.
McGuire, W. J., & Millman, S. Anticipatory belief lowering following forewarning of a persuasive attack. *Journal of Personality and Social Psychology,* 1965, 2, 471-479.
McGuire, W. J., & Papageorgis, E. Effectiveness of forewarning in developing resistance to persuasion. *Public Opinion Quarterly,* 1962, 26, 24-34.
McLeod, J., Harburg, E., & Price, K. O. Socialization, liking and yielding of opinion in imbalanced situations. *Sociometry,* 1966, 29, 197-212.
Miller, G. R., & Hewgill, M. A. Some recent research on fear-arousing message appeals. *Speech Monographs,* 1966, 33, 377-391.

Mills, J. Opinion change as a function of the communicator's desire to influence and liking for the audience. *Journal of Experimental Social Psychology*, 1966, 2, 152-159.

Mills, J., & Aronson, E. Opinion change as a function of the communicator's attractiveness and desire to influence. *Journal of Personality and Social Psychology*, 1965, 1, 173-177.

Mills, J., & Jellison, J. M. Effect on opinion change of how desirable the communication is to the audience the communicator addressed. *Journal of Personality and Social Psychology*, 1967, 6, 98-101.

Mills, J., & Jellison, J. M. Effect on opinion change of similarity between the communicator and the audience he addressed. *Journal of Personality and Social Psychology*, 1968, 9, 153-156.

Mischel, W., & Grusec, J. Determinants of the rehearsal and transmission of neutral and aversive behavior. *Journal of Personality and Social Psychology*, 1966, 3, 197-205.

Mischel, W., & Liebert, R. M. The role of power in the adoption of self-reward patterns. *Child Development*, 1967, 38, 673-683.

Moore, J. C., Jr. Social status and social influence: process considerations. *Sociometry*, 1969, 32, 145-158.

Moreno, J. L. *Who shall survive?* (rev. ed.). Beacon, N. Y.: Beacon House, 1953.

Mouton, J. S., Blake, R. R., & Olmstead, J. A. The relationship between frequency of yielding and the disclosure of personal identity. *Journal of Personality*, 1956, 24, 339-347.

Mowrer, O. H. *Learning theory and behavior*. New York: Wiley, 1960.

Myers, A. Team competition, success, and the adjustment of group members. *Journal of Abnormal and Social Psychology*, 1962, 65, 325-332.

Nardin, T. Communication and the effect of threats in strategic interaction. *Papers*, Peace Research Society (International), 1968, 9, 69-86.

Newcomb, T. M. An approach to the study of communicative acts. *Psychological Review*, 1953, 60, 394-404.

Nord, W. R. Social exchange theory: an integrative approach to social conformity. *Psychological Bulletin*, 1969, 71, 174-208.

Oakes, W. F. Effectiveness of signal light reinforcers given various meanings on participation in group discussion. *Psychological Reports*, 1962, 11, 469-470.

Orne, M. T. On the social psychology of the psychological experiment: with particular reference to demand characteristics and their implications. *American Psychologist*, 1962, 17, 776-783.

Osgood, C. E., Suci, G. J., & Tannenbaum, P. H. *The measurement of meaning*. Urbana: University of Illinois Press, 1957.

Osgood, C. E., & Tannenbaum, P. H. The principle of congruity in the prediction of attitude change. *Psychological Review*, 1955, 62, 42-55.

Oskamp, S., & Perlman, D. Effects of friendship and disliking on cooperation in a mixed-motive game. *Journal of Conflict Resolution*, 1965, 10, 221-226.

Parke, R. D., & Walters, R. H. Some factors influencing the efficacy of punishment training for inducing response inhibition. *Society for Research in Child Development Monographs*, 1967, 32 (1, Serial No. 109).

Pepitone, A. Motivational effects in social perception. *Human Relations*, 1949, 3, 57-76.

Piccolino, E. B. Depicted threat, realism, and specificity, variables governing safety poster effectiveness. Unpublished doctoral dissertation, Illinois Institute of Technology, 1966.

Pivnick, W., & Tedeschi, J. T. Parental occupation, coercive power, and behavioral compliance. *Psychonomic Science*, 1972, 26, 83-85.

Powell, F. A. The effect of anxiety-arousing messages when related to personal, familial, and impersonal referents. *Speech Monographs*, 1965, 32, 102-106.

Powell, F. A., & Miller, G. R. Social approval and disapproval cues in anxiety-arousing communications. *Speech Monographs*, 1967, 34, 152-159.

Pruitt, D. G. Definition of the situation as a determinant of international action. In H. C. Kelman (Ed.), *International behavior: a social psychological analysis*. New York: Holt, Rinehart & Winston, 1965. Pp. 393-432.

Rasmussen, G., & Zander, A. Group membership and self-evaluation. *Human Relations*, 1954, 7, 239-251.

Raven, B. H. Social influence on opinions and the communication of related content. *Journal of Abnormal and Social Psychology*, 1959, 58, 119-128.

Raven, B. H., & French, J. R. P., Jr. Group support, legitimate power, and social influence. *Journal of Personality*, 1958, 26, 400-409.(a)

Raven, B. H., & French, J. R. P., Jr. Legitimate power, coercive power, and observability in social influence. *Sociometry*, 1958, 21, 83-97.(b)

Rosekrans, M. A. Imitation in children as a function of perceived similarity to a social model and vicarious reinforcement. *Journal of Personality and Social Psychology*, 1967, 7, 307-315.

Rosenbaum, M. E., & Levin, I. P. Impression formation as a function of source credibility and order of presentation of contradictory information. *Journal of Personality and Social Psychology*, 1968, 10, 167-174.

Rosenbaum, M. E., & Tucker, I. F. Competence of the model and the learning of imitation and non-imitation. *Journal of Experimental Psychology*, 1962, 63, 183-190.

Rosenblith, J. F. Imitative color choices in kindergarten children. *Child Development*, 1961, 32, 211-223.

Rosenhan, D., & White, G. M. Observation and rehearsal as determinants of prosocial behavior. *Journal of Personality and Social Psychology*, 1967, 5, 424-431.

Rosenthal, R. *Experimenter effects in behavioral research*. New York: Appleton-Century-Crofts, 1966.

Rosenthal, D., & Cofer, C. N. The effect on group performance of an indifferent and neglectful attitude shown by one group member. *Journal of Experimental Psychology*, 1948, 38, 568-577.

Rosnow, R. L., & Robinson, E. J. *Experiments in persuasion*. New York: Academic Press, 1967.

Sampson, E. E., & Bunker, G. L. The effects of power and congruity on small group behavior. Unpublished report, University of California, Berkeley, 1966.

Sampson, E. E., & Insko, C. A. Cognitive consistency and performance in the autokinetic situation. *Journal of Abnormal and Social Psychology*, 1964, 68, 184-192.

Sampson, E. E., & Kardush, M. Age, sex, class, and race differences in response to a two-person non-zero-sum game. *Journal of Conflict Resolution*, 1965, 9, 212-220.

Sapolsky, A. Effect of interpersonal relationships upon verbal conditioning. *Journal of Abnormal and Social Psychology*, 1960, 60, 241-246.

Schachter, S. Deviation, rejection, and communication. *Journal of Abnormal and Social Psychology*, 1951, 46, 190-207.

Schachter, S. *The psychology of affiliation.* Stanford, Cal.: Stanford University Press, 1959.

Schachter, S., Ellertson, N., McBride, D., & Gregory, D. An experimental study of cohesiveness and productivity. *Human Relations,* 1951, 4, 229-238.

Schachter, S., Nuttin, J., DeMonchaux, C., Maucorps, P. H., Osmer, D., Kuijker, H., Rommetveit, R., & Israel, J. Cross-cultural experiments on threat and rejection. *Human Relations,* 1954, 7, 403-439.

Schelling, T. C. *Arms and influence.* New Haven, Conn.: Yale University Press, 1966.

Schlenker, B. R., Bonoma, T. V., Tedeschi, J. T., Lindskold, S., & Horai, J. Interpersonal attraction and compliance to threats and promises. Mimeographed manuscript, State University of New York at Albany, 1970a.

Schlenker, B. R., Bonoma, T. V., Tedeschi, J. T., & Pivnick, W. P. Compliance to threats as a function of the wording of the threat and the exploitativeness of the threatener. *Sociometry,* 1970b, 33, 394-408.

Schulman, G. I. Asch conformity studies: conformity to the experimenter and/or to the group. *Sociometry,* 1967, 30, 26-40.

Scodel, A. Induced collaboration in some non-zero-sum games. *Journal of Conflict Resolution,* 1962, 6, 335-340.

Simon, H. A., & Stedry, A. C. Psychology and economics. In G. Lindzey & E. Aronson (Eds.), *Handbook of social psychology,* 2nd ed. Vol. 5. Reading, Mass.: Addison-Wesley, 1969. Pp. 269-314.

Simons, H. W., Berkowitz, N. N., & Moyer, R. J. Similarity, credibility, and attitude change: a review and a theory. *Psychological Bulletin,* 1970, 73, 1-16.

Singer, J. D. Threat perception and the armament-tension dilemma. *Journal of Conflict Resolution,* 1958, 2, 90-105.

Singer, J. D. Inter-nation influence: a formal model. *American Political Science Review,* 1963, 57, 420-430.

Singer, R. P. The effects of fear-arousing communications on attitude change and behavior. Unpublished doctoral dissertation, University of Connecticut, 1965.

Smith, E. E. The power of dissonance techniques to change attitudes. *Public Opinion Quarterly,* 1961, 25, 626-639.

Smith, W. P., & Leginski, W. A. Magnitude and precision of punitive power in bargaining strategy. *Journal of Experimental Social Psychology,* 1970, 6, 57-76.

Snider, M. The relationship between fear arousal and attitude change. Unpublished doctoral dissertation, Boston University Graduate School, 1962.

Solomon, L. The influence of some types of power relationships and game strategies upon the development of interpersonal trust. *Journal of Abnormal and Social Psychology,* 1960, 61, 223-230.

Spielberger, C. D., & DeNike, L. D. Descriptive behaviorism versus cognitive theory in verbal operant conditioning. *Psychological Review,* 1966, 73, 306-326.

Stinchcombe, A. L. Bureaucratic and craft administration of production. *Administrative Science Quarterly,* 1959, 4, 168-187.

Stotland, E., & Patchen, M. Identification and changes in prejudice and in authoritarianism. *Journal of Abnormal and Social Psychology,* 1961, 62, 265-274.

Stotland, E., Zander, A., & Natsoulas, T. Generalization of interpersonal similarity. *Journal of Abnormal and Social Psychology,* 1961, 62, 250-256.

Swingle, P. G. Effects of the emotional relationship between protagonists in a two-person game. *Journal of Personality and Social Psychology*, 1966, 4, 270-279.

Tannenbaum, P. H. The congruity principle revisited: studies in the reduction, induction, and generalization of persuasion. In L. Berkowitz (Ed.), *Advances in experimental social psychology*. Vol. 3. New York: Academic Press, 1967. Pp. 271-320.

Tedeschi, J. T. A theory of influence within dyads. *Proceedings of the XVIth International Congress of Applied Psychology*, Amsterdam, August 1968.

Tedeschi, J. T. Compliance as a function of source esteem and threat credibility. Mimeographed manuscript, State University of New York at Albany, 1970.

Tedeschi, J. T., Bonoma, T. V., & Brown, R. A paradigm for the study of coercive power. *Journal of Conflict Resolution*, 1971 *XV*, 197-223.

Tedeschi, J. T., Horai, J., Lindskold, S., & Gahagan, J. P. The effects of threat upon prevarication and compliance in social conflict. *Proceedings of the 76th Annual Convention of the American Psychological Association*, 1968, 399-400.

Thibaut, J. W., & Kelley, H. H. *The social psychology of groups*. New York: Wiley, 1959.

Thibaut, J. W., & Strickland, L. H. Psychological set and social conformity. *Journal of Personality*, 1956, 25, 115-129.

Thibaut, J. W., & Riecken, H. W. Authoritarianism, status, and the communication of aggression. *Human Relations*, 1955, 8, 95-120.

Thrasher, J. D. Interpersonal relations and gradations of stimulus structure as factors in judgmental variation: an experimental approach. *Sociometry*, 1954, 17, 228-241.

Tittle, C. R. Crime rates and legal sanctions. *Social Problems*, 1969, 16, 409-423.

Tolman, E. C. A cognition motivation model. *Psychological Review*, 1952, 59, 389-400.

Tornatzky, L., & Geiwitz, P. J. The effects of threat and attraction on interpersonal bargaining. *Psychonomic Science*, 1968, 13, 125-126.

Torrance, E. P. Some consequences of power differences on decision making in permanent and temporary three-man groups. *Research Studies*, State College of Washington, 1954, 22, 130-140.

Tuden, A. Trends in political anthropology. *Proceedings of the American Philosophical Society*, 1969, 113, 336-340.

Udy, S. H., Jr. "Bureaucracy" and "rationality" in Weber's organization theory. *American Sociological Review*, 1959, 24, 791-795.

Vidulich, R. N., & Kaiman, I. The effects of information source status and dogmatism upon conformity behavior. *Journal of Abnormal and Social Psychology*, 1961, 63, 639-642.

Vogel-Sprott, M. Varied effects of noncontingent punishment as a function of the consistency and contingency of punishment on a response. *Psychological Reports*, 1969, 24, 591-598

Vogler, R. E. Awareness and the operant conditioning of a cooperative response. *The Journal of Psychology*, 1968, 69, 117-127.

Wallace, D., & Rothaus, P. Communication, group loyalty, and trust in the PD game. *Journal of Conflict Resolution*, 1969, 13, 370-380.

Walster, E., Aronson, E. & Abrahams, D. On increasing the persuasiveness of a low prestige communicator. *Journal of Experimental Social Psychology*, 1966, 2, 325-342.

Walster, E., & Festinger, L. The effectiveness of "overheard" persuasive communications. *Journal of Abnormal and Social Psychology*, 1962, 65, 325-342.

Walters, R. H. Some conditions facilitating the occurrence of imitative behavior. Paper presented at the Miami University Symposium on Social Behavior, Oxford, Ohio, 1967.

Weber, M. *The theory of social and economic organization*. New York: Oxford University Press, 1947.

Weber, M. *Wirtschaft und Gesellschaft*. Tubingen: Mohr, 1956.

Weiss, R. F., Buchanan, W., & Pasamanick, B. Social consensus in persuasive communication. *Psychological Reports*, 1964, 14, 95-98.

Weiss, R. F., Weiss, J. J., & Chalupa, L. M. Classical conditioning of attitudes as a function of source consensus. *Psychonomic Science*, 1967, 9, 465-466.

Weiss, W. A. A "sleeper" effect in opinion change. *Journal of Abnormal and Social Psychology*, 1953, 48, 173-180.

Weiss, W. Opinion congruence with a negative source of one issue as a factor influencing agreement on another issue. *Journal of Abnormal and Social Psychology*, 1957, 54, 180-186.

Whiting, J. W. M. Resource mediation and learning by identification. In I. Iscoe & H. W. Stevenson (Eds.), *Personality development in children*. Austin: University of Texas Press, 1960. Pp. 112-126.

Wilson, W., & Miller, N. Shifts in evaluations of participants following intergroup competition. *Journal of Abnormal and Social Psychology*, 1961, 63, 428-431.

Wright, P. Attitude change under direct and indirect interpersonal influence. *Human Relations*, 1966, 19, 199-211.

Wyer, R. S., Jr. Effects of incentive to perform well, group attraction, and group acceptance on conformity in a judgmental task. *Journal of Personality and Social Psychology*, 1966, 4, 21-26.

Zajonc, R. B., & Marin, I. C. Cooperation, competition, and interpersonal attitudes in small groups. *Psychonomic Science*, 1967, 7, 271-272.

Zimbardo, P. G., Weisenberg, M., Firestone, I., & Levy, B. Communicator effectiveness in producing public conformity and private attitude change. *Journal of Personality*, 1965, 33, 233-256.

Zipf, S. G. Resistance and conformity under reward and punishment. *Journal of Abnormal and Social Psychology*, 1960, 61, 102-109.

Index

Abelson, R. P., 230
Abrahams, E., 261, 394
Achievement, 127
    and internal-external control,119-21
    and race, 138-39
Activation of commitments, 10-14
Adams, H., 312
Adams, J. S., 203
Adler, A., 106
Adrenalin and emotion, 211
Agreement, 77-78
Aggression and status, 387
Aiken, E. G., 300
Albert, S. M., 184
Alienation, and subjective power, 127
Allen, M. K., 369
Allen, V. L., 366
Allport, G., 106
Alpert-Haber measure of test anxiety, 115
Alternative coalitions, 259
Alternatives
    access to, 266
    availability of, 258
    external, 265-67
    SEU in, 289
    utilization of, 247-48, 265-67
    value of, 266
Ambivalence, 233-34
Analysis of variance and covariance, 187
Anchoring, 313
Anderson, A. J., 329
Anxiety
    and environmental stress, 128
    and internal-external control, 114

Anxiety reduction
    and external control, 116
    as reinforcer, 199
Approval, 226
Argyle, M., 330
Arkoff, A., 257
Aronfreed, J., 362, 368, 379
Aronson, E., 14, 200, 220, 261, 262, 269, 318, 375, 382, 394, 401
Arousal
    and adrenalin, 212
    and sensory input, 107
Arrowood, A. J., 259, 266
Asch, S. E., 23, 58, 367, 393
Aspiration, level of, 309
Assimilation, 73
Atkinson, J. W., 115, 122, 123
Attitude, 219
    defined, 217
    formation, 176-77, 179
    and positive sentiment sharing, 208
Attitude change, 73-74, 262
    vs conformity, 221-22
    defined, 217
    reinforcements in, 219
    and social influence, 217
Attitude similarity, 313
    and attraction, 372
Attraction, 27, 371-81
    and expectation, 372
    and frequency of influence attempts, 312
    interpersonal, 311-14
Attraction-influence relationship, 224-31

Attributions, 4, 22
Authority, 7
    defined, 38, 382
    and information control, 23
    and knowledge, 382
    legitimacy of, 38-39, 101
    and power, 101
    rationality of, 101
    and source, 382
Autokinetic phenomenon and conformity, 29
Awareness of influence relationship, 9

Bachrach, P., 5-6, 15, 38, 101
Back, K., 223, 377
Backman, C. W., 208
Balance and social influence, 229-31
Balance theory, 205, 208
Bandura, A., 18, 25, 26, 249, 351, 279
Baratz, M. S., 5-6, 15, 38, 101
Bargaining, 275-76
Barker, R. G., 16, 23
Baron, R. A., 33, 378
Bass, B. M., 386, 396
Bateson, N., 11, 320
Baumrind, D., 135
Bavelas, A., 300
Beatties, M., 113
Becker, L. A., 184
Becker, S., 312, 331, 372
Bee, H. L., 137
Behavior
    contravalent, 269
    modification, 14
    objects, 16
    settings, 16
    therapy, 18
Behavioral contagion, 26
Behavioral criterion, 117
Behavioral preditions, 117-22
Bennis, W. G., 396
Berger, J., 304
Berger, P. L., 53, 55, 65
Bergin, A. E., 260
Bergman, J. T., 267, 269
Berlo, D. K., 52
Berkowitz, L., 11, 320, 363
Berscheid, E., 199, 201, 202, 203, 206, 207, 230, 394
Bettelheim, B., on hopelessness in Nazi Germany, 128
Bialer, I., 119

Bilateral threat, 255-56
Bierstedt, 101
Blau, P. M., 20, 36, 37, 38-39, 199, 203, 246, 247, 275, 279, 319, 382, 384, 398
Black, A. E., 135
Black Power and threats, 373
Blake, R. R., 388
Bonoma, 315, 326, 329, 365, 373, 392
Boomerang effect, 229-30
Bortner, R. W., 127
Bossard, J. H. S., 208
Boulding, K. E., 58
Bovard, E. W., 201
Boye, D., 207
Brainwashing, 23
Bramel, D., 312
Brehm, J. W., 217, 263, 269, 376
Briggs, B. W., 219
Brock, T. C., 184, 204, 375
Brown, R., 302
Bruner, J. S., 106, 132
Brush, C. A., 228
Bunker, G. L., 360
Burnstein, E., 278
Burnstein, R., 127
Buss, A. H., 204
Butterfield, E. C., 114-15
Byrne, D., 199, 202, 208, 316

California Psychological Inventory, 114
Cambodia Crisis, 78-80
Canon, L. K., 183, 184
Cantril, H., 353
Capability, 13
    and prestige, 390
Caplow, T. A., 257
Carlsmith, J. M., 14, 220, 262, 263, 264, 269, 382, 401
Carter, L., 300
Carter, R. F., 71, 77
Cartwright, D., 15, 20, 29, 55, 101-02, 332, 381
Caudill, W., 386
Causal attribution, 110-11
Causality, 122-23, 125, 126
Cause, concept of, 4
Centrality
    and communication, 329-30
    and influence, 330
Chaffee, S. H., 71, 88
Chambliss, W. J., 362

Index

Chein, I., 5, 6, 101
Chertkoff, J. N., 258
Cherulnik, P. K., 266
Choice
    expected condition, 269-70
    perceived freedom of, 269
Chu, G. C., 355, 362
Clapp, W. F., 129
Clark, K. B., 139
Coalition, 256-59
    and dissatisfaction, 321
    formation, 259, 277
    and relative power, 319
    revolutionary, 259
Coates, B., 378
Coercion, 263, 316
    and conflict intensity, 325
Coercive persuasion, 23
Cognition, 208
Cognitive clarity, 200
Cognitive complexity, 71, 161
Cognitive consistency theory, 222
Cognitive determinants, 211-17
Cognitive development, 33
Cognitive dissonance theory, 208-11
Cognitive map, 56
Cognitive structure, 70-73, 171, 172-73
Cognitive style, 71-73
Cohen, A. R., 230, 315
Cohen, B. P., 280, 304
Cohesiveness, 223
Coleman, J. S., 119-20, 138-39
Collectivities, 67-68
Collins, B. E., 264, 395
Commitment, 264
    and attraction, 376
    and social influence, 225-26
Common value system, 59
Communication, 80-93
    availability of, 327-30
    constraint models of, 81-83
    facilitative functions of, 327-28
    frequency and status, 303-04
    hypotheses on, 24
    and influence attempts, 329, 348-51
    kinds of, 347-48
    nondirected, 350
    "overheard," 395
    patterns of, 84-87
    and propinquity, 329-30
    relevance of, 350
    structure of infamilies, 83-93
    tacit, disadvantages of, 294
Communicator
    attractiveness of, 173-74
    credibility of, 169-73, 260-62
    factors of, 176
    persuasive effect of, 170
    power of, 174-76
    prestige of, 23
Companionate love, 198
Comparison level, 40
    for alternatives, 36
    concept of, 32-33
Competence
    in children, 135-37
    induced, 301
    measure of, 108-09
    motive, 107, 108
    and power, 108
Complex information, 166-67
Complexity
    hierarchial vs flexible, 158
    and information theory, 160-61
    incidence of, 159
    level of, 157
    measurement of, 160-62
    openness vs closedness, 158-59
    perceptual vs executive, 157
    as personality and stimulus variable, 156
    social vs nonsocial, 158
    and social influence, 162-63
    theory, 152-60
Compliance, 221, 222, 225, 289-90
    and accommodative source, 326
    and attraction, 373
    and behavior, 31
    and exploitiveness, 373
    and internal causes, 327
    and persuasion, 327
Conceptual structure, 33
Conclusions of message, 176-79
Conditioning, 219
    verbal, 351
Confidence, 182
Conflict
    defined, 325
    intensity, 323-27
    in social interactions, 324
Conflicting interests, 276
Conformity, 58, 217-18, 267, 273, 318, 350, 365-71
    vs attitude change, 221-22

and attraction, 376-80
and esteem, 402-03
among high-status individuals, 303
and minority judgment, 367
and prestige, 397
and social influence, 217
and status, 281, 383-84, 387-88
Confusion by similarity, 347
Congruency, 62, 63
Consalvi, C., 281
Consensual validation, 25, 41, 29, 59
Consensus, 53-54, 57
Consonant relationship, 209
Contiguity power, 26
Contracts and conflict levels, 325-26
Control
    over behavior, 17-18
    environmental, 15-17, 132-33
    ideology, 118, 121, 113
    and power, 101
    roundabout, 15
    sense of, 120-21
Controlled influence, 15
Cooper, J., 220, 318
Cooperation, 313
    and threats, 329
Coordination, 61-62
Corbin, 267
Core characteristics, 105
Corrective powers, 328
Cosentino, J., 332
Costs, 289-90
    source bases, 290-91
    target based, 290-91, 311
Cottingham, D. L., 363
Counterattitudinal behavior, 264
Counterconditioning, 18
Counterinfluence techniques, 36-37
Crandall, V. C., 120, 137, 137n, 138
Crandall, V. J., 114
Crano, W. D., 185
Credibility, 6n, 260
    and status, 383
Crutchfield, R. S., 366
Cue control, 296
Cullen, P., 365
Cultural deprivation, 139
Cumming, M. E., 141
Curiosity, 10

Dabbs, J. M., Jr., 362
Dahl, R. A., 3-4, 5, 6, 7, 16, 20, 310
Daniels, L. R., 11, 320
D'Antonio, W. V., 102-03
Darley, J. M., 200, 206, 207
Davé, P. N., 123
Davidson, J., 210
Davis, A. H., 256, 329
Davis, K. E., 203, 210, 317, 318
Davis, W. L., 117, 118-19
de Charms, R., 106, 123, 124, 125-26, 132, 320
Dean, D. G., 127
Debt, 275
Deception and power tactics, 270-74
Deceptive behavior, 253
Decision-making and threats, 353
Decision theory, 14-15, 352
Decreasing marginal utility, 243
DeKadt, E. J., 19
Delusion of sufficiency, 347
Demand creation, 246-47, 251, 260-65, 269
    through manipulation of situation, 262-65
    through persuasion, 260-62
Demand curve, 241-43
Dembo, T., 122
Dependence, 320
Dependency, 265
    defined, 36
    and manipulation, 319-20
Depersonalization and internal conflicts, 331
Deprivation, 17
Desensitization therapy, 18
Deterrence, 10, 12
Deutsch, K., 2, 25, 28, 29
Deutsch, M., 255, 256, 307, 325
Deviance, 268
Devaluating product, 248
Dilemma of love, 36
Dillehay, R. C., 312
Direct anxiety, 200
Dissonance theory, 186, 209, 220-21
Dittes, J. E., 201, 281
Dixon, T. R., 370
Doob, L. W., 219, 331
Domain of power, 5
Dozier, G., 142

Drive, 105
Driver, M. J., 155, 156, 157, 161, 16 165n, 167, 180, 185
Durrell, L., 223, 228
Dyadic interaction, 39
Dyadic relationships, 206
D'Zurilla, T. J., 109

Ebbesen, E. B., 262
Ecological control, 16
Edwards, W., 122
Effectance, concept of, 106
Effectance drive, 106-07
Effective response style, 109
Efran, J. S., 388
Ehrlich, H. J., 102-03
Emerson, R. M., 35-36, 246, 247, 319
Emotion, generation of, 214-16
Endler, N. S., 366
Endorsement and status, 282
Environment, control of, 33, 296
Environmental complexity, 156
Environmental stimulation, 133
Environmental stimulus, 163
Equity 320
Equity theory, 203
Erikson, E., 141
Ervin, C. R., 202
Escape, 200
Escoffery, A. S., 118
Esteem
    defined, 398
    and influenceability, 358
Evan, W. M., 384
Evans, J. W., 117
Exchange, 241
    actual rate of, 244-45
    processes, 239
    rates, 242
    terms of, 245
    theories of, 202-05
    unreciprocated relationships, 275
Expectancy, 122, 351
    effect of on performance, 263
    vs hope, 129
Expected value
    of mendations, 364-65
    of message, 359-71
    of promises, 364-65
    of threats, 359-62
    of warnings, 362-64
Expert influence, 24
Expertise, 260-61
    as basis of influence, 305
    of source, 304-05, 382-83
Exploitation
    justification of, 203
    rationalization of, 204
Expressive cues and modeling, 369
External causality and expectancy, 111
External control and anxiety, 115, 116
Externality and conformity, 33
Extinction and reinforcement, 111-12
Extrinsic motive dimensions, 108

Factor analytic study of maturity, 109
Factor structure, 75
Faley, T., 310, 385
Faucheux, C., 265, 276
Fear arousal, 363-64
Feather, N. T., 114, 124
Federal Reserve Board, 15
Feshback, S., 363
Festinger, L., 25, 29, 55, 122, 183, 202, 208, 209, 220, 221, 223, 224, 226, 228, 263, 297, 377, 395
Finck, H. T., 216
Fischer, C. S., 271, 325
Fisher, R., 6, 12, 294, 307
Flattery, 273-74
Florquist, C. C., 317, 318
Floyd, J., 318
Fluctuation, 243
Force, 6, 7, 101
Forced association, 206-07
Forced-choice activity preference scale, 128
Forced-choice questionnaire and expectancy measure, 112
Forewarning
    and conformity, 377
    and influence, 396
Formica, R., 200
Fouriezos, N. T., 299
Frame of reference, 56, 69-70, 75
Frankie, G., 379
Freedman, J. L., 14, 183, 184, 220
French, J. R. P., Jr., 21, 24, 27, 31, 38, 101, 312, 326, 347, 361, 387, 398

French Test of Insight, 123

Gahagan, J. P., 315, 331, 365
Galton, Francis, 198
Gambler's fallacy, 111
Gamson, W. A., 7, 12, 29, 257, 258, 319
Geller, J. D., 121
Generalized expectancy, 110
Generation gap, 141
Gerard, H. B., 25, 28, 29, 33, 200, 246, 247, 248, 296
Gergen, K. J., 187, 240, 273, 309, 317, 318, 331, 377, 385
Gestalt principle of constancy, 22
Gestalt principles of perceptual organization, 206
Gibbs, J. P., 362
Gilmore, J. B., 220
Glass, D. C., 203, 210, 211
Goldberg, C., 294, 401
Golden, B. W., 261, 401
Goldfried, M. R., 109
Goldstein, K., 128
Good, S., 137
Goranson, R. E., 320
Gore, P. M., 33, 117-18, 300
Gottesfeld, H., 142
Gough Adjective Check List, 114
Gouldner, A. W., 326, 382
Graduated Reduction in International Tensions (GRIT), 315
Gray, L. N., 362
Group anxiety, 30
Grinker, R. R., 128
Group cohesiveness, 30
Group manipulation, 29
Group set, 25, 28
Gross, A. E., 300
Grusec, J., 379, 397
Guetzkow, H., 299
Guilford-Zimmerman Ascendency Scale, 300
Gumpert, P., 273
Gunn, R. L., 386
Gurin, P., 113, 118

Halle, L. J., 16
Hamblin, R. L., 332
Hammock, T., 269
Hammond, P., 269
Hamsher, J. H., 121

Hardt, R. H., 142
Harris, M. B., 349, 350
Harsanyi, J. C., 5, 275, 276
Hartup, W. W., 378
Harvey, O. J., 33, 34, 129, 154, 281, 383
Hastorf, A. H., 204, 300
Hawkins, C., 280
Haythorn, W., 300
Heath, D. H., 109
Heider, F., 22, 34, 35, 122, 205, 206, 208, 229, 297
Helmrich, R. L., 264
Hempel, C. G., 60
Hendrick, I., 106
Herriott, R. E., 140
Herrschaft, 382
Hersch, P. D., 114, 115
Hess, R. D., 136
Hetherington, E. M., 369, 379
Higbee, 363
Hollander, E. P., 39, 279, 281, 282, 302, 303, 333
Holmes, J. G., 264, 265
Homans, G. C., 2, 20, 36, 198, 203, 275, 279, 310, 311, 347, 398
Hook, L. H. 331
Hope, 128-29
Horai, J., 254, 310, 315, 359, 365, 373, 392
Hornstien, H., 255-56, 308
Hovland, C. I., 23, 73, 74, 77, 81, 169, 170, 176, 229, 261, 262, 375, 394, 400, 402
Howells, L. T., 331
Hoy, E., 366
Hunt, J. Mc V., 132, 139
Hunt, D. E., 142
Hurwitz, J. I., 304, 314
Hutson, A. C., 379
Hutt, M. L., 299
Hymovitch, B., 304, 315, 346, 377

Identification, 222
    and behavior, 31
    process of, 25
I-E scale, 126, 127, 128
Imitation, 349
    and reinforcement, 378
    and sex, 379
Impression Formation Test (IFT), 154, 161, 180

Index

Impression management communications, 296
Incentive for nomination, 369
Incentive theory, 220
Independence of family, 127
Independent action, 267
Indifference, 319
Indirect anxiety reduction, 200
Inducements, 10-14, 263-64
Inequity, 268
Influence, 7, 17
    attempts, 331, 348-51
    attraction to, 26
    base, 20
    coercive, 316, 324
    cost of, 306, 310
    defensive, 298
    defined, 102
    distinction between types, 12
    exercise of, 292
    exchange theory of, 21
    means of, 8-10
    and mental health professionals, 386
    modes of, 291-98, 316
    nondirective persuasion, 316
    potential, 20
    and prestige
    relationships, 16
    resource-relevant, 308
    self-confidence as factor, 298-302
    social, 19-28
    and status, 303
    and trust, 324
Influenceability, 13, 347-58
Information control, 23, 296
    dependence, 22
    filtering of, 296, 297
    nature of, 183
    receptivity, 185
    supportive and nonsupportive, 185-86
    task-relevant, 305
    utility and nonutility of, 183-84
Informational influence, 21-22, 27, 28, 29
Ingratiation, 272-74, 316-18
Initiating agent and power, 104
Insko, 378
Institutionalization and power disparities, 37
Intellectual Achievement Responsibility Questionnaire, 114, 120, 137

Intention, 13
Intention to influence, 9
Intentionality, 102
Interaction, frequency of, 311-12
Internal arousal level, 107
Internal-external control, 110-22
    concept of, 32-33
    and political activism, 117-18
    and smoking, 119
    and social class, 116-17
    and social influence, 121
Internalization, 222
    and behavior, 31
International relations and prestige, 389
Interpersonal attraction, 197-99
    and social influence, 197, 223-31
Interpersonal expectations, 32
Interpersonal outcome, 32
Interpersonal relations, 210
Interpersonal unit of analysis, 60-65
Intransigence, 268

Jacobs, L., 201
Jaffee, C. L., 305
James, W. H., 111, 112, 119
Janda, K. F., 247
Janis, I. L., 23, 219, 220, 229, 363, 375
Jecker, J., 204
Jellison, J. M., 375, 395
Johnson, H. H., 400, 402
Jones, E. E., 33, 203, 210, 220, 246, 247, 248, 264, 272, 273, 274, 296, 316, 317, 318, 320, 385
Jones, R. G., 273, 317, 318, 376, 385
Julian, J. W., 279, 282, 303
Justice, distributive, 321

Kagan, J., 26, 71, 77, 133-34
Kanareff, V., 368
Kaplan, A., 21, 398
Kardush, M., 365
Katahn, M., 115
Katkovsky, W., 114, 120, 137, 138
Katz, D., 364
Katz, I., 139
Kaufman, D. R., 273
Kaufman, H., 372
Kaye, D., 219
Kelley, H. H., 22, 32, 36, 39, 74, 161, 199, 229, 246, 247, 248, 256, 259, 265, 266, 274, 276, 281, 310,

Kelley, H. H. (continued)
    315, 318, 319, 324, 329, 375, 377
Kelman, H. C., 25, 30-31, 33, 169, 222, 225, 261, 262, 394, 400, 402
Kendon, A., 330
Kepner, C. M., 378
Kiesler, C. A., 267, 349, 376, 382
Kiesler, S. B., 349, 376, 382
Kipnis, D., 316, 327, 328, 332
Kirschner, P., 219
Kite, W. R., 300, 324
Kitt, A., 59
Koslin, 262
Krauss, R. M., 255, 256, 307, 313, 325
Krebs, D. L., 349
Kuhn, A., 1, 17, 324

Labeling of groups, 67-68
Ladwig, G. W., 116-17, 127
Lamberth, J., 202
Landy, D., 204
Lane, W. P., 332
Language
    and influence, 328
    and physical arrangement, 330
Lanyon, R. I., 109
Lanzetta, J., 300, 368
Lao, R. C., 113, 118, 120-21
Lasswell, H. D., 2, 21, 23, 383, 398
Latent power, defined, 103n
Lawler, E. J., 278
Lazarus, A. A., 18
Leadership
    frequency of attempts, 299, 305
    and physical arrangement, 331
Learning
    and attraction, 380
    theory, 25, 218-19
Leavitt, H. J., 329
Lefcourt, H. M., 110, 116, 127
Leff, W. B., 362
Lefkowitz, M., 388
Leginski, W. A., 307
Legitimacy, 7
    and authority, 37-40
    power of, 38
Legitimate authority, source of effectiveness, 40
Lerner, M. J., 312, 372
Level-of-aspiration theory, 32

Leventhal, G. S., 267, 269, 300
Leventhal, H., 362
Levin, I. P., 387
Levinger, G., 300, 326, 361, 387
Lewin, K., 29, 34, 70, 122
Liberty, D. G., Jr., 127
Lichtman, C. M., 266
Liebert, R. M., 369
Liking, 225-31, 311-12
    defined, 197-98
    and imitation, 378
Lindblom, E. C., 16
Linder, D. E., 220, 264
Lindskold, S., 299, 301, 310, 315, 326, 365, 373
Line-judgement tasks, 29
Lippitt, R., 26, 301, 316
Littig, L. W., 123, 369
Litwin, G. H., 123
Locus of Control Scale, 114
Loh, W. D., 262
Lott, A. J., 199, 312, 372
Lott, B. E., 312, 372
Lubin, S. C., 228
Luckmann, T., 53, 55, 65
Lumsdaine, A. A., 262, 394
Lyons, M., 259

Macht, 2, 4
Mac Lean, G., 315
Maddi, S. R., 105, 107
Maladjustment and control scores, 115-16
Mandell, W., 176
Mandler-Sarason Test Anxiety Questionnaire, 123
Manifest power, 103, 105, 108-09
Manipulation, 14-19, 182
    and demand creation, 262-65
    and internal-external control, 121
Manipulatory influence, 9
Manipulatory modes, 296-97
Marak, G. E., Jr., 300
March, J. G., 15
Marginal utility, 306
Marlowe, D., 187, 309, 331
Martin, J. D., 362
Marx, K., 57
Mastery and individual control, 126-27
Matthews, G., 370
Matthews, J. W., 320
Mausner, B., 280, 403

Maximum rates of exchange, 243
Mayer, T. F., 280
McCauley, C., 269
Mc Connell, J. V., on control, 218-19
Mc Ghee, P. E., 120
Mc Leod, J. M., 75, 77
Mc Luhan, M., 82
Measurement procedures, 69-76
Mendations, 13, 14, 294-95, 296, 348, 393-97
    and attraction, 374-76
    and esteem, 400-402
    expected value of, 364-65
    and modeling, 368
    and SEV, 356
    and status, 385-87
Merton, R. K., 59, 67
Message
    complexity, 163-68
    explicit vs. implicit conclusions, 176-79
    expected value of, 359-71
    matching source and target of, 167
    primacy-recency of, 179-81
    theory of complexity, 163-66
    types, 350-51, 354
Milgram, B., 331
Miller, A. G., 121
Miller, J. C., 230
Miller, G. R., 394
Mills, J., 9, 375, 395
Minimum necessary share (MNS), 271
Minton, H. L., 112, 114, 121
Mirels, H. L., 113
Mischel, W., 397
Misrepresentation, 272
Model selection, 25
Modeling, 365-71
    and aggressive behavior, 378-79
    and attraction, 376-80
    and esteem, 402-03
    as form of power, 349
    and prestige, 397
    and status, 387-88
Moore, J. C., 280
Morality and weakness, 322
Morrison, H. W., 326, 361, 387
Moscovici, S., 328, 330
Mothering and infant control, 133
Mothers of Invention, 231
Motivated behavior, 105

Motivation, 185
    for achievement, 123-24
    and personal power, 35
    and power, 105-08
Motivational base and interaction, 40
Motivational withdrawal, 248
Motive as reinforcer, 30
Moulton, R. W., 127
Mowrer, O. H., 128, 372
Multi-variance analysis of variance, 187
Mundy, D., 329
Murphy, L., 134

Nazi Germany and hopelessness, 128
Need values, 110
Negative slope, 242-43
Newcomb, T. M., 53-54, 61, 62, 63, 208, 225, 226, 227, 297
Nietzsche, F., 326
Nominalistic erratic, 3
Nondecision, 10
Norm
    contractual, 275-78
    defined, 275
    formation, 274-82, 326
        frequency of, 277
        and power tactics, 277
    function of, 39
Normative influence, 25, 28, 29
Nurturance and imitation 379-80

Oakes, W. F., 403
Obligations, 275-76, 365
    and source status, 381
OEO, 142
Ofshe, R. and L., 258
Opinion
    change and attraction, 375
    divergence, 318
    value of, 202
Origin-Pawn variable, 125-26
Osgood, C. E., 77, 297, 315
Other-enhancement, 273
Outcome blockage, 246-47, 254-59
    by coalition formation, 256-59
    by individual, 254-56
Outcome devaluation, 248
Outcomes, values, 265

Pallack, M. S., 382
Paradigm state of scientific inquiry, 1

Paradox of Unconditional Omnipotence, 5
Parent-child relationship, 134-35
Parental behavior, 135-39
Parsons, T., 10, 12, 22, 31, 38, 324, 382, 384
Paskel, V., 368
Pepitone, A., 269, 392
Perceived influence and status, 386
Perception and attraction, 374
Perceptual judgements and attraction 377-78
Performance
  differences in, 278
  status, 279-80
Peripheral personality characteristics, 105
Perry, F. A., 279
Personal causation and behavior, 106
Personal control, 118
  factors, 113, 120-21
Personal-ideological distinction, 113
Personal power, 130-43
  defined, 104
  in early childhood, 134-37
  increasing, 142-43
  in infancy, 132-34
  through life span, 140-42
  motivational base of, 105-06
  in school years, 137-40
Perspective, 57
Persuasion, 10, 14, 217
  and attraction, 374-75
  and conflict intensity, 327
  use of in demand creation, 260-62
Persuasive communications, 33
Phares, E. J., 117, 118, 121
Phillips, L., 108
Physical arrangements, 330-34
Piaget, J., 34, 107, 132
Pituitary-adrenal response, 201
Pivnick, W. P., 329, 392
Pluralistic ignorance, 63
Polansky, N., 26, 301, 316
Political activism and internal-external control, 117-18
Political coalitions, 254
Poprick, M. A., 402
Positive slope, 244
Potential power, 108-09
  defined, 104
Potter, S., 271
Powell, F. A., 394

Power
  aspects of, 103
  capabilities, 276-79
  coercive, 4-8, 307, 313, 327
  cognitive approach to, 35
  concept of, 2
  as concept, 100ff
  as control, 102-03
  defined, 3
  as dependency, 35
  disparities, 37
  distribution of, 7
  goals, 107
  imprecise, 308
  interaction, 104
  as interpersonal causation, 3-4
  measure of, 34-35, 102-03
  and motivation, 103, 300
  motive
    dimension, 108
    and self-determination, 107
  network, extension of, 247-48, 265-67
  referent, 24-27
  relative, 314-22
  relationship causation, 4
  resources, 12
  reward, 313, 327
  social, 24
  of source, 174
  tactics, 240
    consequences of use, 253
    and deception, 270-74
    effectiveness of, 252-53
    and outcome blockage, 254-59
    as shifting supply and demand curves, 248-53
    use of, 245-48, 252
  variables, 103-05
  Weber's concept of, 4-5
Powerlessness, 127
Predictions and status, 383
Preferences, transivity of, 288
Preparadigm stage of scientific inquiry, 1
Prestholdt, P., 203, 204, 312
Prestige
  and influenceability, 358
  of source, 306-09, 389-97
Preston, A., 114, 120

Primacy effect of message, 179-81
Principal of Sisyphus, 16-17
Prisoner's Dilemma, 310, 313
Promises, 13, 293-94, 295, 348
    and attraction, 372-74
    as communication, 351
    credibility of, 354, 365
    and esteem, 399-400
    expected value of, 364-65
    and prestige, 391-93
    and SEV, 354
    and social reinforcement, 369
    and status, 384-85
Propinquity, 208, 225, 311
    and communication, 329-30
    and social influence, 225
Propriate strivings, 106
Pruitt, D. G., 280, 389
Punishment, 310
    and avoidance responses, 362
    capability of
    contingent, 361
    magnitude of, 362
    and proximity, 331
Psychasthenia scale, 115

Rabbie, J. M., 200
Race as factor in achievement, 138-39
Radloff, R., 329
Raven, B. H., 21, 22, 24, 25, 27, 31, 101, 347, 367, 377, 386, 387, 398
Ray, W. J., 115
Razran, G. H. S., 219
Real-world vs. laboratory research, 150-51
Reciprocity, 12, 26, 320, 326
Redl, F., 26, 301, 316
Reference group behavior, 58-59
Referent power, 24-27
Reification, 66-67
Reinforcement, 222
    allocation of, 321
    and attitude similarity, 42
    and attraction, 199
    control, 296
    experiences and behavior, 110
    principal of, 198
    schedule and task structure, 111-12
Reinforcement-dissonance controversy, 220
Reinforcers, 199
Relative factor salience, 75
Relationships, power-relevant, 4, 6

Reputation, 295
Resistance forces, 34-37
Resources
    conditions of, 20
    disposable, 306, 307-08
Response complexity, 153-54
Response properties, 8
Rewards, 289-90
Richter, C. P., 128
Riecken, H. W., 386
Rights, 275
    and source esteem, 381
Risk, 266
Risk-taking, 123
Risky-shift phenomenon, 14
Ritchie, D. E., 118-19
Robinson, E. J., 385
Rokeach, M., 158
Role Concept Repertoire (REP), 154, 161
Role position, 302
Role-prescriptions, 37
Romantic love, 198, 216
Rose, A. M., 16
Rosen, S., 26, 301, 316, 326
Rosenbaum, M. E., 387
Rosenberg, M. J., 220
Rosenblith, J. F., 379
Rosnow, R. L., 385
Ross, L. E., 369
Rossi, P. H., 103
Rotter, J. B., 32-33, 110, 111, 112, 113, 115, 116, 117-18, 121, 122, 300
Rotter I-E scale, 126
Rotter Interpersonal Trust scale, 121
Russell, B., 100, 102

St. John, N. H., 140
Sampson, E. E., 360, 365, 378
Sanction, 5-7
Saplosky, A., 380
Sarason Test Anxiety Scale, 115
Sarnoff, I., 200
Satiation, 17, 243
Satisfaction, units of, 289-90
Scarcity, 249
    of outcome, 240
Schachter, S., 198, 199, 200, 211, 213, 214, 227, 234, 268-69, 377
Scheff, T. J., 52, 63
Scheibe, K. E., 114, 115
Scheler, M., 57

Schellenberg, J. A., 265
Schelling, T. C., 294, 391
Schlenker, B. R., 313, 315, 326, 329, 365, 373, 392
Schloper, J., 11, 320
Schmitt, C., 22
Schneider, J. M., 128
Schroder, H. M., 33, 155, 156, 161, 163, 165n, 185
Schulman, G. I., 280
Scientific knowledge, subdivisions of, 1
Sears, P. S., 122
Secondary reinforcement principals, 17
Secrest, L., 119
Seeman, M., 117, 127
Selective exposure, 182-86
Self-change and internal-external control, 118-19
Self-confidence
   chronic, 301
   and influence, 298-302
Self-descriptive achievement scales, 114
Self-determination, 106
Self-esteem and behavior justification, 210
Self-evaluation and affiliative behavior, 200
Self-perception, 260-61
Self-presentation, 273
Semantic differential techniques, 74, 373
Semantic judgements, 74-76
Sensory feedback, 107
Sentence Completion Test (SCT), 154, 161
Sentiment relations, 205, 206
Serial learning, 369
Sex and reinforcement, 369-70
Shaw, M. E., 330
Sheffield, F. D., 262, 394
Sherer, W. C., 312
Sherif, M., 73, 74, 77
Shibutani, T., 58-59, 94
Shifts, actual and perceived, 270
Shipman, V. C., 136
Shomer, R. W., 256, 329
Skill vs chance, 124
Skill-Chance Preference Scale, 127-28
Shriver, B., 300
Siblings and competence, 138
Simmel, G., 6
Simon, R. M., 102, 280
Simulation of Business and Industrial Games (SOBIG) laboratory, 175
Singer, J. E., 34, 211, 228, 389
Situation, factors of, 323-34

Situational congruency, 116
Situational determinants, 111
Skinner, B. F., 17
Smith, M. B., 130
Smith, W. P., 307, 329
Smoking and internal-external control, 119
Social adjustment, 108
Social approval, 12
   as reinforcer, 201-05
Social arrangements, 330-34
Social categories, 67-68
Social class and internal-external control, 116-17
Social comparison, theory of, 25
Social engineering, 142-43
Social influence
   antecedents of, 217-22
   and balance, 229-31
   bases of, 27
   and commitment, 225-26
   defined, 217
   occurance of, 28
   and interpersonal attraction, 197, 223-31
   and liking, 225-31
   multidimensional view of, 152
   and personal attraction, 42
   and propinquity, 225
Social judgments, scaling of, 73-74
Social learning theory, 110
Social power
   defined, 28, 104
   and expertise, 24
   relativity of, 40
   tactical use of, 239-83
Social psychological theory, 1
Social psychology, 41
Social reality, 50
   acceptance of, 55
   as cognitive system variable, 52-53
   concepts of, 56-59
   content of, 54-55
   defined, 51
   development of, 55-56
   as social system variable, 53-54
   validity of, 25
Social reinforcement, 365-71, 402-03
   and modeling, 376-80
   and prestige, 397
   and status, 387-88
Social reference scales, 73
Social relationships as exchanges, 240-45

Social responsibility, 320
Social status
    and children's personal power, 136
    and internal-external control, 116
    and locus of control, 116
Socially mediated response, 25
Socialization and personal power, 140-41
Sorrentino, R. M., 282
Source
    capacity of, 20
    characteristics of, 19-28
    esteem, 21-24, 27, 397-403
    expertise, 304-05
    prestige of, 306-09
    status of, 302-04
    value position of, 20
Space of free movement concept, 34
Speigel, J. P., 128
Staats, A. W. and C. K., 219
Status, 275-76
    conferral, 37
    congruence, 360-61
    as debt, 279
    defined, 381
    as differential distribution, 278
    differentiations, 304
    disparities in, 278
    emergence, 274-82
    and influence, 279-82
    and influenceability, 358
    and juries, 280
    reallocation of, 279
    of source, 302-04, 381-89
    use of, 281
Steiner, I. D., 273
Stimulus complexity, 155-56, 160
Stires, L. K., 273, 274
Stone, V. A., 88
Stoops, J. W., 262
Stotland, E., 128
Straits, B. C., 119
Streufert, S., 155, 156, 157, 161, 163, 165n, 167, 174, 180, 185, 186
Strickland, B. R., 25, 118, 264, 265, 300
Strodtbeck, F. L., 126-27, 280, 304, 331
Structural relations, 62-65
Subjective expected utility (SEU), 288-90, 300, 301, 303, 305, 306, 308, 310, 312, 314
Subjective expected value (SEV), 351-58, 374
Subjective power, 103, 109-10, 113, 126-29

Subjective probability, 122-25, 130
Suedfeld, P., 185
Supply curve, 243-44
Sykes, G. M., 203, 204
Systems Blame, 118

Tannenbaum, P. H., 75, 77, 297, 401
TAT, 123, 124
Target
    accessibility of, 310, 311
    characteristics of, 28-40, 168
    choice of, 309-23
    cognitions, 32-34
    complexity of, 168-86
    motivations, 28-32
    and power, 104
    resistance, 40
    set, 28
Taylor Manifest Anxiety Scale, 115
Teachers and children's competence, 140
Tedeschi, J. T., 6, 13, 16, 254, 299, 301, 310, 313, 315, 319, 324, 326, 329, 331, 354, 359, 365, 373, 385, 392, 399
Terry, C., 280
Thematic apperception measure and power, 107
Thibaut, J., 22, 25, 28-29, 32, 36, 39, 199, 246, 247, 248, 265, 273, 274, 276, 310, 386
Thomas, L. E., 118
Threat, 13, 19, 221, 292-94, 310, 348
    amount of, 263-64
    and attraction, 372-74
    bilateral, 307
    as communication, 351
    credibility of, 354
    as deterrant, 271
    and esteem, 399-400
    expected negative value of, 361-62
    expected value of, 359-62
    potential, 259
    and prestige, 391-93
    and proximity, 332
    and SEV, 354
    and social reinforcement, 369
    and status, 384-85
Tipton, L. P., 71
Tittle, 362
Tolman, E. C., 122
Torcivia, J. M., 402
Torrance, E. P., 304, 388

Transituational reinforcers, 199, 202
Trustworthiness, 261-62, 393-94
Turner, E. A., 14
Turner, J., 262

Uesugi, T. K., 259
Unilateral threat, 255-56
Unit relations, 205-06
Unmasking, 317
Upward Bound, 142
Utility, 353

V scale (achievement related values), 126-27
Valins, S., 216
Valuation, 249
Values
    base, 21
    of behavioral outcome, 240
    scope, 21
Vanderveer, R., 316
Vannoy, J. S., 154
Variety, 107
Verbal discriminations, 13
Veroff, J., 107-08, 300
Viek, P., 128
Vinacke, W. E., 257, 259, 266
Vogel-Sprout, M., 361

Wackman, D. B., 70, 74
Waddell, C. M., 369
Walster, E., 199, 201, 202, 203, 204, 261, 312, 394, 395
Walters, R. H., 18, 25, 26, 349
Warnings, 13, 292, 294-95, 296, 348
    and attraction, 374-76

    and esteem, 400-02
    expected value of, 362-64
    and prestige, 393-97
    and status, 385-87
Warren Commission Report, 121
Warren, W., 119
Watson, D., 115, 116, 315
Weak ordering, 352n, 353
Weber, M., 4-5, 28, 38, 100, 382
Weiss, W., 169, 170, 261, 394, 400, 402
Weltanschauung, 58
White, B. L., 106-07, 133, 134-35
White, R., 106, 132
Whiting, J. W. M., 302
Whorf, B. L., 82
Willerman, B., 318
Witkin, H. A., 154
Withdrawal, 248, 265, 267-70
    deceptive variant of, 271-72
    occurance of, 267-70
Wolfe, R. N., 113-14
Wolosin, R. J., 278
Wolpe, J., 18
Woodruff, A. B., 119
Wright, H. F., 16
Wright, J. C., 14
Wurster, C. R., 386

Zander, A. F., 55, 304, 314, 332, 346, 381
Zappa, F., 231
Zelditch, M., Jr., 304, 384
Ziller, R. C., 332
Zimbardo, P. G., 200, 228, 232, 262
Zipf, S. G., 361, 365
Zojonc, R. B., 70, 77